DEATHQUEST III

ROBERT M. BOHM

UNIVERSITY OF CENTRAL FLORIDA

AN INTRODUCTION TO THE THEORY & PRACTICE OF CAPITAL PUNISHMENT IN THE UNITED STATES

Deathquest III: An Introduction to the Theory and Practice of Capital Punishment in the United States, Third Edition

Copyright © 1999, 2003, 2007
Matthew Bender & Company, Inc., a member of the LexisNexis Group
Newark, NJ

ISBN-10: 1-59345-315-9
ISBN-13: 978-1-59345-315-2

Phone   877-374-2919
Web Site www.lexisnexis.com/anderson/criminaljustice

Library of Congress Cataloging-in-Publication Data

Bohm, Robert M.
    Deathquest III: an introduction to the theory and practice of capital punishment in the United States /
    Robert M. Bohm. -- 3rd ed.
        p. cm.
    Includes index.
    ISBN 1-59345-315-9 (softbound)
    1. Capital punishment--United States. I. Title. II. Title: Death quest III. III. Title: Deathquest 3
       IV. Title: Death quest 3.
    HV8699.U5B65 2007
    364.660973--dc22   2007015423

Cover design by Tin Box Studio, Inc./Cincinnati, Ohio   EDITOR Janice Eccleston
                                                      ACQUISITIONS EDITOR Michael C. Braswell

DEDICATION

To my nieces and nephews:
Lisa, Traci, Allison, Daniel, Kami, Blythe, Weston,
Kyler, Kallie, Jackson, and Bella

ACKNOWLEDGMENTS

I would like to thank all of my friends and colleagues for their support, help, understanding, and inspiration. Although there are too many people to list here by name, many of them are cited in the pages of this book. The others know who they are.

Foreword

by Donald A. Cabana

Professor, University of Southern Mississippi
Author of *Death at Midnight: The Confession
of an Executioner*
Former warden at various correctional facilities
throughout the South

"Vengeance is mine, saith the Lord;
and that means that it is not the
Lord Chief Justice's."
—George Bernard Shaw, 1922

On an oppressively humid July night in 1987, I stood at the window of the gas chamber at the Mississippi State Penitentiary, staring at Connie Ray Evans. Strapped into a cold, steel chair nicknamed the "Black Death" by some forlorn, condemned prisoner many years before I became warden, I was preparing to give the order that would end Connie Evans's life. This was my second execution in just five weeks. Still numb from the first one, I realized as I gazed into the eyes of this next victim that my senses were all but dulled. This one, I knew, would be even more difficult than the first. I had permitted myself to become close to Connie Ray Evans. I came to recognize him as more than just a prison number waiting his turn on death row. In the end, standing there that hot summer night, I realized I was about to execute a friend. My mind was haunted by questions: How had Connie Ray Evans and I gotten there? What goes so wrong that a normal 18-year-old kid spends the last seven years of his life awaiting a date with the executioner?

At a 1790s meeting of the American Philosophical Society held at the home of longtime friend Benjamin Franklin, Dr. Benjamin Rush delivered a paper condemning the young nation's embrace of capital punishment. Rush, signer of the Declaration of Independence, father of American psychiatry, and social reformer, asked the same question: How had America arrived at the use of such a barbaric sanction? He dared to believe that we could be better than that.

Two centuries later, on a sweltering August day in Boston, champion libertarian and death penalty opponent Henry Schwarzschild delivered a message eerily similar to Rush's earlier admonition. Insisting that it is useless to discuss a hypothetical society that applies capital punishment in a fair, rational, consistent manner, Schwarzschild asserted that such an idyllic society is nonexistent. It is necessary, then, to remember that people are not infallible, therefore rendering the legal system imperfect. For that reason alone, he concluded, the use of capital punishment should be relegated to the writings of historical scholars.

Deathquest would win the wholehearted approval of both Rush and Schwarzschild, indeed no small achievement. Professor Bohm has crafted an exhaustive introductory work that should be required reading, not just for students of criminal justice but for any thoughtful, enlightened citizenry as well. Absent the emotional histrionics that characterize so much capital punishment literature, this work forges a detailed, fact-based discussion of what many believe to be the most contentious social issue in America today. While the quality of Professor Bohm's book is unassailable, of even greater importance to the reader is the manner in which he "tells the story." This is not a textbook filled with charts, graphs and data, however impressive and necessary we perceive such material to be. It is, in the final analysis, a book about people—people not so very different from the rest of us. America's death rows are filled with hope and despair, dreams and nightmares, optimism and resignation. While the purpose of this work is not to beatify death row prisoners, it does force the reader to come to grips with the stereotypical images that we so often assign to them.

As any thoughtful reader will quickly conclude, Professor Bohm has skillfully succeeded in painting the death penalty issue in realistic hues and shades of gray. Very rarely can we attribute consummate good or evil to any particular individual or community, and so it is with those on death row.

The death penalty has been a force in every major civilization since the dawn of history. So has the debate and controversy that surrounds it. For our part, executions are not new to the American scene. They have been part of our machinery of justice since the pre-colonial era, brought to Jamestown, Plymouth, and Boston by the earliest European settlers. Capital punishment is not a topic of discussion that falls within the purview of researchers or policymakers alone. The major religious denominations, civil rights organizations and other social- and reform-minded groups have all focused attention on the troublesome issues that arise from the capital punishment debate.

This book will foster renewed, vigorous examination of the multiple realities that are capital punishment, and the impact the execution process has each time America leads one of its citizens to the execution chamber. Whether discussing the early history of executions in this country, or retributive arguments, or our present enthrallment with sanitized lethal injection, Professor Bohm writes with acuity and a forcefulness that compels the reader to revisit longheld beliefs. This is not, after all, a book of abstract ideas or fictitious characters. Rather, when Professor Bohm forces us to confront the stark reality of the gallows, the grisly nature of the electric chair, or the sterility of the lethal injection table, he engages us in a self-examination of who we are as a society. The calculated, methodical, politically convenient approach to justice that has long been part of the execution protocol is laid bare in this book, in all of its disturbing reality.

This work will ensure that we never view state-ordered killing in quite the same way again.

Table of Contents

Introduction

At one level, the death penalty is a minor issue. The media keep the public aware of all sorts of horrible crimes, but relatively few people are directly affected by those crimes, either as perpetrators or victims, or as family and friends of perpetrators and victims. Very few people are sentenced to die for their crimes, and fewer people, still, are ever executed. The 3,300-plus inmates currently on death rows throughout the United States represent less than two-tenths of one percent of the approximately 2 million inmates in all prisons and jails. Moreover, the only reason there are as many as 3,300 death row inmates is that some of them have been awaiting execution for more than 20 years.

Certainly, for me, the death penalty was a minor issue prior to the mid-1980s, and I am a criminal justice professor! I had not given much thought to the issue because other subjects, such as the causes and prevention of crime, were more important to me. (I suppose that even then I did not believe that the death penalty was an important tool in preventing crime.) Then, one day, an article in the local newspaper caught my eye. It mentioned a Gallup poll that showed that 75 percent of the American public supported the death penalty. What struck me as interesting was that such a large percentage of the public agreed about anything. Soon thereafter, I began my effort to understand why the death penalty in the United States was so strongly supported. I wanted to know what was motivating the "deathquest" of the American people.

Not long into my investigation, I became aware that, at another level, the death penalty represents two profound concerns of nearly everyone: the value of human life and how best to protect it. I also discovered that people differ greatly in the ways they believe those concerns should be addressed. For most people who support the death penalty, the execution of killers (and people who commit other horrible acts) makes sense. Death penalty supporters frequently state that executions do prevent those executed from committing heinous crimes again, and that the example of executions probably prevents most people who might contemplate committing appalling crimes from doing so. In addition, many death penalty supporters simply believe that people who commit such crimes deserve to die, that they have earned their ignominious fate.

For opponents, the death penalty issue is about something else entirely. It is a benchmark of the "developing moral standards" of American civilization.[1] As Winston Churchill once said, "The mood and temper of the public with regard to the treatment of crime and criminals is one of the most unfailing tests of the civilization of any country." Put somewhat differently, for many opponents, the level of death penalty support in the United States is a rough estimate of the level of maturity of the American people. The not-so-subtle implication is that a mature, civilized society would not employ the death penalty. Opponents maintain that perpetrators of horrible crimes can be dealt with effectively by other means, and that it makes little sense to kill some people, however blameworthy they are, to teach other people not to kill. These opponents argue that although the perpetrators of terrible crimes may deserve severe punishment, that punishment need not be execution.

The death penalty issue can be and has been addressed on many different levels. Only superficially is it a minor issue. Rather, it is a complex concern that encompasses fundamental questions of who we are as a people and how we deal with some of our most vexing social problems.

One of the more unexpected findings of my research is that most people have a relatively strong opinion about the death penalty, even though they know little about it. What they think they know, moreover, is often wrong. For those reasons, I decided to prepare and teach a college class on the death penalty. Not only did I believe that such a class would be a good vehicle for teaching critical-thinking skills in general, but also I was curious to know whether information about the death penalty (an entire semester's worth) would have any effect on people's opinions about it.

This book is a product of more than two decades of preparing and teaching my class. My principal goal, both in teaching and in writing this book, is to educate students so that whatever their death penalty opinions are, they are informed ones.

I believe it only fair to admit that I am an opponent of the death penalty. Years of study have convinced me that it is a penal practice we can do without. However, as I do in my classes, I will present in this book, as best I can, both sides of all issues. I will let the reader decide whether I have succeeded in the effort and interpret what I write in light of my biases. The reader should be forewarned that most of the literature and research on the death penalty has been produced by its opponents. For the most part, supporters have not felt the need to justify their position. As noted previously, for most of them, supporting the death penalty is just common sense.

The book is divided into 10 chapters. The first four are the least controversial, as they present only facts about the death penalty in the United States. The first chapter traces the history of the death penalty in the United States from 1608 until 1972—which may be called the pre-modern death penalty era, referring to the era prior to *Furman v. Georgia* (1972). The second chapter focuses on the role of the U.S. Supreme Court in the practice of capital punishment. Many of the Court's decisions that have shaped death penalty jurisprudence are described. The third chapter addresses the death penalty systems of the federal government and the military. Similarities and differences between those two systems and the systems of the 37 death penalty states are highlighted. The third chapter also examines the death penalty from a global perspective. The fourth chapter provides a detailed analysis of execution methods employed in the United States, outlines the legal history of the concept of "cruel and unusual punishment," and briefly describes California's execution process and what it is like to witness an execution.

Chapters five through nine examine the arguments and counterarguments employed by proponents and opponents of the death penalty. The fifth chapter addresses the issue of general deterrence. People who believe in the general deterrent effect assume that either the threat of executions or executions themselves prevent other people from committing capital crimes. Incapacitation and the economic costs of capital punishment are the subjects of the sixth chapter. Incapacitation refers to the goal of execution preventing convicted murderers or other capital offenders from committing other crimes. In the second section of this chapter, the economic costs of capital punishment are compared to the economic costs of alternative punishments, especially life imprisonment without opportunity of parole, or LWOP. The seventh chapter explores the subject of miscarriages of justice in capital cases. Incidents of wrongful arrests, wrongful charges or indictments, wrongful convictions, wrongful sentences, and wrongful executions are discussed, as are the reasons for those miscarriages of justice. The chapter ends with suggestions about what can be done about them. The eighth chapter addresses two of the major problems the Supreme Court found with pre–modern death penalty statutes: that they did not prevent the death penalty from being imposed arbitrarily and in a discriminatory fashion. The major focus of the chapter is the modern record and whether the procedural reforms that have been implemented since *Furman v. Georgia* was decided in 1972 have, indeed, eliminated arbitrary and discriminatory application of the death penalty. The ninth chapter examines the subjects of retribution and religion in relation to the death penalty. Emphasized in the section on retribution are the effects of capital punishment on the families of murder victims and death row and executed inmates.

The tenth and final chapter of the book focuses on American death penalty opinion. This chapter is divided into three major sections. The first section provides the history of death penalty opinion, describing what is called here "the too simple and, therefore, misleading death penalty opinion question period." The second section surveys the present period and chronicles "the more complex and revealing death penalty opinion question period." This section begins with a description of research that tested the hypothesis that death penalty support is largely a product of ignorance about the way capital punishment is actually administered. The final section, and the conclusion to the book, addresses the future of American death penalty opinion and the effect it may have on the practice of capital punishment in the United States.

Three remarks about terminology should prove helpful. First, the terms "death penalty" and "capital punishment" are used interchangeably. They refer to the same thing. Second, frequent use is made of the terms "pre-*Furman*" (pre-modern) and "post-*Furman*" (modern) to denote different historical periods. *Furman* refers to the 1972 landmark Supreme Court decision, *Furman v. Georgia*—the first time that capital punishment was held to be unconstitutional. The pre-*Furman* era, for purposes of this book, spans the period from 1608, the year the first person in America was executed by legal authority, to June 29, 1972, the day *Furman* was decided. The "modern" era of capital punishment, the post-*Furman* period, covers everything about the death penalty in the United States that has occurred since June 29, 1972. Third, the term "death-eligible" is used frequently. The definition provided by law professors Baldus and Woodworth is employed: "A death-eligible case refers to one in which the facts are sufficient under state law to sustain a capital murder conviction and death sentence, whether or not the state actually seeks a death sentence or the jury actually imposes a death sentence in the case."[2]

Notes

[1] See, for example, Kohlberg and Elfenbein, 1975.
[2] Baldus and Woodworth, 1998:386.

CHAPTER 1

History of the Death Penalty in the United States: The Pre-*Furman* Period (1608-1972)

The Death Penalty in Colonial Times

Captain George Kendall, a councilor for the Virginia colony, was executed in 1608 for being a spy for Spain—and so began America's experience with capital punishment.[1] The death penalty was just another one of the punishments brought to the New World by the early European settlers.

Death Penalty Laws. The crimes for which the death penalty was legally imposed varied from colony to colony. At one extreme was the law of the Puritans of the Massachusetts Bay Colony, which listed 12 death-eligible crimes: (1) idolatry, (2) witchcraft, (3) blasphemy, (4) murder, (5) manslaughter, (6) poisoning, (7) bestiality, (8) sodomy, (9) adultery, (10) man-stealing, (11) false witness in capital cases, (12) conspiracy and rebellion.[2] Each of these capital crimes, except conspiracy and rebellion, was accompanied by a Biblical quotation as justification. For example, following murder was this Biblical passage, in the language of the statute: "If any person committ any wilfull murther, which is manslaughter, committed upon premeditated mallice, hatred, or Crueltie, not in a mans necessarie and just defence, nor by meere casualtie against his will, he shall be put to death."[3]

At the other extreme was the law of the Quakers who were far less punitive than their neighbors to the north. In the Royal Charter of South Jersey (1646), capital punishment was originally forbidden altogether, but the prohibition ended in 1691.[4] William Penn's Great Act of

1682 (Pennsylvania) allowed capital punishment only for treason and murder.[5] The Quakers, however, were the exception. Most of the British colonies had statutes similar to those of the Massachusetts Bay Colony.

Today it may seem as if the statutes of the colonies listed too many capital crimes (crimes for which death could be imposed), but for colonial times, the number was relatively modest. In Great Britain, death could be imposed for more than 50 crimes, including burglary, robbery, and larceny. Later, during the reign of George II (1727–1760), the number of capital crimes was increased to nearly 100, and under George III (1760–1820), the death penalty could be imposed for almost 150 capital crimes (some authorities maintain it was closer to 200 capital crimes).[6] Moreover, for some of the moral or religious offenses, such as blasphemy, idolatry, adultery, sodomy, and bestiality, few offenders were ever executed in the colonies.[7] The main reason for the relatively small number of capital crimes in colonial America was the great need for able-bodied workers. It made little sense to execute people at a time when workers were so scarce, and people could be made to work. The British colonies might have had even fewer capital crimes if long-term confinement facilities had been available.[8] (The first prison was not established until 1790.)

Executions and Saving Souls. Executions in colonial America, though rare events, had a significant religious component that they lack today. They provided an especially dramatic occasion for saving souls. To be sure, executions served other purposes as well. They were considered just retribution—"an eye for an eye"—and a general deterrent to crime. They were also a stark reminder of what the state had the power to do to people who violated its laws. However, their role in saving souls was part of a morality lesson central to the clergy's social control of the colonists.[9]

The twin beliefs that human beings were inherently depraved, victims of original sin or the fall from grace, and that they could be influenced by the devil or demons anchored the religious view of the world that dominated colonial America. Believers were taught that to avoid eternal damnation they must spend their lives fending off devilish enticements, controlling their evil natural urges, and seeking salvation. Fortunately, for sinners, religious doctrine guaranteed that repentance was possible for anyone, anytime prior to death, no matter how despicable their behavior. In this view, capital punishment both hastened a criminal's effort to repent and expiated the community's collective guilt for past crimes.[10]

It was primarily for these religious reasons that condemned offenders typically were not executed for a week or two or, in some cases, several weeks, after conviction.[11] So important was repentance and assuaging the community's collective guilt that the government was willing to forfeit some of the retributive and deterrent effect of the punishment by temporally separating the connection between the crime and punishment. The delay was also costly to the government because it had to house and feed the condemned person during the interim and it increased the possibility that the condemned person would escape. Another reason for delaying the execution was to provide authorities a chance to publicize the impending execution, allowing spectators to make plans to attend.[12]

A minister would regularly visit the condemned prisoner while the prisoner awaited execution (as could anybody else who wanted to do so). The minister's purpose was to prepare the condemned prisoner for death and the afterlife. If the minister were successful, as he apparently frequently was, the condemned prisoner would repent and accept Christ as his or her savior.[13] Condemned prisoners were usually allowed to attend church on the day of worship just prior to their execution, where they were often the subjects of the sermon.[14] As part of the ritual, condemned prisoners would often rise during the service and confess their guilt and proclaim their newfound faith to the congregation and especially its most influential members. Not only did such proclamations please the ministers who convinced condemned offenders to make them, but they also gave condemned prisoners their best opportunity of receiving executive clemency. (Influential congregants might petition the executive on behalf of the condemned person.) However, having nothing to lose by making the declarations, there was always some question about the condemned person's sincerity.[15]

The ritual continued on hanging day beginning with the procession to the gallows, followed by a sermon (or sermons), sometimes the singing of hymns, and the condemned prisoner's last words.[16] The entire ceremony was public, outdoors, and could take several hours to complete.[17] No other public event in colonial America drew larger crowds than executions and, unlike public executions in the nineteenth century that were criticized for being drunken, irreverent, and rowdy events, public executions in colonial America were generally solemn occasions.[18] They were considered a particularly wholesome experience for children.[19] Having an audience many times larger than they normally had, ministers took advantage of public hangings to preach about the consequences of sin and the power of salvation.[20] They also might use the occasion to instruct spectators (and others who might later read about it) about the perils of resisting religious and secular authority.[21] The same messages were also frequently conveyed by the condemned prisoner's last words. The sermon remained a part of the execution ritual until public executions were finally abandoned in the twentieth century.[22] Allowing the condemned prisoner to make a final statement is a ritual that is still practiced today.

Penitence is no longer an ostensible goal of capital punishment. The reason is that during the colonial period criminals were not viewed as fundamentally different from the rest of the population, as they are more likely to be today. The belief prevalent during the colonial period was that everyone was inherently evil, plagued by the curse of original sin, and that criminals were simply less able to control their primal urges or fend off the devil. Crime was considered a failure of will. Because crime triggered collective guilt, criminal repentance was a common goal. Today, criminals are routinely viewed as lacking the virtue of law-abiding citizens, as fundamentally different and alien to the rest of society. No longer is there a sense of collective guilt when a crime is committed; therefore, penitence is no longer such a major concern. In addition, with the current separation of church and state, religion no longer has the influence in secular affairs as it did during colonial times.[23]

The Death Penalty Imposed. Although Captain Kendall's was the earliest recorded lawful execution in America, his punishment and the circumstances surrounding it differed from most of those that followed. First, his was an execution for a relatively unusual offense (spying/espionage), and, second, he was shot instead of hanged.[24] More than twenty years would pass before the first murderer, John Billington, was executed in 1630. He was executed in the Massachusetts colony. In between Kendall and Billington, Frank Daniell (1622), Cornish Richard (1624), and Hayle Thomas (1626) were executed for theft, sodomy (buggery/bestiality), and rape, respectively. All four men were hanged in the Virginia colony.[25] Of the 162 colonists executed in the seventeenth century (for which the offense is known—85 percent of the total), nearly 40 percent were executed for murder, about 25 percent for witchcraft, and nearly 15 percent for piracy. No other crimes accounted for more than eight percent of all executions. Most of the executed were hanged (88 percent); 10 percent were shot; an alleged witch was pressed to death, and a convicted arsonist was burned.[26]

Since Kendall's execution in 1608, more than 19,000 executions, performed in the United States under civil (as opposed to military) authority, have been confirmed by M. Watt Espy, the leading historian of capital punishment in the United States. Espy estimates that between 20,000 and 22,500 people have been executed by legal authority since 1608.[27] This estimate does not include the approximately 10,000 people lynched in the nineteenth century.[28] Only 1,553 of the 19,000 executions—less than ten percent of the total—occurred during this country's first two centuries. Compared to more recent times, colonial Americans used the death penalty sparingly. More executions were conducted in the 1930s (1,676) than in the entire 1600s (162) and 1700s (1,391).[29]

Nearly all of the people executed during the past four centuries in America have been adult men; only about three percent (approximately 568) have been women.[30] Ninety percent of the women were executed under local, as opposed to state, authority, and the majority (87 percent) was executed prior to 1866.[31] A quarter of all women executed met their fates during the 1600s (42) and 1700s (100).[32] The first woman executed in America was Jane Champion in the Virginia colony in 1632.[33] She was hanged for murdering and concealing the death of her child, who allegedly was fathered by William Gallopin and not her husband.[34] The most women executed in any single year in America were the 14 women hanged for witchcraft in Massachusetts in 1692.[35]

About two percent (approximately 366) of the people executed have been juveniles; that is, individuals who committed their capital crimes prior to their 18th birthdays.[36] Most of them (69 percent) were black, and nearly 90 percent of their victims were white.[37] The first juvenile executed in America was Thomas Graunger in Plymouth colony in 1642 for the crime of bestiality.[38] He was 16 at the time of his crime and execution.[39] The youngest nonslave executed in the United States was Ocuish Hannah, who was hanged for a murder she committed when she was 12 years old. Hannah was executed in New London County, Connecticut, on December 20, 1786.[40] At the time the Bill of Rights was ratified in 1791, American law only prohibited the execution of children under the age of seven. Besides murder, juveniles in America have been executed for sodomy with animals, arson, robbery, assault, and rape. The U.S. Supreme Court ended the practice of executing juvenile capital offenders on March 1, 2005, when, in the case of *Roper v. Simmons* (543 U.S. 551), it ruled that executing capital offenders under the age of 18 violated the U.S. Constitution's Eighth and Fourteenth Amendments (more about this later).

Death Penalty Abolitionists. There have probably always been people opposed to capital punishment, but even though their numbers have often been small, they have not been without influence. Quakers, for example, have always opposed capital punishment, and, because of their early presence and influence in Pennsylvania, that state, and especially the city of Philadelphia, may be considered the birthplace of the American death penalty abolitionist effort.

Among the first people in the United States to organize others against the death penalty was Dr. Benjamin Rush (1747–1813), a Philadelphia physician and signer of the Declaration of Independence.[41] Rush was among the founders (in 1787) of the Philadelphia Society for Alleviating the Miseries of Public Prisons.[42] (In 1833, the Philadelphia Society changed its name to the Pennsylvania Prison Society. That same organization exists under the changed name today.) Rush questioned the Biblical support for capital punishment and the belief that it was a general deterrent to crime. He did not believe that the example of executions dissuades people from carrying out crimes they have contemplated committing. To the contrary, he thought that capital punishment might increase crime.[43] This made Rush one of the first Americans to suggest that the death penalty might have a counterdeterrent or "brutalizing effect" (more about this in Chapter 5). Reflecting Enlightenment philosophy, Rush maintained that the social contract was violated whenever the state executed one of its citizens. He was greatly influenced by Cesare Beccaria's argument against the death penalty in *On Crimes and Punishments*, first published in Italy in 1764 and translated and published in New York in 1773.[44] People had opposed the death penalty for centuries, but Beccaria gave abolitionist sentiment an authoritative voice and renewed energy.[45]

In the late eighteenth century, Dr. Rush attracted the support of such prominent Americans as Benjamin Franklin and William Bradford, who was Pennsylvania and later United States Attorney General. Other prominent Americans who opposed the death penalty early on were James Madison, DeWitt Clinton, future governor of New York, and Thomas Jefferson, who opposed the death penalty for all crimes except murder.[46] It was at Franklin's home in Philadelphia that Rush became one of the first Americans to propose confinement in a "House of Reform" as an alternative to capital punishment.[47] According to one commentator, the paper delivered by Rush at Franklin's home was "the first reasoned argument in America favoring the abolition of capital punishment."[48] The houses of reform envisioned by Rush would be places where criminals could learn to be law-abiding citizens through moral education. At least in part because of the efforts of Rush and his colleagues, in 1790, the Walnut Street Jail in Philadelphia was converted into the world's first penitentiary—an institution devoted primarily to reform.[49]

Pennsylvania became the first state in legal proceedings to consider degrees of murder based on culpability, largely as a result of Bradford's efforts.[50] Before this change, the death penalty was mandated for anyone convicted of murder (and many other crimes), regardless of circumstance. Like Rush, Bradford did not believe that capital punishment deterred crime, citing the example of horse stealing, which at the time was a capital offense in Virginia and the most frequently committed crime in the state. Because of the severity of the penalty, convictions for the crime were hard to obtain.[51] Pressure from abolitionists also caused Pennsylvania in 1794 to repeal the death penalty for all crimes except first-degree murder.[52]

Many people were drawn to Rush's ideas, and petitions to abolish the death penalty were introduced in several state legislatures. Between 1794 and 1798, Virginia and Kentucky joined Pennsylvania in abolishing the death for all crimes except first-degree murder; New York and New Jersey abolished the penalty for all crimes except murder and treason.[53] At the time, New York and New Jersey had not yet divided murder into degrees, as had the other three states.[54] Because treason against a state rarely occurred, in practice, murder was the only capital crime in those two states.[55] Virginia and Kentucky, both slave states, confined the reforms to free people; slaves in those states were still subject to a long list of capital crimes.[56] When New Jersey, Virginia, and Kentucky severely restricted the scope of capital punishment, they also appropriated funds for the construction of their first prisons; Pennsylvania and New York had established prisons earlier.[57] Still, half a century would pass before the first state abandoned capital punishment entirely.

A driving force of the abolitionists' efforts was the belief that the death penalty was no longer needed. Although conceding that the penalty may have been necessary in the more barbaric past, abolitionists argued that society had progressed to a higher stage of civilization rendering the death penalty obsolete. This idea was not peculiar to the United States. It was a sensibility held by death penalty abolitionists throughout Europe and Russia as well.[58] The American abolitionists bolstered their position by pointing out that the newly created prisons could accomplish whatever purposes capital punishment had previously served.[59] Indeed, the prison was crucial to the abolitionist argument because it provided a legitimate alternative to capital punishment.[60] If prisons had not been available, the abolitionist position would have been much weaker. Death penalty proponents, on the other hand, were less sanguine about humanity and the possibility of progress. They were pessimistic about human nature and generally assumed that neither the individual nor society could improve enough to safely eliminate the death penalty from society's arsenal of punishments.[61] They were distrustful of the prison's ability to protect them and did not believe that long-term imprisonment was punishment enough for the most heinous crimes.

It is important to keep in mind that the histories of the death penalty and the death penalty abolitionist movement in the United States are the same in many places because all of the significant changes in the practice of capital punishment—culminating in its complete abolition in some jurisdictions—are the result of abolitionist efforts. Those efforts created: (1) degrees of murder, which distinguish between murders heinous enough to warrant death and those murders that do not, (2) a reduction in the number of offenses warranting the death penalty (except for the federal government, as described in Chapter 3), (3) the hiding of executions from public view, and (4) a decreased annual number of executions (but that trend may be changing). Although abolition of the death penalty has been their unremitting goal, abolitionists have been far more successful reforming its practice.

The Death Penalty in the Nineteenth Century

Between 1800 and 1865, use of the death penalty increased significantly. The number of executions rose almost 60 percent over the number from the entire seventeenth and eighteenth centuries (from 1,553 to 2,443). Although after the Civil War, and until 1880, the number of executions dropped by two-thirds (to 825), from 1880 until the turn of the century, the number of executions increased to about a thousand each decade.[62]

In 1812, New Hampshire joined the five states that had limited the death penalty to murder and treason between 1794 and 1798. Ohio followed suit in 1814.[63] However, most of the death penalty legislation during the first quarter of the nineteenth century was in the opposite direction. For example, in 1807, rape, arson, and horse stealing were made capital crimes in Indiana. It added receiving a stolen horse to the list in 1808.[64] New York, which had limited the death penalty to murder and treason in 1796, added residential arson to its list of capital crimes in 1808 and, following a prison riot, arson in a prison in 1817.[65] Pennsylvania legislators refused to abolish the death penalty for all crimes when the governor proposed it in both 1809 and 1811.[66]

The period between 1825 and 1850 was a time of reform in America. The increase in the number of executions, plus general abolitionist sentiment, spurred anti-death penalty activity, resulting in the organization of several abolitionist societies (especially along the eastern seaboard) and the founding of the American Society for the Abolition of Capital Punishment in 1845.[67] Two of America's greatest poets wrote anti-death penalty poems during the 1840s. John Greenleaf Whittier penned, "The Human Sacrifice," in 1843, and Walt Whitman's "The Dialogue: A Brief Statement of the Argument for the Abolition of the Death Penalty" was published in a popular magazine in 1845.[68] By the late 1840s, death penalty opposition became so prevalent in some northern states that it had become difficult to empanel juries in capital cases. Horace Greeley, the influential founder and editor of *The New York Tribune* and ardent death penalty and slavery opponent, delighted in reporting that 80 percent of the people in a recent capital case jury pool were dismissed because of their opposition to the death penalty.[69] By 1850, death penalty abolitionist societies were working in Tennessee, Ohio, Alabama, Louisiana, Indiana, and Iowa.[70] Two other reform movements—anti-saloon and anti-slavery—also gave a boost to the death penalty abolitionists.

Hiding Executions from the Public. Between 1800 and 1850, American death penalty abolitionists helped change public sentiment about public executions, especially among many northern-state social elites. Whereas in 1800, public hangings were mostly solemn events regularly attended by members of all social classes and touted as having important educational value, by mid-century, members of the upper classes were staying away from them because in their minds they had become tasteless, shocking, rowdy, sometimes dangerous, carnival-like spectacles.[71] This view, however, may have been more a matter of perception than reality, as eyewitness accounts suggested that decorum at public executions had not changed that much.[72] In any event, the elite began to view those who attended executions as contemptible "rabble out for a good time" and concluded that any educational value public hangings once had was being lost on the less respectable crowd.[73] Another problem with public hangings during this period was that attendees were increasingly sympathizing with the condemned prisoners, weakening the position of the state. Indeed, some of those who met their fate on the gallows became folk heroes.[74] Still, another change was increasing acceptance of the belief that public executions were counterproductive because of the violence they caused. Stories were circulated about the violent crimes being committed just before or just after a pubic hanging by attendees of the event.[75]

For these reasons, Connecticut, in 1830, became the first state to ban public executions. Pennsylvania became the second state to do so in 1834.[76] In both states, only a few authorized officials and the relatives of the condemned were allowed to attend. By 1836, New York, New Jersey, Massachusetts, Rhode Island, and New Hampshire had enacted similar policies.[77] By 1860, all northern states and Delaware and Georgia in the South had shifted the site of executions from the public square to an enclosed jail yard controlled by the sheriff and deputies.[78] By 1890, some states had moved executions to inside the jail or a prison building.[79] Some states were so intent on hiding executions from the public that they banned members of the media from attending them, and those people who were allowed to witness executions were expressly forbidden to divulge to anyone what they had seen. State statutes stipulated that anyone who disclosed or published anything about the execution, "beyond the statement of the fact that such convict was on the day in question duly executed according to law," committed a misdemeanor subject to fine or incarceration.[80] These were not trivial changes because executions were among the best-attended public events and continued to be well into the nineteenth century in those states that had not banned public executions.[81] The last public execution was held in Galena, Missouri, in 1937.[82]

In states that hid executions from the public, apparently, legislators were willing to sacrifice any general deterrent effect of witnessing executions to escape the "public disorder, rioting, and even murder" that sometimes accompanied the public spectacles, especially the botched executions and last–minute reprieves.[83] This accusation may be a bit overblown, however, because the movement to ban public executions coincided with other developments that were substitutes, albeit less dramatic substitutes, for personally witnessing an execution. The most important arguably was the proliferation of newspapers—the so-called "penny press."[84] In those states that allowed journalists to attend, the newspapers carried vivid descriptions of jail-yard hangings, allowing the public to at least experience the executions vicariously.[85] A second development was a dramatic increase in the number of people that attended capital trials. Observing a capital trial in a way replaced witnessing a public hanging. For people unable to attend the trials, the newspapers carried daily accounts that helped to satisfy their curiosity.[86] The third development was increased public participation in the clemency process. In the eighteenth century, only a few prominent citizens typically signed clemency petitions, but, by the middle of the nineteenth century, the process had become more democratic. It was not unusual for governors to receive clemency petitions, both for and against, signed by hundreds or even thousands of people.[87] In sum, although most people were banned from personally witnessing public hangings, early nineteenth century Americans still could participate indirectly in the execution process by reading about it in newspapers, attending or reading about capital trials, and signing petitions for clemency.[88]

From Mandatory to Discretionary Capital Punishment Statutes. In 1837, Tennessee became the first state to enact a discretionary death penalty statute for murder; Alabama did the same four years later, followed by Louisiana, five years after that.[89] All states before then employed mandatory death penalty statutes that required anyone convicted of a designated capital crime to be sentenced to death. The reason for the change, at least at first and in the South, undoubtedly was to allow all-white juries to take race into account when deciding whether death was the appropriate penalty in a particular case.[90] Between the Civil War and the end of the nineteenth century, at least 20 additional jurisdictions changed their death penalty laws from mandatory to discretionary ones. Illinois was the first northern state to do so in 1867; New York was the last state to make the change in 1963.[91] The reason most northern states switched from mandatory to discretionary death penalty statutes, and another reason for southern states to do so, was to prevent jury nullification, which was becoming an increasing problem.[92] Jury nullification refers to a jury's knowing and deliberate refusal to apply the law because, in this case, a mandatory death sentence was considered contrary to the jury's sense of justice, morality, or fairness.[93] Many jurors during this period were being influenced by new scientific claims that criminality was not freely chosen but rather a product of biological and environmental factors beyond the criminal's control.[94] If that were true, it seemed unfair to hold offenders completely responsible for criminal behavior they could not fully control. Discretionary death penalty statutes allowed juries the option of imposing a sentence of life in prison instead of death.[95] For the same reason, the insanity defense was being increasingly used (some critics contended overused) in capital cases to allow defendants to escape the death penalty without being acquitted outright.[96] This new deterministic view of criminal behavior that was coming from university-based social scientists in the late nineteenth century not only undermined the retributive and deterrent bases for capital punishment, but it challenged the legitimacy of the death penalty itself.[97] In the case of retribution, how could it be just to execute a person for a crime he or she did not freely choose to commit? In the case of deterrence, how could people be prevented from committing crime if crime were caused by uncontrollable biological, especially genetic, factors?[98] By 1963, as noted, mandatory capital punishment laws were removed from all penal codes, except for a few rarely committed crimes in a handful of jurisdictions.[99]

This change from mandatory to discretionary death penalty statutes, which introduced unfettered sentencing discretion into the capital-sentencing process, was considered, at the time, a great reform in the administration of capital punishment. Ironically, it was unfettered sentencing discretion that the Supreme Court declared unconstitutional in its *Furman* decision in 1972.[100] (The *Furman* decision is discussed in detail in Chapter 2.)

States Abolish the Death Penalty. In 1846, the state of Michigan abolished the death penalty for all crimes, except treason, and replaced the penalty with life imprisonment. The law took effect the next year, making Michigan, for all intents and purposes, the first English–speaking jurisdiction in the world to abolish capital punishment.[101] Sociology professor John Galliher and his colleagues relate that the mostly Puritan-Yankee colonists and later citizens of Michigan have always had an aversion to capital punishment, and that aversion contributed to the state's eventual abolition of the penalty.[102] Prior to abolition, what became the state of Michigan only conducted 11 executions. Eight of the 11 executions occurred in the 1770s under colonial rule; the other three while Michigan was a U.S. territory. Two of the latter three executed were Native Americans, and both were executed in 1821. The other, Stephen Simmons, was executed in 1830, seven years before Michigan gained statehood. Simmons in a drunken rage killed his wife in Detroit. A public outcry against the death penalty followed Simmons' execution, while the execution of the Native Americans drew little interest. Simmons, incidentally, is the only non-Native American ever executed in Michigan under state or territorial authority.[103] Michigan has resisted the death penalty despite high murder rates and large minority and immigrant populations.[104]

The first state to outlaw the death penalty for all crimes, including treason, was Rhode Island, in 1852; Wisconsin was the second state to do so a year later.[105] Although no other states abolished the death penalty during this period, by 1860, no northern state punished by death any crime except for murder and treason. Furthermore, those states that had divided the crime of murder into degrees limited the death penalty to first-degree murders.[106] The last person executed for the crime of rape in the northern states was probably Horace Carter, a white man hanged in Massachusetts in 1825.[107] Opponents of the death penalty, who initially benefited from general abolitionist sentiment, saw concern with capital punishment wane as the Civil War approached, and attention shifted to the growing anti-slavery movement.[108]

Not until well after the Civil War did Iowa, in 1872, and Maine, in 1876, become the next states to abolish the death penalty. Legislatures in both states reversed themselves, however, and reinstated the death penalty in 1878, in Iowa, and in 1883, in Maine. Maine reversed itself again in 1887 and abolished capital punishment and, to date, has not reinstated it.[109] Colorado abandoned capital punishment in 1897, but the move apparently was unpopular with many of its citizens. At least partially in response to three lynchings of blacks by whites within two years of abolition, the death penalty was restored in 1901.[110]

From Local to State–Authorized Executions. A major change took place in the legal jurisdiction of executions during the time of the Civil War. Before the war, all executions were conducted locally—generally in the jurisdiction in which the crime was committed—but on January 20, 1864, Sandy Kavanagh was executed at the Vermont State Prison. He was the first person executed under state, as opposed to local, authority.

This shift in jurisdiction was not immediately adopted by other states. After Kavanagh, there were only about two state- or federally-authorized executions per year well into the 1890s; the rest were locally authorized.[111] That pattern would shift dramatically during the next 30 years. In the 1890s, about 90 percent of executions were imposed under local authority, but by the 1920s, about 90 percent were imposed under state authority.[112] Today, all executions are imposed under state authority, except those conducted in Delaware and Montana and by the federal government and the military.

The Death Penalty in the
First Half of the Twentieth Century

As the United States entered the twentieth century, a new age of reform began. It was called the "Progressive Period."[113] Death penalty abolitionists benefited from the critical examination of American society that characterized the era and achieved a series of successes, albeit in most cases, temporary ones.[114]

States Abolish and Reinstate the Death Penalty. During the first two decades of the twentieth century, six states outlawed capital punishment entirely (Kansas, 1907; Minnesota, 1911; Washington, 1913; Oregon, 1914; South Dakota, 1915; Missouri, 1917), and three states (Tennessee, 1915; North Dakota, 1915; Arizona, 1916) limited the death penalty to only a few rarely committed crimes, such as treason or the first-degree murder of a law enforcement official or prison employee. Tennessee also retained capital punishment for rape.[115] In addition, seventeen other states nearly abolished the death penalty or at least seriously considered abolition, some of them several times. They included California, Connecticut, Colorado, Illinois, Indiana, Massachusetts, Nebraska, New Hampshire, New Jersey, New York, North Carolina, Ohio, Pennsylvania, Utah, Vermont, Virginia, and West Virginia.[116] The momentum, however, failed to last. By 1920, five of the states that had abolished the death penalty earlier had reinstated it (Arizona, 1918; Missouri, 1919; Tennessee, 1919; Washington, 1919; Oregon, 1920).[117]

The Progressive era death penalty abolition movement in eight of the abolition states has been attributed to the support of the state's governor, or the state's press, or both during a time of economic prosperity.[118] Some of the abolition-state governors were affiliated with the Anti-Capital Punishment Society of America.[119] On the other hand, the press apparently played little role in the states that restored the death penalty other than by publicizing taunts made by non-repentant convicted murderers. In each of the states that reinstated the death penalty, a convicted murderer acknowledged that he might not have killed had there been a death penalty. After being sentenced to life imprisonment, others bragged that the state would have to feed and care for them the rest of their lives.[120] These types of remarks angered many citizens who began pushing for the death penalty's reinstatement. The movement to re-establish the death penalty was also a function of the reluctance of some states to abolish the death penalty in the first place. In Oregon and Arizona, for example, legislatures passed death penalty abolition bills by very small margins,[121] Some states considered abolition an experiment, which many people thought was failing.[122] Lynching played a major role in at least four states. State officials began to believe that vigilante violence was a reaction to the death penalty's abolition and that without capital punishment lynchings were bound to occur. In those states, many state officials considered the death penalty the lesser of two evils.[123] Another factor that has been used to explain the death penalty's reinstatement during this period is the post-World War I economic depression. During this time there were frequent complaints about job shortages and the threat of unemployed workers.[124] Punitive attitudes toward criminals tend to increase during periods of economic hardship.[125] The economic recession also exacerbated the fear of minorities. Three of the states that restored the death penalty (Tennessee, Arizona, and Missouri) had the largest minority populations, while two of the states that did not reinstate the death penalty (South Dakota and Minnesota) had the smallest non-white populations.[126]

In the South, the white establishment undoubtedly used the death penalty to terrify and subdue the black population. As the seventeenth century English philosopher John Locke noted early on, Political power is "a right of making laws with penalties of death."[127] Most of the capital crimes in the southern states at the beginning of the Civil War remained capital crimes for nearly a century, long after they had been removed from the penal codes of the northern states.[128] For example, as of 1954, rape was a capital crime in 18 states, 16 of them in the South; robbery was a capital crime in nine states, eight of them in the South; arson was a capital crime in five states, all of them in the South, and burglary was a capital crime in four states, again all of them in the South.[129] Persons executed for those crimes were overwhelmingly black. For example, between 1870 and 1950, 701 of the 771 people (whose race was known) executed for rape were black; 31 of the 35 executed for robbery were black; and 18 of the 21 executed for burglary were black.[130] Although the racial disparity was smaller for those executed for murder, blacks still outnumbered whites.[131] Also, augmenting capital punishment in the South was lynching, which reached its peak in the late nineteenth and early twentieth centuries.[132] At its zenith, lynchings outnumbered executions: 82 to 6 during the 1870s and 92 to 40 during the 1890s.[133] The last public mass lynching in the United States occurred in northeast Georgia in 1946.[134]

Finally, it has been argued that the reinstatement of capital punishment during this period was at least partly the result of a media-inspired panic about the threat of revolution.[135] The Russian Revolution occurred in 1917, the same year the United States entered World War I. Just before the war, the United States had experienced intense class conflict as socialists, and especially the IWW or Industrial Workers of the World ("Wobblies"), increased in number and mounted the first serious challenge to capitalist dominance.[136] Within this frenzied atmosphere, a crime in 1920 involving two foreign anarchists received unprecedented worldwide media coverage. Nicola Sacco and Bartolomeo Vanzetti maintained their innocence but nevertheless were convicted of a robbery and murder. They were electrocuted in 1927. Surrounding circumstances and the trial record suggest that Sacco and Vanzetti were indeed innocent, and that they were sentenced to death because they were anarchists and foreigners.[137] According to at least one observer, the threat of the death penalty has been used to terrify and subdue dissidents,[138] and that may have been a motivating factor in the case against Sacco and Vanzetti.

The death penalty abolitionist movement fell on hard times during Prohibition and the Great Depression (roughly 1920 to 1940). Only the determined efforts of members of the American League to Abolish Capital Punishment, founded in 1925, and a few high-profile abolitionists, such as attorney Clarence Darrow, newspaper publisher William Randolph Hearst, industrialist Henry Ford, and Lewis E. Lawes, the abolitionist warden of New York's Sing Sing State Prison, kept the movement alive.[139] Death penalty abolitionists also received unexpected support from Franklin D. Roosevelt, who, during his first term as president, publicly expressed his opposition to capital punishment.[140]

Despite the efforts of determined abolitionists, more capital offenders were executed during the 1930s than in any other decade in American history; the average was 167 executions per year.[141] The most executions in any single year occurred in 1935 when 199 offenders were put to death.[142] This was a dramatic reversal from earlier in the century when the number of executions fell from 161 in 1912 to 65 in 1919. The 65 executions in 1919 were the fewest in 50 years.[143] Furthermore, of the 10 states that abolished capital punishment for all crimes after 1850, only three—Minnesota, Maine, and Wisconsin—had not restored the death penalty entering the 1950s.[144] No state abolished the death penalty between 1918 and 1957. In contrast, after World War II, most of the advanced western European countries abolished the death penalty or severely restricted its use. Great Britain did not join them until 1969.[145]

The Death Penalty from 1950 to 1972

Beginning in the 1950s, partly as a result of the lingering horrors of World War II and the movement by many allied nations either to abolish the death penalty or to restrict its use, the number of executions in the United States began to drop precipitously—from 1,289 in the 1940s to 715 during the 1950s[146]—and there were only 191 executions from 1960 through 1976.[147] The American abolitionist movement was able to claim some modest achievements in the late 1950s. Besides resurrecting debate in some state legislatures, the (then) territories of Alaska and Hawaii abolished the death penalty in 1957.[148] Delaware did the same in 1958, only to reinstate it three years later in 1961.[149] However, the degree to which these victories can be attributed directly to the efforts of death penalty abolitionist organizations themselves is questionable.[150] To be sure, abolitionists such as Sara Ehrmann, Donal MacNamara, Hugo Bedau, and Doug Lyons worked tirelessly for the cause during this period, but they did so more as individuals than members of strong and effective death penalty organizations.[151] The fact is that death penalty abolitionist organizations during this period and, for that matter, throughout history, have been largely impotent primarily because of a lack of funding. It is hard to raise money for a cause that benefits one of the most despised groups in society whose media images are overwhelmingly negative.[152] The drive to abolish the death penalty in the 1960s was spearheaded by the American Civil Liberties Union (ACLU) and, especially, the NAACP Legal Defense and Educational Fund (LDF), neither of which was a death penalty abolitionist organization. Thus, Professor Haines attributes death penalty abolitionism during this period more to the civil rights movement (because of the lead of LDF attorneys) than to prior death penalty abolitionist efforts.[153] (More about the role of the LDF later.) Also during the 1950s, because of the extraordinary media attention devoted to them, two cases in particular influenced the ways in which many Americans viewed capital punishment. What is interesting is that the two cases had very different effects. The Rosenberg case, involving alleged treason, seemed to influence the public toward favoring capital punishment. The Chessman case, on the other hand, had the opposite and, for the time, the more sustained effect.

The Case of Ethel and Julius Rosenberg. Ethel and Julius Rosenberg were prosecuted for espionage during the summer of 1950 in an atmosphere of anti-Communist hysteria,[154] allegedly having given atomic bomb secrets to Soviet agents. Their guilt, and especially the evidence against them, continues to be the subject of much debate. There was a worldwide campaign of protest following their convictions. Among the notables who championed their cause were Albert Einstein, Jean-Paul Sartre, Pablo Picasso, and the sister of Bartolomeo Vanzetti. Appeals to both President Truman, just before he left office in 1953, and President Eisenhower were turned down. At the last moment, Supreme Court Justice Douglas granted a stay of execution, and Chief Justice Vinson sent out special jets to return the vacationing justices to Washington. The full Court canceled Douglas's stay, and the Rosenbergs were executed on June 19, 1953.

The paradox of the Rosenberg executions is reflected in American death penalty opinion of 1953. Between the first and fifth of November, 1953, Gallup queried the public about the death penalty for the first time in 16 years.[155] Results of the poll indicated that 70 percent of Americans favored the death penalty, 29 percent opposed it, and 1 percent had no opinion. The 70 percent figure was the highest level of support for the death penalty in the United States to that date, and it remained the highest level until the 1980s. To what extent the Rosenberg executions influenced that opinion can only be speculated. What seems clear is that the executions did not generate immediate and overwhelming sympathy for the Rosenbergs or have a dampening effect on American death penalty opinion.

The Case of Caryl Chessman. The decade-long case of Caryl Chessman began in 1948 when, at age 26, he was convicted on 17 counts, including robbery, kidnapping, sexual abuses, and attempted rape. Under California's "Little Lindbergh" law, capital punishment was mandatory for kidnapping "with bodily harm."[156] Chessman was "self-taught in law" and defended himself. He admitted committing many crimes, but he denied guilt in the kidnappings for which he was sentenced to death.[157]

Chessman had an unusually long stay on death row, due to the death penalty post-conviction process. A relatively large segment of the public found this well-publicized experience with capital punishment objectionable and turned against the death penalty.

For purposes of this account, Chessman's story begins on May 3, 1954, a day that held both good and bad news for him. The good news was that his book, *Cell 2544, Death Row*, was published. The book was the first of four and would receive critical acclaim, become a best seller (more than 500,000 copies sold), be translated into many languages, and bring to Chessman's situation unprecedented worldwide attention. The bad news was that California Governor Goodwin J. Knight denied Chessman a reprieve from his execution, scheduled for May 14.[158] The day before he was scheduled to die in San Quentin's gas chamber, however, Chessman won a writ of habeas corpus "on grounds that a false transcript of his first trial had been presented to an appeals court."[159] A writ of habeas corpus claims that a federal constitutional right has been violated and, thus, the claimant is being held illegally.[160] The writ was subsequently denied, and Chessman was rescheduled to die on July 30. The day before this execution, to allow the U.S. Supreme Court the opportunity to act on Chessman's petition for a writ of review, California Supreme Court Justice Jesse W. Carter granted him a stay.

On March 3, 1955, San Quentin Warden Harley O. Teets impounded the manuscript of Chessman's second prison-written book, *Trial by Ordeal*. Teets charged that Chessman violated regulations when he attempted to send the book out of the prison without official clearance.[161] The book nevertheless was published by Prentice-Hall on July 11.[162] Criminologist Robert Johnson relates that the book was a study of "the media distortion of capital offenders, particularly of the type likely to enrage decent citizens."[163] Chessman was "branded the 'Red Light Bandit' during his lengthy tenure on San Quentin's death row, [and] he summarized [in the book] the public image of the condemned fostered by sensationalist journalism."[164]

The Supreme Court granted Chessman a new hearing in San Francisco's U.S. District Court on October 17, 1955. The Court ruled five to three that "Chessman's plea that his 1948 trial records had been 'fraudulently prepared' should not have been summarily dismissed."[165] Nearly a year later, on November 22, 1956, to prevent the setting of an execution date and to allow Chessman to make another appeal to the U.S. Supreme Court, the U.S. Circuit Court of Appeals in San Francisco granted Chessman a stay of mandate.[166]

State authorities had banned Chessman's writing for publication.[167] When a manuscript of his third book, *The Face of Justice*, was found in his cell on February 14, 1957, Chessman, then 35, was placed in solitary confinement. Another copy of the manuscript, however, was smuggled out of prison to his literary agent.

On April 8, 1957, the Supreme Court granted Chessman another hearing, to be held on May 13. This hearing would decide whether Chessman had been denied due process of law, as guaranteed by the Fourteenth Amendment, on the issue of his alleged fraudulent trial transcript. Then, on June 10, the U.S. Supreme Court granted him another stay of execution so that a lower court could review Chessman's lack of representation by an attorney at a Federal District Court hearing the previous year.[168] (That was the hearing to determine whether the state court records of his first trial were fraudulent.) Superior Judge Walter R. Evans ruled in Los Angeles on February 28, 1958, that the record of Chessman's original trial was "adequate for purposes of appeal," and Chessman lost his chance for a new trial on this issue.[169]

By the time Chessman lost another appeal to the U.S. Supreme Court for release on a writ of habeas corpus on April 6, 1959, his execution had been stayed six times, and he was running out of legal maneuvers.[170] On July 7, the California Supreme Court upheld the 11-year-old death verdict by denying his latest appeal for a rehearing, and on August 10, Chessman was ordered to die on October 23.[171] California Governor Edmund G. Brown rejected Chessman's plea for clemency four days before the scheduled execution.

It looked like the end of the line for Chessman, but he had not yet run out of luck. Two days before his execution, the U.S. Supreme Court granted his seventh stay to allow him to file a petition challenging the California Supreme Court's decision on July 7 to affirm his conviction.[172] On December 14, though, the Supreme Court, by an eight to zero vote, rejected that petition. The Court also dismissed a November 30 appeal for a new trial filed by psychiatrist Karl Menninger, writer Aldous Huxley, and 21 others. In Los Angeles, on December 21, Judge Herbert V. Walker ordered Chessman to be executed on February 19, 1960. It was Chessman's eighth execution order.[173]

On February 19, just 10 hours before Chessman was to die, Governor Brown gave Chessman, then 38, a 60-day reprieve. Brown's reasons for granting an eighth stay in 12 years were twofold. First, Brown had received a telegram from Assistant Secretary of State Roy R. Rubottom, Jr., relaying a Uruguayan government warning that if Chessman were executed, President Eisenhower might encounter hostile demonstrations there during his upcoming visit. Second, as a death penalty opponent, Brown wanted the state legislature to consider abolishing capital punishment in California.[174]

Brown's action was decried. Senator Clair Engle and others protested that "justice to an individual should be based on the facts of the case and 'not rest on international reaction'." But throughout the United States, Latin America, and Western Europe, opponents of the death penalty continued to protest on Chessman's behalf, and the Vatican newspaper, *L'Osservatore Romano*, pleaded for Chessman's life—but to no avail. Appeals for a stay of execution were rejected by U.S. Supreme Court Justice Hugo L. Black on February 13, the U.S. Circuit Court of Appeals in San Francisco on February 15, and the California Supreme Court on February 17-18.[175] Chessman was finally executed in the gas chamber at San Quentin on May 2, 1960.[176]

Denying his guilt to the end, Chessman won the support of death penalty opponents universally. Pleas to save his life were made not only by Menninger and Huxley, but also by Albert Schweitzer, Pablo Casals, Brigitte Bardot, and thousands of others.[177] The execution cost California around half-a-million dollars, and it prompted anti-United States demonstrations throughout the world.[178] Additionally, in each of Gallup's death penalty polls following Chessman's execution, the percentage of Americans in favor of the penalty declined (and the percentage opposed increased) until, in 1966, public support for capital punishment reached an all-time low of 42 percent.[179] In addition to the case of Caryl Chessman, the civil rights movements of the 1960s also helped galvanize abolitionist sentiment, as protests against the misuse of government authority continued to grow. Four states abolished the death penalty (Michigan, in 1963, for treason; Oregon, 1964; Iowa, 1965; and West Virginia, 1965), and two states (New York, 1965 and Vermont, 1965) sharply reduced the number of death-eligible crimes.[180] In 1965, alone, legislatures in twenty states debated bills to abolish the death penalty.[181]

Challenging the Legality of Capital Punishment. Although specific methods of execution had been legally challenged as early as 1890, and procedural issues before that, the fundamental legality of capital punishment itself was not subject to challenge until the 1960s.[182] It had long been argued that the Constitution or, more specifically, the Fifth Amendment, authorized capital punishment and that a majority of the framers of the Constitution did not object to it. The Fifth Amendment reads as follows:

> No person shall be held to answer for a *capital*, or otherwise infamous *crime*, unless on a presentment or indictment of a grand jury, except in cases arising in the land or naval forces, or in the militia, when in actual service in time of war or public danger; nor shall any person be subject for the same offense to be twice put in *jeopardy of life* or limb; nor shall be compelled in any criminal case to be a witness against himself, nor be *deprived of life*, liberty, or property, without due process of law, nor shall private property be taken for public use without just compensation (emphasis added).

The three explicit references to capital punishment in the amendment have not only been taken as prima facie evidence that the framers of the Constitution did not object to its use, but they also show that the framers expected it to be used because of the guidelines they provided (that is, "with due process of law").

Referral to capital punishment and the aforementioned guidelines is repeated in the Fourteenth Amendment, which was ratified shortly after the Civil War. The Fourteenth Amendment states in part:

> No State shall make or enforce any law which shall abridge the privileges or immunities of citizens of the United States; nor shall any State *deprive any person of life*, liberty, or property, without due process of law; nor deny to any person within its jurisdiction the equal protection of the laws (emphasis added).

Given such evidence, it made little sense to argue that capital punishment violated the Constitution. That conventional wisdom was challenged in 1961.

In an article published in the *University of Southern California Law Review*, Los Angeles antitrust lawyer Gerald Gottlieb, an affiliate with his local American Civil Liberties Union (ACLU) branch, suggested that "the death penalty was unconstitutional under the Eighth Amendment because it violated contemporary moral standards, what the U.S. Supreme Court in *Trop v. Dulles* (356 U.S. 86, 1958) referred to as 'the evolving standards of decency that mark the progress of a maturing society.'"[183] In *Trop* and in *Weems v. United States* (217 U.S. 349), the latter decided in 1910, the Court departed from the fixed or historical meaning it had always used in deciding whether a particular punishment was cruel and unusual in violation of the Eighth Amendment. The Court opined in *Weems* that the cruel and unusual punishment provision "would only offer paper, illusory protection if it was restricted solely to the intent of the Framers."[184] The Court consequently declared that the meaning of the Eighth Amendment is not limited by the Framers' intent, but that it changes with evolving social conditions—specifically, "the evolving standards of decency that mark the progress of a maturing society."[185] Neither *Trop* nor *Weems* were death penalty cases. Professor Gottlieb applied to the practice of capital punishment the Court's logic from two cases not concerned with the death penalty. The key question raised by Gottlieb's interpretation, of course, was whether the United States, in fact, had evolved or progressed to the point where standards of decency no longer permitted capital punishment.

Professor Gottlieb took an extreme position toward the death penalty, calling for its complete abolition. Most of the other attacks on the penalty during this period were more moderate, seeking only its reform. A 1961 *University of Texas Law Review* article by Professor Walter Oberer criticized the common practice of "death qualifying," a process that eliminates death penalty opponents from capital juries.[186] Professor Oberer argued that death qualification "purged the jury of its more compassionate members and produced a homogenous jury more likely to convict."[187]

Also, in 1961, in a speech delivered at Villanova Law School, Supreme Court Justice Tom Clark voiced his opposition to capital punishment.

Such a public declaration by a sitting justice was not unprecedented. Robert Jackson had done it in 1946 and Felix Frankfurter did it in 1948 and again in 1950.[188] Politicians were also expressing their opposition to the death penalty. In the 1960s, there was not much political liability to taking a principled public stand against capital punishment.[189]

Two years before the Gottlieb and Oberer articles were published, in 1959, drafters of the American Law Institute's Model Penal Code suggested two legal reforms in the way capital punishment was administered.[190] The first was a bifurcated (two–part) trial consisting of a guilt phase, where guilt or innocence was the principal issue to be determined, and a penalty phase, where the imposition of either a life or death sentence was the sole issue. California had implemented such a trial process in 1957; the only other states to have split trials by the early 1960s were Connecticut, New York, Pennsylvania, and Texas.[191] The second reform was the use of enumerated aggravating and mitigating circumstances to guide and restrict the sentencing authority's (judge or jury) discretion during the penalty phase of the bifurcated trial. Both of those procedural reforms would later be incorporated into the new, that is, post-*Furman*, death penalty statutes (examined in detail in Chapter 2).

Problems with the administration of capital punishment had long been a focus of attack by death penalty opponents, but they were also a source of consternation to proponents of the penalty who wanted it "done right." By the 1960s, some reform in the process of putting capital offenders to death seemed necessary, as at least three members of the Supreme Court agreed. In a rare published dissent from a denial of certiorari in Alabama and Virginia rape cases, *Rudolph v. Alabama* and *Snider v. Cunningham*, 375 U.S. 889 (1963) (hereafter referred to as the *Rudolph* case), Justice Arthur Goldberg, joined by Justices Brennan and Douglas, suggested that the entire Court ought to determine whether or not the death penalty for a rapist who has not taken a life was unconstitutional under the Eighth Amendment.[192] (A writ of certiorari is an order from a higher court to a lower court whose decision is being appealed to send the records of the case forward for review. It is a dominant avenue to the U.S. Supreme Court.)

Rudolph's attorneys chose not to challenge the constitutionality of capital punishment for rape, but Justice Goldberg felt compelled to comment, anyway. In his written dissent from the certiorari denial, he posed three questions he thought the Court should address:

1. "In light of the trend both in this country and throughout the world against punishing rape by death, does the imposition of the death penalty by those States which retain it for rape violate 'evolving standards of decency that mark the progress of [our] maturing society,' or 'standards of decency more or less universally accepted?'"

2. "Is the taking of human life to protect a value other than human life consistent with the constitutional proscription against 'punishments which by their excessive . . . severity are greatly disproportioned to the offenses charged?'"

3. "Can the permissible aims of punishment (e.g., deterrence, isolation, rehabilitation) be achieved as effectively by punishing rape less severely than by death (e.g., by life imprisonment); if so, does the imposition of the death penalty for rape constitute 'unnecessary cruelty?'" [193]

Goldberg's position in *Rudolph* was part of a broader strategy to get his colleagues on the Court to either restrict the death penalty or abolish it.[194] He personally considered the death penalty an abomination, maintaining that it was applied arbitrarily, haphazardly, capriciously, and in a discriminatory way against disadvantaged minorities.[195] In the summer of 1963, less than a year after he joined the Court, he asked his new law clerk, Alan Dershowitz, who later would become a Harvard law professor, to research precedent to support an argument that the death penalty constituted cruel and unusual punishment in violation of the Eighth Amendment. With Dershowitz's help, Goldberg prepared and circulated a memorandum imploring his fellow justices to grant a review of six pending death penalty appeals (four murders and two rapes) so that they could rule on the death penalty's constitutionality. Unfortunately, for Goldberg, a majority of the Court was not prepared for such a drastic move.[196] Chief Justice Earl Warren was particularly irate because he believed the memorandum, if published, would turn the public against the Court and jeopardize its desegregation decisions.[197] If not for that, Warren probably would have been sympathetic to a review of the death penalty. He revealed after his retirement in 1968 that he had been repulsed by the death penalty all his life.[198] Even Justices Brennan and Douglas, who joined Goldberg in the *Rudolph* dissent, did not vote to review the cases.[199] Thus, Goldberg's ruminations in *Rudolph* had little immediate effect, but they did hearten a small group of abolitionist lawyers with the NAACP Legal Defense and Educational Fund (LDF) by suggesting that the Supreme Court might be ready at a later date to consider the constitutionality of the death penalty for rape where the victim does not die. For the LDF lawyers it seemed the appropriate time to begin preparing for a test case on the matter.[200]

The NAACP Legal Defense and Educational Fund, founded in 1939 by the National Association for the Advancement of Colored People, is a coalition of lawyers, clients, staff, consultants, and expert advisors that had as its original goals to dismantle racial segregation and attack racial discrimination in the United States through the courts.[201] It played a major role in the black civil rights movement of the 1950s and 1960s by winning challenges to protective covenants that segregated neighborhoods by race and the segregation of public schools from elementary schools to universities.[202] From 1940 until 1961, future U.S. Supreme Court Justice Thurgood Marshall headed the Fund. When John F. Kennedy appointed him to the U.S. Court of Appeals for the Second Circuit in 1961, Marshall handed off the reins of the Fund to Jack Greenberg, a white man who received his law degree from Columbia Law School.[203]

Fund lawyers turned their attention to the death penalty in the 1960s primarily because of the racially discriminatory way it was being administered. Later, however, when they began accepting clients actually facing execution, they realized that they needed to raise issues having nothing to do with race. With this change in focus, there was no longer any reason not to take on the cases of white death row inmates, too, so they did.[204] In attempting to achieve judicial abolition of the penalty, Fund lawyers Michael Meltsner, Frank Heffner, and LeRoy Clark plotted a general strategy to convince the Court that the death penalty was employed in a discriminatory way against minorities and to otherwise block all executions by challenging the legal procedures employed in capital cases (the "moratorium strategy").[205] If successful, their plan would accomplish three goals. First, it would make those who were still executed appear to be unlucky losers in a death penalty lottery. Second, if the death penalty were used only rarely, it would show that the penalty was not really needed for society's protection. Third, if all executions were blocked, the resulting logjam of death row inmates would lead to an inevitable bloodbath if states ever began emptying their death rows by executing en masse. The LDF lawyers did not believe the country could stomach the gore and would demand abolition of the penalty.[206] The Fund's ambitious plan would be very expensive but fortunately for the Fund attorneys and other cooperating lawyers, Greenberg was able to use a million dollar grant from the Ford Foundation to help finance the project.[207] In 1967, Greenberg appointed Jack Himmelstein, a 26-year-old Harvard Law School graduate, to manage the capital project.[208]

The intellectual leader and "front man" of the capital project was Anthony G. Amsterdam. Amsterdam had become acquainted with the LDF lawyers at a 1963 conference where he lectured about the legal defense of civil rights demonstrators. Amsterdam had graduated from the University of Pennsylvania Law School in 1960 and was the first non-Harvard Law School graduate to clerk for U.S. Supreme Court Justice Felix Frankfurter.[209] In 1961, he served as an Assistant United States Attorney in the District of Columbia and, in 1962, he joined the faculty of the University of Pennsylvania Law School.[210] Amsterdam has been described as "a man of rare intelligence and force" and as "a well-programmed legal computer"—a "lawyer's lawyer."[211] He served as an "advisor-at-large" to hundreds of civil rights and civil liberties lawyers, was involved in lawsuits and projects supported by the American Civil Liberties Union, the Lawyer's Committee for Civil Rights Under Law, and the Lawyer's Constitutional Defense Fund, and served as a consultant to the American Law Institute, the President's Commission on Law Enforcement and Administration of Justice (the National Crime Commission), the National Advisory Commission on Civil Disorders (the Kerner Commission), and the American Bar Association—to name a few.[212] He became an LDF consultant after 1963 and between 1965 and 1972 managed the LDF's growing docket of capital cases.[213] From 1963 until 1972, Amsterdam and/or LDF attorneys represented more than 300 death-row inmates.[214] Amsterdam and Himmelstein's first joint project for the LDF was the creation of a "how-to" manual dubbed the "Last Aid Kit." The "Kit" included petitions for habeas corpus, applications for stays of execution, and legal briefs that contained every significant constitutional argument against the death penalty—everything a lawyer would need to present to a court to postpone an execution. The "Kit" was distributed to hundreds of lawyers.[215]

The defendant selected for the LDF's first test case was William L. Maxwell, a 22–year–old black man who in 1961 was charged in Arkansas with the rape of a white woman.[216] Maxwell was convicted of the crime and sentenced to die the following year. His initial appeal to the Arkansas Supreme Court claimed that there was a pattern of racial discrimination in the way Arkansas juries handled rape cases. The appeal was denied. Maxwell's attorney, with the help of LDF lawyers, then drafted a writ of habeas corpus for review by the federal courts. In each of the courts—first the U.S. District Court, then the Court of Appeals for the Eighth Circuit, and, finally, the U.S. Supreme Court—the writ was rejected. This all occurred during 1964 and 1965.

In 1966, a second writ of habeas corpus was presented to the U.S. District Court on Maxwell's behalf and, this time, the court agreed to a hearing. Although his lawyers were able to show, using social scientific evidence, that there was a pattern of racial discrimination in death cases for rape in some Arkansas counties, the result was the same. The court rejected all of Maxwell's claims and refused his request for a stay of execution. The court's ruling was affirmed by the Court of Appeals for the Eighth Circuit. Maxwell, however, was not finished. In 1967, he won a stay of execution from the U.S. Supreme Court, and the Court sent the case back to the Eighth Circuit appellate court for further review. In 1968, the appellate court again denied Maxwell's claim and upheld his death sentence.[217]

Still, Maxwell persevered. In 1968, Maxwell petitioned the U.S. Supreme Court a third time, and the Court agreed to hear arguments about Arkansas's lack of guidleines in jury sentencing and its single-verdict procedure. Amsterdam and his LDF team of Jack Greenberg, James M. Nabrit III, Michael Meltsner, and Elizabeth DuBois, wrote the brief, and Amsterdam argued the cause on March 4, 1969. Following oral arguments, the Court voted 8-to-1 to declare Arkansas's death penalty unconstitutional, but the decision was never announced and no one outside the Court knew of it.[218] Because of unusual circumstances (the unexpected resignation of Justice Abe Fortas on May 14, 1969, and the retirement of Chief Justice Earl Warren that June), the Court ordered *Maxwell v. Bishop* to be reargued at the beginning of the next term on October 13, 1969.[219] The reargument, however, was postponed until May 4, 1970, when President Richard Nixon had trouble getting his first two nominees to replace Fortas confirmed. The Senate rejected both Clement Haynsworth, chief judge of the Fourth U.S. Circuit Court of Appeals, and G. Harrold Carswell, a U.S. District Court judge from Tallahassee, Florida. The Senate finally confirmed Nixon's third nominee for the post, Judge Harry A. Blackmun of the Eighth U.S. Circuit Court of Appeals. However, Blackmun had written the Eighth Circuit's opinion in *Maxwell v. Bishop*, so he could not sit on the case as a Supreme Court justice. Thus, the Court was left with only eight justices to decide *Maxwell*.[220]

One of the consequences of the Maxwell case, as well as two other death penalty cases decided by the Supreme Court in 1968 (*Witherspoon v. Illinois* and *United States v. Jackson*—both discussed in the next chapter), was the unofficial suspension of all executions until some of the more problematic issues with the death penalty could be resolved. The last execution in the United States was held in June of 1967, when Luis Jose Monge was executed in Colorado's gas chamber.[221] The moratorium on executions would last 10 years until 1977, when Gary Gilmore requested to be executed by the state of Utah (more about this in Chapter 4).

Conclusion

William Maxwell's fate was finally determined by the U.S. Supreme Court on June 1, 1970 (*Maxwell v. Bishop*, 398 U.S. 262). The Court, however, did not directly address Maxwell's principal claim that racial discrimination on the part of jurors, who had total discretion in the sentencing decision, infected death cases for rape in at least some Arkansas counties. Instead, the Court vacated Maxwell's death sentence on the more narrow grounds that several prospective jurors in Maxwell's case were improperly removed during voir dire because of their general opposition to the death penalty. As for the problem of juror discretion and, presumably, the racial discrimination that it sometimes allowed, the Court, in footnote four of the *Maxwell* decision, announced that it would address that issue early in the 1970 term. The Court had already granted certiorari in the two test cases: *Crampton v. Ohio* and *McGautha v. California*. What the Court could not know at this time was that it was embarking on a road that would eventually lead to the complete abolition of capital punishment in the United States.

Discussion Questions

1. What general lessons can be learned from the history of the death penalty in the United States?

2. Should religion play as large a role in capital punishment as it did in colonial America? Why or why not?

3. Should the death penalty be reserved primarily for adult men? Why or why not?

4. Why do people oppose capital punishment? How could they be so wrong?

5. Why do people support capital punishment? How could they be so wrong?

6. Should the public be allowed to view executions? Should executions be televised? Why or why not?

7. Which are fairer: mandatory or discretionary death penalty laws? Why?

8. Should executions be carried out in the local jurisdictions where capital defendants are convicted and sentenced or at some other location in the state? Defend your answer.

9. Is the threat of the death penalty in the United States used to terrify and subdue political dissidents? Explain.

10. Why is the United States the only western industrialized nation to routinely employ capital punishment?

11. What can be learned from the cases of Ethel and Julius Rosenberg and Caryl Chessman?

12. Do you agree or disagree with Professor Gottlieb's argument that the death penalty is unconstitutional under the Eighth Amendment if it violates contemporary moral standards, or "the evolving standards of decency that mark the progress of a maturing society"? Why?

13. Is the death penalty inappropriate for rape? Why or why not?

Notes

[1] Espy and Smykla, 1987.
[2] Vila and Morris, 1997:8–9; Bedau, 1982:7.
[3] Exodus 21.12; Numbers 35.13, 14, 30, 31 (cited in Vila and Morris, ibid., p. 8).
[4] Bedau, op. cit., p. 7.
[5] Ibid.

[6] Vila and Morris, op. cit., p. 8; Thompson, 1975:22–23; Bedau, op. cit., p. 6; for the 200 number, see Banner, 2002:7.

[7] Banner, ibid., pp. 6-7.

[8] Filler, 1967:105.

[9] See, for example, Banner, op. cit.

[10] Ibid., p. 14-15.

[11] Ibid., p. 17.

[12] Ibid.

[13] Ibid., pp. 18-19.

[14] Ibid., p. 19.

[15] Ibid., pp. 19-20.

[16] Ibid., p. 24.

[17] Ibid.

[18] Ibid., p. 25 and 27.

[19] Ibid., p. 28.

[20] Ibid., p. 33-34.

[21] Ibid., p. 34-35.

[22] Ibid., p. 35.

[23] Ibid., pp. 22-23.

[24] Espy and Smykla, op. cit.

[25] Ibid.

[26] Ibid.

[27] Updated from personal correspondence.

[28] Bedau, op. cit., p. 3.

[29] Schneider and Smykla, 1991:6, Table 1.1.

[30] Streib, 2006.

[31] Schneider and Smykla, op. cit., p. 14.

[32] Ibid., Table 1.7.

[33] Ibid., p. 14.

[34] Schwarz, 1999.

[35] Streib, 2002.

[36] Streib, 2005.

[37] Streib, 1989:39.

[38] Streib, 1988:251.

[39] Streib, 1989. op. cit., p. 39.

[40] Schneider and Smykla, op. cit., p. 15.

[41] Bedau, op. cit., p. 13.

[42] Filler, op. cit.

[43] Gorecki, 1983:85; also see Filler, op. cit., p. 106.

[44] Filler, op. cit., p. 105; but see Kania, 1999 for a different view of the social contract.

[45] Ancel, 1967:5–6.

[46] Banner, op. cit., p. 88.

[47] Bedau, op. cit., p. 13; Ralph, 1996:413.

[48] Filler, op. cit., p. 106.

[49] See Grimes, 1996:494; Bedau, op. cit.

[50] Paternoster, 1991:6; Filler, op. cit., p. 107.

[51] Filler, op. cit., pp. 106–107.

[52] Bedau, op. cit., p. 4; Bowers, 1984:7; Banner, op. cit., p.98; Hood, 2002:9.

53 Banner, op. cit., p. 98.

54 Ibid., pp. 98-99.

55 Ibid., p. 99.

56 Ibid.

57 Ibid.

58 Ibid., pp. 107-108.

59 Ibid., p. 100-101.

60 Ibid., p. 110.

61 Ibid., pp. 106-107.

62 Schneider and Smykla, op. cit., p. 6, Table 1.1.

63 Banner, op. cit., p. 131.

64 Ibid.

65 Ibid.

66 Ibid.

67 Bedau, op. cit., p. 21.

68 Atwell, 2004:3.

69 Haney, 2005:101-102; Vila and Morris, op. cit., pp. 62-65. Apparently, Greeley and other abolitionists did not consider what effect those dismissals would have on the verdicts of the jurors who remained.

70 Filler, op. cit., p. 112.

71 Banner, op. cit., p. 146.

72 Ibid., p. 152-153.

73 Ibid.

74 Ibid., p. 148.

75 Ibid., p. 149.

76 Banner, op. cit., p. 154. There is some discrepancy about the first state to ban public executions, Banner cites Connecticut, in 1830, while Bowers, 1984: 8 and Filler, op. cit., p. 109, cite Pennsylvania in 1834.

77 Banner, ibid.

78 Banner, op. cit., pp. 146 and 154.

79 See, for example, *Holden v. Minnesota*, 137 U.S. 483 (1890).

80 See, for example, *In re Medley* [Colorado], 134 U.S. 160 (1890); *Holden v. Minnesota*, 137 U.S. 483 (1890).

81 Banner, op. cit., p. 25.

82 Bedau, op. cit., p. 13. Some controversy surrounds this issue. Author Perry Ryan contends that the last public execution took place not in Galena, Missouri, in 1937 but in Owensboro, Kentucky, in 1936. Perry reasons that because a stockade was built around the scaffold in Galena, Missouri, to keep children out and adults had to get tickets from the sheriff (they were free to any adult who wanted one), the execution in Galena, Missouri, was not truly a public one. Banner (2002:156) cites Perry and writes that the last person publicly executed in the U.S. was Rainey Bethea in Owensboro, Kentucky, in 1936. Criminologist Robert Johnson claims that there were public executions in Mississippi in the 1940s (1990:19). Former Mississippi Prison Warden Don Cabana corroborates Johnson's claim that the last public execution in Mississippi was held in the late 1940s. Cabana adds that the condemned was strapped into the portable electric chair set up in the Jackson County courthouse. Anyone who could get into the courtroom could view the execution (Personal communication, September 29, 2005).

83 Bowers, ibid.; Denno, 1994:564.

[84] Banner, op. cit., p. 162.

[85] Ibid.

[86] Ibid., pp. 163-164.

[87] Ibid., pp. 164-165.

[88] Ibid., p. 166.

[89] Ibid., pp. 214-215, see endnote 14.

[90] Ibid, p. 215.

[91] Ibid.

[92] Ibid.

[93] Garner, 2000:694.

[94] Banner, op. cit., p. 208.

[95] Ibid., p. 214.

[96] Ibid.

[97] Ibid., pp. 208-211.

[98] Ibid., p. 217.

[99] Ibid.; Acker and Lanier, op. cit.

[100] Ibid., p. 85.

[101] Bedau, op. cit., p. 21; Bowers, op. cit., p. 9; Filler, op. cit., p. 113.

[102] Galliher et al., 2002:11.

[103] Ibid., pp. 11-12.

[104] Ibid., pp. 12-14.

[105] Bedau, ibid.; Bowers, ibid.; Galliher et al., 2002, op. cit.; Hood (2002:9) writes that Rhode Island retained the death penalty for murder of a prison guard by a convict serving a life sentence.

[106] Banner, op. cit., p. 131.

[107] Ibid., p. 132; Gorecki, op. cit., p. 86.

[108] Bowers, op. cit., p. 10.

[109] Ibid.

[110] Bedau, op. cit., p. 24.

[111] Bowers, op. cit., pp. 43 and 50.

[112] Ibid., pp. 54-55.

[113] Zinn, 1990:341.

[114] For one of the most comprehensive examinations of the history of capital punishment in a single state (Texas, 1923-1990), see Marquart et al., 1994.

[115] Bedau, op. cit., p. 23, Table 1-2; Bowers, op. cit., p. 10.

[116] Banner, op. cit., pp. 222-223.

[117] Bedau, op. cit., p. 23, Table 1-2; Bowers, op. cit., p. 10.

[118] Galliher et al., 1992:559.

[119] Ibid.

[120] Ibid., p. 574.

[121] Ibid.

[122] Ibid.

[123] Ibid.

[124] Ibid., p. 575.

[125] See Rusche and Kirchheimer, 1968; Rothman, 1980.

[126] Galliher et al., op. cit.

[127] Locke, 1988:268.

[128] Banner, op. cit., p. 228.

[129] Ibid., pp. 228-229.

[130] Ibid., p. 230.

[131] Ibid.

[132] Ibid.

[133] Ibid.

[134] Haines, 2006.

[135] See, for example, Filler, op. cit., p. 119; Galliher et al., op. cit.

[136] Zinn, op. cit., p. 350.

[137] Ibid., p. 367.

[138] Ancel, op. cit., pp. 13-14.

[139] See Filler, op. cit., pp. 119-20; Banner, op. cit., p. 224; Haines, 1996, op. cit., pp. 10-11.

[140] Banner, op. cit., p. 224.

[141] Schneider and Smykla, op. cit., p. 7; Gorecki, op. cit., p. 92.

[142] Paternoster, op. cit., p. 10, Table 1-2.

[143] Banner, op. cit., p. 223.

[144] See Bedau, op. cit.

[145] Zimring and Hawkins, 1986:12.

[146] Schneider and Smykla, op. cit., p. 6, Table 1-1.

[147] Bedau, op. cit., p. 25, Table 1-3; Banner (2002:208) notes that the rate of executions had been declining since the 1880s.

[148] Bowers, op. cit., p. 10; Bedau, op. cit., p. 23, Table 1-2.

[149] Bowers, ibid.; Bedau, ibid.

[150] Haines, 1996, op. cit., p. 42.

[151] Ibid.

[152] Ibid., p. 43.

[153] Ibid.

[154] See Zinn, op. cit., pp. 424-426.

[155] See Bohm, 1991:116, Table 8.1.

[156] Facts on File, hereafter abbreviated FOF, 1961:156.

[157] FOF, ibid.; 1955:152.

[158] Ibid.

[159] FOF, 1955: 168.

[160] Bohm and Haley, 1997:234.

[161] FOF, 1956: 80.

[162] FOF, op, cit., p. 243.

[163] Johnson, 1989: 23. Chessman was arrested on suspicion of being Los Angeles's "Red Light Bandit"—a man who impersonated a police officer and used a red spotlight as he robbed couples parked at a "lovers' lane."

[164] Ibid.

[165] FOF, 1956: 345.

[166] FOF, 1957: 400.

[167] FOF, 1958: 60.

[168] Ibid., p. 192.

[169] FOF, 1959: 76.

[170] FOF, 1960: 123.

[171] Ibid., p. 308.

[172] Ibid., p. 348.

[173] Ibid., p. 439.

[174] Ibid., p. 68.

[175] Ibid.

[176] FOF, 1961: 156.

[177] Ibid.

[178] On the cost of the execution, see Bedau, 1982: 193 fn. 21; on the demonstrations, see FOF, ibid.

[179] See Bohm, op, cit.

[180] Bedau, op. cit., p. 23, Table 1-2.

[181] Banner, op. cit., p. 244.

[182] The challenges to specific methods of execution addressed whether such methods as electrocution violated the "cruel and unusual punishment" standard of the Eighth Amendment. See Chapter 2. For early procedural challenges, also see Chapter 2.

[183] Gottlieb, 1961; Paternoster, 1991:41; Meltsner, 1973:23.; Banner, op. cit., p. 248.

[184] Paternoster, ibid., p. 51.

[185] Ibid., p. 52.

[186] Paternosrer, ibid., p. 41; Meltsner, op. cit., p. 24.

[187] Paternoster, ibid.

[188] Banner, op. cit., pp. 238-239.

[189] Ibid., p. 241.

[190] Paternoster, ibid.; Meltsner, op. cit., p. 21.

[191] Meltsner, ibid., p. 109.

[192] Paernoster, ibid., p. 42; Meltsner, ibid., p. 28.

[193] *Rudolph v. Alabama*, 375 U.S. 889 (1963).

[194] Meltsner, op. cit., pp. 31-32.

[195] Meltsner, ibid., p. 32; Banner, op. cit., p. 248.

[196] Meltsner, ibid., pp. 32-33.

[197] Banner, op. cit., p. 250.

[198] Ibid., p. 239.

[199] Meltsner, op. cit., p. 33; Banner, ibid., p. 250.

[200] Meltsner, ibid., pp. 30 and 60. For a fascinating description of the "road to *Furman*" by one of the LDF lawyers who was there from the beginning, see Meltsner, 1973.

[201] Ibid.

[202] See Banner, op. cit., p. 247.

[203] Meltsner, op. cit.

[204] Banner, op. cit., pp. 251-252.

[205] Meltsner, op. cit., pp. 60 and 65-66.

[206] Ibid.

[207] Ibid., p. 109.

[208] Ibid., pp. 110-111.

[209] Ibid., pp. 78-79.

[210] Ibid., pp. 79-80.

[211] Ibid., p. 80.

[212] Ibid., pp. 83-84.

[213] Ibid., pp. 84-86.

[214] Ibid., pp. 85-86.

[215] Ibid., "About the Author."

[216] Ibid., p. 112.

[217] See Paternoster, ibid., pp. 42–45.

[218] Banner, op. cit., p. 255. In *The Brethren* (1979:205-206), the authors wrote that the vote was 6 to 3, not 8 to 1.

[219] Meltsner, ibid., pp. 186-187.

[220] Ibid., pp. 186-197.

[221] Coyne and Entzeroth, 1994:95.

CHAPTER 2

Capital Punishment and the Supreme Court

For more than 150 years, the United States Supreme Court ("the Court") has exercised its responsibility to regulate capital punishment in the United States and its territories. The Court's authority is given in the U.S. Constitution, Article III, Section 1, and the Judiciary Act of September 24, 1789. Article III, Section 1 of the Constitution states, "The judicial Power of the United States, shall be vested in one supreme court, and in such inferior Courts as the Congress may from time to time ordain and establish." The Court was officially organized on February 2, 1790, and handed down it first opinion in 1792.[1]

The Court's appellate jurisdiction in death penalty cases originally derived from its power of judicial review. Judicial review refers to "a court's power to review the actions of other branches or levels of government; esp., the courts' power to invalidate legislative and executive actions as being unconstitutional."[2] Although the U.S. Constitution does not provide for it, there was precedent for judicial review before the Constitution was adopted. For example, prior to 1789, state courts had ruled against legislation that conflicted with state constitutions.[3] Moreover, many of the founding fathers expected the Court to engage in judicial review. For instance, in the *Federalist Papers*, both Alexander Hamilton and James Madison emphasized its importance. Hamilton wrote, "Through the practice of judicial review the Court ensured that the will of the whole people, as expressed in their Constitution, would be supreme over the will of a legislature, whose statutes might express only the temporary will of part of the people."[4] Madison averred, "Constitutional interpretation must be left to the reasoned judgment of independent judges rather than to the tumult and conflict of the political process."[5] He added, "If every constitutional question were to be decided by public political bargaining, the Constitution would be reduced to a battleground of competing factions, political passion and partisan spirit."[6] The Court's power of judicial review was formally confirmed in 1803, when Chief Justice John Marshall invoked it in *Marbury v. Madison* (5 U.S. 137). Marshall argued, "The Supreme Court's responsibility to overturn unconstitutional legislation was a necessary consequence of its sworn duty to uphold the Constitution. That oath could not be fulfilled any other way."[7] He famously asserted, "It is emphatically the province of the judicial department to say what the law is."[8]

The Court received additional review authority with the ratification of the Fourteenth Amendment in 1868. In part, the amendment reads as follows: "No State shall make or enforce any law which shall abridge the privileges or immunities of citizens of the United States, nor shall any State deprive any person of life, liberty, or property, without due process of law; nor deny to any person within its jurisdiction the equal protection of the laws." The main purpose of this "Civil War Amendment" was to extend all of the rights of citizenship to African Americans. Whether the Fourteenth Amendment extended the procedural safeguards described in the Bill of Rights to people charged with crimes at the state level was debatable. Before the passage of the amendment, the Bill of Rights applied only to people charged with federal crimes; individual states were not bound by its requirements. It was not until the 1960s that the Court began to selectively incorporate most of the procedural safeguards contained in the Bill of Rights and apply them to the states. Before then, many Supreme Court justices, perhaps a majority of them, did not believe that the Fourteenth Amendment applied the Bill of Rights to the states. There are at least three explanations for this state of affairs.[9] First, there is little evidence that supporters of the Fourteenth Amendment intended it to incorporate the Bill of Rights. Second, by 1937, a series of court decisions had established the precedent that the due-process clause of the Fourteenth Amendment did not require states to follow trial procedures mandated at the federal level by provisions in the Bill of Rights. The Court had held that due process was not violated if procedures followed in state courts were otherwise fair. Third, there was the states' rights issue. Because the administration of justice is primarily a state and local responsibility, many people resented what appeared to be unwarranted interference by the federal government in state and local matters. Indeed, the Constitution, for the most part, leaves questions about administering justice to the states, unless a state's procedure violates a fundamental principle of justice. This last qualification explains why some of the early appeals in state death penalty cases cited Fourteenth Amendment violations.

Finally, appellate jurisdiction has been conferred on the Court by various statutes under authority given Congress by the Constitution.[10] These statutes give appellate jurisdiction to the Court in cases appealed from federal courts of appeals, federal district courts in certain circumstances, and the high court of a state, providing the claim involves a federal law or the Constitution.

Pre–1968 Death Penalty Cases

With the appointment of Jack Himmelstein to manage the LDF's capital punishment project in 1967, the legal assault on the death penalty's constitutionality accelerated. In 1968, for the first time in American history, no one was executed. Thus began an unofficial moratorium on executions until some of the significant legal issues with the death penalty could be resolved. For these reasons, 1968 is a good place to demarcate the Court's decisions in capital punishment cases. Prior to 1968, none of the capital cases reviewed by the Court challenged the constitutionality of capital punishment, itself. That would come later.

A search of three Supreme Court decision databases—U.S. Supreme Court Center (www.justia.us), FindLaw (www.findlaw.com/casecode/supreme.html), and LexisNexis Academic (https://web.lexis-nexis.com/universe)—using the keywords of "death penalty," "capital punishment," "cruel and unusual punishment," and "execution," and the investigation of citations found in individual cases revealed 65 pre-1968 death penalty cases reviewed by the Court. However, while doing additional research for this book, other pre-1968 death penalty cases not included in the 65 were discovered. Therefore, the pre-1968 cases found must be considered only a subset of an unknown number of such cases. That said, it is probably safe to say that, compared to the number of post-1968 cases, the Court was relatively reticent when it came to interfering in the practice of capital punishment during the earlier period. Two additional points are worth noting. First, throughout its history, the Court has rejected as unworthy of review the vast majority of cases appealed to it. Appeals to the Court are heard at the discretion of the Court, in contrast to appeals to the U.S. circuit courts, which review cases as a matter of right. Second, there are many noncapital cases (i.e., cases that did not involve either a capital charge or a death sentence) that have influenced death penalty jurisprudence. None of the pre-1968 cases reviewed here are noncapital cases and only a very few of the post-1976 death penalty cases examined are.

The pre-1968 death penalty cases are grouped into categories and presented in chronological order within the categories. They provide a good summary of the types of death penalty issues that the Court was willing to address before 1968. The categories are: (1) clemency, (2) jurisdiction, (3) methods of execution, (4) ex post facto, (5) sentencing, (6) the Fifth Amendment (double jeopardy), (7) juries, and (8) the Fourteenth Amendment (equal protection and due process). Unless indicated otherwise, the case descriptions come from the court decisions.

Clemency. What were probably the first two death penalty cases reviewed by the Court involved clemency. In the case of *United States v. Wilson* (32 U.S. 150), decided by the Court in 1833, the issue was whether a capital defendant could refuse to accept a pardon. George Wilson and an accomplice had been indicted on six counts of robbing the U.S. mail and, in some of those counts, putting the life of the mail carrier in jeopardy. The U.S. attorney refused to prosecute three of the counts but proceeded on one of them. At the arraignment, both Wilson and his accomplice pleaded not guilty to the charges. They were subsequently tried, found guilty, and sentenced to death. Wilson's accomplice was executed about a month later. Following Wilson's sentencing, he withdrew his not guilty plea and pleaded guilty to all counts except those the U.S. attorney elected not to prosecute. Before Wilson's date with the executioner, President Andrew Jackson had received numerous petitions from respected citizens to grant Wilson executive clemency. Jackson pardoned Wilson stipulating that the pardon was only for the crime for which Wilson was sentenced to death. Jackson attached the condition knowing that Wilson could still be sentenced to twenty years imprisonment for the crimes for which he pleaded guilty and an even more severe punishment in the criminal courts of Pennsylvania.

At Wilson's subsequent sentencing hearing for a crime for which he changed his plea to guilty (that crime was on the same day, at the same place, and on the same carrier as the crime for which he was previously sentenced to death, except in the latter case the carrier's life was not put in jeopardy), the court asked Wilson whether he wanted to avail himself of his presidential pardon. The court was confused as to whether the crime before it was the same crime for which Wilson had received a pardon or a different crime. Wilson answered that he was not interested in using his pardon to avoid sentence in this particular case, presumably because it only could be punished by imprisonment and a fine. Wilson's response befuddled and divided the court, so it sought clarification from the Supreme Court. The Court ruled that if a defendant does not bring the fact of his or her pardon to the attention of the court by way of plea, motion, or otherwise, the court cannot recognize the pardon nor can it affect the judgment of law.

In *Ex parte Wells* (59 U.S. 307), decided in 1855, the issue was whether the President of the United States had the authority to grant conditional pardons or commutations as opposed to absolute pardons. The Court held that he did. The President's power of pardon is given in Article II, Section 2, of the United States Constitution. The relevant portion of which is: "The President . . . shall have the Power to grant Reprieves and Pardons for Offences against the United States, except in Cases of Impeachment." William Wells was convicted of murder in the District of Columbia in December 1851, and was sentenced to be hung on April 23, 1852. On the day of his scheduled execution, President Fillmore granted Wells a conditional pardon, commuting his death sentence to life imprisonment in the penitentiary in Washington. On the same day, Wells signed a document, witnessed by the jailer and warden, accepting the pardon with its condition. While in prison, Wells petitioned the

District of Columbia circuit court for a writ of habeas corpus, which was granted. After hearing the arguments of counsel, the circuit court upheld the President's power to commute Wells' death sentence to life imprisonment and ordered that Wells be remanded to the penitentiary. Wells then sought a writ of habeas corpus from the Court, which the Court granted, deciding to hear his claim as an appeal from the circuit court. Wells' attorney claimed that his client' pardon was absolute, the pardon's condition was null and void, and Wells was entitled to be discharged from prison. Wells' attorney reasoned

> . . . that a President granting such a [conditional] pardon assumes a power not conferred by the constitution—that he legislates a new punishment into existence, and sentences the convict to suffer it; in this way violating the legislative and judicial powers of the government, it being the province of the first, to enact laws for the punishment of offences against the United States, and that of the judiciary, to sentence convicts for violations of those laws, according to them.

The Court responded,

> We think this [interpretation] is a mistake arising from the want of due consideration of the legal meaning of the word pardon. It is supposed that it was meant to be used exclusively with reference to an absolute pardon, exempting a criminal from the punishment which the law inflicts for a crime he has committed. But such is not the sense or meaning of the word, either in common parlance or in law.

The Court affirmed the circuit court's refusal of Wells' application for the writ of habeas corpus and, in doing so, affirmed the President's right to grant conditional pardons or commutations to people convicted of federal offenses.

In *Biddle v. Perovich* (274 U.S. 480, 1927), the Court ruled that President Taft had the authority to commute Perovich's sentence from death to life imprisonment, without the defendant's consent.

Jurisdiction. The Court appears to have reviewed its third death penalty case, *Ex parte Milligan* (71 U.S. 2), in 1866. The issue before the Court in this case was the problem of military power over civilians. Lambdin P. Milligan was a Southern sympathizer living in Indiana as a civilian during the Civil War.[11] Milligan was a member of the "Copperheads," a northern political group that sought peace at any price, and was believed to be a member of a secret society known as the Order of American Knights or Sons of Liberty, whose purpose was "overthrowing the Government and duly constituted authorities of the United States." He was arrested by the military in 1864, and later that month a military commission tried him on five charges: (1) "Conspiracy against the Government of the United States"; (2) "Affording aid and comfort to rebels against the authority of the United States"; (3) "Inciting insurrection"; (4) "Disloyal practices"; and (5) "Violation of the laws of war." At trial, Milligan objected to the authority of the military commission to try him. The objection was overruled, the military commission found him guilty of all five charges, and sentenced him to death by hanging.

Milligan sought release from military custody through habeas corpus. Although President Lincoln had authorized such military tribunals during the Civil War, the Court held that trials of civilians by military commissions unauthorized by Congressional authority are unconstitutional in jurisdictions where the civil courts are operating constitutionally. Milligan could have been tried in a federal court in Indiana. The Court ordered that "Milligan was to be delivered from military custody and imprisonment, and if found probably guilty of any offence, to be turned over to the proper tribunal for inquiry and punishment; or, if not found thus probably guilty, to be discharged altogether." Milligan was released whereupon he sued the military for false imprisonment. He won the suit and was awarded five dollars in damages.[12]

Methods of Execution. The Eighth Amendment, which prohibits "cruel and unusual punishment," was not incorporated and made applicable to the states until 1962 (*Robinson v. California,* 370 U.S. 660). For that reason, in none of the pre–1968 cases (nor in any case since) was a particular execution method declared cruel and unusual by the U.S. Supreme Court.[13] Neither, as Law Professor Deborah Denno observes, did the Court review any evidence regarding whether a particular punishment was cruel and unusual.[14]

The first case involving the constitutionality of execution methods was *Wilkerson v. Utah* (99 U.S. 130, 1878), wherein the Court declared that shooting is not a cruel and unusual punishment. However, as Denno points out, the Court did not examine any evidence as to whether or not shooting was cruel because the plaintiff did not raise the issue. *Wilkerson* instead challenged the application of Utah's death penalty statute on the grounds that the statute did not specify the method of execution. The Court emphasized that for a punishment to be considered cruel and unusual in violation of the Eighth Amendment it had to involve torture or unnecessary cruelty, something that the Court apparently opined shooting did not.

Electrocution as a permissible form of execution was the subject of *In re Kemmler* (136 U.S. 436, 1890). Although admitting that electrocution was unusual, since it had never been used before, a unanimous Court decided that: "The punishment of death is not cruel, within the meaning of that word as used in the Constitution." The Court's decision specified what constitutes "cruelty" in connection with legal punishments. According to the Court, "punishments are cruel when they involve torture or lingering death. . . . [i]t implies there [is] something inhuman and barbarous, something more than the mere extinguishment of life." The Court also provided examples of punishments it would consider as manifestly cruel and unusual: "burning at the stake, crucifixion, breaking on the wheel, or the like."

In a related case, *Louisiana ex rel. Francis v. Resweber* (329 U.S. 459, 1947), the Court held that a second electrocution, conducted after the first one had failed to kill the defendant, is not in violation of the Eighth Amendment's prohibition. The case involved the botched execution of Willie Francis, a 16-year-old black youth sentenced to die in Louisiana's electric chair for the murder of a popular white druggist.[15] Francis was strapped into the state's portable electric chair, but when the switch was thrown, the device malfunctioned (it did not produce enough current) and death did not result. Francis was removed from the chair and returned to his prison cell. The chair was fixed and his execution rescheduled. Francis stated:

> [T]he experience was in all "plumb miserable." His mouth tasted "like cold peanut butter," and he saw "little blue and pink and green speckles." Added Francis: "I felt a burning in my head and my left leg, and I jumped against the straps."[16]

Francis challenged Louisiana's plan for a second attempt, arguing that it would constitute both torture and the degradation of a human being. The Court denied Francis's claim and maintained that the botched execution was "an unforeseeable accident," "an innocent misadventure," and unintentional on the part of the state—and therefore not a form of torture prohibited by the Eighth Amendment. Justice Burton dissented, seeming to agree with Francis that executing a person after a first attempt had failed was nothing less than imposing "death by installments."

Ex Post Facto. Ex post facto refers to having a retroactive effect. In a legal context, it (1) declares criminal an act that was not illegal when it was committed, (2) increases the punishment for a crime after it is committed, or (3) alters the rules of evidence in a particular case after the crime is committed. Although the first meaning of the term is the most common, the cases in this section involve the second meaning. Article I, Sections 9 and 10 of the U.S. Constitution forbid ex post facto laws.

In the case of *In re Medley* (134 U.S. 160, 1890), James J. Medley had been sentenced to death in Colorado for murdering his wife. He applied to the Court for a writ of habeas corpus, claiming the state's new death penalty law, enacted in 1889, varied substantially from the death penalty law in force at the time the crime was committed. He complained that the changes in the new law under which he was sentenced were prejudicial and injurious to him, and, therefore, ex post facto in violation of Article I, section 10 of the U.S. Constitution.

The Court addressed two of his complaints. The first dealt with the provision in the new statute that allowed the state of Colorado to hold Medley in solitary confinement pending his execution. On that issue, the Court held that holding Medley in solitary confinement "was an additional punishment of the most important and painful character," and is forbidden by the ex post facto provision of the United States Constitution. The second complaint addressed that part of the new statute that required

> the particular day and hour of the execution of the sentence within the week specified by the warrant shall be fixed by the warden, and he shall invite to be present certain persons named, to-wit, a chaplain, a physician, a surgeon, the spiritual adviser of the convict, and six reputable citizens of the state of full age, and that the time fixed by said warden for such execution shall be by him kept secret, and in no manner divulged except privately to said persons invited by him to be present as aforesaid, and such persons shall not divulge such invitation to any person or persons whomsoever, nor in any manner disclose the time of such execution; and . . . that any person who shall violate or omit to comply with the requirements of . . . the act shall be punished by fine or imprisonment.

The Court objected that under the new law the prisoner was "to be kept in utter ignorance of the day and hour when his mortal life [was to] be terminated by hanging, until the moment arrive[d] when this act [was] to be done." The Court ruled that this provision was "a departure from the law as it stood before," and was "an additional punishment to the prisoner [causing an immense mental anxiety], and therefore ex post facto." It added, "it confers upon the warden of the penitentiary a power which had heretofore been solely confided to the court and is therefore a departure from the law as it stood when the crime was committed." The Court concluded that Colorado's new death penalty statute, as applied to crimes committed before it came into force, violated the U.S. Constitution. It, therefore, ordered the release of Medley from his current sentence, warrant, and the custody of the warden of the Colorado penitentiary.

In *Rooney v. North Dakota* (196 U.S. 319, 1905), John Rooney, who had been convicted of murder during a robbery, complained of changes in North Dakota's new death penalty statute of 1903, that was enacted between the time he committed his crime and the verdict was rendered, and the time he was sentenced to death. Specifically, in the new law, "close confinement in the penitentiary for not less than six months and not more than nine months, after judgment and before execution, was substituted for confinement in the county jail for not less than three months nor more than six months after judgment and before execution." In addition, the new law substituted "hanging within an inclosure [sic] at the penitentiary, by the warden or his deputy. . . for hanging by the sheriff within the yard of the jail of the county in which the conviction occurred."

The Court ruled that the two changes in the new statute of which Rooney complained were "not repugnant to the constitutional provision declaring that no state shall pass an ex post facto law." The Court surmised that the provisions at issue "did not create a new offense, nor aggravate or increase the enormity of the crime for the commission of which the accused was convicted, nor require the infliction upon the accused of any greater or more severe punishment than was prescribed by law at the time of the commission of the offense." The substitution of close confinement in the penitentiary prior to execution for confinement in the county jail, the Court maintained, was immaterial. They both amounted to the same thing : "such custody, and only such custody, as [would] safely secure the production of the body of the prisoner on the day appointed for his execution." "Close confinement" was not "solitary confinement." The Court also believed that at least one of the changes in the law actually was favorable to Rooney. He was to receive three more months of life. Not only was that a benefit in its own right, the extra time gave Rooney additional opportunity to obtain a pardon or commutation from the governor.

In 1912, Joe Malloy was found guilty without a recommendation for mercy of a murder he committed in 1910. He was sentenced to die by electrocution under South Carolina's new death penalty statute of 1912. The state supreme court affirmed the judgment. In *Malloy v. South Carolina* (237 U.S. 180, 1915), Malloy sought a reversal on the ground that the new death penalty statute had materially changed the punishment for death, making his punishment ex post facto in violation of Article I, section 10 of the U.S. Constitution.

At the time Malloy committed his crime, the punishment for murder without a recommendation of mercy in South Carolina was "death by hanging within the county jail, or its inclosure [sic], in the presence of specified witnesses." The new law, as noted, prescribed electrocution instead of hanging, and also fixed the place of execution inside the penitentiary and allowed more invited witnesses than had the previous statute. The Court ruled that the new statute did not increase the punishment for murder without a recommendation of mercy; it only changed the method of producing death, which abated "some of the odious features incident to the old method." Other changes in the statute, the Court opined, were "nonessential details in respect of surroundings." Consequently, the Court affirmed the judgment of the state supreme court.

Sentencing. In *Calton v. Utah* (130 U.S. 83, 1889), the jury was instructed as to what constituted murder in the first and second degrees. It was not informed, however, of its right, under the penal code of Utah, to recommend life imprisonment at hard labor in the penitentiary in place of the punishment of death. The Court opined that if the jury's attention had been called to the statute, it may have made such a recommendation, and thereby enabled the court to reduce the punishment to life imprisonment. The Court ruled that the trial court erred in not directing the attention of the jury to the alternative sentence and reversed the judgment, with directions for a new trial, and for such further proceedings as may not be inconsistent with its opinion.

In *Craemer v. Washington* (168 U.S. 124, 1897), Henry Craemer had been charged by information with murder in the first degree, murder in the second degree, and manslaughter. Only the first charge carried the death penalty. In convicting Craemer of murder in the second degree and manslaughter, the jury returned a verdict of simply "guilty as charged." Before he was sentenced, Craemer, alleging that he could not be tried upon an information for his life, appealed his conviction to the Washington Supreme Court and, when unsuccessful there, to the U.S. Supreme Court, which denied his appeal. In the meantime, the original judge in the case had been replaced. The new judge sentenced Craemer to death. Craemer was unable to appeal the sentence to the Washington Supreme Court because the next term of the court did not start until after the date Craemer was to be executed. The only course of action open to Craemer was to appeal his sentence to the federal circuit court, which refused his writ of habeas corpus. The Court affirmed the decision of the federal circuit court, but Craemer apparently escaped execution, anyway.[17]

The petitioner in *Robinson v. United States* (324 U.S. 282, 1945) was indicted and convicted in a federal district court for violating the Federal Kidnapping Act by transporting in interstate commerce a person whom he had kidnapped and held for a reward. The jury recommended and the court imposed the death penalty. The circuit court of appeals affirmed, and the Court granted certiorari on the sole question of the court's statutory authority to impose the death sentence. The act authorizes the death sentence when recommended by a jury "provided that the sentence of death shall not be imposed by the court if, prior to its imposition, the kidnapped person has been liberated unharmed." The indictment charged, and there was evidence before the jury, to the effect that the kidnapping victim yielded to capture only after the petitioner had twice violently struck her on the head with an iron bar; that while held in custody her lips were abrased and made swollen by repeated applications of tape on her mouth; and that wounds resulting from these assaults were not healed when she was liberated after six days' captivity. No evidence was introduced, nor did the indictment charge, that the injuries inflicted were permanent, or that the victim still suffered from them when Robinson was sentenced nine years after commission of the offense. The trial court charged the jury that in determining whether the victim had been "liberated unharmed" they were limited to a consideration of her condition at the time she was liberated, and that they were not authorized to recommend the death penalty if at the time of her liberation she had recovered from her injuries. The Court had to determine only whether the injuries inflicted had to be permanent or in existence at the time of sentence to authorize the infliction of the death sentence. While the Court admitted that Congress did not make clear what it meant by harm, that is, it did not unmistakably mark some boundary between a pin prick and a permanently mutilated body, it did not doubt that a kidnapper who violently struck the head of his victim with an iron bar, as evidence showed that this petitioner did, came within the group Congress had in mind. The Court therefore ruled that the trial court committed no error of which the petitioner could complain.

In *Williams v. New York* (337 U.S. 241, 1949), a jury in a New York state court found Williams guilty of murder in the first degree. The jury recommended life imprisonment, but the trial judge imposed a sentence of death. In giving his reasons for imposing the death sentence the judge discussed in open court the evidence upon which the jury had convicted stating that he had considered this evidence in the light of additional information made available to him through the court's "Probation Department, and through other sources." Consideration of this additional information was pursuant to the New York Criminal Code which provides: "Before rendering judgment or pronouncing sentence the court shall cause the defendant's previous criminal record to be submitted to it, including any reports that may have been made as a result of a mental, phychiatric (sic) or physical examination of such person, and may seek any information that will aid the court in determining the proper treatment of such defendant." The New York Court of Appeals affirmed the conviction and sentence over the contention that as construed and applied the controlling penal statutes are in violation of the due process clause of the Fourteenth Amendment in that the sentence of death was based upon information supplied by witnesses with whom the accused had not been confronted and as to whom he had no opportunity for cross-examination or rebuttal. The Court held that the due-process clause does not render a sentence void merely because a judge gets additional out-of-court information to assist him in the exercise of his awesome power of imposing the death sentence. Note that in this case a Fourteenth Amendment violation was claimed; therefore, the case could have been included in the section of Fourteenth Amendment cases. It was included here because it dealt with a sentencing issue.

The Fifth Amendment (Double Jeopardy). In 1916, Robert Stroud (the "Bird Man of Alcatraz") was convicted of first-degree murder and sentenced to hang for the killing of a prison guard at the Leavenworth Federal Penitentiary in Kansas. Stroud was serving the remainder of a 12-year sentence he received for his 1908 conviction in Alaska for killing the man who had beaten his female companion.

Stroud originally had been serving his sentence at McNeil Penitentiary in Seattle but was transferred to Leavenworth in 1912 for stabbing another inmate who had allegedly stolen food from him and for generally being disobedient.[18] Stroud appealed the judgment of the federal district court in his 1916 trial to the circuit court of appeals, which reversed judgment and granted Stroud a new trial after the U.S. district attorney confessed error. Stroud's new trial was held in 1917. The new trial jury found him "guilty as charged in the indictment without capital punishment." Stroud then appealed that judgment to the Court and, after the United States Solicitor General confessed to error, reversed the judgment of the district court and remanded the case for further proceedings. The district court vacated the former sentence and ordered a new trial. Stroud's third trial ended with the jury finding Stroud guilty of first-degree murder but made no recommendation about dispensing with capital punishment. The judge sentenced Stroud to death.

Stroud appealed to the Court alleging that the results of the last trial placed him in double jeopardy in violation of the Fifth Amendment. In *Stroud v. U.S.* (251 U.S. 15, 1919), the Court observed that the convictions and sentences in the former trials were reversed only after Stroud had appealed those judgments. Once error was found in those proceedings, the Court continued, the only recourse for the appellate courts was to award new trials. The Court concluded that because Stroud, himself, initiated the actions which resulted in new trials, he was not placed in second jeopardy within the meaning of the Constitution.

As a postscript, Stroud was never executed. Through the tireless work of his mother who had gained the support of several women's organizations, President Woodrow Wilson commuted Stroud's death sentence to life in prison in solitary confinement. He was transferred to Alcatraz in his 26th year of confinement, in 1942, and died at the age of 73 after serving 54 years in prison, the last 42 in solitary confinement.[19]

Juries. *Winston v. United States, Strather v. United States*, and *Smith v. United States* (172 U.S. 303, 1899) were three cases of indictments returned and tried in the District of Columbia Supreme Court for murders committed after the passage of the act of Congress of January 15, 1897. The act stipulated, in part, that "in all cases where the accused is found guilty of the crime of murder or of rape . . . the jury may qualify their verdict by adding thereto 'without capital punishment'; and whenever the jury shall return a verdict qualified as aforesaid the person convicted shall be sentenced to imprisonment at hard labor for life." Upon review, the Court maintained that the instructions of the judge to the jury in each of the three cases led the jury to understand that the act of Congress did not intend or authorize the jury to qualify their verdict by the addition of the words "without capital punishment," unless mitigating or palliating circumstances were proved. The Court held that the instructions were erroneous in matter of law, as undertaking to control the discretionary power vested by Congress in the jury, and as attributing to Congress an intention unwarranted either by the express words or by the apparent purpose of the statute. The Court reversed the judgment in each of the three cases and remanded them to the court of appeals, with directions to reverse the judgment of the District of Columbia Supreme Court and to order a new trial.

Alfred Aldridge, a black man, was convicted by an all-white jury and sentenced to death in the District of Columbia Supreme Court for the first-degree murder of one of the District's white police officers. The conviction was affirmed by the court of appeals, and the Court granted certiorari on the question about the trial court's voir dire of prospective jurors. In this interracial case, the trial court refused to ask prospective jurors whether they had racial prejudices. In *Aldridge v. United States* (283 U.S. 308, 1931), the government argued "that it would be detrimental to the administration of the law in the courts of the United States to allow questions to jurors as to racial or religious prejudices." To which the Court replied,

> We think that it would be far more injurious to permit it to be thought that persons entertaining a disqualifying prejudice were allowed to serve as jurors and that inquiries designed to elicit the fact of disqualification were barred. No surer way could be devised to bring the processes of justice into disrepute. We are of the opinion that the ruling of the trial court on the voir dire was erroneous.

The Court reversed the judgment.

In the case of *Norris v. Alabama* (294 U.S. 587, 1935), Clarence Norris, a black man and one of the "Scottsboro Boys" (discussed later in *Powell v. Alabama*), moved at the onset of his trial to quash his indictment for rape and his trial venire because qualified "Negroes" were systematically excluded from both his grand and petit juries, "solely because of their race and color"—a long-standing, though unconstitutional practice in the counties in which he was indicted and tried. Norris was indicted in Jackson County and, because of a change of venue, was tried in Morgan County. The trial judge denied both motions, and Norris was convicted and sentenced to death. On appeal, the Alabama Supreme Court affirmed the judgment of the trial court. The U.S. Supreme Court granted certiorari and, after reviewing the evidence and arguments, reversed the judgment of the Alabama Supreme Court, asserting that the practice violated the equal protection clause of U.S. Constitution's 14th Amendment, and remanded the cause for further proceedings not inconsistent with its opinion.

The same issue was raised again in *Patton v. Mississippi* (332 U.S. 463, 1948). Patton, a black man, was indicted for the murder of a white man in the Lauderdale County, Mississippi circuit court by an all-white grand jury, He was convicted by an all-white petit jury and sentenced to death by electrocution. He filed a timely motion to quash the indictment alleging that, although there were blacks in the county qualified for jury service, the venires for the term from which the grand and petit juries were selected did not contain the name of a single black person. He claimed that the absence of any blacks on the venires was due to the "systematic, intentional, deliberate and invariable practice on the part of administrative officers [of the county] to exclude Negroes from the jury lists, jury boxes and jury service, and that such practice has resulted and does now result in the denial of the equal protection of the laws to this defendant as guaranteed by the 14th amendment to the U.S. Constitution." The petitioner introduced evidence showing "without contradiction that no Negro had served on the grand or petit criminal court juries for thirty years or more." According to the U.S. Census, the 1940 adult black population of Lauderdale County was 12,511 (36 percent) out of a total adult population of 34,821. The trial court overruled the motion to quash, and the Mississippi Supreme Court affirmed the trial court's decision.

Upon review, the Court held:

> . . . the State wholly failed to meet the very strong evidence of purposeful racial discrimination made out by the petitioner upon the uncontradicted showing that for thirty years or more no Negro had served as a juror in the criminal courts of Lauderdale County. When a jury selection plan, whatever it is, operates in such way as always to result in the complete and long-continued exclusion of any representative at all from a large group of negroes, or any other racial group, indictments and verdicts returned against them by juries thus selected cannot stand . . . our holding does not mean that a guilty defendant must go free. For indictments can be returned and convictions can be obtained by juries selected as the Constitution commands.

The Court reversed the judgment of the Mississippi Supreme Court and remanded the case for proceedings that were not inconsistent with its opinion. This case also could have been reviewed in the Fourteenth Amendment category.

The Fourteenth Amendment (Equal Protection and Due Process). The Court reviewed many Fourteenth Amendment challenges charging violations of due process of law. In many cases, those appeals on Fourteenth Amendment grounds served as unofficial proxies for alleged violations of provisions of the Fourth, Fifth, Sixth, and Eighth Amendments. The reason is conveyed by the Court, which frequently wrote: "It has been well settled for years that the first ten amendments apply only to the procedure and trial of causes in the federal courts, and are not limitations upon those in state courts."[20]

In *McElvaine v. Brush* (142 U.S. 155, 1891), Charles McElvaine, who was sentenced to death for murder in New York, contended that being held in solitary confinement pending his execution, as provided by the New York death penalty statute, constituted cruel and unusual punishment in violation of the federal constitution's Eighth Amendment. In his petition, McElvaine acknowledged that the first ten amendments to the U.S. Constitution "were not intended to limit the powers of the states in respect of their own people, but to operate on the federal government only." Nevertheless, he argued that,

> so far as those amendments secure the fundamental rights of the individual, they make them his privileges and immunities as a citizen of the United States, which cannot now, under the fourteenth amendment, be abridged by a state; that the prohibition of cruel and unusual punishments is one of these; and that that prohibition is also included in that 'due process of law' without which no state can deprive any person of life, liberty, or property.

The Court responded that the "general rule of decision is that this court will follow the adjudication of the highest court of a state in the construction of its own statutes, and there is nothing in this case to take it out of that rule." It added that "the record does not disclose that the petitioner is restrained of his liberty in violation of the constitution and laws of the United States."

James W. Finley was tried, convicted, and sentenced to death for violating Section 246 of the California state penal code: "Every person undergoing a life sentence in a state prison of this state, who, with malice aforethought, commits an assault upon the person of another with a deadly weapon or instrument, or by any means or force likely to produce great bodily injury, is punishable with death." The California Supreme Court affirmed the sentence. In *Finley v. California* (222 U.S. 28, 1911), Finley argued that "246 is repugnant to the 14th Amendment of the U.S. Constitution in that it denies to him the equal protection of the laws, because it provides an exceptional punishment for life prisoners." The California Supreme Court "sustained the law on the ground that there was a proper basis for classification between convicts serving life sentences in the state prison, as defendant was when he committed the crime . . . and convicts serving lesser terms." In affirming the judgment of the state supreme court, the Court reasoned that for convicts serving life sentences, there "manifestly" "could be no extension of the term of imprisonment as a punishment for crimes they might commit, and whatever other punishment should be imposed was for the legislature to determine."

In 1913, 29-year-old pencil factory manager Leo Frank was tried, convicted, and sentenced to death in Atlanta, Georgia, for the murder of his 13-year-old employee Mary Phagan. The day after he was sentenced, his counsel filed a written motion for a new trial, which was amended about two months later to include 103 different grounds. Among them were several contending that Frank did not have a fair and impartial trial, because it was conducted in a charged atmosphere of virulent anti-Semitism. The motion argued that the disorder both inside and outside the courtroom "amounted to mob domination" that intimidated the presiding judge and the jury. The trial court denied the motion, whereupon the cause was appealed to the state supreme court, which affirmed the conviction. After the decision by the Georgia Supreme Court, an "extraordinary motion" was made on Frank's behalf on the basis of newly discovered evidence. That motion was refused, and again the case was brought before the state supreme court, which again affirmed the action of the trial court. Other motions were then brought before various state courts and a petition was made to the U.S. Supreme Court, all without success. Persevering, a petition for a writ of habeas corpus was presented to the U.S. District Court for the northern district of Georgia on the ground that Frank was being confined in violation of the U.S. Constitution, "especially that clause of the 14th Amendment which declares that no state shall deprive any person of life, liberty, or property without due process of law." The district court refused to award the writ. That decision was appealed to the Court and, in *Frank v. Mangum* (237 U.S. 309, 1915), the Court affirmed the decision of the district court. But the legal maneuverings did not end there.

Facing execution, Frank sought clemency from Georgia governor John Slaton, who, after reviewing the trial transcripts and knowing he was committing political and perhaps actual suicide, commuted Frank's death sentence to life imprisonment.[21] Following his decision, Governor Slaton, who had found numerous discrepancies in the trial transcript, stated "he would rather live in fear of his life than have a guilty conscience." Community members burned the governor in effigy, threatened his life, and eventually forced him to leave Georgia. As for Frank, on the night of August 16, 1915, a group of armed men forcibly took Frank from the prison where he was being held and lynched him. Later, it was discovered that another man's lawyer told the judge in Frank's original trial that his client, Jim Conley, also an employee of the pencil factory, had confessed to him several times that he, and not Leo Frank, had killed Mary Phagan. The judge kept this information to himself during Frank's trial and sentenced Frank to death, anyway. In 1982, Alonzo Mann, who was a 14-year-old pencil factory employee at the time of Phagan's murder, told investigators that he had witnessed Conley commit the murder but kept silent because Conley threatened to kill him if he revealed what he saw. In 1986, Frank was issued a posthumous pardon by the state of Georgia because of "blatant due-process violations."[22] No one was ever charged with a crime for Frank's lynching.[23]

In *Moore v. Dempsey* (261 U.S. 86, 1923) the Court responded to an appeal from an order of the District Court for the Eastern District of Arkansas dismissing a writ of habeas corpus. The appellants were five black men who were convicted of first-degree murder and sentenced to death by an Arkansas court. The ground of the petition for the writ was that the defendants did not receive a fair trial; that they "were hurried to conviction under the pressure of a mob without any regard for their rights and without according to them due process of law."

The circumstances of the original case were as follows. On the night of September 30, 1919, a number of black people were meeting in a church to discuss hiring an attorney to protect them from being extorted by white landowners. During the meeting, a group of white men, presumably representing the white landowners, attacked and shot at the blacks. In the disturbance that followed, a white man was killed. The news of the killing incited white community members who went on a rampage killing many black people. During the rampage, a white man, Clinton Lee, was killed. The five black defendants were indicted for Lee's murder. The black defendants claimed that other whites killed Lee.

The Governor, in the meantime, appointed a "Committee of Seven" to investigate what the committee called the "insurrection" in the county. All the while, the newspapers were daily publishing inflammatory articles. In one of the articles, it was made public that at least one member of the committee believed that what had occurred was "a deliberately planned insurrection of the negroes against the whites, directed by an organization known as the 'Progressive Farmers' and 'Household Union of America' established for the purpose of banding negroes together for the killing of white people."

Shortly after the five black men were arrested, a lynch mob marched to the jail but was prevented from lynching the black men by the presence of U.S. troops and "the promise of some of the Committee of Seven and other leading officials that if the mob would refrain . . . they would execute those found guilty in the form of law." The Committee's own statement indicated that mob violence was prevented because the "Committee gave our citizens their solemn promise that the law would be carried out."

The Court reversed the district court's dismissal of the writ of habeas corpus and ordered the district court to conduct a hearing. In doing so, the Court wrote: ". . . it does not seem to us sufficient to allow a Judge of the United States to escape the duty of examining the facts for himself when if true as alleged they make the trial absolutely void."

Powell v. Alabama (287 U.S. 45, 1932) involved the so-called "Scottsboro Boys"—nine young black men, ranging in age from 13 to 21, arrested for the alleged rapes of two white women.[24] One remarkable aspect of the case was that it took only one week to arrest, indict, arraign, try, convict, and sentence the defendants to death.[25] Another conspicuous aspect was that none of the defendants was represented by counsel until the day of the trial. Even then, it was not until the morning of the trial that a reluctant Scottsboro attorney offered to represent the young men.

On appeal, the Alabama Supreme Court reversed the conviction of one of the defendants but affirmed the convictions of the other seven (see note 25). Those defendants appealed their convictions to the Court, which reversed all seven convictions, holding that because of the special circumstances involved ("the ignorance and illiteracy of the defendants, their youth, the circumstances of public hostility, the imprisonment and the close surveillance of the defendants by the military forces, the fact that their friends and families were all in other states and communication with them necessarily difficult, and above all they stood in deadly peril of their lives"), the defendants were denied their right to the effective assistance of counsel required by the due process clause of the Fourteenth Amendment. Upon retrial, however, the eight "Scottsboro Boys" were reconvicted and, although they escaped execution, five of the eight served between 10 and 20 years in prison.[26] The *Powell* decision was narrowly drawn—it applied only to cases in which defendants were indigent, incapable of defending themselves because of their ignorance, illiteracy, or other similar handicap, and the death penalty was a possible sentence—but it was still important because it was the first in a series of cases that would extend the Sixth Amendment right to the effective assistance of counsel.

The question in *Brown v. Mississippi* (297 U.S. 278, 1936) was whether convictions based solely on coerced confessions violated due process of law as required by the Fourteenth Amendment. Three black men were indicted on March 30, 1934, for a murder committed five days earlier. They were arraigned the next day, and all three pleaded not guilty. Their trial commenced the following day and ended one day later. All three defendants were convicted and sentenced to death. Their convictions were based solely on their confessions, which, according to their testimony during the trial, were false and obtained through physical torture.

One of the suspects was taken from his home by a deputy sheriff accompanied by several white men to the house of the murdered man. There they accused him of the crime, which he vehemently denied committing, whereupon they hung him by the neck to a tree. After letting him dangle for a few moments, they cut him down and again asked him if he had committed the crime, which again he denied. They then hung him again, cut him down after a few moments, and posed the question to him anew. Again, he protested his innocence. After that, they tied him to a tree and whipped him, but he still refused to confess. They finally released him and with some difficulty he returned home. A day or two later, the aforementioned deputy sheriff together with another officer went to the suspect's home again, this time to arrest him. Following the arrest, the two deputies transported the suspect to a jail in an adjoining county. Along the way, the deputies stopped the car, removed the suspect, and severely whipped him again, declaring that they would continue to whip him until he agreed to confess to the murder, which he did. The suspect was then transported to the jail. The other two suspects were arrested and taken to the same jail. There the same deputy sheriff, along with the jailer and other white men, made the suspects strip and lean over chairs, whereupon their backs were cut to pieces by leather straps with buckles on them. The deputy sheriff advised the suspects that the beatings would continue until they agreed to confess to the murder, which they did. The next day the sheriff, some deputies, and other men came to the jail to hear the "free and voluntary confessions" of the three suspects.

In court, the sheriff testified that he had heard about the beatings but stated that he had no personal knowledge of them. He also admitted that one of the defendants was limping badly and did not sit down when making his confession because, as the defendant told it, he was strapped so badly he could not sit down. Finally, the sheriff noted that the rope burns around one of the defendant's neck was visible for anyone to see. During the trial the defendants were called to testify as to how the confessions were obtained, which they did truthfully. Interestingly, the deputy sheriff and two others who had administered the beatings were put on the stand and admitted to their roles in the torture. Not a single witness who was introduced denied that the beatings took place. Nevertheless, the so-called "free and voluntary confessions" were admitted in evidence over the objections of the defendants' counsel, which, incidentally, was only appointed the previous day. As noted, all three defendants were convicted and sentenced to death based solely on their confessions. The trial court's decision was challenged in the state supreme court as a violation of the Fourteenth Amendment's due process clause. The state supreme court upheld the lower court's judgment and chose not to enforce the defendants' constitutional rights. However, the U.S. Supreme Court reversed the state supreme court's judgment citing a violation of a fully established federal right.

Frank Palko was indicted in Connecticut for first-degree murder. The jury in his case found him guilty of second-degree murder, and he was sentenced to life imprisonment. The state of Connecticut appealed and won a new trial. At the new trial, Palko was convicted of first-degree murder and sentenced to death. Before the jury was impaneled for the new trial, as well as during later stages of the case, Palko objected that the second trial effectively put him twice in jeopardy for the same offense and, thus, violated the Fourteenth Amendment. The trial judge overruled his objections. The Connecticut Supreme Court affirmed the judgment, which Palko then appealed to the Court. In *Palko v. Conneticut* (302 U.S. 319, 1937), the Court held that the Fourteenth Amendment's due process clause absorbed fundamental rights and applied them to the states. The Court concluded, however, that the protection from double jeopardy was not a fundamental right, as the freedoms of speech, press, religion, and peaceable assembly were, and affirmed the judgment.

In *Watts v. Indiana* (338 U.S. 49, 1949), the Court elected to review a case after the Indiana Supreme Court rejected the petitioner's claim that "confessions elicited from him were procured under circumstances rendering their admission as evidence against him a denial of due process of law." Robert Watts was arrested on November 12, 1947, on suspicion that he had committed a criminal assault earlier that day. Later the same day, a dead woman was found near where Watts committed the alleged assault. The police immediately suspected that Watts had committed the murder and began questioning him about it. They took him from the county jail to state police headquarters, where six to eight officers questioned him in relays off and on for six days, with only a break on Sunday. During the lengthy interrogation, he did not receive much food, and he was deprived of sleep. At about 3 o'clock on the sixth day, Watts finally made an incriminating statement. However, the statement did not satisfy the prosecutor who had been called in, so the prosecutor turned Watts over to another interrogator for additional questioning, which produced a more incriminating statement from Watts.

Although Indiana law required that Watts be given a prompt preliminary hearing before a magistrate, "with all the protection a hearing was intended to give him," Watts was denied the preliminary hearing during the entire time he was being interrogated. He also "was without friendly or professional aid and without advice as to his constitutional rights."

In reversing the decision of the Indiana Supreme Court, the Court held that the due process clause of the Fourteenth Amendment bars "police procedure which violates the basic notions of our accusatorial mode of prosecuting crime and vitiates a conviction based on the fruits of such procedure." It opined:

> A confession by which life becomes forfeit must be the expression of free choice. A statement to be voluntary of course need not be volunteered. But if it is the product of sustained pressure by the police it does not issue from a free choice. When a suspect speaks because he is overborne, it is immaterial whether he has been subjected to a physical or a mental

ordeal. Eventual yielding to questioning under such circumstances is plainly the product of the suction process of interrogation and therefore the reverse of voluntary.

It added that, while "mindful of the anguishing problems which the incidence of crime presents to the States . . . the history of the criminal law
proves overwhelmingly that brutal methods of law enforcement are essen-
tially self-defeating, whatever may be their effect in a particular case."[27]

In *Alcorta v. Texas* (355 U.S. 28, 1957), a Texas state court had
convicted Alvaro Alcorta of murdering his wife and sentenced him to
death. At his trial, Alcorta admitted he had killed his wife but claimed
it occurred in a fit of passion when he saw his wife, whom he had already
suspected of marital infidelity, kissing another man in a parked car
late at night. Had the jury believed him, it could have returned a verdict
of guilty of "murder without malice" which, under Texas law, carried a
maximum sentence of five years' imprisonment. The jury did not believe
him and sentenced him to death. At the trial, the other man testified that
he and Alcorta's wife were simply friends and that their "relationship"
amounted to nothing more than his driving her home from work a
few times. The Texas Court of Criminal Appeals affirmed the judgment
and sentence. However, in a subsequent habeas corpus proceeding, the
other man confessed of having had sexual intercourse with Alcorta's wife
several times. He also testified that he had told the prosecutor about it
before the trial and that the prosecutor advised him not to volunteer the
information unless he was asked and then he should tell the truth.
The prosecutor admitted that these statements were true. Nevertheless,
both the trial court and the Texas Court of Criminal Appeals denied
Alcorta's petitions for writs of habeas corpus. Having exhausted state
remedies, Alcorta appealed to the Court, which held that Alcorta had
been denied due process of law. It reversed the judgment denying the
writ of habeas corpus and remanded the cause to the Texas Court of
Criminal Appeals.

In *Ciucci v. Illinois* (356 U.S. 571, 1958), Vincent Ciucci, a Chicago
grocery store owner, was charged in four separate indictments with murdering his wife and three children, all of whom were found dead in a
burning building with bullet wounds in their heads. In three successive
trials, Ciucci was convicted of the first-degree murder of his wife and
two of his children. At each of the trials the prosecution introduced into
evidence the details of all four deaths. At the first two trials, involving
the death of the wife and one of the children, the jury fixed the penalty
at 20 and 45 years imprisonment, respectively. At the third trial, which
involved the death of the second child, the penalty was fixed at death.
Before the third trial, Ciucci objected that he was being subjected to double jeopardy and moved to exclude testimony about the other deaths.
The trial court overruled both objections. On appeal, the state supreme

court affirmed the conviction. Ciucci then appealed to the Court, claiming that his third trial violated the due process clause of the Fourteenth Amendment. In his brief, Ciucci appended several articles from Chicago newspapers describing how the prosecutor was dissatisfied with the prison sentences in the first two trials, and his intention to prosecute Ciucci until he obtained a death sentence. However, none of that material was part of the record certified to the Court from the state supreme court, so the Court could not consider it in the appeal. In affirming the judgment of the state supreme court, the Court ruled "the State was constitutionally entitled to prosecute these individual offenses singly at separate trials, and to utilize therein all relevant evidence, in the absence of proof establishing that such a course of action entailed fundamental unfairness." It added, "Prosecution is allowed to try the accused with repeated trials (three) and convictions on the same evidence, until it achieves its desired result of a capital verdict." The Court did leave open the opportunity for Ciucci to institute "such further proceedings as may be available to him for the purpose of substantiating the claim that he was deprived of due process."

Leslie Irvin, an Evansville, Indiana pipe fitter, was tried, convicted, and sentenced to death for the murder, in 1954, of gas station attendant Whitney Wesley Kerr. Shortly after Irvin's arrest, the prosecutor of Vanderburgh County and Evansville police officials issued widely publicized press releases stating that Irvin had confessed to six murders that had recently been committed in the Evansville area. The local news media had extensively covered the six murders, which had created quite a stir throughout Vanderburgh County, where Evansville is located, and in adjoining Gibson County. When Irvin was indicted in Vanderburgh County, his appointed attorney sought a change of venue, which was granted, but to adjoining Gibson County. Irvin's attorney then moved for a change of venue from Gibson County, claiming that the widespread and inflammatory publicity had also highly prejudiced the residents of that county against Leslie, but that motion was denied. The jury pool for Irvin's trial consisted of 430 persons; 268 of whom were excused for cause because they had already decided that Irvin was guilty. Of the 12 who were finally selected to serve on the jury, 8 had admitted that they thought Irvin was guilty, but each indicated that he or she could still render an impartial verdict. After the state supreme court sustained Irvin's conviction, he applied to a federal district court for a writ of habeas corpus, claiming that he had not received a fair trial in violation of the Fourteenth Amendment. The district court denied his application for the writ on the ground that he had not exhausted his state remedies. The Seventh Circuit Court of Appeals affirmed the dismissal. After another round in the federal courts, the Court granted certiorari. In *Irvin v. Dowd* (366 U.S. 717, 1961), the Court held that Irvin was "not accorded a fair and impartial trial, to which he was entitled under the due process clause of the 14th Amendment." The Court voided his conviction and vacated the judgment denying him the writ of habeas corpus. It remanded the case to the district court for further proceedings affording the state a reasonable time to retry Irvin. The case is important because it was the first time the Court overturned a murder conviction because of pretrial publicity.[28]

Edward Griffin was convicted and sentenced to death in California for the first-degree murder of Essie Mae Hodson, the female companion of one of his drinking buddies, after he sexually assaulted her.[29] On automatic appeal, the California Supreme Court affirmed the judgment. The judgment was appealed to the Court on the ground that the prosecutor's comments and the trial judge's instructions to the jury about Griffin's failure to take the stand and testify during the guilt stage of his trial violated the self-incrimination clause of the Fifth Amendment, made applicable to the states by the Fourteenth Amendment in *Malloy v. Hogan* (378 U.S. 1, 1964). In *Griffin v. California* (380 U.S. 609, 1965), the Court reversed the California Supreme Court's affirmation of Griffin's conviction and death sentence.

"Skinny" Gilbert was tried, convicted, and sentenced to death for a 1964 armed robbery of a California bank and the murder of a police officer who entered the bank during the robbery. The California Supreme Court affirmed the judgment. The Court granted certiorari to hear Gilbert's allegations about four constitutional errors made in his case. Specifically, Gilbert claimed that (1) the admission of handwriting exemplars taken from him after arrest violated his Fifth and Sixth Amendment rights; (2) the admission during the guilt stage of his trial of his co-defendant's pre-trial statements to the police detailing his [Gilbert's] role in the crimes—statements that in his co-defendant's appeal were held to have been improperly admitted—violated his right to due process of law; (3) the admission of testimony identifying him from photographs seized by police from his locked apartment pursuant to a warrantless search was a violation of his Fourth Amendment rights; and (4) the admission of witness testimony that identified him at a lineup, which occurred 16 days after his indictment and after appointment of counsel, who was not notified, violated his Sixth Amendment right to have counsel present during a pretrial lineup.

In *Gilbert v. California* (388 U.S. 263, 1967), the Court ruled on the four claims. First, it held that the taking of handwriting exemplars did not violate Gilbert's constitutional rights. The Court reasoned that a handwriting exemplar, as opposed to the content of what is actually written, is not protected by the Fifth Amendment's privilege against compelled self-incrimination. It also maintained that Gilbert's Sixth Amendment right to counsel was not violated because the taking of handwriting exemplars is not a "critical" stage of criminal proceedings entitling him to the assistance of counsel. Second, regarding the admission of his co-defendant's statements, the Court found no problem with the California Supreme Court's judgment that any error involving the statements was harmless. Third, as for the claim of a Fourth Amendment violation in the search and seizure of the photographs from his apartment, the Court observed that the facts submitted were not clear enough to permit resolution of that question. Therefore, it vacated certiorari on that issue as improvidently granted. Fourth, the Court determined that the admission of the in-court identifications of Gilbert without first ascertaining whether they were tainted by the illegal lineup procedure was constitutional error. The Court opined that a post-indictment pretrial lineup is a "critical" stage in criminal proceeding and the denial of counsel at that stage violates the Sixth Amendment's right to counsel. However, the Court added that because the record did not allow an informed judgment about whether the in-court identifications at the two stages of the trial [the guilt stage and the penalty stage] had an independent source, Gilbert was entitled only to a vacation of his conviction, "pending proceedings in California courts allowing the State to establish that the in-court identifications had an independent source or that their introduction in evidence was harmless error." As for the witnesses' testimony that they identified Gilbert at the lineup, which was a direct result of an illegal procedure, the Court ruled that "the State [was] not entitled to show that such testimony had an independent source but the California courts must, unless 'able to declare a belief that it was harmless beyond a reasonable doubt', grant [Gilbert] a new trial if such testimony was at the guilt stage, or grant appropriate relief if it was at the penalty stage." (See Chapter 7 for a discussion of harmless and serious or prejudicial errors in capital cases.)

Some of the pre-1968 death penalty cases set precedent for post-*Furman* capital jurisprudence, but other cases, perhaps most of them, are mostly of historical interest. All of them, however, revealed troubling flaws in the death penalty systems of many jurisdictions. After *Furman* (1972) and *Gregg* (1976), the issues addressed by the Court were very different than most of those reviewed prior to 1968. (*Gregg v. Georgia*, which is discussed at greater length later in this chapter, is the case in which the Court approved new death penalty statutes.) Prior to 1968, the issues involved (1) clemency, (2) jurisdiction, (3) methods of execution, (4) ex post facto, (5) sentencing, (6) the Fifth Amendment (double jeopardy), (7) juries, and (8) the Fourteenth Amendment (equal protection and due process). After *Furman* and *Gregg*, they have dealt primarily with issues pertaining to the new death penalty statutes, such as (1) the constitutionality of the new death penalty statutes, (2) what crimes are capital, (3) mitigating circumstances, (4) aggravating circumstances, (5) the appellate process, (6) capital juries, (7) who may or may not be executed, and (8) assistance of counsel, Before turning to the post-*Furman* Court decisions, consider some important cases that paved the way for both *Furman* and *Gregg*.

1968 Cases: *U.S. v. Jackson* and *Witherspoon v. Illinois*

The Supreme Court decided two cases in 1968 that dealt with the discretionary roles of the prosecutor and the jury in the processing of a capital case. The problem addressed in the first case, *U.S. v. Jackson* (390 U.S. 570, 1968), was the provision in the federal kidnapping statute that required a jury recommendation to impose the death penalty.[30] Congress made kidnapping punishable by death in 1934, following a rash of professional kidnappings, the most notorious of which was the 1932 kidnapping of the Lindbergh child (the kidnapping statute was known as the Lindbergh law).[31] Under the statute, a defendant could escape a death sentence by waiving the right to a jury trial or by entering a guilty plea. By being able to dangle the prospect of a death sentence before a defendant, prosecutors gained considerable leverage in the plea bargaining process and, apparently, still do.[32] The Court opined that the provision impermissibly encouraged defendants, particularly innocent defendants, to waive their right to a jury trial to escape the chance of a death sentence. The Court ruled the provision unconstitutional.

In *Witherspoon v. Illinois* (391 U.S. 510, 1968), the Court rejected the common practice of excusing prospective jurors simply because they were opposed to capital punishment.[33] In Witherspoon's case, 47 jurors, nearly half the jurors called for the trial, were successfully challenged for that reason.[34] Witherspoon, who was convicted in 1960 of killing a Chicago police officer,[35] argued that such a practice—referred to as "death qualification"—deprived him of his right to a jury that was representative of the community.[36] Research shows that death–qualified jurors are less concerned with due process and more inclined to believe the prosecution than are excludable jurors. Death-qualified jurors are also significantly less knowledgeable and have more misconceptions about the death penalty and the death-sentencing process than do excludable jurors. Death-qualified jurors are more likely to believe that the focus of the penalty phase of a bifurcated trial should be only on the nature of the crime rather than mitigation, and that the death penalty deters murder. They are less likely to believe that innocent people are convicted of capital crimes, that the death penalty is unfair to minorities, and that life without parole really means that a prisoner will not be released from prison. Most troublesome, death-qualified jurors have been found to be more conviction–prone.[37]

Little of this evidence was available when the Court decided *Witherspoon*, but the Court, nonetheless, agreed with Witherspoon's argument and held that prospective jurors could be excused only for cause. That is, jurors could be excused only if they would automatically vote against imposition of the death penalty, regardless of the evidence presented at trial, or if their attitudes toward capital punishment prevented them from making an impartial decision on the defendant's guilt. The *Witherspoon* decision was especially important because it drew attention to the composition of capital juries. The discretion exercised by such juries was frequently identified as a principal source of the arbitrariness and discrimination that occurred in the imposition of the death penalty.[38] During the 1980s, the Supreme Court would reconsider its *Witherspoon* decision three different times.

Death Penalty Cases: 1969–1977

As noted in Chapter 1, by 1969, opponents of capital punishment, and especially the NAACP Legal Defense Fund lawyers, believed that the time was right for an assault on the death penalty's constitutionality. The Supreme Court had announced, in footnote four of *Maxwell v. Bishop* (1970),that it would address early in the 1970 term the issue of juror discretion in capital cases and the problems it created. The Court had already granted certiorari in the two test cases: *Crampton v. Ohio* and *McGautha v. California* (both cases were consolidated under 402 U.S. 183). Before turning to those two cases, however, first consider the 1969 case of *Boykin v. Alabama* (395 U.S. 238).

Boykin v. Alabama. The same day that Amsterdam argued the appeal in *Maxwell v. Bishop* (March 4, 1969), the U.S. Supreme Court heard the appeal of Edward Boykin, Jr.[39] Boykin, a 27-year-old black man, had been sentenced to death after pleading guilty to five counts of robbery committed during the spring of 1966. At the time, Alabama was one of the few states that still provided the death penalty as the maximum punishment for robbery. On appeal, Boykin's new attorney (his original court-appointed attorney dropped out of the case after sentencing) maintained that to execute a person for robbery constituted cruel and unusual punishment in violation of the Eighth Amendment. Another argument made on Boykin's behalf was that the trial judge failed to make sure that Boykin understood the possible consequences of his guilty plea. On February 8, 1968, the Alabama Supreme Court rejected both arguments, and six months later the U.S. Supreme Court agreed to review the Alabama Court's decision.[40] Amsterdam and his legal team (Jack Greenberg, James A. Nabrit III, Michael Meltsner, and Melvyn Zarr) wrote an amicus curiae brief urging reversal.[41] In June of 1969, the Supreme Court granted Boykin a new trial. In doing so, however, the Court bypassed the Eighth Amendment claim and ruled more narrowly that the trial judge had erred in not inquiring about Boykin's understanding of the nature and consequences of his guilty plea.[42]

The Boykin appeal is important for two reasons. First, it was the first time the U.S. Supreme Court agreed to consider the constitutionality of the death penalty itself and not simply the procedures used to impose it.[43] Second, the LDF attorneys hoped that the arguments set forth in the Boykin brief would eventually become the basis for the death penalty's complete abolition on Eighth Amendment grounds.[44] In the brief, Amsterdam argued:

> The American people . . . accept the death penalty *only* on the statute books—in theory, that is, but not in practice. The evidence demonstrates that Americans will not in fact tolerate its general, even-handed application. Our society accepts the death penalty . . . solely because it is applied "sparsely, and spottily to unhappy minorities." The numbers selected are so few, their plight so invisible, and their background so unappealing, that "society can readily bear to see them suffer torments which would not for a moment be accepted as penalties of general application to the populace." (emphasis in the original)[45]

McGautha v. California* and *Crampton v. Ohio. Dennis McGautha was sentenced to death for killing a store owner's husband during an armed robbery; James Crampton, for the first–degree murder of his wife.[46] Oral arguments in the cases were heard before the full Supreme Court in November of 1970. A final decision was rendered on May 3, 1971.

The defendants' lawyers argued that unfettered jury discretion in imposing death for murder resulted in arbitrary or capricious sentencing (that is, sentences not governed by principle; fickle or fanciful sentencing) and, hence, violated the Fourteenth Amendment right to due process of law. McGautha's trial–court judge, following the procedure used in California at the time, instructed the jury as follows: "Now, beyond prescribing the two alternative penalties [death or life imprisonment], the law itself provides no standard for the guidance of the jury in the selection of the penalty, but, rather, commits the whole matter of determining which of the two penalties shall be fixed to the judgment, conscience, and absolute discretion of the jury."[47]

Jurors in Crampton's case were instructed to "consider all the evidence and make your finding with intelligence and impartiality, and without bias, sympathy, or prejudice, so that the State of Ohio and the defendant will feel that their case was fairly and impartially tried."[48] They were also instructed that, unless they recommended mercy, a conviction for first–degree murder would result in a death sentence. The importance of Crampton's case to the issue at hand was not so much the jury instructions, though they provided little guidance on how to arrive at a decision, but, rather, whether bifurcated trials were required in capital cases. McGautha's trial was bifurcated; Crampton's was not.[49]

McGautha's claim, which was joined for decision with Crampton, was rejected by a vote of six to three. In rejecting the claim, the Court tacitly approved (1) unfettered jury discretion in death sentencing, and (2) capital trials in which guilt and sentence were determined in one set of deliberations. Regarding unfettered jury discretion, Justice Harlan, for himself, Chief Justice Burger, and Justices Stewart, White, Black, and Blackmun, reasoned that: "In light of history, experience, and the present limitations of human knowledge, we find it quite impossible to say that committing to the untrammeled discretion of the jury the power to pronounce life or death in capital cases is offensive to anything in the Constitution."[50] That conclusion was based on the underlying belief that it was impossible to adequately guide capital sentencing discretion:

> Those who have come to grips with the hard task of actually attempting to draft means of channeling capital sentencing discretion have confirmed the lesson taught by . . . history. . . . To identify before the fact those characteristics of criminal homicides and their perpetrators which call for the death penalty, and to express these characteristics in language which can be fairly understood and applied by the sentencing authority, appear to be tasks which are beyond present human ability.[51]

Abolitionists were disappointed but not surprised by the decision. Some abolitionists remained hopeful because in the majority opinion there was a suggestion that the Court had not foreclosed entirely the possibility of a successful Eighth Amendment challenge.[52] Indeed, on June 28, 1971, less than 60 days after its *McGautha* decision, the Supreme Court agreed to review four cases that challenged the death penalty's constitutionality. In its review orders, the Court stipulated that it would entertain only one question: "Does the imposition and carrying out of the death penalty in this case constitute cruel and unusual punishment in violation of the Eighth and Fourteenth Amendments?"[53] The four test cases were *Aikens v. California*, *Branch v. Texas*, *Furman v. Georgia*, and *Jackson v. Georgia*.

Aikens, Branch, Furman, and Jackson. The four test cases were not selected at random. The Court had chosen them from the nearly 200 pending death penalty appeals.[54] *Aikens* and *Furman* were murder cases; *Jackson* and *Branch* were rape cases.[55] All four of the defendants were black, while all of their victims were white.[56] Aikens, Furman, and Jackson were chosen because LDF attorneys represented them; thus, the Court knew their Eighth Amendment challenges would be well presented.[57] Jackson was also picked because the victim had suffered no special injury, thus making his death sentence appear disproportionately severe for rape.[58] By choosing both murder and rape cases, the Court left itself the option of declaring the death penalty unconstitutional for rape but not for murder.[59]

Earnest James Aikens, Jr. was indicted in California on first-degree murder charges for the stabbing deaths of Kathleen Nell Dodd and Mary Winifred Eaton. Dodd, a 25-year-old pregnant housewife with two small children, was raped and murdered in 1962. Eaton, in her sixties, was raped and murdered in 1965. Aikens pleaded not guilty to both charges. He, his court-appointed counsel, and the district attorney agreed to consolidate the two cases and try them before a judge. At his trial in 1969, he was found guilty on both charges and sentenced to death for the Eaton murder, but could only be sentenced to life in prison under California law for the Dodd murder because he was only 17 years old at the time of the murder. Also, during the sentencing phase of the trial, the state introduced evidence of a third rape and murder he allegedly had committed in 1962 for which he was neither charged nor convicted.[60]

Elmer Branch was sentenced to die in Texas for raping a 65-year-old woman. He did not have a weapon when he raped her and did not make any threats, but he did press his arm against her throat when she tried to scream. Following the rape, he asked her for money, and she gave him the contents of her purse. Before he left, they had a brief conversation about her feelings toward black people, and he told her that if she told anyone, he would come back and kill her. Branch had an IQ of 67 and the equivalent of five and a half years of grade school education.[61]

William Henry Furman was sentenced to die on September 20, 1968, in Savannah, Georgia, for the August 1967, murder of William J. Micke, Jr., a 30-year-old Coast Guard petty officer and the father of four children and the stepfather of six others. Furman, 25 years old at the time of the murder and with an IQ of 65, shot Micke during a burglary attempt at Micke's home.[62] It is instructive to note that Furman's court-appointed trial attorney was paid a total of $150 to defend him. The trial judge denied his attorney's request for additional funds to hire an investigator and to pay for the additional time and expenses needed to prepare Furman's defense. The entire trial—from jury selection to the jury's rendering a death sentence—was completed in one day, between 10 A.M. and about 5 P.M. Furman's trial attorney made no mention of his client's mental impairments. (Furman was diagnosed as "mentally deficient" with convulsive disorder and psychotic episodes.) According to Justice Brennan, "the jury knew only that he [Furman] was black and that, according to his statement at trial, he was 26 years old and worked at 'Superior Upholstery'."[63]

Lucious Jackson, Jr. was sentenced to die in Georgia for the rape of a 20-year-old woman in 1968. At the time of the crime, he was an escaped convict from a prison work gang. He was serving a three-year sentence for auto theft. He entered the victim's home after her husband had left for work, held scissors against her neck, and demanded money. When she could find none, they battled over the scissors. She lost the battle, and he raped her, holding the scissors against her throat. During the three days Jackson was at large, he had committed other crimes— burglary, auto theft, and assault and battery.[64]

Furman v. Georgia. On January 17, 1972, less than nine months after the *McGautha* decision, Furman's lawyers argued to the Supreme Court that unfettered jury discretion in imposing death for murder resulted in arbitrary or capricious sentencing. However, Furman's lawyers, per the Court's stipulation and unlike McGautha's, claimed that unbridled jury discretion violated both their client's Fourteenth Amendment right to due process and his Eighth Amendment right not to be subjected to cruel and unusual punishment. Furman's challenge proved successful and, on June 29, 1972—the last day of the term—the U.S. Supreme Court set aside death sentences for the first time in its history. Furman's sentence was commuted to life imprisonment. He was paroled in 1984.

In September 2006, Furman, age 64, was indicted on a 2004 burglary charge. He had broken into a house in Macon, Georgia that was occupied by a mother and her 10-year-old daughter. The mother, unbeknown to Furman, called 911. When the police arrived, they arrested him. Furman had a pair of the girl's panties in his pocket. He was denied bond because of a bail-jumping charge related to a 2005 possession of burglary tools arrest. Since his 1984 release from prison, Furman has worked in construction in Macon, Georgia, and has had a few arrests for alcohol and weapons violations.[65]

In its decision in *Furman v. Georgia*, *Jackson v. Georgia*, and *Branch v. Texas* (all three cases were consolidated under 408 U.S. 238, 1972, and are referred to here as the *Furman* decision; the *Aikens* case had been dropped on June 7 and will be discussed later),the Court held that the capital punishment statutes in the three cases were unconstitutional because they gave the jury complete discretion to decide whether to impose the death penalty or a lesser punishment in capital cases. Although nine separate opinions were written (a very rare occurrence), the majority of five justices (Douglas, Brennan, Stewart, White, and Marshall) pointed out that the death penalty had been imposed arbitrarily, infrequently, and often selectively against minorities. The majority agreed that the statutes provided for a cruel and unusual punishment in violation of the Eighth and Fourteenth Amendments. (The four dissenters—all Nixon appointees—were Chief Justice Burger and Justices Blackmun, Powell, and Rehnquist. Justices Burger and Blackmun noted, however, that had they been legislators they would have voted to abolish or severely restrict the death penalty.[66]) The *Furman* decision totaled 50,000 words and 243 pages and at the time was the longest decision in Supreme Court history.[67] A practical effect of *Furman* was the Supreme Court's voiding of 40 death penalty statutes and the sentences of more than 600 death row inmates in 32 states.[68] Depending on the state, the death row inmates received new sentences of life imprisonment, a term of years, or, in a few cases, new trials.[69]

An interesting question is why the Supreme Court entertained the Furman challenge to unbridled jury discretion in capital cases in the first place, having just the year before rejected the same claim made in *McGautha*. The answer lies in the constitutional right that was challenged. As Professor Raymond Paternoster relates:

> The position that the plurality in *Furman* appeared to be tak-
> ing . . . was that while *the process* of having defendants sen-
> tenced to death by juries lacking formal guidance is consistent
> with the Fourteenth Amendment's requirement of due process,
> *the product*, an arbitrary and freakish pattern of death sen-
> tencing, is condemned by the Eighth Amendment (emphasis
> in original).[70]

The argument was persuasive enough to change the positions of Justices White and Stewart, who voted against McGautha (who lost by a 6-
3 margin) but in favor of Furman (who won on a 5-4 vote). Making no
difference was the change in the composition of the Court between the
two cases. Although Lewis Powell replaced Hugo Black and William Rehnquist replaced John Harlan, Powell and Rehnquist voted against Furman
just as Black and Harlan voted against McGautha.

Another factor that may have influenced the Court's *Furman* decision was the Fourth U.S. Circuit Court of Appeals' decision in *Ralph v.
Warden* (438 F. 2d 786, 4th Cir. 1970). On December 11, 1970, the court
became the first federal court to declare the death penalty unconstitutional in violation of the Eighth Amendment's prohibition of cruel and
unusual punishment.[71] William Ralph had been convicted of rape in
Maryland in 1961, and sentenced to die. Although he did not employ violence, and the victim showed no visible signs of trauma, Ralph did
threaten to kill her and her young son, who was asleep in another room,
if she resisted.[72] Following years of litigation, Ralph's court-appointed attorney, supported by Amsterdam and an LDF amicus brief, presented the
Eighth Amendment claim to the appeals court.[73] In deciding the case, the
court relied on Amsterdam's *Boykin* theory of the Eighth Amendment (that
the public would be appalled by the less arbitrary application of the death
penalty).[74] The court concluded that the death penalty was not necessarily
unconstitutional for all rapes, but it was for rapes where the victim's life
was neither taken nor endangered.[75] It also pointed out that death was an
excessive penalty for rape because only a few jurisdictions authorized it,
and even in those it was seldom imposed.[76] The court's *Ralph* opinion only
applied to death row inmates convicted of certain forms of rape. Some
critics questioned whether the victim, in fact, was not endangered. What
if the victim had not submitted voluntarily, and what about pregnancy and
disease? Despite the criticism, the *Ralph* case did demonstrate that the
Eighth Amendment's cruel and unusual punishment prohibition could be
applied successfully in capital cases.[77]

Also consequential to the *Furman* decision may have been California's preemptive action. Between *McGautha* and *Furman*, the California Supreme Court decided *People v. Anderson* (6 Cal. 3d 628, 493 P.2d
880, 1972), in which by a vote of 6-to-1 it ruled the state's death penalty
cruel and unusual, in violation of the state constitution. The decision not
only invalidated the state's death penalty, but it rendered moot the

Aikens' appeal to the U.S. Supreme Court.[78] Because he no longer faced execution, the Court granted an LDF motion to dismiss Aikens' appeal.[79] Nevertheless, *Aikens* probably influenced *Furman* by allowing Aiken's legal team to continue to hone its arguments in preparation for *Furman*. Amsterdam argued the cause for both petitioners, and five of the eight members of his legal team who helped with the *Aikens* brief also assisted on the six-member team that wrote the *Furman* brief. The five members of both teams were LDF lawyers Michael Meltsner, Jack Greenberg, James M. Nabrit III, Jack Himmelstein, and Elizabeth B. DuBois.[80] Thus, another factor that may have influenced the *Furman* decision was Amsterdam and his team's skilled advocacy. As one commentator put it, they simply convinced the justices to change their minds.[81]

It is important to note that the Court did not declare the death penalty itself unconstitutional. It held as unconstitutional only the statutes under which the death penalty was then being administered. Actually, the five justices in the majority split on this issue. Justices Brennan and Marshall maintained that capital punishment itself violated the Eighth and Fourteenth Amendments. Justices Douglas, Stewart, and White, on the other hand, rejected the position that capital punishment was inherently unconstitutional and argued that only the way it was being applied under current statutes made it unconstitutional. The Court seemed to be implying that if the process of applying the death penalty could be changed to eliminate the problems cited in *Furman*, then it would pass constitutional muster. Both Justices White and Burger believed that mandatory or automatic death sentences were still probably constitutional.[82] Justice Stewart, on the other hand, was fairly certain that the states would not reenact the old, "barbaric" mandatory death penalty statutes[83]—the last of which (except for a few rarely committed crimes in a few jurisdictions) was abolished in 1963.

Ignoring for the moment the Court's suggestion that the death penalty could be salvaged, death penalty opponents were jubilant on that June day in 1972. LDF lawyers knew their work did not end with *Furman*. There was still much to do to ensure that states followed the Court's directive. They understood that capitulation to the Court's decree would not come automatically, and that it would have to be fought for in most of the states that had their capital punishment statutes invalidated. To implement *Furman* and to make sure the death sentences of all death row inmates were vacated, each state's highest court had to take action, which in many states required the prodding of the LDF lawyers and those that assisted them throughout the country.[84] Nevertheless, on that June day in 1972, LDF attorneys could take pride in what they had accomplished. In seven years of hard work, they had achieved what had eluded American abolitionists for two centuries.[85] Many people believed, as Justices Stewart and Burger predicted privately, that there would never be another execution in the United States.[86]

Justices Stewart and Burger and all those who shared their belief, of course, were wrong! The backlash against *Furman* was immediate and widespread. Many people, including those who had never given the death penalty issue much thought, were incensed at what they perceived as the Supreme Court's arrogance in ignoring the will of the majority and its elected representatives. They clamored to have the penalty restored. Obliging their constituents, the elected representatives of 36 states proceeded to adopt new death penalty statutes designed to meet the Court's objections. Florida was the first jurisdiction to reinstate the death penalty after *Furman*. The Florida legislature met in special session to approve the new law in December of 1972, only five months after the *Furman* decision.[87] (Currently, 39 jurisdictions, which includes 37 states, the federal government, and the military, have death penalty statutes; 14 jurisdictions, including 13 states and the District of Columbia, do not.) The new death penalty laws took two forms. Twenty-two states removed all discretion from the process by mandating capital punishment upon conviction for certain crimes ("mandatory" death penalty statutes).[88] Other states provided specific guidelines that judges and juries were to use in deciding if death were the appropriate sentence in a particular case ("guided discretion" death penalty statutes).[89] Georgia was the first jurisdiction to impose a post-*Furman* death sentence. Chester Thomas Atkins was sentenced to death in early May 1973, about six weeks after Governor Jimmy Carter signed the state's post-*Furman* "guided discretion" death penalty statute into law. Atkins' death sentence was overturned six months later by the state supreme court.[90]

The legislative response to *Furman* caused the LDF lawyers to begin preparing to take on the new death penalty statutes. In doing so, their immediate mission was to extend the then five-year-old moratorium, but their ultimate goal was to abolish the death penalty once and for all.[91] There was reason to be optimistic about both goals. In the first place, it was unlikely the Court would approve the new "guided discretion" statutes when, just a few years earlier, Justice Harlan maintained in *McGautha* that it was humanly impossible to create adequate guidelines to channel juror discretion. Second, because of the moratorium and the subsequent growth of the death row population, a resumption of executions could cause a bloodbath—something few people wanted. Third, the Court was getting weary of deciding death penalty cases every year. Fourth, as noted previously, Justices Stewart and Burger did not think there would be any more executions in the United States. Fifth, Justice Powell, who voted with the *Furman* minority, believed that either Justice Stevens, who was new to the Court since *Furman*, or Justice Blackmun would join the four justices left from the *Furman* majority and vote to bring closure to the issue. Sixth, Justice Powell also assumed that Justices Stewart and White, who, in their *Furman* decisions, voted to strike down the death penalty, as then applied, but expressed their belief that it could be fixed, would vote to totally abolish the death penalty if given another chance.[92] How could the death penalty be reinstated under those circumstances? The answer is that it could and it was. As it turned out, each of the reasons was wrong. In retrospect, the legal strategy backfired. It produced only a fleeting victory. Given the scope of the public reaction to *Furman*, the Court was put in a difficult position when the new death penalty laws were challenged four years later. The LDF lawyers' strategy of invoking an "evolving standards" argument was hard to defend in light of the backlash.[93] Had the public response to *Furman* been milder, perhaps the outcome in the subsequent cases might have been different.[94] Justices Stewart and White suggested as much in later decisions.[95] The lesson of *Furman* was that death penalty abolition had to be won in the legislatures and not in the courts.

Another response to the *Furman* decision, though its importance probably was not fully appreciated at the time, was the enactment of the first true life without opportunity of parole (LWOP) statutes. Afraid of the prospects of a punishment scheme without a capital option and responding to public dissatisfaction with murderers sentenced to "life" being paroled early, law-and-order legislators, with the support of prosecutors, pushed through the first LWOP statutes in Alabama, Illinois, and Louisiana.[96] Other states followed. At this writing, all but two states, Alaska and New Mexico, have LWOP statutes, and Alaska does not have a death penalty.[97] Passage of the LWOP statutes following *Furman* soon became a classic case of "be careful of what you wish for." When the death penalty was reinstated in 1976, prosecutors no longer wanted the LWOP statutes because they wanted to use the possibility of parole to convince jurors to sentence defendants to death. Prosecutors frequently used the possibility of parole as a scare tactic by warning jurors that if a capital defendant were not executed, he or she would pose a future danger to society. At the same time, death penalty abolitionists began to realize that LWOP could be promoted as a viable option to death sentences.[98]

Woodson v. North Carolina and Gregg v. Georgia. The constitutionality of the new death penalty statutes was quickly challenged, and on July 2, 1976, the Supreme Court announced its rulings in five test cases. The five cases were chosen because they were "relatively straightforward," the facts were clear, and there were no side issues, such as racial prejudice.[99] All five cases involved felony murders, none of which was especially brutal and, perhaps most important, each case was selected from a state that had one of the five different types of new death penalty laws.[100] In *Woodson v. North Carolina* (428 U.S. 280) and *Roberts v. Louisiana* (428 U.S. 325), the Court rejected, by a vote of five to four, mandatory statutes that automatically imposed death sentences for defined capital crimes. In the North Carolina case, the state's brief defending the law pointed out that the state enacted the law to eliminate "all sentencing discretion" so that "there would be no successful *Furman*-based attack" on it.[101] Justice Stewart explained why the Court rejected the mandatory statutes. First, Stewart admitted that "it is capricious to treat similar things differently," and that mandatory death penalty statutes eliminated that problem.[102] He added, however, that it also "is capricious to treat two different things the same way."[103] Therefore, to impose the same penalty on all convicted murderers, even though all defendants are different, is just as capricious as imposing a penalty randomly.[104] To alleviate the problem, then, some sentencing guidelines were necessary.[105] Thus, in *Gregg v. Georgia* (428 U.S. 153), *Jurek v. Texas* (428 U.S. 262), and *Proffitt v. Florida* (428 U.S. 242) (hereafter referred to as the *Gregg* decision), the Court, by a vote of seven to two (Justices Marshall and Brennan dissented), approved guided discretion statutes that set standards for juries and judges to use when deciding whether to impose the death penalty. Justice Harlan's *McGautha* opinion notwithstanding, the Court's majority concluded that the guided discretion statutes struck a reasonable balance between giving the jury some direction and allowing it to consider the defendant's background and character and the circumstances of the crime. In doing so, they would respect the defendant's basic human dignity, as required by the Eighth Amendment, and prevent jury nullification—the practice of a jury's refusal to convict guilty defendants to avoid imposing unjust death sentences.[106] The Court also approved three other major procedural reforms in *Gregg*: bifurcated trials, automatic appellate review of convictions and sentences, and proportionality review. Proportionality review is a process whereby state appellate courts compare the sentence in the case before it with sentences imposed in similar cases in the state. Its purpose is to identify sentencing disparities and aid in their elimination.[107] Ironically, in the case that would set the standards for the modern death penalty, no mitigating evidence was presented during the new, special sentencing hearing. Mitigating evidence, along with aggravating evidence (to be discussed later) are the hallmarks of guided discretion statutes. The jury heard absolutely nothing about Gregg's background and character. In fact, in a trial that lasted only four days, Gregg's court-appointed attorney presented no evidence at all (except to put Gregg on the witness stand to testify that he did not commit the murders with which he was charged).[108]

In any event, the primary justification for the unique procedural safeguards approved in *Gregg* was the "death is different" principle created by Supreme Court Justice William Brennan and first articulated in *Furman v. Georgia*.[109] In *Furman*, the Court observed that death is "an unusually severe punishment, unusual in its pain, in its finality, and in its enormity."[110] Later, in *Gardner v. Florida* (420 U.S. 349, 1977), the Court elaborated:

> [F]ive Members of the Court have now expressly recognized
> that death is a different kind of punishment from any other
> which may be imposed in this country. From the point of
> view of the defendant, it is different both in its severity and its
> finality. From the point of view of society, the action of the sov-
> ereign in taking the life of one of its citizens also differs dra-
> matically from any other legitimate state action. It is of vital
> importance to the defendant and to the community that any
> decision to impose the death sentence be, and appear to be,
> based on reason rather than caprice or emotion.[111]

As a result of those decisions, the death penalty, unlike any other punishment prescribed by law, requires special procedures that ensure its
lawful application. Law Professor Margaret Jane Radin refers to those special procedures as "super due process."[112]

Professor Paternoster has noted that the Court in *Gregg* and *Woodson* attempted to cleverly reconcile two seemingly irreconcilable goals:
consistency in application and consideration of individual circumstances.[113] Whereas in *Woodson*, mandatory statutes would guarantee
consistency in application; they would preclude "individualized" sentencing decisions. In *Gregg*, guided discretion statutes would allow for
the consideration of factors peculiar to the case but would necessarily
produce disparities in sentencing. If one of the two goals had to be sac-
rificed for the other, the Court apparently opted (if it ever considered
the dilemma) for the consideration of individual circumstances over consistency in application. Inconsistency in application, however, was
one of the problems cited by the Court in *Furman*.

It is also noteworthy that the Court approved the guided discretion
statutes on faith, assuming that the new statutes and their procedural
reforms would rid the death penalty's administration of the problems
cited in *Furman*. Because guided discretion statutes, automatic appellate review, and proportionality review had never been required or
employed before in death penalty cases, the Court could not have
known whether they would make a difference. Now, more than 30 years
later, it is possible to evaluate the results. Law Professors Steiker and
Steiker claim the statutes have not made much (positive) difference:[114]

> The Supreme Court's death penalty law, by creating an impres-
> sion of enormous regulatory effort, while achieving negligible
> effects, effectively obscures the true nature of our capital sen-
> tencing system. The pre–*Furman* world of unreviewable sen-
> tencer discretion lives on, with much the same consequences
> in terms of arbitrary and discriminatory sentencing patterns.[115]

One of the problems was that the Court, which endorsed the aforementioned reforms, did virtually nothing to guarantee that defendants
benefited from them. For example, despite the emphasis placed on the

presentation of mitigation evidence during the penalty phase of the bifurcated trial, the Court ignored the fact that many attorneys in capital cases
lacked the training, experience, and resources to do so effectively.[116]

The Court actually accepted several different types of guided discretion statutes that varied in the restrictions placed on judges and
juries. Some of those statutes were modeled after ones proposed in the
American Law Institute's Model Penal Code of 1959.[117] Two of the most
common types of guided discretion statutes are "aggravating versus mitigating" and "aggravating only"; a third type, " structured discretion," is
one of the most frequently used types of guided discretion statutes.[118]
Aggravating circumstances (or factors) or "special circumstances," as they
are called in some jurisdictions, refer "to the particularly serious features
of a case, for example, evidence of extensive premeditation and planning
by the defendant, or torture of the victim by the defendant."[119] Mitigating circumstances (or factors), or "extenuating circumstances," refer
"to features of a case that explain or particularly justify the defendant's
behavior, even though they do not provide a defense to the crime of murder" (e.g., youth, immaturity, or being under the influence of another person).[120] An example of each type of statute is presented next.

Aggravating versus Mitigating Death Penalty Statutes. Florida's
current death penalty statute is an example of the "aggravating versus mitigating" type. It is the most widely used type of death penalty statute.[121]
Under it, at least one aggravating factor must be found before death may
be considered as a penalty. If one or more aggravating factors are found,
they are weighed against any mitigating factors. If the aggravating factors
outweigh the mitigating factors, then the sentence is death. If the mitigating factors outweigh the aggravating factors, the sentence is life
imprisonment without possibility of parole. If the aggravating and mitigating factors are of equal weight, a death sentence may be imposed.[122]

Following are the aggravating and mitigating circumstances listed in
Florida's death penalty statute:

Aggravating Circumstances

1. The capital felony was committed by a person previously
   convicted of a felony and under sentence of imprisonment or placed on community control or on felony probation.

2. The defendant was previously convicted of another capital felony or of a felony involving the use or threat of violence to the person.

3. The defendant knowingly created a great risk of death to
   many persons.

4. The capital felony was committed while the defendant was engaged, or was an accomplice, in the commission of, or an attempt to commit, or flight after committing or attempting to commit, any: robbery; sexual battery; aggravated child abuse; abuse of an elderly person or disabled adult resulting in great bodily harm, permanent disability, or permanent disfigurement; arson; burglary; kidnapping; aircraft piracy; or unlawful throwing, placing, or discharging of a destructive device or bomb.

5. The capital felony was committed for the purpose of avoiding or preventing a lawful arrest or effecting an escape from custody.

6. The capital felony was committed for pecuniary gain.

7. The capital felony was committed to disrupt or hinder the lawful exercise of any governmental function or the enforcement of laws.

8. The capital felony was especially heinous, atrocious, or cruel.

9. The capital felony was a homicide and was committed in a cold, calculated, and premeditated manner without any pretense of moral or legal justification.

10. The victim of the capital felony was a law enforcement officer engaged in the performance of his official duties.

11. The victim of the capital felony was an elected or appointed public official engaged in the performance of his official duties if the motive for the capital felony was related, in whole or in part, to the victim's official capacity.

12. The victim of the capital felony was a person less than 12 years of age.

13. The victim of the capital felony was particularly vulnerable due to advanced age or disability, or because the defendant stood in a position of familial or custodial authority over the victim.

14. The capital felony was committed by a criminal street gang member, as defined in s. 874.03.

15. The capital felony was committed by a person designated as a sexual predator pursuant to s. 775.21 or a person previously designated as a sexual predator who had the sexual predator designation removed.

Mitigating Circumstances

1. The defendant has no significant history of prior criminal activity.

2. The capital felony was committed while the defendant was under the influence of extreme mental or emotional disturbance.

3. The victim was a participant in the defendant's conduct or consented to the act.

4. The defendant was an accomplice in the capital felony committed by another person and his or her participation was relatively minor.

5. The defendant acted under extreme duress or under the substantial domination of another person.

6. The capacity of the defendant to appreciate the criminality of his or her conduct or to conform his or her conduct to the requirements of law was substantially impaired.

7. The age of the defendant at the time of the crime.

8. The existence of any other factors in the defendant's background that would mitigate against imposition of the death penalty.[123]

Two issues about Florida's death penalty statute in particular, and aggravating versus mitigating death penalty statutes in general, are worthy of note. First, until June 2002, Florida was one of only three death penalty states (the others were Alabama and Delaware) where a jury's sentencing recommendation was only advisory.[124] In other words, a judge was legally entitled to ignore the jury's recommendation and impose the sentence (either life or death) that he or she believed was most appropriate.[125] Thus, between 1972 and May 2002, Florida judges overruled 167 jury decisions to sentence defendants to life in prison and instead sentenced the defendants to death. However, most Florida judges stopped overruling juries, even though the law allowed it, because so many of those death sentences had been overturned on appeal by the Florida Supreme Court.[126] In Alabama, more than 20 percent of recent death row inmates were sentenced to death by trial judges who overrode jury sentences of life without parole.[127] None of this may matter anymore, because in June 2002, the U.S. Supreme Court ruled in *Ring v. Arizona* (536 U.S. 584) that the Sixth Amendment right to a jury trial requires that juries and not judges determine whether or not death is the appropriate penalty in a capital case. That decision ended the practice in Delaware and may end the practice in Florida and Alabama of making the jury's decision in capital cases only advisory. As of this writing, however, both states have withstood several *Ring* challenges to their override provisions.

The second issue is that the weighing of aggravating versus mitigating factors was not intended as a simple exercise in adding and subtracting. Jurors are not supposed to count the number of aggravating factors and then subtract them from the number of mitigating factors, or vice versa. Not all factors necessarily count equally. It is conceivable that a single aggravating factor could outweigh several mitigating factors, or, again, vice versa.

Aggravating Only Death Penalty Statutes. Georgia's post-*Furman* capital statute is an example of the "aggravating only" type. In Georgia, if a jury finds at least one statutory aggravating factor, then it may, but need not, recommend death. Two exceptions are the offenses of aircraft hijacking or treason, for which the death penalty may be imposed without finding at least one of the statutory aggravating factors. In all capital cases, the jury may also consider any mitigating factor, although mitigating factors are not listed in the statute as they are in some states. The judge must follow the jury's recommendation.[128] The aggravating factors listed in Georgia's death penalty statute are similar to those in Florida's death penalty statute.

Structured Discretion Statutes. Texas's current death penalty statute is an example of the "structured discretion" type. It is the most unusual type of guided discretion statute, employed only in Texas, Oregon, and Virginia.[129] In Texas, aggravating or mitigating factors are not listed in the statute. Instead, during the sentencing phase of the trial, the state and the defendant or the defendant's counsel may present evidence as to any matter that the court deems relevant to sentence, that is, any aggravating or mitigating factors. The court then submits the following issues to the jury:

1. whether there is a probability that the defendant would commit criminal acts of violence that would constitute a continuing threat to society; and

2. (if raised by the evidence) whether the defendant actually caused the death of the deceased or did not actually cause the death of the deceased but intended to kill the deceased or another or anticipated that a human life would be taken.

During penalty deliberations, juries in Texas must consider all evidence admitted at the guilt and penalty phases. Then, they must consider the two aforementioned issues. To answer "yes" to the issues, all jurors must answer "yes"; to answer "no" to the issues, 10 or more jurors must answer "no." If the two issues are answered in the affirmative, jurors are then asked if there is a sufficient mitigating factor (or factors) to warrant that a sentence of life imprisonment without parole rather than a death sentence be imposed. To answer "no" to this issue, all jurors must answer "no"; to answer "yes," 10 or more jurors must agree. If the jury returns an affirmative finding on the first two issues and a negative finding on the third issue, then the court must sentence the defendant to death. If the jury returns a negative finding on either of the first two issues or an affirmative finding on the third issue, then the court must sentence the defendant to life imprisonment without parole.[130]

Answering the first issue in the affirmative might prove difficult for many people. Despite decades of trying, social scientists remain incapable of predicting, with a reasonable degree of accuracy (a debatable standard), future human behavior, criminal or otherwise. Given what might seem the difficulty in getting all 12 jurors to answer "yes" to the two issues of aggravation and "no" to the issue of mitigation, one might surmise that states with structured discretion statutes would have a hard time sentencing offenders to death. That conclusion, however, would be wrong: Texas has executed more people than any other state under its structured discretion statute, executing nearly four times more people than any other state.[131] Apparently, getting all members of a jury to answer in the ways necessary to return a death sentence can be relatively easy.

Automatic Appellate Review. Each of the guided discretion statutes approved in *Gregg* also provided for automatic appellate review of all convictions and death sentences. This reform was added to ensure that death sentences were applied in a constitutionally acceptable manner. Prior to *Furman*, many death row inmates did not take advantage of the appellate process. During the 1960s, for example, one–quarter of the prisoners executed had no appeals at all, and two-thirds of their cases were never reviewed by a federal court.[132]

The review is typically conducted by the state's highest appellate court. Florida requires its Supreme Court to complete the review within two years after the filing of a notice of appeal.[133] In some states, the duties of the reviewing court are specified by statute, while in other states they are not. Georgia is an example of a state whose death penalty statute explicitly outlines the obligations of the Georgia Supreme Court in reviewing death sentences. The statute specifies that the reviewing court must determine:

1. Whether the sentence of death was imposed under the influence of passion, prejudice, or any other arbitrary factor; and

2. Whether, in cases other than treason or aircraft hijacking, the evidence supports the jury's or judge's finding of a statutory aggravating circumstance . . . ; and

3. Whether the sentence of death is excessive or dispro-
    portionate to the penalty imposed in similar cases, con-
    sidering both the crime and the defendant.[134]

At the beginning of 2005, 37 of the 38 states with capital punishment
statutes provided for an automatic review of all death sentences, regardless of the defendant's wishes.[135] South Carolina allows the defendant
to waive sentence review if the court deems the defendant competent;
also, the federal jurisdiction does not provide for automatic appellate
review. Most of the 37 states automatically review both the conviction
and the sentence. Idaho, Montana, Oklahoma, South Dakota, and Tennessee require review of the death sentence only. In Idaho, review of
conviction has to be filed through appeal or forfeited. In Indiana and Kentucky, a defendant can waive review of the conviction. In Virginia, a
defendant can waive an appeal of trial court error but cannot waive a
review of the death sentence for arbitrariness and proportionality. Mississippi has not addressed whether a defendant can waive the right to
automatic appellate review. In Wyoming, neither case law nor statute
preclude waiver of appeal. Arkansas requires review of specific issues
relating to both capital convictions and sentences.[136] The rationale for
not allowing defendants to waive the automatic review is that the state
has an independent interest in making sure that the death penalty is
administered lawfully. On the other hand, the rationale for waivers is that
the defendant's autonomy and freedom of choice ought to prevail. If
either the conviction or the sentence is overturned, then the case is usually sent back to the trial court for additional proceedings or for retrial.
It is possible that the death sentence may be reimposed as a result of this
process. Although the Supreme Court does not require it (*Pulley v. Harris*, 465 U.S. 37, 1984), some states, as noted previously, provide for proportionality review during the review process.

Post–1976 Death Penalty Cases

This section of the chapter is devoted to many (but not all) of the
Supreme Court cases decided after capital punishment was reinstated
in 1976. Since that time, the Court has been engaging in a time–consuming effort to fine tune the way capital punishment is applied.
According to Law Professor Franklin Zimring, in the century before *Furman*, the Supreme Court "only rarely reviewed state death sentences,"
but in the two decades after 1976, "the substantive law and procedure
in state death penalty cases became the most frequent business of that
court."[137] Some of the issues have been so controversial that the Court
has changed positions on them several times. The cases address nine
basic and, frequently, interrelated issues: (1) the constitutionality of death

penalty statutes, (2) what crimes are capital, (3) mitigating circumstances, (4) aggravating circumstances, (5) the appellate process, (6) capital juries, (7) who may or may not be executed, (8) assistance of counsel, and (9) other procedural issues. Many of the cases addressed multiple issues but generally only the most important issue is examined. For the most part, cases in each subsection are presented in chronological order and only brief descriptions of the Court's holdings are provided.

The Constitutionality of Death Penalty Statutes. Not long after the Supreme Court rendered its decisions in *Woodson* and *Gregg*, the constitutionality of the new death penalty statutes was challenged in *Harry Roberts v. Louisiana* (431 U.S. 633, 1977). The Supreme Court had rejected mandatory death penalty statutes as unconstitutional in *Woodson v. North Carolina* (1976) and *Roberts v. Louisiana* (1976), but the new rewritten Louisiana statute still mandated the death penalty for the killing of a special category of victim: a police officer. Consistent with its earlier ruling, the Court held that even mandatory death penalty statutes that are confined to a special category of victim are unconstitutional.

Ten years later, in *Sumner v. Shuman* (483 U.S. 66, 1987), the Court considered the death penalty mandated for a special category of offender. The Nevada legislature had (1) established the punishment of life imprisonment without possibility of parole, and (2) amended its death penalty statute to require the penalty for a murder committed by an inmate serving a life sentence without possibility of parole. In *Sumner v. Shuman*, the Court declared the provision unconstitutional. The Court's decisions in *Harry Roberts v. Louisiana* and *Sumner v. Shuman* seem to confirm the Court's opposition to mandatory death penalty statutes, even if they are confined to a special category of victim or offender.

Still, the Court is not necessarily opposed to mandatory provisions in otherwise nonmandatory statutes. In *Blystone v. Pennsylvania* (494 U.S. 299, 1990), for example, the Court upheld Pennsylvania's statute that mandates a death sentence if the jury finds at least one aggravating circumstance and no mitigating circumstance.

The most sweeping challenge to the constitutionality of the new death penalty statutes was *McCleskey v. Kemp* (481 U.S. 279, 1987) wherein the Court considered evidence of racial discrimination in the application of Georgia's death penalty statute. Recall that in the *Furman* decision, racial discrimination was cited as one of the problems with the pre-*Furman* statutes. The most compelling evidence was the results of an elaborate statistical analysis of post-*Furman* death penalty cases in Georgia. That analysis showed that Georgia's new statute produced a pattern of racial discrimination based on both the race of the offender and the race of the victim. In *McCleskey*, the Court opined that evidence such as the statistical analysis—which showed a pattern of racial discrimination—is not enough to render the death penalty unconstitutional. By a vote of five to four, it held that state death penalty statutes are constitutional even when statistics indicate they have been applied in racially biased ways.[138] The Court ruled that racial discrimination must be shown in individual cases—something McCleskey did not show in his case. For death penalty opponents, the *McCleskey* case represented the best, and perhaps last, chance of having the Supreme Court again declare the death penalty unconstitutional.

What Crimes Are Capital. The Supreme Court has repeatedly emphasized that the death penalty should be reserved for the most heinous crimes. In two cases decided in 1977, the Court, for all intents and purposes, limited the death penalty to only "aggravated" or capital murders. (To date, all post-*Furman* executions have been for that type of murder.) The Court ruled in *Coker v. Georgia* (433 U.S. 584) that the death penalty is not warranted for the crime of rape of an adult woman in cases in which the victim is not killed. The Court held that the death penalty for such a rape was "grossly disproportionate and excessive punishment." At the time of the decision, Georgia was the only state that authorized the death penalty for the rape of an adult woman and, in 9 out of 10 rape convictions in Georgia since 1973, juries had not imposed the death penalty. Likewise, in *Eberheart v. Georgia* (433 U.S. 917), the Court, for the same reasons, held that the death penalty is not warranted for the crime of kidnapping in cases in which the victim is not killed. Traditionally, both rape and kidnapping have been capital crimes, regardless of whether the victim died.

The federal 1994 Violent Crime Control and Law Enforcement Act expanded the federal death penalty to about 50 crimes—46 of which involve murder. The four exceptions are treason; espionage; drug trafficking in very large amounts; and attempting, authorizing or advising the killing of any public officer, juror, or witness in a case involving a continuing criminal enterprise—regardless of whether such a killing actually occurs.

As of 2006, 12 states had death penalty statutes that listed capital crimes which do not necessarily involve murder. They were:

- California: train-wrecking, treason, and perjury causing an execution

- Colorado: treason

- Florida: capital drug-trafficking and capital sexual battery

- Georgia: aircraft hijacking and treason

- Idaho: kidnapping with aggravating factors, perjury resulting in death

- Kentucky: kidnapping with aggravating factors

- Louisiana: aggravated rape of victim under age 12 and treason

- Mississippi: aircraft piracy

- Montana: capital sexual assault

- Oklahoma: rape, sodomy or lewd molestation involving children younger than 14

- South Carolina: convicted twice of raping children younger than 11

- South Dakota: kidnapping with aggravating factors[139]

Oklahoma and South Carolina, in June 2006, became the latest states to add capital offenses that do not involve murder. Both states passed legislation allowing the death penalty for certain sex crimes involving children. Law Professor David Bruck, commenting on this latest legislation, noted how stupid it was, arguing that it put a child rape victim's life in jeopardy. According to Bruck, "The last message you want to give an offender who has the life of a child in his hands is you might as well kill the child because he's already got the death penalty."[140] So far, no one has been executed for any of those crimes, although one inmate is on Louisiana's death row after being convicted in 2003 of raping an 8-year-old girl.[141] If and when the statutory provisions are challenged, though, it seems unlikely that the Supreme Court would allow the execution of offenders convicted of any of the crimes.

Mitigating Circumstances. One of the changes to death penalty statutes approved by the Court in *Gregg* was the requirement that sentencing authorities (either juries or judges) consider mitigating circumstances before determining the sentence. The main purpose of considering mitigating factors is to temper the desires for retribution and punishment with mercy, to realize that all people who kill do not deserve the death penalty.[142] The requirement to consider mitigating factors has been the subject of several challenges. The first test was in 1978 in the cases of *Lockett v. Ohio* (438 U.S. 586) and *Bell v. Ohio* (438 U.S. 637). In those cases, one of the issues was whether defense attorneys could present only mitigating circumstances that were listed in the death penalty statute. The Court held that trial courts must consider any mitigating circumstances that a defense attorney presents, and not just those listed in the statute.

In *Eddings v. Oklahoma* (455 U.S. 104, 1982), the trial judge refused to consider three mitigating circumstances: a turbulent family history, beatings by a harsh father, and serious emotional disturbance.

The only mitigating circumstance the judge found was Eddings' youth; he was 16 at the time of the crime. The judge held that the single mitigating circumstance did not outweigh the aggravating circumstances and sentenced Eddings to death. The Court reversed and remanded maintaining that although the sentencer and reviewing court could determine the weight given to any mitigating circumstance, they could "not give it no weight by excluding it from their consideration."

The issue before the Court in *Skipper v. South Carolina* (476 U.S. 1, 1986) was the admissibility of a specific mitigating circumstance: the defendant's good behavior in jail while awaiting trial. Such testimony by correctional officers is very persuasive with jurors because it shows that if they choose LWOP rather than death, the defendant is not likely to pose a future danger, and may even contribute positively to the prison environment.[143] Consistent with its earlier rulings in *Lockett, Bell*, and *Eddings*, the Court held that convicted murderers trying to escape a death sentence in favor of life in prison may present such evidence and it must be considered a legitimate mitigating circumstance in sentencing deliberations.

A year later, in *Hitchcock v. Dugger* (481 U.S. 393, 1987), the Court again revisited *Lockett, Bell,* and *Eddings* when a Florida court refused to consider evidence of nonstatutory mitigating circumstances. The Court reemphasized that the sentencing authority may not refuse to consider any relevant mitigating evidence. Also in 1987, the Court heard *California v. Brown* (479 U.S. 538), in which the petitioner challenged the trial judge's instruction that the jury not be swayed by "mere sympathy, passion, prejudice or public opinion." The petitioner argued that such an instruction undermined his ability to present mitigating evidence and, hence, violated both his Eighth and Fourteenth Amendment rights. The Court rejected the argument.

In 1988, in *Mills v. Maryland* (486 U.S. 367), the Court considered jury instructions that required the jury to be unanimous in its finding of a mitigating circumstance. In other words, before a Maryland juror (and jurors in other "weighing" states as well) could weigh a mitigating circumstance against aggravating circumstances, all 12 members of the jury had to agree that the mitigating circumstance did exist. If they did not, the mitigating circumstance could not be used in sentencing deliberations. The Court ruled that jury unanimity on the presence of a mitigating circumstance is not required before an individual juror may weigh it against aggravating factors. The issue arose again in 1990 in the case of *McKoy v. North Carolina* (494 U.S. 433), and the Court held that sentencing instructions, which prevent the sentencing jury from considering any mitigating factor that the jury does not unanimously find, violates the Eighth Amendment.

In *Walton v. Arizona* (497 U.S. 639, 1990) the Court ruled that states may adopt a preponderance of the evidence standard for proving mitigating factors (as Arizona did), though such a standard is not required. Preponderance of the evidence is evidence that outweighs the opposing evidence, or sufficient evidence to overcome doubt or speculation. It is a less stringent standard of proof than beyond a reasonable doubt (which is required for proving aggravating circumstances). In *Walton*, the Court determined that a state may adopt any standard for proving mitigating factors so long as the adopted standard does not lessen the prosecution's burden of proving all the elements of its case beyond a reasonable doubt. In North Carolina, Tennessee, and Ohio, for example, mitigating factors need only be proven to a juror's personal satisfaction.

In *Parker v. Dugger* (498 U.S. 308, 1991), the issue, in part, was whether appellate courts must independently (of trial courts) consider mitigating circumstances. The Florida Supreme Court reviewed Parker's death sentence and disallowed two of the aggravating circumstances on which the trial judge based his sentencing decision. However, relying on the trial court's finding of no mitigating circumstances and the existence of other aggravating circumstances, the Florida Court upheld Parker's death sentence. The Florida Court would have found that the trial record supported a showing of nonstatutory mitigating circumstances had it independently reviewed the evidence. The U.S. Supreme Court held that the Florida Supreme Court and, by implication, other reviewing courts, must conduct an independent reweighing of mitigating (and aggravating) evidence before rendering a decision.

In *Delo v. Lashley* (507 U.S. 272, 1993), the Court considered a Missouri case in which no evidence was presented to support the existence of a mitigating circumstance—the defendant's lack of prior criminal activity. The trial court judge refused to instruct the jury about the mitigating circumstance following the penalty phase of the trial because defense counsel provided no supporting evidence. The Supreme Court denied relief, holding that without supporting evidence, the Missouri trial court is not required to instruct the jury of the mitigating circumstance.

In *Deck v. Missouri* (544 U.S. 622, 2005), the Court ruled that the Fifth and Fourteenth Amendments are violated when a capital defendant is made to wear visible shackles during a capital trial's penalty phase, as Deck was made to do, unless that use is "justified by an essential state interest" such as courtroom security, which it was not. The problem, according to the Court, is that "the offender's appearance in shackles almost inevitably implies to a jury that court authorities consider him a danger to the community (which is often a statutory aggravator and always a relevant factor); almost inevitably affects adversely the jury's perception of the defendant's character; and thereby inevitably undermines the jury's ability to weigh accurately all relevant considerations when determining whether the defendant deserves death. The same rule also applies to the use of visible shackles during a capital trial's guilt phase for similar reasons.

In sum, this line of cases clearly shows that the U.S. Supreme Court requires trial courts to consider any mitigating circumstances that a defense attorney presents, whether or not a mitigating circumstance is listed in a state's death penalty statute. The only qualification to this requirement is that the mitigating circumstance must be supported by evidence. Although the requirement serves the desired purpose of narrowing death eligibility, it also "invites arbitrary and even invidious decisionmaking."[144] The problem, according to Law Professors Steiker and Steiker, is that the "unconstrained consideration of any kind of mitigating evidence . . . gives those with a mind to discriminate the opportunity to discriminate."[145] They further claim that, "although such discretion cannot be used to render a defendant death-eligible contrary to community standards, it can be used to exempt favored defendants from the death penalty or to withhold severe punishment for crimes against despised victims."[146]

Aggravating Circumstances. The "trigger" for any death sentence is the finding of at least one aggravating circumstance, generally "beyond a reasonable doubt."[147] Without such a finding, death may not be imposed. Death penalty states vary in the number of aggravating circumstances listed in their statutes. New Mexico has the fewest with 7; California and Delaware have the most with 22.[148] Most death penalty statutes list between 8 and 12 aggravating circumstances, but the trend is toward an increase in the number of statutory aggravating circumstances.[149] It is important to note that aggravating circumstances differ widely in their significance; therefore, their content is more important than how many there are in determining the number of death-eligible offenses.[150] There are three broad types of aggravating circumstances: (1) those that focus on offender characteristics, (2) those that focus on the manner in which the murder was committed, and (3) those that focus on victim characteristics.[151]

As was the case with mitigating circumstances, the aggravating circumstance requirement has generated a series of constitutional challenges. Ironically, although the aggravating circumstance requirement, like the mitigating circumstance requirement, was intended to narrow death-eligibility, it has not done so very well. Law Professors Steiker and Steiker observe, "States have adopted, and the Court has sustained, aggravating circumstances that arguably encompass every murder."[152] Research shows that "virtually all persons sentenced to death in Georgia before *Furman* would have been deemed death eligible under Georgia's post-*Furman* statute."[153]

Law Professor Jonathan Simon and Public Defender Christina Spaulding suggest that aggravating circumstances also have a largely unrecognized but important symbolic role.[154] Simon and Spaulding contend that the aggravating factors in all current death penalty statutes serve not only their ostensible legal purpose of narrowing the range of offenders eligible for the death penalty, but also the legislative purpose of recognizing and valorizing certain kinds of subjects and situations. In the latter context, aggravators have symbolic capital as "tokens of our esteem" as they validate the worth of potential victims. Types of potential victims "honored" in this way include public employees (such as peace officers, parole agents, and government investigators), private employees (such as newspaper reporters in the state of Washington),[155] and victims of crimes that have caused particular angst for some groups, such as drive-by shootings, car jackings, or gang activity. This is what has occurred with the aggravating factors in Illinois's death penalty statute, for example, which have ballooned from seven in the 1977 statute to 21 today.[156] Simon and Spaulding argue that public employees and other people not specifically covered by the aggravators are being dishonored by exclusion. This "popular punitiveness" or "punitive kitsch," as Simon and Spaulding call it, is being promoted for a popular audience to evoke empathy for people "just like me" and vengeance against those who threaten "us." A practical effect of these new aggravators is the forcing of prosecutors to seek the death penalty in cases where it ordinarily might not be pursued.[157]

One of the first tests involving aggravating circumstances was *Godfrey v. Georgia* (446 U.S. 420, 1980). The Court held that the aggravating factor under which Godfrey had been sentenced to death (his offense, in the language of the statute, was "outrageously or wantonly vile, horrible or inhuman in that it involved torture, depravity of the mind, or an aggravated battery to the person") was too broad and vague, and as a result, it reversed Godfrey's death sentence. It is worth noting that the Court did not rule that the statutory aggravating factor was unconstitutional on its face (many other states have similar aggravating circumstances in their statutes), only in the way it was applied in Godfrey's case. The problem was twofold. First, the trial judge did not explain the meaning of the aggravating circumstance to the jury, and second, the Georgia Supreme Court did not apply a clarifying interpretation of the meaning it had developed in earlier cases. Thus, in the words of the Court, "There is no principled way to distinguish this case, in which the death penalty was imposed, from the many cases in which it was not." For such a statutory aggravating circumstance to withstand constitutional challenge, a state high court must adequately clarify its meaning and that meaning must be applied independently to the facts of the case, as the Tennessee Supreme Court has done with the "especially heinous, atrocious, or cruel" aggravating circumstance in its statute (see *Bell v. Cone*, 543 U.S. 447, 2005).

In *Barefoot v. Estelle* (463 U.S. 880, 1983), the Court addressed the issue of using psychiatric evidence to predict future dangerousness. Such a prediction is a component (and aggravating circumstance) in Texas's post–*Furman* death penalty statute. Barefoot claimed that (1) "psychiatrists, individually and as a group, are incompetent to predict with an acceptable degree of reliability that a particular criminal will commit other crimes in the future and so represent a danger to the community," (2) "psychiatrists should not be permitted to testify about future dangerousness in response to hypothetical questions and without having examined the defendant personally" (as they did in Barefoot's case), and (3) "in the particular circumstances of this case, the testimony of the psychiatrists was so unreliable that the sentence should be set aside." The Supreme Court rejected all three claims and held that such psychiatric evidence predicting future dangerousness is admissible. Subsequent examination of 155 Texas death penalty cases in which prosecutors used experts to predict defendants' future dangerousness showed that the experts were wrong 95 percent of the time.[158] Currently, Texas is one of only three death penalty states in which the prediction of future dangerousness plays a significant role in juries' life and death decisions. In six other death penalty states, the prediction of future dangerousness has a limited role, and in the other 28 death penalty states, the prediction of future dangerousness has no role in capital sentencing procedures.[159]

The Court considered two other cases in 1983 involving aggravating circumstances. In *Zant v. Stephens* (462 U.S. 862), the issue was whether a death sentence must be vacated if one of the three statutory aggravating circumstances found by the jury was subsequently held to be unconstitutional, even though the two other aggravating circumstances were valid. The Court noted that the answer depended on the function of aggravating circumstances in a particular state's death penalty statute. In Georgia, for example, where the case originated, the jury is instructed not "to give any special weight to any aggravating circumstance, to consider any multiple aggravating circumstances any more significant than a single such circumstance, or to balance aggravating against mitigating circumstances pursuant to any special standard." Consequently, "in Georgia, the finding of an aggravating circumstance does not play any role in guiding the sentencing body in the exercise of its discretion, apart from its function of narrowing the class of persons convicted of murder who are eligible for the death penalty." For those and other reasons, the Supreme Court did not vacate the death sentence in the Georgia case. The outcome likely would have been different had the case occurred in a state in which aggravating circumstances played a more important role.

In *Barclay v. Florida* (463 U.S. 939, 1983), the principal issue was whether a nonstatutory aggravating circumstance was admissible. The nonstatutory aggravating factor in this case was racial hatred. Barclay was a member of the Black Liberation Army, whose avowed purpose was "to kill white persons and to start a revolution and a racial war." The Court upheld Barclay's death sentence, implying that the sentencing authority may consider virtually any factor in aggravation (that would be properly before it) once it has found at least one statutory aggravating circumstance.

In 1987, the Court addressed for the first time the use of victim–impact statements in death penalty cases. The case was *Booth v. Maryland* (482 U.S. 496). Victim–impact statements typically describe the harm done to and the suffering of victims and their family members. In accordance with Maryland law, victim–impact information was contained in the presentence investigation report. Booth's defense attorney moved to suppress the victim–impact statement, claiming it was both irrelevant and unduly inflammatory and, thus, its use violated the Eighth Amendment. The trial court judge denied the motion. The Supreme Court ruled five to four to vacate Booth's death sentence, holding that the introduction of victim–impact statements at the sentencing phase of a capital trial risked arbitrary and capricious imposition of the death penalty and, thus, violated the Eighth Amendment. The Court opined that victim-impact statements improperly refocused the death decision from the defendant and his or her crime to the "character and reputation of the victim and the effect on his family." Two years later, in *South Carolina v. Gathers* (490 U.S. 805, 1989), the Court, again by a five to four decision, reversed Gathers's death sentence. It reasoned that the prosecutor's argument that the death penalty should be imposed because of the personal characteristics of the victim—that he was a religious person and a registered voter—violated *Booth v. Maryland*. By 1991, however, the composition of the Court had changed. Justices Souter and Kennedy had replaced Justices Brennan and Powell. Consequently, in *Payne v. Tennessee* (501 U.S. 808, 1991), this time by a six to three decision, the Court reversed itself in both *Booth v. Maryland* and *South Carolina v. Gathers*. Justices Souter and Kennedy joined the *Booth* and *Gathers* minority, while the *Booth* and *Gathers* majority had lost Justices Brennan and Powell. The Court ruled that the introduction of victim–impact evidence and prosecutorial argument on that subject at the sentencing phase of a capital trial does not violate the Eighth Amendment. The Court decided that "evidence about the victim and about the impact of the murder on the victim's family is relevant to the jury's decision as to whether or not the death penalty should be imposed." The Court reasoned that it was only fair that the defendant's mitigating evidence be counterbalanced by evidence about the loss of the victim to his or her family and to society as a whole.

It is important to note that *Payne* allows victim-impact statements but does not require them. At this writing, 33 of the 37 death penalty states, the U.S. government, and the military authorize the use of victim-impact statements.[160] Most of those jurisdictions have no limitations on their use other than the Court's admonition in *Payne* that a statement not be so "unduly prejudicial that it renders the trial fundamentally unfair."[161] Based on data from the Capital Jury Project, victim-impact evidence has been used in about half of all capital trials since the *Payne* decision in 1991, but the data also show that it does not have much of an influence on sentencing outcomes.[162]

In *Brown v. Sanders* (546 U.S. __, 2006), the Court created a new rule for the handling of a subsequently invalidated aggravating circumstance in a jury's weighing process. The California Supreme Court invalidated the aggravating circumstance in this case. The Court held, "An invalidated sentencing factor . . . will render the sentence unconstitutional by reason of its adding an improper element to the aggravation scale in the weighing process unless one of the other sentencing factors enables the sentencer to give aggravating weight to the same facts and circumstances."

The Appellate Process. Many of the capital cases that address the appellate process involve the Court's effort to reduce the amount of time between imposition of sentence and execution. That time interval currently averages more than 10 years.[163] The Court first signaled its intention in *Barefoot v. Estelle* (463 U.S. 880, 1983). Not only did *Barefoot* allow psychiatric evidence predicting future dangerousness, it also approved acceleration of the appeals process in capital cases. Specifically, it allowed courts of appeal to deny an application for a stay of execution on habeas appeal—something they rarely did before *Barefoot*. The Court also provided detailed procedural guidelines for handling such appeals.

Professor Haines is among those who consider 1983 a pivotal year in the struggle against the death penalty. In the seven years between *Gregg* and *Barefoot*, the Supreme Court decided in favor of 14 of the 15 death-sentenced inmates whose appeals were fully argued before it.[164] Haines argues that by 1983 a majority of the Supreme Court justices had become frustrated trying to regulate death-sentencing procedures.[165] Those justices were no longer interested in telling states how to administer the penalty phase of capital trials.[166] The Court's *Barefoot* decision was only one among a number of cases that signaled the Court's new attitude. For at least a decade after 1983, most of the cases decided by the Supreme Court went against death-row inmates.[167] However, during the first few years of the twenty-first century, the Court's attitude appears to have changed, and it seems willing again to police the capital process.[168]

In *Pulley v. Harris* (465 U.S. 37, 1984), as mentioned previously, the Court decided that there was no constitutional obligation for state appellate courts to provide, upon request, proportionality review of death sentences. Recall that proportionality review, as required in Georgia's post–*Furman* death penalty statute, and as recommended in *Gregg* as a desirable reform, is a means by which the appellate court can compare the sentence in the case before it with penalties imposed in similar cases in the state. Its purpose is to reduce arbitrariness and discrimination in death sentencing. Since *Pulley*, many states have eliminated the proportionality review requirement from their statutes, while some states simply no longer conduct the reviews. Other states continue to conduct proportionality reviews but never find a death sentence to be disproportionate.[169] For example, as of the mid-1990s the Georgia Supreme Court had found only one death sentence to be disproportionate in the more than 300 it had reviewed, and it had not found any death sentences to be disproportionate since *Pulley*.[170] A recent examination of Georgia's death penalty system found its proportionality review process deficient because the Georgia Supreme Court "only reviews cases in which a death sentence has been imposed [a valid proportionality review also requires comparing sentences in which the death penalty was sought but not imposed and cases in which the death penalty could have been sought but was not], only expands that review to cases where the death penalty was not imposed upon a claim by the defendant that his/her sentence is disproportionate to that of his/her co-conspirator, and explains its proportionality review in a cursory manner."[171]

Further streamlining was accomplished in *Antone v. Dugger* (465 U.S. 200, 1984). In this case, the Court announced that it would no longer consider issues raised for the first time pursuant to last-minute pleas for stays of execution when the issues could have been raised on previous petitions for habeas relief. The Court's ruling was aimed at the popular practice employed by some appellate attorneys of stalling executions by raising constitutional issues one at a time.

In 1989, in *Murray v. Giarratano* (492 U.S. 1), the Court hastened the process by ruling that neither the Eighth nor the Fourteenth Amendment requires the appointment of counsel to indigent death row inmates seeking state post–conviction relief. Chief Justice Rehnquist, writing for the majority, explained that the right to counsel at the trial stage and for an initial appeal of the judgment and sentence of the trial court does not carry over to discretionary appeals. He reasoned that "the additional safeguards imposed by the Eighth Amendment at the trial stage of a capital case are . . . sufficient to assure the reliability of the process by which the death penalty is imposed." Nevertheless, by 1995, all states with death row inmates had passed legislation providing appointed counsel for indigent death row inmates in state habeas corpus post-conviction proceedings.[172] In state habeas corpus post-conviction proceedings, unlike in direct-appeal proceedings, a new lawyer, who is not associated with the previous proceedings, is allowed to thoroughly examine the trial's fairness by looking outside the formal record of the case.[173]

In the 1990s the Supreme Court made it more difficult for innocent defendants to obtain relief. For example, in 1992, in *Sawyer v. Whitley* (505 U.S. 333), the Court ruled that to show "actual innocence" on a successive petition for a writ of *habeas corpus*, a defendant must show, by clear and convincing evidence, that "but for a constitutional error, no reasonable juror would have found the [defendant] eligible for the death penalty." In 1993, in *Herrera v. Collins* (506 U.S. 390), the Court decided that a claim of actual innocence based on newly discovered evidence is not grounds for granting a further hearing in federal court. Chief Justice Rehnquist maintained that judges are not empowered "to correct errors of fact," even if a mistake could lead to the execution of an innocent person, and that the federal courts should intervene only when state courts violate constitutional procedures. The proper procedure for making claims of actual innocence after the "judicial process has been exhausted" is by filing a request for executive clemency. Clemency, wrote Rehnquist, "is the historic remedy for preventing miscarriages of justice"; it has "provided the 'fail safe' in our criminal justice system."

In dissent, Justice Blackmun, who was joined, in part, by Justices Stevens and Souter, responded that "nothing could be more contrary to contemporary standards of decency, or more shocking to the conscience, than to execute a person who is actually innocent." Justice Blackmun argued that to rely on executive clemency to correct miscarriages of justice is to "make judicial review under the Eighth Amendment meaningless." He further suggested that "to obtain relief on a claim of actual innocence, the petitioner must show that he probably is innocent." Justice Blackmun ended his dissent with a warning to those who would reduce procedural safeguards to speed up the process:

> Of one thing, however, I am certain. Just as an execution without adequate safeguards is unacceptable, so too is an execution when the condemned prisoner can prove that he is innocent. The execution of a person who can show that he is innocent comes perilously close to simple murder.

In 1995, in *Schlup v. Delo* (513 U.S. 298), the Court abandoned the "clear and convincing" standard for demonstrating actual innocence and replaced it with the new standard of "probable innocence." "Probable innocence" means that it is "more likely than not" that the inmate is innocent.

The Court made it harder for federal judges to overturn tainted convictions and sentences in state courts again in 2000, in *Williams (Terry) v. Taylor* (529 U.S. 362). A 5-4 majority held that it is not enough that a state court acted incorrectly. The law requires a hands-off approach by federal judges unless a state court clearly is wrong about some Supreme Court precedent or "unreasonably applies that principal to the facts of the prisoner's case." In other words, a federal court can save a prisoner from execution only if the state court decision against the prisoner was not only wrong but unreasonably wrong.

Capital Juries. Challenges involving capital juries have occupied a considerable amount of the Court's time. Among the first was *Beck v. Alabama* (447 U.S. 625, 1980), in which the issue was whether a conviction–minded jury must be allowed to consider a verdict of guilt of a lesser included noncapital offense. Under Alabama's death penalty statute, the trial judge was prohibited from giving the jury this option. Instead, the jury was given the choice of either convicting the defendant of the capital crime, in which case it was required to impose the death penalty, or acquitting the defendant. (In Alabama, if the defendant is convicted and the death penalty is imposed, the trial judge must hold a hearing to consider aggravating and mitigating circumstances. After hearing the evidence, the judge may refuse to impose the death penalty and, instead, may sentence the defendant to life imprisonment without possibility of parole. As noted previously, this jury override provision may change as a result of *Ring v. Arizona*, 2002.) The Court held in *Beck* that the death penalty may not be constitutionally imposed after a jury verdict of guilt of a capital offense when the jury was not permitted to consider a verdict of guilt of a lesser included noncapital offense when the evidence would have supported such a verdict. In *Hopper v. Evans* (456 U.S. 605, 1982), the Court qualified its ruling in *Beck*, holding that *Beck v. Alabama* applies only when the evidence supports a verdict of a lesser sentence and not in the case where the defendant makes it crystal clear that he or she killed the victim, intended to kill the victim, and would do the same thing again in similar circumstances.

The Court further qualified its *Beck* decision in *Hopkins v. Reeves* (524 U.S. 88, 1998). In this case, the Court held, "*Beck* does not require state trial courts to instruct juries on offenses that are not lesser included offenses of the charged crime under state law." Prior to jury deliberations in his felony-murder case, Reeves, who was attempting to escape a death sentence, asked the trial court to instruct the jury to consider convicting him of second-degree murder or manslaughter instead of felony murder. The trial court refused on the ground that the Nebraska Supreme Court had consistently ruled that those two crimes are not lesser-included offenses of felony murder. Reeves was convicted and sentenced to death. After exhausting state remedies, Reeves filed a federal habeas corpus petition claiming that trial court's failure to give the requested instructions violated *Beck*. As noted, the Court ruled that it did not. The Court explained that this case differed from *Beck* in two important respects. In Beck, Alabama law prohibited instructions on offenses that state law clearly recognized as lesser-included offenses of the charged crime. Nebraska law, on the other hand, did not provide for second-degree murder or manslaughter as lesser-included offenses for felony murder. Second, in Alabama, juries were restricted to a choice between conviction of a capital offense and death or acquittal. In Nebraska, on the other hand, the jury did not impose sentence (which will change as a result of *Ring v. Arizona*, 2002) and the three-judge sentencing panel had a choice between death or life imprisonment.

The Court revisited its *Witherspoon* decision in a series of cases. Recall that in *Witherspoon v. Illinois* (1968) the Court held that during the voir dire, prospective jurors may not be removed from the jury for cause simply because they voiced general objections to the death penalty or expressed conscientious or religious scruples against its imposition. In the first case, *Adams v. Texas* (448 U.S. 38, 1980), the Court decided that prospective jurors can be excluded from capital juries if their views on capital punishment would not allow them to obey their oath and follow the law of Texas without conscious distortion or bias. Texas law at that time required prospective jurors to state under oath that the mandatory penalty of death or life imprisonment would not affect their deliberations on any issue of fact. The law mandated a sentence of life imprisonment or death on conviction of a capital felony.

In *Wainwright v. Witt* (469 U.S. 412, 1985), the Court reconsidered its decisions in *Witherspoon* and *Adams* and held that potential jurors in capital cases should be excluded from jury duty in a manner no different from how they are excluded in noncapital cases. The Court opined that no longer does a juror's automatic bias against imposing the death penalty have to be proved with unmistakable clarity. Instead, the question of exclusion from a jury should be determined by the interplay of the prosecutor and the defense attorney and the decision of the judge based on his or her first-hand observations of the prospective juror. If the judge determines that a prospective juror's beliefs would bias the juror's ability to impose the death penalty, then the juror should be excluded.

The Court's final word on this issue (so far) came in *Lockhart v. McCree* (476 U.S. 162, 1986). In this case, the Court ruled that prospective jurors whose opposition to the death penalty is so strong that it would prevent or substantially impair the performance of their duties as jurors at the sentencing phase of the trial may be removed for cause. Stated differently, as long as jurors can perform their duties as required by law, they may not be removed for cause because they are generally opposed to the death penalty.

This series of cases modifying the Court's *Witherspoon* decision addressed the issue of what to do with prospective jurors who are opposed to capital punishment. Another interesting issue is what to do with prospective jurors who would automatically impose the death penalty following a defendant's conviction in a capital case. That issue was considered in *Morgan v. Illinois* (504 U.S. 719, 1992). During jury selection, Morgan's attorney requested the judge to ask all prospective jurors the following question: "If you found Derrick Morgan guilty, would you automatically vote to impose the death penalty no matter what the facts are?" The judge refused to ask the jurors this "life qualifying" or "reverse-*Witherspoon*" question. The jury found Morgan guilty and sentenced him to death. Morgan appealed the court's refusal to ask the reverse-*Witherspoon* question, and the Supreme Court reasoned that "a juror who will automatically vote for the death penalty in every case will fail in good faith to consider the evidence of aggravating and mitigating circumstances as the instructions require him to do." Thus, ruled the Court, a prospective juror who would automatically vote for the death penalty may be challenged for cause.

In *Bullington v. Missouri* (451 U.S. 430, 1981), the Court considered the issue of whether a death sentence could be imposed following a retrial when a jury had imposed life imprisonment at the first trial. The Court held that it could not because to do so would violate the Fifth Amendment's prohibition of double jeopardy. In *Sattazahn v. Pennsylvania* (537 U.S. 101, 2003), the Court considered a similar issue. During the penalty phase of Sattazahn's capital trial, the jury reported to the trial judge that it was hopelessly deadlocked 9-3 for life imprisonment. The court discharged the jury and entered a life sentence as Pennsylvania law required. Sattazahn then appealed his first-degree murder conviction to the Pennsylvania superior court, which reversed the conviction and remanded for a new trial. At his second trial, Sattazahn was convicted and sentenced to death. The Pennsylvania Supreme Court affirmed the death sentence, noting that the death sentence in the second trial, after he was sentenced to life imprisonment in the first trial, neither violated the Fifth Amendment's double jeopardy clause nor the Fourteenth Amendment's due process clause. In a 5-4 ruling, the Supreme Court agreed, opining that "the life sentence at issue did not amount to an acquittal based on findings sufficient to establish legal entitlement to the life sentence or that the government failed to prove one or more aggravating circumstances beyond a reasonable doubt." The Court also maintained that the Fourteenth Amendment's due process clause does not provide greater double-jeopardy protection than does the double jeopardy clause of the Fifth Amendment.

In *Spaziano v. Florida* (468 U.S. 447, 1984), the jury override provision of Florida's death penalty statute was challenged. Recall that in Florida (as well as in Alabama, Delaware, and Indiana at the time), a trial judge was allowed to overrule the jury and impose a death sentence, even if all jurors voted for a life sentence, or impose a life sentence, even if all jurors voted for a death sentence. A majority of jurors in Spaziano's case recommended life imprisonment after he was found guilty of first–degree murder. The trial judge, however, who conducted his own independent weighing of the aggravating and mitigating circumstances in the case, overrode the jurors' recommendation and sentenced Spaziano to death. On appeal, the Supreme Court upheld Florida's override provision, maintaining that a sentencing judge may disregard the jury's recommendation of life imprisonment and impose the death penalty. In *Harris v. Alabama* (513 U.S. 504, 1995), the Court upheld Alabama's override provision.

However, in *Ring v. Arizona* (536 U.S. 584, 2002) the constitutionality of the jury override provisions in the capital punishment statutes of Florida, Alabama, and Delaware (Indiana had since eliminated jury override from its death penalty statute) were thrown into doubt. In a 7-2 decision, the Court ruled that the Sixth Amendment right to a jury trial requires that juries and not judges determine whether or not death is the appropriate penalty in a capital case. That means that a jury and not a judge (in a jury trial) must find capital aggravating factors beyond a reasonable doubt. The decision invalidated the death sentencing statutes in Arizona, Idaho, Montana, Colorado, and Nebraska, which gave the trial judge or sentencing judges (in Colorado and Nebraska a three-judge panel decided the sentence) sole responsibility for determining the appropriate sentence. The fate of the 168 death row inmates in those five states at the time of the decision is uncertain. Some are likely either to have their sentences commuted to life imprisonment or be resentenced. Others, however, will get no relief. In *Schriro v. Summerlin* (542 U.S. 348, 2004), the Court ruled that *Ring* did not apply retroactively to cases already final on direct review. The Court maintained that a new rule, as created in *Ring*, applies to convictions that are final only in limited circumstances. According to the Court, "New substantive rules generally apply retroactively, but new procedural rules generally do not," and *Ring* created a procedural rule. *Ring* neither altered the range of conduct nor the class of persons subject to the death penalty in Arizona. It only changed the method of determining whether the defendant engaged in that conduct. The only procedural rules that can be applied retroactively are "watershed rules" that address "the fundamental fairness and accuracy of the criminal proceeding," and Ring did not announce a watershed rule of criminal procedure. At this writing, it is not entirely clear what the effect of the *Ring* decision will be on the death sentencing practices of Florida and Alabama, but, as mentioned previously, both states have withstood several *Ring* challenges to their override provisions. Days after the *Ring* decision, Delaware changed its law to conform with the ruling.

The issue in *Caldwell v. Mississippi* (472 U.S. 320, 1985) was whether a death sentence is valid when the sentencing jury is led to believe that responsibility for determining the appropriateness of a death sentence rests not with the jury but with the appellate court which later reviews the case. The prosecutor at Caldwell's trial urged the jury not to view itself as determining whether the defendant would die, because a death sentence would be reviewed for correctness by the state supreme court. The Court vacated the petitioner's sentence, arguing that the prosecutor's suggestion to the sentencing jury that the appellate court would correct an inappropriate death sentence created an intolerable risk of unreliable sentencing.

Another series of cases in this area deals with procedures that may contribute to unacceptable forms of juror discrimination in the imposition of the death penalty. In *Batson v. Kentucky* (476 U.S. 79, 1986), a non-death penalty case, the Court considered the relatively common prosecutorial practice of using peremptory challenges to eliminate black people from trial juries in capital cases involving black defendants. This practice resulted in black defendants frequently being tried by all-white juries. In *Batson*, the Court held that "the Equal Protection Clause forbids the prosecutor to challenge potential jurors solely on account of their race or on the assumption that black jurors as a group will be unable impartially to consider the State's case against a black defendant." Thus, under *Batson*, once the defendant establishes a prima facie case showing race was a factor in a prosecutor's decision to exercise a peremptory challenge, the burden shifts to the prosecutor to provide a neutral, legitimate explanation to justify his or her striking of the juror. However, in *Purkett v. Elem* (514 U.S. 765, 1995), another non-death penalty case, the Court held that once the prosecutor provided a race-neutral explanation, the trial court must decide whether the opponent of the strike has proved purposeful racial discrimination. According to the Court, this does not demand an explanation by the prosecutor that is persuasive or even plausible, only one that is facially valid. If discriminatory intent is not inherent in the prosecutor's explanation, then the explanation offered is considered race neutral.

Batson and *Elem* were put to the test in the case of *Miller-El v. Dretke* (545 U.S. 231, 2007, 2005). In this case, the Court ruled that Thomas Miller-El, a black defendant, was entitled to a new trial because of strong evidence of racial bias during jury selection at his original trial. Prosecutors peremptorily struck 10 of 11 qualified black venire members. The Court found the prosecutors' race-neutral explanations for striking the black venire members improbable and a pretext designed to conceal racial bias. Also indicative of decisions based on race were the prosecution's shuffling of the venire panel (rearranging the order in which venire panel members were seated and questioned), its asking different questions to black and nonblack panel members about their views on the death penalty and minimum acceptable sentences, and, perhaps most telling, the widely known practice of the Dallas County District Attorney's Office to exclude black venire members from juries—a practice that had been going on for decades. The Court surmised that some of the evidence is open to judgment calls, but when viewed cumulatively "its direction is too powerful to conclude anything but discrimination."

The Court applied its *Batson* logic to the selection of grand juries in *Vasquez v. Hillery* (474 U.S. 254, 1986). In this case, the Court ruled that indictment by an all-white grand jury from which black individuals were systematically excluded created an intolerable risk that a defendant's indictment was a result of discrimination, thereby violating the Equal Protection Clause. The Court added that even though a defendant is subsequently lawfully convicted, that fact does not cure the taint attributed to a grand jury selected on the basis of race.

At issue in the case of *Turner v. Murray* (476 U.S. 28, 1986) was whether a defendant in an interracial murder case has a right to question prospective jurors about racial prejudice. In this case, the defendant was denied that opportunity. The Court ruled on appeal that failure to voir dire a jury about racial bias in an interracial murder case created an intolerable risk of discrimination.

In *J.E.B. v. Alabama* (511 U.S. 127, 1994), a noncapital case, the Equal Protection Clause was held to prohibit discrimination in jury selection on the basis of gender, or an assumption that an individual will be biased in a particular case solely because that person happens to be a woman or a man. The Court's decision suggests that the Court will not tolerate gender discrimination in capital jury selection for the same reason it will not tolerate racial discrimination.

At issue in *Simmons v. South Carolina* (512 U.S. 154, 1994) was South Carolina's new sentencing option in capital cases: life imprisonment without possibility of parole. Research shows that citizens are confused and skeptical about this sentencing option. Many citizens believe that even when offenders are sentenced to life imprisonment without possibility of parole, they may still be paroled. Concerned that the jury might not understand that "life imprisonment" did not carry with it the possibility of parole in Simmons's case, his defense attorney asked the trial judge to clarify the issue by defining the term "life imprisonment" in accordance with the South Carolina statute. The judge refused. On appeal, the Court ruled that a defendant has a right to inform the jury of the real consequences of a "life" sentence when the state argues that the defendant would be dangerous in the future (as the state did in Simmons's case), and "life" means life without possibility of parole, as a matter of state law. However, in *Ramdass v. Angelone* (530 U.S. 156, 2000) the Court made clear that where an offender may some day be paroled, the state is under no obligation to explain to the jury what a life sentence means. Also, in *California v. Ramos* (463 U.S. 992, 1983), the Court held that a capital sentencing instruction about the Governor's power to commute a life sentence without possibility of parole (a "Briggs Instruction") did not violate the Constitution. The Court suggested that focusing the jury's attention on a defendant's probable future dangerousness if ever released was a desirable goal.

The Court reiterated its decision in *Simmons v. South Carolina* in 2001 in *Shafer v. South Carolina* (532 U.S. 36). In *Shafer*, the Court maintained that whenever a defendant's future dangerousness is raised by the prosecution, the defendant has the right to an accurate jury instruction that a life sentence means no possibility of parole. The jury in *Shafer* was given the ambiguous instruction that "life imprisonment means until death of the offender," and that "[p]arole eligibility or inel-igibility is not for your consideration." The Court returned Shafer's case to South Carolina because the instructions misled the jury.

In yet a third South Carolina case, *Kelly v. South Carolina* (534 U.S. 246, 2002), the Court in a 5-4 decision held that a South Carolina trial court again had violated *Simmons v. South Carolina* by refusing to inform Kelly's sentencing jury that he would never be eligible for parole if the jury sentenced him to life imprisonment instead of death. During the sentencing phase of Kelly's trial, the prosecution did not state outright that Kelly posed a future danger but rather told the jury that "murderers will be murderers" and that Kelly had planned jail escapes when previously incarcerated. On appeal, Kelly contended that the issue of future dangerousness had been raised by the state. The South Carolina Supreme Court believed otherwise and maintained that escape attempts were not the type of evidence of future dangerousness intended by *Simmons*. The Supreme Court reversed that decision and ordered a new sentencing trial for Kelly.

Note that when a state does not argue that a defendant would be dangerous in the future, there is no obligation to explain to sentencing juries parole eligibility and minimum sentence requirements associated with life imprisonment sentences. Only a few death penalty statutes have such a requirement.[174]

In another case dealing with sentencing instructions the issue was how far a judge must go to clarify jury questions. In *Weeks v. Angelone* (528 U.S. 225, 2000) the Court decided that a trial judge's refusal to do more than to refer the jury to pattern instructions he had given before deliberations was permissible and constitutionally sound. Pattern instructions are a uniform set of scripted instructions.

Who May or May Not Be Executed. The Supreme Court has established limits on who may or may not be executed and has estab-lished the principle that the Eighth Amendment requires at least a rough correspondence between the punishment imposed, the harm done, and the blameworthiness of the defendant.[175] In the extreme, this means that the Court would not allow an execution for jaywalking, how-ever intentional. The cases that the Court has decided were not as easy. The first of the cases addressed the issue of whether a participant in a felony murder who did not kill, attempt to kill, or intend to kill may be executed. Many states include the crime of felony murder in their homicide statutes. In a felony murder, it is possible to find a defendant guilty of murder even though he or she did not intend to kill and may or may not have caused a death. Many states hold such a defendant guilty of first–degree murder because he or she committed a specified felony that caused a death. For example, prior to Governor Ryan's mass com-mutation in 2003, 60 percent of Illinois's death row inmates had been convicted of a felony murder.[176] Illinois's felony-murder statute lists

16 felony-murder offenses punishable by death.[177] It has been esti-mated that, nationwide, about 40 percent of all capital indictments are for felony murder.[178]

The Supreme Court first addressed the issue in *Enmund v. Florida* (458 U.S. 782, 1982). Enmund was the driver of the getaway car in a rob-bery in which the victims were murdered. Enmund did not himself kill and was not present at the killings, but the fact that he helped the killers escape was enough under Florida law to make him "a constructive aider and abettor and hence a principal in first–degree murder upon whom the death penalty could be imposed." Enmund was sentenced to death for his role in the crime. In addressing Enmund's blameworthiness, the Court ruled that to impose the death penalty on someone who did not kill or intend to kill violated the Eighth Amendment. The Court reversed the judgment upholding Enmund's death penalty and remanded the case for further proceedings in light of its ruling.

The Court revisited its *Enmund* decision in 1987 in the case of *Tison v. Arizona* (481 U.S. 137). As in *Enmund*, Raymond and Ricky Tison were participants in felony murders—in this case, involving robbery and kidnapping. Also like Enmund, the Tison brothers did not do the killing or intend to kill. Unlike Enmund, however, the Tisons were major par-ticipants in the crimes and showed a "reckless indifference to human life." The Court held that even though the killing and intent to kill were absent, the other circumstances were sufficient to support a judgment of death.

In 1986, in *Ford v. Wainwright* (477 U.S. 399), the Court considered the issue of whether states may execute people who have literally gone crazy on death row. Writing for the majority, Justice Marshall noted that the Court had never decided whether the Constitution forbids the execution of the insane, even though for centuries no jurisdiction has approved the practice. This does not mean that insane persons have never been executed. To the contrary, as attorney Stephen Bright observes, "'insane' has been so narrowly defined as to allow people with severe mental illness to be put to death."[179] Justice Powell defined insanity for Eighth Amendment purposes as the condition under which people "are unaware of the punishment they are about to suffer and why they are to suffer it." In a recent Florida case, a circuit judge acknowledged the men-tal health problems of the death row inmate in the case before him, but concluded that they were not severe enough to prevent his impending execution. The judge opined that to meet the threshold of incompetency to be executed the inmate "would have to virtually be unable to clean him-self, feed himself, or otherwise function."[180] Nevertheless, consistent with common–law heritage, the Court in *Ford* held that states are barred from executing people who have become insane while on death row. The implication is that death row inmates must first be cured of their insan-ity before they are executed.[181]

An important question raised by the *Ford* decision is whether a state can forcibly medicate death row inmates who have become insane while on death row for the sole purpose of rendering them competent for execution? However, when a case (*Singleton v. Norris*, 124 S. Ct. 74, 2003) addressing that question was appealed to the U.S. Supreme Court, the Court refused to grant *certiorari*. As a result, Charles Singleton was executed in Arkansas on January 6, 2004, and the Eighth U.S. Circuit Court of Appeals' decision in the case (*Singleton v. Norris*, 319 F. 3d 1018, 8th Cir. 2003) remains precedential.[182] The Eighth Circuit ruled:

> In order to justify the forcible medication of an inmate when that medication would render the prisoner competent for execution, the state must (1) present an essential state interest that outweighs the individual's interest in remaining free from medication, (2) prove that there is no less intrusive way to fulfill the essential interest, and (3) prove by clear and convincing evidence that the medication is medically appropriate. Medication is medically appropriate where it is in the best medical interest of the inmate, where the medication is likely to render the inmate competent, and where the severity of the side effects of the medication does not overwhelm its benefits.

The court held that "the interest in carrying out Singleton's capital punishment sentence outweighed Singleton's substantial liberty interest in remaining free of unwanted medication," despite Singleton's argument "that medication could not be in his best interest when it would ultimately render him eligible for execution." Although the state has an essential interest in exacting punishment, the decision has been criticized because the state's interest may be achieved by another punishment besides the death penalty, such as life imprisonment without opportunity of parole.[183] In dissent, one of the Eighth Circuit judges observed:

> At the end of the day, the state executed a person who was mentally ill. Artificial sanity is not the same as true sanity. Treatment is not synonymous with being cured; antipsychotic drugs merely mask mental illness. Competency in Singleton's case was a fiction maintained only by powerful antipsychotic medications.[184]

The issue in *Penry v. Lynaugh* (492 U.S. 302, 1989) was whether the Eighth Amendment categorically prohibits the execution of a capital offender who is mentally retarded. Court testimony indicated that Penry, who was 22 years old when he allegedly committed the brutal rape and murder for which he was convicted and sentenced to death, had the reasoning capacity of a 7-year-old. The Court provided the following rationale in upholding Penry's death sentence:

> In sum, mental retardation is a factor that may well lessen a
> defendant's culpability for a capital offense. But we cannot con-
> clude today that the Eighth Amendment precludes the execu-
> tion of any mentally retarded person of Penry's ability convicted
> of a capital offense simply by virtue of his or her mental retar-
> dation alone. So long as sentencers can consider and give
> effect to mitigating evidence of mental retardation in imposing
> sentence, an individualized determination whether "death is the
> appropriate punishment" can be made in each particular case.
> While a national consensus against execution of the mentally
> retarded may someday emerge reflecting the "evolving standards
> of decency that mark the progress of a maturing society," there
> is insufficient evidence of such a consensus today.

By 2002, a national consensus against the execution of the mentally
retarded had emerged. Results of a 2002 Gallup poll showed that only
13 percent of respondents favored the death penalty for the mentally
retarded who are convicted of capital crimes, 82 percent opposed it, and
5 percent didn't know or refused to answer. Among subgroups, only 18
percent of males, 9 percent of females, 13 percent of whites, and 14 percent of nonwhites favored the death penalty for mentally retarded capital offenders.[185] Furthermore, by 2002, eighteen death penalty states had
prohibited the execution of the mentally retarded. In 1989, when
Penry was decided, only Maryland and Georgia prohibited their execution. The Court was swayed by these developments and in June
2002, in the case of *Atkins v. Virginia* (536 U.S. 304), ruled 6-3 that it
is cruel and unusual punishment to execute the mentally retarded.
The Court reasoned that the death penalty's two social purposes—retribution, i.e., "just deserts," and deterrence of capital crimes by prospective offenders—are not served by the execution of mentally retarded
capital offenders. Regarding retribution, the Court believed the lesser
culpability of mentally retarded offenders by virtue of their cognitive
and behavioral impairments did not merit that form of retribution;
regarding deterrence, the Court averred that those impairments make
it less likely they can process the information of execution as a possible penalty and, therefore, control their behavior based on that information. The Court also surmised that exempting the mentally retarded
from execution would not lessen the death penalty's deterrent effect for
offenders who are not mentally retarded. The Court was especially
concerned that mentally retarded offenders faced a special risk of
wrongful execution because they might unwittingly confess to crimes
they did not commit, be less able to meaningfully assist their attorneys,
be poor witnesses, and their demeanor may create an unwarranted
impression that they lacked remorse for their crimes. A problem with
the *Atkins* decision is that the Court did not set a standard for what constitutes mental retardation. That issue was left to the states to decide.

It is presumed that the standard definition of mental retardation, which is an IQ of 70 or below and significant limitations in adaptive skills, will be used. The decision is likely to spare the lives of dozens, if not hundreds, of convicted killers. It is estimated that 12 to 20 percent of the death row population is mentally retarded, and that at least 27 mentally retarded defendants have been executed under post–*Furman* statutes.[186] Ironically, on August 5, 2005, a Virginia jury found Daryl Atkins (the petitioner in *Atkins v. Virginia*) mentally competent, despite his IQ of 59, and he was rescheduled for execution.[187]

In 1988 and 1989, the Court decided three cases that dealt with the age of the offender at the time the crime was committed. At issue was the question of whether the Constitution permitted the execution of juveniles, i.e., individuals who committed their capital crimes prior to their eighteenth birthday. The Court held in *Thompson v. Oklahoma* (487 U.S. 815, 1988) that the Constitution prohibited the execution of a person who was under 16 years of age at the time of his or her offense. In this particular case, the Court stipulated that the decision applied only when a state had not specifically legislated the death penalty for such minors. The next year, in the cases of *Stanford v. Kentucky* and *Wilkins v. Missouri* (collectively as 492 U.S. 361), the Court determined that the Eighth Amendment did not prohibit the execution of persons who were 17 (in *Stanford*) or 16 (in *Wilkins*) years of age at the time of their offenses. The three decisions together meant that the Supreme Court would allow the executions of 16 and 17 year olds but would not allow the execution of persons who were under 16 years of age at the time of their offenses.

By 2002, however, it was clear that a national consensus had developed about the desirability of executing juveniles. In a 2002 Gallup poll, for example, only 26 percent of respondents favored the death penalty for juveniles, 69 percent opposed it, and 5 percent didn't know or refused to answer. Among subgroups, only 31 percent of males, 21 percent of females, 25 percent of whites, and 29 percent of nonwhites favored the death penalty for juveniles.[188] However, the Supreme Court was slow to move. Toward the end of 2002, the Court by a 5 to 4 vote declined to hear another appeal by Kevin Stanford (the appellate in *Stanford v. Kentucky*) who had been sentenced to die for abducting, sodomizing, and killing a gas-station attendant when he was 17.[189] Nevertheless, by 2005, 18 death penalty states prohibited the death penalty for juveniles, and the 20 death penalty states that had not prohibited it, infrequently imposed it. More importantly, by 2005, Justice Anthony Kennedy had changed his mind on the issue. Based on these developments, the Court, in *Roper v. Simmons* (543 U.S. 551, 2005), affirmed by a 5 to 4 vote the decision of the Missouri Supreme Court and ruled that the Eighth and Fourteenth Amendments forbid the imposition of the death penalty on offenders who were under the age of 18 at the time their crimes were committed. The Missouri Supreme Court had accepted Simmons's claim that the Court's reasoning in *Atkins v. Virginia* applied to the execution of juveniles. The Court identified three differences between juvenile offenders and adult offenders that diminished the former's culpability: (1) "Juveniles' susceptibility to immature and irresponsible behavior means 'their irresponsible conduct is not as morally reprehensible as that of an adult'"; (2) "Their own vulnerability and comparative lack of control over their immediate surroundings mean juveniles have a greater claim than adults to be forgiven for failing to escape negative influences in their whole environment"; and (3) "The reality that juveniles still struggle to define their identity means it is less supportable to conclude that even a heinous crime committed by a juvenile is evidence of irretrievably depraved character." The Court concluded:

> When a juvenile commits a heinous crime, the State can exact forfeiture of some of the most basic liberties, but the State cannot extinguish his life and his potential to attain a mature understanding of his own humanity. While drawing the line at 18 is subject to the objections always raised against categorical rules, that is the point where society draws the line for many purposes between childhood and adulthood and the age at which the line for death eligibility ought to rest.

Assistance of Counsel. Not only do capital defendants have a Sixth Amendment right to counsel, they also have the right to the "effective assistance of counsel."[190] It was not until 1984, however, that the Court provided any guidelines for determining when counsel is ineffective. The case was *Strickland v. Washington* (466 U.S. 668).

Strickland's claim of ineffective assistance of counsel was denied, but the Court did create a two-pronged test for determining when counsel is ineffective at either the guilt or penalty phase of a bifurcated capital trial. First, the defendant must show (and the burden of proof is on the defendant) that his or her attorney's performance was deficient based on "prevailing professional norms." The Court emphasized, however, that:

> Judicial scrutiny of counsel's performance must be highly deferential, and a fair assessment of attorney performance requires that every effort be made to eliminate the distorting effects of hindsight, to reconstruct the circumstances of counsel's challenged conduct, and to evaluate the conduct from counsel's perspective at the time. A court must indulge a strong presumption that counsel's conduct falls within the wide range of reasonable professional assistance.

If the Court agrees with the defendant on this first claim, then the defendant must also show that his or her attorney's deficient performance contributed to the adverse outcome of the case. The Court stressed that "the ultimate focus of inquiry must be on the fundamental fairness of the proceeding whose result is being challenged." Thus, "a court need not first determine whether counsel's performance was deficient before examining the prejudice suffered by the defendant as a result of the alleged deficiencies. If it is easier to dispose of an ineffectiveness claim on the ground of lack of sufficient prejudice [i.e., adverse outcome], that course should be followed." Professor Paternoster observes that the second prong of the test "requires that a court reviewing an attorney's performance for effectiveness must, with hindsight, determine if the outcome of the trial would have been different had counsel not been incompetent."[191] In Strickland's case, that was easy. Strickland had pleaded guilty to three capital murder charges. In cases in which the defendant does not plead guilty, however, it may be more difficult to show. In sum, the Court's holding in *Strickland* seems to suggest that it is unnecessary for defense lawyers in capital cases to be effective; it is only necessary for them not to be ineffective.[192]

In *Burger v. Kemp* (483 U.S. 776, 1987), the petitioner claimed that his well-respected and experienced court-appointed trial lawyer was constitutionally inadequate because, in part, he failed to develop and present any mitigating evidence at either of the two state-court sentencing hearings. The evidence that might have been disclosed would have shown that Christopher Burger had "an exceptionally unhappy and unstable childhood." After talking with Burger's mother, a psychologist who the trial lawyer retained, and other people who knew his client, Burger's trial lawyer decided his client's interests would not be served by presenting what mitigating evidence was available. He also decided that it would not be wise to put his client, his client's mother, or the psychologist on the witness stand and expose them to cross-examination. Burger had never expressed remorse for his crime, and the psychologist believed that Burger might have bragged about it on the witness stand. The trial lawyer did not think his client's mother's testimony would be helpful and might even be counterproductive. As it was, no evidence had been produced at trial establishing that Burger had any prior criminal record. His mother, however, knew her son had committed at least one prior petty offense, had been involved with drugs, had a violent temper, and had other problems with law enforcement officers. All that could have come out during cross-examination. Citing *Strickland v. Washington*, the Court concluded that petitioner had not established "in light of all the circumstances, the identified acts or omissions [of counsel] were outside the wide range of professionally competent assistance." It further noted that petitioner did not show that "the justice of his sentence was rendered unreliable by a breakdown in the adversary process caused by deficiencies in counsel's assistance."

In *Wiggins v. Smith* (539 U.S. 510, 2003), the Court held, "The performance of Wiggins' attorneys at sentencing violated his Sixth Amendment right to effective assistance of counsel." The principal concern of the Court was not whether trial counsel should have presented a mitigation case (according to the Court, they presented a "halfhearted mitigation case"), but whether trial counsel's investigation supporting their decision not to introduce mitigating evidence about the severe physical and sexual abuse Wiggins suffered at the hands of his alcoholic, absentee mother and a series of foster parents, his time spent homeless, and his diminished mental capacities was reasonable under prevailing professional norms. The Court concluded that counsel did not conduct a reasonable investigation; that their failure to investigate thoroughly "stemmed from inattention, not strategic judgment." Wiggins' trial attorneys chose not to hire a forensic social worker at the state's expense to investigate his background. The only significant mitigating factor the jury heard was that Wiggins had no prior convictions. The Court reasoned that had the jury heard about the other mitigating factors, it may have returned with a sentence other than death.

In the case of *Florida v. Nixon* (543 U.S. 175, 2004), Nixon's public defender was faced with overwhelming evidence of his client's guilt. Therefore, he adopted the strategy of conceding his client's guilt at the guilt phase of the capital trial to preserve credibility for penalty phase evidence of his client's mental instability and defense pleas to save his client's life. When he attempted to explain his strategy to his client, Nixon was unresponsive, neither approving nor protesting the proposed strategy. Nixon gave little, if any, assistance or direction to his attorney in the preparation of his case. Nixon was convicted and sentenced to death. The Florida Supreme Court reversed holding that conceding that a defendant is guilty without the defendant's express consent automatically constitutes ineffective assistance of counsel requiring a new trial. The Court ruled that the Florida Supreme Court erred and reversed its decision, noting, "Counsel's failure to obtain the defendant's express consent to a strategy of conceding guilt in a capital trial does not automatically render counsel's performance deficient." In explaining its ruling and, at the same time, acknowledging the special problems faced by defense attorneys in capital trials, the Court wrote:

> Attorneys representing capital defendants face daunting challenges in developing trial strategies: Prosecutors are more likely to seek the death penalty, and to refuse to accept a plea to a life sentence, when the evidence is overwhelming and the crime heinous. Counsel therefore may reasonably decide to focus on the trial's penalty phase, at which time counsel's mission is to persuade the trier that his client's life should be spared. Defense counsel must strive at the guilt phase to avoid a counterproductive course. Mounting a "defendant did not commit the crime" defense risks destroying counsel's penalty phase credibility and may incline the jury against leniency for the defendant. In a capital case, counsel must consider in

conjunction both the guilt and penalty phases in determining how best to proceed. When counsel informs the defendant of the strategy counsel believes to be in the defendant's best interest and the defendant is unresponsive, counsel's strategic choice is not impeded by any blanket rule demanding the defendant's explicit consent.

In *Rompilla v. Beard* (543 U.S. 1086, 2005), the Court held: "Even when a capital defendant and his family members have suggested that no mitigating evidence is available, his lawyer is bound to make reasonable efforts to obtain and review material that counsel knows the prosecution will probably rely on as evidence of aggravation at the trial's sentencing phase." In this case, the Court found defense attorneys deficient because they failed to carefully examine the court file of Rompilla's prior rape and assault conviction even though they knew the prosecution intended to seek the death penalty by proving that Rompilla had a prior history of violent felony convictions. Had they carefully examined the file, which was a public record readily available at the courthouse, they would have discovered, just like Rompilla's postconviction attorney did, a number of mitigation leads that were not identified by the defendant or his family members. That mitigation evidence, then, taken as a whole, might have convinced the jury to return a verdict other than death.

In *In Re Berger* (498 U.S. 233, 1991), the Court determined that appointed counsel representing a capital defendant before the U.S. Supreme Court is limited to $5,000 in fees, even though 21 U.S.C. § 848 (q) (10) prescribes no such limitation.

Other Procedural Issues. Other procedural issues that do not fit well into any of the other categories are briefly described in this last section. The first three cases involve the role of psychiatrists in capital cases. In *Estelle v. Smith* (451 U.S. 454, 1981), the Court held that a defendant's statements to a psychiatrist during a competency evaluation may not be used against the defendant in a capital sentencing proceeding unless, prior to the evaluation, the defendant was "informed of his right to remain silent and the possible use of his statements." In *Ake v. Oklahoma* (470 U.S. 68, 1985), the issue was whether the Constitution requires that an indigent defendant have access to psychiatric examination and assistance necessary to prepare an effective defense based on his or her mental condition, when sanity at the time of the offense is seriously in question. In *Ake*, the Court held that "when a defendant has made a preliminary showing that his insanity at the time of the offense is likely to be a significant factor at trial, the Constitution requires that a State provide access to a psychiatrist's assistance on this issue if the defendant cannot otherwise afford one." In *Powell v. Texas* (492 U.S. 680, 1989), the Court ruled that the Sixth Amendment is violated if a state psychiatrist conducts a pretrial evaluation without notice to defense counsel.

In *Darden v. Wainwright* (477 U.S. 168, 1986), the Court decided that a Florida prosecutor's reference to a capital murder defendant as "an animal" at a sentencing trial did not violate the defendant's right to a fair trial.

In *Minnick v. Mississippi* (498 U.S. 146, 1990), the Court held that once counsel is requested, police interrogation must cease, and any reinitiation of interrogation without presence of counsel, irrespective of whether the accused has consulted with counsel, is prohibited.

The facts in *Arizona v. Fulminante* (499 U.S. 279, 1991) were as follows. After Fulminante's 11-year-old stepdaughter was murdered in Arizona, Fulminante left the state. He was subsequently convicted of an unrelated federal crime and imprisoned in New York. A fellow inmate, who was really a government agent posing as an organized crime figure, told Fulminante that Fulminante was getting rough treatment from other inmates because of rumors he was a child murderer and promised to protect him in exchange for the truth. Fulminante confessed to the government agent that he had killed his stepdaughter and provided details of the crime. Subsequently, Fulminante was indicted in Arizona for first-degree murder. The trial court denied his motion to suppress his confession and he was convicted and sentenced to death. On appeal, the Arizona Supreme Court held that the confession was coerced in violation of the 5th and 14th Amendments and remanded the case for a new trial without the confession. The Court affirmed that decision but also noted that the erroneous admission of a coerced confession may, in some cases, be a harmless error, but that under the circumstances of this case, it was not. (For a discussion of errors in capital cases, see Chapter 7.)

A Note on the Appellate Process under Post–*Furman* Statutes

In addition to automatic appellate review, defendants sentenced to death also have a dual system of collateral review; that is, they may challenge their convictions and/or sentences through both state post–conviction proceedings and federal habeas corpus petitions.[193] Steps in the dual system of collateral review in death penalty cases are:[194]

Stage 1:
    Step 1: Trial and Sentence in State Court
    Step 2: Direct Appeal to State Appeals Court
    Step 3: U.S. Supreme Court for Writ of Certiorari

Stage 2:
    Step 1: State Post–conviction
    Step 2: State Court of Appeals
    Step 3: U.S. Supreme Court for Writ of Certiorari

Stage 3:
    Step 1: Petition for Writ of Habeas Corpus in U.S. District
             Court
    Step 2: Certificate of Probable Cause and Request for Stay
             of Execution
    Step 3: U.S. Circuit Court of Appeals
    Step 4: U.S. Supreme Court for Writ of Certiorari
    Step 5: Request for a Stay of Execution

A state appellate court has at least five options when a conviction and/or death sentence has been appealed to it: (1) it can vacate the conviction (and therefore the sentence) and remand the case to the trial court for additional proceedings or for retrial, (2) it can affirm the conviction and remand the case to the trial court for resentencing, (3) it can reduce the sentence to life imprisonment or life imprisonment without opportunity of parole, (4) it can affirm both the conviction and sentence,[195] or (5) it can reverse both the sentence and conviction and order the defendant to be freed, although this option occurs rarely. If the state appellate court affirms both the conviction and the sentence, an appeal may be made to the U.S. Supreme Court through a writ of *certiorari*. If the appeal to the Supreme Court is unsuccessful, the capital defendant may then return to state post–conviction proceedings and begin the appeals process anew. Even if the defendant's appeal is denied in the state appellate courts, because of the dual system of collateral review, the defendant may appeal to the appropriate U.S. District Court through a writ of *habeas corpus*. If the appeal is denied in the U.S. District Court, that decision may be appealed to the appropriate U.S. Circuit Court of Appeals. However, in order to appeal a district court's decision to a federal court of appeals, either the district court or the court of appeals must grant the inmate permission in the form of a certificate of appealability, or COA.[196] If the COA is granted but relief in the court of appeals is denied, a third appeal may be made to the U.S. Supreme Court.

Until recently, it was possible for people sentenced to death to employ this dual system of collateral review numerous times (see, for example, the case of Caryl Chessman in Chapter 1). Now, however, because of Supreme Court decisions, the passage of the Antiterrorism and Effective Death Penalty Act of 1996, and similar measures by state legislatures, access to both the federal and state appellate courts has been made more difficult. Proponents of these types of decisions and legislation believe that most appeals are frivolous and are simply delaying tactics, and they hope that the new rules will greatly reduce the long delays in executions and the high costs associated with the entire capital punishment process.[197] But what if many of the appeals are not frivolous and delaying tactics? What if the delays in executions are greatly reduced because death row inmates are unable to have their claims heard in the federal courts?

At least 28 percent and as many as 68 percent of all convictions or sentences in death penalty cases from 1973 through 2004 have been overturned on appeal.[198] Many appeals may, indeed, be frivolous and delaying tactics, but the evidence shows that many of them are not. The reversals, as described in more detail in Chapter 7, have resulted from fundamental constitutional errors such as coerced confessions; ineffective assistance of counsel; denial of the right of an impartial jury; prosecutors withholding exculpatory evidence, suborning perjury, and use of tainted evidence; and unconstitutional jury instructions.[199] The percentage of death penalty cases overturned by the appellate courts since the reestablishment of capital punishment has far exceeded the percentage of appellate reversals of all other noncapital felony cases— in most states, this probably does not exceed one percent.[200] However, the number of death penalty appeal reversals has been decreasing dramatically in recent years, not because of greater fairness in the system or fewer constitutional errors, but rather because death row inmates are simply less likely to prevail. Nearly all constitutional errors today are subject to harm analysis and "proving that an error was harmful is difficult or impossible."[201]

In sum, despite a very elaborate process that includes guided discretion statutes and bifurcated trials, a large number of convictions and/or sentences in death penalty cases are reversed on appeal or during post-conviction review—a reversal rate many times higher than in noncapital cases. The errors that are discovered, moreover, are not insignificant legal technicalities but are the result of violations of fundamental constitutional protections. Under such circumstances, a likely result of restricting the access of death row inmates to the appellate process is miscarriages of justice. In other words, without the ability to challenge arrests, charges, indictments, convictions, sentences, and pending executions in the appellate courts, there likely will be an increase in the number of innocent people or people not legally eligible for execution involved in the capital punishment process. The subject of miscarriages of justice in capital cases is examined in detail in Chapter 7.

Conclusion

As the list of cases and appeals reversals indicate, over the past three decades the Supreme Court has been actively refining the procedures approved in *Gregg*. Its faith in its ability to make the system of capital punishment a just and constitutionally acceptable one remains strong. With Justices Marshall and Brennan no longer members of the Court, it is only on rarest of occasions that any doubts are expressed—but they are expressed. On February 22, 1994, for example, in a rare written dissent from the Court's refusal to hear the appeal of a Texas inmate scheduled to be executed the next day, Justice Harry A. Blackmun asserted that he had come to the conclusion that "the death penalty experiment has failed" and that it was time for the Court to abandon the "delusion" that capital punishment could be administered in a way that was consistent with the Constitution. Blackmun proclaimed, "From this day forward, I no longer shall tinker with the machinery of death." What is interesting is that, unlike Justices Marshall and Brennan, who always opposed capital punishment, Justice Blackmun, despite personally opposing the penalty, had supported the administration of capital punishment for more than 20 years.[202] He believed the death penalty was "basically a legislative discretionary matter."[203]

Justice Blackmun is the exception. The majority of the current Court continues to make adjustments to the process. To summarize the general elements of that process: Bifurcated trials are required in capital cases. Guided discretion statutes are constitutional; mandatory statutes of any kind are not. For practical purposes, capital punishment is permissible only in cases of aggravated murder. (At the state level it is also permissible for a few other rarely committed crimes, such as treason. At the federal level, it is authorized for about 50 crimes.) It is not a permissible penalty unless there is at least one aggravating circumstance, generally proved "beyond a reasonable doubt." A person who participated in a crime that resulted in death but who did not actually kill or plan to kill anyone may be found guilty of aggravated murder if he or she was a major participant and showed a reckless regard for the value of human life. Juries must be allowed to convict a capital defendant of an included noncapital offense instead of the capital one. During the penalty phase of bifurcated trials, courts must allow the presentation of any mitigating evidence that is supported by evidence and victim–impact statements. The presentation of aggravating evidence is initially limited only to factors listed in the statutes. However, after one statutory aggravating factor has been found, any factor in aggravation can be considered. Automatic appellate and proportionality reviews, though desirable, are not required. Death penalty opponents may be excluded from juries in capital cases if they are opposed to the death penalty, no matter what the circumstances. Prospective jurors who would automatically vote for the death penalty may be challenged for cause. Executing people who have gone crazy on death row or who are mentally retarded is not permitted. Execution of persons who were under 18 years of age at the time of their offense is prohibited. Execution by lethal injection, firing squad, hanging, electrocution, or lethal gas is not cruel and unusual punishment and, thus, is allowable for capital crimes.

Discussion Questions

1. Are any of the current execution methods cruel and unusual punishments?

2. Do you agree with the Court's decision in *Louisiana ex rel. Francis v. Resweber*? Why or why not?

3. Do you agree with the Court's *Witherspoon* decision?

4. Do you agree with Justice Harlan in *McGautha* that it is impossible to adequately guide capital sentencing discretion?

5. Do you agree with the Court's *Furman* decision?

6. Which are fairer: mandatory or discretionary death penalty laws?

7. Do you agree with Justice Brennan that "death is different"?

8. Does the death penalty require "super due process"?

9. Do the guided-discretion death penalty statutes adequately reconcile the goals of consistency in application and consideration of individual circumstances?

10. Which type of guided-discretion death penalty statute is fairest?

11. Is automatic appellate review necessary?

12. Do you agree with the Court's decision in *McCleskey v. Kemp*?

13. Should any crimes besides aggravated murder be death-eligible?

14. Do you agree with Professors Steiker and Steiker that the "unconstrained consideration of any kind of mitigating evidence . . . gives those with a mind to discriminate the opportunity to discriminate . . . [by exempting] favored defendants from the death penalty or [by withholding] severe punishment for crimes against despised victims"?

15. Has the requirement of finding at least one statutorily enumerated aggravating circumstance adequately narrowed death-eligibility?

16. Can future dangerousness be accurately and adequately predicted?

17. Should a prediction of future dangerousness be a basis for sentencing someone to death?

18. Should victim-impact statements be admissible at the penalty phase of a capital trial?

19. Should proportionality review be required of all death penalty jurisdictions?

20. Should appointment of counsel be required for appeals beyond the automatic appeal?

21. Should a person's opinion about the death penalty (either in favor or opposed) affect whether he or she serves as a juror in a capital case?

22. Should a judge be allowed to overrule a jury sentence in a capital case (as is allowed in Alabama and Florida)?

23. Should a participant in a crime in which a capital murder is committed be death-eligible, even though the participant did not kill or intend to kill?

24. Should inmates who have become insane while on death row be executed anyway?

25. At what age should a person be death-eligible? Should there be an age limit for death-eligibility?

26. Should mentally retarded offenders be death-eligible? At what IQ level, if any, should a capital offender be death-eligible?

27. What are the steps in the dual system of collateral review?

28. Should we be concerned about the reversal rate of convictions and death sentences in capital cases?

29. What, if anything, should be learned from Justice Blackmun's recent mea culpa?

30. What are the general elements of the capital punishment process in the United States?

Notes

[1] Supreme Court of the United States, "About the Supreme Court," "A Brief Overview of the Supreme Court" at www.supremecourtus.gov/about/about.html

[2] Garner, 2000.

[3] Supreme Court of the United States, "About the Supreme Court," "The Court and Constitutional Interpretation," op. cit.

[4] Ibid.

[5] Ibid.

[6] Ibid.

[7] Ibid.

[8] Ibid.

[9] Cox, 1987:239-249.

[10] Supreme Court of the United States, "About the Supreme Court," "A Brief Overview of the Supreme Court," op. cit.

[11] See The Supreme Court Historical Society, "History of the Court," "The Chase Court, 1864-1873" at www.supremecourthistory.org/02_history/subs_history/02_c06.html

[12] Ibid.

[13] Denno (1997) notes that courts have relied on *In re Kemmler* to dismiss challenges not only to electrocution but to the other four methods of execution as well. See the discussion of *In re Kemmler* below and in Chapter 4. In October 2001, the Georgia Supreme Court by a vote of 4-3 became the first appellate court in the United States to rule that electrocution violated the Eighth Amendment's prohibition against cruel and unusual punishment. The Court held that electrocution "inflicts purposeless physical violence and needless mutilation that makes no measurable contribution to accepted goals of punishment," www.clarkprosecutor.org/html/death/updates.htm; "Georgia Bans the Electric Chair," *The Orlando Sentinel* (October 6, 2001), p. A19.

[14] Denno, 1997; 1998.

[15] See Denno, 1994:607–612; Paternoster, 1991:39.

[16] Andersen, 1983:32.

[17] Craemer's name was not listed in the Espy File, see Espy and Smykla, 1987.

[18] Gaddis, 1979.

[19] Ibid.

[20] See, for example, *Gaines v. Washington*, 277 U.S. 81, 1928; *Spies v. Illinois*, 123 U.S. 131, 1887, and cases cited.

[21] See Radelet, Bedau, and Putnam, 1992:304; Dinnerstein, 1968.

[22] Ibid.

[23] Bedau, 1987:218, fn. 6.

[24] See Carter, 1969; Paternoster, 1991, op. cit. p. 68, fn. 3. It is generally believed that the charges against the "Scottsboro Boys" were fabricated. See Haines, 1996:210, n. 1.

[25] Only eight of the suspects were indicted; the 13-year-old was not.

[26] Haines, op. cit.

[27] Also see *Turner v. Pennsylvania* (388 U.S. 62, 1949) for a similar decision under similar circumstances.

[28] The Indiana Law Blog, 2005.

[29] *People v. Griffin*, 60 Cal. 2d 182.

[30] See Nakell and Hardy, 1987:20.

[31] Meltsner, 1973:115.

[32] See Leyte-Vidal and Silverman, 2006:271.

[33] Nakell and Hardy, op. cit.

[34] Meltsner, op. cit., p. 119.

[35] Ibid., p. 118.

[36] Death qualification received judicial approval as early as 1820. In *United States v. Cornell* (25 F. Cas. 650, 1820), Circuit Justice Joseph Story reluctantly denied a motion for a new trial in this murder case. One of the exceptions raised by counsel was that two potential jurors disqualified themselves because they were Quakers and had conscientious scruples about "taking away life." The two Quakers stated that they could not be impartial in a capital cause. In response to the counsel's exception and endorsing death qualification, Justice Story wrote:

> To insist on a juror's sitting in a cause when he acknowledges himself to be under influences, no matter whether they arise from interest, from prejudices, or from religious opinions, which will prevent him from giving a true

verdict according to law and evidence, would be to subvert the objects of a trial by jury, and to bring into disgrace and contempt, the proceedings of courts of justice.

[37] See Haney, 2005:109; also see Sandys, 1998; Dillehay and Sandys, 1996; Thompson, 1989; Luginbuhl and Middendorf, 1988; Moran and Comfort,1986; Horowitz and Seguin,1986; Cowan et al.,1984; Fitzgerald and Ellsworth,1984; Gross, 1984; Haney, 1984; Jurow, 1971; Goldberg, 1970; Bronson, 1970.

[38] See Nakell and Hardy, op. cit., p. 20.

[39] Meltsner, op. cit., p. 168.

[40] Ibid., pp. 169-170.

[41] *Boykin v. Alabama*, 395 U.S. 238, 1969.

[42] Meltsner, op. cit., p. 184.

[43] Ibid., p. 170.

[44] Ibid., p. 185.

[45] Ibid., p. 182.

[46] Paternoster, op. cit., pp. 45–46.

[47] *McGautha v. California*, 602 U.S. 183 at 190, 1971.

[48] Ibid., p. 195.

[49] Acker, 1996:143–144. In 1971, only six states used bifurcated trials in capital cases: California, Connecticut, Georgia, New York, Pennsylvania, and Texas, see *McGautha v. California*, op. cit., p. 208, n. 19.

[50] *McGautha v. California*, op. cit., p. 207.

[51] Ibid., p. 204.

[52] Meltsner, op. cit., p. 242.

[53] Ibid., p. 246.

[54] Banner, op. cit., 258.

[55] Meltsner, op. cit., p. 246.

[56] Ibid.

[57] Meltsner, ibid.; Banner, op. cit.

[58] Banner, ibid.

[59] Ibid.

[60] See *People v. Aikens*, 70 C2d 369, 1969.

[61] *Furman v, Georgia*, 408 U.S. 238, 1972; Meltsner, op. cit., p. 248.

[62] *Savannah Morning News*, August 12, 1967, p. 8B; September 21, 1968, p. 1A.

[63] Haney, 2005, op. cit., p. 21.

[64] *Furman v, Georgia*, 408 U.S. 238, 1972; Meltsner, op. cit.

[65] Sturrock, 2006.

[66] Meltsner, op. cit., p. 305.

[67] Woodward and Armstrong, 1979:220.

[68] Anderson, op. cit., p. 38; Meltsner, op. cit., pp. 292-293. Woodward and Armstrong (1979:430) wrote the *Furman* decision "struck the laws in 35 states."

[69] Meltsner, ibid., p. 293.

[70] Paternoster, op. cit., p. 54.

[71] Meltsner, op. cit., p. 231.

[72] Ibid., p. 232.

[73] Ibid.

[74] Ibid., p. 231.

[75] Ibid., p. 232.

[76] Ibid.

[77] Ibid., pp. 232-233.

[78] *Aikens v. California*, 406 U.S. 813, 1972.

[79] Meltsner, op. cit., p. 287.

[80] See *Aikens v. California*, 1972; *Furman v. Georgia*, 1972.

[81] See Banner, op. cit., p. 266.

[82] Woodward and Armstrong, op. cit., pp. 217 and 220.

[83] Ibid., p. 218.

[84] Haines, 1996, op. cit., p. 50.

[85] Ibid., p. 44.

[86] Woodward and Armstrong, op. cit., pp. 218-219.

[87] Cole, 1984.

[88] See Bowers and Steiner, 1999:612, n. 25; Haines, 1996, op. cit., p. 46 reports that 16 states enacted "mandatory "death penalty statutes following *Furman*.

[89] Haines, ibid. indicates that 13 states enacted "guided-discretion" death penalty statutes following *Furman*.

[90] Liebman et al., 2000: n. 136

[91] Haines, 1996, op. cit., p. 50. On extending the moratorium, Amsterdam and the LDF attorneys fought each individual death sentence and were successful in blocking all executions until January 1977, when Gary Gilmore, at his own request, was executed by the state of Utah. The first "non-volunteer" executed was John Spinkelink, who was executed by Florida in May 1979. Woodward and Armstrong, op. cit., p. 442, n.

[92] Woodward and Armstrong, op. cit., p. 432.

[93] Haines, 1996, op. cit., p. 54.

[94] Ibid., p. 44.

[95] Ibid., p. 54.

[96] "A Matter of Life and Death," 2006.

[97] Death Penalty Information Center, "Life Without Parole."

[98] "A Matter of Life and Death," 2006, op. cit.

[99] Woodward and Armstrong, op. cit., p. 431.

[100] Ibid.

[101] Ibid., p. 439.

[102] Ibid.

[103] Ibid.

[104] Ibid.

[105] Ibid.

[106] Acker, op. cit., p. 145.

[107] For a detailed examination of proportionality review, see Bienen, 1996.

[108] Haney, 2005, op. cit., p. 22.

[109] Also see Steiker and Steiker, 1998:55; Bedau, 1987.

[110] *Furman v. Georgia*, 408 U.S. 238 at 287-289,1972.

[111] *Gardner v. Florida*, 420 U.S. 349 at 357, 1977. Also see *Woodson v. North Carolina* 428 U.S. 280, 1976, and *Gregg v. Georgia*, 428 U.S. 153, 1976.

[112] Radin, 1980.

[113] Paternoster, op. cit., pp. 75-76; also see Steiker and Steiker, op. cit.

[114] Steiker and Steiker, ibid.; also see Acker, op. cit.; Mello, 1989.

[115] Steiker and Steiker, ibid., p. 70. Much of the death penalty research that has been conducted over the past 30–plus years on this matter is presented in subsequent chapters of this book.

[116] Haney, 2005, op. cit., pp. 21 and 24.

[117] Acker and Lanier, 1997; Nakell and Hardy, op. cit.

[118] Acker and Lanier remark, "It is futile in the post-*Furman* era to embark on a discussion of 'the death penalty' from a procedural standpoint, for there are almost as many variations on capital-sentencing laws as there are capital-punishment jurisdictions" (1998:89).

[119] Baldus and Woodworth, 1998:394.

[120] Ibid.

[121] Acker and Lanier, op. cit., p. 101. Twenty-one of the 38 death penalty states have some type of balancing statute, see Bowers and Steiner, 1999:618, n. 49.

[122] See *Kansas v. Marsh*, 2006.

[123] Online Sunshine View Statutes, 2006.

[124] See Acker and Lanier, op. cit., p. 98; Bowers and Steiner, 1998:309.

[125] Until June 2002, juries were excluded entirely from the capital sentencing process in five states—Arizona, Colorado, Idaho, Montana, and Nebraska. That practice was held to be unconstitutional by the Supreme Court in *Ring v. Arizona*. Only a few states (e.g., Kentucky and Texas) give juries sentencing responsibility in noncapital cases, see Acker and Lanier, ibid.; Bowers and Steiner, ibid.

[126] Gibson, 2002; Stevenson, 2004:110, n. 65.

[127] Stevenson, ibid., p. 89.

[128] Coyne and Entzeroth, op. cit., pp. 264-265.

[129] Acker and Lanier, op. cit., p. 103.

[130] Coyne and Entzeroth, 2001, pp. 329-331; Tex. Code Crim. Proc. art. 37.071 (2005) at http://web.lexis-nexis.com.ucfproxy.fcla.edu/universe/document?_m=4164cdf8d5273c4a209fe1084b5efa11&_docnum=5&wchp=dGLbVtz-zSkVb&_md5=ddb2b83eb42f6124ad1f2b4a8e4e9a06.

[131] See The Death Penalty Information Center, "Executions" (accessed September 13, 2006).

[132] Andersen, op. cit.

[133] Online Sunshine View Statutes, op, cit.

[134] Official Code of Georgia Annotated, Title 17, ch. 10, art. 2 § 17-10-35 (2006) at http://web.lexis-nexis.com.ucfproxy.fcla.edu/universe/document?_m=7b314b53852cd0791721d62e4eb3fdee&_docnum=26&wchp=dGLbVtb-zSkVA&_md5=9c24e549dd02a8e0a8897fa3f8a68f3f.

[135] See Bonczar and Snell, 2005. Actually 36 of 37 death penalty states provide for automatic appellate review because, at this writing, New York's death penalty statute has been ruled unconstitutional.

[136] Ibid.

[137] Zimring, 2003:9.

[138] Justice Powell, who wrote the opinion in *McCleskey*, has since stated that his vote in *McCleskey* was his biggest and most regrettable mistake as a Supreme Court Justice. See Cavender, 1995:128.

[139] Bonczar and Snell, op. cit., p. 2, Table 1; Tim Talley, "Oklahoma Oks death penalty for repeat child molesters," *The Orlando Sentinel* (June 10, 2006), p. A8.

[140] Cited in Talley, ibid.

[141] Ibid.

[142] Sundby, 2005:14.

[143] Sundby, op. cit., p. 19.

[144] Steiker and Steiker, op. cit., p. 63.

[145] Ibid.

[146] Ibid.

[147] Acker and Lanier, op. cit., p. 102; *Tuilaepa v. California* (512 U.S. 967, 1994).

[148] Snell, op. cit., p. 2, Table 1; Acker and Lanier, op. cit., p. 92; 11 Del. C. § 4209 (2006); Cal Pen Code § 190.2 (2006); Idaho Code § 19-2515 (2006); O.C.G.A. [Ga.] § 17-10-30 (2006); KRS [Ky.] § 532.025 (2006); La.R.S. 14:30 (2006); Md. Criminal Law Code Ann. § 2-303 (2006); Miss. Code Ann. § 97-3-19 (2006); § 565.032 R.S.Mo. (2006); R.R.S.Neb. § 29-2523 (2006); N.J. Stat. § 2C:11-3 (2006); RSA [NH] 630:5 (2006); N.C. Gen. Stat. § 15A-2000 (2006); Utah Code Ann. § 76-5-2002 (2006); Rev. Code Wash. (ARCW) § 10.95.020 (2006); Wyo. Stat. § 6-2-102 (2006).

[149] Ibid.

[150] Acker and Lanier, op. cit., p. 92.

[151] Ibid., pp. 92–93.

[152] Steiker and Steiker, op. cit., p. 57.

[153] Ibid., p. 58.

[154] Simon and Spaulding, 1999.

[155] Sundby, op. cit., p. 11.

[156] Turow, 2003:67-68.

[157] Simon and Spaulding, op. cit.

[158] Texas Defender Service, 2004:xiii.

[159] Ibid., p. xii.

[160] Logan, 2006:163.

[161] Ibid.; also see Lanier and Breslin, 2006; Karp and Warshaw, 2006. In some jurisdictions, prosecutors have not allowed co-victims to make victim-impact statements because the co-victims are opposed to the death penalty (Reed and Blackwell, 2006:261-262). Some states, such as Delaware, Georgia, Idaho, and Indiana, allow members of the victim's family to sit with the prosecution at counsel table during a capital trial (Stevenson, op. cit., p. 101, n. 4).

[162] Karp and Warshaw, ibid., p. 283 and 290; Eisenberg et al., 2006:298 and 304.

[163] Bonczar and Snell, op. cit., p. 11, Table 11.

[164] Haines, 1996, op. cit., p. 74.

[165] Ibid., p. 73.

[166] Ibid., p. 74.

[167] Ibid., p. 75.

[168] Steiker and Steiker, 2006.

[169] Bright, 1997:14.

[170] Ibid.

[171] American Bar Association, 2006.

[172] Dow, 2005:22.

[173] Ibid., p. 61.

[174] Acker and Lanier, op. cit., pp. 99–100.

[175] See McCord, 2000, about the Court's attempt to minimize "overinclusion," and Hoffmann, 1993:124, for the correspondence between the punishment and blameworthiness.

[176] Turow, op. cit., p. 68.

[177] Ibid., p. 69.

[178] Walker, 2006:267. The Constitution Project (2005:xvii and xxv) recommends that felony murder should not be death eligible or an aggravating circumstance.

[179] Bright, op. cit., p. 19.

[180] Cox, 1999.

[181] For a detailed description of the *Ford* case, see Miller and Radelet, 1993.

[182] Brunsvold, 2004.

[183] Ibid., p. 1306.

[184] Ibid., pp. 1309-1310.

[185] Jones, 2002..

[186] Owens, 2002; Bright, op. cit., p. 17.

[187] Lindsey, 2005.

[188] Jones, 2002, op. cit.; also see Vogel and Vogel, 2003.

[189] McCaffrey, 2002.

[190] See *McMann v. Richardson*, 397 U.S. 759, 771, note 14, 1970.

[191] Paternoster, 1991, op. cit., p. 88.

[192] Ibid., p. 89; also see Mello and Perkins, 1998.

[193] Paternoster, op. cit., p. 202.

[194] From Paternoster, ibid.; also see Cook and Slawson, 1993:19; Freedman, 1998:418.

[195] See Paternoster, ibid., pp. 202–204; Liebman et al., 2000: n. 44.

[196] Dow, 2002b:18.

[197] It has been claimed that "in a capital case, the lawyer for the accused has a professional obligation to assert at every level of the proceedings what otherwise might be deemed a frivolous claim" if that claim "might conceivably persuade even one judge in an appeals court or in the Supreme Court" or "might increase the chances of a desirable plea agreement or might favorably influence a governor or other official in making a decision regarding clemency," see Freedman, 2003.

[198] Approximately 7,500 death sentences were imposed in the United States from 1973 through 2004. See Pastore and Maguire (2006:Table 6.0002.2004) for the lower figure and Liebman et al., op. cit., for the higher figure. State reversal rates vary widely, from highs of 54 percent in Mississippi and 53 percent in North Carolina to lows of 13 percent in Texas and 5 percent in Virginia, see Lofquist (2002:1513-1514). Dow (2002b, op. cit., p. 14 and 27) claims that since the late 1980s more than 90 percent of death penalty cases have been affirmed by state courts of appeals (i.e., fewer than 10 percent have been reversed), and, in Texas and Virginia, the number exceeds 98 percent (i.e., fewer than 2 percent have been reversed). Hammel (2002:116-117) also notes the dramatic decrease in appellate reversals in Texas. From 1974 to 1995, according to Hammel, the reversal rate in Texas death penalty appeals was about 30 percent compared to the low single digits in more recent years.

[199] Scheck et al. 2001; Liebman et al. 2000; Paternoster 1991:208-209.

[200] White, 1987:10.

[201] Dow, 2005, op. cit., pp. xxii-xxiii and 44.

[202] *Callins v. Collins*, 510 U.S. 1141 (1994); Meltsner, op. cit., p. 198..

[203] Ibid.

CHAPTER 3

The Death Penalty
at the Federal Level,
in the Military,
and Globally

It is important to understand that there are 39 separate death penalty systems in the United States. Thirty-seven states have a death penalty system, as do the federal government and the military. No two systems are exactly alike. In this chapter, the death penalty systems of the federal government and the military are examined. Also briefly explored is the international context in which the death penalty in the United States exists.

The Death Penalty at the Federal Level

Except for the judicial branch, the federal government (that is, the executive and legislative branches) historically has played a limited role in the administration of capital punishment in the United States. Its principal responsibility has been the execution of offenders found guilty of committing federal capital crimes. In addition, the president has granted an occasional pardon or commutation, and Congress has tinkered with federal death penalty legislation. Beginning in the 1990s, however, Congress has become much more active in death penalty matters. Two major initiatives have been the expansion of the number of federal crimes punishable by death and the changing of the ways capital crimes are handled. Those congressional initiatives will be examined following a brief description of the role of the federal courts in capital punishment.

Capital Punishment and the Federal Courts. The federal courts represent one-half of the dual court system in the United States.[1] The other half is the state court system. The federal court system consists

115

of three levels of courts. At the bottom are 94 district courts. The U.S. district courts are further divided into 13 circuits, with at least one federal district court in each state, one each in the District of Columbia and the Commonwealths of Puerto Rico and the Northern Mariana Islands, and one each in the U.S. territories of the Virgin Islands and Guam. Violations of federal capital punishment statutes are first adjudicated in federal district courts, as are claims first made in federal post-conviction proceedings.

The middle level of the federal court system is comprised of 13 U.S. circuit courts of appeals. Twelve of them have jurisdiction over death penalty appeals from U.S. district courts in the particular geographic areas assigned to them. The Court of Appeals for the Federal Circuit is the only court of appeals that does not hear appeals in death penalty cases.

At the top of the federal court system is the United States Supreme Court—the "court of last resort." Under its appellate jurisdiction, the Court hears death penalty cases appealed from U.S. circuit courts of appeals or from the high court of a state. It hears appeals from the high court of a state only when claims under federal law or the Constitution are involved. This means that the Supreme Court rules only on death penalty cases in which (1) the constitutionality of a state or federal death penalty statute is challenged, or (2) a capital defendant claims that his or her constitutional rights were violated. Such violation might be improper guilt phase or penalty phase court procedures or improper procedures of the appellate court.

For a case to be heard by the Supreme Court, at least four of the nine justices must vote to hear the case (the "rule of four"). (It takes five justices to stay, or stop, an execution.) The Court next issues a writ of *certiorari* to the lower court whose decision is being appealed, ordering it to send the records of the case forward for review. The Court will issue a writ of *certiorari* only if the defendant in the case has exhausted all other avenues of appeal and the case involves a substantial federal question as defined by the appellate court.

When the Supreme Court decides a case it has accepted on appeal, it can take one of four actions:

1. affirm the verdict or decision of the lower court and "let it stand";

2. modify the verdict or decision of the lower court, without totally reversing it;

3. reverse the verdict or decision of the lower court, requiring no further court action; or

4. reverse the verdict or decision of the lower court and remand the case to the court of original jurisdiction, for either retrial or resentencing.

Appeals to the Supreme Court are heard at the discretion of the Court, in contrast to appeals to the U.S. circuit courts, which review cases as a matter of right. The high Court's refusal to hear a case generally ends the process of direct appeal.

In some cases, a death row inmate whose appeal has been denied may still try to have the Supreme Court review his or her case on constitutional grounds by filing a writ of *habeas corpus*. A writ of *habeas corpus* is a court order directing a law officer to produce a prisoner in court to determine if the prisoner is being legally detained or imprisoned. The *habeas corpus* proceeding does not test whether the prisoner is guilty or innocent. Recent changes making it more difficult to get *habeas* petitions heard by the Court are discussed in a later section of this chapter.

Federal Capital Crimes. Prior to the 1990s, the most significant act of Congress regarding the death penalty may have been its effort to reduce the number of federal capital crimes. In the latter part of the nineteenth century, Congress reduced the number of federal crimes punishable by death from 60 to only 3 nonmilitary offenses: murder, rape, and treason.[2] A hundred years later, it has reversed course and added numerous new crimes. The 1994 federal crime bill (the Violent Crime Control and Law Enforcement Act), for example, expanded the number of federal crimes punishable by death to about 50. (Estimates vary depending on whether statutes or offenses are counted, and how offenses are counted.) The bill also reinstated the death penalty for federal crimes already on the books that likely would have been held unconstitutional had they been tested. The new law brings the earlier statutes into compliance with guidelines established by the Supreme Court (see the discussion in Chapter 2). The federal crimes for which the death penalty is now available as a sentencing alternative are:[3]

- aircraft hijacking (either domestic or international) where death results

- alien smuggling where death results

- assassination of the President or Vice President

- assassination of a member of Congress, cabinet member, Supreme Court justice, and major Presidential or Vice Presidential candidates

- attempting, authorizing, or advising the killing of any public officer, juror or witness in a case involving a continuing criminal enterprise—regardless of whether such a killing actually occurs

- carjacking where death results

- destroying federal property with explosives or by arson where death results

- destroying aircraft, motor vehicles, or their facilities where death results

- destroying property used in interstate commerce with explosives or by arson where death results

- drive-by shooting where death results

- drug trafficking in large quantities (even where no death results)

- espionage

- first-degree murder on federal land or property

- genocide

- gun murders during federal crimes of violence and drug trafficking crimes

- hostage-taking where death results

- kidnapping where death results

- killing or attempted killing by a drug kingpin of a public officer or juror to obstruct justice

- mailing injurious articles (e.g., explosives) where death results

- murder at a U.S. international airport

- murder by a federal prisoner serving a life sentence

- murder by an escaped federal prisoner

- murder for hire involving interstate travel or the use of interstate facilities

- murder in aid of racketeering activity

- murder involving firearms or other dangerous weapons during attack on federal facilities

- murder of a federal witness, victim, or informant

- murder of a state correctional officer by a federal prisoner

- murder of a U.S. citizen abroad

- murder by terrorism of a U.S. citizen abroad

- murder of federal jurors and court officers

- murder of federal law enforcement officials or employees

- murder of foreign officials or internationally protected people on U.S. soil

- murder of state or local officials assisting federal law enforcement officials

- murder within the special maritime and territorial jurisdiction of the United States

- robbery of a federally insured bank where death results

- sexual abuse committed within federal territorial jurisdiction where death results

- child molestation committed within federal territorial jurisdiction where death results

- torture where death results outside the United States

- train sabotage where death results

- transporting or receiving explosives with intent to kill where death results

- treason

- use of weapons of mass destruction (e.g., biological weapons or poison gas) where death results

- violating a person's federally protected rights based on race, religion, or national origin where death results

It is interesting to note that all but four of the crimes involve murder. The four exceptions are treason; espionage; drug trafficking in large quantities; and attempting, authorizing, or advising the killing of any public officer, juror or witness in a case involving a continuing criminal enterprise—regardless of whether such a killing actually occurs.

Federal Capital Punishment Procedures. When the Supreme Court in *Furman* (1972) invalidated existing death penalty statutes, it also invalidated the federal death penalty law. Congress did not create procedures that would meet the requirements of *Furman* until 1988 in a new statute that allowed the death penalty for murder in the course of a drug-kingpin conspiracy. Six people have subsequently been sentenced to death under this conspiracy law; only one of them, Juan Raul Garza (discussed later), as of April 10, 2006, has been executed.[4] Using the long record of reforms summarized in Chapter 2, Congress incorporated into its new law many of the desirable features of state death penalty statutes already approved by the Supreme Court. Congress further refined federal death penalty procedures in the Federal Death Penalty Act of 1994. Among the features the current federal death penalty law shares with some states are:

- requiring a minimum of two attorneys be appointed to represent federal capital defendants (at least one of the attorneys must have experience in capital defense work)

- requiring the government to inform the defendant of its intention to seek death within a reasonable time before trial or before the court accepts a defendant's guilty plea

- requiring the government, before trial or plea, to list the aggravating circumstances that it proposes to prove to justify a death sentence

- the weighing of statutorily enumerated aggravating and mitigating circumstances (no method or standard for weighing is prescribed)

- giving the government the burden of establishing aggravating circumstances beyond a reasonable doubt

- requiring unanimity on the part of jurors in the finding of an aggravating circumstance

- requiring that a sentence other than death be imposed if no aggravating circumstance is found to exist

- requiring only a single juror to find a mitigating circumstance before it can be weighed

- allowing victim-impact evidence

- the right to appeal both the conviction and the death sentence*

- exempting from the federal death penalty persons less than 18 years of age at the time of the offense, mentally retarded and insane persons, and pregnant women (but only while they are pregnant)

A few features unique to the federal death penalty statute are:

- requiring authorization from the U.S. attorney general before federal prosecutors can file capital charges

- requiring the court to consider the federal public defender's recommendation about which attorneys are qualified for appointment in capital cases

- three different sets of aggravating circumstances: those for espionage and treason; those for homicide; and those for nonhomicide drug offenses

- requiring federal judges in capital sentencing proceedings to instruct the jury that "in considering whether a sentence of death is justified, it shall not consider the race, color, religious beliefs, national origin, or sex of the defendant or of any victim"

- requiring a jury that recommends death to furnish the court with a certificate signed by each juror swearing that discrimination played no part in the decision and that the same sentencing recommendation would have been made regardless of the race, color, religious beliefs, national origin, or sex of the defendant or any victim

- restricting the federal government's ability to impose the death penalty on Native Americans (capital prosecution of persons subject to the criminal jurisdiction of an Indian tribal government where federal jurisdiction is based solely on Indian country and where the offense occurred within the boundaries of Indian country is prevented, unless the governing body of the Indian tribe waives its sovereign immunity)

---

*There are three grounds for appeal: (1) the death sentence was imposed under the influence of passion, prejudice, or any other arbitrary factor, (2) the admissible evidence and information adduced does not support the special finding of the existence of the required aggravating factor, or (3) the proceedings involved any other legal error requiring reversal which was properly preserved for appeal under the rules of criminal procedure. No relief may be provided for any error that the government proves to be harmless beyond a reasonable doubt.

Federal Executions. After the U.S. government was founded, more than a decade would pass before it conducted the first federal execution. On June 25, 1790, Thomas Bird was hanged for murder in Maine.[5] Until recently, federal prisoners were usually executed in the state where the crime occurred because the federal government did not have its own site for executions. Prior to 1937, all federal prisoners were hanged but, after that date, they were executed using the method of the state in which the crime was committed.[6] In states without a death penalty, a federal judge could choose another state to conduct the execution. All that changed in 1995, when the federal Bureau of Prisons converted an old cellblock at the U.S. Penitentiary in Terre Haute, Indiana, into the first national death-row facility in American history.

Renovations of the two-story housing unit of the redbrick federal prison built in the 1940s were made at a cost of $475,000.[7] The special unit was designed to confine male offenders sentenced to death by the federal courts. It includes 50 single-cells, upper tier and lower tier corridors, an industrial workshop, indoor and outdoor recreation areas, a property room, a food preparation area, attorney and family visiting rooms, and a video-teleconferencing area that is used to facilitate inmate access to the courts and their attorneys. The small brick death house, where executions are conducted, is located near the housing unit and is surrounded by chain-link fencing and razor wire. The death-row facility did not become operational until July 13, 1999, the date it received the first group of death row inmates. The government delayed opening the facility until then because it decided that it took at least 20 inmates to be cost effective. Henceforth, most federal executions will take place in Terre Haute. However, in some cases, federal executions will still be conducted near the jurisdiction in which the crime was conducted.[8] The first three people executed at the Terre Haute facility were Timothy McVeigh on June 11, 2001, Juan Raul Garza on June 19, 2001, and Louis Jones, Jr. on March 18, 2003.

Since Bird's execution in 1790, and including McVeigh, Garza, and Jones, the U.S. government has executed 339 men and four women. Although most of those executed were convicted of murder or crimes involving murder, some were convicted of rape, kidnapping, rioting, piracy, spying and espionage. McVeigh, Garza, and Jones were executed by lethal injection, the only method now used by the U.S. government. The 340 other federal executions were by hanging (81 percent), electrocution (17 percent), and lethal gas (2 percent).

The execution of McVeigh was the first federal execution in nearly 40 years. The last federal execution before him occurred on March 15, 1963, when Victor H. Feguer was hanged at Iowa State Penitentiary for kidnapping and murdering an Iowa physician. The prison billed the U.S. government $28.75 for the rope. Between 1931 and 1963, the U.S. government executed 68 people (about 20 percent of the total), two of whom were women. (This includes more than 30 people executed under federal jurisdiction because their crimes occurred in the District of Columbia.) Between 1871 and 1910, by contrast, the U.S. government executed 175 people (more than 50 percent of the total). Between 1790 and 1870, there were 71 federal executions (about 20 percent of the total) and between 1911 and 1931, there were 26 (8 percent). Under its modern death penalty statute, the federal government has executed relatively few capital or potentially capital offenders. For example, from 1995 through 2000, 682 cases eligible for the federal death penalty were submitted to the U.S. Attorney General, who authorized prosecutors to seek the death penalty in 159 or 23 percent of the cases. Of those 159 cases, 51 or 32 percent were resolved through a plea bargain. The remaining cases were tried, but most defendants avoided the death penalty.[9]

Of the three most recent people executed by the federal government, Timothy McVeigh is by far the more infamous.[10] In interviews for the book, *American Terrorist: Timothy McVeigh & the Oklahoma City Bombing* by authors Lou Michel and Dan Herbeck, McVeigh confessed to the April 19, 1995, bombing of the Alfred P. Murrah Federal Building in Oklahoma City, Oklahoma. The death toll from the 9:02 a.m. explosion was 168, including 19 children. More than 500 other people were wounded. Until the horrific tragedy of September 11, 2001, the disaster at Oklahoma City was considered the worst act of domestic terrorism in American history and McVeigh, the worst mass murderer in American history.

McVeigh's trial began on April 24, 1997, in a federal courthouse in Denver, Colorado. (The trial was moved from Oklahoma because of a concern that McVeigh could not get a fair trial there.) He was convicted on June 2, 1997, of all eleven counts for which he was indicted: conspiracy to use a weapon of mass destruction, use of such a weapon, destruction of government property with explosives, and eight counts of first-degree murder—one for each of the eight federal law enforcement officers killed in the blast. McVeigh was sentenced to death by the jury on June 13, 1997, and by the trial judge two months later on August 15.

Not coincidentally, the explosion in Oklahoma City occurred on the two-year anniversary of the government debacle at Waco, Texas, which left some 80 people dead. Revenge for Waco and the tragedy at Ruby Ridge, Idaho, in 1992 was the principal motivating factor in the bombing. However, McVeigh had been compiling a list of grievances against the U.S. government for years. Among them were U.S. military actions against smaller nations, no-knock search warrants, crooked politicians, overzealous government agents, high taxes, political correctness, and gun laws. McVeigh believed that the bombing was necessary to send a message to an out-of-control U.S. government that he claimed was using military tactics to turn the U.S. into a police state. He was concerned about a new American tyranny and wanted to teach the U.S. government a lesson. It has been estimated that the McVeigh case cost taxpayers more than $100 million (the defense spent nearly $20 million, and the government spent more than $80 million).

Juan Raul Garza, the second person executed by the federal government in nearly 40 years, was the first person executed under the 1988 federal "drug kingpin" statute, which allows the death penalty to be imposed on murders resulting from large-scale illegal drug operations.[11] Garza was sentenced to death in Texas in August 1993 for murdering a man by shooting him five times in the head and neck and ordering the murders of two other men. The victims, like Garza, were drug traffickers; the murders motivated by Garza's desire to gain control of marijuana distribution networks.

President Clinton twice delayed Garza's execution within a week of his scheduled execution date (the second time just three days before he left office) because of concern about the results of a Justice Department study that showed large racial and geographical disparities in the application of the federal death penalty. The study revealed that 80 percent of federal defendants charged with capital offenses between 1995 and 2000 were minorities; half of them were African American. The study also found that just 5 of the 94 U.S. attorney districts accounted for about 42 percent of all cases in which prosecutors sought the death penalty. Deputy Attorney General Eric Holder remarked that he could not "help but be both personally and professionally disturbed by the numbers . . . [and] that no one reading [the] report [could] help but be disturbed, troubled, by [the] disparity."[12] Though not part of the study, Garza's attorney in court filings cited 26 cases involving similar crimes to Garza's where prosecutors did not seek the federal death penalty.

Garza's petition for clemency was considered and denied by newly-elected President Bush. Following the clemency denial, newly-appointed Attorney General John Ashcroft told the press that besides the three murders for which he was convicted, Garza was responsible for at least five more deaths, including four in Mexico for which he was not prosecuted. Ashcroft also stated that there was no racial bias in Garza's case, pointing out that the prosecutor was Hispanic as were seven of the eight victims. As for the racial disparities found in the aforementioned Justice Department study, Ashcroft explained that they were not the result of racial bias but were rather a product of legitimate law-enforcement strategies and differing policies in the nation's 94 federal districts. According to Ashcroft, "In areas where large-scale, organized drug trafficking is largely carried out by gangs whose membership is drawn from minority groups, the active federal role in investigating and prosecuting these crimes results in a high proportion of minority defendants in potentially capital cases . . ."[13] What Ashcroft failed to note was that black and Hispanic gang members frequently face death sentences, while white mobsters almost never do. According to a recent Federal Death Penalty Resource Counsel study, since 1988, when the federal death penalty was restored (and until 2000), 700 defendants had been charged with potentially death–eligible federal crimes; the Attorney General authorized 211 (30 percent) of them to be prosecuted as death penalty cases. At least 40 of the death penalty cases (nearly 20 percent) involved black or Hispanic gang members but only one of the cases involved a white mobster. Because of the high priority given organized crime by the FBI in recent years, 1500 organized crime figures have been convicted since 1996. Not one of them faced a death sentence, even when multiple murders were committed.[14] (Chapter 8 provides an extended discussion of arbitrary and discriminatory application of the death penalty at the state level.)

As of April 11, 2007, 50 people were under a federal death sentence. All but one of them were male, 50 percent were black, 40 percent were white, 8 percent were Latino, and 2 percent were Native American.[15]

The Racial Justice Act and the Fairness in Death Sentencing Act. Justice Powell suggested in the *McCleskey* decision (described in Chapter 2) that claims of racial discrimination would be best presented to legislative bodies for corrective action. Congress thereupon commissioned a review of research on racial discrimination in capital charging and sentencing. The resulting General Accounting Office (GAO) report confirmed that such discrimination was a problem—especially when it was based on the race of the victim.[16] (Findings of the GAO report are described in more detail in Chapter 8.) In an effort to rectify the situation, two pieces of legislation were proposed: the Racial Justice Act and the Fairness in Death Sentencing Act.

The legislation was intended to give offenders sentenced to death the right to challenge as racially discriminatory their individual death sentences, much in the same way that individuals may challenge racially discriminatory outcomes under federal employment or housing laws.[17] The two pieces of legislation would allow a black defendant or a defendant whose victim was white the opportunity to present evidence showing a pattern of racially discriminatory charging or sentencing. The state could rebut the evidence by showing, by a preponderance of the evidence, that the pattern of racially discriminatory charging or sentencing could be explained by identifiable and pertinent nonracial factors. If the state failed in its rebuttal, the defendant would be entitled to have his or her death sentence set aside.[18]

Both proposals were vigorously opposed by state attorneys general and by prosecutors who claimed that (1) racial discrimination did not exist, making legislation unnecessary, and (2) passage of the legislation would result either in the use of quotas or the de facto abolition of the death penalty.[19]

The Racial Justice Act stalled and was set aside. The House of Representatives passed the Fairness in Death Sentencing Act in 1990 and again in 1994, but the Senate in a House–Senate Conference Committee rejected the act both times.[20] When Congress enacted death penalty measures as part of the Violent Crime Control and Law Enforcement Act later in 1994, it included no provisions regarding racial discrimination in charging or sentencing.[21]

The Antiterrorism and Effective Death Penalty Act of 1996. In the mid-1990s, Congress turned its attention to what some of its members believed was the abuse of the writ of *habeas corpus* in death penalty cases. Recall that a writ of *habeas corpus* claims that a federal constitutional right has been violated and, thus, the claimant is being held illegally. It is a primary avenue to the U.S. Supreme Court. Critics maintain that abuse of the writ has contributed to the long delays in executions (currently averaging more than 10 years after conviction) and to the high costs associated with capital punishment.

In part to speed up the process and reduce costs, Congress passed the Antiterrorism and Effective Death Penalty Act of 1996, and President Clinton signed it into law on April 24. The law requires that second or subsequent *habeas* petitions be dismissed when the claim has already been made in a previous petition. It also requires that new claims be dismissed unless the Supreme Court hands down a new rule of constitutional law and makes it retroactive to cases on collateral review. Under the act, the only other way the Supreme Court will hear a claim made for the first time is when the claim is based on new evidence not previously available. Even then, the new evidence must be of sufficient weight, by a clear and convincing standard of proof, to convince a judge or jury that the capital defendant was not guilty of the crime or crimes for which he or she was convicted.

The act made the federal appellate courts "gatekeepers" for second or subsequent *habeas corpus* petitions. Now, to file a second or subsequent claim, a capital defendant must first file a motion in the appropriate appellate court, announcing his or her intention. A panel of three judges must hear the motion within 30 days and decide whether the petitioner has a legitimate claim under the act. If the claim is denied, the new law prohibits any review of the panel's decision, either by a rehearing or writ of *certiorari* to the Supreme Court. So far, the U.S. Supreme Court has upheld the constitutionality of the new law.[22]

The Innocence Protection Act of 2004. The issues of innocent people being wrongly convicted of capital crimes and inadequate legal representation of capital defendants fared better in Congress than did the issue of racial discrimination in the administration of the death penalty. On October 30, 2004, President Bush signed into law a crime bill dubbed the "Justice For All Act of 2004." The Innocence Protection Act of 2004 is a part of that crime bill. The Innocence Protection Act was not an easy sell. It was first introduced in the Senate, albeit in a much tougher form, in early 2000, by Senator Patrick Leahy of Vermont. Leahy's motivation for introducing the legislation was what he called "the growing national crisis in the administration of capital punishment."[23] He noted that, since the reinstatement of capital punishment in the 1970s, 85 people [at the time] had been released from death rows after being found innocent. He implored his colleagues to join him in finding ways to minimize the risk of executing innocent people. It took four years for what critics contend is a watered-down version of Leahy's original bill to become law.

The Innocence Protection Act has three major sections. The first is entitled "Exonerating the Innocent Through DNA Testing." This section "establishes rules and procedures governing applications for DNA testing by inmates in the Federal system."[24] According to these rules and procedures:

> A court shall order DNA testing if the applicant asserts under penalty of perjury that he or she is actually innocent, and the proposed DNA testing may produce new material evidence that supports such assertion and raises a reasonable probability that the applicant did not commit the offense. Motions filed more than 5 years after enactment and 3 years after conviction are presumed untimely, but such presumption may be rebutted upon good cause shown. Penalties are established in the event that testing inculpates the applicant. Where test results are exculpatory, the court shall grant the applicant's motion for a new trial or resentencing if the test results and other evidence establish by compelling evidence that a new trial would result in an acquittal.[25]

In addition, this section "prohibits the destruction of DNA evidence in a Federal criminal case while a defendant remains incarcerated, with certain exceptions."[26] Specifically:

> The government may destroy DNA evidence if the defendant waived the right to DNA testing; if the defendant was notified after his conviction became final that the evidence may be destroyed and did not file a motion for testing; if a court has denied a motion for testing; or if the evidence has already been tested and the results included the defendant as the source. If the evidence is large or bulky, the government may remove and preserve a representative sample. Intentional violations of these evidence-retention provisions to prevent evidence from being tested or used in court are punishable by a term of imprisonment. Nothing in this section supersedes any law requiring that evidence be preserved.[27]

This section also includes "The Kirk Bloodsworth Post-Conviction DNA Testing Grant Program" and "Incentive Grants to States to Ensure Consideration of Claims of Actual Innocence." The former, named after the first death row inmate to be exonerated by DNA evidence, authorized $5 million in grants through 2009 to help states pay for the costs of post-conviction DNA testing. The latter provides states with funding to establish procedures for providing post-conviction DNA testing and preserving DNA evidence.[28]

The second major section of the Innocence Act is entitled "Improving The Quality of Representation in State Capital Cases." Its purpose is to increase the reliability of capital trial verdicts. The first part of this section "authorizes a grant program, to be administered by the Attorney General, to improve the quality of legal representation provided to indigent defendants in State capital cases."[29] The second part "authorizes grants to improve the representation of the public in State capital cases," that is, to improve the work of prosecutors in capital cases. Congress authorized $75 million a year for five years to implement these programs. Each one has an evaluation component.[30]

The Innocent Act's third major section is entitled "Compensation Of the Wrongfully Convicted." This section "increases the maximum amount of damages that the U.S. Court of Federal Claims may award against the United States in cases of unjust imprisonment from a flat $5,000 to $50,000 per year in non-capital cases, and $100,000 per year in capital cases."[31] The section also "expresses the sense of Congress that States should provide reasonable compensation to any person found to have been unjustly convicted of an offense against the State and sentenced to death."[32]

The Death Penalty in the Military

Information on the military's use of the death penalty is scarce. What little is available suggests that, historically, the military has used the death penalty mostly for crimes committed during wartime.[33] In this section of the chapter, three topics are addressed: (1) the history of military executions, (2) military capital offenses, and (3) military capital punishment procedures.

Military Executions. Although there are no official records on the subject, it is believed that executions by the military were relatively common during both the American Revolution and in the early years of the nation. It is also believed that many death sentences were never carried out because of subsequent pardons. It is presumed that the crime for which most soldiers were sentenced to death during this period was desertion.

Official War Department records of military executions were first kept during the Civil War by the Union Army. Those records show 267 executions for the following offenses:

desertion	141
murder	72
rape	23
mutiny	20
theft	4
multiple offenses	4
spying	3

The list shows that more than half of the executions were for desertion. More Union soldiers would have been executed for desertion had President Lincoln not pardoned many of them, deciding "to take the risk on the side of mercy." There is no record of executions by the Confederate Army. Either no such records were kept, or they were destroyed before the war's end.

During World War I, the U.S. military executed 35 of the 145 soldiers sentenced to death. All of the soldiers executed were black. They were executed for murder and mutiny (19), rape (11), murder and rape (3), and murder (2). Ten of the executions were conducted in France and the remaining 25 in the United States. All executions took place at dawn following the day the trial ended. Because executions were carried out so quickly, there was no time to review the records of a case, as required by law, or enough time for condemned soldiers to petition the President for clemency or a pardon.

During World War II, the Army executed 147 soldiers. The Navy, the Air Force, and the Marine Corps executed none. The crimes for which soldiers were executed were murder (76), rape (52), murder and rape (18), and desertion (1). Although only one soldier was executed for desertion, 2,864 soldiers were tried for the offense and 49 of them were sentenced to death. All of those death sentences, except the one, were later commuted to life imprisonment. The one execution involved what has been called "the most widely publicized [case] of cowardice and desertion in modern times." The soldier violated Articles of War #52—desertion to avoid hazardous duty—and was executed by firing squad in France on January 31, 1945. In addition to American soldiers, 14 German prisoners of war were hanged at the United States Disciplinary Barracks, Fort Leavenworth, Kansas, in July and August 1945, for murdering other POWs.

Criminologist J. Robert Lilly has researched the records of 18 American soldiers executed by the U.S. Army in England from 1943 to 1945.[34] Eight of the executions were for murder, six were for rape, and four were for murder/rape.[35] Fifty-six percent (10) of the 18 soldiers executed, and 80 percent of all U.S. soldiers executed in the European Theater, were African-American even though African-Americans comprised no more than 10 percent of the soldiers in the European Theater and in the Army, generally.[36] Combined with the three Latinos executed, minorities accounted for 72 percent (13) of the 18 executions studied by Lilly. He found that only nonwhite soldiers were executed for rape. He also discovered evidence of racial discrimination at nearly every stage of the process.[37]

After World War II and until 1961, the military executed only 12 soldiers, although many more had been sentenced to death. All but the 12 had their sentences commuted. Eleven of the 12 executed were African-American.[38] The U.S. military's last execution was on April 13, 1961. Private John Bennett was hanged at the United States Disciplinary Barracks, Fort Leavenworth, Kansas, for the rape and attempted murder of an 11-year-old Austrian girl. Bennett was the 464th Army soldier executed since 1861. By contrast, the Navy has executed no more than 26 sailors during its history (not counting deaths from flogging which was outlawed in 1850). The last executions by the Navy were in 1849, when two sailors were hanged for mutiny. Similarly, the Air Force has executed only three airmen in its history: one in 1948 and two in 1954. The Coast Guard has carried out no executions, and no information is available on the Marines.

As of January 1, 2007, nine soldiers occupied the military's death row: all were male, six were African-American, two were white, and one was Asian.[39] So far, the military has not executed anyone since 1961.

Military Capital Offenses. Offenses for which death is a potential punishment in the military can be divided into three general categories: (1) offenses that could be committed at any time, (2) offenses committed during time of war, and (3) offenses that are "grave breaches" of the law of war. There are 10 potentially capital offenses that could be committed at any time:

1. mutiny or sedition

2. misbehavior before the enemy

3. subordinate compelling surrender

4. forcing a safeguard

5. aiding the enemy

6. espionage

7. improperly hazarding a vessel

8. premeditated murder

9. felony murder

10. rape

The five potentially capital offenses committed during time of war are:

1. desertion

2. assaulting or willfully disobeying superior commissioned officer

3. improper use of countersign

4. spying

5. misbehavior of sentinel

For purposes of the military's death penalty, "time of war" refers to a period of war declared by Congress or the factual determination by the President that the existence of hostilities warrants a finding that a "time of war" exists (examples of the latter are the Korean and Vietnam wars). The death penalty is mandatory for soldiers convicted of spying in time of war; however, given the Supreme Court's consistent post-*Furman* record of rejecting mandatory death penalty statutes, it is doubtful the military's mandatory provision could withstand constitutional scrutiny if ever challenged.

The third category of offenses for which the death penalty is a possible sanction is "grave breaches" of the law of war. The law of war to which this provision refers is the Geneva Convention Relative to the Treatment of Prisoners of War. Potentially capital crimes under the law of war are:

1. willful killing, torture, or inhuman treatment, including biological experiments

2. willfully causing great suffering or serious injury to body or health

3. unlawful deportation or transfer or unlawful confinement of a protected person

4. compelling a protected person to serve in the forces of a hostile power

5. willfully depriving a protected person of the rights of fair and regular trial prescribed in the present Convention

6. taking of hostages and extensive destruction and appropriation of property, not justified by military necessity and carried out unlawfully and wantonly

Military Capital Punishment Procedures. The Supreme Court has upheld the military death penalty process in *Loving v. United States* (1996).[40] Private Loving had been sentenced to death in 1988 for the murder of two taxi drivers. He appealed, arguing that his death sentence violated the Eighth Amendment's prohibition against cruel and unusual punishment and the separation of powers doctrine. The latter requires that Congress, and not the President, set military death penalty policy. The statute under which Loving was convicted and sentenced contained a list of aggravating factors—at least one of which had to be found before a death sentence could be imposed—issued by President Reagan in 1985 by executive order. President Reagan was responding to the ruling of the Court of Military Appeals in *U.S. v. Matthews* (1983), wherein the court held the military's death penalty unconstitutional because it was imposed in an arbitrary manner. Specifically, the statute "failed to narrow effectively the class of defendants eligible for capital punishment." Recall that the Supreme Court reached the same conclusion about the civilian death penalty in *Furman v. Georgia* in 1972. President Reagan issued the aggravating factors to satisfy the Court on this issue. In *Loving*, the Court ruled nine to zero that Congress had granted the President that power in 1951 under the *Uniform Code of Military Justice,* and it denied Private Loving's claim.

The military's death penalty process has much in common with some of the schemes approved by the Supreme Court in *Gregg*. Chief among them is that the members of the military court (the military's counterpart to the civilian jury) must unanimously find, beyond a reasonable doubt, at least one statutorily enumerated aggravating circumstance before it may consider a death sentence. Any aggravating circumstance that is found must be weighed against any mitigating circumstances that are presented at trial. Like its civilian counterpart, the military court must allow the presentation of any mitigating factor that is supported by evidence. If the members of the military court unanimously find that the aggravating circumstance or circumstances substantially outweigh any mitigating circumstances, then a death sentence may be imposed; if the mitigating circumstances are found to outweigh the aggravating circumstance or circumstances, then a death sentence may not be imposed.

The military's aggravating factors, many of which are unique to the military, are:

1. that the offense was committed before or in the presence of the enemy, except that this factor shall not apply in the case of a violation of Article 118 [premeditated murder and felony–murder] or 120 [rape];

2. that in committing the offense the accused—

    (A) knowingly created a grave risk of substantial damage to the national security of the United States; or

(B) knowingly created a grave risk of substantial damage to a mission, system, or function of the United States, provided that this subparagraph shall apply only if substantial damage to the national security of the United States would have resulted had the intended damage been effected;

3. that the offense caused substantial damage to the national security of the United States, whether or not the accused intended such damage, except that this factor shall not apply in case of a violation of Article 118 [premeditated murder and felony-murder] or 120 [rape];

4. that the offense was committed in such a way or under circumstances that the life of one or more persons other than the victim was unlawfully and substantially endangered, except that this factor shall not apply to a violation of Articles 104 [aiding the enemy], 106a [espionage], or 120 [rape];

5. that the accused committed the offense with the intent to avoid hazardous duty;

6. that, only in the case of a violation of Article 118 [premeditated murder and felony-murder] or 120 [rape], the offense was committed in time of war and in territory in which the United States or an ally of the United States was then an occupying power or in which the armed forces of the United States were then engaged in active hostilities;

7. that, only in the case of a violation of Article 118(1) [premeditated murder]:

   (A) the accused was serving a sentence of confinement for 30 years or more or for life at the time of the murder;

   (B) the murder was committed: while the accused was engaged in the commission or attempted commission of any robbery, rape, aggravated arson, sodomy, burglary, kidnapping, mutiny, sedition, or piracy of an aircraft or vessel; or while the accused was engaged in the commission or attempted commission of any offense involving the wrongful distribution, manufacture, or introduction or possession, with intent to distribute, of a controlled substance; or, while the accused was engaged in flight or attempted flight after the commission or attempted commission of any such offense.

   (C) the murder was committed for the purpose of receiving money or a thing of value;

(D) the accused procured another by means of compulsion, coercion, or a promise of an advantage, a service, or a thing of value to commit the murder;

(E) the murder was committed with the intent to avoid or to prevent lawful apprehension or effect an escape from custody or confinement;

(F) the victim was the President of the United States, the President-elect, the Vice President, or, if there was no Vice President, the officer in the order of succession to the office of President of the United States, the Vice-President-elect, or any individual who is acting as President under the Constitution and laws of the United States, any member of Congress (including a delegate to, or resident commissioner in, the Congress) or member-of-Congress elect, justice or judge of the United States, a chief of state or head of government (or the political equivalent) of a foreign nation, or a foreign official . . . if the official was on official business at the time of the offense and was in the United States or in a place described in Mil. R. Evid. . . . ;

(G) the accused then knew that the victim was any of the following persons in the execution of office: a commissioned, warrant, noncommissioned, or petty officer of the armed services of the United States; a member of any law enforcement or security activity or agency, military or civilian, including correctional custody personnel; or any firefighter;

(H) the murder was committed with intent to obstruct justice;

(I) the murder was preceded by the intentional infliction of substantial physical harm or prolonged, substantial mental or physical pain and suffering to the victim. For purposes of this section, 'substantial physical harm' means fractures or dislocated bones, deep cuts, torn members of the body, serious damage to internal organs, or other serious bodily injuries. The term 'substantial physical harm' does not mean minor injuries, such as a black eye or bloody nose. The term 'substantial mental or physical pain or suffering' is accorded its common meaning and includes torture;

(J) the accused has been found guilty in the same case of another violation of Article 118 [premeditated murder and felony-murder];

(K) the victim of the murder was less than fifteen years of age;

8. that only in the case of a violation of Article 118(4) [felony-murder], the accused was the actual perpetrator of the killing or was a principal whose participation in the burglary, sodomy, rape, robbery, or aggravated arson was major and who manifested a reckless indifference for human life;

9. that, only in the case of a violation of Article 120 [rape]:

    (A) the victim was under the age of 12; or

    (B) the accused maimed or attempted to kill the victim;

10. that, only in the case of a violation of the law of war, death is authorized under the law of war for the offense;

11. that, only in the case of a violation of Article 104 [aiding the enemy] or 106a [espionage]:

    (A) the accused has been convicted of another offense involving espionage or treason for which either a sentence of death or imprisonment for life was authorized by statute; or

    (B) that in committing the offense, the accused knowingly created a grave risk of death to a person other than the individual who was the victim.

Other key features of the military's capital punishment procedure are listed next. Some of the procedures are the same as those in other death penalty jurisdictions, and some of them are unique to the military.

• Before arraignment, the prosecution must provide written notice to the defense of aggravating factors that the prosecution intends to prove.

• Court members (the military's equivalent to civilian jurors) do not need to possess any specific requirements other than being the best qualified by reason of age, education, training, experience, length of service, and judicial temperament. They do not have to hold any particular rank.

• Although the UCMJ requires only five court members, including a military judge, defense counsel is likely to insist on a 12-person panel (because of Supreme Court decision, a panel should never be fewer than six). The accused may not elect to be tried by a military judge alone.

- Capital defendants are entitled to individual military counsel, preferably one with experience defending capital cases. They may also retain civilian counsel. The military is not required to appoint "ABA qualified" civilian defense counsel at government expense.[41]

- A guilty plea may not be accepted for an offense for which the death penalty may be adjudged.

- The panel members must find unanimously that the accused is guilty of a death eligible offense.

- The panel members must find unanimously beyond a reasonable doubt that at least one qualifying aggravating factor exists.

- The panel members must unanimously concur that any aggravating factors substantially outweigh any mitigating factors.

- The panel members must unanimously vote for the death penalty as the sentence for the accused. (It is the duty of the military judge in a capital case to ensure that the members are informed and understand that they may propose lesser sentences and, if so propose, must vote on such sentences before reaching a vote for death.)

- If death is adjudged, the president (military judge and one of the court members) shall announce which aggravating factors were found by the members.

- A death sentence includes a dishonorable discharge or dismissal, as appropriate. Confinement is a necessary incident of a death sentence but not part of it.

- Convictions and death sentences may be appealed first to the particular branches' court of criminal appeals (e.g., the Army Court of Criminal Appeals); next, to the United States Court of Appeals for the Armed Forces; and finally, to the United States Supreme Court.

- The President of the United States must approve all military executions. The President may also grant a commutation or pardon.

- Execution is by lethal injection.

The *Uniform Code of Military Justice* was recently amended to provide life without opportunity of parole (LWOP) as an alternative to the
death penalty for any soldier whose capital crime occurred on or after
November 17, 1997. Prior to the LWOP alternative, a soldier sentenced
to life imprisonment was eligible for parole in ten years.[42]

The Death Penalty in a Global Context[43]

Globally, the death penalty is trending toward abolition. At the
beginning of the twentieth century, only 3 countries—Costa Rica, San
Marino, and Venezuela—had abolished the death penalty for all crimes.
By 1977, only 14 countries had abolished the death penalty for all
crimes. Another 2 countries had abolished it for all but exceptional capital crimes, such as those committed during wartime. As of March 2007,
89 countries had abolished the death penalty for all crimes; another 10
countries had abolished it for all but exceptional crimes; and 29 countries had abolished it in practice (that is, they retain the death penalty
but have not carried out an execution for at least 10 years and are
believed to have a policy or established practice of not using the death
penalty). More than 40 countries have abolished the death penalty since
1990. The most recent are: Bhutan, Greece, Samoa, Senegal and Turkey
in 2004, Liberia and Mexico in 2005, the Philippines in 2006, and Alba-
nia in 2007. Since 1985, only 4 abolitionist countries have reintroduced
the death penalty. Two of those countries, Nepal and the Philippines, have
since abolished it again; and the two others, Gambia and Papua New
Guinea, have not executed anyone since reintroducing the penalty. So,
as of this writing, more than half of the countries in the world—128 of
them—have abolished the death penalty in law or practice.

On the other hand, only 69 countries and territories have retained
the death penalty. However, the number of countries that actually execute anyone in a given year is much smaller. All of the United States' major
allies except Japan have abolished the death penalty.

Executions Worldwide. During 2005, at least 2,148 prisoners
were executed in 22 countries and, in 53 countries, at least 5,186 people were sentenced to death. Another 19,474 to 25,546 are estimated
to be condemned to death and awaiting execution. The actual numbers
are assumed to be higher. China, Iran, Saudi Arabia, and the United States
accounted for 94 percent of the known executions in 2005, with China
estimated to have executed about 82 percent of the total. The list of
countries that executed at least one person in 2005 is instructive.
Besides China, Iran, Saudi Arabia, and the United States, they included,
in alphabetical order, Bangladesh, Belarus, Indonesia, Iraq, Japan, Jordan, Kuwait, Libya, Mongolia, North Korea, Pakistan, Palestinian Authority, Singapore, Somalia, Taiwan, Vietnam, and Yemen.

Since 2000, the following execution methods have been employed. Lethal injection has been used to execute in China, Guatemala, the Philippines, Thailand, and the United States. The United States has also executed by electrocution. Prisoners in Egypt, Iran, Japan, Jordan, Pakistan, Singapore and other countries have been hanged. Shooting has been the preferred method of execution in Belarus, China, Somalia, Taiwan, Uzbekistan, Viet Nam and other countries. Beheading has been used in Saudi Arabia and Iraq, and prisoners have been executed by stoning in Afghanistan and Iran.

International Treaties Prohibiting the Death Penalty. In recent years, many countries have committed to abolishing the death penalty by ratifying international treaties prohibiting the practice. Currently, there are four such treaties:

- The Second Optional Protocol to the International Covenant on Civil and Political Rights, which was adopted by the UN General Assembly in 1989. Fifty-seven countries have ratified this treaty. An additional 7 countries have signed the Protocol, indicating their intention to become parties to it at a later date.

- The Protocol to the American Convention on Human Rights to Abolish the Death Penalty, which was adopted by the General Assembly of the Organization of American States in 1990. This treaty has been ratified by 8 countries and signed by 1 other in the Americas.

- Protocol No. 6 to the European Convention for the Protection of Human Rights and Fundamental Freedoms (known as the European Convention on Human Rights), which was adopted by the Council of Europe in 1982. It has been ratified by 45 European countries and signed by 1 other.

- Protocol No. 13 to the European Convention for the Protection of Human Rights and Fundamental Freedoms (the European Convention on Human Rights), which was adopted by the Council of Europe in 2002. It has been ratified by 36 European countries and signed by 8 others.

Protocol No. 6 to the European Convention on Human Rights is an agreement to abolish the death penalty in peacetime. Its influence on the international debate about the death penalty is considered enormous because it has provided "the foundation for external judgments about the penal policies of other nations."[44] The Second Optional Protocol to the International Covenant on Civil and Political Rights and the Protocol to the American Convention on Human Rights provide for the total abolition of the death penalty but allow states wishing to do so to retain the death penalty in wartime as an exception. Protocol No. 13 to the European Convention on Human Rights provides for the total abolition of the death penalty in all circumstances with no exceptions permitted. The United States has taken reservations to the death penalty abolition provisions of treaties that it has ratified or signed. Reservations are statements that modify or exclude the applications or certain provisions for that country.

In addition, three human rights treaties that have been ratified by the United States ban arbitrary and discriminatory punishments. The International Covenant on Civil and Political Rights, mentioned above, prohibits any arbitrary use of the death penalty. The United Nations Convention Against Torture and Other Cruel, Inhuman or Degrading Treatment or Punishment bans torture and the infliction of severe pain or suffering based on any kind of discrimination. And the International Convention on the Elimination of All Forms of Racial Discrimination (the Race Convention), as the name implies, forbids racial discrimination in the law's administration. International agencies and courts have found the United States in violation of each of these treaties. The United States, in turn, has adamantly denied the accusations.

The Death Penalty Viewed Globally. The United Nations Commission on Human Rights has repeatedly condemned the death penalty in the United States. It has implored the U.S. government to halt all executions until states are brought into compliance with international standards and laws.

In Europe, the death penalty is viewed as a human rights violation. Admittance into the European Union requires abolition of the death penalty, and membership in the Council of Europe necessitates renouncing it. In 2001, the Council of Europe's 602-member parliamentary assembly passed a resolution to remove the United States and Japan as observers at the organization unless significant progress toward abolishing executions and repealing the death penalty was made by January 1, 2003. When both countries failed to comply by that date, the Assembly passed another resolution requiring the United States and Japan "to make more of an effort" to place a moratorium on executions "with a view to abolishing the death penalty," or risk losing their observer status.

The European Union also considers a universal moratorium on executions and the death penalty's abolition as key factors in relations between the European Union and third countries. Member countries are to take this into account when finalizing agreements with third countries. Consequently, some foreign businesses, particularly those operated by governments, may make economic decisions based on a state's use of the death penalty. In a 1998 letter to then-Texas Governor George Bush, a European Union official wrote, "Many companies, under pressure from shareholders and public opinion to apply ethical business practices, are beginning to consider the possibility of restricting the investment in the U.S. to states that do not apply the death penalty."

The most direct way in which the United States has been alienating its allies is the execution of foreign nationals, especially when they have not been accorded their rights under the Vienna Convention on Consular Relations. The United States, along with almost all of the other countries of the world, has long been a party to the Vienna Convention. Article 36 of this Convention requires officials in the United States and other countries that have ratified the Convention to inform foreign nationals placed under arrest of their rights to confer with their home country's consular officials. This provision is binding on all states under the U.S. Constitution but has been systematically ignored, partly because the police generally are unaware of the law. Cases in which countries fail to comply with Article 36 can be referred to the International Court of Justice, which can forward those cases to the U.N. Security Council for "appropriate action"—whatever that means. In February 2005, President Bush signed a memorandum affirming the United States would comply with the 2004 decision of the International Court of Justice to have state courts review and reconsider the effect of Vienna Convention violations in the cases of 51 Mexican nationals on U.S. death rows. However, in March 2006, the United States announced its withdrawal from the Vienna Convention's Optional Protocol Concerning the Compulsory Settlement of Disputes, the international legal instrument that empowers the International Court to interpret and apply the treaty's terms. As of this writing, 121 foreign citizens representing 32 nationalities were imprisoned on U.S. death rows.

Until March 2005, when the Supreme Court decided *Roper v. Simmons* (543 U.S. 551), the most flagrant U.S. deviation from the consensus of international law was its execution of juvenile offenders. The execution of offenders who were under 18 years of age at the time of their crime is directly prohibited by the International Covenant on Civil and Political Rights, by the U.N. Convention on the Rights of the Child, and the American Convention on Human Rights. So broad is the acceptance of this prohibition that it is widely considered a norm of customary international law.

Ironically, former Supreme Court Justice Sandra Day O'Connor, during a speech in 2003, argued that international law was important in American jurisprudence, and that the United States needed to improve its image abroad. She noted how the Supreme Court cited international law in its recent decision banning the execution of the mentally retarded, as it had done in many cases over its history.[45] Justice O'Connor stated, "I suspect that over time we will rely increasingly, or take notice at least increasingly, on international and foreign courts in examining domestic issues." She added that doing so "may not only enrich our own country's decisions, I think it may create that all important good impression."

The U.S. position on the death penalty is also affecting the war on terrorism. In 2000, the European Union adopted the Charter of Fundamental Rights, which, among other things, prohibits the extradition of offenders to any country where the death penalty might be imposed unless a firm guarantee is given that the death penalty will not be imposed. This includes those suspected of carrying out terrorist acts against the United States post 9/11. This impediment to extradition may cause the United States to expand the practice of forcibly taking suspects from other countries without resort to the courts, a practice referred to as "rendition."

Countries that have retained the death penalty, such as the United States and Japan, continue to oppose death penalty abolitionist efforts. They resent attempts to make the issue one of international morality. They consider such attempts as insulting and culturally imperialistic. In the United States, Supreme Court Justice Antonin Scalia, in his dissent in *Atkins v. Virginia* (536 U.S. 304, 2002), called the practices of the "so-called 'world community'" irrelevant, maintaining that its "notions of justice are (thankfully) not always those of our people." Death penalty proponents in the United States argue that European and other countries have a convoluted interpretation of human rights. As one death penalty advocate has put it:

> What the DP is, is a punishment for a human rights violation, not a human rights violation itself. Anyone with any amount of moral judgment and coherence would recognize and respect that difference. All abolitionists are trying to do is protect human rights violators at the expense of their victims by trying to pass off the just punishment of human rights violations as a human rights violation itself, an analysis that one would have to be totally lacking in sound moral judgement [sic] to accept since it is so obviously contradictory as well as morally and logically skewed.[46]

Death penalty opponents, on the other hand, counter that the views expressed above are arrogant and dismissive of the position of most countries of the world, including all of our allies except Japan. They observe that the U.S. position on the death penalty is especially important because other retentionist countries can point to the United States as a champion of human rights that continues to impose the death penalty.

The international movement away from the death penalty raises serious questions for the United States:

- How likely is it that sanctions will be invoked against the U.S. if it continues to ignore the growing international consensus?

- What damage is being done to the U.S.'s leadership and credibility in the field of human rights?

- Are the rights of U.S. citizens abroad being endangered because the U.S. has failed to follow international treaties and the decisions of international courts?

The answers to these questions may profoundly affect the United States' place in the world community and the course of human rights for years to come.

Conclusion

With the exception of the federal courts, neither the federal government nor the military plays a significant role in the practice of capital punishment. At this writing, the federal government, which has executed three people under post-*Furman* statutes, and the military, which has executed none, account for less than 0.3 percent of all post-*Furman* executions. Yet, together, they have made many more crimes death-eligible than has any of the states.

The position of the United States on the death penalty is contrary to the position of all other western-industrialized nations and all U.S. allies, except Japan. Retaining the death penalty may have significant political and economic repercussions. As Law Professor Richard Wilson observes, "[T]he United States risks bitter resentment and legitimate claims of hypocrisy by the community of nations if it continues to aggressively apply the death penalty while asserting a commitment to human rights at home and abroad."[47]

Discussion Questions

1. What are four actions the Supreme Court can take when it decides a case it has accepted on appeal?

2. Do you agree with the list of federal capital crimes? Should any of the crimes be removed from the list? Should any crimes be added to the list?

3. Should the federal government have executed Timothy McVeigh and Juan Raul Garza? Why or why not?

4. Do you agree with the changes in federal *habeas corpus* made in the Antiterrorism and Effective Death Penalty Act of 1996?

5. What are major procedural differences among the death penalty statutes of the death penalty states, the federal government, and the military?

6. What accounts for the differences identified in question five?

7. Should the United States be concerned about world opinion about its use of the death penalty? Why or why not?

8. Why does the United States remain the only western industrialized nation in the world to employ the death penalty?

Notes

[1] Material in this section is from Bohm and Haley, 2007:Chap. 8.

[2] Gorecki, 1983:86; Filler, 1967:117.

[3] The list is from the published law itself—Public Law 103-322, September 13, 1994; Snell, 1997:4, Table 2; Coyne and Entzeroth, 1998:151-155.

[4] Death Penalty Information Center, April 10, 2006.

[5] Material about Bird and pre-*Furman* federal executions is from Death Penalty Information Center, 2001, www.deathpenaltyinfo.org/feddp.html; Santich, 2001; Gillespie, 2003:91-102.

[6] Banner, 2002:189.

[7] Material about the national death-row facility is from Michel and Herbeck, 2001:371-373.

[8] In the case of *United States v. Sampson*, 300 F. Supp. 2d 278 (D. Mass. 2004), for example, the court selected New Hampshire as the place of execution because Massachusetts, where the trial took place, does not have a death penalty or execution facilities. Also see 18 U.S.C. § 3596 (a).

[9] Word, 2002.

[10] More than 1,000 reporters registered for credentials to cover McVeigh's execution; only 75 reporters registered for credentials for Garza's execution. Most of the material about McVeigh is from Michel and Herbeck, 2001; also see Gillespie, 2003:91-97.

[11] Material about Garza is from www.aclu.org/death-penalty/garza_factsheet.html; http://ccadp.org/juanraulgarza~news.htm.

[12] For a copy of the federal study, see www.usdoj.gov/dag/pubdoc/dpsurvey.html.

[13] Cited in "Study: No racial bias in executions." *The Orlando Sentinel* (June 7, 2001), p. A3.

[14] Cited in "Death Penalty Often a Subjective Pursuit." *The Orlando Sentinel* (June 14, 2001), p. A16; for information about the Federal Death Penalty Resource Counsel, see www.capdefnet.org.

[15] Death Penalty Information Center, April 11, 2007.

[16] U.S. General Accounting Office, 1990.

[17] Baldus and Woodworth, 1998:410; Acker, 1996:150-151.

[18] Ibid.

[19] Baldus and Woodworth, op. cit., pp. 410-411.

[20] Baldus and Woodworth, 1998:410; Acker, 1996:150-151.

[21] Acker, op. cit., p. 151.

[22] See *Felker v. Turpin*, 518 U.S. 1051, 1996.

[23] Leahy, 2004a.

[24] Justice For All Act of 2004: Section-By-Section Analysis" at Leahy, 2004b.

[25] Ibid.

[26] Ibid.

[27] Ibid.

[28] Ibid.

[29] Ibid.

[30] Ibid.

[31] Ibid.

[32] Ibid.

[33] Unless indicated otherwise, information in this section is from Turney, 2000; Einwechter, 1998; Montgomery, 1994; Wyble, 1985.

[34] Lilly, 1996.

[35] Ibid., p. 497, Table 1.

[36] Ibid., p. 497; Lilly, Davies, and Ball, 1995:2.

[37] Lilly, 1993:13.

[38] Lilly, 1997:11.

[39] Death Row U.S.A. (Winter 2007).

[40] The following account of the *Loving* case is from Lilly, 1996:511–12; also see Visger, 2005, for a discussion of the military capital process.

[41] ABA (American Bar Association) guidelines require lead trial defense counsel in capital cases to have at least five years criminal defense experience, to have tried no fewer than nine jury trials of serious and complex cases (one of which was a capital case), or to have completed in the last year a CLE course in defending capital cases.

[42] Death Penalty Information Center, op. cit., /military.html#facts.

43 Unless indicated otherwise, material in this section is from Amnesty International at http://web.amnesty.org/pages/deathpenalty-index-eng; the Death Penalty Information Center at www.deathpenaltyinfo.org/article.php?did=127&scid=30; the Council of Europe at http://assembly.coe.int/Main.asp?link=/Documents/AdoptedText/ta03/ERES1349.htm; Hood, 2002.

[44] Zimring, 2003:29.

[45] Wilson, 2003.

[46] Pro Death Penalty Webpage at http://www.wesleylowe.com/cp.html.

[47] Wilson, op. cit., p. 150.

CHAPTER 4

Methods of Execution

Introduction: Cruel and Unusual Punishment

Human beings historically have been quite creative in the methods they have legally employed to put people to death. At one time or another, execution methods have included "flaying and impaling, boiling in oil, crucifixion, pulling asunder, . . . burying alive, and sawing in half."[1] None of those methods has ever been used legally in the United States, but beheading, pressing to death, drawing and quartering, breaking on the wheel, drowning, and burning at the stake were used as late as the 18th century.[2] The last execution method—burning at the stake— was reserved for two classes of crimes, both referred to legally as "petit treason." The first class included the murdering of an owner by a slave or a slave plotting a revolt; the second was the murder of a husband by a wife. Both classes of crimes had in common a challenge to traditional hierarchical authority and were considered especially disruptive of the social order. Burning was employed infrequently.[3]

As noted in Chapter 1, deterrence was a primary goal of the death penalty during the colonial period. To increase deterrence, colonial Americans sometimes employed "enhancements" to an execution. The "gibbet" was one of those enhancements. If a crime were particularly heinous and authorities wanted to magnify and extend the deterrent message beyond the actual execution, they might take the corpse from the gallows and cover it in tallow or pitch to slow down the body's decomposition.[4] Then they would enclose the corpse in a "gibbet"—an iron cage with bars that permitted easy viewing—and hang it in a public place, subjecting it to the weather, insects, and birds of prey.[5] People, as they engaged in their daily routines, would pass the hanging corpse and literally watch it decompose. Sometimes, executions would be followed by dismemberment of the body—another "enhancement." A head might be severed from a corpse and placed on the end of a pole for public viewing, or, in some cases, not only would the head be severed from the body but also the remaining body would be cut into quarters. The body parts would be displayed in different parts of the county allowing more people to be exposed to the message being conveyed.[6] These death penalty "enhancements," along with burning the body, were especially terrifying to most colonial Americans and, thus, presumably effective deterrents to crime, because, according to Christian theology, if the integrity of a person's corpse had been violated and the corpse had not been properly buried, that person would be denied resurrection at the final judgment.[7]

Commenting on these early methods of execution, Professor Hugo Adam Bedau observed, "It is curious that any of these barbarous and inhumane methods of execution survived so long, for the English Bill of Rights (1689) proscribed "cruel and unusual punishments."[8] Such punishments were also prohibited by several American state constitutions and by the Eighth Amendment of the United States Constitution.

A Fixed or Historical Meaning. For approximately 120 years after the adoption of the Bill of Rights, the Supreme Court employed a fixed or historical meaning for the concept of cruel and unusual punishment. The Court interpreted the concept's meaning in light of the practices authorized and used at the time that the Eighth Amendment was adopted in 1791. Thus, only the most barbarous punishments and tortures were prohibited. Capital punishment itself was not prohibited because there was explicit reference to it in the Fifth Amendment, and it was in use when the Eighth Amendment was adopted.

The Court, in *Wilkerson v. Utah* (1878), provided examples of punishments that were prohibited by the Eighth Amendment because they involved "torture" or "unnecessary cruelty." They included punishments in which the criminal "was embowelled alive, beheaded, and quartered." The Court expanded the meaning of cruel and unusual punishment in *In re Kemmler* (1890) to include punishments that "involve torture or lingering death . . . something more than the mere extinguishment of life," such as "burning at the stake, crucifixion, breaking on the wheel, or the like."

A New Meaning. In 1910, in the noncapital case of *Weems v. United States,* the Court abandoned its fixed or historical interpretation of cruel and unusual punishment and created a new one. Weems was a U.S. Coast Guard disbursing officer in the Philippines convicted of making two false accounting entries amounting to 612 pesos (equivalent to about 13 U.S. dollars in 2007).[9] He was fined and sentenced to 15 years of hard labor and forced to wear chains on his ankles and wrists. After completing his sentence, he was to be under surveillance for the rest of his life, he was to lose his rights to parental authority and guardianship of persons and property, he was to notify public authorities whenever he changed his place of residence, and he was to lose his voting rights and the right to hold office as well. Weems argued that his punishment was disproportionate to his crime and, therefore, cruel and unusual.[10]

The Court agreed with Weems and broke with tradition, holding "that (1) the meaning of the Eighth Amendment is not restricted to the intent of the Framers, (2) that the Eighth Amendment bars punishments that are excessive, and (3) that what is excessive is not fixed in time but changes with evolving social conditions."[11] Thenceforward, the Court no longer used the fixed or historical interpretation; it chose instead to interpret the concept in the context of "evolving social conditions."

The Court further clarified its position nearly 50 years later in another noncapital case, *Trop v. Dulles* (1958). As punishment for desertion during World War II, Trop was stripped of his U.S. citizenship.[12] The Court reviewed the case on appeal and ruled that the punishment was cruel and unusual because it was an affront to basic human dignity. It noted that the "dignity of man" was "the basic concept underlying the Eighth Amendment," and it held that Trop's punishment exceeded "the limits of civilized standards." Referring to the earlier *Weems* case, the Court emphasized that "the limits of civilized standards . . . draws its meaning from the evolving standards of decency that mark the progress of a maturing society." Those evolving standards are, in turn, determined by "objective indicators, such as the enactments of legislatures as expressions of 'the will of the people,' the decisions of juries, and the subjective moral judgments of members of the Supreme Court itself."[13] In short, it appears that as long as a punishment has been enacted by a legislature, imposed by a jury, and approved of by the Supreme Court, it will not be considered cruel and unusual. The Supreme Court has never declared an execution method cruel and unusual punishment.[14]

What about Long Stays on Death Row? Do long stays on death row constitute cruel and unusual punishment? According to the U.S. Supreme Court, apparently not. In November 1999, the Court refused to hear appeals from two convicted killers who claimed that their long stays on death row subjected them to cruel and unusual punishment. Carey Dean Moore had been on Nebraska's death row for 19 years, while Askari Abdullah Muhammad had been a resident of Florida's death row for 24 years. Justice Stephen Breyer, who voted to hear the appeals, wrote: "Where a delay, measured in decades, reflects the state's own failure to comply with the Constitution's demands, the claim that time has rendered the execution inhuman is a particularly strong one." On the other hand, Justice Clarence Thomas, who voted not to hear the appeals, blamed his colleagues for making the review of capital punishment cases so time consuming. Thomas argued that "[c]onsistency would seem to demand that those who accept our death penalty jurisprudence as a given also accept the lengthy delay between sentencing and execution as a necessary consequence."[15] Similar unsuccessful claims had been made earlier by Clarence Lackey (in 1995), who had served 17 years on Texas's death row, and William Elledge (in 1998), who had been confined on Florida's death row for 23 years.[16] A provocative argument has been made that the lengthy delays on death row serve the prison bureaucracy's interests of achieving a smooth execution process by rendering condemned inmates completely docile, unwilling to resist being executed.[17]

What about the Execution of Elderly and Infirm Death Row Inmates? The Supreme Court also has ruled that it is not cruel and unusual punishment to execute elderly and infirm death row inmates. In 2004, 74-year-old James Hubbard was executed in Alabama for a murder he had committed in 1977, shortly following his release from prison after serving 19 years for a 1957 killing. Hubbard's lawyer argued to the Supreme Court that to execute someone so old and mentally incompetent was cruel and unusual.[18] After serving 20 years on Mississippi's death row, 77-year-old John Nixon, Sr. was executed in 2005, for a murder he was convicted of committing in 1985. He did not pursue an appeal based on his age.[19] Finally, in 2006, 76-year-old Clarence Ray Allen was executed in California after being sentenced to death in 1982 for hiring a hit man who killed a witness and two bystanders. Allen was blind and mostly deaf, had diabetes, and almost died of a heart attack a few months prior to his execution. Four large correctional officers had to assist him into the death chamber, where they lifted him out of his wheelchair and placed him on the gurney. The Supreme Court had rejected Allen's requests for a stay of execution, and Governor Schwarzenegger had rejected his clemency appeal. Allen's lawyer had argued unsuccessfully to the Supreme Court that his client's execution would constitute cruel and unusual punishment because Allen was a frail old man, who had spent 23 years on death row.[20]

What about Conditions on Death Row? Conditions of death row confinement are another area that has been subjected to Eighth Amendment claims. In *Rhodes v. Chapman* (1981), the Supreme Court held that "the Constitution does not mandate comfortable prisons." Conditions may be "restrictive and even harsh." To rise to the level of an Eighth Amendment violation, prison conditions must "involve the wanton and unnecessary infliction of pain." The Court established a two-part analysis to govern Eighth Amendment challenges to conditions of confinement. First, under the objective component, an inmate must show that the condition of which he complains is sufficiently serious to violate the Eighth Amendment, that it is "extreme," and that it "poses an unreasonable risk of serious damage to his future health."[21] It also must be so grave that it violates contemporary standards of decency.[22] Second, under the subjective component, an inmate must show that prison officials "acted with a sufficiently culpable state of mind," that they acted with "deliberate indifference."[23] In other words, a prison official can be held liable under this standard if he or she "knows of and disregards an excessive risk to inmate health or safety; the official must both be aware of facts from which the inference could be drawn that a substantial risk of serious harm exists, and he must draw the inference."[24]

In two cases decided by federal appellate courts in 2004, death row conditions were challenged on Eighth Amendment grounds. The first case, *Gates v. Cook*, addressed death row conditions at the Mississippi State Penitentiary in Parchman. In the class-action suit, it was claimed that "prisoners housed on Death Row are knowingly and deliberately subjected to profound isolation, lack of exercise, stench and filth, malfunctioning plumbing, high temperatures, uncontrolled mosquito and insect infestations, a lack of sufficient mental health care, and exposure to psychotic inmates in adjoining cells." Reiterating the trial court's findings of fact, the Fifth U.S. Circuit Court of Appeals described in detail the conditions in which Mississippi death row inmates had to live:

1. **Sanitation.** Inmates have been subjected to cells that were extremely filthy with chipped, peeling paint, dried fecal matter and food encrusted on the walls, ceilings, and bars, as well as water from flooded toilets and rain leaks. Inmates are routinely moved from cell to cell and are forced to clean their new cells that may have been left in horrendous sanitation by the prior occupants, especially if the occupant were mentally ill. Adequate cleaning supplies and equipment are not routinely made available for inmates to clean their cells. These filthy conditions contribute to the infestation of pests and play a role in the mental well being of inmates.

2. **Heating and Cooling.** The summer temperatures in the Mississippi Delta average in the nineties with high humidity, and Death Row is primarily not an air-conditioned facility. There are industrial type fans in the hallways to help with air circulation, and most inmates have smaller fans. Relief from the heat can be obtained by keeping the windows open in the cell using fans. But keeping the windows open increases the mosquito population in the cells since there are holes in the cell window screens and the screen gauge is not sufficient to keep mosquitoes out. The ambient temperature in the cells is within reasonable limits except during the summer months. The ventilation is inadequate to afford prisoners a minimal level of comfort during the summer months. The probability of heat-related illness is extreme on Death Row, and is dramatically more so for mentally ill inmates who often do not take appropriate behavioral steps to deal with the heat. Also, the medications often given to deal with various medical problems interfere with the body's ability to maintain a normal temperature. The inmates are not afforded extra showers, ice water, or fans if they don't have fans when the heat index is 90 or above. The heat problem extends to all of Death Row and possibly throughout Parchman.

3. **Pest Control.** The heat problem also exacerbates the problem of pest control. Mosquitoes in Mississippi, and the Delta in particular, are a problem that cannot be eliminated. But the problem must be addressed and the impact lessened, especially with the incidence of West Nile virus, a mosquito-born disease increasing in Mississippi. Inadequate screening on the cell windows causes the inmates to choose between suffering from the heat or increasing the mosquitoes in their cells. The problems of heat and mosquitoes must be addressed to provide the inmates with conditions that would meet minimal constitutional standards. The problem of roaches and other vermin will be met by adhering to the ACA [American Correctional Association] standards and by meeting the sanitation goals the court will set.

4. **"Ping-Pong" Toilets and Plumbing.** Fecal and other matter flushed by a toilet in one cell will bubble up in the adjoining cell unless the toilets are flushed simultaneously. This has been a problem since the unit opened. Parchman officials have identified the problem as one of calibration, especially if the water is shut off. The toilets must be recalibrated to work properly. Recalibration has helped, but not eliminated, the problem of ping-pong toilets. No one in civilized society should be forced to live under conditions that force exposure to another person's bodily wastes.

5. **Lighting.** The lighting in the cells is grossly inadequate. While 20 foot-candles [a foot-candle is a unit of measure of the intensity of light falling on a surface] is the appropriate level of lighting for the cells, the maximum foot-candles . . . was seven or eight, with the typical cell being in the 2-4 foot-candle range.

6. **Laundry.** The inmates' laundry is returned foul smelling, necessitating the inmates to wash their clothes in their cells.

7. **Mental Health Issues.** The extremely psychotic prisoners [on Death Row] scream at night, throw feces, and generally make life miserable for the other inmates and guards. . . . The mental health care afforded the inmates on Death Row is grossly inadequate. . . . What mental health services are provided generally take place at the inmate's cell within hearing of other inmates and guards. This results in the failure of inmates to tell the mental health specialists anything of substance. Moreover, com-

prehensive mental health evaluations are consistently inadequate. Inmates are also prescribed psychotropic drugs with only sporadic monitoring. This can result in life-threatening situations due to the toxicity of these drugs.

8. **Exercise.** The exercise facilities provided are adequate. While, in general, the use of "flip-flops" is understandable as a security measure, such shoes do not allow effective exercise. The inmates should be given access to sneakers prior to entering the exercise pen and should be given access to water and shade while exercising.

The trial court concluded that the aforementioned conditions constituted Eighth Amendment violations and ordered injunctive relief. The appeals court vacated in their entirety three of the injunctions, vacated four of the injunctions to the extent they did not apply exclusively to conditions on Death Row, and affirmed three of the injunctions. Following are the injunctions affirmed by the court:

1. If defendants wish to continue the practice of moving inmates from cell to cell [on Death Row], they will insure that the cell to which an inmate is moved is clean prior to the move. While an inmate should be required to keep his own cell clean, he should not be required to clean the cell of another inmate in order to inhabit it.

2. Adequate cleaning supplies and equipment shall be provided inmates in order that they may clean their cells at least weekly.

3. The defendants shall insure that the new vendor for medical services complies with the ACA and the National Commission on Correctional Healthcare medical and mental health standards. Each inmate on Death Row shall be given a comprehensive mental health examination in private. These comprehensive examinations shall be conducted on a yearly basis. Those inmates diagnosed with psychosis and severe mental health illnesses shall be housed separately and apart from all other inmates. The medication levels of all inmates receiving psychotropic medications shall be monitored and assessed in accordance with appropriate medical standards. All inmates receiving mental health counseling or evaluation shall meet with the mental health professionals in a private setting.

In the other case, the class-action suit, *Chandler v. Crosby*, the Eleventh U.S. Circuit Court of Appeals ruled against 365 Florida death row inmates at Union Correctional Institution in Raiford. The inmates claimed that the high temperatures in their cells during the summer months combined with high humidity and inadequate ventilation amounted to cruel and unusual punishment in violation of the Eighth Amendment. To deal with the heat, inmates would stand in toilets, drape themselves in wet towels, and sleep naked on the concrete floors.[25] In the ruling the court observed "while no one would call the summertime temperatures at the Unit pleasant, the heat is not unconstitutionally excessive." It cited the district court's finding that "the building mass remains at a relatively constant temperature" during July and August, "between approximately eighty degrees at night to approximately eighty-five or eighty-six degrees during the day." Furthermore, temperatures during the two months climbed past ninety degrees only nine percent of the time in 1998 and 1999. During the same time period, the temperature reached ninety-five degrees or higher only seven times, and there were no recorded temperatures that exceeded 100 degrees. The court noted, "at the hottest times of the day, it is cooler in the cells than it is outdoors." It concluded "the temperatures and ventilation on the . . . Unit during the summer months are almost always consistent with reasonable levels of comfort and slight discomfort which are to be expected in a residential setting in Florida in a building that is not air-conditioned."

Death row in Oklahoma also has no air conditioning, despite very hot summer temperatures. However, in Oklahoma, the entire death row facility is underground, which undoubtedly gives relief from the summer heat but allows for no natural light. Thus, a death sentence in Oklahoma means never seeing sunshine again. That may help explain why about one-third of all Oklahoma death row inmates do not pursue any appeals.[26]

Turning to methods of execution, for a century after the ratification of the Eighth Amendment, hanging was the only legally authorized method of execution in the United States. The one exception was that spies, traitors, and deserters convicted under federal statutes could be shot.[27] Five methods of execution are currently authorized in various jurisdictions in the United States: (1) hanging, (2) firing squad, (3) electrocution, (4) lethal gas, and (5) lethal injection.

Hanging

Hanging was one of the first lawful execution methods used in the United States. Although its use declined dramatically after the introduction of the electric chair in 1890, more people—at least 70 percent of the total—have been executed by hanging than by any other method.[28]

In colonial America, hanging had a dual role. Its primary role, of course, was as an execution method. However, it also was employed as a means of mitigating a death sentence, which, at the time, was the sentence for most serious crimes.[29] The second use for hanging—"simulated hanging"—was first employed in the Massachusetts colony in 1693 for offenders convicted of a second burglary or robbery.[30] Such offenders were required to sit upon the gallows for an hour with a noose around their necks, after which they were taken down and whipped.[31] If they were convicted of either offense a third time, they were executed.[32]

The slow and agonizing deaths caused by hangings prior to the nineteenth century were meant to be instructive for the public and degrading to the person executed. Quicker and more dignified methods of execution were firing squad and beheading.[33] In the nineteenth century, British master hangmen discovered the "long drop"—a fall sufficiently long to break the neck and cause relatively quick and painless death.[34] The long drop proved a more humane technique than the previous strangulation method, but in some cases it still took up to 20 minutes to cause death.[35]

Until they eventually abolished capital punishment, England and other European countries employed professional hangmen who were often pariahs in their own communities.[36] The American colonies tried several different arrangements. For example, in the seventeenth century, the Massachusetts colony excused Thomas Bell from taking his turn on the night watch in exchange for his serving as the colony's hangman.[37] Maryland had such a hard time appointing a hangman that it finally employed convicted criminals to serve in the position for a number of years or for life in exchange for death sentence reprieves.[38] However, by the end of the seventeenth century, all of the colonies had made executions the responsibility of the county sheriff, the arrangement that most colonies had adopted in the first place.[39] The sheriff was responsible for the entire execution, from building the gallows to disposal of the corpse.[40] When the sheriff could not induce someone with money or liquor to serve as hangman, he did the job himself.[41]

There were numerous botched hangings. At least 170 legal hangings performed in the United States between 1622 and 2002 were botched.[42] Before routine use of the long drop, most of the flawed hangings resulted in slow and painful strangulation. An improperly administered long drop (that is, if the drop were too long) could cause decapitation. As late as the 1960s, for example, at the state prison in Walla Walla, Washington, a hanging resulted in the inmate's head nearly being torn off and witnesses to the execution being spattered with blood.[43]

Two states (New Hampshire and Washington) still allow hanging;[44] however, both states also authorize lethal injection. New Hampshire authorizes hanging only if lethal injection cannot be given (see note 81). In Washington, the choice is the condemned prisoner's to make. If the prisoner fails to choose, the method is hanging. The first person executed by hanging in the United States since 1965 was child-killer Westley Allan Dodd, on January 5, 1993, in the state of Washington.[45]

Firing Squad

Execution by firing squad currently remains an option in two states: Idaho and Oklahoma.[46] Idaho authorizes firing squad only if lethal injection is "impractical." In Oklahoma, firing squad is authorized only if both lethal injection and electrocution are held to be unconstitutional. Also, in Utah, execution by firing squad is available for those inmates who chose that option before legislation passed in March 2004 banned it.

Firing squads in Utah consisted of five volunteer marksmen. Four of them were given rifles with live rounds and one of them was given a rifle with blanks.[47] The rifle with blanks maintained the fiction that none of the shooters would know who fired the fatal shot. In reality, the kick produced by live rounds is easily distinguishable from the kick produced by blanks, and any firearms expert would have no trouble telling the difference. The inmate was seated and strapped to a chair with a hood over his head and a bull's-eye over his heart. Following a signal from the warden, the shooters fired at the bull's-eye. There is no solid evidence, but it is presumed that a competently performed execution by firing squad caused a quick death with little or no pain. When given a choice between death by firing squad and death by hanging, most inmates chose the former. Botched executions by firing squad were rare.

The most celebrated recent execution by firing squad was the January 17, 1977, execution of Gary Gilmore in Utah.[48] Gilmore was the first person executed in the United States in a decade and the first person executed under post-*Furman* statutes. Unlike most death row inmates, Gilmore had voluntarily waived his right to appeal and demanded that the state of Utah carry out his sentence. His case was appealed anyway without his consent, and he received three stays of execution. While in prison, he twice tried to commit suicide. His last words were "Let's do it."

The last person executed by firing squad in the United States was John Albert Taylor, in 1996. He was also executed in Utah. Fewer than 150 people have been executed legally by firing squad in the United States since 1608.[49]

Electrocution

In October 2001, the Georgia Supreme Court by a vote of 4–3 became the first appellate court in the United States to rule that electrocution violated the Eighth Amendment's prohibition against cruel and unusual punishment. The court held that electrocution "inflicts purposeless physical violence and needless mutilation that makes no measurable contribution to accepted goals of punishment."[50] A year earlier the U.S. Supreme Court refused to review a challenge to Alabama's use of the electric chair, and canceled its review of Florida's practice after the state legislature passed new legislation providing for lethal injection as the primary means of execution. Alabama then followed Florida's lead and gave condemned inmates the option of lethal injection or electrocution.[51] As a result, Nebraska is the only state that still uses electrocution as the sole method of execution, though it remains an option in nine other states.[52] Alabama, Florida, South Carolina, and Virginia authorize a choice of electrocution or lethal injection.[53] Arkansas, Kentucky, and Tennessee offer the same choice to death row inmates whose offenses occurred before July 4, 1983, March 31, 1998, and January 1, 1999, respectively. For those whose capital offenses occur after those dates, there is no choice—execution is by lethal injection. Finally, Illinois and Oklahoma authorize electrocution if lethal injection is ever held to be unconstitutional. (If both electrocution and lethal injection are ever held to be unconstitutional, Oklahoma authorizes firing squad, as previously noted.) Although many states have recently abandoned electrocution, between 1930 and 1972 it was the method employed by 25 states; hanging was employed in 13 states and lethal gas in 11.[54] During the twentieth century, more people were executed by electrocution than by any other method.[55]

The history of electrocution as a method of capital punishment is both fascinating and instructive.[56] The electric chair is an American invention and an unintended product of a corporate battle between the Westinghouse and Edison companies. In the late 1880s, competition was fierce over which of the two companies would "electrify" American cities. Westinghouse was successfully touting its alternating current (AC), while Edison was promoting, somewhat less successfully than Westinghouse, its direct current (DC). A problem with Edison's direct current was that low transmission voltages reduced its range to just a mile beyond the generator that produced it. There was no such problem with alternating current. In addition, alternating current proved cheaper than direct current to transmit. Trying to beat its competition, Edison staged public demonstrations during which animals were electrocuted with Westinghouse's alternating current to show how dangerous their competitor's product was.

The governor of New York, meanwhile, dissatisfied with hanging as the state's method of execution, appointed a three-member commission to determine and recommend to the legislature "the most humane and practical method [of execution] known to modern science." One of the commission members was Dr. Alfred P. Southwick, a dentist from Buffalo, who believed that electrocution would be preferable to hanging. Before his appointment to the commission, Dr. Southwick (later known as the "father of electrocution") had witnessed a man touch an electric generator and die what appeared to be a fast and painless death. Southwick also witnessed and conducted the electrocution of animals in demonstrations like those performed by the Edison company. Southwick enlisted the help of Edison, who already was an American hero, to persuade the other commission members to endorse electrocution as the new method of execution. Edison personally opposed capital punishment, but he agreed to help Southwick, who had convinced him that the issue was not whether capital punishment should be employed, but rather what form it should take.

The commission did recommend that hanging be replaced with electrocution. Interestingly, the commission also considered lethal injection (as well as the guillotine and the garrote) as an alternative to hanging but rejected injection because of protests from the medical profession. Doctors feared that people would associate death with the hypodermic needle and the practice of medicine. On June 4, 1888, the legislature, with little opposition, enacted New York's Electrical Execution Act. The act provided that anyone sentenced to die after January 1, 1889, would be electrocuted instead of hanged. The act did not, however, stipulate what type of current would be employed. That matter was left to the Medico-Legal Society of New York to decide. Following a number of experiments on animals, it was decided that Westinghouse's alternating current (AC) would be used.

William Kemmler became the first person to die by legally authorized electrocution on August 6, 1890. Kemmler had been convicted of the brutal first-degree murder of his girlfriend, who he believed was involved with another man. Although there was little doubt about his guilt, his appeals drew much public interest. In an effort to block the ultimate test of alternating current's lethality, Westinghouse retained for Kemmler one of the nation's leading lawyers, W. Bourke Cockran, and reportedly spent more than $100,000 on the appeals.

The case ultimately reached the Supreme Court. Kemmler's lawyer, however, failed to convince the Court that death by electrocution was cruel and unusual. The Court refused to decide Kemmler's claim, arguing that the Eighth Amendment did not apply to the states (*In re Kemmler* [1890]).[57] By taking that position, the Court did not have to scrutinize the New York state legislature's conclusion that electrocution produced "instantaneous, and, therefore, painless death."

Eyewitness reports of Kemmler's execution belie the legislature's conclusion. Kemmler did not die "instantaneously"[58]—a second jolt of electricity had to be administered four-and-a-half minutes after the first one. During the second jolt, witnesses observed Kemmler's hair and flesh burning and blood on his face. His body emitted a horrible stench. Whether his death was a "painless" one is uncertain. Electricians blamed faulty equipment for the botched execution. Among the problems were the failure to provide enough power, an uninterrupted current, and adequate contact between the electrodes and Kemmler's body. Reaction to the bungled execution was mixed. Some commentators argued that death by electrocution was worse than hanging; others believed it was not. It was even suggested that the execution was intentionally sabotaged to deter further use of the alternating current. Not surprisingly, West-inghouse stated that "[t]hey could have done better with an axe." Experts on electricity, such as Thomas Edison and Nikola Tesla, publicly debated whether electrocution was so horrible that it should never have been invented. Both proponents and opponents of capital punishment called for repeal of New York's Electrical Execution Act, but to no avail.

Nearly a year after Kemmler's execution, New York electrocuted four men in one day and a fifth man later that year. Despite continued reports of flawed electrocutions, numerous other states were quick to adopt the new method and, as noted at the beginning of this section, electrocution became the method used by a majority of executing states between 1930 and 1972.[59]

Botched electrocutions are not a thing of the past. Following are three more recent newspaper accounts.[60]

- The state's [Georgia's] first try at executing Alpha Otis Stephens in the electric chair failed today, and he struggled to breathe for eight minutes before a second jolt carried out his death sentence.[61]

- [In Michigan City, Indiana] five jolts of electricity instead of the prescribed two were needed today to execute William E. Vandiver. . . . A prison doctor said Vandiver, 37, was still breathing after the first round of 2,300 volts and second of 500 volts were applied at 12:03 a.m. Three more blasts of current were applied before he was pro-nounced dead 17 minutes later.[62]

- The replacement of a worn sponge in the headpiece of the electric chair by two maintenance workers at Florida State Prison led to the botched execution of Jesse Tafero. Their action triggered an eruption of smoke and flames from Tafero's head. . . . When the first jolt of 2,000–volt electricity hit Tafero, the sponge in the headpiece gave off a combustible gas, which shot smoke and flames from the top of the leather hood hiding Tafero's face. The flames— described as 3 inches to a foot long—horrified witnesses. Tafero's attorney described the flawed execution as tor-ture. . . . Between the jolts, witnesses observed Tafero seemingly gasping for air.[63]

Lethal Gas

Seeking a more humane method of execution, in 1921 the Nevada legislature passed a "Humane Death Bill."[64] The legislation replaced hanging with death by lethal gas, which had gained attention because of its use in World War I. The condemned inmate was to be executed in his or her cell, while asleep and without any warning. Governor Emmet Boyle, who personally opposed the death penalty, nevertheless signed the legislation, believing that, upon challenge, it would be ruled unconstitutional as a cruel and unusual punishment.

The first person sentenced to die under the new legislation was Gee Jon, who was convicted of a gangland murder. Jon was a member of a "tong," in this case an organized Chinese crime association. Jon appealed his death sentence to the Nevada Supreme Court, which, to the surprise of Governor Boyle, upheld the constitutionality of lethal gas. When prison officials realized the impracticality of executing Jon in his cell while he slept, they quickly built a chamber for the purpose, and on February 8, 1924, Jon became the first person to be lawfully executed with a lethal dose of cyanide gas.

By 1937, Arizona, California, Colorado, North Carolina, and Wyoming had passed legislation requiring executions to be carried out using lethal gas. By 1970, 10 states (which, in addition to the aforementioned, included Maryland, Mississippi, Missouri, and New Mexico) used lethal gas as their sole method of execution, but by 1992, Maryland was the only state to do so.[65] Maryland abandoned lethal gas for lethal injection in 1994, except for inmates whose sentence was imposed before the change in statute. They have a choice between lethal gas and lethal injection.

Lethal gas is currently an option in only five states.[66] California and Missouri authorize both lethal gas and lethal injection.[67] If the condemned inmate refuses to choose, the method is lethal gas. Arizona authorizes lethal injection for persons whose capital sentence was imposed after November 15, 1992; for those who were sentenced before that date, the condemned prisoner may select lethal injection or lethal gas. If the condemned prisoner refuses to choose, the method is lethal injection. Maryland authorizes lethal injection for those sentenced after March 25, 1994; for those who were sentenced before that date, the condemned prisoner may select lethal injection or lethal gas. Wyoming authorizes lethal gas if lethal injection is ever held to be unconstitutional.

A newspaper account of the 1979 execution of Jesse Bishop in Nevada describes death by lethal gas:

> After a metal door to the 10-by-10 death chamber clanged shut, three volunteer guards flipped switches to activate the device that lowered cyanide pellets into acid beneath the death seat. Only one of the switches was live, so none of the guards knew which one would kill Bishop. . . . [When the] cyanide pellets fell into the acid bath, unleashing deadly gas, Bishop wrinkled his nose, seemed to search the room and breathed deeply several times. His eyes rolled upward, his head fell on his chest and then snapped back. He took another deep breath and closed his eyes—for the last time. Bishop's face reddened, saliva ran from his mouth and his body shuddered. After a series of convulsive jerks, it was over.[68]

Lethal Injection

In the continuing quest to find more humane and publicly acceptable methods of execution, Oklahoma became the first jurisdiction in the United States to authorize lethal injection as an execution method.[69] The legislation, passed on May 11, 1977, replaced electrocution with the "continuous, intravenous administration of a lethal quantity of an ultra-short-acting barbiturate in combination with a chemical paralytic agent."[70] The three chemicals most commonly used in lethal injections are (1) sodium thiopental or sodium pentothal, a common anesthetic used in surgery, which is the ultrashort-acting barbiturate that is supposed to induce a deep sleep and loss of consciousness in about 20 seconds, (2) pancuronium bromide, also known as Pavulon, a total muscle relaxant, which in sufficient dosages stops breathing by paralyzing the diaphragm and lungs, and (3) potassium chloride, which induces cardiac arrest and stops the inmate's heartbeat permanently.[71] Economic matters played a major role in Oklahoma's change to lethal injection. Legislators were concerned that the electric chair, which had not been used since 1966, would be too expensive to return to good working order. The cost of fixing the chair was estimated to be $62,000.[72] Execution by lethal gas was rejected because of the estimated $300,000 cost of a gas chamber.[73] Lethal injection was estimated to cost less than $15 per execution.[74] Also favoring the use of lethal injection was the argument that persons executed by this method could donate all of their bodily organs for medical transplants. Other execution methods limited this possibility.

Texas, Idaho, and New Mexico were quick to follow Oklahoma in adopting lethal injection as their method of execution. In Florida, however, a 1979 bill calling for the replacement of electrocution with lethal injection was defeated in the state legislature. Opposed to the legislation were medical doctors, and especially anesthesiologists, who argued that, among other things, no assurances could be given that the barbiturates would not wear off before death occurred, causing the condemned inmate to wake up and slowly suffocate to death. (The Florida legislature grudgingly approved lethal injection as an option to electrocution in January 2000. The legislature wanted to avoid legal challenges to the use of the electric chair.[75]) The 1980 annual meeting of the American Medical Association saw a resolution passed urging doctors not to be participants in executions by lethal injection beyond pronouncing an inmate dead. To participate in any other way would constitute a violation of the Hippocratic Oath and international medical principles, and would represent "a corruption and exploitation of the healing profession's role in society." The resolution was mostly symbolic, however, because no state's death penalty statute required that a licensed doctor perform the lethal injection. Nevertheless, a 1994 study by the American College of Physicians, Human Rights Watch, the National Coalition to Abolish the Death Penalty, and Physicians for Human Rights found that 29 of the then 37 capital punishment states required the presence or participation of a physician at all executions, and that no licensing boards in any of the states were enforcing the prohibition.[76] In a survey published in the *Annals of Internal Medicine* in 2001, 41 percent of the 413 doctors who responded to the survey indicated that they would perform at least one of ten functions of administering a lethal injection and 25 percent would perform five or more.[77] Thus, it appears that many doctors would be willing to participate in an execution despite the fact that it violates the Hippocratic Oath to do no harm and is prohibited by medical societies. For doctors willing to participate in executions, death penalty states provide them with a handy rationalization. The laws in all death penalty states stipulate that the medical techniques used in lethal injection executions are not medical techniques, and the medical personnel who participate in them are not medical personnel for the purpose of executing prison inmates.[78]

The first person executed by lethal injection was Charles Brooks, Jr., in Texas, on December 7, 1982. He was sentenced to die on December 14, 1976, for the murder of David Gregory in Forth Worth. Brooks was also the first black man to be executed in the United States since 1967 and the first person executed in Texas since 1964.[79]

Until recently, the only challenge to lethal injection as an execution method that the Supreme Court has been willing to hear was *Heckler v. Chaney* (470 U.S. 821, 1985). In this case, inmates in Oklahoma and Texas claimed that the Food and Drug Administration (FDA), as required by law, had not approved the drugs used in lethal injections for that purpose. The plaintiffs claimed that to use approved drugs for unapproved purposes violates the misbranding prohibition of the Federal Food, Drug, and Cosmetic Act. The plaintiffs wanted the FDA to approve the drugs for the purpose of human execution; the FDA refused to do so. The Court dodged the issue, maintaining that the FDA's discretionary authority in refusing the plaintiffs' demands was not subject to judicial review.

Lethal injection has now become the sole or principal method of execution in all but one executing jurisdiction in the United States (the exception is Nebraska). However, there is no uniform policy for conducting lethal injections among executing jurisdictions. There are differences in procedure, in the number of drugs used, in the amount of drugs used, who performs the injections, how well the executioners are trained, and how much the executioners are paid—to name just a few differences.[80] In some jurisdictions, lethal injections are performed on a table attached to the floor with wings on the sides of the table for the inmate's arms. South Carolina uses a gurney with wings that is wheeled into the same execution chamber that contains the state's electric chair. A curtain is used to separate the two. North Carolina requires that the inmate's arms be flat against his or her body while lying on a hospital–like gurney. Some jurisdictions begin the procedure only after all appeals and requests for a stay of execution have been exhausted. Other jurisdictions insert the tubes while the inmate is awaiting final word from the governor and the U.S. Supreme Court. In some jurisdictions prisoners make their final statements in their cells before they are taken to the execution chamber; in other jurisdictions final statements are made on the table in the execution chamber minutes before execution.

Most jurisdictions employ prison employees with some emergency medical training to insert the needles. A common problem with inmates who have been intravenous drug users is finding suitable veins. Frequent drug injections can leave scarring on the blood vessels. Minor surgery is sometimes needed to expose a viable vein. However, generally, the execution team just keeps searching the inmate's body until a viable vein is found. In Texas, condemned inmates have had to help the execution team find a viable vein, and in Louisiana the execution team had to insert the needle into an inmate's neck after failing to find a viable vein in the inmate's arm.

Some jurisdictions employ lethal injection machines; in other jurisdictions the warden or governor selects the executioners who inject the drugs. When executioners are used to inject the drugs, their identities are kept confidential. They generally perform their duties from behind a curtain or a one–way glass mirror, or inside a separate room. In North Carolina, each of three executioners has a syringe. Each of the executioners injects each of the three drugs (see above), but with each drug one of the injections is detoured into a "dummy bag" instead of the inmate's body. This practice conceals who is actually administering the lethal drugs to the inmate. Oklahoma pays three executioners $300 each per execution, while Florida pays its lone executioner $150 per execution.

Most jurisdictions use the three aforementioned lethal drugs; however, North Carolina and New Jersey use only two. North Carolina uses sodium thiopental and pancuronium bromide; New Jersey uses sodium thiopental and potassium chloride. Louisiana injects all three drugs into one IV inserted into the left arm, which is closest to the heart. If a problem arises, a second IV is inserted into the right arm. Texas and Florida insert IVs into both arms, but inject the drugs only into the left arm unless there is a problem, in which case they are injected into the right arm. Oklahoma inserts IVs into both arms and alternates the injection of the three drugs from arm to arm—left, right, left. Arizona injects all three drugs into both arms. It is standard procedure to flush the IV lines with a saline solution between injections to prevent the chemicals from crystallizing before they reach the inmate's bloodstream. In some jurisdictions the entire procedure takes only a few minutes, while in other jurisdictions the procedure can take thirty minutes or longer. An inmate is usually pronounced dead within five to ten minutes following the injection. Because medical ethics, as noted previously, prohibit doctors from participating in executions, most jurisdictions use doctors only to verify the inmate's death. In Texas this practice allows the prison system to avoid an autopsy that is otherwise required by state law.

Theoretically, death by lethal injection should be a more humane method of execution than any of the other methods then or now in use. The popular image is one in which the condemned inmate painlessly falls asleep (forever) on a hospital gurney. Perhaps the New York legislature of 100 years ago, in its rejection of lethal injection as a less humane method of execution than electrocution,[81] showed an insight still valid today. Despite the creation of elaborate machines to administer the lethal drugs, problems still arise.[82] Consider, for example, the following newspaper account of the 1988 execution of Raymond Landry in Texas:

> Prison officials began administering the lethal dosage [to Landry] at 12:21 a.m. Landry was not pronounced dead until 24 minutes later. In between, a tube attached to a needle inside his right arm began leaking, sending the lethal mixture shooting across the death chamber toward witnesses. "There was something of a delay in the execution because of what officials called a 'blowout'. . . . The syringe came out of the vein and the warden ordered the (execution) team to reinsert the catheter into the vein." The leak occurred two minutes after the injections began.[83]

Another problem that could occur in lethal injections, although it would be nearly impossible to detect, is that an inadequate dose of sodium pentothal (the anesthetic used in lethal injections) would cause the inmate to retain consciousness and suffer great pain during the injections of the second and third chemicals.[84] A similar problem would occur if the three chemicals were administered out of sequence.

The problem of an inadequate dose of sodium pentothal and its inter-action with pancuronium bromide was the subject of recent challenges to lethal injection in Florida and California. Both challenges followed the April 2005 publication of an article in *The Lancet*, a prominent British medical journal, that claimed "methods of lethal injection are flawed and some inmates might experience awareness and suffering during execution."[85] The article's authors reported that toxicology reports from Arizona, Georgia, North Carolina, and South Carolina "showed that post-mortem concentrations of [sodium] thiopental in the blood were lower than that required for surgery in 43 of 49 executed inmates (88%); 21 (43%) inmates had concentrations consistent with awareness."[86] They noted "without anaesthesia, the condemned person would experience asphyxiation, a severe burning sensation, massive muscle cramping, and finally cardiac arrest" because of the other drugs commonly used in executions.[87] Following their examination of protocol information from Texas and Virginia, whose officials refused to provide toxicology reports, the authors also found that "executioners had no anaesthesia training, drugs were administered remotely with no monitoring for anaesthesia, data were not recorded and no peer-review was done."[88] The authors added, in contrast to medical applications, "anaesthesia in execution has not been subjected to clinical trials, governmental regulation, extensive training of practitioners, standardization, or the supervision of peer-review and medico-legal liability."[89] Critics have questioned the study's methodology and the conclusion that some inmates might have experienced awareness and suffering during the execution.[90] The major criticism is that concentrations of sodium pentothal in the blood as long as twelve hours after an execution (at the time autopsies were performed) do not accurately reflect the concentrations of the drug at the time of death, that concentrations decrease over time. In a reply to their critics, the authors of the original study countered that research shows that after death, concentrations of sodium pentothal in the blood actually increase, not decrease. They surmised, "post-mortem concentrations of [sodium] pentothal in blood, including those taken after execution, might actually overestimate concentrations in life."[91]

In Florida, Clarence Hill's January 24, 2006 execution was halted just moments before the deadly chemicals were to be injected into his body, when U.S. Supreme Court Justice Anthony Kennedy issued a temporary stay. The next day the full court confirmed the stay and agreed to hear Hill's civil-rights claim (in *Hill v. McDonough*) that Florida's lethal injection method caused inmates to suffer excessive pain during the procedure and, thus, violated the U.S. Constitution's Eighth Amendment. Recall that the Court had previously ruled that any execution method that involved "something more than the mere extinguishment of life" constituted cruel and unusual punishment. Hill's attorneys argued that if a condemned inmate were not unconscious because of an inadequate dose of sodium pentothal, then the pancuronium bromide, which paralyzes muscles, would render the inmate helpless to respond to his or her suffocating and the excruciating pain caused by the potassium chloride. It would also make it impossible for those witnessing the execution to recognize and prevent the gratuitous pain and suffering.[92] At this writing, the U.S. Supreme Court had not decided the case but when it does, it may decide to ban the second drug in the sequence, pancuronium bromide, because it serves no purpose other than keeping the inmate quiet while the potassium chloride kills.[93] In other words, the pancuronium bromide only has a cosmetic role, creating the serene appearance of dying associated with lethal injection executions. It is instructive to note that the American Veterinary Medical Association has banned pancuronium bromide for animal euthanasia because it can conceal any signs of whether the anesthetic has failed to work.[94]

In California, Michael Morales's lawyers made a similar claim in U.S. District Court and, as a result, on February 21, 2006, his execution was postponed indefinitely. The federal judge who heard the case, rather than wait until the Supreme Court decided the Florida case, ruled that the state could execute Morales either with an overdose of barbiturates alone (something no other state did) administered by someone medically qualified to give intravenous drugs or, if the state wanted to use the standard three-drug combination, a qualified anesthetist had to be present at the execution. To comply with the judge's order, prison officials hired two anesthetists (one for back up), but, just hours before the execution, they both refused to participate when they learned they would have to intervene if Morales regained consciousness. They had believed their role was only to verify that the execution protocol was humane. After the anesthetists' refusal to participate, prison officials tried to find a medical professional willing to administer the barbiturate overdose before Morales's death warrant expired. They were unable to do so. Consequently, the federal judge declared he would hold a hearing on California's lethal injection protocol at a later date.[95]

The judicial decisions in Florida and California have influenced impending executions in other jurisdictions. For example, on March 7, 2006, a U.S. District Court judge for the District of Columbia issued a stay of execution, pending the outcome of the Florida case, for three co-defendants on federal death row, who were scheduled to die in May.[96] Also, on April 10, 2006, a U.S. District Court judge ordered North Carolina prison officials to provide medically trained personnel to supervise the execution of Willie Brown, Jr., who was scheduled to die on April 21.[97] Stays of executions have also been granted to inmates in Maryland, Missouri, and another inmate in Florida, for similar reasons. Other inmates that have raised lethal injection challenges have been denied and executed.[98] Even Clarence Hill, who made the initial challenge, was executed by lethal injection (using the controversial 3-chemical cocktail) in Florida on September 20, 2006, after the Supreme Court, by a 5-4 vote, refused to grant him another stay. His latest challenges had been rejected as "stalling tactics," with the clear message that complicated issues should not be raised at the last minute.[99]

As noted, lethal injection is the method of execution provided by the most states (36), at least as an option, as well as by the U.S. military and the U.S. government.[100] For the military, the government, and in the following 22 states, it is the sole method of execution: Colorado, Connecticut, Delaware, Georgia, Illinois, Indiana, Kansas, Louisiana, Mississippi, Montana, Nevada, New Jersey, New Mexico, North Carolina, Ohio, Oklahoma, Oregon, Pennsylvania, South Dakota, Texas, Utah, and Wyoming. In Arkansas, lethal injection is the authorized mode of execution for those convicted after July 4, 1983; for Arizona, after November 15, 1992; for Kentucky, after March 31, 1998; for Maryland, after March 24, 1994; for New Hampshire, if it can be given; and for Tennessee, after January 1, 1999. Lethal injection is one of two options in the following eight states: Alabama, California, Florida, Idaho, Missouri, South Carolina, Virginia, and Washington.

Lethal injection is also the method by which the most people have been executed under post-*Furman* statutes (since 1976). As of April 12, 2007, 1,070 people had been executed in the United States under post-*Furman* statutes. The number of executions by method employed was as follows: lethal injection (901); electrocution (153); lethal gas (11); hanging (3); firing squad (2).[101]

California's Execution Process[102]

When Execution Order Is Received. As soon as the execution order is received, the condemned inmate is moved into a special security area of the prison. Based on hourly checks, staff document his/her behavior and bring anything unusual to the warden's attention. The inmate receives priority visiting privileges; no visitors are turned away without authorization of the warden. Every effort is made to accommodate visits by the inmate's attorney including weekend or holiday visits if necessary.

Pre-Execution Reports. Two reports are prepared within three weeks of the established execution date. The first is 20 days before execution; the second is seven days before execution. Each report includes:

- Psychiatric report—Results and interpretation of examinations, interviews and history of the inmate by three psychiatrists which will be used to determine the inmate's sanity.

- Chaplain report—Comments on the inmate's spiritual and emotional well-being.

- Summary of behavior—Observations noted by case worker and custody staff.

- Cover letter from warden—Includes firsthand information from interviews, observations or communication with the inmate and his/her family or friends.

The seven-day pre-execution report discusses any changes that have occurred since the first report.

Sanity Review Requests. Within 30 to seven days before the execution, the inmate's attorney may submit current psychiatric information that may have a bearing on the sanity of the condemned inmate. This information will be provided to the panel of psychiatrists to consider in completion of the pre-execution psychiatric reports.

Last 24 Hours. During the day before the execution, the warden will make special arrangements for visits by approved family members, spiritual advisors, and friends. About 6 p.m. the day before the execution, the inmate will be moved to the death watch cell which is adjacent to the execution chamber. From then on, a three-member staff unit will provide a constant death watch. Soon after he is rehoused, the inmate will be served his last dinner meal. The prison makes every effort to provide the meal requested by the inmate. Between 7 and 10 p.m., the inmate may be visited by the assigned state chaplain and the warden. The inmate may read, watch television, or play the radio. He can request special food items and coffee or soft drinks. The family, spiritual advisors and friends the inmate has selected as witnesses may arrive up to two hours before the scheduled execution. About 30 minutes before the scheduled execution, the inmate is given a new pair of denim trousers and blue work shirt to wear. He is escorted into the execution chamber a few minutes before the appointed time and is strapped onto a table. [The chairs previously used for lethal gas executions have been removed.] The inmate is connected to a cardiac monitor which is connected to a printer outside the execution chamber. An IV is started in two usable veins and a flow of normal saline solution is administered at a slow rate. [One line is held in reserve in case of a blockage or malfunction in the other.] The door is closed. The warden issues the execution order.

The Execution. In advance of the execution, syringes containing the following are prepared:

- 5.0 grams of sodium pentothal in 20-25 cc of diluent

- 50 cc of pancuronium bromide

- 50 cc of potassium chloride

Each chemical is lethal in the amounts administered. At the warden's signal, sodium pentothal is administered, then the line is flushed with sterile normal saline solution. This is followed by pancuronium bromide, a saline flush, and finally, potassium chloride. As required by the California Penal Code, a physician is present to declare when death occurs. After all witnesses have left, the body is removed with dignity and care. Typically, the family claims the body. If not, the State makes the arrangements.

Chamber Description. The California execution chamber is a self-contained unit at San Quentin State Prison which includes:

- Witness area—Entered via a door to the outside, the witness area has a view of the chamber through five windows.

- Execution chamber—An octagonal vacuum chamber, approximately 7-1/2 feet in diameter. It is entered through a large oval door at the rear of the chamber.

- Anteroom—Contains three telephones. One is kept open for use by the Governor; the other is for use by the State Supreme Court and Attorney General's Office; the third is connected to the Warden's office. The lethal injections are administered from the anteroom. The area also includes the valves and immersion lever used for executions by lethal gas.

- Chemical room—Includes storage cabinets and a work bench, plus the chemical mixing pots, pipes and valves used for executions by lethal gas.

- Two holding cells—Each contains a toilet and room for a mattress.

- Kitchen/officers' area—Includes a sink, cabinet, counter area and resting area for staff.

Witnesses. Up to 50 individuals may witness an execution. The following are specified in the Penal Code:

Warden 1
Attorney General 1
Reputable citizens 12
Physicians 2
Inmate family/friends 5 (if requested)
Inmate spiritual advisor 2 (if requested)

State procedures also allow for:

News media representatives 17
State-selected witnesses 9
Staff escorts 4

A Note on Witnessing an Execution

Many death penalty states do not allow citizens to witness an execution unless they have a direct relationship to the case. However, in at least 16 death penalty states, state law requires that a certain number of people serve as official witnesses to ensure that the execution is carried out in a dignified and humane way. For example, Pennsylvania requires six witnesses, Missouri requires eight witnesses, and Florida requires twelve witnesses.[103]

At Florida State Prison, the warden selects the witnesses to an execution. He allows 30 witnesses but usually only one or two of them are from the waiting list. A dozen places are reserved for the news media—six for the print media and six for television and radio. The warden lets trade organizations such as the Florida Press Association select the media witnesses. The warden chooses the twelve official witnesses. His first priority is law enforcement officers and prosecutors who were involved in the case and victims' relatives. Other witnesses include prison personnel, state officials, and a medical staff member to care for witnesses who need medical attention. Typically, an inmate's attorney and religious advisor witness an execution but rarely are they counted as official witnesses. The few citizens selected from the waiting list in Florida do not have to provide a reason why they want to witness an execution. Currently, there is no shortage of volunteers. Arizona has a waiting list of nearly 80 people; Florida's list has about 100. However, the Florida prison warden believes that with the state's recent shift from electrocution to lethal injection, interest in viewing an execution will drop substantially.[104]

Witnesses are generally asked to arrive anywhere from 20 minutes to two hours before the scheduled execution. Once they get to the prison, they are escorted into the witness room by prison guards. In Oklahoma, relatives of the victim are placed in a different room than relatives of the prisoner; in other death penalty states all the witnesses sit together. Some execution chambers have a one-way mirror that only allows the witnesses to see the condemned. Others have a clear window that allows the condemned to see the witnesses as well. Once the IVs are inserted into the prisoner's arms, the curtain or blind covering the window is opened. In California, a recent 9th U.S. Circuit Court of Appeals ruling allows witnesses to "view executions from the moment the condemned is escorted into the execution chamber."[105] Complete silence in the witness area is required in some states. In some cases, the witness room is not large enough to hold all the relatives that want to witness the execution, so an overflow room in another part of the prison may be used to allow family witnesses to view the execution via closed-circuit TV. In Illinois, family members can only view the execution through closed-circuit TV. Once the execution is completed, the curtain or blind is closed and prison staff escort the witnesses out of the witness room. Official witnesses are then required to sign a document attesting to the fact that they witnessed the execution and that it took place. In some cases, members of the media and families may be taken to a press area for a press conference. The witnesses are then escorted out of the prison.[106]

Conclusion

Law Professor Deborah Denno argues that if the Supreme Court were willing to hear Eighth Amendment challenges to all current execution methods, to consider available evidence demonstrating the cruelty of those methods, and to apply both the "death is different" and "evolving standards of decency" criteria, it would be forced to conclude that all current methods of execution are unconstitutional.[107] Denno believes that if the Court were to follow such a course, it would also have to declare the death penalty itself unconstitutional because no method of punishment could meet the required standards. Denno may be overly optimistic on the latter point.

In the future, death penalty jurisdictions may require executions to be conducted using methods designed (and possibly approved) for human euthanasia. For example, an execution during which the condemned prisoner dies by inhaling carbon monoxide from a mask and tank—a preferred method of euthanasia expert, Dr. Jack Kevorkian—might meet the required criteria. Criminal justice futurist Gene Stephens predicts that executions may one day be conducted using ultrasound which would literally "dematerialize" the condemned inmate. An added benefit to ultrasound is that it would eliminate the costs of disposing of the body.[108] If the death penalty continues to be employed, the future will likely bring execution methods which are now beyond imagination.

Discussion Questions

1. Do you agree with the Supreme Court's definition of "cruel and unusual punishment"? Why or why not?

2. Are any of the current execution methods cruel and unusual punishments? Why or why not?

3. Should execution methods be cruel (and/or unusual)?

4. Are long stays on death row cruel and unusual punishment? Why or why not?

5. Is execution of the elderly or infirm cruel and unusual punishment? Why or why not?

6. What conditions of death row confinement, if any, do you think constitute cruel and unusual punishment? Why?

7. Should we be concerned about botched executions? What should be done about them?

8. Would you change anything about the execution process? If yes, what would you change and why?

9. Would you like to witness an execution? Why or why not?

Notes

[1] Bedau, 1982:14; also see Denno, 1994:566, fn. 87.
[2] Bedau, ibid.; Denno, ibid., p. 563.
[3] Banner, 2002:71.
[4] Ibid., p. 72.
[5] Ibid.
[6] Ibid., pp. 74-75.
[7] Ibid., pp. 81-82.
[8] Bedau, op. cit., p. 15.
[9] *Weems v. United States* (217 U.S. 349, 1910); Meltsner, 1973:173-175; Paternoster, 1991:51.

[10] Ibid.

[11] Paternoster, op. cit., p. 52.

[12] *Trop v. Dulles* (356 U.S. 86, 1958); Paternoster,, ibid.

[13] *Trop v. Dulles*, ibid.; Paternoster, ibid., p. 53.

[14] Banner, op. cit., p. 235; also see Denno, 1997, 1998.

[15] "High Court Rejects Killers' Cases," *The Orlando Sentinel* (November 9, 1999), p. A-7.

[16] Federman and Holmes, 2005, pp. 338-339.

[17] Ibid., p. 328.

[18] "Alabama inmate becomes oldest executed since '41," 2004.

[19] "Man executed in Mississippi is the oldest to die since 1970s," 2005.

[20] Thompson, 2006.

[21] See *Hudson v. McMillian*, 1992; *Helling v. McKinney*, 1993; also see Johnson, 2003; 1990; 1989, for a description of conditions on death row.

[22] Ibid.

[23] See *Hudson v. McMillian*, 1992; *Wilson v. Seiter*, 1991.

[24] See *Farmer v. Brennan*, 1994.

[25] Word, 2004b.

[26] Dow, 2002b:12.

[27] Bedau, op. cit.

[28] Percentage calculated by dividing 16,000 hangings cited in Denno, op. cit., p. 680, by the more liberal 22,500 total execution estimate of Espy.

[29] Banner, 2002:62 and 64.

[30] Ibid., p. 65.

[31] Ibid.

[32] Ibid.

[33] Denno, op. cit., p. 679.

[34] Ibid.

[35] Ibid.

[36] Banner, op. cit., p. 36.

[37] Ibid.

[38] Ibid.

[39] Ibid.

[40] Ibid.

[41] Ibid., p. 37.

[42] Denno, op. cit., p. 686; Death Penalty Information Center, June 3, 2002.

[43] Denno, ibid., p. 682.

[44] Death Penalty Information Center (accessed September 16, 2006).

[45] Denno, 1994, op. cit., p. 683.

[46] Death Penalty Information Center, op. cit.

[47] See Denno, 1994, op. cit., pp. 687-688.

[48] See, for example, Mailer, 1979.

[49] Calculated from Espy and Smykla, 1987 and Death Penalty Information Center, op. cit.

[50] www.clarkprosecutor.org/html/death/updates.htm; "Georgia Bans the Electric Chair," *The Orlando Sentinel* (October 6, 2001), p. A19.

[51] "Electric Chair in Alabama Upheld." *The Orlando Sentinel* (February 23, 2000), p. A-5.

[52] Death Penalty Information Center, op. cit. In May 2000, a Nebraska district court judge upheld Nebraska's death penalty statute, but ruled that the procedure used during electrocutions constituted cruel and unusual punishment. The court objected to the practice of Nebraska prison officials of using four separate jolts of electricity to execute

inmates. According to the statute, a current of electricity is to be administered continuously until the inmate dies. "Procedure of Execution Ruled Cruel and Unusual." *The Orlando Sentinel* (May 9), p. A-6.

[53] On July 20, 2006, murderer and rapist Brandon Hedrick was executed by electrocution in Virginia. Hedrick, who chose electrocution because he was afraid of lethal injection, was the first person in the United States to die in the electric chair in two years. "Convicted killer put to death by electric chair in Virginia," 2006.

[54] Paternoster, op. cit., p. 23.

[55] Denno, 1994, op. cit., p. 557.

[56] The following account is from Denno, 1994, op. cit.; Bedau, 1982, op. cit., pp. 15-16; Paternoster, op. cit., pp. 14-15.

[57] The Court made the Eighth Amendment applicable to the states in 1962, see *Robinson v. California*(370 U.S. 660).

[58] The specific cause of death from electrocution is presumed to be extensive electrical damage to the nervous system.

[59] It is interesting that electrocution is considered an acceptable method for human executions but unacceptable for animal euthanasia. According to the American Veterinarian Medical Association, "electrocution [is] an unacceptable method unless it is preceded by an injury inducing immediate unconsciousness, such as a blow to the head, because electrocution alone will not lead to unconsciousness for 10-to-30 seconds or longer" (cited in Denno, 1997, op. cit.). For an explicit description of the execution by electrocution of John Evans in Alabama, see Canan, 1989.

[60] Denno ,1997, op. cit., Appendix 2A, provides descriptions of 14 botched electrocutions since 1976.

[61] *The Anniston* (Alabama) *Star*, December 12, 1984.

[62] Ibid., October 16, 1985. Heart death cannot be ensured with voltages of less than 2,000 volts. Current exceeding six amps can cause excessive burning of the flesh, see Denno, 1997, op. cit.

[63] *Charlotte* (North Carolina) *Observer*, May 10, 1990.

[64] See Bedau, op. cit., p. 16.

[65] Denno, 1997, op. cit.

[66] Death Penalty Information Center, op. cit.

[67] For detailed descriptions of executions by lethal gas at San Quentin in California, see Kroll, 1989.

[68] *The Anniston* (Alabama) *Star*, October 22, 1979. Because of the pain and agony experienced by Jesse Bishop, Nevada changed its method of execution from lethal gas to lethal injection. As was the case with electrocution, it is interesting that lethal gas is considered an acceptable method for human executions but unacceptable for animal euthanasia. Dr. Richard Traystman, Director of the Anesthesiology and Critical Care Medicine Research Laboratories at Johns Hopkins Medical School, states, "[W]e would not use asphyxiation, by cyanide gas or by any other substance, in our laboratory to kill animals that have been used in experiments—nor would most medical research laboratories in this country use it" (cited in Denno, 1997, op. cit.). For a description of eight botched executions by lethal gas since 1976, see Denno, 1997, op. cit., Appendix 2A.

[69] See Bedau, op. cit., pp. 17-19.

[70] Ibid., p. 17.

[71] Denno, 1997, op. cit.; Denno, 2002.

[72] Denno, 1997, ibid.

[73] Ibid.

[74] The cost of drugs used in lethal injections in the mid-1990s averaged about $70 per execution. See ibid.

[75] Taylor and Stutzman, 2000.

[76] Recer, 1994.

[77] Cited in "Some Doctors Willing to Kill," *The Orlando Sentinel* (November 20, 2001), p. A15.

[78] Federman and Holmes, op. cit., pp. 342.

[79] Reinhold, 1982.

[80] Information about the differences in the ways lethal injections are administered among jurisdictions is from Kunerth, 2000; Taylor and Stutzman, 2000; Denno, 2002, op. cit.

[81] In 1953, the British Royal Commission on Capital Punishment concluded that lethal injection as a method of capital punishment was deficient for four reasons: (1) it "could not be administered to individuals with certain 'physical abnormalities' that make veins impossible to locate, and that even 'normal' veins can be flattened by cold or nervousness, conditions oftentimes characteristic of an execution setting"; (2) it "is difficult unless the subject fully cooperates and keeps 'absolutely still'"; (3) "although a qualified [*sic*] injection requires medical skill, the medical profession was opposed to participating in the process"; and (4) "because of all such problems, the Commission concluded that it was likely that executioners would have to implement intramuscular (rather than intravenous) injection even though the intramuscular method would be slower and more painful." Cited in Denno, 1997, op. cit.

[82] Denno, 1997, op. cit., Appendix 2C, provides descriptions of 22 botched executions by lethal injection since 1976. For an update through April 2006, see Radelet, 2006b.

[83] *The Anniston* (Alabama) *Star*, December 13, 1988.

[84] Denno, 1997, op. cit.

[85] Koniaris et al., 2005.

[86] Ibid.

[87] Ibid.

[88] Ibid.

[89] Ibid.

[90] See Groner, 2005; Heath et al., 2005; Weisman et al., 2005.

[91] Zimmers et al., 2005.

[92] Lytle and Kennedy, 2006.

[93] Denno, 2002, op. cit.

[94] "Executions by Lethal Injection," 2005.

[95] McCarthy, 2006; Kravets, 2006.

[96] "Three Men," 2006.

[97] "Federal Judge Requires," 2006.

[98] "Lethal Injections," 2006.

[99] Leusner and Tseng, 2006.

[100] Death Penalty Information Center, op. cit.

[101] Death Penalty Information Center, op. cit.

[102] California Department of Corrections and Rehabilitation, "Lethal Injection Procedures" at www.cya.ca.gov/ReportsResearch/lethalInjection.html (accessed March 31, 2006).

[103] Hansen, 2000; Taylor, 2000.

[104] Ibid.

[105] Mintz, 2002.

[106] Howstuffworks: "How Lethal Injection Works," 2002; also see Gillespie, 2003:4-8.

[107] Denno, 1997, op. cit.; 1998; also see Gottlieb, 1961.

[108] Stephens, 1990. Another possibility is the return to a method employed in antiquity. For example, in 399 B.C., Socrates was condemned to drink a cup of hemlock, an execution method that produced a relatively dignified and presumably painless death.

CHAPTER 5

General Deterrence
and the Death Penalty

The next several chapters consider rationales or justifications for capital punishment, as well as arguments against its use. Available evidence is presented and evaluated. This chapter examines general deterrence—the belief that people in general can be prevented from engaging in crime by punishing specific individuals and making examples of them. In the context of this book, the broad deterrence question is whether or not executions prevent people other than the person executed from committing capital crimes.[1]

Another type of deterrence is specific or special deterrence—the prevention of individuals from committing crime again by punishing them. Special or specific deterrence does not apply to capital punishment because execution precludes the determination of whether a punished individual returns to crime. When people want to forever prevent prisoners from reoffending, they desire incapacitation and not specific or special deterrence. Capital punishment ensures incapacitation, which is one of the most compelling rationales in support of the death penalty. Incapacitation is the subject of the next chapter. Subsequent chapters address the costs of capital punishment, miscarriages of justice, arbitrariness and discrimination in the death penalty's administration, retribution, and religious arguments. The last chapter is devoted to public opinion about the death penalty.

The Relative Importance of General Deterrence

Until recently, general deterrence was the reason cited most often when people were asked why they supported the death penalty.[2] This was a curious finding because other research found that retribution was the primary basis of death penalty support.[3] Professors Phoebe Ellsworth and Lee Ross contend that the reason for the paradox is that deterrence is more scientific or socially desirable than retribution: "people mention it [deterrence] first because its importance is obvious, not because its importance is real."[4] Ellsworth and Ross's contention is supported by their finding that compelling evidence of no deterrent effect would not have much effect on people's death penalty support. In other words, a majority of death penalty supporters would not change their opinion even if it were proven to them that their belief in general deterrence was wrong.

Deterrence no longer seems to be an important rationale for death penalty proponents. According to a 2006 Gallup poll, 64 percent of respondents did not think that the death penalty deterred crime.[5] When asked their reasons for supporting the death penalty in a 2003 Gallup poll, only 11 percent of respondents chose "Deterrent for potential crimes/Set an example," while 50 percent chose "An eye for an eye/They took a life/Fits the crime/They deserve it" (that is, retribution).[6]

Arguments and Counterarguments

Philosopher Ernest Van den Haag explains why one should believe in the general deterrent effect of the death penalty. In the first place, he says, "our penal system rests on the proposition that more severe penalties are more deterrent than less severe penalties."[7] If this is true, he asserts, the corollary is that "the most severe penalty—the death penalty—would have the greatest deterrent effect."[8] He adds that "arguments to the contrary assume either that capital crimes never are deterrable (sometimes because not all capital crimes have been deterred), or that, beyond some point, the deterrent effect of added severity is necessarily zero."[9]

Professor Van den Haag's first assumption—more severe penalties are more deterrent than less severe penalties—is generally correct. Beyond a point, though, added severity may reduce deterrence. In England during the eighteenth century, for example, there were about 150 capital crimes (some put the number at more than 200). Many of the crimes were so petty that juries chose not to convict clearly guilty defendants rather than having to condemn them to die. The practice is called jury nullification.[10] Such a practice likely reduces any general deterrent effect.

Professor Van den Haag's corollary—the most severe penalty, the death penalty, would have the greatest deterrent effect—is based on a debatable assumption and a testable proposition with no scientific evidence to support it. Is the death penalty the most severe penalty? For many, it may be; but for others, it may not. The prospect of spending the rest of one's life in prison may be more terrifying to some people than death, as it apparently was for Gary Gilmore.

Taking the opposite position to Van den Haag, Cesare Beccaria, the eighteenth century philosopher whose ideas are the basis of much of the criminal justice process in the United States today, claimed that life imprisonment (he called it "perpetual servitude") is probably a greater deterrent than death:

> To anyone raising the argument that perpetual servitude is as painful as death and therefore equally cruel, I will reply that, adding up all the moments of unhappiness of servitude, it may well be even more cruel; but these are drawn out over an entire lifetime, while the pain of death exerts its whole force in a moment. And precisely this is the advantage of penal servitude, that it inspires terror in the spectator more than in the sufferer, for the former considers the entire sum of unhappy moments, while the latter is distracted from the thought of future misery by that of the present moment.[11]

Although Beccaria could never have imagined the prolonged process now operative in the United States—a process that takes an average of more than 10 years to complete[12]—he still may be correct that life imprisonment is a more severe punishment (and better deterrent) than execution. In any case, he did not think much of capital punishment, calling it a "useless prodigality of torments" that "never made men better."[13] He believed that "the death penalty cannot be useful, because of the example of barbarity it gives men."[14]

Abolitionists maintain that the important question is not whether capital punishment is the severest punishment, but rather what punishment should be the severest allowed by law. As noted in the last chapter, not all punishments are legally allowed. The United States Constitution prohibits cruel and unusual punishments. Interestingly, how a person answers the question of what punishment should be the severest allowed by law may be what ultimately divides people on the death penalty issue.

Even if it were agreed that the death penalty is the severest penalty (and that at least some capital crimes are deterrable), the problem remains that there is no scientific evidence showing conclusively that the death penalty has any marginal effect. There is no evidence that capital punishment deters more than an alternative noncapital punishment, such as life imprisonment without opportunity for parole.[15] Instead, statistics indicate that capital punishment makes no discernible difference on homicide or murder rates.

Evidence

When considering the deterrence question, it is useful to distinguish between pre- and post–1975 studies because, until 1975, there were no scientific data showing that capital punishment had a significant (or greater than a chance) effect on homicide or murder rates.[16] This finding held, despite more than 40 years of research and dozens of studies.

Pre–1975 Studies. The pre–1975 studies generally employed one of three basic research designs.[17] The first type compares murder rates of states with and without a capital punishment statute. For example, Professor Thorsten Sellin compared the average annual homicide death rates (per 100,000 population) in contiguous states with and without capital punishment for the years 1920 through 1963.[18] If capital punishment had a marginal deterrent effect, one would expect that states without capital punishment would have higher homicide rates than states with capital punishment—all other things being equal. States next to each other were compared in an effort to control for other possibly influential factors. Sellin found no persuasive evidence of deterrence. The following are among his findings:

- The average annual homicide death rates for Michigan (without capital punishment), Indiana (with capital punishment), and Ohio (with capital punishment) during the time period were all 3.5.

- Rates for Minnesota (without capital punishment), Wisconsin (without capital punishment), and Iowa (with capital punishment) were 1.4, 1.2, and 1.4, respectively; rates for North Dakota (without capital punishment), South Dakota (with capital punishment), and Nebraska (with capital punishment) were 1.0, 1.5, and 1.8, respectively.

- Rates for Maine (without capital punishment), New Hampshire (with capital punishment), and Vermont (with capital punishment) were 1.5, 0.9, and 1.0, respectively.

- Rates for Rhode Island (without capital punishment), Massachusetts (with capital punishment), and Connecticut (with capital punishment) were 1.3, 1.2, and 1.7, respectively.

Again, those data fail to reveal a marginal deterrent effect for the death penalty.[19]

Sellin also employed his comparative method to the specific cases of police killings and prison murders.[20] Regarding police killings, Sellin wanted to test whether or not capital punishment provided police officers an added measure of protection. It was (and still is) assumed by many people that the threat of execution deters criminals from carrying guns and using them when they face arrest.[21] Sellin examined rates of municipal police killings for contiguous states per 10 years and 100,000 population for the years 1919 through 1954. As with his previous comparisons of general homicide rates for contiguous states, Sellin did not find that the availability of capital punishment had any discernible effect on the rate of police killings. Specifically, he reported that the rate of police killings in 82 cities in abolition states was 1.2, while the rate in 182 cities in death penalty states was 1.3.[22] Sellin observed in an editorial postscript to his study that from 1961 through 1963, 140 police officers were killed in the United States: 9 in abolition states and 131 in death penalty states. When he computed the average annual risk for the three years per 10,000 police in abolition states and contiguous death penalty states, he found a rate of 1.312 in the abolition states and 1.328 for the bordering death penalty states—not a significant difference.[23]

With regard to prison murders, Sellin researched whether, if capital punishment were an effective deterrent to murder, it would be reasonable to assume that inmates and correctional staff in prisons in abolition states would be in greater jeopardy for their lives than inmates and correctional staff in prisons in death penalty states because in abolition states there is no death penalty threat to deter would-be killers. The answer he found was that the evidence did not support the intuitive belief.[24] To the contrary, in 1965, there were 61 prison killings in the 37 jurisdictions that responded to his survey—8 of the victims were staff members and 53 were inmates. All of the staff members and 85 percent of the inmates were killed in death penalty states. Wendy Wolfson, who examined prison killings in 52 jurisdictions in the United States in 1973, has reported similar findings.[25] Of the 124 prison killings in 1973, 11 of the victims were staff members and 113 were inmates. Ninety-one percent of the staff member victims and 95 percent of the inmate victims were killed in death penalty jurisdictions. These data clearly show that prison staff members and inmates are no safer in prisons in death penalty states than in prisons in abolition states. The threat of death does not seem to effectively deter prison killings.[26]

The principal criticism of studies such as Sellin's is that the comparative results are weak evidence of deterrence (or its absence), because contiguous states are not necessarily comparable in all important respects. In attempting to overcome the criticism, studies have been conducted that compare several important factors that could affect the murder rates in the contiguous states.[27] Examples of such factors include probability of apprehension, probability of conviction, labor force participation, unemployment rate, population aged 15 through 24, real per-capita income, nonwhite population, civilian population, per-capita government expenditures (state and local), and per-capita police expenditures (state and local).[28] When those factors are compared for the contiguous states, no apparent reason emerges for the absence of a deterrent effect for capital punishment. Still, the criticism remains that the early comparative studies fail to account for the simultaneous influence of the other possible influential factors. That criticism would later be addressed using newer, more powerful statistical analytic techniques.

A second type of research design compares murder rates before and after the abolition and/or reinstatement of the death penalty.[29] If capital punishment has a deterrent effect, one would expect higher murder rates in states following abolition of the death penalty or lower rates following its reinstatement—all other things being equal. But before-and-after studies reveal no apparent deterrent effect for capital punishment.

A particularly interesting example of the "before-and-after" methodology using cross-national comparisons is a study by Professors Dane Archer, Rosemary Gartner, and Marc Beittel.[30] The researchers examined homicide rate changes for selected countries one year, five years (where possible), and the maximum possible years before and after abolition of the death penalty. The countries (dates of abolition, except for extraordinary crimes, are in parentheses) were: Austria (1968), Canada (1967), Denmark (1930), England and Wales (1965), Finland (1949), Israel (1954), Italy (1890), Netherland Antilles (1957), Norway (1905), Sweden (1921), and Switzerland (1942). In some countries, homicide rates increased following abolition, and in other countries, the rates decreased, but there were more decreases than increases. In short, these data do not show that capital punishment has a consistent or, for that matter, any deterrent effect. Fluctuations in homicide rates before and after abolition are probably a function of factors other than capital punishment. A problem with before-and-after studies is that they fail to control for other possibly influential factors.

The third type of research design examines short-term murder trends just before and just after highly publicized executions of convicted murderers.[31] If capital punishment has a deterrent effect, one would expect murder rates to decrease after these executions—all other things being equal. Some of the studies do reveal a short-term deterrent effect,[32] but in no case does the decrease in homicides last very long. Moreover, replications and reanalyses of these studies tend to show brutalizing, rather than deterrent, effects of execution publicity (more about brutalizing effects later).[33] This method does not provide any evidence of a long-term deterrent effect for capital punishment. The major problem with this method, like the other two, is the failure to adequately control for other possibly influential factors on homicides or murders.

In sum, none of the studies using any of the three research designs produced evidence to support a belief in the (long-term) deterrent effect of the death penalty. If the death penalty were an effective deterrent to homicides or murders (or any other crimes), one might expect to see at least some supportive evidence in at least some studies.

Ehrlich Finds a General Deterrent Effect. In 1975, Economics Professor Isaac Ehrlich published the first scientific study to report a deterrent effect for capital punishment.[34] Ehrlich began his article with two major criticisms of Sellin's research. The first was that Sellin compared different states on the basis of whether they had death penalty statutes rather than on whether they actually employed the death penalty. The second was that Sellin failed to control for a variety of factors that could influence homicide or murder rates

Ehrlich used a sophisticated statistical analytic technique—multiple regression analysis—to examine the simultaneous effect of several variables on homicide rates during the years 1933 to 1969. Among the variables were arrest and conviction rates for murder, unemployment rates, labor force participation rates, per-capita incomes, and proportions of the general population between 14 and 24 years of age. His key variable—execution risk—was measured by dividing the number of executions by convictions for murder in the United States during the time period selected. Ehrlich concluded that "an additional execution per year over the period in question may have resulted, on average, in seven or eight fewer murders."[35]

Ehrlich's findings drew considerable attention. For example, the solicitor general of the United States introduced Ehrlich's prepublished results in *Fowler v. North Carolina* (428 U.S. 904, 1976) as evidence in support of the death penalty.[36] The study was cited in the majority's opinion in *Gregg v. Georgia* (1976), to support the more modest contention that scientific evidence concerning the death penalty's general deterrent effect was "inconclusive."[37] Ehrlich's research continues to inform the opinions of some Supreme Court members who believe that capital punishment deters many types of murder.[38] Finally, Ehrlich's research inspired additional studies (see Yunker, 1976; Cloninger, 1977; Wolpin, 1978; Layson, 1985), including another one by Ehrlich himself (1977), that have found a statistically significant general deterrent effect for the death penalty.[39] Each of those studies, however, is considered methodologically inferior to Ehrlich's first study.

Most of the attention devoted to Ehrlich's first study was critical, and numerous methodological flaws with his research were cited.[40] Among the problems were: (1) the failure to compare the effectiveness of capital punishment with that of particular prison terms (the marginal effect issue), (2) his finding of a deterrent effect does not hold if the years between 1965 and 1969 are omitted from his statistical model, (3) his use of aggregate United States data ignores important regional differences, and (4) despite his criticism of Sellin's failure to control for possibly influential factors on homicide or murder rates, in accounting for the increase in homicides during the 1960s, Ehrlich fails to consider the possible influences of racial discord, the Vietnam conflict, the sexual revolution, and increased handgun ownership—to name only a few possible factors. Regarding the third and fourth problems, although the homicide rate in the United States did indeed increase during the 1960s, the increase was as great in those states with capital punishment as it was in those states without it. More generally, Ehrlich's model also omitted such variables as the decline in time served in prison for murder and the availability and quality of emergency medical care, both of which might significantly affect the murder rate.

One of the first and most forceful critiques of Ehrlich's research came from a panel established in 1975 by the National Academy of Sciences.[41] The panel's final report was based in part on several commissioned papers. One of the more influential was by Professor Lawrence R. Klein, a past president of the American Economic Association, and his colleagues, Professors Brian Forst and Victor Filatov.[42] Most of the problems listed earlier, as well as several others, were first described in this paper. Klein and his colleagues were more generous than the full panel would be in their assessment of Ehrlich's research. They wrote, "The deterrent effect of capital punishment is definitely not a settled matter, and this is the strongest social scientific conclusion that can be reached at the present time."[43] The panel's report emphasized that Ehrlich's research provides "no useful evidence on the deterrent effect of capital punishment" and that "the current evidence on the deterrent effect of capital punishment is inadequate for drawing any substantive conclusions."[44] Although not all members agreed, the report concluded on a pessimistic note: "research on this topic is not likely to produce findings that will or should have much influence on policy makers."[45]

Critiques of Ehrlich's research have prompted a new wave of deterrence studies, many of them conducted by economists like Ehrlich. Since 1995, more than a dozen studies (some published and some posted on the Internet as working papers) have reported finding a deterrent effect for capital punishment.[46] Some of them have even found additional murders associated with pardons, commutations, and exonerations.[47] Critical analyses of these newer studies have faulted them for some of the same problems that invalidated Ehrlich's earlier research, plus some new ones. First, the newer studies, like most of the older ones, generally do not distinguish between different types of murder. Included in the general category are crimes of passion and jealousy and intimate partner homicides, crimes that are less likely to be deterred. One study discovered that capital punishment was an especially effective deterrent to intimate partner homicides.[48] This finding contradicts what is known about homicide and fails to account for the steadily declining incidence of intimate partner homicide since the early 1970s, despite fluctuations in executions over the period.[49] Another new deterrence study showed that murders were more prevalent in rural areas than in cities, which is contrary to most evidence on the subject.[50] Second, none of the studies controls for autoregression, which is the tendency for

results in time-series analyses to be influenced by what happened in preceding years. Thus, the best predictor of next year's murder rate is last
year's murder rate, not the relatively few executions that occurred.[51]
Third, few of the studies statistically control for law enforcement's
ability to clear capital crimes. Many studies show that police effectiveness at detection and apprehension is far more important for deterrence than are a few, poorly publicized executions.[52] Fourth, the studies
ignore large amounts of missing data, which likely biases the results. For
example, most of the studies use homicide rates from the FBI; yet, the
FBI is missing Florida's homicide data for four years in the 1980s and
another four years in the 1990s.[53] Fifth, all of the studies are indirect tests
of the deterrence hypothesis. None of them measures whether murderers were aware of the likelihood of execution in the state where the
murder was committed, and the few studies that examine newspaper
accounts of executions fail to ascertain whether murderers regularly read
newspapers.[54] Sixth, the deterrent effect found in most of the studies
disappears when Texas executions are eliminated from the model.
Apparently, none of the other executing states has enough executions
to make a difference.[55] Seventh, none of the studies determines the marginal effect of executions, that is, whether executions have a greater
deterrent effect than life without opportunity of parole (LWOP). For the
more than 100 death row inmates that since 1976 have voluntarily
given up their appeals because they preferred death to LWOP, LWOP
clearly was considered a harsher punishment. Furthermore, the dramatic
recent decrease in homicide rates in New York, Texas, and California
seems to demonstrate the deterrent superiority of LWOP over executions
because in capital cases LWOP sentences are much more frequently given
than death sentences. On February 24, 2004, for instance, 3,163 California inmates were serving LWOP sentences, while 635 inmates were
awaiting execution on death row.[56] Eighth, the studies fail to consider
alternate explanations for variations in the murder rate. For example,
none of the studies controls for the differences between homicides committed with guns and those that are not (the rate of non-gun homicides
has not varied much since the early 1970s), gun availability, and the influence of the crack cocaine epidemic in the late 1980s and early 1990s
on gun violence.[57]

Ehrlich's research also inspired numerous studies that failed to find
a deterrent effect for the death penalty. Professors Peter Passell (1975),
William J. Bowers and Glenn L. Pierce (1975), Brian Forst (1977), Scott
H. Decker and Carol W. Kohfeld (1984, 1986, 1987, 1988, 1990), Carol
W. Kohfeld and Scott H. Decker (1990), Jon Sorensen, Robert Wrinkle,
Victoria Brewer, and James Marquart (1999), and William C. Bailey all
used Ehrlich's multiple regression analytic approach, but none of them
found a statistically significant deterrent effect. Professor Bailey, a soci-
ologist at Cleveland State University and the most prolific researcher in

this area, has conducted numerous studies on the possible deterrent effect of capital punishment using multiple regression analysis. His research on the possible deterrent effect on first-degree murder reviewed: (1) executions versus imprisonment (1974; 1977a), (2) the role of celerity or swiftness in the use of the death penalty (1980), (3) actual executions in each of five states—California, North Carolina, Ohio, Oregon, and Utah—(1979a; 1979d; 1979b; 1979c; 1978, respectively), (4) executions in Chicago and Washington, D.C. (1984a; 1984b, respectively), (5) executions during the 1950s (1983), (6) execution publicity (1990; and with Peterson, 1989), and (7) executions for assaults against the police (with Peterson, 1987; 1994). He also looked for a deterrent effect of executions on rape (1977b) and noncapital felonies (1991). In none of those studies did Bailey find a statistically significant deterrent effect.

Five Counterarguments to Studies that Show No General Deterrent Effect

The first three counterarguments to studies that show no general deterrent effect of capital punishment are from a 1980 report by the Committee on the Judiciary of the United States Senate: "[T]he value of these [deterrence] studies is seriously diminished by the unreliability of the statistical evidence used, the contrary experience of those in the field of law enforcement, and the inherent logic of the deterrent power of the threat of death."[58] The fourth counterargument that undermines the value of the deterrence studies is the observation that, from the mid-1960s through the 1970s, the homicide rate increased as the number of executions decreased.[59] A fifth counterargument is that the death penalty's deterrent effect has been reduced to nothing in recent years (and thus does not show up in the research) because it has not been imposed often or quickly enough to have the desired effect.

Regarding the first point—that "the value of the studies is seriously diminished by the unreliability of the statistical evidence used"—the report noted that "those who are, in fact, deterred by the threat of the death penalty and do not commit murder are not included in the statistical data."[60] It added that "even those favoring abolition agree that the available evidence on the subject of deterrence is, at best, inadequate."[61]

That the available evidence on the subject of deterrence is, at best, inadequate may have been true in 1980, but it is no longer, as the previous section makes clear. As Professor William J. Bowers explains:

> The evidence that capital punishment has no deterrent advantage over imprisonment is now stronger and more consistent than when the Court last considered this issue in *Gregg*. Indeed, a comprehensive review of previous studies and

> recent analyses of refined statistical data both support the
> contention that the death penalty has a "brutalizing" rather than
> a deterrent effect—that executions can be expected to stim-
> ulate rather than to inhibit homicides.[62]

In 1989, following a comprehensive review of death penalty research by
a panel of distinguished scholars, the American Society of Criminology—the largest association of criminologists in the nation—passed a resolution condemning capital punishment and calling for its abolition.
Among the reasons for the Society's position was the absence of "consistent evidence of crime deterrence through execution."[63] Additionally,
a recent survey of 67 current and past presidents of the top three criminology professional organizations—the American Society of Criminology,
the Academy of Criminal Justice Sciences, and the Law and Society Association—found that about 80 percent of them believe that the death
penalty is no greater a deterrent to homicide than long imprisonment."[64]

The second counterargument is that most law enforcement officials
continue to favor capital punishment because they believe it is an
effective deterrent to violent crime.[65] Law enforcement officials, it is
assumed, are in the best position to judge the utility of capital punishment because they are the people "most frequently called upon to deal
with murderers and potential murderers."[66] This second counterargument, however, appears to be wrong. Most police chiefs do not believe
that the death penalty is an effective deterrent to violent crime. A 1995
Hart Research Associates poll found that two-thirds of U.S. police chiefs
do not believe that the death penalty significantly reduces the number
of homicides. The police chiefs rated the death penalty last among
seven effective ways of reducing violent crime. Only one percent of the
chiefs selected "expand death penalty." By contrast, 31 percent of the
chiefs chose "reducing drug abuse," 17 percent selected "better economy, jobs," 16 percent opted for "simplifying court rules," 15 percent preferred "longer prison sentences," 10 percent wanted "more police
officers," and three percent chose "reducing guns."[67]

The third counterargument, which simply generalizes the second,
is that "[t]here is an inherent logic in the deterrent power of the threat
of death."[68] This logic, moreover, is frequently supported by anecdotal
evidence. For example, in the mid-1990s, California Senator Dianne Fein-
stein said the following about a woman convicted of first-degree armed
robbery in the 1960s:

> . . . I saw that she carried a weapon that was unloaded into a
> grocery store robbery. I asked her the question: "Why was the
> gun unloaded?" She said to me: "So I would not panic, kill some-
> body, and get the death penalty." That was firsthand testimony
> directly to me that the death penalty in place in California in
> the sixties was in fact a deterrent."[69]

During a bank robbery in New York in the 1970s, one of the robbers reportedly told FBI agents:

> I'll shoot everyone in the bank. The Supreme Court will let me get away with this. There's no death penalty. It's ridiculous. I can shoot everyone here, then throw my gun down and walk out and they can't put me in the electric chair. You have to have a death penalty, otherwise this can happen everyday.[70]

While the death penalty was suspended during the 1970s because of the *Furman* decision, a couple in Kansas were held as hostages during a bank robbery. Rather than leave them alive as potential witnesses, the robbers decided to kill them. The wife escaped and the husband survived after being shot in the head twice. Later, they commented, "Thank God that we lived so that we can tell you that capital punishment does make a difference."[71] During a debate in the mid-1990s, Harvard Law Professor Alan Dershowitz, a death penalty opponent, conceded, "Of course, the death penalty deters some crimes. That's why you have to pay more for a hitman in a death penalty state, than a non-death penalty state."[72] Contradicting the argument made previously about prison murders, five federal prison officials were murdered during the 1980s when the federal death penalty was suspended. Inmates already serving a life sentence for murder committed three of the prison killings. Norman Carlson, former director of the U.S. Bureau of Prisons, remarked:

> . . . in the case of someone serving a nonrevokable life sentence, execution is the only sanction which could possibly serve as a deterrent. . . . We must impose the death penalty on prisoners sentenced to life who murder guards or other inmates in order to bring some semblance of security to our Federal prison system.[73]

Even without evidence, the deterrent power of capital punishment makes intuitive sense. Defense attorney Anthony Amsterdam agrees that "the real mainstay of the deterrence thesis . . . is not evidence but intuition" but argues that the intuitive belief is misguided:

> You and I ask ourselves: Are we not afraid to die? Of course! Would the threat of death, then not intimidate us to forbear from a criminal act? Certainly! Therefore, capital punishment must be a deterrent. The trouble with this intuition is that the people who are doing the reasoning and the people who are doing the murdering are not the same people. You and I do not commit murder for a lot of reasons other than the death penalty.[74]

In addition, there are intuitive reasons for believing that capital punishment provokes violence and other calamity; that it has a "brutalizing effect." For example, if persons are to be dissuaded from killing by fear of capital punishment, then why have executions been banned from public view since the late 1930s? Why are executions not televised? The first chapter noted that executions were hidden from public view to avoid the rowdiness and violence that frequently accompanied them; the same is said of televised executions.[75] Similarly, if capital punishment is an effective deterrent, then why are prison inmates not allowed to view executions? Executions are almost always scheduled for late at night when most inmates are asleep. The reason? To avoid violent reactions.[76] Professor Bowers remarks, "Our experience is that those who should benefit most react instead with anger, resentment, and hostility, if not overt violence, to the 'lesson' of an execution."[77]

The fourth counterargument—that because the homicide rate increased as the number of executions decreased from the mid-1960s through the 1970s, there must be a general deterrent effect—is also suspect. It underscores the need for rigorous scientific inquiry into conclusions based on common sense. Amsterdam states the problem with the counterargument succinctly:

> This is ridiculous [as evidence for general deterrence] when you consider that crime as a whole has increased during this period; that homicide rates have increased about *half* as much as the rates for all other FBI Index crimes; and that whatever factors are affecting the rise of most noncapital crimes (which *cannot* include cessation of executions) almost certainly affect the homicide-rate rise also (emphasis in original).[78]

Professor Bowers further notes, "[C]ompared with yearly changes in the national homicide rate from 1962 on, states with reduced executions tended to have reduced homicide rates and those with increased executions tended to have increased homicide rates."[79] Law Professor and now U.S. District Court Judge Paul Cassell counters that states with increased homicide rates have greater numbers of executions simply because they need them more [for deterrence?] than states with much lower homicide rates.[80] Furthermore, when comparing 1966 and 1999 state murder rates—two years when nationwide murder rates were about the same—Cassell reports states that aggressively employed the death penalty during that period generally saw their murder rates decline, while states not using the death penalty generally saw their murder rates increase.[81]

The fifth and related counterargument is that the death penalty's deterrent effect has been reduced to nothing in recent years (and thus does not show up in the research) because it has not been imposed often or quickly enough to have the desired effect. In California, for example, only 10 of the 717 defendants (1.4 percent) sentenced to death between 1977 and 2004 have been executed. By contrast, 13 death row inmates committed suicide during that period.[82] Such critics claim that a return to the "good old days" of more frequent and swifter executions would produce deterrence.[83] Evidence from the good old days, however, belies that hope.

During the 1930s, for example, there were a total of 1,676 executions in the United States.[84] That represents 167 executions per year, 14 executions per month, and the most executions in any single decade of the twentieth century. The most executions in any single year since 1930, the first year records were kept by the U.S. government, were the 199 recorded in 1935.[85] Furthermore, although data on the celerity of executions are not available for this period, data on celerity for 1951–1960 show that the average time between death sentence and execution was 14.4 months (the range was from 4.6 to 46.1 months); the average for 2004 was 132 months.[86] If capital punishment had a deterrent effect, and the frequency and celerity of executions were important, then one might expect a relatively low murder rate for the decade. The evidence shows, though, that homicide rates were higher in the 1930s than in the 1940s, 1950s, and early-to-mid-1960s—decades that had fewer executions.[87] Historical evidence provides no reason to believe that increasing the frequency and celerity of executions would dramatically increase the death penalty's deterrent effect.[88]

Assumptions and Problems with Deterrence Theory

According to Professor Bowers, "Deterrence theory assumes that potential offenders exercise rational judgment in deciding whether to kill and that they are predictably sensitive to the actual range of variation in certainty and severity of legal punishment for murder at the time of the decision to act."[89] Additional assumptions of deterrence theory are that potential killers "know what constitutes a capital murder," "that they view death as less acceptable than the other punishments imposed for capital murder," and "that the deterrence message is not neutralized by other confounding or contrary messages conveyed by capital punishment."[90] "From what we know about murder," Bowers surmises, "there is reason to doubt these assumptions."[91] Nevertheless, studies based on economic models of crime, such as the aforementioned study by Ehrlich (1975), rest on some of those dubious assumptions.

Most murderers, especially capital murderers, probably do not rationally calculate the consequences of their actions before they engage in them. Many murderers who end up on death row killed someone during the course of an armed robbery. Many never intended to kill but did so because of unexpected circumstances. Any who may have calculated the consequences of their actions before engaging in their crimes probably did not consider that the punishment might be death. And even if would-be killers knew that execution was the possible penalty for their actions, it likely would not deter them anyway. As Professor Bowers notes, "Police statistics reported to the Federal Bureau of Investigation and execution records from the National Bureau of Prisons indicate that only a small fraction of criminal homicides have resulted in executions—no more than two percent per year since 1930."[92] The chance of being executed for criminal homicide is very remote.

A problem is that the objects of deterrence theory—rational human beings—frequently do not calculate the consequences of their actions. The point is moot, however, because most people, whether they calculate consequence or not, do not kill. Without dismissing the tragedy of even a single murder victim, according to data from the Federal Bureau of Investigation, in recent years there have been only about 16,000 murders and nonnegligent manslaughters committed annually in the United States. Precise figures are not available, but it is estimated that only 10 to 25 percent of them, or about 1,600 to 4,000, are capital crimes and thus death-eligible.[93] In a well-armed country of nearly 300 million people, one might expect many more murders. The point is that most people do not kill, and the reasons they do not kill generally do not include fear of the death penalty.

Those killers who do take into account the possible consequences of their actions commit crimes that usually are impossible for the police to detect.[94] When they are caught, the chances of their being convicted are small and their chances of being executed even less.[95] As noted earlier, 75-90 percent of all killers are not eligible for the death penalty. Consider the prototypical rational killer, the professional "hit person," who would be the most likely candidate for execution. According to a study by Sarah Dike, "during 1919-1968, there were 1,004 gangland murders in Chicago, 23 convictions, 4 sentences to life imprisonment, and no death sentences imposed."[96]

Critics of the death penalty point out that even if the penalty deterred some would-be killers, it does not logically follow, nor does available evidence support, that capital punishment is a more effective deterrent to capital crimes than is an alternative, noncapital punishment.[97]

The Counterdeterrent or Brutalizing Effect

Most of the replications of Ehrlich's research not only show no deterrent effect for the death penalty, but many of them actually found a counterdeterrent or brutalizing effect. In other words, the death penalty may actually cause murders rather than deter them! The idea that executions can provoke murders is an old one,[98] and for years, psychiatrists have provided anecdotal evidence of such an effect. One variant of this phenomenon is called the "suicide–murder syndrome," which is illustrated by the case of Pamela Watkins. Watkins was "a babysitter in San Jose who had made several unsuccessful suicide attempts and was frightened to try again. She finally strangled two children so that the state of California would execute her."[99] Gary Gilmore was probably another example of this syndrome. Another variant of this phenomenon has been termed the "executioner syndrome."[100] Those afflicted with the problem believe their killing performs a public service by eliminating a problem. Still another variant stems from the pathological desire to die by execution.[101] Finally, from what is known about capital murderers, it is likely that some of them kill to gain the attention and notoriety that being executed might bring: Their executions provide them a stage that would not be available to them under different circumstances. That certainly seems to be true about serial killer Danny Rolling, who was sentenced to die in 1994 for five murders, three rapes, and three burglaries in what became known as the "Gainesville [Florida] Student Murders." Rolling confessed he wanted to be a criminal "superstar" and the "world's greatest rapist."[102]

Among those who believe most strongly in the death penalty's counterdeterrent or brutalizing effect are Professor Bowers and Professor Glenn L. Pierce, of the Center for Applied Social Research at Northeastern University. They attempted to replicate Ehrlich's research, and discovered that Ehrlich's finding of a deterrent effect for the death penalty appeared only "if the period of analysis is extended beyond 1965 to include years when executions had dwindled to one or two or had actually ceased, and only if logarithmic values of the variables are used, giving disproportionate weight to these recent years in the regression analysis."[103] When the analysis is limited to the period 1935 to 1963, however, a period when executions actually took place, their research revealed:

- that execution risk tends to make a positive contribution to the homicide rate as measured by the FBI . . . and by the Census Bureau . . .

- that the number of executions imposed (a better index of possible brutalizing effects) makes a stronger and more consistent positive contribution to the FBI homicide rate . . .; and

- that the evident brutalizing effects become even stronger and more statistically significant with the more reliable census measure of willful homicide.[104]

Later, in an analysis of the 692 executions and all of the homicides in New York state between 1906 and 1963, Bowers and Pierce found that each execution "adds roughly three more to the number of homicides in the next nine months of the year after the execution."[105]

Professor Bowers provides the following explanation for his findings:

> The lesson of the execution . . . may be to devalue life by the example of human sacrifice. Executions demonstrate that it is correct and appropriate to kill those who have gravely offended us. The fact that such killings are to be performed only by duly appointed officials on duly convicted offenders is a detail that may get obscured by the message that such offenders deserve to die. If the typical murderer is someone who feels that he has been betrayed, dishonored, or disgraced by another person—and we suggest that such feelings are far more characteristic of those who commit murder than is a rational evaluation of costs and benefits—then it is not hard to imagine that the example executions provide may inspire a potential murderer to kill the person who has greatly offended him. In effect, the message of the execution may be lethal vengeance, not deterrence.[106]

Bowers maintains that the brutalization effect requires a different type of identification process than does the deterrent effect. If executions are to achieve deterrence, would-be killers must identify with criminals who are executed. If they do not, deterrence cannot work. If executions brutalize, on the other hand, would-be killers must identify their victims with executed criminals and themselves with state-sanctioned executioners. Bowers describes the process:

> The potential murderer will not identify personally with the criminal who is executed, but will instead identify someone who has greatly offended him—someone he hates, fears, or both—with the executed criminal. We might call this the psychology of "villain identification." By associating the person who has wronged him with the victim of an execution, he sees that death is what his despised offender deserves. Indeed, he himself may identify with the state as executioner and thus justify and reinforce his desire for lethal vengeance.[107]

Bowers adds that capital punishment may provoke homicides in other ways, such as through the psychology of suggestion or imitation.[108] To that, Professor Van den Haag counters, "It is possible that all displays of violence, criminal or punitive, influence people to engage in unlawful imitations. This seems one good reason not to have public executions. But it does not argue against executions."[109] Van den Haag seems to be implying that only the viewing of executions is suggestive, but knowledge of them is not. For Van den Haag, media representations of executions must be inconsequential, yet there is considerable evidence that the media influences many types of behavior, including criminal behavior.[110] Consequently, if displays of or knowledge of violence do influence people to engage in unlawful imitations, as Professor Van den Haag concedes in part, then it seems reasonable to conclude that executions, as a form of violence, could provoke some people to commit violent acts. If Professor Van den Haag is correct, then the imitation of violence may help account for the relatively high violent crime rate in the United States.

Murder versus Capital Punishment

Beyond the imitation of violence, some people equate capital punishment with murder. Beccaria wrote, "It seems to me absurd that the laws, which are an expression of the public will, which detest and punish homicide, should themselves commit it, and that to deter citizens from murder, they order a public one."[111] Professor Van den Haag's reply is that capital punishment is not murder:

> Legally imposed punishments . . . although often physically identical to the crimes punished, are not crimes or their moral equivalent. The difference between crimes and lawful acts is not physical, but legal . . . [Finally,] whether a lawful punishment gives an "example of barbarity" depends on how the moral difference between crime and punishment is perceived. To suggest that its physical quality, ipso facto, morally disqualifies the punishment, is to assume what is to be shown.[112]

On the other hand, Amsterdam writes that "the advocates of capital punishment can and do accentuate their arguments with descriptions of the awful physical details of such hideous murders as that of poor Sharon Tate," who was brutally killed by members of the infamous Manson family.[113] He argues that there are two main problems with justifying capital punishment by citing the heinousness of murders:

> First, the murders being described are not murders that are being done by us, or in our name, or with our approval; and our power to stop them is exceedingly limited even under the most exaggerated suppositions of deterrence. . . . Every execution, on the other hand, is done by our paid servants, in our collective name, and we can stop them all. Please do not be bamboozled into thinking that people who are against executions are in favor of murders. If we had the individual or the collective power to stop murders, we would stop them all— and for the same basic reason that we want to stop executions.

> Murders and executions are both ugly, vicious things, because they destroy the same sacred and mysterious gift of life which we do not understand and can never restore. Second, please remember therefore that descriptions of murders are relevant to the subject of capital punishment only on the theory that two wrongs make a right, or that killing murderers can assuage their victims' sufferings or bring them back to life, or that capital punishment is the best deterrent to murder. The first two propositions are absurd, and [for the third] the evidence is overwhelmingly against it.[114]

Albert Camus, the French philosopher, once wrote that an execution

> is not simply death. It is just as different. . . from the privation of life as a concentration camp is from prison. . . . It adds to death a rule, a public premeditation known to the future victim, an organization . . . which is itself a source of moral sufferings more terrible than death . . . [Capital punishment] is . . . the most premeditated of murders, to which no criminal's deed, however calculated . . . can be compared. . . . For there to be an equivalency, the death penalty would have to punish a criminal who had warned his victim of the date at which he would inflict a horrible death on him and who, from that moment onward, had confined him at his mercy for months. Such a monster is not encountered in private life.[115]

Whether or not capital punishment is the same as murder, or—as Amsterdam and Camus argue—worse, is an ethical issue that likely defies a definitive answer. Yet, it seems a critical issue to resolve because how one stands on the issue probably determines, to a large extent, one's position on capital punishment in general.

Conclusion

In 2000, during the third presidential debate between Republican George W. Bush and Democrat Al Gore, the debate's moderator, Jim Lehrer, asked both candidates whether they believed the death penalty was a deterrent. Bush replied that he thought it was and added that it was the only reason to support the death penalty. Gore did not disagree with him.[116] Apparently, both candidates were unaware of the more than a half century of research and dozens of studies investigating the intuitively appealing belief in the death penalty's deterrent effect. Had they been, they would have known that, with the exception of a handful of thoroughly discredited older analyses or the newer studies that have also been criticized for various problems, no evidence existed of the hypothesized effect. They also may have known about evidence of a counterdeterrent or brutalizing effect. Still, in fairness to both men, perhaps capital punishment both deters *and* brutalizes, producing the absence of a discernible deterrent effect by canceling each other out. In the final analysis, none of this may matter if results of a recent opinion poll are to be believed: Only 11 percent of death penalty proponents polled selected deterrence as a reason for their position.

The irony is that although capital punishment has virtually no effect on crime, capital or otherwise, it continues to be a favored political "silver bullet"—a simplistic solution to the crime problem used by aspiring politicians and some law enforcement officials.[117] A problem is that, as long as politicians and law enforcement officials can gain political currency by perpetuating the belief in the death penalty's deterrent effect, attention will be diverted from more constructive and (it is hoped) more effective approaches to the prevention and control of violent behavior.[118] This may be yet another way that capital punishment contributes to an increase in violent crime rather than the expected decrease.

Discussion Questions

1. Is the death penalty a greater general deterrent to capital crime than an alternative noncapital punishment such as life imprisonment without opportunity of parole?

2. Is the death penalty a general deterrent to noncapital crimes?

3. Regarding the first two questions, does it matter?

4. Is the death penalty the most severe penalty?

5. Does the death penalty provide an added measure of protection for police officers?

6. Does the death penalty provide an added measure of protection for correctional officers?

7. Why have executions been banned from public view since the late 1930s?

8. Why are executions not televised?

9. Why are prison inmates not allowed to view executions?

10. In what ways, if any, could the general deterrent power of capital punishment be increased?

11. Does the death penalty have a counterdeterrent or "brutalizing" effect? (Does the death penalty cause capital crimes?)

12. Is capital punishment murder?

Notes

[1] Available evidence indicates that capital punishment does not deter noncapital felonies; specifically, murder and nonnegligent manslaughter, rape, assault, robbery, burglary, grand larceny, or vehicle theft, see Bailey, 1991.

[2] Ellsworth and Ross, 1983:121, fn. 15.

[3] See, for example, Bohm, Clark, and Aveni, 1991; Gallup Report, 1985; Kohlberg and Elfenbein, 1975.

[4] Ellsworth and Ross, op. cit., p. 149.

[5] Sourcebook of Criminal Justice Statistics Online, Table 2.57.2006 at www.albany.edu/sourcebook/pdf/t2572006.

[6] Sourcebook of Criminal Justice Statistics 2003, p. 147, Table 2.55 (online).

[7] Van den Haag, 1982:326.

[8] Ibid., p. 327.

[9] Ibid.

[10] O.J. Simpson's criminal trial jury was accused of jury nullification when they acquitted him.

[11] Beccaria, 1975:48-49.

[12] Bonzcar and Snell, 2005:11, Table 11.

[13] Beccaria, op. cit., p. 45.

[14] Ibid., p. 50.

[15] See, for example, Peterson and Bailey, 2003; Paternoster, 1991:Chap. 7; Zimring and Hawkins, 1986:Appendix; Conrad in Van den Haag and Conrad, 1983:133-4; Waldo, 1981; Glaser, 1979.

[16] Specifically, statistical significance refers to the unlikelihood that relationships observed in a sample, that is, a subset of a larger group, can be attributed to sampling error alone. Sampling error refers to the difference between the measure of a population (the larger group) and the measure of a sample (the subset of the larger group).

[17] See Peterson and Bailey, op. cit.; Paternoster, op. cit., Chap. 7; Zimring and Hawkins, op. cit., Appendix; Zeisel, 1982.

[18] Sellin, 1967:135-38. Sellin also conducted a year-by-year comparative analysis of contiguous states from 1920 to 1955, see Sellin, 1959.

[19] Also see Bye, 1919; Sutherland, 1925; Vold, 1932; 1952; Schuessler, 1952; Reckless, 1969. For examples of a similar type of analysis using data for the 1973-1984 and 1980-1995 periods, see Peterson and Bailey, 1988; 1998. Other recent examples using this methodology are Cheatwood, 1993 and Harries and Cheatwood, 1997, who examined comparable counties, and the Death Penalty Information Center, www.deathpenaltyinfo.org/deter.html. These studies found no deterrent effect for capital punishment either.

[20] Sellin, 1959, op. cit.; 1967, op. cit., pp. 138-154.

[21] Sellin, 1967, op. cit., p. 138.

[22] Sellin, op. cit., p. 55; 1967, op. cit., p. 146.

[23] Sellin, 1967, op. cit., pp. 152-153. For multivariate analyses that found the same non-deterrent results, see Bailey and Peterson, 1987; 1994.

[24] Sellin, 1967, op. cit., pp. 154-160.

[25] Wolfson, 1982:159-173.

[26] Based on the results of a 1950 survey by the International Penal and Penitentiary Commission, Sellin (1959:70) also notes that "countries without the death penalty reported no more serious disciplinary problems [in prisons] than the countries which had retained the penalty."

[27] See, for example, Baldus and Cole, 1975.

[28] See Bedau, 1982:123, Table 4-2-2.

[29] See, for example, Bye, op. cit.; Schuessler, op. cit.; Sellin, 1959, op. cit.; Reckless, op. cit.; Cochran et al., 1994; Bailey, 1998.

[30] Archer et al., 1983; also see Sellin, 1959, op. cit., pp. 38-50 for cross-national comparisons.

[31] See, for example, Sellin, 1959, op. cit.; King, 1978; Bailey, 1990; Peterson and Bailey, 1991; Thompson, 1999.

[32] See, for example, Dann, 1935; Savitz, 1958; Phillips, 1980; McFarland, 1983; Stack, 1987. Both Dann (1935) and Savitz (1958) overlooked seasonal variations in homicides, see Bowers, 1988:66. For a detailed critique of Phillips (1980), see Bowers, 1988:72-79. McFarland (1983) attributed the short-term decline in homicides following Gary Gilmore's execution in Utah, which was confined to only certain parts of the United States, to the abnormally severe winter conditions in those parts of the country. Bailey and Peterson (1989) replicated Stack's research, correcting some of Stack's coding errors, and failed to find a statistically significant relationship between execution publicity and homicide rates.

[33] See Bowers, op. cit.

[34] See Ehrlich, 1975.

[35] Ibid., p. 414.

[36] Zimring and Hawkins, op. cit., p. 175.

[37] Bowers, 1984:281, fn. 13.

[38] Peterson and Bailey, 1998, op. cit.; Haney and Logan, 1994:87-90. Some of the Supreme Court justices apparently are ignoring the bulk of the evidence showing that capital punishment has no marginal deterrent effect, see Haney and Logan, op. cit., p. 89, and the review of studies below.

[39] Wolpin (1978) reported that each execution may deter four murders; Layson (1985), about 18; Ehrlich (1977), 20-24; Yunker (1976), 156; and Cloninger (1977), 560.

[40] See, for example, Peterson and Bailey, 2003, op. cit.; Paternoster, op. cit., Chap. 7; Zimring and Hawkins, op. cit., pp. 175-181; Bowers, 1988, op. cit.; 1984, op. cit., pp. 280-282, 332-333; Andersen, 1983:35; Zeisel, 1982, op. cit.; Beyleveld, 1982; Klein, Forst, and Filatov, 1982; Barnett, 1981; Waldo, op. cit.; Friedman, 1979; Forst, 1977; Passell and Taylor, 1977; Bowers and Pierce, 1975. For Ehrlich's reply to Beyleveld's critique, see Ehrlich, 1982.

[41] See Zimring and Hawkins, op. cit., pp. 179-181.

[42] Klein, Forst, and Filatov, op. cit.

[43] Ibid., p. 158.

[44] Cited in Zimring and Hawkins, op. cit., p. 180.

[45] Ibid.

[46] See Fagan, 2005; Shepherd, in press, 2004; Liu, forthcoming; Zimmerman, forthcoming, 2004; Deshbakhsh et al., 2003; Mocan and Giddings, 2003, 2001; Katz et al., 2003; Yunker, 2002; Cloninger and Marchesini, 2001; Ehrlich and Liu, 1999; Brumm and Cloninger, 1996.

[47] Mocan and Giddings, ibid

[48] Shepherd, forthcoming.

[49] Fagan, op. cit.

[50] The study was by Deshabkhsh et al., op. cit., and the criticism by Turow, 2003:60.

[51] Fagan, op. cit.

[52] Ibid.

[53] Ibid.

[54] Ibid.

[55] Ibid.; Berk, 2005; also see Shepherd, forthcoming.

[56] Fagan, ibid.

[57] Ibid.

[58] Committee on the Judiciary, United States Senate, 1982:312.

[59] See, for example, King, 1982, who recognizes that other factors were also involved.

[60] Committee on the Judiciary, U.S. Senate, op. cit.

[61] Ibid.

[62] Bowers, 1984, op. cit., p. 190; also see Zimring and Hawkins, op. cit., Appendix.

[63] Petersilia, 1990:1.

[64] Radelet and Akers, 1996. In 1975, the Massachusetts Supreme Judicial Court reviewed the deterrence literature, including Ehrlich's study, and concluded that "there is simply no convincing evidence that the death penalty is a deterrent superior to lesser punishments" (*Commonwealth v. O'Neal*, 339 N. E. 2d 676, 1975 at 252).

[65] Committee on the Judiciary, U.S. Senate, op. cit.

[66] Ibid. Another group that should have some expertise on the deterrent value of capital punishment is prison inmates. Professors Wilcox and Steele (2003:475) found that only about 25 percent of the prison inmates they surveyed believed that the death penalty was a deterrent. Nearly 80 percent of the inmates who had committed more than three violent crimes did not believe the death penalty deterred violent crime (also see Steele and Wilcox, 2003).

[67] Cited in the Death Penalty Information Center, op. cit.

[68] Committee, ibid.

[69] Cassell, 2004:190.

[70] Ibid., p. 191.

[71] Ibid.

[72] Ibid.

[73] Ibid., p. 192.

[74] Amsterdam, 1982:357.

[75] Bowers, 1988, op. cit., p. 49. For a thoughtful discussion about televising executions, see Leighton, 1999; also see Sarat, 2002:187-208.

[76] Bowers, 1988, ibid.

[77] Ibid.

[78] Amsterdam, op. cit., p. 356; also see Bowers, 1984, op. cit., p. 333. A similar argument could be made about the observation that Harris County, Texas sentences to death more capital defendants than 36 of the then-38 death penalty states and, as a result, its murder rate has fallen more than 70 percent in the last 20 years, see Marquis, 2004:126.

[79] Bowers, ibid.; for a cross-national perspective, see Archer et al., op. cit.; also see Death Penalty Information Center, op.cit.

[80] Cassell, op. cit., p. 192.

[81] Ibid., pp. 192-194.

[82] Sundby, 2005:38.

[83] Cited in Peterson and Bailey, 2003, op. cit.

[84] See Schneider and Smykla, 1991:6, Table 1.1; Zimring and Hawkins, op. cit., p. 30, Table 2.2.

[85] Bedau, op. cit., p. 25, Table 1-3.

[86] Peterson and Bailey, 2003, op. cit., p. 177; Bonczar and Snell, op. cit.

[87] See Zahn, 1989:219, Figure 10.1.

[88] However, Peterson and Bailey warn that "because the celerity question has received so little attention, we are not able to conclude, 'with confidence', that prompt executions are/are not effective in preventing murder," see Peterson and Bailey, 2003, op. cit., p. 274.

[89] Bowers, 1984, op. cit., p. 272.

[90] Bowers, 1988, op. cit., p. 50. Peterson and Bailey write that "deterrence theory rests upon the premise that individuals weigh the costs and rewards associated with alternative sanctions, and choose behaviors that yield the greatest gain at the least cost. Thus, crime occurs when illegal actions are perceived either as more profitable (rewarding) or less costly (painful) than conventional alternatives. . . . [M]urder is discouraged because the threat of one's own death presumably outweighs the rewards gained from killing another," see Peterson and Bailey, 2003, op. cit., p. 252; also see Sellin, 1959, op. cit., p. 20.

[91] Bowers, 1984, op. cit.

[92] Ibid., pp. 272-273. Liebman et al. (2000:6) report that during the years 1973-1995 only twelve death sentences were imposed for every 1,000 homicides. Also, in a study conducted by researchers on behalf of the Commission on sentencing decisions in Illinois it was found that during the study period (1988-1997) there were 5,310 cases in which an Illinois defendant was convicted of first-degree murder. Only 115 (about two percent) of those cases resulted in the imposition of a death sentence, see Governor's Commission on Capital Punishment, 2002.

[93] Baldus et al., 1990:22; Andersen, op. cit., p. 32. Professors Paternoster and Brame (2003) found that 22 percent of the Maryland murders they reviewed were death eligible.

[94] Van den Haag and Conrad, op. cit., p. 84.

[95] As Henry Schwarzschild, former director of the ACLU's Capital Punishment Project, observes: "the deterrent value [of capital punishment] (which very likely does not exist at all in any case) is reduced to invisibility by the overwhelming likelihood that one will not be caught, or not be prosecuted, or not be tried on a capital charge, or not be convicted, or not be sentenced to death, or have the conviction or sentence reversed on appeal, or have one's sentence commuted," see Schwarzschild, 1982:366.

[96] Cited in Van den Haag and Conrad, op. cit., p. 92.

[97] See, for example, Professor John Conrad: "Punishment certainly deters some potential offenders, but we must not rely on increasing severity to make a corresponding decrease in the number of crimes committed. If we cannot do more to reduce the economic and social causes of crime, we must increase the risks of apprehension by the police. With crime clearance rates as low as they are, it is idle to suppose that dramatic increases in the severity of punishment will seriously affect the incidence of any type of crime," see Van den Haag and Conrad, op. cit., p. 103.

[98] See Bowers, 1984, op. cit., pp. 273-274; 1988, op. cit., pp. 57-61; Sellin, 1959, op. cit., pp. 65-69.

[99] Amsterdam, op. cit., p. 357; also see Bedau, op. cit., p. 98; Sellin, ibid. Another example of the suicide-murder syndrome is the case of Daniel Colwell, who, in October 1998, was sentenced to die in Georgia's electric chair. Colwell confessed that, unable to kill himself, he shot two strangers (Mitchell and Judith Bell) in a parking lot so that the state would help him commit suicide. Diagnosed as a paranoid schizophrenic, Colwell had been released from a mental health program just two days before he committed the 1996 murders, see "Georgia Killer Is Granted His Wish to be Executed," 1998. Still another example of the phenomenon is the case of John Blackwelder, who was executed in Florida on May 26, 2004. Blackwelder stated that he killed a fellow inmate so that he would get the death penalty because he couldn't stand the idea of spending the rest of his life in prison, and he could not commit suicide. Blackwelder was serving an LWOP sentence for a series of sex convictions. He was diagnosed as a pedophile who had impulse control disorder and anti-social personality disorder, see Word, 2004. Sellin remarks that such cases once must have been relatively frequent "because Denmark, by an ordinance of December 18, 1767, deliberately abandoned the death penalty in cases where 'melancholy and other dismal persons (committed murder) for the exclusive purpose of losing their lives'," see Sellin, ibid., p. 67. In some cases, the motivation for such actions was religious, explains Sellin: "by murdering another person and thereby being sentenced to death, one might still attain salvation whereas if one were to take one's own life, one would be plunged into eternal damnation," see Sellin, ibid.

[100] See Bedau, ibid.

[101] See Sellin, op. cit., p. 65.

[102] Leusner, 2006.

[103] Bowers, 1984, op. cit., p. 333.

[104] Ibid.

[105] Bowers and Pierce, 1980:481; also see Bailey, 1984a; Cochran et al., 1994, who found a brutalization effect for killings involving strangers; Thompson, 1997; Cochran and Chamlin, 2000; Shepherd, forthcoming. For the most sophisticated analysis to date to find a brutalization effect involving different types of murders, see Bailey, 1998.

[106] Bowers, 1984, op. cit., p. 274.

[107] Ibid.

[108] Ibid., p. 275.

[109] Van den Haag, op. cit., p. 328.

[110] For a review of the literature on the subject, see Surette, 1992:Chap. 5.

[111] Beccaria, op. cit., p. 50.

[112] Van den Haag, op. cit., pp. 327-328.

[113] Amsterdam, op. cit., p. 348.

[114] Ibid., pp. 348-349.

[115] Cited in Amsterdam, op. cit., pp 347-348. By contrast, prisoners in Japan are informed of their execution only moments before they are hanged. They are given only enough time to clean their cells, write a final letter, and receive last rites. Relatives are informed of the execution only after the fact. They are given 24 hours to claim the body. French, 2002.

[116] Turow, op. cit., p. 57. At the end of 2005, President Bush remained convinced that the death penalty deters, see "White House: Bush thinks," 2005.

[117] Philosopher Ernest Van den Haag claims that, beyond deterrence, capital punishment, or at least the threat of capital punishment, has some technical advantages that should not be overlooked:

> By threatening it, prosecutors may persuade accomplices to testify against murderers, or persuade the murderers themselves to plead guilty in exchange for a life sentence. Also, in a hostage situation police can promise the criminal that the prosecution will not ask for the death penalty if he releases his hostages. Without the death penalty the criminal can threaten to kill his victims, while police can only threaten incarceration. See Van den Haag, 1998:155.

[118] Bowers, op. cit., p. 164.

CHAPTER 6

Incapacitation and Economic Costs of Capital Punishment

Incapacitation and Capital Punishment

Incapacitation refers to preventing convicted murderers (or other capital offenders) from killing (or committing other crimes) again by executing them. Though it is arguably the most defensible of all rationales in support of the death penalty, the Supreme Court considers it only a secondary consideration.[1] Furthermore, only seven percent of recent supporters of capital punishment chose incapacitation—"They will repeat their crime/Keep them from repeating it"—as a reason for their support. The percentage of death penalty supporters to choose incapacitation dropped from 19 percent in 1991 to the seven percent in 2003. In both polls incapacitation ranked well below retribution at 50 percent.[2]

Are Executions Necessary? Death penalty opponents concede that capital punishment permanently removes a threat to society, but they question whether such a drastic measure is necessary. They argue that if an alternative penalty, such as life imprisonment without possibility of parole, accomplishes the same purpose, it would be preferable because of the other costs associated with the death penalty (e.g., a possible brutalizing effect, execution of innocent persons, etc.).

A key question, then, is whether the death penalty is necessary to protect society from the possible future actions of those who have already committed capital crimes. For proponents of the penalty, the answer to the question is a resounding yes. They argue that "some criminals are incorrigibly anti-social and will remain potentially dangerous to society for the rest of their lives."[3] They add that "mere imprisonment offers these people the possibility of escape or, in some cases, release on parole through error or oversight."[4] And even if they are never released, prisoners still may pose a threat to the victims' survivors or others. For example, while imprisoned challenging his conviction and death sentence, the murderer of a woman's husband sent her a threatening letter telling her that if she did not stop speaking to the media about him he would "take care of her," and he knew people on the outside who would do it for him.[5] Although inmate correspondence is supposed to be censored, apparently sometimes it is not.

Escapes, Errors, Oversights, and Other Mistakes. As for the possibility of escape, on July 28, 1980, four death row inmates disguised as guards escaped from Georgia's maximum-security prison at Reidsville. Among them was Troy Leon Gregg, the appellant in *Gregg v. Georgia* (1976). Gregg and the other three inmates escaped by using a hacksaw to cut the bars on their fourth-floor cells and a window in an exercise area. They then walked along the ledge of the building and gained access to fire escapes. The escapees had altered their prison-issue blue pajamas to look like guards' uniforms. On their way to the front gate, they were challenged by real guards but were allowed to continue on their way after saying they were making "security checks." Prison officials learned of the escape from a reporter for *The Albany Herald*, who Gregg had telephoned a couple hours later. Gregg told the reporter that they had to get out because they could not stand the inhuman conditions on death row anymore. He added that they would rather die than stay there another day. Three of the escapees were captured the next day in rural North Carolina. Gregg's body was found later that day in a lake a few miles away from where the other escapees were captured. Gregg had been beaten to death.[6] Another escape occurred on May 31, 1984. Six death-row inmates, who had murdered a total of 17 people, took 13 prison personnel hostage, put on the guards' uniforms and, using a fake bomb (actually a television set), bluffed their way out of Mecklenburg Correctional Center in Boydton, Virginia. All of the escapees—known collectively as the "Mecklenburg 6"—were recaptured without incident, the last of them after 19 days of freedom.[7] Death penalty proponents can also point to death-row inmate Martin Gurule, who escaped from the Texas prison in Huntsville in November 1998. Gurule was the first Texas death-row inmate to escape since 1934. Gurule and six other death-row inmates cut through a fence surrounding an outdoor recreation yard and climbed to a rooftop. Prison guards did not notice that the men were missing because they had created dummies out of pillows and sheets that made them appear to be asleep in their bunks. A guard noticed the men dropping from the rooftop about 12:20 a.m., immediately sounded an alarm, and fired as many as 20 rounds. When the shooting began, the six other inmates surrendered, but Gurule ran about 30 yards and scaled two ten-foot chainlink fences topped with rolled razor wire that rim the perimeter of the prison. Gurule was free for a week. His bloated corpse was found beneath a bridge about a mile from the prison. He probably drowned.[8] More recently, on November 3, 2005, convicted double murderer and death-row inmate Charles Victor Thompson escaped from the Harris County Jail in Houston, Texas. He was awaiting return to death row after attending a resentencing hearing on October 28, where he was again sentenced to death. After meeting with an attorney in a jail visiting room, Thompson put on civilian clothes that authorities believe he wore during his hearing and somehow smuggled back to his cell. Thompson left the locked prisoner's booth in the visiting room and waved a fake ID badge as he passed at least four jail employees. Thompson was then let into the jail's visitor's lobby, from which he walked out the door and into the street. He was captured without incident outside of a liquor store 200 miles away in Shreveport, Louisiana, on November 6. He was drunk and talking on a pay phone.[9] Troy Gregg and the other three Georgia death-row imates, the "Mecklenburg 6," Gurule, and Thompson show that a few death-row inmates have escaped.

As for release decisions made by parole-board members, it is ironic and perhaps somewhat hypocritical that parole authorities are distrusted because of decision errors they have made.[10] A similar distrust is not generally voiced about prosecutors who decide whom to charge with capital crimes, or with judges and juries who decide whether defendants charged with capital crimes are guilty and should be executed. Mistakes made by any of those decision makers can and have caused the deaths of innocent people. Attorney Anthony Amsterdam asks the pertinent question and supplies a thoughtful answer:

> Are we really going to kill a human being because we do not trust other people—the people whom we have chosen to serve on our own parole boards—to make a proper judgment in . . . [a] case at some future time? We trust this same parole board to make far more numerous, difficult, and dangerous decisions: hardly a week passes when they do not consider the cases of armed robbers, for example, although armed robbers are much, much more likely statistically to commit future murders than any murderer is to repeat his crime. But if we really do distrust the public agencies of law—if we fear that they may make mistakes—then surely that is a powerful argument 'against' capital punishment. Courts which hand out death sentences because they predict that a man will still be criminally dangerous 7 or 25 years in the future cannot conceivably make fewer mistakes than parole boards who release a prisoner after 7 or 25 years of close observation in prison have convinced them that he is reformed and no longer dangerous.[11]

As for mistakes made by courts in capital cases, remember that as a result of automatic appellate reviews, direct and discretionary appeals, collateral post–conviction proceedings in state and federal courts, and occasional gubernatorial commutations, nearly 100 death row inmates have their sentences vacated each year.[12] That represents between approximately 60 percent and 80 percent of the death sentences imposed each year (between 2001 and 2004).[13]

Why Not Execute All Capital Offenders? To ensure that no convicted capital offender killed again, all convicted capital offenders would have to be executed. There are several problems with such a strategy. First, as will be described in detail in the next chapter, innocent people, wrongfully convicted of capital crimes, have been executed. If all convicted capital offenders were executed to prevent any one of them from killing again, it would be impossible to rectify the injustices done to the innocent people executed, their families and friends, and to a society that considered such acts immoral. At least 400 Americans were wrongly convicted of crimes punishable by death in the twentieth century, and 123 Americans have been released from death row because of evidence of their innocence since 1973 (through March 2007),[14] and all of them would have died if this strategy were implemented.

To prevent such miscarriages of justice and still retain the death penalty it is necessary to identify convicted capital offenders who are innocent and spare them from death. This is no easy task because nearly all convicted capital offenders claim they are innocent, even though only a small percentage of them really are. Generally, it is only after considerable effort that proof of innocence is ever discovered, and rarely is such effort expended on death row inmates. For those family members and friends who would like to try, the financial and psychological resources necessary for such an endeavor are often not available.

Selecting the Very Worst. Some death penalty proponents argue that the chances of executing an innocent person could be greatly reduced if death eligibility were reserved for the "worst of the worst" among all those currently sentenced to die. The key issue, of course, is identifying the very worse. The Supreme Court has wrestled with this issue since it approved guided-discretion statutes in 1976 and, as noted previously, has limited the death penalty almost entirely to people convicted of an aggravated murder. At the same time, the response of many state legislatures and Congress has been to expand death eligibility by increasing the number of aggravating factors or death-eligible crimes.

Suppose, nevertheless, that death eligibility was narrowed to reduce the chances of executing an innocent person. For what type of offender, or, specifically, what type of murderer should capital punishment be reserved? Law Professor Robert Blecker has recently suggested a few ways to narrow death eligibility. His views are particularly interesting because they are based on the opinions of more than 100 imprisoned "street criminals" most of whom were murderers who he interviewed in a Virginia prison from 1986 to 1999.[15]

From his interviews, Professor Blecker, himself a qualified supporter of the death penalty, concludes that to narrow death eligibility death penalty statutes need to be revised to eliminate the overly broad aggravating factor that has put more people on death row than any other: murder during the course of a robbery. He would substitute in its stead the following three aggravating factors: killing an unresisting victim, killing from a pecuniary motive, and killing to eliminate an innocent witness. He would also modify a standard mitigating factor that he and the inmates he interviewed consider too broad: killing under the influence of alcohol or any other drug. He argues that "mitigation should be limited to a drug that significantly diminished the killer's mental capacity and self-control [such as crack and PCP], and then only if the killer was not aware while sober of the drug's probable effect on him and did not get high to summon the courage to kill."

The Constitution Project recommends limiting the death penalty to five types of murder: (1) the murder of a police officer while engaged in official duties; (2) murder in a correctional facility; (3) multiple murders; (4) murder involving torture; and (5) murder affecting the judicial system, such as the murder of witnesses, jurors, judges, prosecutors, or investigators.[16]

Such revisions to current death penalty statutes likely would reduce the number of people sentenced to death and, in turn, the chances of executing an innocent person. However, there are no changes or revisions that would eliminate entirely the chances of executing an innocent person. Such a risk is inherent in the process.

LWOP as an Alternative. An alternative to capital punishment, and one that eliminates entirely the possibility of executing an innocent person, is true life imprisonment without possibility of parole (LWOP). Ironically, neither death penalty opponents nor death penalty proponents are enthusiastic about LWOP. For many death penalty opponents, LWOP is the "lesser of two evils." It is endorsed only because it is a tolerable alternative to the death penalty.[17] Death penalty foe Henry Schwarzschild, former director of the American Civil Liberties Union Capital Punishment Project, described LWOP as "mindless," "humanly and economically wasteful," and "morally repellant in its very assumptions," and was willing to withhold his opposition to it only as "a reluctant gesture of legislative realism."[18] Opponents such as Joseph Ingle, a minister to death row inmates, believe that LWOP suffers from the same problem as the death penalty. Both penalties write off the offender as worthless and beyond redemption. Both penalties amount to human garbage disposal.[19] Professor Bedau, another death penalty opponent who considers LWOP a politically expedient "trade-off," would substitute for both LWOP and the death penalty "life imprisonment without the *probability* of parole." He would allow persons convicted of capital crimes to be sentenced to no more than 10 years in prison before they became eligible for parole. He would also require them to work in prison industry and give half of their pay to a victim's family fund. Bedau maintains the death penalty is unnecessary from a utilitarian perspective because there is no evidence that capital punishment has a marginal deterrent effect, and keeping most elderly offenders incarcerated is neither beneficial nor cost-effective.[20] Still, the availability of LWOP has reduced the number of death sentences sought and won. Prosecutors have used LWOP in plea negotiations as an inducement to get death-eligible defendants to plead guilty and avoid execution.[21]

For their part, proponents of capital punishment object to LWOP, claiming that "even if they [convicted capital offenders] are successfully imprisoned for life, prison itself is an environment presenting dangers to guards, inmates and others."[22] They argue that LWOP inmates, without the threat of the death penalty, would have nothing to lose if they killed in prison.

Available evidence suggests, however, that the threat posed by inmates serving life sentences is probably more imagined than real. Wardens and superintendents of correctional institutions in the United States have long held that "lifers are generally . . . among the best behaved prisoners,"[23] and Amsterdam relates that "Warden Lawes of Sing Sing [Prison] and Governor Wallace of Alabama, among others, regularly employed murder convicts as house servants because they were among the very safest of prisoners."[24] It is important to emphasize that this evidence may not apply to LWOP inmates because they have no hope of release (this is why Professor Sellin advises against LWOP sentences) nor to capital murderers—yet a recent study found that capital murderers sentenced to LWOP were no greater threat to other prisoners or correctional staff than death-sentenced inmates or other murderers sentenced to terms of imprisonment.[25]

The fact is that LWOP inmates do have something to lose if they kill or commit other infractions in prison. They have numerous privileges, which they could lose for violations. Among those privileges are visits from family and friends, access to mail and the telephone, being able to buy items from the commissary, being able to take educational and vocational classes, being able to participate in recreational activities, etc. They also can be removed from the general prison population and placed in isolation cells. Correctional authorities attest to the effectiveness that the threat of lost privileges has in controlling LWOP inmates: "[E]xperience with LWOP inmates in the Alabama penal system has shown that they commit about one-half as many infractions as other inmates."[26] LWOP inmates behave in prison because it is the only life they have. They become "institutionalized to the routines and limits of prison life."[27]

Another reason to recommend LWOP as an alternative to the death penalty is that some death-sentenced inmates rehabilitate themselves while in prison and contribute to society. For example, San Quentin death row inmate and Crips street gang co-founder Stanley "Tookie" Williams was nominated for the 2001 Nobel Peace Prize. Williams, who was convicted in 1981 for killing four people, was nominated for his series of children's books and his international peace efforts. His latest book, *Life in Prison*, describes daily life behind bars in San Quentin. It is targeted at sixth-graders and intended to keep them out of street gangs. His Internet Project for Street Peace links at-risk California and South African youths through e-mail and chat rooms. The project allows these youths to share their experiences and transform their lives.[28] In 2005, Williams received a "Presidential Call to Service Award" from President Bush for his more than 4,000 hours of community service.[29] In December 2005, Williams was executed.

Death penalty opponents claim that historically only a small number of imprisoned capital offenders have killed other inmates and prison personnel. Inmates not sentenced to death, they contend, commit most prison killings. The available evidence suggests that such a contention is only partially true (depending on what offenses are considered capital and what is considered a small number).

For example, Sellin examined fatal and nonfatal prison assaults that occurred in 1965,[30] reporting that 603 victims were assaulted in the 37 jurisdictions that responded to his survey. Sixty-one of the assault victims died—8 staff members and 53 inmates. There were 59 killers, and 34 percent of them were serving time for capital offenses (11 for murder, 6 for robbery, 1 for assault, 1 for rape, and 1 for kidnapping). At the time, all of the listed offenses were death-eligible in at least some jurisdictions; today, only aggravated murder is. If the crimes that currently are not death-eligible are excluded, the largest group of killers was inmates convicted of robbery, accounting for 32 percent of the total. The second largest group of killers, accounting for 27 percent of the total, was inmates convicted of murder (only 18 percent were convicted of capital murder). Therefore, even if convicted murderers do not account for the largest number of prison killings, at least in 1965 they did account for more than one in four of them (or about one in five if only capital murderers are included).

The problem with this knowledge, observes Sellin, is that it does not help in the prediction of which convicted murderers will kill in prison and which ones will not. Evidence shows that at least 90 percent of convicted capital offenders probably will not kill again. But to prevent all prison killings by convicted capital offenders, it would be necessary to execute all of them (before they could kill), even though that strategy would not have prevented nearly three out of every four of the prison killings in 1965.

The prediction problem has been addressed in a study of life-sentenced Texas capital murder defendants.[31] The study found that the likelihood of repeat murder by a life-sentenced Texas capital murder defendant was about 0.2 percent over a 40-year period. (Texas law at the time required capital murderers to serve at least 40 years of flat time before they become eligible for parole. Texas is now an LWOP state.) The likelihood of future assaultive behavior in general was approximately 16 percent. Six factors were significantly related to future violent behavior among the incarcerated murderers. Three of the factors were related to the circumstances of the offense and three factors were related to the characteristics of the offender. The offense factors were involvement in a robbery/burglary murder, the presence of multiple victims in the original offense, and a previously attempted murder or assault. The offender factors were prison gang membership, having served a prior prison term, and age at time of entering prison. The age factor was the most influential predictor of prison violence. The younger the inmate the higher was the risk of violence.

Another recent study examined the prison behavior of 39 former Indiana death row inmates who were transferred to the general prison population between 1972 and 1999 following modifications to their death sentences.[32] The average number of years served by the inmates was 16. During that period, 14 inmates (36 percent) were involved in 24 violent acts (3.8 per 100 inmates). Only seven of the violent acts caused serious injury. Six inmates committed them. There was one murder. About a quarter of the violent acts was committed on death row and about 20 percent, including the murder, occurred in the general prison population. As was the case in the previously described Texas study, the likelihood of prison violence decreased as the length of incarceration increased. Disciplinary records showed that more than 20 percent of the former death row inmates had no disciplinary write-ups following their transfer to the general prison population, and 60 percent had four or fewer disciplinary infractions. On the other hand, nearly 80 percent of the inmates had at least one disciplinary write-up while in the general prison population, and 40 percent had five or more disciplinary infractions. Not all former death-row inmates make model prisoners.

Another problem with LWOP as an alternative to capital punishment is that it is unnecessary for most convicted capital offenders who will not kill again, even if they are released from prison. Based on the 1953 Report of the Royal Commission on Capital Punishment, Appendix 15, for foreign countries; a study of parolees from Pennsylvania from 1914 to 1952; and a study of parolees from California from 1945 to 1954, Sellin stated, "It is generally agreed that those who are allowed to return to the community after serving a term of years for a capital crime, behave themselves better than do other criminals similarly released."[33] He elsewhere noted, "The conclusion seems inescapable that the murderer who is not executed but instead sentenced to life imprisonment is not nearly so great a danger to the prison community, nor to the outside world when he is paroled or pardoned, as are many other classes of prisoners, who are regularly released after serving much shorter periods of imprisonment."[34]

Other data support Sellin's conclusion. For example, Bedau reports that of 2,646 murderers released in 12 states between 1900 and 1977, only 88 (approximately 3 percent) were reincarcerated after conviction for a subsequent felony and only 16 (approximately .6 percent) were reincarcerated after conviction for committing a subsequent criminal homicide.[35] He also used data from the National Council on Crime and Delinquency's Uniform Parole Reports to show that, between 1965 and 1975, 11,404 inmates originally convicted of "willful homicide" were released from prison nationwide. One year after release, only 170 (approximately 1.5 percent) were reincarcerated after conviction for the commission of a subsequent felony and only 34 (approximately .3 percent) after conviction for the commission of a subsequent criminal homicide.[36]

Admittedly, there are problems with those data. A problem with the figures from the National Council on Crime and Delinquency is that they only cover one year after release—certainly too short a time to draw any definitive conclusions about the future risks of released murderers (the amount of time on release in the first study cited above was not mentioned). A more recent study with a longer follow–up period discovered that 8 (4.9 percent) of 164 paroled Georgia murderers committed subsequent murders within 91 months of release.[37] A second problem is that the data includes both capital and noncapital murderers. Without separating the two groups, it is impossible to know whether one group is a greater risk than the other of committing subsequent homicides. A third problem is that the data includes only those recidivists who were caught and convicted. The actual number of released capital offenders who kill again, though probably very small, is unknown.

The *Furman*–Commuted Inmates. The first and second problems just discussed can be meaningfully addressed, thanks to a natural experiment created by the Supreme Court in 1972. The *Furman* decision resulted in all death row inmates in the United States at that time having their sentences automatically commuted to life imprisonment *with* opportunity for parole. Some of those death row inmates have since been paroled. An examination of their post–release criminal behaviors can provide a relatively good measure of the risks posed by capital offenders who, but for the luck of *Furman*, might have been executed. Because each of the studies described below defines recidivism as reconviction or reincarceration, they share, with the previous data, the problem of not showing the proportion of subsequent killers who are not reconvicted or reincarcerated. Death penalty opponents assume the number is very small.

The 26 states that responded to a 1987 survey by the National Clearinghouse on Prisons and Jails reported 457 living *Furman*-commuted inmates, of whom 185 (40.6 percent) were paroled.[38] Eight parolees died during the 14-year period and are excluded from the following analysis, reducing the percentage of *Furman*-commuted inmates paroled to 38.7 percent. Only 35 (19.7 percent) of the paroled inmates recidivated (were reincarcerated). Of those who did recidivate, 3 (8.6 percent) had committed murder, and 8 (23 percent) had committed a violent crime (3 murders, 3 robberies, 1 rape, and 1 kidnapping). The largest number of parolees was returned to prison for parole violations (12 or 34.3 percent). Other parolees were reimprisoned for burglary (6 or 17.1 percent), drug offenses (5 or 14.2 percent), and other property offenses (4 or 11.4 percent). Also worthy of note is that 29 (16.4 percent) of the 177 paroled *Furman*-commuted inmates successfully completed their parole terms and regained (in applicable states) their civil rights.

Another study tracked down 558 of the *Furman*-commuted inmates and discovered that only about one percent of them murdered again. Conversely, more than 98 percent of them did not kill again either in prison or in the free community upon release.[39]

A third study examined the postrelease behavior of 28 *Furman*-commuted inmates in Texas over the 14-year period of 1973 to1986.[40] Only 7 (25 percent) of the 28 recidivated. The average time they spent in the community was 4.1 years. One of the parolees (3.6 percent) committed a murder; 4 of them (14 percent) committed felonies (1 murder, 1 rape, 2 burglaries); and 3 of them (11 percent) were reincarcerated for technical parole violations. The one recidivist murderer killed his girlfriend and then committed suicide within 12 months of his release from prison.

A fourth study focused on the experiences of the 23 *Furman*-commuted death row inmates in Kentucky, of whom 17 were paroled.[41] The average follow-up period was 42 months. None of the parolees was rearrested for a murder; only 2 (12 percent) were rearrested for violent crimes (robberies); and only 4 (24 percent) for any new crime (2 for robbery, 1 for burglary, and 1 for drug possession). In all, 35 percent of the parolees were rearrested, 29 percent were reconvicted and reimprisoned, and 6 percent were put in jail. One of the parolees (6 percent) obtained his final release from parole supervision and 11 (65 percent) had been placed on inactive supervision.

More recently, Texas executed Kenneth McDuff, who is believed to be the only murderer ever freed from death row and then returned to it after killing again. McDuff was executed in 1998 for the 1992 rape and killing of a young woman who he abducted from a convenience store. He originally was sent to death row in 1968 for the killing of three teenagers. He was a *Furman*-commuted inmate.[42]

Conclusion. Three arguments for the execution of all capital offenders are: (1) execution is the only way to guarantee they won't kill again, (2) life imprisonment provides opportunity for escape, parole, or additional murders, and (3) LWOP is costly.

The data just presented show that murderers, including capital murderers, do sometimes kill again even after having been imprisoned for many years, but the data also reveal that the number of such repeat killers is very small. A somewhat larger percentage of paroled death row inmates commit other offenses. However, most individuals are returned to prison for parole violations rather than for committing new crimes. Most convicted capital offenders will not kill again, even if they are released from prison, and a large majority of them will not be arrested for any new crimes.

For those who claim that life imprisonment provides the opportunity for escape or parole through error or oversight, or that life prisoners are a threat to other inmates and correctional personnel, Anthony Amsterdam responds, "You cannot tell me or believe that a society which is capable of putting a man on the moon is incapable of putting a man in prison, keeping him there, and keeping him from killing while he is there."[43]

Some people oppose LWOP because they believe it would be too costly; they assume that the death penalty is cheaper than LWOP. If they have in mind only the costs of the eventual execution, they are right, but if they consider the entire process of capital punishment, including trials, appeals, and executions, then they are wrong. The financial costs of capital punishment are the subject of the next section.

The Economic Costs of Capital Punishment versus Life Imprisonment[44]

One of the most common myths about capital punishment is that it is cheaper than alternative punishments such as life imprisonment without opportunity for parole. Political Science Professor John Culver claims, for example, that "the execution of an individual in his or her 30s is less expensive than maintaining that person in prison for 30 or more years until a natural death occurs."[45] In a recent Gallup poll, 20 percent of supporters of capital punishment selected as a reason for their support that it "save[d] taxpayers money/[c]ost associated with prison." It was the second most frequently selected reason behind retribution at 48 percent.[46]

The principal purpose of this section is to compare the economic costs of capital punishment with the economic costs of alternative punishments. Implicit in the analysis are comparisons of three types: (1) capital punishment versus an alternative punishment applied after a successful plea bargain, (2) capital punishment versus an alternative punishment imposed after a trial only, and (3) capital punishment versus an alternative punishment imposed after a trial and post-conviction review. Assuming the same alternative punishment, the comparisons are listed in descending order from largest to smallest cost differential. The first comparison reveals the largest cost differential because the costs of the alternative punishment do not include trial or post-conviction review expenses, all of which are invariably incurred in capital cases (unless post-conviction proceedings are waived). Also briefly discussed are past practices and their costs (which may help explain why some people believe in the myth), financial and other ramifications of recent efforts to streamline the process, the costs of mistakes, "start-up" costs for jurisdictions contemplating reinstatement of the death penalty, and some of the consequences if capital punishment were to be replaced with LWOP in the future.

Economic Costs of Capital Punishment under Pre–*Furman* Statutes. Prior to the *Furman* decision in 1972, the economic costs of capital punishment were not an issue. The death penalty was not an expensive punishment relative to LWOP because capital cases were disposed of quickly, no extraordinary procedures were followed, reversals were relatively rare, and the costs associated with executions alone were minimal. Regarding the relatively quick disposal of capital cases, in 1934, for example, Doc Williams was executed in Florida 33 days following his apprehension and only 45 days after the crime was committed.[47] Data from 1956 to 1960 show that the average time between death sentence and execution was 14.4 months; however, by year-end 2005, the average had risen to 147 months.[48] A primary reason for the 921 percent increase in time between sentence and execution in capital cases is the super due process now required by the Supreme Court's "death is different" doctrine.[49] Super due process, as noted previously, refers to the unique procedural safeguards afforded people charged with capital crimes. Those safeguards apply primarily to the trial and post-conviction stages of the process.

Economic Costs of Capital Punishment under Post–*Furman* Statutes. Although the actual death-causing procedure may be relatively inexpensive, the process of getting to that point is quite costly under post-*Furman* statutes. The Supreme Court requires that defendants charged with capital crimes be provided with super due process, and super due process is expensive. Below are some recent estimates of the economic costs of capital punishment.

- The average cost of California's 11 executions during the past 27 years was about $2.3 million, and the death penalty costs California taxpayers $114 million annually.[50]

- New Jersey's death penalty cost taxpayers at least $253 million since 1983, approximately $11 million a year, even though New Jersey has not executed anyone during that period. The $253 million is "over and above the costs that would have been incurred had the state utilized a sentence of life without parole instead of death." Since 1982 and through the end of 2005, New Jersey had conducted 197 capital trials and had imposed 60 death sentences, of which 50 were reversed. At the end of 2004, it was estimated that it took $2.3 million to $3.2 million to pursue a death prosecution in New Jersey.[51]

- Indiana taxpayers spent an average of $741,000 over 16 years to execute a 30-year-old capital offender. The figure includes jails costs, prosecutor's and defender's fees from murder trial through appeals, and execution costs. It cost $622,000 to lock up the same person for life, estimated to be 47 years in prison. That includes appeals and health care costs. It cost $506,000 to imprison a person for 65 years with a 50 percent reduction for good behavior.[52]

- In the state of Washington between 1993 and 2003, a death penalty trial cost, on average, $432,000. That was more than twice as much as the average $153,000 cost of a non-death penalty trial.[53]

- The average cost of a death penalty case in Kansas was $1.2 million. A life-without-parole sentence could save Kansas taxpayers between $400,000 and $500,000 per trial.[54]

The average cost per execution in the United States (that is, the entire process) is estimated to range from about $2.5 million to $5 million (in 2000 dollars).[55] Extraordinary cases can cost much more. The state of Florida, for example, reportedly spent $10 million to execute serial murderer Ted Bundy in 1989.[56] Orange County, California spent more than $10 million just to convict serial killer Randy Kraft the same year. (At this writing, Kraft remains on California's death row.)[57] As noted in Chapter 3, the federal government spent more than $100 million to execute mass murderer Timothy McVeigh in 2001.

If an inmate sentenced to LWOP lives 31 years,[58] and the average annual cost of imprisonment for the first 21 years is about $23,400 per inmate, and the average annual cost of imprisonment for the last 10 years is $70,000 per inmate,[59] then the cost of that LWOP sentence is roughly $1 million (assuming the LWOP sentence was the result of a successful plea bargain), making capital punishment, on average, two and one-half to five times more expensive than LWOP imposed as a result of plea bargaining. If the LWOP sentence is imposed after a trial and includes other post–conviction proceedings, then the difference will be much smaller. Nevertheless, the costs of a death sentence will probably always be more expensive than the costs of an LWOP sentence because super due process is required only in capital cases.[60] In North Carolina, for example, the cost differential between a capital case culminating in an execution and a noncapital case resulting in a 20-year sentence has been estimated to be between $163,000 and more than $216,000.[61] Another consideration, as Richard Dieter, Executive Director of the Death Penalty Information Center, points out, is that "death penalty costs are accrued upfront, especially at trial and for the early appeals, while life-in-prison costs are spread out over many decades." "A million dollars spent today," Dieter notes, "is a lot more costly to the state than a million dollars that can be paid gradually over 40 years."[62]

Why is super due process so expensive? That question is answered in the next sections. It must be emphasized that many of the costs reported are estimates, that there can be great variation in the costs of specific services among different jurisdictions, that cost estimates are not available for every part of the process, and that not every cost or part of the process occurs in every case. Some costs can be duplicated when retrials or resentencings follow the vacation of a conviction or capital sentence on appeal or during the post-conviction review process.

It should also be remembered that whenever a capital trial does not result in a death sentence and execution, the added costs associated with the death penalty process have been incurred without any "return" on the state's investment of resources. In other words, the enormous costs of capital punishment are not a product of the number of executions but rather the number of people death penalty jurisdictions attempt to execute.[63] This last point is an especially important one because, as Professor Jon Sorensen argues, the high costs of capital punishment, such as the $11 million a year New Jersey spends on the sanction despite no executions, can be explained at least in part by the large number of capital trials that do not result in executions. Sorensen maintains that if 50 percent of death penalty trials produced executions, the cost savings of LWOP would "wash out" and capital punishment would be "cost effective."[64] Whether Sorensen is right about this, the fact remains that the number of capital trials that produce executions is currently decreasing not increasing.[65]

One final introductory point is that the death penalty's availability creates a pressure to seek it that is difficult to resist and would not exist in its absence. As Professor Herbert Haines explains:

> How is a prosecutor to explain to [a] grieving family why she decided to seek death for another accused murderer but not for the killer of their loved one? How is she to apply it sparingly, knowing that her opponent in some future election will accuse her of being soft on criminals? Elected officials striving to appear moderate sometimes call for limited death

penalty laws intended only for the "worst of the worst" killers. But limited death penalties beg to be expanded, especially in election years. Capital punishment, then, often seems to have a built-in momentum that demands that it be used and drives up its cost.[66]

The following analysis is divided into five general stages of the capital punishment process: (1) pretrial, (2) trial, (3) posttrial, (4) imprisonment, and (5) execution.

The Pretrial Stage. The costs of capital punishment begin to mount soon after a potentially capital crime (in most cases, an aggravated murder) has been reported to the police. The investigation of potentially capital crimes tends to be more rigorous than the investigation of other felonies. When the crime may be a capital offense, forensic experts examine the crime scene more carefully, and this greater attention and time result in an added but unknown cost.[67]

Investigation of the case frequently continues through trial and can last several years.[68] The investigation of potentially capital crimes has been estimated to take three to five times longer than for other felonies, primarily because the prosecution as well as the defense must prepare for both stages of the bifurcated trial—the guilt and penalty phases.[69] Because defense counsel can present any relevant mitigating evidence during the penalty phase of a capital trial (see *Lockett v. Ohio*, 1978), a thorough investigation of possible mitigators is time–consuming and expensive. Investigators working for the state of North Carolina were paid $22.16 per hour in 1991-92.[70] In 2002, the District Attorney's Office in Fulton County, Georgia spent an additional $43,000 on overtime for investigators in a single case.[71] Experienced private investigators, who frequently are hired by the defense, are paid between $75 and $200 an hour.[72] In 2003, investigation costs for death-sentence cases in Kansas were found to be about 3 times greater than for non-death cases.[73]

Once a suspect has been identified and arrested, a bond hearing is held. The costs of those processes probably do not differ greatly for potentially capital crimes and other serious felonies, but estimates of the costs have not been reported. If bond is denied, however, and the suspect is incarcerated—which is nearly always more likely with potentially capital crimes—then additional costs will be incurred as a result of the tighter security that will be provided through the entire process.[74] There are no estimates for those extra security costs, either.

If the prosecutor believes that there is evidence to convict the suspect of the crime, and the crime is an aggravated murder (or other capital offense), then the prosecutor will seek an indictment for capital murder in jurisdictions that employ grand juries.[75] In those jurisdictions that do not use grand juries, formal charges are filed through an information. The costs of each capital indictment are believed to be "enormous" (though no dollar figure has been cited) because each indictment must be prepared, even though only about 20 percent of them will reach trial.[76]

The most expensive part of the pretrial process frequently involves the motions filed in death penalty cases. Defense counsel has both a professional and an ethical obligation to represent his or her client's interests by filing nonfrivolous motions which, at a minimum, create and preserve the defendant's record for appeal.[77] Extensive amounts of time can be devoted to researching and writing pretrial motions. The prosecution must respond to the motions as well as prepare and file its own. In North Carolina, at least 34 different motions have been made in capital litigation, not to mention 11 more motions made during the penalty phase of the trial.[78] Those motions are in addition to the more standard ones that are frequently filed by both sides in other felony cases.[79] Typical motions filed in capital cases involve voir dire, jury composition, death qualification process challenges, change of venue, and challenges to the death penalty's constitutionality in general and to the state's death penalty statute in particular.[80] It is estimated that two to six times more motions are filed in death penalty cases than in other felony cases.[81] Between five and seven motions typically have been filed in noncapital cases in New York.[82] In a single North Carolina capital case in 1991, the cost of pretrial motions was $115,247.[83]

A big part of the expense of motions is the cost of experts who are paid for their research/consulting and for their testimony at trial. Both the defense and the prosecution employ experts. Among the experts used in capital cases are: (1) psychiatrists, who have been paid $100 to $150 an hour or $500 to $1,000 a day;[84] (2) medical examiners, who have been paid $700 to $1,000 a day;[85] (3) polygraph experts, who have been paid $200 to $300 a day for courtroom testimony and $150 to $250 per examination;[86] (4) experts on eyewitness identification, who have been paid about $100 an hour or about $500 a day for courtroom testimony;[87] and (5) forensic scientists, juristic psychologists, and criminologists, who (in 1996) were paid a maximum of about $130 an hour in Florida (Orange County) unless special circumstances existed.[88] Defense expert witnesses alone can easily cost more than $40,000 in capital cases.[89]

The Trial Stage. Approximately 95 percent of criminal cases never reach trial, but instead are resolved through plea bargaining. Capital cases are an exception; they are rarely plea bargained.[90] Because "death is different," death penalty cases go to trial 10 times more often than do other felony cases.[91]

The most striking difference between a capital trial and trials for other serious felonies is that capital trials are bifurcated, that is, divided into two separate stages: a guilt phase and a penalty phase. In bifurcated trials, all of the expenses of the guilt phase can possibly be duplicated in the penalty phase.[92] In 2003, trial costs for death-penalty cases in Kansas were about 16 times greater than for non-death penalty cases. The average death penalty trial cost about $508,000, while the average trial in a non-death penalty case cost about $32,000. Trials involving a death sentence averaged 34 days, including jury selection; non-death penalty trials averaged about 9 days.[93] An average capital trial in California in 1983 was about 3.5 times or 30 days longer than an average noncapital murder trial, which required approximately 12 days.[94] A 1999 capital murder trial in Suffolk County, New York cost 3.5 times what it would have cost had the death penalty not been sought.[95] The average death penalty trial in Texas in 1992 lasted 14 weeks and cost $265,640.[96] The average death penalty trial in North Carolina in 1991–92 lasted 14.6 days and cost $84,099,[97] with the range being a low of $24,777 and a high of $179,736.[98] By contrast, the average noncapital murder trial in North Carolina lasted 3.8 days and cost $16,697,[99] with a range of $7,766 to $30,952.[100] The cost difference in a death penalty murder trial compared to a non-death penalty murder trial in Harris County, Texas, in 2005, was estimated to be $57,000.[101]

The guilt phase of the bifurcated capital trial in North Carolina was considerably more expensive than the penalty phase. The costs of the guilt phase ranged from $9,802 to $137,500; the average guilt phase cost $52,290 and lasted 10.6 days.[102] The guilt phase, in other words, accounted for about 62 percent of the costs and 73 percent of the time spent on the entire trial. The cost of a capital trial's guilt phase in North Carolina may be atypical, however. Paternoster claims that the penalty phase, and not the guilt phase, is "the single greatest cost inflator of a capital trial."[103] He explains that in most capital trials, the prosecutor's overwhelming evidence makes the defendant's guilt obvious, so there is little to contest. Law Professor David Dow corroborates Paternoster's explanation by noting that during the 1990s, 99 percent of capital murder defendants in Houston, Dallas, and San Antonio were convicted; the conviction rate in Virginia, Alabama, Mississippi, and Louisiana ranged from more than 75 percent to more than 90 percent; and the conviction rate in Florida and California exceeded well over 50 percent.[104] Consequently, defense counsel focuses on saving his or her client's life in the penalty phase of the trial. To aid the effort, counsel is allowed to present mitigating evidence on his or her client's behalf, which requires a considerable, but unknown amount of time.

Among the specific costs of the guilt phase of a capital trial are voir dire, attorney hours, expert testimony, witnesses, and court costs. Most of those expenses involve payments for time expended on the case. However, in a 2002 case conducted in Fulton County, Georgia, the District Attorney's Office spent about $34,000 for equipment, graphic design for court exhibits, and expert testimony.[105] Many prosecutors and defense attorneys believe that jury selection is the key element in a capital case. As an Erie County, New York, district attorney observed, "All you have to do is find one person that doesn't want to go for the death penalty, and you've defeated it."[106] It is estimated that voir dire during the selection of the jury takes five times longer in capital cases than in other felony cases[107] and, in 1985, increased the cost of a capital trial by nearly $90,000.[108] Jury selection in capital cases typically takes six weeks to complete and can take longer than the guilt phase of the trial.[109] In two capital cases in New York, jury selection took ten weeks in the first case and seven weeks in the second case.[110] The average cost of empaneling a jury in capital cases in Texas in 1992 was $17,220.[111] A survey of 20 California capital murder trials conducted in the early 1980s found that jury selection was the most expensive part of a capital trial.[112]

A major reason voir dire in capital cases is so costly is that many death penalty jurisdictions require that jurors not only be questioned individually, but that they also remain sequestered until the full jury is selected or until they are dismissed.[113] In a recent case in Fulton County, Georgia, selecting and sequestering the jury cost $87,000, which included $63,600 for hotel rooms, dinners and drinks for jurors; $6,000 for juror lunches and beverages; $2,500 for juror transportation; $765 for entertainment expenses; and $14,300 to copy the questionnaires used to select the jury. The amount did not include the overtime paid to sheriff's deputies who guarded the jury and the court.[114] Many jurisdictions allow defendants to waive the individual questioning and sequestering of jurors requirements. Although data on the frequency of such waivers are not available, they are probably not requested very often. Other reasons that voir dire in capital cases takes longer and is more expensive are: (1) the increased number of peremptory challenges allowed in capital cases,[115] (2) the increased number of jurors who are likely to be dismissed for cause,[116] (3) the increased number of jurors who try to disqualify themselves,[117] and (4) in some jurisdictions, the need to select jurors for both the guilt and penalty phase of the trial.[118]

Many states require that capital defendants have two attorneys; no state requires two attorneys in noncapital cases.[119] Attorneys can spend from 300 to 1,000 hours on capital cases.[120] In North Carolina in 1991–92, for example, defense attorneys and prosecutors spent an average of 613 and 282 hours, respectively, on capital cases.[121] By contrast, they spent an average of 150 and 61 hours, respectively, on noncapital cases.[122] The demands of capital cases can be so great; they can devastate an attorney's regular practice.[123]

In the early 1990s, public defenders in North Carolina were paid an average of $68.31 an hour; assistant public defenders received an average of $48.34 an hour.[124] District attorneys, on the other hand, were paid an average of $83.10 an hour and assistant district attorneys received an average of $55.63 an hour.[125] Based on those hourly rates, the average cost of a public defender in North Carolina capital cases in 1991–92 was about $42,000 per case; the average cost of an assistant district attorney (assuming most capital cases are handled by ADAs) was about $16,000 per case (it would be about $23,000 if handled by a DA).[126] In 2002, the Fulton County, Georgia district attorney assigned four prosecutors to a capital case. Not including time spent preparing for the case, the prosecutors' salaries exceeded $74,000 for the two months of trial and jury selection.[127]

The cost of defense counsel through sentencing in Maryland in 1982 was estimated to range from $50,000 to $75,000 per capital case.[128] In 2002, Fulton County, Georgia paid a defense attorney in a capital case $164,000 in fees and expenses.[129] In 1993, the Connecticut Public Defender's Office spent $138 to defend an average noncapital case (this included plea bargains) and approximately $200,000 to defend each death penalty case.[130] Private defense fees in a California capital trial involving three defendants cost the state $1.1 million.[131] Florida increased its fees for appointed defense attorneys in capital cases in January 1998. The hourly rate for the lead attorney was raised from $50 to $120, while assisting attorneys may receive as much as $100 an hour.[132] Florida also set a $3500 cap on the amount it would pay for defense services in capital cases.[133] Some states pay less. For example, in the 1990s, court-appointed attorneys in Alabama were being paid only $20 an hour for out–of–court time in capital cases, with a limit of $2,000 per case; Mississippi was limiting payment to $1,000 a case.[134] In 2005, Alabama paid on average $20,416 for the defense of indigents charged with capital crimes, which included the costs of two defense attorneys, an investigator, and a mitigation specialist. That $20,416 average was about 16 times as much as the $1,300 average Alabama paid for indigent defense in class-A felony cases. Since 2000, Alabama taxpayers have paid more than $14 million to defend people charged with capital murder.[135] From 1995 through 1999, the New York Capital Defender's Office spent more than $34 million on 37 defendants charged with capital crimes. The costs included the Defender Office's annual budget and money paid to court-appointed defense attorneys, defense investigators, and defense experts. For fiscal year 1999, $14.75 million was allocated for capital defense costs.[136] In 1998, defense expenses in three capital cases cost Indiana taxpayers more than $2 million.[137] In two recent capital cases in New York, defense expenditures were nearly $600,000 and $900,000, respectively. The district attorneys in those cases spent nearly $800,000 and $750,000, respectively.[138] In the capital prosecutions of John Muhammad and Lee Boyd Malvo in Virginia, it was reported that Muhammad's attorneys were paid $790,726 and Malvo's attorneys, more than $781,000 for their work and expenses. The costs did not include appeals.[139] The federal government spent $13.8 million in public funds to hire private attorneys and cover other costs to defend Timothy McVeigh.[140]

The hourly or daily rates of expert witnesses for in-court testimony were described previously and are not repeated here.

A larger number of witnesses are usually called in capital trials. Those witnesses must be interviewed, their testimony must be prepared, and the other side must depose them. All of this requires considerable attorney time. Total costs for two defense attorneys, three prosecutors, investigators, and expert witnesses in capital cases in Texas in 1992 averaged $150,452 ($112,400 for the two defense attorneys, investigators, and expert witnesses and $38,052 for the three prosecutors).[141]

Court costs are estimated to be 3.5 times greater in capital cases than they are in other felony cases.[142] In North Carolina in 1991–92, superior court judges were paid an average of $631 a day; court reporters, an average of $191 a day; deputy court clerks, $146 a day; and bailiffs, $125 a day.[143] Two bailiffs were generally assigned to each capital trial.[144] In Texas in 1992, the average cost per judge in a capital case was $23,968.[145] Courtroom space in North Carolina was estimated to cost $174 a day.[146] In sum, the total per day cost of a capital trial in a North Carolina Superior Court in 1991–92 was estimated to be $1,416; the cost of a capital trial per day in California in 1983 was approximately $2,186, not including extra security or transcript costs.[147] In 1999, a criminal court case in New York City cost about $3,800 per day. At that rate, court costs in two death penalty cases in Queens totaled approximately $725,000. In Suffolk County, where the daily rate was $3,556, the court costs in one capital case were almost $650,000.[148]

As mentioned earlier, all of the expenses of the guilt phase could be duplicated in the penalty phase. The penalty phase will require, at a minimum, additional expenditures for attorney time, expert testimony, witnesses, and court costs.[149] Some jurisdictions require separate juries for the penalty phase of a capital trial, in which case the costs of voir dire also could be duplicated.

Capital trials can force local governments to make difficult choices. For example, a recent study in Illinois found that capital trials could increase county spending by as much as 1.8 percent per trial. Such trials are often financed through increased property taxes or funds taken from police and highway appropriations.[150] A *Wall Street Journal* article reported that the Texas county where the three men convicted of the 1998 murder of James Byrd were tried was forced to raise property taxes 6.7 percent for two years to cover trial costs.[151] During the early 1990s, two capital trials in Jefferson County, Florida caused the county to put a freeze on employee raises and cut the library budget by 20 percent.[152] Some counties have almost been bankrupted by capital trial costs.[153] County officials in Kentucky and Georgia have been jailed for contempt because they refused to provide funding for expert defense testimony in capital cases.[154] In some death-eligible cases, prosecutors forego capital trials altogether rather than incur the expense. Some defense attorneys have used the high costs of capital trials as leverage when negotiating a plea deal for their clients.[155] The costs of capital punishment are thus a source of its arbitrary and discriminatory application (discussed in Chapter 8). Counties that can afford it may seek the death penalty in all cases that warrant it, while "poor" counties may have to pick and choose among death-eligible cases, pursuing the death penalty in only some cases or not at all. "Poor" counties simply may not be able to afford the death penalty.[156]

The Posttrial Stage. At least one authority believes the posttrial stage generally is the most expensive part of the entire process.[157] However, a 2003 report from Kansas found that pre-trial and trial expenses accounted for 49 percent of the total costs, appeals accounted for 29 percent of the total, and the remaining 22 percent goes for incarceration and execution costs.[158] Automatic appeal of conviction and/or death sentence to the state supreme court is required in nearly all jurisdictions with capital punishment statutes.[159] If the appellant wins, the costs of the original trial, or at least part of those costs, could be replicated at the retrial or resentencing.[160]

In 2003, appeals in Kansas death penalty cases were 21 times more expensive than appeals in non-death penalty cases.[161] It is estimated that a typical capital appeal requires from 500 to 2,000 hours of attorney time, not including travel, photocopying, etc.[162] In North Carolina in 1991–92, appellate defenders received an average of $61.89 an hour; assistant appellate defenders were paid an average of $43.80 an hour.[163] Appointed appellate defense attorneys in California received an average of $60 per hour in 1985.[164] North Carolina Supreme Court justices were paid an average of $96.92 an hour, while their law clerks received an average of $28.02 an hour.[165] The average cost of a North Carolina Supreme Court justice for a capital appeal was estimated to be $1,887; the average cost of a court clerk was $2,083.[166] The average cost of the North Carolina attorney general for a capital appeal was estimated to be $5,261.[167]

Some states also provide proportionality review, although the Supreme Court does not require it (see *Pulley v. Harris,* 1984). Proportionality review is a process whereby state appellate courts compare the sentence in the case being reviewed with sentences imposed in similar cases in the state.[168] Its purpose is to identify disparities in sentencing. To perform proportionality review, data must be gathered and analyzed, and a report must be written. In 2006, the New Jersey Administrative Office of the Courts estimated that each proportionality review costs an average of $93,018 in additional salary costs for court staff.[169] Many death penalty states do not conduct proportionality reviews because of the expense.

Besides the automatic appellate review, capital defendants may contest their conviction and/or sentence through both state and federal post–conviction proceedings. Including the automatic appeal, there are at least nine or ten possible levels of review following the guilt and penalty phase of a capital trial.[170] The average cost of the state post-conviction process for capital cases in Texas in 1992 was $94,240,[171] the biggest expense being for attorney time. The U.S. Constitution does not require the appointment of attorneys for indigent capital defendants beyond the automatic appeal, that is, for state post-conviction collateral review (see *Murray v. Giarratano,* 1989), but many jurisdictions provide them anyway.[172] It has been estimated that attorneys spend an average of 700 to 1,000 hours on state post-conviction proceedings in capital cases.[173] A 1986 American Bar Association survey found that lawyers spent an average of 963 hours on state post-conviction appeals.[174] Specific cost averages in Texas were as follows:

1. defense costs = $15,000,

2. prosecution costs = $29,000,

3. cost of reproducing the trial record[175] = $20,000, and

4. court of criminal appeals (three-day estimate) = $30,240.[176]

The cost of state post-conviction proceedings in two North Carolina cases was considerably higher—$293,393 and $216,387 per case—although that may be due to the inclusion of stages such as clemency/commutation proceedings not included in the Texas costs.[177] Specific costs in the more expensive North Carolina case included the following (years in which expenses were incurred are in parentheses):

1. state motion for appropriate relief = $29,957 (1985-87),

2. petition for certiorari to North Carolina Supreme Court = $6,188 (1987-88),

3. state motion hearing = $2,057 (1988),

4. motion for stay of execution in North Carolina Supreme Court = $833 (1989),

5. motions in North Carolina Supreme Court = $3,642 (1990),

6. motions in North Carolina Superior Court = $115,247 (1991), and

7. clemency/commutation proceedings = $84,888 (1991-92).[178]

Federal post-conviction proceedings for Texas capital appellants averaged six years and cost about $1.7 million per appellant.[176] Unlike the situation for state post-conviction proceedings, the federal government requires legal representation for capital defendants pursuing federal habeas corpus appeals.[180] The federal courts have (or had) three options in meeting this statutory requirement.[181] First, they may appoint attorneys from the private bar. Those attorneys submit vouchers for payment to the Administrative Office of the United States Courts, which allocates funds according to provisions in the Criminal Justice Act (1994).[182] Although the act does not prescribe any limitation on the amount that can be paid for services, in *In re Berger* (1991), the Court limited appointed counsel representing capital defendants before the Supreme Court to $5,000 in fees. A second option is to appoint attorneys employed by federal public defender organizations, which are funded through grants made available by the Judicial Conference of the United States.[183] A problem with these first two options is that neither one guarantees the appointment of attorneys with expertise in capital jurisprudence.[184]

The third and best option (for capital defendants) was the appointment of attorneys employed by Post-Conviction Defender Organizations (PCDOs), which were originally called Death Penalty Resource Centers. Congress created those agencies in 1988.[185] They dealt only with capital cases and related post-conviction issues and employed full-time, salaried attorneys, investigators, and support staff.[186] In the mid-1990s, they operated in 20 of the then-38 death penalty states.[187] The Judicial Conference funded PCDOs through grants that were contingent upon the receipt of state funding for any state court work PCDOs did. In fiscal year 1994, the 20 PCDOs received nearly $20 million for their work on capital cases.[188]

Because of the success of PCDO attorneys in getting convictions and death sentences overturned, the agencies came under fire from death penalty proponents, who won the day. On January 6, 1996, President Clinton signed into law HR-1358 (Pub. L. No. 104-91, 110 Stat. 7). The law provided a budget of approximately $262 million for the Federal Judiciary's Defender Services but stipulated that none of the money was to be spent on PCDOs after April 1, 1996—to allow for an orderly end to the program.[189] After the 1996 fiscal year ended on September 30, no further federal funding of the PCDOs was to be provided.[190]

With the demise of PCDOs, the federal courts are left with only the first two options of providing attorneys for capital defendants pursuing federal habeas corpus relief. The debate in Congress suggested that the abolition of PCDOs would save the government about $20 million annually,[191] but the Chief Judge of the U.S. Court of Appeals for the Eighth Circuit, Richard Arnold, disagrees. He predicts "that elimination of the PCDOs will significantly increase delays in handling an ever-increasing death penalty caseload by creating an insufficient pool of qualified and experienced attorneys to handle the petitions."[192] He estimates that "the cost of representing death row inmates would rise from the current expenditure of $21.2 million to 'between $37 million and $51.1 million' with the elimination of the PCDOs."[193]

It has been estimated that attorneys in capital cases spend an average of 700 to more than 1,000 hours on federal post-conviction proceedings.[194] The 1986 American Bar Association survey found that lawyers spent an average of 1,037 hours on federal post-conviction litigation.[195] In Texas, defense attorneys received an average of $92,300 for their federal post-conviction work in capital cases, while it cost the Texas attorney general's office an average of $19,600 per capital case challenged on federal habeas corpus.[196] The remainder of the estimated $1.7 million per federal post-conviction capital case went for court costs and outlays.[197]

Cost estimates of federal post-conviction proceedings for North Carolina capital prisoners included the following (years on which estimates are based are in parentheses):

1. *certiorari* petition to the U.S. Supreme Court = $7,885 (1984),

2. motion for stay of execution in the federal district court = $757 (1989),

3. federal district court habeas proceedings = $17,383 (1989-90), and

4. federal appellate proceedings = $24,556 (1990-92).[198]

Imprisonment. Under current practices, convicted capital offenders serve a long prison term on death row (now averaging more than 10 years), in addition to being sentenced to death.[199] Put somewhat differently, because of super due process protections, capital offenders typically serve more than 20 percent of what otherwise might be a 50-year-LWOP sentence before they are executed.

It almost certainly is more expensive to house inmates on death row than to confine them with the general population in a maximum-security prison.[200] Reasons are added security precautions, which include single cell confinement. Although one source suggests that the difference in the annual costs of confinement is not great—approximately $1,000 to $2,000 per inmate, in 2005, it cost the state of Florida $26,422 to house an inmate on death row, and $18,108 to house an inmate in a major prison—a more than $8,300 difference. The difference in Texas was about $7,600, $22,477 on death row (in 2002) compared to $14,877 (in 2005) in the general population of a maximum-security prison. In 2005, it reportedly cost California about $90,000 more a year to house an inmate on death row than in the general prison population.[201] In 2006, the New Jersey Department of Corrections estimated that the state would save between $974,430 and $1,299,240 per inmate over each inmate's lifetime, if it were to abolish the death penalty. The Department's figures were based on an annual cost of $72,602 to house an inmate on New Jersey's death row versus an annual cost of $40,121 to house an inmate in the general population of New Jersey's maximum-security prison. It was estimated that a life sentence would be 30 to 40 years.[202] An additional and unique cost of confinement for death row inmates involves the death watch—the period just before the execution, generally 24 hours, when the condemned inmate is watched by the guards who will also take part in the execution process.[203] The extra costs of the death watch have not been estimated.

Execution. Executions themselves are fairly inexpensive, regardless of the method employed. The electricity needed for an electrocution costs about 31 cents; the sodium cyanide pellets used in executions by lethal gas were about $250; and the chemicals needed for a lethal injection cost anywhere from $71.50 to $700.[204] At the end of 2003, the cost of the drugs used in Texas executions was $86.08.[205] The prices of the bullets and rope used in shooting and hanging executions have not been reported, but must be minimal. The costs of the execution apparatuses also vary considerably and are not very expensive when averaged over a large number of executions. An electrocution system was about $35,000; the cost of a gallows, about $85,000; a gas chamber was around $200,000; and a lethal injection system was around $30,000. These costs do not include payments to the "execution technicians," which may range from $150 to $500 per execution.[206]

One last cost of capital punishment involves disposal of the body—a potential cost for any inmate who dies in prison. If the family of the executed offender does not make final arrangements, burial or cremation is left to the state. This final cost has not been estimated, but it is unlikely to be very expensive.

Streamlining the Appellate and Post–Conviction Process. Proponents of capital punishment argue that the costs of the penalty could be reduced significantly if the appellate and post–conviction process were streamlined. They contend that most of the legal challenges filed by death row inmates or their attorneys are without merit—that they are nothing more than desperate attempts to keep the inmate alive. The evidence presented in Chapter 2, however, shows that many of the habeas corpus petitions filed by death row inmates or their attorneys do have merit. Nevertheless, it is true that, until recently, it was possible for death row inmates to employ the dual system of collateral review numerous times, but this is no longer the case. The Supreme Court began placing restrictions on the federal review process in state capital cases in the 1980s.[207]

In addition, as explained in Chapter 3, the passage of the Antiterrorism and Effective Death Penalty Act of 1996 (and similar measures by state legislatures) has made access to both the federal and state courts during the post-conviction process more difficult. However, while the recent restrictions on federal *habeas corpus* in capital cases may reduce costs at the federal level, they may not reduce costs overall. Costs likely will be shifted to the states and counties where post-conviction motions in state courts will be litigated more extensively.[208]

The Costs of Mistakes. Mistakes made in capital cases (see Chapter 7) can add another monetary cost to the process. For example, Freddie Lee Pitts and Wilbert Lee were pardoned in Florida in 1975 after spending 12 years apiece on death row for a murder that somebody else committed.[209] In 1997, after years of failed efforts, Pitts and Lee received a few hundred thousand dollars each as compensation from the state for its mistakes. Bobby Joe Leaster, received a check from Massachusetts for $75,000 in 1992. The money was the first installment of the $1 million annuity the state pays him for wrongly imprisoning him for 15 years for a murder he did not commit.[210] Leaster was released from prison in 1986 after prosecutors declined to pursue a retrial. Because of the state's fiscal problems, it took several attempts before Massachusett's legislators approved the indemnification measure. The Ford Heights Four won a $36 million settlement from the Illinois county that wrongfully convicted them. They had spent 18 years in prison before DNA tests exonerated them in 1996.[211]

Twenty states, the District of Columbia, and the federal government have statutory provisions for indemnifying the wrongly convicted (in capital and non-capital cases). Most of those states are far from generous. A list of compensating states and the amounts they allow is provided in Chapter 7. Until the end of 2004, when Congress passed the Innocence Protection Act, the federal government limited compensation to a maximum of $5,000 regardless of the amount of time served. The new law now provides a maximum of $100,000 a year. The law also recommends that states "should provide reasonable compensation to any person found to have been unjustly convicted of an offense against the State and sentenced to death."[212] Nevertheless, in many states that provide compensation, attorney expenses for preparing the necessary legal documents can take a third of the money. Getting the money from the state, even after it has been awarded, as noted previously, seldom is easy.[213] Regardless, mistakes made in capital cases can prove costly to the jurisdictions that make them.

"Start–Up" Costs. Another cost of capital punishment is the substantial start-up expense incurred when a jurisdiction decides to reinstate the death penalty. Those expenses are of three types: (1) building and facility costs, (2) judicial and attorney training costs, and (3) equipment costs.[214] Because the costs of execution equipment were described previously, only the first two types of start-up costs are examined here.

Building and facility costs vary greatly, but jurisdictions can expect to spend hundreds of thousands and, in some cases, millions of dollars to construct death rows and execution chambers. For example, in 1993, the Wisconsin Department of Corrections estimated that "a new twelve-unit death row, including a lethal injection death chamber" would cost $1.4 million to construct.[215] An estimated $144,600 would have to be spent on one-time start-up overhead costs, and about $500,000 annually for security personnel.[216]

When New York reinstated the death penalty in 1995, the legislature appropriated a little more than $1 million for start-up costs: $389,000 for a 12-cell death row, $190,000 to convert an old correctional hospital into a three-cell death row for women, and $475,000 for a death chamber, injection room, and three holding cells.[217] Florida spent $9.5 million in 1992 to build a new 336-unit death row,[218] and in 1996 the federal government spent $500,000 to build a lethal injection chamber at the new federal death row in Terre Haute, Indiana.[219]

Because "death is different," special training is needed for judges and attorneys involved in death penalty cases. A few jurisdictions require such training. When the New York legislature reinstated capital punishment in 1995, it appropriated about $3.5 million for a new agency for training capital defense attorneys, and another $2 million for the training of capital prosecutors.[220] Kansas reinstated the death penalty in 1994, then budgeted $1.4 million for a death penalty defense agency.[221] In 1995, the Wisconsin legislature contemplated the reenactment of capital punishment and considered spending $60,000 to $70,000 to bring in national experts for a one-time seminar to train 50 to 100 lawyers.[222] It also estimated that attorney and judicial training costs for the first two years after reenactment would be about $400,000 and then $200,000 annually, thereafter.[223] In short, attorney and judicial training in capital jurisprudence involves both substantial start-up costs and ongoing expenses to keep both lawyers and judges abreast of changes in capital punishment law.

The LWOP Alternative. Currently, 36 of 37 death penalty states plus the federal government and the U.S. military have LWOP. The only death penalty state without it is New Mexico.[224] As of the mid-1990s, LWOP was the only alternative to capital punishment in 16 death penalty jurisdictions in the United States; in 12 jurisdictions, the alternative to capital punishment was either LWOP or a lesser punishment, usually life imprisonment with parole eligibility.[225] The preceding discussion shows that it is less costly to sentence capital offenders to LWOP than it is to sentence them to death—as much as two and one-half to five times less costly on average.

The greatest savings occur when LWOP sentences are imposed following a guilty plea (but see note 126). In such cases, the substantial costs of the bifurcated trial, the automatic appeal, and post-conviction processes are eliminated. The most expensive outcome is when lengthy and complicated death penalty trials are followed by a sentence of LWOP. This outcome is typical because the death penalty is frequently not imposed following a capital trial and, even when it is imposed, it is rarely carried out. As Dieter observes, "the death penalty without executions is just another name for life-without-parole; and this is the most expensive form of life-without-parole because the sentences that are obtained occur after the high costs of death penalty trials."[226]

If LWOP sentences were imposed after a non-death penalty trial (and post–conviction review), they would be cheaper than capital punishment because the Supreme Court has ruled that LWOP sentences do not require the super due process procedures necessary when the penalty is death.[227] Thus, the replacement of death sentences with LWOP sentences would reduce financial expenditures considerably.

Critics fear that such a strategy would have the undesirable effect of exacerbating the current prison–overcrowding crisis, but this has not been a problem. For example, according to information from a *New York Times* study, only about 2.5 percent of the nation's more than 1.4 million prison inmates in 2005 were serving LWOP sentences.[228] If all death sentences were changed to LWOP, the 125 to 170 offenders sentenced to death each year (since 2001), together with the approximately 3,400 current death row inmates, would hardly be noticed among the more than 1.4 million inmates now confined in American prisons.

Another concern is the medical costs of an increasing number of elderly inmates if the death penalty were replaced with LWOP. At the end of 2003, there were 110 death row inmates aged 60 or older—almost 3 times the number in 1994.[229] The oldest person on death row is probably LeRoy Nash, who in 2005 was 89-years-old. Nash, who is on Arizona's death row and has been in prison for more than half his life, suffers from heart disease, deafness, and arthritis.[230] In many states, elderly prisoners who are not on death row are housed in geriatric facilities inside prisons, or they are placed in "end of life" programs. These options are not available to death row inmates because current policy requires them to be segregated from the general prison population and housed in individual cells on death row.[231] This policy, of course, could be changed. Although the costs of medical care for elderly prison inmates is unknown (but presumably high), national estimates put the annual costs of elderly inmates at about $70,000, or about 3 times the approximately $23,400 per inmate regardless of age.[232] Thus, there certainly would be added medical expenses if the death penalty were replaced with LWOP, but, as above, the number of elderly LWOP inmates who otherwise would have been sentenced to death if that penalty were available represents only a tiny fraction of the overall prison population.

In sum, death sentences could be replaced with LWOP at considerable cost savings to the taxpayer, with negligible impact on the current prison overcrowding crisis. LWOP sentences would also allow for the correction of miscarriages of justice when they were discovered and would eliminate any brutalizing effect of capital punishment—to name just a few benefits. North Carolina passed legislation that allows prosecutors to offer capital defendants the chance to plead guilty and accept an LWOP sentence.[233] Prosecutors previously did not have that option. The legislation likely will save the state millions of dollars by eliminating the costs of a capital trial and appellate and post-conviction review. Whether such a strategy is desirable for other reasons is another matter.

Conclusion. The evidence clearly shows that capital punishment systems in the United States are always more expensive than punishment systems without capital punishment because super due process is required in the former but not in the latter. Still, for some people, the cost issue is a red herring because there are so few capital prosecutions—only 10 to 15 each year in Illinois, for example.[234] Even if the costs of capital cases exceeded the costs of non-capital cases by one or two million dollars, observe these cost skeptics, the overall annual cost to the state of Illinois, for example, would pale in comparison to its more than $50 billion annual state budget.[235] Nevertheless, if the ultimate penal sanction is supported because of the belief that it is cheaper than non-capital punishments, then this chapter establishes why such a belief is mistaken. Thus, a fair question in the capital punishment debate is whether the death penalty is worth the extra cost.

Discussion Questions

1. Is the death penalty necessary to adequately protect society from the possible future actions of those who have already committed capital crimes?

2. Is the death penalty necessary to protect prison guards and other inmates?

3. Why not execute all capital offenders?

4. Do you agree with Professor Blecker's strategy for narrowing death eligibility? Should death eligibility be narrowed?

5. Should Stanley "Tookie" Williams have been eligible for the Nobel Peace Prize? Why or why not?

6. Should capital punishment be replaced with LWOP?

7. Which costs more: capital punishment or LWOP? How much more? Why?

8. In a society with limited resources, is capital punishment worth the costs?

9. Why is "super due process" so expensive?

10. Could and should the costs of capital punishment be significantly reduced? (If answered in the affirmative, how?)

11. Should the cost of capital punishment matter?

Notes

[1] Bowers and Steiner, 1999:623-624.

[2] See *Sourcebook of Criminal Justice Statistics 2003*, p. 147, Table 2.55 (online); Gallup and Newport, 1991.

[3] Committee on the Judiciary, 1982:315; also see Rosenbluth, 2006; Van den Haag, 1982.

[4] Ibid.

[5] Levey, 2006:40-41; also see Wagner, 2006:77.

[6] "4 in Death Row in Georgia Flee Jail in Disguise," *New York Times* (1857-Current file); Jul 29, 1980; *ProQuest Historical Newspapers The New York Times* (1851-2003) p. A10; "3 Convicted Killers Recaptured in North Carolina; 4th Is Found Dead," *New York Times* (1857-Current file); Jul 31, 1980; *ProQuest Historical Newspapers The New York Times* (1851-2003) p. A12.

[7] "Escape from Death Row" at www.courttv.com/onair/shows/thesystem/a_f_episodes/escape_death_row.html.

[8] "Man Escapes from Texas' Death Row." *The Orlando Sentinel* (November 28, 1998), p. A-1; "Fugitive Inmate Found Dead." *The Orlando Sentinel* (December 4, 1998), p. A-6.

[9] "'Strenuous security' as escapee returns to jail" at http://msnbc.msn.com/id/9922969/.

[10] California has sentenced inmates to LWOP for more than 25 years, and not one inmate with such a sentence has ever been released from prison, see Dieter, 1993:13.

[11] Amsterdam, 1982:354. Zimring (2003:48) points out the irony in the death penalty position of political conservatives, who are more likely to support the death penalty than are political liberals: "If you do not trust government bureaucracies with your tax dollars and racial policies in public schools, how can you trust them to choose appropriate targets for death sentences and believe that government officials can protect against the execution of the innocent? If the government screws up every other major responsibility it administers, why should the death penalty be any different?"

[12] Calculated from Bonczar and Snell, 2005:8-9.

[13] Ibid.

[14] Radelet et al., 1992; The Death Penalty Information Center at www.deathpenaltyinfo.org/article.php?did=412&scid=6.

[15] Material in this section is from Blecker, 2001.

[16] The Constitution Project, 2005:xxiv-xxv.

[17] Haines, 1996:139-140.

[18] Cited in ibid., p. 227, n. 49.

[19] Ibid., p. 138.

[20] Cited in ibid., p. 139.

[21] Ibid., p. 207.

[22] Committee on the Judiciary, op. cit.; also see Van den Haag, op. cit.

[23] Sellin, 1959:72.

[24] Amsterdam, op. cit.

[25] Sorensen and Wrinkle, 1996.

[26] Paternoster, 1991:279.

[27] Ibid.

[28] Harris, 2000. For additional examples of death row inmates who were rehabilitated, see Guin, 2002.

[29] Furillo, 2005.

[30] Sellin, 1967:154–160.

[31] Sorensen and Pilgrim, 2000.

[32] Reidy et al., 2001.

[33] Sellin, 1959, op. cit., p. 76.

[34] Ibid., pp. 77–78.

[35] Bedau, 1982:176, Table 4-5-1.

[36] Ibid., p. 177, Table 4-5-2.

[37] Heilbrun et al., 1978.

[38] Vito et al., 1991.

[39] Marquart and Sorensen, 1989:26.

[40] Marquart and Sorensen, 1988.

[41] Vito and Wilson, 1988.

[42] "Killer once freed from death row is executed," *The Orlando Sentinel* (November 18, 1998), p. A16; but also see the cases of Robert Massie and Carl Bowles, who killed again following release or escape from prison to which they were sent for a previous murder or murders, Marquis, 2005:518–519 .

[43] Amsterdam, op. cit.

[44] A version of this section appeared as "The Economic Costs of Capital Punishment: Past, Present, and Future," in Acker et al., 2003. It is reprinted with permission of the publisher.

[45] Culver, 1985:574.

[46] *Sourcebook of Criminal Justice Statistics, 2003*, op. cit.; but see Longmire, 1996, for the finding that cost effectiveness does not greatly affect death penalty attitudes.

[47] McGovern, 1982, p. 10.

[48] Peterson and Bailey, 1998; Snell, 2006, p.11, Table 11.

[49] On "super due process," see Radin, 1980.

[50] "Death Penalty in California is Very Costly," 2006.

[51] "Death Penalty Has Cost New Jersey Taxpayers $253 Million," 2005.

[52] "Indiana Editorial Calls For End to 'Costly; Death Penalty," 2005; also see Dickson, 2006:280.

[53] Larranaga and Mustard, 2004.

[54] "Kansas Study Concludes Death Penalty is Costly Policy," 2003.

[55] Liebman et al., 2000, n. 74; also see New York State Defenders Association 1982; Garey, 1985; Spangenberg and Walsh, 1989; Hoppe, 1992; Dieter, 1992; Cook and Slawson, 1993. Between 1995, the year New York reinstated the death penalty, and 1999, New York spent an estimated $68 million on 37 death penalty cases. More than half of those cases resulted in plea deals and life sentences. Eight cases were still pending. Of the nine trials completed, five ended with death sentences and four with life without parole. By the time the first death row inmate is executed, the costs to New York of the five cases could reach $238 million. See "Death Penalty Expenses Adding Up," *New York Daily News* (October

20, 1999) at www.th-record.com/1999/10/20/executio.htm. In 2004, the state supreme court ruled New York's death penalty unconstitutional. As of this writing, New York had not enacted new death penalty legislation.

[56] Muwakkil, 1989:6.

[57] "'Hanging Judge' Calls for End to the Death Penalty," 2005.

[58] Because of the conditions of prison life, such as violence, HIV and other diseases, poor diets, and poor health conditions, it has been estimated that an inmate sentenced to LWOP will live an average of 31 years in prison, see Brooks and Erickson, op. cit. At year-end 2005, the median age of a death row inmate at time of arrest was 27 (the median age of death row inmates was 41), see Snell, op. cit., p. 7, Table 7.

[59] The $23,400 average annual cost of imprisonment does not include additional expenses that may be incurred because of the medical problems of elderly inmates. Although those costs are unknown, it has been estimated that the annual costs of elderly inmates is about $70,000, or about 3 times the approximately $23,400 per inmate regardless of age. See Villa, 2005; *American Correctional Association 2005 Directory*, p. 362. The annual cost of confining an inmate on death row generally is somewhat greater than the annual cost of housing an LWOP inmate among the general population of a maximum security prison, see Brooks and Erickson, 1996:883. One source suggests that the difference in the annual costs of confinement is not great—approximately $1,000 to $2,000 per inmate. See Brooks and Erickson, ibid. In 2005, it cost the state of Florida $26,422 to house an inmate on death row, and $18,108 to house an inmate in a major prison—a more than $8,300 difference. See "Death Row Fact Sheet," Florida Department of Corrections at www.dc.state.fl.us/oth/deathrow/index.html and "Inmate Cost Per Day, Florida Department of Corrections at www.dc.state.fl.us/pub/statsbrief/cost.html. In 2005, it reportedly cost California about $90,000 more a year to house an inmate on death row than in the general prison population. See "'Hanging Judge' Calls for End to the Death Penalty," op. cit.

[60] Paternoster, op. cit.; also see *Harmelin v. Michigan*, 1991.

[61] Cook and Slawson, op. cit., pp. 97–98.

[62] Dieter, 2005.

[63] Haines, 1996, op. cit., p. 170.

[64] Sorensen, 2004.

[65] See, for example, "A Matter of Life and Death: The Effect of Life-Without-Parole Statutes on Capital Punishment," 2006.

[66] Haines, 1996, op. cit., p. 170.

[67] Spangenberg and Walsh, op. cit.; New York State Defenders Association, op. cit. Assistant District Attorney for Harris County, Texas, Bill Hawkins (2006:258) claims that the police investigation of a death-eligible homicide has "no impact on the criminal justice system," it "does not require more of or less of the police."

[68] Spangenberg and Walsh, op. cit., p. 49; Garey, op. cit., p. 1252.

[69] Spangenberg and Walsh, ibid.; Garey 1985, ibid.; Brooks and Erickson, op. cit., p. 893.

[70] Cook and Slawson, op. cit., p. 44, Table 5.3.

[71] "Georgia Judge Notes Expensive Bottom Line in Capital Cases," 2002.

[72] Spangenberg and Walsh, op. cit.

[73] "Kansas Study Concludes Death Penalty is Costly Policy," op. cit.

[74] Spangenberg and Walsh, ibid., p. 48; Brooks and Erickson, op. cit., p. 901.

[75] Grand juries are involved in felony prosecutions in about half the states and in the federal system, see Bohm and Haley, 2007:296.

[76] Spangenberg and Walsh, op. cit., p. 49.

[77] Garey, op. cit., p. 1251, n. 134.

[78] Cook and Slawson, op. cit., pp. 28–29, n. 47.

[79] Ibid., p. 30, n. 47.

[80] Garey, op. cit., pp. 1249–1250; Cook and Slawson, op. cit., pp. 28–29, n. 47.

[81] Garey, op. cit., p. 1248; Spangenberg and Walsh, op. cit., p. 50.

[82] New York State Defenders Association, op. cit., p. 12.

[83] Cook and Slawson, op. cit., p. 81, Table 7.6.

[84] Spangenberg and Walsh, op. cit.; Garey, op. cit., p. 1253.

[85] Ibid.

[86] Ibid.

[87] Ibid.

[88] Author's own experience.

[89] Brooks and Erickson, op. cit., p. 895.

[90] In some cases, the threat of the death penalty may encourage guilty pleas, thus providing substantial cost savings in comparison to capital cases that go to trial. However, the death penalty is not often used in that way, see Brooks and Erickson, op. cit., pp. 890–891. In some states, state law restricts such plea bargains. Moreover, if this were an avowed purpose of the death penalty, it is unlikely "the courts would uphold the constitutionality of such an intentional interference with the right to trial." See Dieter, 2005, op. cit. If capital punishment were replaced with LWOP, on the other hand, it is unlikely that defendants would plead guilty to LWOP (what would they have to lose if they went to trial?). Consequently, in jurisdictions that provide for both capital punishment and LWOP sentences, the availability of capital punishment, as at least a threat, may sometimes reduce costs.

[91] Spangenberg and Walsh, op. cit.; Garey, op. cit., p. 1247, n. 114.

[92] Spangenberg and Walsh, op. cit., p. 52; Brooks and Erickson, op. cit., p. 897.

[93] "Kansas Study Concludes Death Penalty is Costly Policy," op. cit.

[94] Garey, op. cit., p. 1258 and p. 1258, n. 175.

[95] "New York Death Penalty Trial 3.5 Times More Costly than Non-Capital Trial," 1999.

[96] Hoppe, op. cit.

[97] Cook and Slawson, op. cit., pp. 59 and 61, Tables 6.2 and 6.3.

[98] Ibid., p. 59, Table 6.2.

[99] Ibid., pp. 59 and 61, Tables 6.2 and 6.3.

[100] Ibid., p. 59, Table 6.2.

[101] Hawkins, 2006:261.

[102] Cook and Slawson, op. cit., pp. 59 and 61, Tables 6.2 and 6.3.

[103] Paternoster, op. cit., p. 198; also see Garey, op. cit., p. 1259.

[104] Dow, 2002a:4-5.

[105] "Georgia Judge Notes Expensive Bottom Line in Capital Cases," op. cit.

[106] See "Death Penalty Expenses Adding Up," *New York Daily News* (October 20, 1999) at www.th-record.com/1999/10/20/executio.htm.

[107] Spangenberg and Walsh, op. cit.; Garey, op. cit., p. 1257.

[108] Garey, ibid.

[109] Brooks and Erickson, op. cit., p. 896, n. 134.; Assistant District Attorney for Harris County, Texas, Bill Hawkins (2006:259) reports that jury selection in capital cases in his county averages close to three weeks, compared to one day in non-death capital cases. On taking longer than the guilt phase, see Leyte-Vidal and Silverman, 2006:271.

[110] "Death Penalty Expenses Adding Up," op. cit.

[111] Hoppe, op. cit.

[112] Kaplan, 1983:571.

[113] Spangenberg and Walsh, op. cit., p. 51; Garey, op. cit., p. 1255.

[114] "Georgia Judge Notes Expensive Bottom Line in Capital Cases," op. cit.

[115] Spangenberg and Walsh, ibid., p. 52; Garey, ibid., p. 1256.

[116] Garey, ibid.

[117] Ibid., p. 1257, n. 173.

[118] Spangenberg and Walsh, op. cit.; Garey, ibid.; Brooks and Erickson, op. cit., p. 897.

[119] Spangenberg and Walsh, op. cit., p. 54; Cook and Slawson, op. cit., p. 15.

[120] Spangenberg and Walsh, ibid., p. 53.

[121] Cook and Slawson, op. cit., p. 61, Table 6.3.

[122] Ibid.

[123] Haines, 1996, op. cit., p. 172.

[124] Cook and Slawson, op. cit., p. 44, Table 5.3.

[125] Ibid.

[126] Although the hourly costs of district attorneys, public defenders, judges, etc. are usually "fixed" (because they receive salaries) and would be the same whether the case was capital or noncapital, the costs of those participants in the process are provided for two reasons. First is to allow the reader to gauge the costs of a capital case (or any case) that goes to trial (and is further reviewed) in comparison to the costs of a capital case that is plea bargained to LWOP. Second is to help in the estimation of some of the "hidden costs" or "opportunity costs" of capital punishment. When district attorneys spend much of their time trying capital cases, when court time is consumed with lengthy death trials, and when appellate courts spend so much of their time reviewing death penalty appeals, other, noncapital cases are affected. For example, other serious cases receive less attention than they would otherwise, or cases that ordinarily would be tried are plea bargained, simply because there is not enough time to do otherwise. On the latter point, see Haines, 1996, op. cit., pp. 171-172, for example.

[127] "Georgia Judge Notes Expensive Bottom Line in Capital Cases," op. cit. Harris County, Texas Assistant District Attorney Bill Hawkins (2006:259) reports that because of experience, "the prosecution of a capital death case does not significantly affect the ordinary operations of the office."

[128] Garey, op. cit., p. 1258.

[129] "Georgia Judge Notes Expensive Bottom Line in Capital Cases," op. cit.

[130] Brooks and Erickson, op. cit., p. 892.

[131] Ibid., p. 894.

[132] Clary, 2001.

[133] Acker and Lanier, 1999:448-449.

[134] Bright, 1997:11.

[135] "Birmingham News Criticizes Costly, Arbitrary Death Penalty, 2005.

[136] "Death Penalty Expenses Adding Up," op.cit.

[137] "Indiana Taxpayers Charged over $2 Million for Defense of Three Capital Cases." 1999.

[138] "Death Penalty Expenses Adding Up," op.cit.

[139] "Partial Costs in the Virginia trials of John Muhammad and Lee Malvo," 2004.

[140] "McVeigh Defense: $13.8 Million." *The Orlando Sentinel* (June 30, 2001), p. A17.

[141] Hoppe, op. cit.

[142] Spangenberg and Walsh, op. cit.; Garey, op. cit.

[143] Cook and Slawson, op. cit., p. 46, Table 5.4.

[144] Ibid., p. 45.

[145] Hoppe, op. cit.

[146] Cook and Slawson, op. cit., p. 46.

[147] Ibid.; Garey, op. cit., p. 1255. See note 126, supra.

[148] "Death Penalty Expenses Adding Up," op.cit.

[149] Spangenberg and Walsh, op. cit., p. 52.

[150] Cited in Governor's Commission on Capital Punishment, 2002:199; also see Haines, 1996, op. cit., p. 170.

[151] Ibid.

[152] "Costly Death Penalty Takes Toll on State Budgets," 2003.

[153] Haines, 1996, op. cit., p. 171.

[154] Ibid.

[155] Ibid.

[156] Dieter, 2005, op. cit.

[157] Paternoster, op. cit., p. 212.

[158] "Kansas Study Concludes Death Penalty is Costly Policy," op. cit.

[159] Spangenberg and Walsh, op. cit. At year-end 2005, the federal government was the only exception. In South Carolina, the defendant, if deemed competent, may waive right of sentence review. Idaho, Montana, Oklahoma, South Dakota, and Tennessee require only review of the sentence. Review of conviction in Idaho has to be filed through appeal or forfeited. An appeal of trial court error may be waived in Virginia but not a review of sentence for arbitrariness and proportionality. The right to waive an automatic review has not been addressed in Mississippi. Neither statute nor case law precludes a waiver of appeal in Wyoming. See Snell, 2006, op. cit., p. 3.

[160] Spangenberg and Walsh, op. cit., p. 53; Brooks and Erickson, op. cit., pp. 897–898.

[161] "Kansas Study Concludes Death Penalty is Costly Policy," op. cit.

[162] Spangenberg and Walsh, ibid., pp. 52–53; Garey, op. cit., p. 1263; Paternoster, op. cit., p. 205.

[163] Cook and Slawson, op. cit., p. 48, Table 5.6.

[164] Garey, op. cit.

[165] Cook and Slawson, op. cit., p. 47, Table 5.5.

[166] Ibid., p. 79, Table 7.5.

[167] Ibid. See note 126, supra.

[168] See, for example, Paternoster, op. cit., pp. 81–82.

[169] New Jersey Death Penalty Study Commission Report (January 2007), p. 32 at www.njleg.state.nj.us/committees/dpsc_final.pdf.

[170] Freedman, 1997; Garey, op. cit. See Chapter 2, note on the appellate process in capital cases.

[171] Hoppe, op. cit.

[172] Spangenberg and Walsh, op. cit., p. 54.

[173] Ibid., p. 55, for both state and federal post-conviction proceedings.

[174] Paternoster, op. cit., p. 205.

[175] In 2006, a study found that the typical trial record in a capital case in California was 9,000 pages, see "Death Penalty in California Very Costly," 2006. In Indiana, trial records in the initial appeal of a capital sentence typically consist of 3,000 to 5,000 pages, or more, and the record presented in subsequent collateral review appeals is usually twice that amount, Dickson, op. cit., p. 279. The cost for preparing 24 copies of the

22,000-page transcript of a 1999 capital trial in New York was $44,478.28, see "Death Penalty Expenses Adding Up," *New York Daily News*, op. cit.

[176] Hoppe, op. cit.

[177] Cook and Slawson, op. cit., pp. 81–82, Tables 7.6 and 7.7.

[178] Ibid., p. 81, Table 7.6. In California, state habeas corpus petitions typically average 200 to 300 pages, plus hundreds of pages of exhibits and declarations, see Gillette, 2006:264.

[179] Hoppe, op. cit.

[180] 21 U.S.C. S 848 (q)(4), 1994; also see Howard, 1996.

[181] See Howard, ibid., p. 903.

[182] 18 U.S.C. S 3006A, 1994.

[183] 18 U.S.C. S 3006A(g)(2)(A), 1994; 28 U.S.C. S 605, 1994.

[184] Howard, op. cit.

[185] Ibid., p. 904.

[186] Ibid.

[187] Ibid.

[188] Ibid.

[189] Ibid., p. 914

[190] Ibid.

[191] Ibid., p. 915.

[192] Ibid.

[193] Ibid.

[194] Spangenberg and Walsh, op. cit., p. 55, for both state and federal post–conviction proceedings.

[195] Paternoster, op. cit.

[196] Hoppe, op. cit.

[197] Ibid.

[198] Cook and Slawson, op. cit., p. 81, Table 7.6.

[199] Some death row inmates have served more than 20 years awaiting execution. For a description of the "living hell" that death row inmates experience, see Johnson, 2003; 1990; 1989; Gillespie, 2003:35-51.

[200] See Spangenberg and Walsh, op. cit., p. 56.

[201] See Brooks and Erickson, op. cit., p. 883; "Death Row Fact Sheet," Florida Department of Corrections at www.dc.state.fl.us/oth/deathrow/index.html; "Inmate Cost Per Day, Florida Department of Corrections at www.dc.state.fl.us/pub/statsbrief/cost.html; Hawkins, 2006, op. cit., p. 261; "'Hanging Judge' Calls for End to the Death Penalty," op. cit.

[202] New Jersey Death Penalty Study Commission Report, op. cit.

[203] See Johnson, 1990, op. cit., Chap. 6.

[204] Denno, 1994:655.

[205] "Death Row Facts," Texas Department of Criminal Justice at www.tdcj.state.tx.us/stat/drowfacts.htm (accessed June 20, 2006).

[206] Denno, 1994, op. cit., p. 655. Denno notes that before 1990, states were increasingly buying "execution trailers" costing $100,000. The trailers included "a lethal–injection machine, a steel holding cell for the prisoner, and additional areas for witnesses, the chaplain, prison employees, and medical personnel," see ibid.

[207] See, for example, *Barefoot v. Estelle*, 1983; *Saffle v. Parks*, 1990; *Clemons v. Mississippi*, 1990.

[208] Brooks and Erickson, op. cit., pp. 900 and 902.

[209] Amsterdam, 1982:349.

[210] *The Charlotte Observer*, November 13, 1992.

[211] Cohen, 1999.

[212] "Justice for All Act of 2004: Section-By-Section Analysis."

[213] Scheck et al., 2001:297-298.

[214] See Brooks and Erickson, op. cit.

[215] Ibid., p. 886.

[216] Ibid.

[217] Ibid., p. 886, n. 62.

[218] Ibid., p. 886.

[219] Ibid., pp. 886–887.

[220] Ibid., p. 887.

[221] Ibid., p. 892.

[222] Ibid., p. 887.

[223] Ibid.

[224] Death Penalty Information Center, www.deathpenaltyinfo.org/lwop.html. In addition, 11 of 12 states without the death penalty plus the District of Columbia have LWOP. Alaska is the only state without the death penalty not to have LWOP.

[225] Acker and Lanier, 1995:55.

[226] Dieter, 2005, op. cit.

[227] *Harmelin v. Michigan,* 1991; Paternoster, op. cit., p. 279.

[228] Calculated from "New York Times Series Examines Life Sentences," 2005; Harrison and Beck, 2006.

[229] "Growing Elderly Population on Death Row," 2005.

[230] Ibid.

[231] Ibid.

[232] Villa, 2005; American Correctional Association 2005 Directory, p. 362.

[233] The Death Penalty Information Center, www.deathpenaltyinfo.org/Changes.html#NC.

[234] Turow, 2003:61-62.

[235] Ibid.

CHAPTER 7

Miscarriages of Justice and the Death Penalty

Professor Austin Sarat writes about a "new abolitionism" that eschews moralistic arguments against the death penalty, as well as those that suggest the penalty is unconstitutional, in favor of arguments about the unfair and inequitable way in which capital punishment is administered. He argues that "new abolitionists" focus on the damage capital punishment has done to core legal values such as due process and equal protection and to the legitimacy of the law, itself.[1] Law Professor David Dow, who has represented more than 30 death row inmates, argues that the commanding issue for death penalty abolitionists today is innocence; that is, wrongfully convicting the innocent, sentencing the innocent to death, and executing them.[2] Innocence is an issue that exposes many of the injustices associated with capital punishment and is arguably the most unfair outcome of the process. Thus, for these new abolitionists (and old abolitionists, too!), when assessing the administration of capital punishment, it is important to distinguish between how the death penalty might be administered ideally, and the way it is administered in practice. To support the death penalty is to support actual practice and not some unobtainable ideal. It is noteworthy, in this regard, that much of the Supreme Court's workload during the past 30 years has been devoted to refining capital punishment procedures—to making the process work "right." The record of that effort clearly shows that the death penalty in the United States remains very much a work in progress.[3]

One of the enduring problems with capital punishment is that it "not merely kills people, it also kills some of them in error, and these are errors which we can never correct."[4] This irrevocability of capital punishment is one reason why "death is different" and why it requires "super due process."

Ironically, super due process sometimes creates a false sense of security. Some people believe that the chances of a miscarriage of justice in the administration of the death penalty (such as a wrongful arrest, a wrongful charge or indictment, a wrongful conviction, a wrongful sentence, or a wrongful execution) have been reduced to a mere possibility, and probably do not occur in any case. The Committee on the Judiciary wrote: "The Court's decision with respect to the rights of the individual . . . have all but reduced the danger of error in these [capital] cases to that of a mere theoretical possibility. Indeed, the Committee is aware of no case where an innocent man has been put to death."[5] But miscarriages of justice are still a possibility because human beings are fallible. Had the committee examined the evidence, which at the time was anecdotal but, in many cases, persuasive, it could have drawn a different conclusion. For example, M. Watt Espy, Jr., the capital punishment historian who has confirmed more than 19,000 legal executions in the United States since 1608, estimates that approximately five percent, or 950, of those executed were innocent.[6]

Definitions of Innocence

To determine whether any innocent people have been victims of miscarriages of justice in capital cases, it is necessary to settle on a definition of "innocence." There are several possibilities.[7] Probably the most conservative definition is one that includes only those cases in which a government official admitted error. A problem is that in the twentieth century, no government official in the United States had ever admitted to being involved in the execution of an innocent person. That does not mean that none had occurred.

The next most conservative definition of innocence includes only officially exonerated defendants who either were completely uninvolved in the capital crime for which they were convicted or were convicted of a capital crime that did not occur. Examples of the latter category are defendants who were convicted of capital rape (when rape was a capital crime) even though sexual relations were consensual, or defendants convicted of capital murder even though the alleged victim was alive.[8] This was the definition of innocence employed by Professors Bedau and Radelet (1987) in their research (which is discussed later) and the definition used in this chapter (unless indicated otherwise).

A more liberal definition of innocence might include capital defendants whose cases were dismissed or who were found not guilty at retrial. A problem with that definition is that such defendants may be legally innocent but factually guilty. Other definitions might include defendants convicted of capital crimes even though those crimes were accidental, committed in self-defense, or the product of mental illness. In none of those examples should the crime have been considered capital in the first place, even though in some cases it was. In short, a more liberal definition of innocence produces a larger number of such people, while a more conservative definition produces a smaller number.

It should also be noted that the best evidence of miscarriages of justice in capital cases are those convicted capital offenders who have been freed prior to their executions. The reason is that once a person has been executed, there is usually little interest in pursuing his or her claim of innocence. Critics may complain that such "freed" individuals should not count because they were not executed, and, furthermore, they show that the system works. However, it should be remembered that, in each case, the freed individual was the victim of a miscarriage of justice (many of them spent years on death row despite their innocence) and in all likelihood would have been executed if not for sheer luck.

Miscarriages of Justice in Pre–*Gregg* (1976) Capital Cases

Some of the allegedly innocent people executed under pre–*Gregg* (1976) statutes have become a part of American folklore. Among the most famous are Nicola Sacco and Bartolomeo Vanzetti, the anarchists who were electrocuted for robbery and murder in Massachusetts, Bruno Hauptmann, the alleged abductor and killer of the Lindbergh baby, in New Jersey, and Julius and Ethel Rosenberg, who were convicted in New York of selling atomic bomb secrets to the Soviet Union. There is lingering doubt about each of those cases, but no definitive proof of their innocence—or guilt. Most cases do not receive such publicity and attention.

Borchard's Research. Yale Law Professor Edwin Borchard conducted the pioneering study of miscarriages of justice in the United States.[9] Responding to a challenge from the district attorney of Worcester County, Massachusetts, who contended that innocent men are never convicted, Borchard accumulated case studies of 65 people whose experiences with the justice system belied the district attorney's belief. The 65 miscarriages of justice included several cases in which men condemned to die were eventually exonerated. Borchard's research, which was published in 1932 in his classic book, *Convicting the Innocent*, exposed for the first time how frequently wrongful convictions occurred in the U.S. criminal justice system.

Bedau's Research. One of the first scholars to publish a study of miscarriages of justice exclusively in capital cases or potentially capital cases in the United States (in 1964) was Professor Hugo Adam Bedau.[10] Bedau reported:

> 74 cases between 1893 and 1962 involving criminal homi-
> cide, and thus the possibility of a death sentence, in which the
> evidence suggested that the following major errors had
> occurred: In each of the 74 cases an innocent person was
> arrested and indicted; in 71, the innocent person was convicted
> and sentenced; in 30 (including 11 in states with no death
> penalty), there was a sentence to prison for life; in 31 cases,
> there was a sentence to death; in *eight an innocent person
> was executed* (emphasis in the original).[11]

Bedau has since added 50 "new" cases to the 74 above. The new cases
cover 1930 to 1980.

Bedau and Radelet's Research. A more recent and ambitious
attempt to document miscarriages of justice in capital cases is the joint
effort by Professor Bedau and Professor Michael L. Radelet.[12] They have
catalogued 416 cases involving 496 defendants who were convicted of
capital or potentially capital crimes in the twentieth century, in many
cases sentenced to death, and who were later found to be innocent.[13]
The 416 cases represent those found through the summer of 1991, when
the research was formally concluded. Among the innocent people
wrongfully convicted were 23 people who were executed (about 5 percent of the total) and another 22 people who were reprieved within 72
hours of execution.[14]

Of the 496 people wrongfully convicted, 84 percent were convicted prior to 1976 and the implementation of super due process. All
but one of the wrongful executions (96 percent) occurred before 1976.
One should not infer from those percentages that super due process has
significantly reduced miscarriages of justice in capital cases, however.
The "prior-to-1976 data" are for seven and one-half decades, while the
"1976-and-after data" are for only about one and one-half decades. The
average number of people wrongfully convicted of capital crimes in the
first six decades of the twentieth century is 59 per decade. The number
of wrongful convictions for the 1980s is also 59.[15] During the first
seven and one-half decades of the twentieth century, there was an average of six wrongful convictions in capital cases discovered each year.
That was about the same number of discovered wrongful convictions
per year during the 1980s with super due process. The yearly average
is based on the number of wrongful convictions discovered by Bedau
and Radelet, which, according to them, may represent only the "tip of
the iceberg."

Miscarriages of Justice in Post–*Gregg* (1976) Capital Cases: Despite Super Due Process

Bedau and Radelet's research reveals that 16 percent of the wrongful convictions in capital cases and one of the 23 wrongful executions occurred between 1976 and the summer of 1991—after the reimposition of the death penalty and super due process and the conclusion of their research. Between 1976 and 1979, 21 wrongful convictions were discovered (an average of seven per year); during the 1980s, 59 wrongful convictions were discovered (almost six per year); and in 1990, only one wrongful conviction was found. Under post–*Gregg* statutes and super due process, according to Bedau and Radelet's research, there has been an average of six or seven discovered wrongful convictions (excluding the one in 1990) in capital cases per year. That average is about the same as the one for the prior period.

Looked at somewhat differently, the Death Penalty Information Center reports that since 1973 (as of March 2007), 123 people in 25 states have been released from death rows because of evidence of their innocence. That represents about one death row inmate released for every 8.5 that have been executed. The average number of innocent death row inmates being released has been increasing according to this source. Between 1973 and 1999 there was an average of 2.96 innocent death row inmates released per year. Between 1999 and 2006, on the other hand, there has been an average of 6.43 death row inmates released per year.[16]

Again, it must be remembered that the averages are based only on those wrongful convictions that have been discovered. It does not appear that super due process protections have made much of a difference in the incidence of wrongful convictions in capital cases.[17] The evidence shows that despite super due process safeguards, miscarriages of justice in capital cases continue. On the other hand, death penalty proponents argue that these data demonstrate that super due process works because it has dramatically reduced, if not eliminated altogether, wrongful executions.[18] None of the 123 people released from death row was executed. Indeed, death penalty proponents maintain that, among the approximately 7,000 defendants sentenced to death under post-*Furman* statutes, there is no incontrovertible evidence that a single innocent person has been executed.[19] Furthermore, death penalty advocates claim that the vast majority of the released death row inmates were not "factually" innocent but rather the objects of procedural errors that required reviewing courts to order retrials and, for a variety of reasons, prosecutors elected not to retry the case.[20] Among the reasons that prosecutors might not retry a case are the following: (1) the prosecutor was barred from using some of the evidence against the defendant by the appellate court; (2) incriminating evidence against the defendant was misplaced or destroyed; (3) witnesses against the defendant, often co-perpetrators, either have or have not received the prosecutor's incentive to testify and thus have no incentive to testify again; (4) key prosecution witnesses cannot be found or are deceased; (5) because of the passage of time, prosecution witnesses may have trouble recalling what occurred, thus injecting doubt into the prosecution's case; and (6) the public may no longer support a prosecution because their feelings about the case have changed or they are no longer interested.[21] In light of these allegations, what does the evidence show? Following are a few examples that have received some publicity.

Examples from News Accounts. Wayne Williams, the so-called Atlanta child murderer, was arrested on June 21, 1981, and later convicted of killing two ex-felons (27 and 21 years old). He was sentenced to two life terms.[22] Police also linked Williams to 21 of 27 child murders, and those cases were then closed. Meanwhile, the unsolved murders of young blacks continued for three more years, until 1984. Police refused to say how many murders occurred following Williams's arrest, but the Fulton County medical examiner's log listed at least 23 that seemed to fit the pattern. Many people feel that Williams was a scapegoat.

In 1984, Larry Hicks of Gary, Indiana, won his freedom two weeks before his scheduled execution. Apparently an innocent bystander, Hicks had been convicted of murder on the testimony of one person in a trial that lasted only a day and a half.[23]

Also in 1984, Earl Charles was nearly executed in Georgia for a double murder. He was freed after proving that he was in Florida at the time.[24]

Randall Dale Adams was released from a Texas prison in 1989 after serving more than 12 years following his 1977 conviction for the murder of a Dallas police officer.[25] Adams, the subject of an award-winning documentary, *The Thin Blue Line*, once came within three days of execution, despite steadfastly maintaining his innocence. In the documentary, the state's key witness against Adams, David Harris, all but confessed to the shooting for which Adams was convicted. The Texas Court of Criminal Appeals set aside Adams's conviction and noted that prosecutors had suppressed evidence and that witnesses had given perjured testimony in the case.

Also in 1989, Timothy Hennis walked away from a New Hanover County, North Carolina, courthouse a free man after serving 844 days on death row at Central Prison in Raleigh.[26] Hennis was convicted of three murders in July, 1986. He was granted a new trial when the North Carolina Supreme Court ruled that the state's use of victim photographs may have inflamed the jury. The jury acquitted him at his second trial.

Leonel Torres Herrera was executed in Texas on May 12, 1993, for the murder of two police officers.[27] Prior to his execution, the Supreme Court rejected evidence (sworn statements) that his then-dead brother had committed the crimes. The Court ruled that Herrera and others like him are not entitled to federal hearings on belated evidence of innocence unless they meet an undefined "extraordinarily high" level of proof. The Court opined that relief in cases such as Herrera's should be sought through executive clemency.

In June, 1993, Anson Avery Maynard's death sentence was commuted to life in prison by North Carolina Governor Jim Martin.[28] Maynard had been convicted of the 1981 killing of his thief-partner, Steven Henry. It was believed that Henry had made a deal to testify against Maynard and that Maynard had killed Henry to keep him silent. Maynard was convicted on the testimony of a man who swore he had witnessed the killing. No physical evidence tied Maynard to the crime. As Maynard awaited his execution, the wife of the man who had testified against him admitted she had lied during her part of the trial in order to protect her husband—who may have been Henry's killer in a drug deal gone bad. Several alibi witnesses then came forward, including a truck driver who corroborated Maynard's claim that he had hitchhiked a ride after his car broke down far from where the crime was committed.

In 1993, a Baltimore County, Maryland, circuit judge overturned Kirk Bloodsworth's conviction for the rape and murder of a nine-year-old girl and ordered him freed from prison.[29] Bloodsworth had served nine years in prison, part of it on death row, despite his continued claim of innocence. His conviction was overturned after DNA testing of the semen on the girl's underpants indicated that someone else had committed the crime. Bloodsworth had been convicted on the testimony of three eyewitnesses who stated that they saw the defendant with the girl shortly before she disappeared. Bloodsworth insisted that he had never met the girl.

Jesse Dwayne Jacobs was executed in Texas on January 4, 1995. Two days prior to the execution, the Supreme Court denied his request for a stay of execution, even though the state of Texas conceded that he did not kill the victim of the kidnapping and murder for which he was convicted in 1987.[30] Jacobs originally confessed to the crime, but later recanted and told authorities that his sister, Bobbie Hogan, had committed the murder. He said that he confessed to the murder because he preferred death to spending the rest of his life in prison. Seven months after Jacobs was convicted of capital murder, his sister was tried and convicted of the same crime. During the sister's trial, the prosecutor, who had also prosecuted Jacobs, told the jury that the sister had pulled the trigger and that Jacobs did not even know that she had a gun. Jacobs was called to testify at his sister's trial and claimed that he was outside when the killing took place in an abandoned house. The Supreme Court has held (in *Enmund v. Florida*, 1982) that the Eighth Amendment prohibits the execution of a person who participated in a crime that led to murder when that person did not actually kill or intend for a killing to occur.

Don Paradis was set free in April 2000 after serving 21 years on
Idaho's death row for a murder he did not commit. With the help of a
New York City corporate attorney working *pro bono* for two decades,
Paradis had his conviction overturned by a federal judge because of
irrefutable evidence that the prosecution had concealed exculpatory evidence. Paradis's attorney estimates that the cost of securing justice for
his client was more than $5 million.[31]

In January 2002, Juan Melendez was released from Florida's death
row after serving nearly 18 years for a murder he did not commit.
Melendez was convicted in 1983 of killing a cosmetology school owner
based on the testimony of two witnesses. There was no physical evidence
linking Melendez to the murder. After Melendez was convicted, the true
killer, Vernon James, confessed to at least four investigators or attorneys,
but the prosecutor in the case did not disclose that confession to
Melendez's defense attorneys. Also, after Melendez's conviction, one of
the witnesses recanted; the other witness is now dead. The witness who
recanted was a paid police informant who had negotiated a deal in
exchange for his testimony—a fact the prosecutor failed to disclose at
the trial. During his prison stay, Melendez, who had always claimed that
he was innocent, had lost several rounds of appeals and had his death
sentence upheld by the Florida Supreme Court before James's confession to the killing was discovered in 1999.[32]

In April 2004, North Carolina Governor Mike Easley pardoned Darryl
Hunt, after vacating the charges against him the previous month. Hunt
had served 18 years in prison for a rape and a murder he did not commit. Hunt was freed from prison in December 2003, when DNA evidence
led police to another man, Willard Brown, who confessed to the crimes
and acting alone. Brown was charged with murder, rape, kidnapping,
and robbery; pled guilty to the charges; and was sentenced to life in
prison plus 10 years.[33] Two eyewitnesses had identified Hunt as the perpetrator in the 1984 crime. Two juries had convicted him and appellate
courts upheld the convictions, even though DNA testing in 1994 proved
that he was not the rapist, Only after Brown was arrested for Hunt's supposed crimes did the prosecutors turn over to Hunt's attorneys hundreds
of pages of police reports they illegally withheld, including a two-page
report of a 1986 interview with Brown, who the police briefly suspected
was the perpetrator in the 1984 crimes. The eyewitnesses, not surprisingly, were mistaken.[34] One eyewitness picked Hunt out of a photo
lineup after spending hours with the lead detective. The second witness
failed to identify Hunt in a live lineup but later picked him out in a photo
lineup.[35] Hunt's attorney observed, ". . . we always ran into so many obsta-
cles, from the courts and the police, from district attorneys, . . . [o]ther
attorneys were very skeptical, and most people in the community were
very dubious about Darryl's innocence."[36]

Wrongful Executions under Post–*Gregg* (1976) Statutes. Documenting cases of innocent persons executed is an extraordinarily difficult task. Once an alleged murderer is dead, it is almost impossible to right the record, so a degree of uncertainty nearly always characterizes such cases. Of particular interest are wrongful executions that have taken place under post-*Gregg* (1976) statutes and super due process. Bedau and Radelet report one (as of the summer of 1991): James Adams, a black man, convicted of first-degree murder in 1974 and executed in Florida in 1984. Following is Bedau and Radelet's description of the facts of the case, as taken from their catalogue of defendants:

> Witnesses located Adams' car at the time of the crime at the home of the victim, a white rancher. Some of the victim's jewelry was found in the car trunk. Adams maintained his innocence, claiming that he had loaned the car to his girlfriend. A witness identified Adams as driving the car away from the victim's home shortly after the crime. This witness, however, was driving a large truck in the direction opposite to that of Adams' car, and probably could not have had a good look at the driver. It was later discovered that this witness was angry with Adams for allegedly dating his wife. A second witness heard a voice inside the victim's home at the time of the crime and saw someone fleeing. He stated this voice was a woman's; the day after the crime he stated that the fleeing person was positively not Adams. More importantly, a hair sample found clutched in the victim's hand, which in all likelihood had come from the assailant, did not match Adams' hair. Much of this exculpatory information was not discovered until the case was examined by a skilled investigator a month before Adams' execution. Governor Graham, however, refused to grant even a short stay so that these questions could be resolved.[37]

Critics have challenged Bedau and Radelet's inclusion of James Adams. They contend that a reading of the trial transcript leaves little doubt that Adams was guilty of the crime for which he was executed. They attribute Bedau and Radelet's mistake to their source of information, which was Adams' Petition for Executive Clemency (the only source they cited) written by his defense attorneys. The Florida Clemency Board found Adams' petition without merit, something that Bedau and Radelet failed to mention.[38] In a personal communication to this author, Professor Radelet took exception to these criticisms.[39] He noted that the Florida Clemency Board, which is comprised of Florida cabinet members; specifically, the Governor, Attorney General, Chief Financial Officer, and Commissioner of Agriculture, is hardly an objective body. He also explained that, in addition to the clemency petition, his and Bedau's inclusion of Adams in their catalogue was based on his reading of the entire trial transcript and all of the appellate briefs for both the prosecution and defense, his conversation with Adams on Florida's death row, conversations with Adams's minister, the retired Philadelphia police detective who investigated the case, his lead attorney, and other attorneys who worked on the case. Only the clemency petition was cited in the notes because, in Radelet's words, it was "the most concise treatment of the case" and "to cite everything else would have been . . . overkill."

Bedau and Radelet also cite the case of Edward Earl Johnson who was executed in Mississippi on May 20, 1987. Although they describe why they doubt his guilt, they did not include him in their catalogue apparently because his case did not meet their conservative definition of innocence.

Besides Leonel Torres Herrera and Jesse Dwayne Jacobs, who were both executed in Texas in 1993 and 1995, respectively (both cases were described previously but were not included in Bedau and Radelet's catalogue of cases because their executions occurred after the summer of 1991 when Bedau and Radelet's research was formally concluded), another post-*Gregg* (1976) execution involved Robert Sullivan, who was convicted in 1973 and executed in Florida in 1983. Enough questions were raised about Sullivan's guilt that Pope John Paul II made a personal plea to Florida Governor Graham to halt the execution. Other people executed after 1976 and the implementation of super due process, despite evidence of their innocence, include (state and date of execution in parentheses): Timothy Baldwin (Louisiana, 1984), Willie Jaspar Darden (Florida, 1988), Walter Blair (Missouri, 1993), Ruben Cantu (Texas, 1993), Robert Nelson Drew (Texas, 1994), Roy Stewart (Florida, 1994), Girvies L. Davis (Illinois, 1995), Barry Fairchild (Arkansas, 1995), Larry Griffin (Missouri, 1995), Bernard Bolender (Florida, 1995), Billy Gardner (Texas, 1995), Dennis Stockton (Virginia, 1995), Joseph O'Dell (Virginia, 1997), David Spence (Texas, 1997), Leo Jones (Florida, 1998), Wilburn Henderson (Arkansas, 1998), Troy Farris (Texas, 1999), Roy Roberts (Missouri, 1999), Bernie Demps (Florida, 2000), Gary Graham (Texas, 2000), and Cameron Willingham (Texas, 2004).[40] It is important to emphasize that the evidence of wrongful execution in each of these cases is not definitive. For example, a previous member of this list, Roger Keith Coleman, who was executed in Virginia in 1992, has been removed. In January 2006, Virginia Governor Mark Warner announced the results of new DNA tests that confirmed Coleman's guilt. The new DNA tests used technology that was not available at the time of Coleman's execution.[41]

Not counting Coleman, as many as 24 people (and likely more) may have been executed in error in the United States since 1976 and the implementation of super due process. That represents about two percent of all executions through March 2007. How could those wrongful executions (and wrongful convictions) occur, especially within the context of super due process? That question is addressed shortly. First, however, it is important to distinguish between two general types of errors that occur in capital cases.

Errors in Capital Cases

Most errors in capital cases are probably never discovered, but of those that are there are two general types: "harmless" errors and "serious" or "prejudicial" errors.[42] A serious or prejudicial error is one that can be shown by the defendant to have likely affected the outcome of the trial or to be the type of error that generally results in reversals. In addition—and this is important—the error has to be properly preserved. A harmless error is one, which by proof beyond a reasonable doubt, did not contribute to the verdict. Appellate courts will reverse convictions and sentences only for serious or prejudicial errors that have been properly preserved.

Prior to the mid-1960s, nearly any mistake, especially a violation of a defendant's constitutional rights, was considered serious or prejudicial even if it did not affect the outcome of the trial. In cases tainted by such error, appellate courts almost always reversed convictions. Critics complained that the practice allowed clearly guilty criminal defendants to escape justice because of minor errors—"legal technicalities"—that probably did not adversely influence the trial's outcome. In 1967, the Supreme Court created the "Chapman rule" in *Chapman v. California* (386 U.S. 18). The rule provided that violations of a defendant's rights do not require remedy (reversal of conviction or sentence) unless the error or errors are serious or prejudicial.

At each appeal stage, what constitutes serious or prejudicial error becomes more restrictive mostly due to the requirement that error be properly preserved. For example, most state direct appeals courts will not grant relief based on error—even if the error affected the outcome of the trial—if three conditions are not met: (1) a timely objection was not made at trial, (2) a motion for a new trial based on the objection is not made in a timely fashion after the trial ends, and (3) the objection is not properly asserted in a timely appeal. Defendants may suffer even though the failure to properly preserve the error is entirely their defense attorneys' fault. Several capital defendants have been executed despite obvious prejudicial errors because of their lawyers' failure to properly preserve their objections (when objections were made in the first place). Even in the case of a claim of innocence based on new evidence, 33 death penalty states require that such a claim be made within six months of the final appeal. Virginia, which has the shortest deadline in the U.S., requires the claim to be made within twenty-one days following conviction. Only seven states allow the motion at any time. Consequently, most prisoners who claim innocence based on new evidence can get state relief only by applying to the governor for executive clemency.[43]

At the state post-conviction stage, serious or prejudicial error is properly preserved when it (1) meets the criteria of the direct appeals stage, (2) involves a state or federal constitutional issue, and (3) was not or could not have been raised on direct appeal. Today, most error discovered by state appellate courts in capital cases is considered harmless and does not result in reversals.

At the federal *habeas corpus* stage, serious or prejudicial error is properly preserved when the error (1) meets the criteria of the direct appeals stage, (2) violates the federal Constitution, (3) does not involve the Fourth Amendment's exclusionary rule, (4) is not based on a new rule of federal law if litigated in 1989 or later, and (5) if litigated in 1993 or thereafter meets an especially high standard of prejudice or harmful error (that the error had "substantial and injurious effect or influence in determining the jury's verdict").

Given the restrictive requirements of serious or prejudicial error, one might suppose that the percentage of death sentences reversed on those grounds would be small. However, that was not the case, at least at first. According to a study of the fully reviewed state death sentences imposed between 1973 and 1995, two-thirds were reversed at one of the appeal stages because of serious or prejudicial errors.[44] The study found that in 82 percent of the reversals by state post-conviction courts the defendant deserved a sentence other than death when the errors were cured on retrial and in seven percent of the reversals the defendant was found to be innocent of the capital crime. Eighty percent of the reversals were due to ineffective assistance of counsel, prosecutor misconduct, unconstitutional jury instructions, and judge/jury bias. Yet, as noted in Chapter 2, the number of reversals in death penalty appeals has been decreasing dramatically in recent years, not because of greater fairness in the system or fewer constitutional errors, but rather because death row inmates are simply less likely to prevail. Nearly all constitutional errors today are subject to harm analysis and "proving that an error was harmful is difficult or impossible."[45] The irony, as Professor Dow observes, it that "it is easier in our system to convict someone who did not commit a crime than to have that conviction set aside once we have evidence of the person's innocence."[46]

Why Wrongful Convictions Occur in Capital Cases

As Law Professor Samuel Gross surmises, "The basic cause for the comparatively large number of errors in capital cases is a natural and laudable human impulse: We want murderers to be caught and punished."[47] Many of the errors that contribute to wrongful convictions in capital cases frequently occur long before the case goes to trial. Some of the sources of those errors are discussed in the following sections.

Shoddy Investigation and Misconduct by the Police. Many wrongful convictions in capital cases are a product of shoddy investigation by the police, who sometimes identify the wrong person as the criminal. According to Professor Gross, "This is the critical stage, where most errors occur."[48] When a capital crime is committed, there is usually great pressure on the police to solve it. When the police are unable to do so within a reasonable amount of time, they sometimes cut corners and jump to conclusions. In particular jeopardy in such cases are people who are innocent of the crime being investigated but who have prior felony records. Individuals with prior felony records often become the focus of criminal investigations, especially when police do not have other leads. Unfortunately for such people, recent exploratory research has discovered that innocent (of the crime being investigated) people with prior felony records who have been wrongly convicted of a capital crime have a much greater chance of being executed than innocent people without prior felony records who have been wrongly convicted of capital crimes.[49]

Law enforcement officers (or others who aid them) may even go so far as to lose, destroy, or manufacture evidence against a suspect. For example, in 1993, the West Virginia Supreme Court of Appeals ruled as invalid hundreds of blood tests that West Virginia prosecutors had used over a 10-year period to link defendants to crime scenes.[50] The state police serologist in every case had lied about, made up, or manipulated evidence to win convictions. There was also evidence that the serologist's supervisors may have ignored or concealed complaints of his misconduct. At least 134 prisoners may have been entitled to new trials because of the falsified testimony that put them in prison.

More recently, an FBI investigation found that an Oklahoma City police crime laboratory chemist had misidentified or misinterpreted evidence or testified improperly in court in at least five of the eight cases reviewed. The investigation was prompted by DNA evidence that disproved her testimony against Jeffrey Pierce who was released from prison in May 2001, after serving 15 years on a rape conviction. Another state investigation focused on 23 capital trials in which her testimony helped gain convictions. Ten of those defendants had already been executed. Most controversial was the case of Malcolm Rent Johnson who was executed for rape and murder on January 6, 2000. At Johnson's trial, she testified that six samples of semen taken from the victim's bedroom were consistent with Johnson's blood type. However, when the evidence was reexamined after Johnson's execution, there was no semen present. This same police chemist, who was involved in about 3,000 cases from 1980 to 1993, had been criticized for years. (In 1994 she stopped doing laboratory work after she was promoted to a supervisory position.) In another case, two appellate courts ruled that this police chemist gave false testimony about semen evidence in the 1992 rape and murder trial of Alfred Brian Mitchell. In August 2001, Mitchell's rape conviction was overturned because of her false testimony (his murder conviction was upheld). State officials and the FBI scrutinized her work in about 1,200 cases, including the cases of three death row inmates. She was fired from her job in September 2001 after a hearing by an administrative panel into her alleged misconduct.[51] Note that in both these examples the errors were discovered (posthumously in Malcolm Johnson's case); how many such errors go undetected cannot be known.

Eyewitness Misidentification and Perjury by Prosecution Witnesses. Eyewitness misidentification is the most important contributing factor to wrongful convictions in noncapital cases.[52] For example, a study of recent DNA exonerations by the Innocence Project discovered that 82 percent of the wrongful convictions were at least in part a result of mistaken identification by an eyewitness or victim.[53] Decades of research show that eyewitnesses are just not very good at identifying criminal offenders especially when the eyewitnesses are under stress or are attempting to identify offenders of a different race. Oftentimes the witnesses who are most certain of their identification are the least likely to be correct.[54] Eyewitness misidentification is probably less common in capital cases, but it still was the second most important factor, accounting for 16 percent of the errors in the capital cases discovered by Bedau and Radelet.

In noncapital cases, the crime victim is often able to identify the offender; in capital cases, that is not possible. Consequently, in capital cases, the police frequently must rely on evidence from other people, such as accomplices, jailhouse snitches, other disreputable characters, and even the defendant himself or herself. Some offenders implicate innocent people to divert suspicion from themselves. Other people, who may or may not have had a role in the crime, perjure themselves for money or for other favors from criminal justice officials, such as the dropping of charges in another unrelated case. It should come as no surprise, then, that perjury by prosecution witnesses is the foremost cause of wrongful convictions in capital cases. Bedau and Radelet identified witness perjury as a factor in 35 percent of the wrongful convictions that they discovered.[55] Furthermore, recent exploratory research shows that when allegations of witness perjury are raised on appeal, innocent capital defendants are 27 times more likely to be exonerated and released from death row than are innocent defendants who did not raise perjury issues on appeal and are eventually executed.[56]

False Confessions. The third most common cause of errors in capital cases is false confessions, which accounted for 14 percent of the errors in the cases discovered by Bedau and Radelet.[57] Police officers in the United States have powerful techniques for extracting confessions:

> They confuse and disorient the suspect, they lie about physical evidence, about witnesses, about statements by other suspects; they pretend that they already have their case sealed and are only giving the suspect a chance to explain his side of the story; they pretend to understand, to sympathize, to excuse; they play on the suspect's fears, his biases, his loyalty to family and friends, his religion; they exhaust the suspect and wear him down; in some cases, they use violence, even torture.[58]

By using such coercive and manipulative methods, the police are often successful in getting guilty defendants to confess. Sometimes, however, they get innocent people to confess, too.

Guilty Pleas by Innocent Defendants. Another source of error in capital cases is guilty pleas by innocent defendants. Because of their fear of being executed, some innocent people charged with capital crimes plead guilty to lesser, noncapital offenses. Radelet and his colleagues list 16 cases of innocent people in the twentieth century who pled guilty to noncapital murder to avoid the possibility of execution.[59]

Prosecutor Misconduct. Prosecutors are the most powerful people in the administration of justice.[60] Not only do they conduct the final screening of each person arrested for a criminal offense, deciding whether there is enough evidence to support a conviction, but in most jurisdictions they also have unreviewable discretion in deciding whether to charge a person with a crime and whether to prosecute the case. In other words, regardless of the amount (or lack) of incriminating evidence, and without having to provide any reasons to anyone, prosecutors have the authority to charge or not to charge a person with a crime and to prosecute or not prosecute a case. If they decide to prosecute, they also determine what the charge or charges will be. (The charge or charges may or may not be the same as the one or ones for which the person was arrested.)

For these reasons and others (such as their authority to decide which cases to "plea–bargain" and what bargain to strike), prosecutors are the most powerful people in the capital punishment process too. They are the gatekeepers of that process and alone decide whether to charge a suspect with a capital crime. (A committee of prosecutors sometimes makes the decision.) They sometimes try to minimize their awesome responsibility by saying that their role is only to give a judge or jury the opportunity to decide whether death is the appropriate punishment in a capital case. However, their role is much more pivotal. Prosecutors are the first authorities to determine who among those arrested is fit to live and who should die.

Ideally, prosecutors are supposed to charge an offender with a crime (capital or otherwise) and to prosecute the case if after full investigation three, and only three, conditions are met: (1) they find that a crime has been committed; (2) a perpetrator can be identified; and (3) there is sufficient evidence to support a guilty verdict. In capital cases, prosecutors must also find at least one statutorily enumerated aggravating factor.

On the other hand, prosecutors are not supposed to charge suspects with more criminal charges or for more serious crimes than can be reasonably supported by the evidence. They are not supposed to prosecute simply because an aroused public demands it. They are not supposed to be influenced by the personal or political advantages or disadvantages that might be involved in prosecuting or not prosecuting a case. Nor, for that matter, are they supposed to be swayed by their desire to enhance their records of successful convictions. It would be naive, however, to believe that those factors do not have at least some influence on some prosecutors' decisions in capital or potentially capital cases.[61] A large body of evidence (presented in the next chapter) shows that prosecutor misconduct is a major source of arbitrary and discriminatory application of the death penalty. Prosecutor misconduct is also a principal cause of wrongful convictions. For example, in a recent study of the 88 cases under post-*Furman* statutes (through December 31, 2000) in which people were completely exonerated of crimes for which they were sentenced to die, thirty instances of prosecutor misconduct were discovered in 27 (31 percent) of the cases.[62] Fourteen instances of prosecutor misconduct involved withholding exculpatory evidence, 12 instances involved the subordination of perjury, and four instances involved the use of improper evidence.[63]

Prosecutors know that legal procedure prohibits them from withholding exculpatory evidence from the defense as was done in the case of Don Paradis, who was mentioned previously, and many others like him. Exculpatory evidence is evidence favorable to the accused that has an effect on guilt or punishment. Examples of possible exculpatory evidence are physical evidence, evidentiary documents (such as a defendant's recorded statements to police, or reports of medical examinations or scientific tests), and lists of witnesses. A prosecutor's concealment or misrepresentation of evidence (typically referred to as a "Brady violation," see *Brady v. Maryland*, 1963) is grounds for an appellate court's reversal of a conviction or sentence. In the study of the 88 exonerations cited above, withholding exculpatory evidence accounted for more than half of all instances of prosecutor misconduct and was a factor in about 16 percent of the 88 cases.[64]

Because suborning perjury is a criminal offense, it is hard to believe that many prosecutors know in advance that their witnesses are lying under oath. Yet, how can prosecutors ignore or not suspect the obvious motives of jailhouse snitches and the questionable incriminating evidence they provide?[65] It is also hard to believe that most prosecutors are not privy to inmate informer argot about their deceptive practices: "'Don't go to the pen—send a friend.' Or: 'If you can't do the time, just drop a dime.' [Or:] 'Trouble? You better call 1-800-HETOLDME.'"[66] Perjury by prosecution witnesses occurred in 13.6 percent of the cases in the aforementioned study of the 88 people sentenced to die who were exonerated. It accounted for nearly 45 percent of all cases of prosecutor misconduct.[67] And, as noted previously, Bedau and Radelet identified witness perjury as a factor in 35 percent of the wrongful convictions that they discovered.[68] In their study, it was the foremost cause of wrongful convictions in capital cases.

Sometimes prosecutors fail to dismiss capital charges against ostensibly innocent defendants. Prosecutors may be reluctant to dismiss charges even when the case is a weak one, especially when there is public clamor for a conviction. Much of this has to do with ego. A sign seen in the Dallas County, Texas, prosecutor's office reads: "Convicting the guilty is easy. It's the innocent that keep us working late."[69] The problem is that not only are some weak cases tried, but, as the quotation suggests, in some cases innocent defendants are convicted. In 20 of the 88 cases (22.7 percent) in which people sentenced to die were exonerated, lack of evidence was the primary reason for release.[70]

DNA analysis has proven to be an important tool in the successful investigation, prosecution, and exoneration of criminal defendants, including defendants facing the death penalty. In ten (11.4 percent) of the 88 cases in the study cited above, DNA evidence was responsible for exoneration.[71] Yet, despite relatively easy access to the technology, many local prosecutors refuse to release crime evidence for DNA analysis unless litigation is threatened or filed. They point out that they have no legal obligation to cooperate because once a trial has been concluded, a convicted defendant has no absolute right to prove his or her innocence. They argue that the offender's interest in proving his or her innocence is outweighed by the state's interest in the finality of judgment.[72] Although refusing to release crime evidence for DNA analysis when possible innocence is at stake may not be prosecutor misconduct in a legal or technical sense, the belief that finality of sentence is more important than the preservation of innocent life is certainly debatable.

In some cases, following the exoneration of an innocent person who was wrongfully convicted and sentenced to death, prosecutors elect not to seek a death sentence when the actual perpetrator is found.[73]

Hopefully, most prosecutors follow the rules. Some do not. What happens to those prosecutors who get caught engaging in misconduct in capital cases? The answer is not much. In a study of 381 murder convictions since 1963 that were reversed because of police or prosecutor misconduct, not one of the prosecutors who broke the law was convicted or disbarred for his or her misconduct. Most of the time, they were not even disciplined. Current laws also protect prosecutors from civil suits even when they knowingly allowed perjured testimony or deliberately concealed evidence of innocence.[74]

Judicial Misconduct or Error. In capital trials, judges are responsible for allowing the jury a fair chance to reach a verdict on the evidence presented. Judges must ensure that their behavior does not improperly affect the outcome of the case. Before juries retire to deliberate and reach a verdict, judges instruct them on the relevant law. This involves interpreting legal precedents and applying them to the unique circumstances of the case.

In her examination of Missouri clemency petitions, sociologist Cathleen Burnett found the following allegations of judicial misconduct or error:

(1) not permitting the defense to present evidence of an alternative theory of the case;

(2) not permitting the defense to present certain mitigating evidence;

(3) denying the right of defense experts to offer evidence;

(4) failing to order a psychiatric examination prior to trial;

(5) prejudging the case;

(6) incorrectly finding fact;

(7) refusing to give certain jury instructions;

(8) failing to admonish the prosecutor for an improper closing argument;

(9) allowing a highly prejudicial photograph during the penalty phase;

(10) failing to permit withdrawal of a guilty plea; and

(11) not having jurisdiction.[75]

Bad Defense Lawyers. Professor Gross claims that despite some of the problems just cited, the capital trial "plays a comparatively minor role in the production of errors in capital cases."[76] Gross says the reason is that capital defendants usually have superior (as compared to other felony defendants) defense counsel: "Capital defendants . . . may be better represented than other criminal defendants. The attorneys who are appointed to represent them may be more experienced and skillful, and their defenders may have more resources at their disposal." [77] The evidence, however, suggests that Gross may be wrong on this point.

Professor Bedau relates that "experienced criminal trial attorneys . . . say that 'no really capable defense lawyer should ever lose a capital case.'"[78] Research shows that "a lawyer's skill is the most important factor determining whether a defendant is sentenced to death or to life in prison."[79] Most capital defendants, though, are not represented by capable defense attorneys, but by those who are inexperienced, overworked, understaffed, less resourceful, less independent, and who frequently lose capital cases.[80]

A good example is the case of John Spinkelink, the third person executed in the United States under post-*Gregg* (1976) statutes and the first person during that period executed against his will. Spinkelink's last appeal was based on a Sixth Amendment claim of counsel ineffectiveness. According to Ramsey Clark, former attorney general of the United States:

> John Spinkelink's trial attorneys were court-appointed. They lacked sufficient resources to prepare and conduct the defense. One publicly stated that the case was beyond his competence. One was absent during part of the jury selection to be with his wife in childbirth. He had not sought a delay in the proceeding or permission of the court to be absent. Spinkelink's lawyers also failed to challenge the composition of the grand and petit juries. Both were later found to underrepresent blacks, women and young people—groups considered by most experienced attorneys to be favorable to the defense in capital cases. The lawyers failed to ask that Spinkelink be tried separately from his co-defendant who was acquitted. Severance was authorized under Florida law and would seem strategically important. Counsel failed to challenge excessive security measures in the courtroom, which are generally thought to be prejudicial to a defendant. . . . They [the prosecution] had (wrongly) informed the jury in their closing argument that the judge could not impose a more severe sentence than the jury recommended. This may have encouraged the jury to ask for a maximum sentence, leaving the judge the full range of punishment alternatives. Counsel failed to obtain a transcript of questions asked prospective jurors, which was necessary in determining if they were constitutionally selected. The Florida Supreme Court ruled that all objections had been waived. With their client facing death, counsel did not request oral argument on appeal in the Supreme Court of Florida.[81]

Spinkelink's experience is not uncommon. A Texas study by the governor's judicial council found that three-quarters of murderers with court-appointed attorneys were sentenced to death, while only about a third of those represented by private lawyers were so sentenced.[82] Another study that compared innocent capital defendants who were eventually exonerated and released from death row and innocent capital defendants who were later executed discovered that defendants with private lawyers at trial were nine times more likely to be exonerated and released from death row than defendants with court-appointed attorneys.[83]

A 1990 *National Law Journal* study showed that criminal defendants in six states of the South—Alabama, Florida, Georgia, Louisiana, Mississippi, and Texas—often wound up on death row after being represented by inexperienced, unskilled, or unprepared court-appointed lawyers.[84] The study found that many poor defendants sentenced to death (and nearly all capital defendants are poor) had lawyers who had never handled a capital trial before, lacked training in life-or-death cases, made little effort to present evidence in support of a life sentence, or had been reprimanded, disciplined, or subsequently disbarred. An investigation published in the *Chicago Tribune* on June 11, 2000, found that in Texas, "attorneys in 40 capital cases 'presented no evidence whatsoever or only one witness during the trial's sentencing phase' [and that in] forty-three cases, the accused were represented by attorneys who were punished for professional misbehavior."[85] One notoriously incompetent Texas attorney, Ron Mock, had so many clients sentenced to death that people referred to a section of Texas's death row as the "Mock Wing."[86] In 2002, the U.S. Supreme Court upheld the death sentence of Gary Cone from Tennessee, even though his attorney presented no mitigating evidence and did not argue for his client's life. It was reported that the attorney was mentally ill and later committed suicide. Nevertheless, the Court ruled 8-1 that the attorney's inaction did not amount to a complete absence of representation, and that the state court did not act unreasonably when it held that the attorney might have been making a tactical decision in not presenting evidence.[87] Consider the following additional examples from the *National Law Journal* study:

- Nine years after John Young was condemned to death in Georgia in 1976, his disbarred lawyer, Charles Marchman Jr., admitted that his drug use, the breakup of his marriage, the discovery of his homosexuality, and other factors prevented him from defending Young adequately.

- James Copeland, on Louisiana's death row, had a lawyer at his second trial who confessed that he never read the first trial's transcript and did little to uncover evidence for life imprisonment.

- Texas lawyer Jon Wood unsuccessfully defended Jesus Romero against the death penalty with 29 words, among them: "You've got that man's life in your hands. You can take it or not. That's all I have to say."

Even an attorney who sleeps through the trial is not necessarily considered ineffective, as is seen in the following description of a capital case in Houston, Texas:

> Seated beside his client—a convicted capital murderer—defense attorney John Benn spent much of Thursday afternoon's trial in apparent deep sleep. His mouth kept falling open and his head lolled back on his shoulders, and then he awakened just long enough to catch himself and sit upright. Then it happened again. And again. And again.

> Every time he opened his eyes, a different prosecution witness was on the stand describing another aspect of the Nov. 19, 1991, arrest of George McFarland in the robbery-killing of grocer Kenneth Kwan.

> When state District Judge Doug Shaver finally called a recess, Benn was asked if he truly had fallen asleep during a capital murder trial. "It's boring," the 72-year old longtime Houston lawyer explained.[88]

Attorney Benn's performance did "not offend the right to counsel guaranteed by the United States Constitution, the trial judge explained, because, '[t]he Constitution doesn't say the lawyer has to be awake.'"[89] Agreeing with the trial judge's assessment was the Texas Court of Criminal Appeals, which rejected McFarland's claim of ineffective assistance of counsel.[90]

Benn is not the only Texas attorney who has fallen asleep during a capital trial. Houston attorney Joe Frank Cannon, who is now dead, also had that reputation. He continually dozed off while defending Calvin Burdine, and the Texas Court of Criminal Appeals again held that "a sleeping attorney was sufficient 'counsel' under the Constitution."[91] However, in August 2001, the 5th U.S. Circuit of Appeals, sitting en banc, reversed a three judge federal panel, which earlier had upheld Burdine's death sentence. The full court ordered a new trial for Burdine because his lawyer dozed off frequently enough and for long enough stretches to deprive Burdine of his right to the effective assistance of counsel.[92] The Texas Attorney General's office appealed the ruling to the U.S. Supreme Court, contending that Burdine had received a fair trial despite his attorney's lapses. In June 2002, the Supreme Court let stand the 5th Circuit's earlier ruling, giving no reason for its refusal to intervene. The Houston district attorney's office plans to retry Burdine and again seek the death penalty.[93] On the other hand, when another one of Cannon's death penalty clients, Carl Johnson, eventually appealed to the United States Court of Appeals for the Fifth Circuit, the court ruled that Johnson was not denied the effective assistance of counsel "notwithstanding the sleeping lawyer."[94] At least the Texas Court of Criminal Appeals is empowered to consider claims of ineffective assistance of counsel; Virginia appellate courts are not.[95]

The *National Law Journal* study discovered a general failure of the states to provide effective assistance of counsel to capital defendants. Not much has changed. At the beginning of the 21st century, only half of the then-38 states with death penalty statutes had adopted minimum guidelines or standards or created an agency to promulgate standards for the appointment of counsel at either the trial or appellate level or both in capital cases.[96] One state that adopted such minimum standards (on July 1, 2000) was Florida, whose guidelines resemble those created by the American Bar Association (ABA) in 1989.

The statement of purpose to Florida's new standards reads in part: "Counsel in death penalty cases should be required to perform at the level of an attorney reasonably skilled in the specialized practice of capital representation, zealously committed to the capital case, who has had adequate time and resources for preparation." Following are the minimum standards in Florida.[97]

A. List of Qualified Counsel
    1. Every circuit shall maintain a list of counsel qualified for appointment in capital cases in each of three categories:
        a. lead trial counsel;
        b. trial cocounsel; and
        c. appellate counsel.
        No attorney may be appointed to handle a capital trial unless duly qualified on the appropriate list.
    2. The conflict committee for each circuit is responsible for approving and removing attorneys from the list pursuant to section 925.037, Florida Statutes. Each circuit committee is encouraged to obtain additional input from experienced capital defense counsel.
    3. No attorney may be qualified on any of the capital lists unless he or she has attended within the last year a continuing legal education program of at least ten hours' duration devoted specifically to the defense of capital cases. Continuing legal education programs meeting the requirements of this rule shall be offered by the Florida Bar or another recognized provider and should be approved for continuing legal education credit by the Florida Bar. The failure to comply with this requirement shall be cause for removal from the list until the requirement is fulfilled.

B. Appointment of Counsel. A court must appoint lead counsel and, upon written application and a showing of need by lead counsel, should appoint cocounsel to handle every capital trial in which the defendant is not represented by retained counsel or the Public Defender. Lead counsel shall have the right to select cocounsel from attorneys on the lead counsel or cocounsel list. Both attorneys shall be reasonably compensated for the trial and sentencing phase. Except under extraordinary circumstances, only one attorney may be compensated for other proceedings.

C. Lead Counsel. Lead trial counsel assignments should be given to attorneys who:
1. are members of the bar admitted to practice in the jurisdiction or admitted to practice *pro hac vice* [for this occasion]; and
2. are experienced and active trial practitioners with at least five years of litigation experience in the field of criminal law; and
3. have prior experience as lead counsel in no fewer than nine jury trials of serious and complex cases which were tried to completion, as well as prior experience as lead defense counsel or cocounsel in at least two cases tried to completion in which the death penalty was sought. In addition, of the nine jury trials which were tried to completion, the attorney should have been lead counsel in at least three cases in which the charge was murder; or alternatively, of the nine jury trials, at least one was a murder trial and an additional five were felony jury trials; and
4. are familiar with the practice and procedure of the criminal courts of the jurisdiction; and
5. are familiar with and experienced in the utilization of expert witnesses and evidence, including but not limited to psychiatric and forensic evidence; and
6. have demonstrated the necessary proficiency and commitment which exemplify the quality of representation appropriate to capital cases.

D. Cocounsel. Trial cocounsel assignments should be given to attorneys who:
1. are members of the bar admitted to practice in the jurisdiction or admitted to practice *pro hac vice*; and
2. who qualify as lead counsel under paragraph (C) of these standards or meet the following requirements:
    a. are experienced and active trial practitioners with at least three years of litigation experience in the field of criminal law; and
    b. have prior experience as lead counsel or cocounsel in no fewer than three jury trials of serious and complex cases which were tried to completion, at least two of which were trials in which the charge was murder; or alternatively, of the three jury trials, at least one was a murder trial and one was a felony jury trial; and

        c. are familiar with the practice and procedure of the criminal courts of the jurisdiction; and

        d. have demonstrated the necessary proficiency and commitment which exemplify the quality of representation appropriate in capital cases.

E. Appellate Counsel. Appellate counsel assignments should be given to attorneys who:

    1. are members of the bar admitted to practice in the jurisdiction or admitted to practice *pro hac vice*; and

    2. are experienced and active trial or appellate practitioners with at least five years of experience in the field of criminal law; and

    3. have prior experience in the appeal of at least one case where a sentence of death was imposed, as well as prior experience as lead counsel in the appeal of no fewer than three felony convictions in federal or state court, at least one of which was an appeal of a murder conviction; or alternatively, have prior experience as lead counsel in the appeal of no fewer than six felony convictions in federal or state court, at least two of which were appeals of a murder conviction; and

    4. are familiar with the practice and procedure of the appellate courts of the jurisdiction; and

    5. have demonstrated the necessary proficiency and commitment which exemplify the quality of representation appropriate in capital cases.

F. Exceptional Circumstances. In the event that the trial court determines that counsel meeting the technical requirements of this rule is not available and that exceptional circumstances require appointment of other counsel, the trial court shall enter an order specifying, in writing, the exceptional circumstances requiring deviation from the rule and the court's explicit determination that counsel chosen will provide competent representation in accord with the policy concerns of the rule.

Clearly, Florida's standards for the appointment of counsel in capital cases, as well as the standards created by other death penalty states, are better than no standards at all. However, none of the standards can be considered particularly rigorous; they are truly minimum standards.

In 2003, the American Bar Association's House of Delegates approved a revised edition of its 1989 guidelines for the appointment and performance of defense counsel in death penalty cases. (These guidelines are provided in Appendix A) The revised edition was created because of deficiencies in the older guidelines. One change in emphasis is illustrative. In the 1989 version, the stated purpose of the guidelines was to ensure "quality legal representation." In the 2003 guidelines, that was changed to "high quality legal representation." However, a year after the new guidelines were approved, no death penalty state had adopted them.[98] The reason is twofold. First, according to critics of the guidelines, they are too expensive to implement.[99] Second, the Supreme Court has not required them. In fact, in *Strickland v. Washington* (466 U.S. 668, 1984), the case that provided a test for determining when counsel is ineffective, the Court adamantly refused to adopt performance guidelines for evaluating counsel in capital cases.[100] It gave three reasons for its position. First, the Court pointed out the purpose of the effective assistance guarantee was "not to improve the quality of legal representation." Second, the Court opined that "no particular set of detailed rules for counsel's conduct can satisfactorily take account of the variety of circumstances faced by defense counsel or the range of legitimate decisions regarding how best to represent a criminal defendant." Third, the Court was concerned that the adoption of specific standards would encourage ineffectiveness claims, which would discourage many attorneys from representing defendants in capital cases.

In addition, and contrary to what Professor Gross reports, defense counsel in capital cases (including those in states with minimum standards) rarely has the resources necessary to mount an effective defense. In the 1990s, for example, attorneys in Alabama were being paid only $20 an hour for out-of-court time in capital cases, with a limit of $2,000 per case; Mississippi was limiting payment to $1,000 a case.[101] As late as 2004, Florida had a $3,500 cap on the payment for defense services in capital cases, meaning that state-funded lawyers in Florida capital cases would be paid an estimated $3.00 an hour.[102] A paralegal working on a federal bankruptcy case is paid more per hour than a defense attorney in a capital case in Alabama, Georgia, Mississippi, and Virginia.[103] It is not unusual for attorneys in capital cases to be compensated at less than minimum wage, and states have been known to appoint attorneys in capital cases who submitted the lowest bids.[104] As Professor Bowers explains:

> Dollar-wise [an appointed attorney] peaks out before going to trial, meaning the trial is his gift to the defendant—it's free—that's his practice he's cutting into. . . . The cap makes hungry, inexperienced guys take cases but attorneys who can command fees can't afford to.[105]

In 1924, famed attorney Clarence Darrow observed, "No court ever interferes with a good lawyer's business by calling him in and compelling him to give his time" to a poor person facing criminal charges; "instead, judges appoint lawyers willing to take the case for what the courts pay."[106] This is as true today as when Darrow said it. Furthermore, some judges will not appoint capable defense attorneys to represent capital defendants even when they have the opportunity to do so. According to a Texas survey of trial judges, for about half the judges, a lawyer's reputation for moving cases quickly, regardless of the quality of the defense, was a factor in the decision to appoint a particular lawyer.[107] Some court-appointed attorneys may be less than zealous in their client's defense because they do not want to antagonize a judge and lose future business.[108] Some jurisdictions have attempted to provide more adequate resources in capital cases, but in none could the provision of those resources be considered generous. Most provide woefully inadequate resources. The Louisiana Supreme Court recently ruled that trial judges in death penalty cases could stop prosecutions of indigent defendants until the state provides the money to pay for an adequate defense.[109] (See Chapter 6 for the economic costs of capital punishment.)

Even if the necessary financial resources *were* provided, that would not compensate entirely for deficient intellectual resources. Defense attorneys, however, are not entirely to blame for this problem. Capital jurisprudence is a highly specialized area of the criminal law, and most attorneys have not received instruction in it.[110] Nevertheless, many judges will appoint any lawyer licensed to practice law to represent a capital defendant, even if the lawyer's practice is limited mostly to real estate or divorce law.[111] Consequently, even when they are conscientious, appointed attorneys in capital cases may make numerous mistakes.

Defense attorneys who lack experience in capital cases are often stymied at the penalty phase of the bifurcated trial. Many attorneys have experience pleading their client's innocence (the focus of the guilt phase), but only those lawyers who have tried several capital cases are experienced in making an affirmative case for their client's life in the penalty phase. As attorney Margot Garey relates:

> Many defense attorneys fail to make the transition and do not adequately prepare or effectively present the defendant's penalty phase trial. For example, a defense attorney may structure a guilt trial strategy that is inconsistent with the penalty phase theory. This situation may negate any effective defense at the penalty proceeding since a consistent trial strategy increases the defendant's believability and credibility. Should a guilty verdict be rendered in the guilt phase, it is imperative that the jury believe the defendant's mitigating circumstances proffered in the penalty phase. Therefore, the defense attorney cannot plan the theory of the guilt phase trial independent of the penalty phase. She must develop and structure a defense theory that will include the penalty phase. Because the preparation required for structuring a bifurcated proceeding is categorically different from that required for a noncapital trial, defense counsel who may be very competent in complex noncapital criminal trials may, without training, be ineffective in capital trials.[112]

An example of the problem of coordinating the guilt and penalty phase of a capital trial is provided by the case of *People v. Lane*.[113] In the guilt phase of Lane's trial, his attorney claimed that that Lane was not the killer despite a videotape clearly showing Lane pulling the trigger at point-blank range. Lane's attorney contended that it was a case of mistaken identity, that Lane was not the person on the videotape. The jury found Lane guilty of capital murder. At the penalty phase, his attorney argued that Lane did the murder because of extenuating circumstances, which jurors took as just another attempt to deceive them (as Lane's attorney tried to do during the guilt phase). Lane's attorney also noted at the penalty phase that others, such as Hitler and Manson, were worse than his client—"assuming, of course, that he had done it." By first denying guilt then arguing mitigation, jurors viewed Lane as a "remorseless manipulator."[114] The jury sentenced Lane to death.

In sum, whether it is the result of a lack of training, experience, or heart, most capital defendants receive what appears to be ineffective legal representation. Critics cynically argue that in practice the courts use the "mirror test" in determining whether a defense attorney is effective in a capital case: If the mirror fogs up because the attorney is breathing, then the attorney is effective. That may be why the Supreme Court has rarely granted relief on the grounds of ineffective assistance of counsel.[115]

Proponents of capital punishment argue the reason the Supreme Court rarely grants relief in ineffective assistance of counsel claims is because most capital defendants have superior defense attorneys, as death penalty opponent Gross suggested at the onset of this section. Proponents argue that death penalty abolitionists do not show that ineffectiveness of counsel is widespread and that the evidence of ineffectiveness is mostly anecdotal and "grossly outdated."[116] They add that just because some defense attorneys in some death penalty states may be ineffective the death penalty in the entire United States need not be abolished. They ask, Why should a state or the federal government, for that matter, that provides effective representation be penalized because of states that do not?[117] Their answer, of course, is they should not.

Furthermore, not all of the problems encountered in a capital defense are a defense attorney's fault. Some capital defendants refuse to cooperate or cooperate fully with their attorneys. For example, some defendants refuse to help their attorneys develop their life story to use as mitigation in the penalty phase. These defendants often want to protect their families from embarrassment by not revealing family secrets of child abuse and molestation. Sometimes defendants refuse to allow their attorneys to claim their clients suffer from mental illness, even when the evidence strongly supports such a claim. Some defendants simply want to be sentenced to death, placing a considerable burden on their attorneys who are required by law to zealously defend them.[118]

Jury Problems. Jury problems that may cause miscarriages of justice in capital cases are described in more detail in the next chapter on arbitrary and discriminatory application of the death penalty. Suffice it to say here that jurors are unlikely to find defendants innocent of their crimes after the police and prosecutors failed to do so. Jurors have less information and experience than the police and prosecutors. Consequently, jurors are less to blame for miscarriages of justice in capital cases than are the police and prosecutors.[119]

The Illusive Hope of Clemency

Clemency generally provides the final opportunity to consider whether a death sentence should be imposed.[120] All 50 states, the federal government, and the military have provisions for granting clemency.[121] They allow the governor of a state or the president of the United States, when federal or military law is violated, to exercise leniency or mercy. Many states have specialized administrative boards or panels authorized to assist the governor in making the clemency decision. In a few states, the governor is not authorized to grant clemency unless an administrative body has first recommended it.[122]

The granting of clemency was much more common in colonial America than it is today. For example, in the eighteenth century, more than half of all condemned prisoners in New York and one-quarter to one-third of condemned prisoners in Virginia escaped execution through clemency.[123] The reason was not that colonial Americans were more lenient than their contemporary counterparts, but rather that clemency had more purposes in the seventeenth and eighteenth centuries that, today, are accomplished in other ways. For instance, in colonial America, there were no criminal appeals so clemency was the only way to correct trial errors, such as the conviction of an innocent person. Today, appellate courts perform that function (in at least some cases).[124] Incidentally, the availability of automatic appellate review under post-*Furman* statutes has given governors a plausible excuse for denying clemency petitions. They can simply state that they are deferring judgments about constitutional issues to appellate court judges.[125] Second, during the colonial period, clemency was the only way to mitigate a death sentence. Today, mitigation is considered during sentencing.[126] Third, clemency served a law enforcement purpose in the colonial period that it does not serve today. It was sometimes granted to offenders who implicated their partners, something that is now accomplished through plea bargaining.[127] Thus, there were important practical reasons for the more liberal use of clemency during the colonial period.

George W. Bush, in his autobiography, *A Charge to Keep*, wrote that decisions about executions are "by far the most profound" that a governor can make. He should know having presided over 152 executions—by far the most by a governor in the U.S. under post-*Furman* statutes—during his six years as Texas governor.[128] Because Texas has conducted more than one-third of all executions under post-*Furman* statutes and nearly three times as many executions as its nearest contender, an examination of its clemency strategy may prove instructive though probably not representative.[129]

The state of Texas maintains the legal fiction that its governor, unlike governors of other states, does not have unfettered authority to grant clemency. In Texas, the governor can grant clemency only to those inmates that the 18-member Board of Pardons and Paroles recommends. Otherwise, the governor must either approve the execution or grant a 30-day stay. However, the governor can control the process because the governor appoints the board that is authorized to approve or deny all clemency applications.[130] A good example of this legal fiction in action involves the case of infamous serial killer Henry Lee Lucas, the only person to whom Bush granted clemency during his tenure as governor. Lucas, who had confessed falsely to hundreds of murders, had been convicted in the 1980s of nine murders for which he was serving six life sentences, two seventy-five-year sentences, and one sixty-year sentence. In yet another murder trial, Lucas was sentenced to death. After the trial and investigations by two successive state attorneys, it became apparent that Lucas was wrongly convicted of the murder for which he was sentenced to death because he had not been in the state of Texas when the victim was killed. When then-Governor Bush became aware of this fact, he let the Board of Pardons and Paroles know that he would not allow Lucas to be executed for a crime he did not commit. The Board of Pardons and Paroles subsequently voted 17 to 1 to commute Lucas's death sentence to life in prison, which Bush approved. Ironically, in denying Karla Faye Tucker's clemency petition, Bush, citing Texas law, stated that he could not commute Tucker's sentence from death to life in prison without the recommendation of the Board of Pardons and Paroles—something he somehow was able to get in the Lucas case.[131]

The Texas Board of Pardons and Paroles does not meet to discuss applications. Instead, members review cases separately and fax in their votes from across the state. The board operates without guidelines and does not have to give explanations for its decisions. *The Dallas Morning News* described the clemency process in Texas as "shrouded in secrecy." In 1999, Federal District Judge Sam Sparks ruled that the clemency system in Texas had the "minimal procedural safeguards" required by the U.S. Supreme Court. He added, however, that

> [i]t is abundantly clear the Texas clemency procedure is extremely poor and certainly minimal. Legislatively, there is a dearth of meaningful procedure. Administratively, the goal is more to protect the secrecy and autonomy of the system

rather than carrying out an efficient legally sound system. The board would not have to sacrifice its conservative ideology to carry out its duties in a more fair and accurate fashion.[132]

Before Governor Bush made a final decision on clemency, usually on the morning of the day of the scheduled execution, he reviewed a document prepared by his legal counsel summarizing the facts of the case. His counsel then briefed him on those facts. Alberto Gonzales, who, at this writing, is the United States Attorney General, prepared the first 57 clemency memos given to then-Governor Bush. An examination of those memos and Bush's handling of them is revealing about the clemency process in Texas at that time.[133]

The clemency memos, which were only three to seven pages long, were the primary source of information used by the governor in making his clemency decisions. Each memo contained a brief description of the crime, one or two paragraphs about the defendant's personal background, and a short legal history. Rarely were recommendations made about whether or not to grant clemency, but many memos reflected a clear prosecutorial bias and an assumption that the governor had no good reason to revisit claims already rejected by appellate courts. Conspicuously missing from nearly all of the memos was any reference to crucial issues in the case, such as ineffective counsel, conflict of interest, mitigating evidence, or evidence of actual innocence.

When speaking about the clemency process throughout his term of office, Bush repeatedly made statements like the following: "I take every death penalty case seriously and review each case carefully." "Each case is major, because each case is life or death." In his autobiography, he revealed, "I review every death penalty case thoroughly." Referring to his legal staff, he wrote, "For every death penalty case, they brief me thoroughly, review the arguments made by the prosecution and defense, raise any doubts or problems or questions." Bush touted the review as a "fail-safe" method for ensuring due process and certainty of guilt. During the 2000 presidential campaign, Gonzales was asked whether Bush ever read death row inmates' clemency petitions. He responded, "I wouldn't say that was done in every case . . . [b]ut if we felt there was something he should look at specifically—yes, he did look from time to time at what had been filed." However, a review of the clemency memos suggests that Governor Bush often allowed executions to proceed "based on only the most cursory briefings on the issues in dispute."

Three types of clemency relevant to capital punishment are reprieve, commutation, and pardon. Reprieve is the most common type of clemency employed in capital cases and the most limited. A reprieve temporarily postpones an execution. It is typically used to allow a death row inmate the opportunity to complete a pending appeal or to give the governor a last-minute chance to review questions about the inmate's guilt.

Commutation involves the substitution of a lesser punishment for the one imposed by the court. A sentence of life imprisonment (with or without the opportunity for parole) is the sentence most likely to be substituted for a death sentence. Sometimes commutations are contingent on certain conditions, such as the inmate waiving his or her right to a new trial or agreeing not to profit from the sale of an account of his or her crime. From 1976 through September 2006, 224 death row inmates had their sentences commuted. That represents about three percent of all death sentences imposed during the period. Illinois governors granted 75 percent of the commutations (172), including 167 in January 2003, by Illinois Governor George Ryan, just days before leaving office(more about this later).[134]

A pardon is the most expansive type of clemency. With a pardon, the prisoner's crime is erased and his or her punishment is terminated. A pardoned individual is freed entirely from the criminal justice system and is treated legally as if he or she had never been charged or convicted of a crime. Pardons are rarely granted to people convicted of capital crimes. From January 1, 1973, through September 2006, only 7 pardons were granted to condemned inmates, including four by Illinois Governor Ryan in January 2003.[135] Also, between January 1, 1973 and September 2006, the Courts cleared 116 capital offenders of the charge that put them on death row, though those exonerations by the courts are not "executive" pardons.[136]

Former Chief Justice Rehnquist considered executive clemency the "fail safe" of the criminal justice system.[137] It is the last, best chance of rectifying miscarriages of justice. Unfortunately for those who would rely on clemency to correct errors made earlier in the process, recent experience contradicts the promise. In a bow to states rights, the federal courts are increasingly deferring to governors the job of correcting substantive problems with death sentences. Yet, governors are being effectively deterred from granting clemency. Few death sentences have been commuted under post-*Furman* statutes because of increased media attention devoted to capital clemency deliberations and the realization by governors that a decision to commute a death sentence is likely to lead to political suicide. The few commutations that have been granted have come mostly from governors not seeking reelection.[138] This is a change from the past. Prior to 1970, governors in death penalty states "routinely commuted up to a third of the death sentences that they reviewed," but since then, with the exception of the 167 death sentences commuted by Illinois governor George Ryan in 2003, only about two death sentences a year (in the entire country) have been commuted.[139] The most common reasons given for granting clemency during the post-*Furman* period are doubts about the offender's guilt, the offender's mental retardation or mental illness, and equitable concerns about offenders who have received harsher sanctions than other participants in the same crime.[140]

What Can Be Done?

The only sure way to put a stop to miscarriages of justice in capital cases is to abolish the death penalty. However, short of total abolition are reforms that could substantially reduce the incidence of miscarriages of justice in capital cases. The following sections describe some of those reforms.

Good Defense Attorneys Can Make a Difference. The most successful capital punishment defense attorney in American history was undoubtedly Clarence Darrow, who, in more than 100 capital trials, never had a client sentenced to death.[141] Most capital defendants do not have attorneys as talented as Darrow. Perhaps The Innocence Protection Act of 2004, which was described in Chapter 3, and the ABA's 2003 capital defense guidelines, which are listed in Appendix A, will help change that. Some death penalty states, as noted previously, have created minimum standards for defense attorneys in capital cases—that, too, is at least a start. It would also help if fees for court-appointed defense attorneys were raised to levels high enough to attract competent lawyers.[142] A handful of states have attempted to address the legal representation problem in capital cases by creating centralized state funded agencies (capital defender offices or CDOs) comprised of defense attorneys who specialize in capital cases. Attorneys in these agencies defend indigent clients charged with capital crimes as well as advise and assist other appointed counsel in capital cases.[143] Some of these agencies appear to be particularly effective in not only reducing the number of people sentenced to death but also the amount of capital litigation generally. Both situations likely reduce the number of wrongful convictions.

For example, in Colorado the CDO is part of the statewide Office of the Public Defender. So successful is the office that prosecutors in Colorado rarely seek the death penalty—only about three times a year on average. Between 1975 and 2000, there were 52 capital trials in Colorado, five people were sentenced to death, and only one person was executed.[144] Connecticut also has a CDO within its public defender office. Although the death penalty is rarely sought in northeastern states, only one person has been executed in Connecticut in the more than a quarter of a century since it reinstated the death penalty.[145] New York reenacted its death penalty statute in 1995. The statute created a CDO that was considered one of the best. In 2000, it had a $15 million budget, 21 experienced trial lawyers, and 17 well-trained investigators. Between 1995 and 2000, there were more than 500 cases in which prosecutors either charged first-degree murder or went to court leaving open the possibility of that charge. However, in only 39 cases (as of February 2000) did prosecutors seek the death penalty, and in only five cases was a defendant sentenced to death. Not one of the five defendants was executed.[146] (In 2004, New York's death penalty statute was declared unconstitutional.

As of this writing, New York had not reenacted a death penalty statute.) It may never be known for sure whether it is the CDOs or some other factor or factors that are responsible for reducing the number of people sentenced to death and death penalty litigation generally in those states with CDOs, but it is instructive that few death penalty states, especially those with the largest number of executions, have adopted the CDO model of legal representation in capital cases.

Adopt the American Bar Association's 2003 Guidelines for the Appointment and Performance of Counsel in Death Penalty Cases. Death penalty states should adopt the ABA's guidelines. The guidelines are listed in Appendix A.

Punish the Misconduct of Defense Attorneys.[147] Most acts of misconduct by defense attorneys in capital cases should result in the attorney being disciplined by the state bar association. Where applicable, such disciplined attorneys should be removed from the roster of attorneys eligible to handle death penalty cases. For egregious cases of misconduct, defense attorneys should be disbarred.

Improve Police Investigations, Interrogations, and the Handling of Evidence.[148] Police should keep an open and objective mind during investigations. They should investigate crimes rather than trying to build a case against a likely suspect. Once a suspect has been identified, the police should continue to pursue all reasonable leads, whether they point towards or away from the suspect. Police should be trained to avoid "tunnel vision" or "confirmatory bias" where the belief that a particular suspect has committed a crime often prevents an objective evaluation of whether there might be others who are actually guilty.

To reduce the number of false confessions, defense counsel should be provided to indigent suspects during police interrogation in potential death penalty cases. When there is doubt about whether the suspect is indigent, defense counsel should be provided. Police should also make a reasonable attempt to determine if a suspect is mentally retarded. If the suspect is deemed mentally retarded, the police should not ask leading questions (mentally retarded suspects are inclined to agree with the police version of events) and suggest that they believe the suspect is guilty.

In potential death penalty cases, the entire police custodial interrogation should be videotaped to help validate the interrogation and confessions. Where videotaping is not feasible during an interrogation, audiotaping should be substituted. Any non-recorded statement by a homicide suspect, e.g., in a patrol car on the way to the police station, should be repeated to the suspect on tape, and the suspect's comments recorded. Interviews with significant witnesses in homicide cases should also be electronically recorded.

To make sure that the police provide all the evidence in their possession to the prosecution: (1) all relevant evidence, including exculpatory evidence and its location, should be listed on schedules by the police, (2) specific police officers or employees should be assigned record-keeping responsibility, and (3) prosecutors should be given certified written copies of the schedules by the police.

Improve Eyewitness Identification Techniques and Procedures.[149] Experts agree that the accuracy of eyewitness identifications could be greatly improved if the following policy reforms were adopted in all jurisdictions. First, videotapes should be made of all lineups, photo spreads, and other identification processes so that later any biases, suggestions, or hints that infected the process could be exposed and evaluated. Second, eyewitnesses should be given explicit instructions that the suspected perpetrator might not be in the lineup or photo spread, and therefore making an identification may not be possible. Third, independent examiners should conduct all lineups and photo spreads. Fourth, to avoid dropping hints, examiners should not know who the suspect is. Fifth, eyewitnesses should be told that they should not assume that the examiner of the lineup or photo spread knows which person is the suspect in the case. Sixth, when the examiner does not know who the suspect is, a sequential procedure should be used. With a sequential procedure the eyewitness views only one lineup member or photo at a time, making a judgment ("yes it is" or "no it isn't" the perpetrator) about each person before looking at another lineup member or photo. Seventh, non-suspect lineup "fillers" should look like the witnesses' descriptions of the suspect and not the person who has been identified as the potential suspect. Eighth, witnesses should be required to rate the certainty of their identifications at the time they make them. This would provide fact finders important information weeks or months after the identifications were made. Ninth, police and prosecutors should be trained not to provide corroborating details to eyewitnesses. Such prompts tend to increase the certainty of identifications but to decrease their reliability. In addition, trial judges should inform jurors that eyewitness testimony should be judged in light of the other evidence in the case. Finally, convictions for murder based on the testimony of a single eyewitness or accomplice, without any other corroboration, should never be death eligible.[150]

Improve the Work and Credibility of Crime Lab Technicians.[151] To promote greater credibility in the work of crime lab technicians, such labs and their budgets should be independent and not under the supervision of a police department or prosecutor's office as is now typically the case. Crime labs should also be accredited by professional organizations and subjected to regulatory oversight and external blind proficiency testing (in which samples are sent in as ordinary evidence to corroborate the validity of results). Prosecutors who introduce scientific evidence should be required to provide all underlying documentation that was used in writing the report as well as the name of the technician or technicians who performed the work. Fundamental questions should be asked about the reliability of the evidence: Have the scientific tests been replicated? What is the error rate of the procedure? Did any controls fail? Have the methods been published in peer-reviewed journals? Agent-technicians who make mistakes should be disciplined. The reports should indicate what, if any, exculpatory inferences can be derived from the evidence. Every public defender's office should have at least one attorney with scientific evidence expertise.

Require DNA Testing.[152] DNA testing should be required in cases in which DNA evidence is available and there is a reasonable probability that the defendant could be exonerated based on it. The testing should be conducted in a timely manner, within seven to fourteen days of the crime, if possible, to ensure that innocent suspects are not incarcerated too long and to improve the chances of catching the guilty. In May 2000, only two states—Illinois and New York—gave inmates the right to use the latest DNA testing.[153] As of September 2006, 40 states gave inmates that right.[154] The federal government and the states also should provide adequate funding for the creation of a comprehensive DNA database. Hopefully, The Innocence Protection Act of 2004, which was described in Chapter 3, is a step in that direction.

Set Rigorous Standards for Jailhouse Snitches/Informants.[155] Before allowing a jailhouse snitch/informant to testify a committee of prosecutors should be able to provide satisfactory answers to the following questions: (1) Is there corroborating evidence to support the statement other than the testimony of another snitch? (2) Does the statement provide details of the crime or lead to evidence that could only be known by the perpetrator? (3) Could the incriminating evidence have been obtained from a source other than the accused, such as press accounts or legal proceedings? (4) Does the snitch/informant have a reputation for being dishonest? And (5) Does the snitch/informant regularly provide incriminating evidence? There should be a presumption that the testimony of a jailhouse snitch/informant is unreliable, and the prosecutor should be required to overcome that presumption before a jury is allowed to hear the evidence. Any deal that police officers or prosecutors make with a snitch/informant should be recorded, preferably videotaped. Additionally, trial judges should inform jurors of the potential hazards of relying on the testimony of a jailhouse snitch/informant. Finally, the uncorroborated testimony of a jailhouse snitch/informant witness about the confession or admission of the defendant should never be the sole basis for imposition of a death penalty.

Improve Police Training.[156] Training manuals should be developed and police who work on homicide cases should receive periodic training in the following areas: (1) the risks of false testimony by in-custody informants ("jailhouse snitches"), (2) the risks of false testimony by accomplice witnesses, (3) the dangers of tunnel vision or confirmatory bias, (4) the risks of wrongful convictions in homicide cases, (5) police investigative and interrogation methods, (6) police investigating and reporting of exculpatory evidence, (7) forensic evidence, (8) the risks of false confessions, and (9) consular rights and the notification obligations during the arrest and detention of foreign nationals.

Punish Police Misconduct.[157] Depending on the seriousness of the misconduct, offending police officers should be reprimanded, suspended without pay, decertified (if applicable) or terminated. Particularly serious misconduct by police officers should be prosecuted in the federal courts.

Guide Prosecutors' Decisions to Seek the Death Penalty.[158] Statewide written protocols should be developed to guide county prosecutors in making death penalty determinations. The guidelines should include the requirement that each county prosecutor establish within his or her office a committee to review homicide cases in which the death penalty may be sought, to assist the prosecutor in making the decision. The governor should appoint a statewide committee to review prior to trial death eligibility decisions made by prosecutors. Where the committee decides that death is not the appropriate sentence in the case, the prosecutor should not be authorized to seek the death penalty. Committee authorization of the death penalty should be required by statute and mandatory.

Improve Disclosure Requirements.[159] The prosecutor should be required to file a certificate with the court at least 14 days before the date set for the trial guaranteeing that all material that is required to be disclosed to the defense has been disclosed. Also, any discussions with a witness or the representative of a witness about benefits, potential benefits or detriments given to a witness by any prosecutor, police official, corrections official or anyone else should be put in writing and disclosed to the defense prior to trial. Both of these requirements could occur in a case management conference before the trial judge. Following conviction, the prosecutor should have a continuing obligation to make timely disclosure to the defendant's counsel, or the defendant if not represented by counsel, of the existence of evidence known to the prosecutor that tends to negate the guilt of the defendant or mitigate the defendant's capital sentence.

Punish Prosecutor Misconduct.[160] For extreme misconduct, prosecutors should be criminally prosecuted. At the least, statutes should be narrowed that grant prosecutors broad immunity from civil suits in cases of intentional misconduct. Another strategy is to create panels comprised of bar association members who would review complaints against prosecutors. For egregious cases of misconduct, prosecutors should be disbarred.

Better Training and Certification of Trial Judges in Capital Cases.[161] Capital case training should be provided for all trial judges who preside over capital cases. The training should be required before a judge hears a capital case. A statewide bench manual covering capital cases should also be developed and used. A digest should be created and made available to trial judges and other participants in capital cases. The digest should contain information about relevant case law and other resources. Trial judges should be certified to hear capital cases by the state supreme court or the chief judges of judicial circuits. Certification should be based on experience and training. Only certified judges should hear capital cases.

Give Trial Judges Veto Power.[162] The trial judge should have to indicate on the record whether he or she agrees with the jury's sentence of death. When the judge does not agree with the jury's death sentence, the defendant must not be sentenced to death. (In most cases, the defendant should be sentenced to LWOP.)

Eliminate Time Limits and Other Constraints on Claims of Actual Innocence.[163] Claims of actual innocence in capital cases based on newly discovered evidence should be heard by a court of record any time after conviction, without regard for other post-conviction matters or timing. Also, state "closed discovery" laws should be repealed. Those laws prevent defense attorneys or journalists from reviewing evidence following a conviction, thus making the detection of miscarriages of justice even more difficult,

Improve the Clemency Process.[164] To make officials more accountable in their decision making, clemency boards should hold public hearings to determine their recommendations to the governor. Governors should meet personally with attorneys and should be required to provide the public with an explanation of their clemency decisions. Better yet, to depoliticize the process, clemency decisions should not be made by governors but, instead, by respected three-judge panels.

Collect Relevant Data.[165] To provide a complete understanding of how a capital punishment system is working, each death penalty jurisdiction should collect detailed and relevant information and create a statistical database about all first degree murder cases in that jurisdiction, and not just the death penalty cases. These data could be used for proportionality reviews, to effectively monitor the system, and for other research purposes.

Innocence Projects and Innocence Commissions.[166] Attorneys Barry Scheck and Peter Neufeld founded the first Innocence Project in 1992. It is a clinical law program for law students that operates out of the Benjamin N. Cardoza School of Law in New York City. The Project provides pro bono legal services to inmates who are challenging their convictions based on DNA evidence. The Project has represented or assisted more than one hundred cases in the U.S., including several death penalty cases, where convictions have been reversed or overturned. As of this writing, a national network of Innocence Projects is operating in 40 states and the District of Columbia, including all but 5 death penalty states (Alabama, Arkansas, Montana, Oregon, and South Dakota).

Innocence Commissions are organizations created to monitor, investigate, and address errors in a jurisdiction's criminal justice system and, in this case, a jurisdiction's capital punishment system. When errors are discovered, the commissions should review the system's failures by asking the following questions: (1) What went wrong? (2) Was the error the result of an individual's mistake or a systemic error? (3) Was there any official misconduct? and (4) What can be done to correct the problem and prevent it from happening again? Innocence Commissions are modeled after the National Transportation Safety Board (NTSB), which investigates airline crashes. To operate properly, Innocence Commissions must have subpoena power, access to first-rate investigative resources, and political independence. North Carolina was the first state to create an Innocence Commission in 2002. California, Connecticut, Illinois, and Virginia are other death penalty states that have established Innocence Commissions.

Assistance and Indemnity.[167] When wrongfully convicted inmates and especially death row inmates are released from prison, they almost always need immediate financial assistance. Most of them also need help with such things as obtaining a driver's license, opening a bank account, and getting meaningful employment. In addition, there is generally a need for counseling to overcome stress, depression, and anger caused by wrongful incarceration. Death penalty jurisdictions should create mechanisms or expand existing ones to help with these needs.

Currently, wrongfully convicted death row inmates may be compensated in one of three ways: lawsuits, private legislation, or private donations. The most common method is by bringing a lawsuit against the state. Such lawsuits are rarely successful, however, primarily because government officials (and their jurisdictions) are generally immune from liability as long as they are acting in their official capacities, and they have not committed a constitutional violation—something that is very hard to prove.[168]

Other methods of litigation also can be pursued if intentional misconduct was the cause of the wrongful conviction and imprisonment. Simple error is not grounds for receiving state compensation in such cases. If it can be shown that the wrongful conviction and imprisonment were the result of a breach of duty, then a common law tort claim can be made. For example, on May 5, 2006, a federal jury awarded Earl Washington Jr. $2.25 million from the estate of Virginia State Police investigator Curtis Reese Wilmore, who died in 1994. The jury ruled that Wilmore deliberately fabricated Washington's confession to a 1982 rape and murder Washington did not commit. Washington's conviction and death sentence were based largely on his confession, in which he got several key details wrong. There was no forensic or physical evidence. Washington, with an IQ of 69, spent 18 years in Virginia prisons—nine and a half of those years on death row.[169] Washington was lucky because it is difficult to prove intentional misconduct and the burden of proof was on him, as it is in all such cases. Other possible grounds for litigation to obtain compensation are charging a criminal offense, claiming eminent domain, or alleging false imprisonment. None of those strategies is likely to prove successful.

Some states address wrongful convictions and imprisonment through a policy of strict liability. Strict liability does not depend on actual negligence or intent to harm but is based on the breach of an absolute duty.[170] As mentioned in Chapter 6, 20 states, the District of Columbia, and the federal government have statutory provisions for indemnifying the wrongly convicted (in capital and non-capital cases). Five of those compensating states (Iowa, Maine, New York, West Virginia, and Wisconsin) and the District of Columbia do not have a death penalty. Following is a list of death penalty states with compensation statutes and the amount or type of compensation provided (as of June 2006).

- Alabama: Minimum of $50,000 for each year served.

- California: $100 a day for each day served.

- Illinois: Maximum of $15,000 for up to 5 years served; $30,000 for 6 to 14 years served; and $35,000 for more than 14 years served.

- Louisiana: $15,000 per year served with a $150,000 maximum.

- Maryland: No cap on compensation described as "actual damages sustained" and reasonable amount for counseling.

- Missouri: $50 per day served; $36,500 maximum per year served.

- Montana: Free tuition, fees, books, room, and board at any school in the state's university system.

- New Hampshire: $20,000 maximum.

- New Jersey: Capped at twice the amount earned the year before incarceration or $20,000, whichever is greater.

- North Carolina: $20,000 a year served, total not to exceed $500,000.

- Ohio: $40,330 per year of incarceration (adjusted based on the Consumer Price Index in odd-numbered years), plus lost wages, prison costs, and attorneys fees.

- Oklahoma: $175,000 maximum.

- Tennessee: $1 million maximum.

- Texas: $25,000 per year of incarceration, total not to exceed $500,000, plus one year of counseling.

- Virginia: 90 percent of the average Virginia income for up to 20 years, $15,000 transition grant, and $10,000 in tuition to enroll in the state's community-college system.[171]

Prior to 2004, the federal government limited compensation to a maximum of $5,000 regardless of the amount of time served. However, the Innocence Protection Act of 2004 raised the amount of compensation in federal capital cases to $100,000 per year of incarceration.[172]

A major purpose of these compensation statutes is to protect the jurisdiction and its officials from frivolous claims. Most of them impose substantial barriers to recovery. Two of those barriers are requirements that the claimant did not by misconduct or neglect cause or bring about his or her own prosecution or enter a guilty plea. As described previously in this chapter, false confessions and guilty pleas by innocent defendants are common causes of errors in capital cases. The wrongfully convicted who wants to file a lawsuit also must hire an attorney, who will take a substantial amount of any compensation that is granted. Although the claimant does not have to prove fault in strict liability cases, he or she still has to prove his or her innocence and, as noted, has the burden of proving—if specified, by either clear and convincing evidence or a preponderance of the evidence—that the wrongful conviction was not in any way his or her fault.

If the claimant is successful in a strict liability case, a court or, in some states, a board of claims determines, within statutory limits, the amount of compensation to be awarded. As noted above, some states have cap limits on awards, while others do not. Some states require the governor to issue a pardon before awarding compensation; other states will only award compensation for DNA exonerations. Some states have time limits for filing claims. California, for example, has the shortest time limit, requiring claims to be filed within 6 months of release. The state, however, currently does not have to inform the freed death row inmate of the statute or the deadline. In most cases, as noted above, attorney fees are deducted from the compensation. Some states also deduct the costs of housing, clothing and feeding the claimant while he or she was imprisoned.

A second method for obtaining compensation is by private legislation. This compensatory method is discretionary and not an obligation of the state. It requires the claimant and/or his or her advocate to lobby the state legislature. This method, like lawsuits, is rarely successful for two principal reasons. First, a sympathetic legislator must be found, and there is little incentive and some political risk for getting involved. Second, with always-scarce resources, there invariably are more worthy projects and causes (in the minds of legislators and the public) than indemnifying an innocent inmate who has spent many years on death row. Some state constitutions (e.g., Missouri's) expressly prohibit seeking compensation through private legislation. Two examples of a successful effort of obtaining compensation by private legislation are the cases, mentioned earlier, of Freddie Lee Pitts and Wilbert Lee, two black men who, in 1975, were finally pardoned by the Florida Cabinet.[173] Pitts and Lee had been tried and sentenced to death twice. They spent 12 years apiece on death row for a murder that somebody else committed. The average amount of time a wrongfully convicted inmate spends on death row before being released, incidentally, is 9 years, but some have spent 15 years or more before being freed. In the case of Pitts and Lee, it was not until 1997, after years of failed efforts, that they received a few hundred thousand dollars each as compensation from the state of Florida for its mistakes. That they received any compensation at all, as noted, is unusual.

Another fortunate exception is Bobby Joe Leaster who, in 1992, finally received a check for $75,000. The money was the first installment of the $1 million annuity the state of Massachusetts will pay him for wrongly imprisoning him for 15 years for a murder he did not commit.[174] Leaster was arrested in 1970 for the killing of a variety store owner during a holdup. After reading a newspaper article about Leaster, an eyewitness to the crime told police he knew the killer, and the killer was not Leaster. Leaster was released from prison in 1986 after prosecutors declined to pursue a retrial. Because of the state's fiscal problems, it took several attempts before Massachusetts's legislators approved the indemnification measure.

A third method of obtaining compensation is through private donations. Like the other methods, this method has a number of problems. First, the released inmate is generally not psychologically prepared to seek private donations. Thus, to be successful, a released inmate must have devoted advocates willing to work for him or her. Second, the released inmate and his or her advocates must find a source of funding willing to donate. Possible sources are religious and civic organizations, as well as private foundations such as the Soros or Ford Foundations. These groups receive many requests to help fund worthy causes with which the freed death row inmate will have to compete. A problem with foundation funding is the application process can be very complicated. Third, it is difficult to raise enough money to pay and sustain the costs of reintegration. Fourth, this method of compensation can have the undesirable effect of keeping the released inmate in a state of childlike dependence rather than promoting his or her independence.

A number of proposals have been made to improve the compensation process for the wrongfully convicted and imprisoned. Following are some of the better ideas. Compensation should be automatic; it should be a part of the release package. A death row inmate who has been freed because of his or her innocence should not have to prove again that he or she is innocent to receive compensation. Any judicial or executive order indicating that the claimant is innocent should suffice. Professor Cathleen Burnett proposes to move the issue of compensation to wrongfully convicted and imprisoned inmates from the formal criminal justice process to a restorative justice process. In restorative justice, the focus is on the miscarriage of justice victim and what he or she needs to have the harm repaired and to be reintegrated into society. A first step should be the creation of a state-level "Wrongful Conviction Office," with staff to help released innocent death row inmates from the moment they leave prison. However, the freed death row inmate should not have to participate, to be left alone, if he or she wishes. If the newly freed death row inmate elects to participate, the Wrongful Conviction Office staff member assigned to him or her will, in consultation with his or her client and other relevant stakeholders, prepare a plan or program for successful reintegration. A mediation setting and, if needed, an arbitration setting rather than a courtroom would be the forum for addressing compensation issues in a restorative justice framework. The specific administrative process could be modeled after the federal government's Victim Compensation Fund of 2001, which was used to assist the 9/11 victims. The case also should be turned over to an innocence commission (see the previous section) to investigate the causes of the miscarriage of justice, not for the purpose of assigning blame, but to prevent a similar calamity from happening in the future. The most difficult issues are probably the amount of compensation to be awarded and from where it comes. As for the first issue, what is the worth of years of a person's life lived in horrible prison conditions? Regarding the source of funds, they could come from the state attorney general's budget, since that office is ultimately responsible for the administration of justice in a particular state, or they could come from the state treasury. Whatever the source, the compensation funds should be tax-free at least at the state level so the state does not benefit from its mistakes.

Moratorium. Short of total abolition some observers, including some respected individuals who support the death penalty in principle, have called for a moratorium on executions until some of the more egregious problems with its administration are fixed. The current moratorium movement, not to be confused with its earlier predecessor of the 1968–1977 era, has lost some of its momentum, having been eclipsed by the events of September 11, 2001. Nevertheless, it still promises to be a force in the debate on capital punishment.

The current moratorium movement is the result of a series of developments that began during the last few years of the twentieth century.[175] The movement started in Illinois with revelations that people convicted of capital crimes and sentenced to die were actually innocent (among the first were Rolando Cruz and Alejandro Hernandez and the Ford Heights Four). In some cases investigations by Northwestern University Journalism Professor David Protess and his students provided the proof of innocence. The movement gained momentum in November 1998, when Northwestern University hosted the first National Conference on Wrongful Convictions and the Death Penalty. Attending were 35 former death row inmates. Some of them told their stories about almost being executed and how they were spared when evidence emerged showing that they had been wrongly convicted.[176]

The most publicized and influential miscarriage of justice in Illinois during this period was the Anthony Porter case. By sheer luck Porter's innocence was discovered, and he was exonerated and released from prison in February 1999, after spending 16 years on death row. He came within two days of his execution in 1998. Porter's attorneys were able to secure a stay of execution for him arguing that he might be mentally incompetent to be executed because he was unable to understand that he was going to be executed and why. His IQ was 51. As a result of the stay, a Northwestern University journalism class that previously had decided not to investigate his case changed its decision. In a few months the students, Professor Protess, and an investigator discovered the real killer and proved that Porter was innocent. The real killer confessed on videotape to the 1982 double murder for which Porter was convicted.[177]

Also in 1999, the *Chicago Tribune* published two major series. The first series documented prosecutor misconduct throughout the United States; the second series examined problems with Illinois's capital punishment system that contributed to such a large percentage of its death row inmates being exonerated because of their innocence. Based largely on the Anthony Porter case, the series by the *Chicago Tribune*, and the fact that Illinois had released thirteen condemned inmates from death row since 1977 while executing twelve, Republican Governor George Ryan, himself a proponent of the death penalty, imposed a moratorium on capital punishment in Illinois in January 2000. In May 2000, Governor Ryan charged a special commission he created with producing a comprehensive report on the administration of capital punishment in Illinois. In April 2002, Governor Ryan received the completed report, which contained 85 recommendations for changes in Illinois' capital punishment system.[178] Declaring the Illinois capital-punishment system to be broken, in January 2003, just days before he was to leave office, Governor Ryan, as noted previously, pardoned four death-row inmates and commuted the sentences, mostly to life in prison without possibility of parole, of the remaining 167 inmates on Illinois' death row.[179]

A second important influence on the current moratorium movement is the American Bar Association (ABA). In February 1997, the ABA adopted a resolution calling for a moratorium on the death penalty until problems with its administration could be resolved. Problems cited by the ABA included ineffective assistance of counsel, racial discrimination, imposition of the penalty on juveniles and the mentally retarded (which is no longer allowed, see *Roper v. Simmons*, 2005 and *Atkins v. Virginia*, 2002), and post–conviction and *habeas corpus* concerns. Former ABA president Martha Barnett, a "reluctant supporter" of the death penalty, made the organization's moratorium effort a high priority. She maintained that defendants should not be executed unless there are guarantees that they received adequate legal representation and the sentence was not the result of racial discrimination. In March 2001, the ABA Section of Individual Rights and Responsibilities issued a group of protocols that identified factors that the Section believed legislatures and commissions should consider when evaluating the fairness of death penalty laws and how those laws could be reformed. Finally, as noted previously, in 2003, the ABA's House of Delegates approved a revised edition of its 1989 guidelines for the appointment and performance of defense counsel in death penalty cases.

Third, besides the state of Illinois and the ABA, other governmental bodies and organizations have joined the moratorium movement. For example, the Republican–controlled Nebraska legislature in 1999 voted for a moratorium on executions and for a study of the fairness of Nebraska's capital punishment system. Although Governor Mike Johanns vetoed the moratorium, the study was approved after legislators overrode the governor's veto of it. Similar studies have been undertaken in Illinois (as noted), Arizona, North Carolina, Maryland, and Indiana. In 1999, legislators in at least nine states introduced moratoria on executions (most were unsuccessful; besides Nebraska and Illinois, states that introduced moratoria bills were Connecticut, Maryland, Montana, New Jersey, North Carolina, Pennsylvania, and Washington).[180] In May 2002, Democratic Governor Parris Glendening imposed a moratorium on executions in Maryland until the state completed a study of whether there was racial bias in the use of the death penalty.[181] Despite the study's finding of racial bias, Glendening's successor, Republican Robert Ehrlich, resumed executions in 2004. In 2005, the New Jersey state legislature passed and Governor Richard Codey signed legislation that provided a one-year moratorium on executions, thus becoming the first state to pass a moratorium legislatively, rather than by executive order.[182] Additionally, more than 700 small towns and cities, church and religious groups, legal organizations, labor organizations, human rights groups, social service agencies, and business groups throughout the United States have passed resolutions calling for a moratorium on the death penalty.[183]

Fourth, in May of 2000, the New Hampshire legislature voted to abolish the death penalty and thus became the first state to do so since the death penalty was reinstated in 1976. New Hampshire Democratic Governor Jeanne Shaheen vetoed the bill.[184]

A fifth development was the winter of 2000 publication and accompanying national publicity of Barry Scheck, Peter Neufeld, and Jim Dwyer's book, *Actual Innocence: Five Days to Execution, and Other Dispatches from the Wrongly Convicted.* The book documents numerous exonerations that resulted from after-the-fact DNA testing. Material in the book came from cases handled by the Innocence Project, which was described earlier. [185]

Sixth was the publication in June 2000 of a study by Columbia University Law Professor James S. Liebman and his colleagues Jeffrey Fagan and Valerie West. The study, discussed previously, showed that two-thirds of the fully reviewed state capital cases between 1973 and 1995 were infected by serious, reversible error. The study received major media attention. It was both lauded and criticized. Such reports are embarrassing the courts.

Seventh was the extensive media publicity surrounding the execution of Gary Graham in Texas on June 22, 2000. Though he claimed he was innocent, there was no DNA evidence to exonerate him. He was convicted on the testimony of a single eyewitness. Graham's execution also reignited the debate about the execution of juveniles.

Eighth were Juan Garza's impending execution by the federal government (the second federal execution under post-*Furman* statutes) and the national media publicity it generated. Just a day after Gary Graham's execution the national media reported claims that the federal capital punishment system discriminated against minorities and that Garza's execution was being rushed. The White House leaked President Clinton's decision to stay Garza's execution at about the same time that the president stated at a news conference that he was disturbed about the racial distribution of the federal death row population. At about the same time the *Washington Post* did an expose on the racial disparities of Maryland's death row and several papers ran stories about recent miscarriages of justice in capital cases in Texas and Virginia. Then, in September 2000, a report issued by the Justice Department showed an apparent pattern of racial discrimination in the federal death penalty's imposition. That led to calls from a number of organizations, including the ABA, for a moratorium on federal executions. The Justice Department responded by announcing it would hire outside experts to study the matter further.

Ninth, members of the U.S. Congress have been active in the moratorium movement. For example, on October 26, 2000, the U.S. Senate passed a non-binding resolution introduced by Vermont Democratic Senator Patrick Leahy. The resolution called for states to improve the quality of legal representation in capital cases and to provide wider access to post-conviction DNA testing. On January 31, 2001, a bill to place a moratorium on executions by the federal government was introduced by Wisconsin Democratic Senator Russell Feingold. The bill urged states to do the same while a National Commission on the Death Penalty reviewed the death penalty's fairness. Senator Feingold together with Illinois Democratic Congressman Jesse Jackson, Jr., also introduced legislation that would give more time to death row inmates to gain access to DNA testing. On March 7, 2001, Senators Leahy, Feingold, Gordon Smith (Oregon Republican), and Susan Collins (Maine Republican), joined Representatives William Delahunt (Massachusetts Democrat) and Ray LaHood (Illinois Republican) to reintroduce the Innocence Protection Act in Congress. The bipartisan legislation sought to address problems of fairness in the death penalty in order to avoid the risk of wrongful convictions and executions. The bill required states to provide qualified and experienced attorneys to all defendants facing the death penalty, and allowed for greater access to DNA testing.[186] Much of the bill was passed as the Innocence Protection Act of 2004, part of the Justice For All Act of 2004.

Tenth, long-time proponents of capital punishment began to express their misgivings about the penalty's administration. For example, former Florida Chief Justice and Miami prosecutor Gerald Kogan has called for a moratorium on the death penalty. Pat Robertson, head of the conservative Christian Coalition, and conservative commentator George Will have also expressed their concerns. This development has led to the creation of the National Committee to Prevent Wrongful Executions. On October 12, 2000, former President Jimmy Carter and his wife Rosalynn called for both a federal and state moratorium of the death penalty. As Governor of Georgia, Carter had signed into law Georgia's post-*Furman* death penalty statute.

Two sitting Supreme Court justices have voiced their concerns about the administration of the death penalty, especially the quality of legal representation. Justice Sandra Day O'Connor (who has since retired) believes that it may be time to require minimum standards for lawyers in capital cases. She also believes such lawyers should be adequately compensated. She remarked in a speech to a women's law group in Minneapolis that "if statistics are any indication, the system may well be allowing some innocent defendants to be executed."[187] Justice Ruth Bader Ginsburg, speaking at the University of the District of Columbia, acknowledged that she supported a proposed moratorium on the death penalty in Maryland. She observed that her experience with death row inmates who have asked the Court for last-minute reprieves demonstrated that not one of them received really good legal help at trial. She also criticized the "meager" amount of money spent to defend poor people. (Maryland lawmakers failed to pass the moratorium.)[188]

Eleventh, the Catholic Church strongly and unequivocally opposes capital punishment and supports a moratorium. Toward the end of 1999, the Catholic Church together with the Reform and Conservative Jewish movements announced a joint campaign against capital punishment in the United States.

Twelfth, world opinion also seems to be playing a role. See the discussion in Chapter 3.

Thirteenth, the media in the United States have increasingly focused on problems with the death penalty and its administration. For example, "The Oprah Winfrey Show," the highest-rated talk show in the country, devoted its entire September 2000 program to the death penalty issue. Oprah presented several innocent men who had been on death row as well as legal experts in favor of a death penalty moratorium.

All of this has affected public support for the death penalty in the U.S., which appears to be waning. In 26 national public opinion polls conducted between February 2000 and May 2006, only 62-69 percent of adults or registered voters nationwide were in favor of the death penalty for a person convicted of murder.[189] This is the lowest level of support recorded in a national poll in more than twenty years, and likely the first time the level of support has fallen below 70 percent during that period.[190] Professor Fan and his colleagues found that the decline in death penalty support was a product of the media's attention on the condemnation of innocent persons (see the material that follows).[191] Moreover, for about a decade and a half, national public opinion polls have shown that when given a choice between the death penalty and life imprisonment with absolutely no possibility of parole (LWOP), no more than about half and sometimes less of the public prefers the death penalty.[192]

The American public is also expressing greater concern about the way the death penalty is being administered, although recently that concern seems to be moderating somewhat. For example, a *USA Today/Gallup* poll conducted in June 2000 found that 41 percent of adults nationwide believed the death penalty is applied unfairly (51 percent believed it is applied fairly).[193] An NBC News/*Wall Street Journal* poll conducted in July 2000 found that 42 percent of registered voters nationwide thought that the death penalty is not applied fairly (42% believed it is applied fairly). Sixty-three percent of the respondents to that poll favored the suspension of the death penalty until questions about its fairness could be studied. Gallup polls conducted in May 2002, May 2003, May 2004, May 2005, and May 2006 discovered that 40 percent, 37 percent, 39 percent, 35 percent, and 35 percent of respondents, respectively, believed the death penalty is applied unfairly (53 percent, 60 percent, 55 percent, 61 percent, and 60 percent, respectively, believed the penalty is applied fairly). A *Newsweek* poll conducted in June 2000 found that more than 80 percent of adults nationwide think that at least some innocent people have been wrongly executed since the death penalty was reinstated in the 1970s: 8 percent think that "many" innocent people have been wrongly executed; 33 percent think that only "some" innocent people have been wrongly executed; and 41 percent think that only a "very few" innocent people have been wrongly executed. A Harris poll conducted in July 2000 revealed that 94 percent of adults nationwide think that innocent people are sometimes convicted of murder. Perhaps even more telling, according to a CNN/*USA Today*/Gallup poll conducted in June 2000, 80 percent of adults nationwide think that in the past five years a person has been executed who was, in fact, innocent of the crime with which he or she was charged. Gallup polls conducted in May 2003, May 2005, and May 2006 show that 73 percent, 59 percent, and 63 percent of respondents, respectively, believe an innocent person has been executed within the past five years.[194] The June 2000 *Newsweek* poll revealed that 82 percent of adults nationwide thought that states should make it easier for death row inmates to introduce new evidence that might prove their innocence, even if that might result in delays in the death penalty process. Ninety-five percent of adults nationwide thought that states should permit DNA testing in all cases where it might prove a person's guilt or innocence, and 88 percent of adults nationwide thought that the federal government should require states to permit DNA testing under those circumstances. To varying degrees, those suggestions have been implemented. It appears that revelations about the quality of justice in capital murder trials, the overturning of convictions as a result of DNA tests, and the resulting moratorium on executions in Illinois, among other factors, have had an impact on public opinions about the death penalty.

Also noteworthy is the dramatic decrease in the number of death sentences imposed annually and, to a somewhat lesser extent, the number of annual executions that have coincided with the moratorium movement. Regarding death sentences, in 1999, 276 individuals were sentenced to death in the United States; in 2000, 232 individuals were sentenced to death; in 2001, 163; in 2002, 168; in 2003, 152; in 2004, 125; in 2005, 123; and, in 2006, 102.[195] As for executions, in 1999, there were 98 executions in the United States; in 2000, 85; in 2001, 66; in 2002, 71; in 2003, 65; in 2004, 59; in 2005, 60; and, in 2006, 53.[196]

Conclusion

Contrary to the beliefs of some death penalty proponents, miscarriages of justice in capital cases, including wrongful executions, do occur and, unfortunately, they happen with some regularity and frequency. Moreover, the evidence suggests that super due process requirements have not had the desired effect of significantly reducing those mistakes. Professor Gross maintains that:

> The basic conclusion is simple. The steady stream of errors that we see in cases in which defendants are sentenced to death is a predictable consequence of our system of investigating and prosecuting capital murder. . . . But what about what happens after trial? Everybody knows that direct and collateral review are more painstaking for capital cases than for any others. Isn't it likely that all these mistakes are caught and corrected somewhere in that exacting process? The answer, I'm afraid, is No. At best, we could do an imperfect job of catching errors after they occur, and in many cases we don't really try. As a result, most miscarriages of justice in capital cases never come to light.[197]

Some death penalty proponents argue that even if some innocent persons are executed, those mistakes, though regrettable, are justified nonetheless by the protection executions provide society.[198] Those who make the argument clearly believe that executions (whether of the guilty or the innocent) have a general deterrent effect. As shown in detail in Chapter 5, however, there is no credible evidence to support such a belief. The view is also misguided for another reason. Most miscarriages of justice in capital cases, especially wrongful convictions, mean that the actual killer has gone free and remains able to prey upon an unsuspecting public.

Finally, some death penalty proponents generalize the preceding argument and maintain that (unspecified) advantages of capital punishment morally justify miscarriages of justice in capital cases. Professor Van den Haag writes:

> Most human activities—medicine, manufacturing, automobile and air traffic, sports, not to speak of wars and revolutions—cause the death of innocent bystanders. Nevertheless, if the advantages sufficiently outweigh the disadvantages, human activities, including those of the penal system with all its punishments, are morally justified.[199]

A Harris survey conducted in 2001 found that 67 percent of Americans support the death penalty. Yet, the same survey discovered that 94 percent of Americans believe that innocent people are sometimes convicted of murder. Those surveyed believe that, on average, 12 percent of those convicted of murder are innocent.[200]

One must wonder whether there is a threshold level for miscarriages of justice at which people who favor the death penalty in general would oppose it.[201] If other, less final punishments can achieve the same purposes as capital punishment—and can do so without the liabilities associated with capital punishment, such as miscarriages of justice—then, morally, the alternative punishments should be preferred.[202]

Discussion Questions

1. Have innocent people been wrongly convicted and executed under post-*Furman* statutes?

2. Do you agree with the harmless error rule? Why or why not?

3. How can wrongful convictions and executions occur, especially within the context of "super due process"?

4. To what type of defense should capital defendants be entitled?

5. Should attorneys who represent capital defendants be required to possess any special qualifications or training? What should the special qualifications or training be?

6. Should we trust capital defendants' lives to juries?

7. If not juries, who should make the decision of whether a convicted capital defendant should live or die?

8. What constitutes effective assistance of counsel?

9. What can be done about miscarriages of justice in capital cases? What do you consider to be the most important reform? Why?

10. Should the state be required to indemnify innocent people wrongly convicted of capital crimes when they have spent years in prison?

11. Should the state be required to indemnify the families of innocent people who have been executed?

12. Do you favor a moratorium on capital punishment? Why or why not?

13. Is the possibility of executing innocent people reason enough to abolish the death penalty?

14. How can the human sacrifice of innocent persons (any persons?) be morally justified in the first years of the twenty-first century?

Notes

[1] Sarat, 2005:9-10; 2002:246-260.

[2] Dow, 2005.

[3] Professor David McCord (2006) makes an interesting argument that if the death penalty were subject to consumer protection laws, the public would have a cause of action for consumer fraud.

[4] Amsterdam, 1982:349.

[5] Committee on the Judiciary, 1982:317; also see Markman and Cassell, 1988.

[6] Personal communication between Espy and the author.

[7] The following discussion is from Radelet and Bedau, 2003.

[8] In 20 of the 350 cases (6 percent) of wrongful convictions in capital cases catalogued by Bedau and Radelet (1987), no crime actually occurred, though a defendant was convicted of a capital offense.

[9] See Scheck et al., 2001:322.

[10] But also see Sellin, 1959:63-65; Bye, 1919:80-81.

[11] Bedau, 1982:234.

[12] Bedau and Radelet, op. cit.; also see Radelet et al., 1992. The Bedau and Radelet study caused great consternation in the Reagan Justice Department. Attorney General Edwin Meese III requested Stephen J. Markman, Assistant Attorney General to Meese, and Paul G. Cassell, Special Assistant United States Attorney, Eastern District of Virginia and former Associate Deputy Attorney General, to write a response. The first draft of their response was an 18-page Department of Justice internal memorandum. See Markman and Cassell, op. cit. For Bedau and Radelet's rejoinder to the Markman and Cassell response, see Bedau and Radelet, 1988.

[13] Most of the information in this chapter about the Bedau and Radelet research is from Radelet et al., 1992, op. cit. Note also that although Radelet et al. report 416 cases, the author's count of cases in their Inventory of Cases revealed only 375.

[14] For an update of this study with additional cases, see Radelet et al., 1996.

[15] The specific number for each decade is as follows: 1900s = 30; 1910s = 93. (This total is misleading because one case had 51 defendants. The "crime"—a race riot between blacks and whites—occurred in Arkansas in 1919. All 51 of the defendants were black; no whites were charged with crimes. Excluding those 51 defendants in the 1910s, the average for the six decades was 51 and not 59.); 1920s = 64; 1930s = 69; 1940s = 41; 1950s = 31; and 1960s = 27. Between 1970 and 1976, before the reimposition of the death penalty and super due process, there were 60 wrongful convictions in capital cases.

[16] Death Penalty Information Center, www.deathpenaltyinfo.org/innoc.html; also see Dieter, 2004. Another source claims that only about 30 of those people are actually innocent, see Marquis, 2005:520.

[17] Theoretically, one might assume that super due process protections would reduce the number of wrongful convictions in capital cases. On the other hand, one might reasonably argue that miscarriages of justice might be easier to detect and, therefore, more numerous the more recently they occur because of the "fresher trail" that is left.

[18] See, for example, Sorensen, 2004 (who may not be a proponent); Marquis, 2005, op. cit.

[19] Ibid.

[20] Ibid.

[21] Ibid.

[22] See *The Anniston* [AL] *Star,* September 9, 1984; "Murders Still Haunt Atlanta." *The Orlando Sentinel*, June 21, 1999, p. 5.

[23] *U.S. News and World Report*, December 17, 1984, p. 45.

[24] Ibid.

[25] See *The Anniston* [AL] *Star*, March 22 and 24, 1989.

[26] *The Charlotte* [NC] *Observer*, September 5, 1989.

[27] See *The Charlotte* [NC] *Observer*, January 26, 1993.

[28] See *The Charlotte* [NC] *Observer*, June 27, 1993.

[29] See *The Charlotte* [NC] *Observer*, June 29, 1993.

[30] See *The Charlotte* [NC] *Observer*, January 3, 1995.

[31] Herbert, 2000.

[32] "Man gets off death row," *The Orlando Sentinel*, January 4, 2002, p. C2; "Man leaves death row after 17 years, hoping to find 'good things'," *The Orlando Sentinel*, January 6, 2002, p. B3; Roman, Ivan, "Freed man relishes his 2nd chance," *The Orlando Sentinel*, January 27, 2002, p. A1.

[33] Holmes, 2004.

[34] The problem of eyewitness misidentification and what to do about it is discussed later in this chapter.

[35] Problems with lineups and how they can be improved are discussed later in this chapter.

[36] Zerwick, 2004.

[37] Bedau and Radelet, op. cit., p. 91. See Markman and Cassell (1988) for a critique of Bedau and Radelet's conclusion and Bedau and Radelet (1988) for a rejoinder.

[38] Cassell, 2004:206-207.

[39] Radelet, 2006.

[40] Harmon and Lofquist, 2005; Lehner, 1996; Death Penalty Information Center, www.deathpenaltyinfo.org/innocothershtml#executed. For a detailed analysis of the Gary Graham case, see Welch and Burr, 2002.

[41] Gelineau, 2006; also see Marquis, 2005, op. cit.

[42] Unless indicated otherwise, material in this section is from Coyne and Entzeroth, 2001:540; Liebman et al., 2000.

[43] Scheck et al., op. cit., pp. 282 and 340.

[44] See Liebman et al., 2000.

[45] Dow, 2005, op. cit., pp. xxii-xxiii and 44.

[46] Ibid., p. 133.

[47] Gross, 1996:499–500. Unless indicated otherwise, most of the information in this section is from Gross, 1996, who based his analysis on data from Bedau and Radelet, op. cit., and Radelet et al., 1992, op. cit.

[48] Gross, 1998:133.

[49] Harmon and Lofquist, op. cit., p. 514.

[50] See *The Charlotte* [NC] *Observer*, November 12, 1993, p. 8A.

[51] Hastings, 2001; Yardley, 2001a and 2001b; "Accusations," 2001; for more examples, see Scheck et al., op. cit., Chap. 5.

[52] Huff et al., 1986; Scheck et al., op. cit.

[53] Scheck et al., op. cit., p. 95.

[54] Ibid., p. 58.

[55] Also see Harmon, 2001.

[56] Harmon and Lofquist, op. cit., p. 511.

[57] On the other hand, the discovery of most miscarriages of justice in capital cases is the result of a confession by the real criminal. On false confessions, also see Drizin and Leo, 2004.

[58] Gross, op. cit., p. 485; also see Scheck et al., op. cit., p. 116; Dow, 2005, op. cit., p. 26.

[59] Radelet et al., 1992, op. cit.

[60] Bohm and Hailey, 2007: 278; also see McCord, 2005:822-823.

[61] For additional reasons why prosecutors do not pursue death sentences in death-eligible cases, both merit-based and non-merit-based, see McCord, 2005, op. cit., pp. 856-864.

[62] Miller and Potter, 2001; also see Scheck et al., op. cit.; Harmon, op. cit.; Liebman et al., op. cit.; Burnett, 2002.

[63] Ibid. Other forms of prosecutor misconduct in capital cases are overzealous and inappropriate arguments to the jury. See Burnett, op. cit., p. 43. For a theory of prosecutor misconduct, see Shoenfeld, 2005.

[64] Miller and Potter, op. cit.; also see Liebman et al., op. cit.

[65] See Scheck et al., op. cit., Chap. 6.

[66] Ibid., pp. 165-167.

[67] Miller and Potter, 2001, op. cit.

[68] Also see Harmon, op. cit.

[69] Lehner, op. cit.

[70] Miller and Potter, op. cit.

[71] Ibid.

[72] Scheck et al., op. cit., pp. xxi-xxii.

[73] Bright, 2004:164-165.

[74] Scheck et al., op. cit., pp. 226 and 233.

[75] Burnett, op. cit., p. 103.

[76] Gross, op. cit., pp. 492-493.

[77] Ibid., p. 496.

[78] Bedau, op. cit., pp. 189-190.

[79] Dow, 2005, op. cit., p. 7.

[80] Bedau, ibid., p. 190; Bowers, 1984:339. Hammel (2002:108) maintains that Texas capital defense attorneys frequently begin with a defeatist attitude and put on passive, reactive, and minimal defenses because they feel (and with good reason) it is inevitable that their clients will be convicted, sentenced to death, and executed.

[81] Quoted in Bowers, ibid., pp. 352-353.

[82] Andersen, 1983:39; also see Harmon, op. cit.

[83] Harmon and Lofquist, op. cit., p. 511.

[84] Coyle et al., 1990; also see Mello and Perkins, 1998:268. Those six states accounted for approximately 50 percent of all post-*Gregg* executions. See Burnett, op. cit., pp. 66-68 for attorney problems alleged in Missouri clemency petitions. For additional examples, see Dow, 2005; 2002b:22-23.

[85] Cited in Scheck et al., op. cit., p. 336; also see Liebman et al., op. cit; Dow, 2005, ibid., pp. 82-84.

[86] Bright, 2004, op. cit., p. 160.

[87] See *Bell v. Cone*, 2002.

[88] Cited in Bright, 1998:130; also see Mello and Perkins, ibid., p. 271.

[89] Bright, ibid.

[90] Ibid.

[91] Ibid., pp. 130–131.

[92] "Court Backs Death-Row Man," 2001.

[93] Weinstein, 2002.

[94] Bright, 1998, op. cit.; also see Dow, 2005, op. cit., pp. 1-24.

[95] Tabak, 2001:756.

[96] See In re Amendment to Florida Rules of Criminal Procedure—Rule 3.112 Minimum Standards for Attorneys in Capital Cases, adopted July 1, 2000; also see Acker and Lanier, 1999.

[97] See In re Amendment to Florida Rules of Criminal Procedure—Rule 3.112 Minimum Standards for Attorneys in Capital Cases, adopted July 1, 2000.

[98] Post, 2004.

[99] Ibid.

[100] Williams, 2005.

[101] Bright, 1997:11.

[102] Acker and Lanier, 1999, op. cit., pp. 448–449; Williams, 2005.

[103] Bright, 2004, op. cit., p. 168.

[104] Bright, 1997b:816–821.

[105] Bowers, op. cit.

[106] Cited in Bright, 2004, op. cit., p. 168.

[107] Ibid.

[108] Ibid., pp. 168-169.

[109] "Death Penalty Prosecutions May Be Halted if Funding Is Inadequate," 2005.

[110] To help remedy that problem, some states, such as Florida, have created capital punishment defense agencies. The attorneys who work in the agencies handle only capital punishment cases and, thus, are able to develop expertise. A problem is that most of the agencies are understaffed and underfunded and, consequently, have only the resources to handle appeals.

[111] Bright, 2004, op. cit., p. 169.

[112] Garey, 1985:1240-1241; also see Wollan, 1989, regarding the complexities of capital jurisprudence. Some inexperienced defense attorneys naively believe that their clients will be acquitted in the guilt stage and, therefore, do not bother to prepare for the penalty stage. See Burnett, op. cit., p. 36.

[113] See Sundby, 2005.

[114] Ibid., p. 35.

[115] Alter, 2000; *Wiggins v. Smith* (539 U.S. 510, 2003); *Rompilla v. Beard* (545 U.S. 374, 2005).

[116] Cassell, op. cit., pp. 209-210.

[117] Ibid., p. 209.

[118] Sundby, op. cit., p. 77.

[119] See Gross, 1998, op. cit., p. 145–146.

[120] Unless indicated otherwise, material in this section is from Kobil, 2003; Acker and Lanier, 2000; Sarat, 2005.

[121] Every judicial system in the world except China's provides for clemency, Sarat, 2006:204, n. 2.

[122] The governor in 35 states can make clemency decisions directly or in conjunction with an advisory board. Boards make clemency decisions in 5 states, and the decision is shared between the governor and an advisory board in 16 states, ibid.

[123] Banner, 2002:54.

[124] Ibid., pp. 56-57.

[125] Ibid., pp. 291-292.

[126] Ibid., p. 58.

[127] Ibid.

[128] Berlow, 2003.

[129] For a description of the Missouri clemency process, see Burnett, op. cit., pp. 162-165.

[130] Yardley, 2000.

[131] Berlow, op. cit.

[132] Yardley, op. cit.

[133] Material on the Texas clemency memos is from Berlow, op. cit.

[134] Dieter, 2006.

[135] Ibid.

[136] Ibid.

[137] Cited in *Herrera v. Collins*, 1993:415.

[138] Banner, op. cit., p. 291.

[139] See Death Penalty Information Center, www.deathpenaltyinfo.org/article.php ?did=126&scid=13; Baldus and Woodworth, 1998:388-389 and Acker and Lanier, 2000, op. cit., pp. 212-213, Table 1 for the pre-1970's figure; also see Dieter, 1996:26. Palacios, 1996:347, claims that "the heyday of commutations was the early and mid-1940s, during which twenty to twenty-five percent of death penalties were commuted."

[140] Acker and Lanier, 2000, op. cit., p. 215. For additional reasons, see Burnett, op. cit., pp. 158 and 169, n. 7; Radelet and Zsembik, 1993.

[141] Cited in Acker and Lanier, 1999, op. cit., p. 430.

[142] Also see Burnett, op. cit., pp. 185-187.

[143] Ibid., p. 437.

[144] Perez-Pena, 2000.

[145] Ibid; Death Penalty Information Center (accessed June 26, 2006).

[146] Perez-Pena, op. cit.

[147] Material in this section is from the Governor's Commission on Capital Punishment, pp. 191-192.

[148] Material in this section is from ibid., pp. 20, 22-25, 30-31; also see The Constitution Project, 2005.

[149] Material in this section is from Scheck et al., op. cit., pp. 98-99; the Governor's Commission on Capital Punishment, pp. 31-40, 129 and 158; also see The Constitution Project, op. cit.

[150] Dow (2005, op. cit., p. 30) reports that Texas law, and the law of other states, makes it impossible to convict someone of a crime based solely on the testimony of a co-conspirator. However, Texas law only requires minimal corroboration of accomplice testimony, ibid., p. 120.

[151] Material in this section is from Scheck et al., op. cit., pp. 158, 161-162, 212-213, 220; also see The Constitution Project, op. cit.

[152] Unless indicated otherwise, material in this section is from Scheck et al., op. cit., p. 351; Governor's Commission on Capital Punishment, pp. 52–60; also see The Constitution Project, op. cit.

[153] Alter and Miller, 2000.

[154] Ferrero, 2006.

[155] Material in this section is from Scheck et al., op. cit., pp. 352–353; Governor's Commission on Capital Punishment, pp. 131 and 158; also see The Constitution Project, op. cit.

[156] Material in this section is from the Governor's Commission on Capital Punishment, pp. 40–42; also see The Constitution Project, op. cit.

[157] Material in this section is from Scheck et al., op. cit., pp. 233–234 and 355; Governor's Commission on Capital Punishment, pp. 42–43.

[158] Material in this section is from Governor's Commission on Capital Punishment, pp. 82–85; also see The Constitution Project, op. cit.

[159] Material in this section is from ibid., pp. 118, 120 and 168; also see The Constitution Project, op. cit.

[160] Material in this section is from Scheck et al., op. cit., pp. 233–234 and 355.

[161] Material in this section is from Governor's Commission on Capital Punishment, pp. 94–99; also see The Constitution Project, op. cit.

[162] Material in this section is from ibid., p. 152; also see The Constitution Project, op. cit.

[163] Material in this section is from ibid., p. 172; also see The Constitution Project, op. cit.

[164] Material in this section is from Burnett, op. cit., pp. 188–189.

[165] Material in this section is from ibid., pp. 189–191.

[166] Material in this section is from Innocence Project at www.innocentproject.org; also see The Constitution Project, op. cit.; Gross et al., 2004.

[167] Unless indicated otherwise, material in this section is from Burnett, op. cit., pp. 194–195; Burnett, 2006.

[168] See, for example, the discussion of *Strickland v. Washington* (466 U.S. 668, 1984) in Chapter 2.

[169] "Jury: Freed inmate to get $2.25 million," 2006; Markon, 2006.

[170] Garner, 2000.

[171] "Table of Compensation Statutes," 2006.

[172] Death Penalty Information Center at www.deathpenaltyinfo.org/article.php?scid=40&did=1234#subC.

[173] See Amsterdam, op. cit.

[174] See *The Charlotte* [NC] *Observer*, November 13, 1992.

[175] Unless indicated otherwise, material in this section is from Tabak, op. cit.

[176] See Alter, op. cit.; Davis, 1998; www.deathpenaltyinfo.org/IllinoisCCP.html.

[177] www.deathpenaltyinfo.org/IllinoisCCP.html; also see Armbrust, 2002.

[178] Ibid.

[179] Davey and Mills, op. cit. Ryan's critics are sure to point out that on September 6, 2006, Ryan was sentenced to 6.5 years in prison for 18 counts of racketeering, conspiracy, fraud and other offenses involving favoritism and kickbacks for state contracts and property leases that enriched Ryan and his friends. Most of the charges were related to Ryan's 8 years as secretary of state during the 1990s. Ryan maintained his innocence throughout the trial, and the verdict is being appealed (Stern, 2006).

[180] Cohen, 1999; www.apbnews.com:80/cjsystem/justicenews/2000/02/04/moratorium 0204_01.html.

[181] "Maryland Halts Executions." *The Orlando Sentinel* (May 10, 2002), p. A15.

[182] "Codey signs bill suspending executions in New Jersey" at www.njadp.org/forms/ codeymor.html.

[183] www.apbnews.com:80/cjsystem/justicenews/2000/02/04/moratorium0204_01.html.

[184] Alter and Miller, 2000.

[185] www.cardozo.yu.edu/innocence_project.

[186] www.deathpenaltyinfo.org/Changes.html.

[187] Healy, 2001.

[188] Gearan, 2002.

[189] The polls can be found at the following sites: PollingReport.com, "Crime/Law Enforcement" at www.pollingreport.com/crime.htm#Death; The Death Penalty Information Center, "Summaries of Recent Poll Findings" at www.deathpenaltyinfo.org/ article.php?scid=23&did=210#gallup200310.

[190] In only five national Gallup polls during that period did public support for the death penalty exceed 69 percent: May 2002 (72 percent), October 2002 (70 percent), May 2003 (70 and 74 percent), and May 2004 (71 percent). Ibid.

[191] Fan et al., 2002.

[192] For example, in a June 1991 Gallup poll, 53 percent of adults nationwide preferred the death penalty to LWOP; in an ABCNews.com poll conducted in January 2000, 48 percent of adults nationwide preferred the death penalty to LWOP; in a May 2001 Gallup poll, 52 percent of adults nationwide preferred the death penalty to LWOP; in a May 2002 Gallup poll, 52 percent of adults nationwide preferred the death penalty to LWOP; in a May 2003 Gallup poll, 53 percent of adults nationwide preferred the death penalty to LWOP; in a May 2004 Gallup poll, 50 percent of adults nationwide preferred the death penalty to LWOP, but in December 2004, a Quinnipiac University poll reported that only 42 percent of adults nationwide preferred the death penalty to LWOP (46 percent preferred LWOP); in a April 2005 CBS News poll, 39 percent of adults nationwide preferred the death penalty to LWOP (39 percent preferred LWOP); and a May 2006 USA Today/Gallup poll, 47 percent of adults nationwide preferred the death penalty to LWOP (48 percent preferred LWOP). PollingReport.com, "Crime/Law Enforcement," op. cit.; Gallup and Newport, 1991; www.pollingreport.com/crime.htm#Death; Jones, op. cit.

[193] The following poll data can be found at PollingReport.com at www.pollingreport.com/crime.htm#Death.

[194] Ibid; also see Unnever and Cullen (2005:14-15, and 29) who found that 74.6 percent of Gallup poll respondents believed that an innocent person had been executed in the last five years. They also found that Americans were more likely to oppose the death penalty if they believed that the penalty was applied unfairly than if an innocent person had been executed. Finally, they discovered that the decrease in death penalty support among African Americans was much greater than it was for whites when either group believed an innocent person had been executed.

[195] The Death Penalty Information Center, op. cit.

[196] Ibid.

[197] Gross, op. cit., p. 497.

[198] See, for example, the Committee on the Judiciary, op. cit.; Markman and Cassell, op. cit.

[199] Van den Haag, 1982:325.

[200] Death Penalty Information Center, www.deathpenaltyinfo.org/Polls. Html#Harris7/01.

[201] See Longmire, 1996, for the finding that evidence of the execution of innocent persons is one of the most effective ways of changing the opinions of death penalty supporters to opponents.

[202] Professor Bedau (1999:47) offers this general substantive due process principle that might apply here: "Society, acting through the authority of its government, must not enact and enforce policies that impose more restrictive–invasive, harmful, violent–interference with human liberty, privacy, and autonomy than are absolutely necessary as the means to achieve legitimate and important social objectives." Bedau (2004:32-33) calls this the "Minimal Invasion principle." For Bedau, the death penalty always violates the principle.

CHAPTER 8

Arbitrariness and Discrimination in the Administration of the Death Penalty

In its *Furman* decision, two of the major problems the Supreme Court found with existing death penalty statutes were that they did not prevent the death penalty from being imposed arbitrarily and in a discriminatory fashion. Professors Nakell and Hardy provide relevant definitions of the two key terms:

- Arbitrariness involves the question of whether discretion permits the death penalty to be applied randomly, capriciously, irregularly, or disproportionately among the qualified defendants without any evident regard for the legal criteria designed to determine the selection. Arbitrariness is random.[1]

- Discrimination involves the question of whether discretion permits the death penalty to be deliberately directed disproportionately against certain qualified defendants, not because of the nature of their crimes, but because they belong to a particular class or group, determined by such considerations as race, sex, nationality, religion, or wealth. Discrimination is deliberate.[2]

Recall from the discussion in Chapter 2 that the Supreme Court approved, on faith, the new guided discretion statutes enacted in the wake of *Furman*. The Court assumed, without any evidence, that the new statutes and other procedural reforms would rid the death penalty's administration of the problems cited in *Furman*, including arbitrariness and discrimination. The purpose of this chapter is to examine the evidence amassed since the Court's 1976 decision and to determine whether the Court's faith was justified.

Arbitrariness in the Administration of the Death Penalty under Post–*Furman* Statutes

As evidence of arbitrary application of the death penalty under post-*Furman* statutes, critics point to the small percentage of all death-eligible offenders who are executed and to the patterns in which the death penalty has been applied across jurisdictions and over time. Sources of that arbitrariness have been identified as: (1) post-*Furman* statutes that justify arbitrariness, (2) jurors' misunderstanding or underestimating their sentencing obligations, (3) rule changes by the Supreme Court, (4) problems in determining murderous intent, (5) the availability and use of plea bargaining, and (6) the appellate courts.

Few Death–Eligible Offenders Are Executed. Only one to two percent of all death-eligible offenders have been executed from 1930 to the present. Thus, not only is the vast majority of capital offenders able to escape execution, but there is no meaningful way to distinguish between the eligible offenders who were executed and those who were not. Even during the peak of executions in the United States in the 1930s, only 20 percent of all death-eligible offenders were executed.

The situation has not changed much under post-*Furman* statutes. Professor Bowers found that:

> of the first 607 sentences imposed on convicted murderers under Georgia's post-*Furman* capital statute—not counting guilty pleas resulting in life sentences—113 were death sentences. . . . That is to say, more than 80 percent of the death-eligible murderers in Georgia—the vast majority—were given life sentences. And Georgia is among the states most likely to impose death sentences; in most other states the percentage of death-eligible murderers receiving death sentences will be even less.[3]

One might assume that the few death-eligible offenders that are executed represent the "worst of the worst," but the "worst of the worst" sometimes escape execution, while murderers who clearly are not among the "worst of the worst" do not. Regarding the first category, in 2003, Gary Ridgway, the so-called "Green River Killer," admitted to killing 48 women during a span of two decades. He was allowed to escape the death penalty by pleading guilty to the murders and, in doing so, gained the distinction of pleading guilty to more murders than any other serial killer in American history. He was sentenced to consecutive life sentences without opportunity of parole for each murder. The prosecutor reluctantly agreed to the plea deal because investigators and victims' relatives wanted the murders resolved and cases closed. Had the victims not been prostitutes, drug addicts, and runaways, perhaps the prosecutor's decision might have been different. However, Ridgeway is not the only serial killer to escape the death penalty. Two more examples are Angelo Buono and Kenneth Bianchi, the so-called "Hillside Stranglers." Bianchi pleaded guilty to 5 murders, and Buono was found guilty of 9 murders. All of the murder victims were young women. Both Bianchi and Buono were sentenced to LWOP in 1983.[4]

Application of the Death Penalty across Jurisdictions and over Time. Arbitrariness is evident in the way the death penalty has been applied across jurisdictions and over time. As attorney Amsterdam, who has defended dozens of capital offenders, describes:

> [T]here is a haphazard, crazy-quilt character about the administration of capital punishment that every knowledgeable lawyer or observer can describe but none can rationally explain. Some juries are hanging juries, some counties are hanging counties, some years are hanging years; and men live or die depending on these flukes. However atrocious the crime may have been for which a particular defendant is sentenced to die, 'experienced wardens know many prisoners serving life or less whose crimes were equally, or more atrocious.'[5]

Consider, for example, the distribution of executions among death penalty jurisdictions. Although 39 jurisdictions in the United States (which includes 37 states, the U.S. government, and the U.S. military) have death penalty statutes, only 34 jurisdictions have executed at least one person under their post-*Furman* statutes.[6] The federal government has executed three people, and the military has executed none under their post-*Furman* statutes at this writing.[7] Nearly half of the executing jurisdictions (16) have executed fewer than 10 people since executions resumed in 1977.[8] Professor Bowers contends, "Capital punishment appears to be not an integral part of the criminal justice process in these states, but an occasional product of chance—an unpredictable occurrence."[9]

Only five of the 34 jurisdictions account for about two-thirds of the 1.070 people executed under post-*Furman* statutes as of April 12, 2007; two states (Texas and Virginia) can lay claim to about 46 percent of the total; and one state (Texas) has executed nearly 37 percent of the total.[10] Still, even Texas executes only a small percentage of its death-eligible offenders.

Regional variation in executions also suggests arbitrariness in application. Historically, capital punishment has been employed mostly in the South. Sixty percent of the approximately 4,000 persons legally executed under state authority in the United States between 1930 and 1980 were in the South. Between 1930 and 1980, the state of Georgia executed more people (366) than any other state.[11] The distribution by region is as follows:

South	2,307 (60 percent)
Northeast	602 (16 percent)
West	511 (13 percent)
North Central	403 (11 percent)
Total	3,823

During the period, 3.75 times more capital offenders were executed in the South than in any other region of the United States.[12] As of April 20, 2007, in excess of seven times more capital offenders were executed in the South than in any other region of the United States under post-*Furman* statutes.[13] More than 80 percent of executions under post-*Furman* statutes have occurred in the South.[14] The post-*Furman* distribution by region is:

South	878	(82 percent)
Northeast	4	(0.4 percent)
West	66	(6 percent)
Midwest	122	(11 percent)
Total	1,070	

There is also regional variation within states. For example, in Florida and Georgia, the probability of receiving a death sentence for felony homicide (death-eligible murder) by judicial circuit or county varied greatly.[15] In Florida, a capital offender was more than four times more likely to be sentenced to death for a felony homicide in the panhandle area of the state than in either the northern or southern regions of the state, and more than twice as likely to be sentenced to death in the panhandle than in the central region of the state. Similarly, in Georgia, a capital offender was nearly nine times more likely to be sentenced to death in either the central or southwest regions than in Fulton County (Atlanta), more than four times more likely to be sentenced to death in either the central or southwest regions of Georgia than in the northern region, and twice as likely to be sentenced to death in the northern region than in Fulton County. A study of Virginia death sentencing practices found that the strongest predictive factor was location of the prosecution. A death sentence was significantly more likely to be sought in lower density areas of the state than in high-density urban areas.[16]

These data do not necessarily indicate arbitrariness if it can be shown that a similar proportion of death-eligible murders are committed in the South or in a particular region of a state. However, in 2004, only 43 percent of [all] homicides occurred in the South[17]—a smaller percentage than might be predicted, given that more than 80 percent of executions occur in the South. But the 43 percent is for all homicides and not just death-eligible homicides, and data separating the two categories are not available. Thus, it is still possible, though improbable, that a much larger proportion of murders are death-eligible in the South than in other regions of the country.

Such disparities are not limited to the South. A study in Nebraska also discovered significant differences in charging and plea bargaining in major urban and non-urban counties. In major urban counties prosecutors were more willing than their counterparts in non-urban counties to waive the death penalty unilaterally or by way of plea bargain. Those practices produced a statewide "adverse disparate impact" on racial minorities, who were more likely to face a death sentence.[18] In Illinois, defendants outside of Cook County were substantially more likely to receive a death sentence than defendants within Cook County. Specifically, after controlling for aggravating factors, 8.4 percent of first-degree murder convictions from rural counties in Illinois resulted in a death sentence. The corresponding percentages for urban counties, collar counties, and Cook County were, respectively, 3.4 percent, 3.3 percent, and 1.5 percent.[19] Similar geographical (county) disparities were found in Ohio and Maryland, in the latter, even after controlling for numerous relevant case characteristics.[20]

Data of regional variation within states suggest that greater numbers of death-eligible homicides do not increase the overall probability of a death sentence, as one might expect. Rather, the data show that the odds of being sentenced to death are either greater in regions with fewer death-eligible homicides or not related to the number of death-eligible homicides at all. It may be that where capital murders are few, those that are committed receive harsher punishment. Another explanation, as noted in Chapter 6, has to do with the costs of capital punishment. Counties that can afford it may seek the death penalty in all cases that warrant it, while "poor" counties may have to pick and choose among death-eligible cases, pursuing the death penalty in only some cases or not at all. "Poor" counties simply may not be able to afford the death penalty.[21]

In Florida, for example, other regions had between 4.5 and nearly 9 times more homicides than the panhandle, yet in the panhandle, the probability of a death sentence was two to four times greater than in other regions of the state. That finding was the exception, however. The overall probability of a death sentence in the central region of Florida was at least twice as great as the probability in either the north or south regions, even though the number of death-eligible homicides in the central region (172) was more than the 140 in the north region and less than the 270 in the south region. In Georgia, the central and southwest regions were nearly nine times more likely than Fulton County to impose a death sentence, yet the 154 death-eligible homicides in Fulton County were greater than the 103 in the southwest region and fewer than the 162 in the central region. In Texas, Harris County (Houston) alone accounts for nearly a third of the state's death row inmates, while Dallas, with a higher murder rate, has only about a quarter of Houston's death row inmates.[22] These combined data show that the application of the death penalty under post-*Furman* statutes, in the words of the Court in its *Furman* decision, has been "rare," "uncommon," and "freakish."

Post–*Furman* Statutes Justify Arbitrariness. Professor Bowers suggests that the post-*Furman* statutes may have an effect different from the one intended by the Court. Rather than reducing or eliminating arbitrary and discriminatory application, the new statutes may facilitate both problems, especially in states such as Texas. He further explains, "Perhaps explicitly enumerated aggravating circumstances do not serve to guide sentencing discretion as much as they become means of justifying arbitrary or discriminatory sentencing practices in places where social or political influences favor such practices."[23]

Jurors' Misunderstanding or Underestimating their Sentencing Obligations. Another troublesome problem with post-*Furman* statutes—a problem that also contributes to arbitrary application—is the failure of many jurors to understand their statutory sentencing obligations. Research shows that jurors commonly misapprehend judges' capital-sentencing instructions, especially those pertaining to mitigating circumstances.[24] Particularly troublesome is evidence from the Capital Jury Project indicating that nearly 75 percent of jurors "acknowledge that sentencing instructions did not guide their decision-making on punishment but served instead as an after-the-fact façade for a decision made prior to hearing the instructions."[25] Many jurors inappropriately made their sentencing decisions before the sentencing phase of the trial began, and oftentimes those decisions were pro-death.[26] Data from the Capital Jury Project also reveal that jurors frequently have mistaken views about the alternatives to a death sentence and, consequently, vote for death even though they would vote for life if they were assured that the defendant would never be released from prison or would not be released for a long time. Many jurors do not believe that LWOP actually means that a defendant will be imprisoned for the rest of his or her life. Many capital jurors believe murderers will be back on the streets far too soon; typically, in about 15 years or less.[27] Judges in many jurisdictions are legally barred from clarifying that issue for jurors.[28]

Many jurors also underestimate their sentencing responsibilities, seeming to believe that they are only to follow a prescribed formula in determining a sentence in capital cases. For them, it is "the law" or "legal instructions" that ultimately determines whether a capital defendant lives or dies. For some jurors, "the law" or "legal instructions" "authorizes" them to impose the death penalty and, at the same time, relieves them of any personal responsibility in making the decision.[29] Other jurors assume that the sentence they impose is only preliminary and non-binding since it will be reviewed and corrected, if necessary, by an appellate court.[30] In *Caldwell v. Mississippi* (1985), the Supreme Court opined that for jurors to believe that "the responsibility for any ultimate determination of death will rest with others" is an "intolerable danger." Such thinking on the part of capital jurors may lead to arbitrarily imposed death sentences.

Rule Changes by the Supreme Court. Arbitrariness is also inevitable whenever the Supreme Court changes the rules by which the penalty is imposed. This is especially true when those changes have a retroactive effect (that is, when they are applied to earlier cases). An example is the Court's 1968 *Witherspoon* decision, which held as unconstitutional the practice of excluding people from capital juries simply because they generally opposed capital punishment. This ruling resulted in dozens of death row inmates having their death sentences set aside because of constitutional errors in jury selection. *Witherspoon* was welcome news to those inmates who received new trials, but the decision did nothing for the dozens who had been executed even though their trials were infected with identical errors.[31]

Similarly, the Court's 1977 *Coker* decision declared capital punishment for rape of an adult woman unconstitutional. *Coker* did nothing for the 455 men (405 of whom were black) who had been executed for rape in the United States since 1930.[32] Had they been tried under the *Coker* standard, they would have met a different fate. The same could be said for the mentally retarded before *Atkins v. Virginia* (2002) and for juveniles under the age of 18 before *Roper v. Simmons* (2005). There are numerous other such examples of changes in death penalty laws. The point is that whether or not an inmate is executed depends, in part, on chance—that is, whether his or her execution date came before or after a crucial Supreme Court decision.

Problems in Determining Murderous Intent. Another source of arbitrariness in the application of capital punishment involves the charge for which a defendant is prosecuted. Generally, whether a defendant is charged with first- or second-degree murder or capital or non-capital murder depends on such considerations as whether or not the defendant acted with "premeditation" or "criminal intent."[33] Determining what a person intended to do before he or she acted is a difficult, if not impossible, task. Former Supreme Court Justice Benjamin Cardoza underscored this dilemma when he wrote "that [he] did not understand the concept of premeditation after several decades of studying and trying to apply it as a judge,"[34] yet whether or not a defendant is tried for his or her life depends on just such a determination.

Availability and Use of Plea Bargaining. A related source of arbitrariness involves whether or not a capital suspect is allowed to plea bargain to a noncapital offense. The plea bargain option creates a particular dilemma for the capital suspect who is innocent (or at least innocent of a capital offense). If the suspect pleads guilty to a noncapital offense and, thus, escapes the death penalty, he or she will still have to serve a prison sentence (in all likelihood), perhaps for a crime that he or she did not commit. On the other hand, if the innocent suspect (or suspect who did not commit a capital crime) elects to be tried for the capital charge, he or she risks the chance of being found guilty and executed. This scenario is more than hypothetical. Julian Bond recounts that "on the date of his death [May 25, 1979], [John] Spinkelink could have already been paroled if he had plea bargained and accepted the uncontested second-degree murder conviction offered him by the state [of Florida]."[35]

The Appellate Courts. As noted previously, at least 28 percent and as many as 68 percent of death sentences imposed under post–*Furman* statutes have been found legally faulty. Many people may believe that appellate review detects and corrects arbitrary and discriminatory application of capital punishment, and, in some cases, it does—at a considerable burden in time and other resources to the appellate courts. Sometimes, though, appellate review becomes another independent source of arbitrariness. The description of John Spinkelink's final appeal to the Eleventh U.S. Circuit Court illustrates how this occurs.[36] Professor Bowers summarizes the lesson to be learned from Spinkelink's experience (as well as an unanticipated consequence):

> The final appeal of Spinkelink . . . reveals arbitrariness at the highest levels of legal authority. Federal judges are not exempt from or immune to personal, social, or situational influences; they are subject to the same pressures and temptations as everyone else who handles capital cases. . . . It is a seductive illusion to believe that the highest courts can intercept arbitrariness wherever it occurs in the handling of capital cases.
>
> Indeed, [for some] the assumption that the federal appellate process can serve as a fail-safe mechanism against arbitrariness and discrimination now sustains the institution of capital punishment in America. But the truth . . . is that the federal courts themselves are an independent source or conduit of such arbitrariness.[37]

Conclusion. Perhaps it is impossible to completely eliminate arbitrary application of the death penalty because of human involvement in the process. Perhaps the Supreme Court, in *Gregg*, was naive to believe that the new guided-discretion statutes and other procedural reforms would eliminate arbitrary imposition of the death penalty.

Either way, faced with evidence from the post–*Gregg* experience, the Court would seem to have two alternatives. First, it could decide that some arbitrariness in the death penalty's application is tolerable (which may be its current unofficial and implicit position, anyway). However, if it were to officially recognize the arbitrariness, then it probably would have to determine how much arbitrariness it will allow. That task might lead down a slippery slope to the second alternative—the abolition of capital punishment. The Court might conclude that arbitrary application of capital punishment is inevitable (intolerable though it may be) as long as the penalty is administered.

Discrimination in the Administration of the Death Penalty under Post–*Furman* Statutes

Only a select few of all murderers eligible for execution are ever actually executed. Consideration of the unique characteristics of those executed, the laws under which they are prosecuted, and the behavior of defense attorneys, prosecutors, and jurors reveals objectionable forms of discrimination. Before turning to evidence of discrimination, however, it is important to distinguish between disparity and discrimination.

Disparity versus Discrimination. Disparity refers to numerical differences based on some characteristic, such as race. There has been a pattern of racial disparity in the imposition of the death penalty in the United States because the penalty has been imposed on blacks disproportionately to their numbers in the population.[38] The Supreme Court holds that as long as racial or other disparities can be justified by relevant legal factors (e.g., that blacks commit a disproportionate number of capital crimes), there is nothing inherently problematical with those disparities in the administration of capital punishment. For the most part, the Court considers it legally irrelevant that disparities may be either wholly or partially products of factors antecedent to the criminal act (e.g., growing up in a racist or psychologically impoverished environment).[39]

Discrimination is a violation of the equal protection clause of the Fourteenth Amendment and of special restrictions on the use of capital punishment under the Eighth Amendment. Discrimination is evident to the Court when the death penalty is intentionally or purposefully imposed on persons because of some characteristic, such as race, and not because of or in addition to legitimate sentencing considerations. Proving intentional discrimination in specific cases is an extremely difficult task.

Discrimination Based on Social Class and the Definition of Murder. The FBI's Uniform Crime Report shows that, since 2000, approximately 16,000 murders and nonnegligent manslaughters have been committed each year. About 20 percent (or 3,200) of them are probably death-eligible. A problem with the murders reported by the FBI is that they represent only a fraction of the people killed intentionally or negligently each year and an even smaller fraction of potentially death-eligible murders. For example, conservative estimates indicate that each year in the United States at least 12,000 lives are lost because of unnecessary surgeries, 98,000 to preventable medical errors, 37,500 to hospital personnel spreading infections in hospitals, 50,000 to occupational disease, 450,000 to tobacco-related diseases, and an unknown number to lethal industrial products.[40]

While the proximate decisionmakers and perpetrators in most of those deaths are not death-eligible, because their actions or inactions are neither intentional nor criminally negligent, a small but significant fraction are. Yet, few of them are defined legally as murderers, especially death-eligible murderers. One reason is that few of the offenders are readily identifiable because their decisions are hidden by the complexities of the workplace environment or by the corporate chain of command. Another more cynical reason is that, by virtue of their class position, the perpetrators of these "white-collar crimes," no matter how malicious and heinous their actions, simply are not considered appropriate candidates for capital punishment in the United States. Justice Douglas wrote in his *Furman* decision, "One searches our chronicles in vain for the execution of any member of the affluent strata of this society."[41] Former San Quentin warden Clinton T. Duffy stated that he knew of no one of means who was ever executed.[42] Finally, as attorney Bryan Stevenson has pointed out, capital punishment really means "them without the capital gets the punishment."[43] The reason wealth matters is that the wealthy are able to hire the best attorneys. In many capital cases, the outcome depends more on an attorney's skill than what actually happened.[44]

The point, however, is not to argue for the death penalty for such offenses and offenders, but to show that an unacceptable form of discrimination is created by the way death-eligible murders are defined.[45] If death-eligible murder also included those actions and inactions just listed that are particularly reprehensible, then the distribution of persons convicted of death-eligible murder would be more evenly divided among social classes.[46]

Discrimination by Gender. The death penalty is rarely inflicted on women, even though women commit roughly one in ten of all criminal homicides (where the gender of the offender is known).[47] (The percentage of women who commit death-eligible homicides is unknown.) Approximately 19,000 people have been legally executed in the United States since 1608, and about 3 percent (approximately 568) of those have been women. Most of them (nearly 90 percent) were executed prior to 1866.[48] Between 1930 and 1980, approximately 4,000 persons were executed by civil authority in the United States—32, or about .8 percent, were women.[49]

It has been estimated that under current death penalty laws if women and men were treated equally, and that no factor other than offense was considered, women would receive between 4 and 6 percent of all death sentences.[50] Under post-*Furman* statutes, however, women have received about 2 percent of all death sentences—2 to 8 death sentences a year—155 between January 1, 1973, and January 1, 2006.[51] The reason for the difference is that from arrest through execution, women are filtered from the process. Women account for about:

- 10 percent of murder arrests,

- 2 percent of death sentences imposed at trial,

- 1.7 percent of persons on death row, and

- 1 percent of persons executed under post-*Furman* statutes (1,070 executions as of April 12, 2007).[52]

Only eleven women have been executed under post-*Furman* statutes as of this writing. At least fourteen years separated the first execution from the other ten. The women executed were Velma Barfield, who was executed in North Carolina on October 2, 1984; Karla Faye Tucker, who was executed in Texas on February 3, 1998; Judy Buenoano, who was executed in Florida on March 30, 1998; Betty Lou Beets, who was executed in Texas on February 24, 2000; Christina Riggs, who was executed in Arkansas on May 2, 2000; Wanda Jean Allen, who was executed in Oklahoma on January 11, 2001; Marilyn Plantz, who was executed in Oklahoma on May 1, 2001; Lois Nadean Smith, who was executed in Oklahoma on December 4, 2001; Linda Lyon Block, who was executed in Alabama on May 10, 2002, Aileen Wuornos, who was executed in Florida on October 10, 2002, and Frances Newton, who was executed in Texas on September 14, 2005. [53]

Approximately 90 percent of the post-*Furman* women sentenced to death but no longer on death rows had their death sentences reversed.[54] As of January 1, 2007, 59 women occupied death rows—about 1.8 percent of the total.[55] They ranged in age from 21 to 72, and had been on death row for as little as a few weeks to nearly twenty years.[56] Thirteen of the women currently on death rows killed their husbands or boyfriends, ten of them killed their children, and two of them killed both their husbands and children.[57]

Law Professor Victor Streib observes that the women who have been executed, both historically and in modern times, share certain distinctive characteristics:

The executed females tended to be very poor, uneducated, and of the lowest social class in the community. Their victims tended to be white and of particularly protected classes, either children or socially prominent adults. Comparatively few executed females committed their crimes with a co-defendant, so they could not claim they were under the domination of another. Most of the executed females manifested an attitude of violence, either from past behavior or present acts, that countered any presumption of nonviolence. Finally, and perhaps most fatally for them, they committed shockingly "unladylike" behavior, allowing the sentencing judges and juries to put aside any image of them as "the gentler sex" and to treat them as "crazed monsters" deserving of nothing more than extermination.[58]

Professor Streib is among the scholars who believe gender discrimination is evident in the application of the death penalty.[59] He identifies two principal sources of this discrimination: (1) the conscious or subconscious attitudes of key actors in the criminal justice process, and (2) death penalty laws, themselves.[60] Streib contends that the aggravating and mitigating circumstances enumerated in death penalty laws bias the application of the death penalty in favor of women. For example, among aggravating factors that generally advantage women over men charged with capital crimes are those that pertain to: (1) previous criminal record (women are less likely than men to have one), (2) premeditation (homicides by women tend to be unplanned and sudden acts), and (3) felony-murders (women are rarely involved in them).[61] Mitigating factors that tend to advantage women involve: (1) committing a capital crime while under extreme mental or emotional disturbance (female murderers are perceived to be more emotionally disturbed than male murderers), and (2) acting under the substantial domination of another person (when both women and men are involved in a capital crime, the man is generally considered the principal actor).[62]

As for the key actors in the criminal justice process, judges (who are predominately male) admit that, in general, they tend to be more lenient toward female offenders. They also tend to believe that women are better candidates for rehabilitation than are men. Jurors also tend to be more lenient toward female offenders, particularly in cases of serious crimes.[63]

Professor Streib describes an ethical dilemma with the practice of reserving execution almost entirely for men:

Making women ineligible for the death penalty, as Russia has done expressly and as the United States has done in practice, seems harder to defend. This practice, while explainable in some of its dimensions, seems at bottom to be unvarnished gender bias—a queasiness among criminal justice officials for putting a woman to death. One need not be a supporter of the death penalty to observe that if men are eligible for it then women should be also. Otherwise, women are lumped in with children and the mentally retarded as not fully responsible human beings.[64]

In short, if women are to be accorded full dignity as human beings, and illegal discrimination is to be avoided, then, as Professor Streib contends, women either must be executed for their capital crimes, or no one should be executed for a capital crime. Apparently, a large percentage of the American public agrees—at least with the first part. According to a 2002 Gallup poll, 68 percent of Americans favor the death penalty for women, 29 percent oppose it, and 3 percent don't know or refused to answer. In the same poll, 72 percent of Americans favored the death penalty in general, 25 percent opposed it, and 3 percent didn't know or refused to answer. Among subgroups, however, 72 percent of males but only 63 percent of females favored the death penalty for women, and 72 percent of whites but only 51 percent of nonwhites favored the death penalty for women. [65]

Discrimination by Age. About 2 percent (approximately 366) of the approximately 19,000 people executed in the United States since 1608 have been juveniles, that is, individuals who committed their capital crimes prior to their 18th birthday. As noted previously, on March 1, 2005, in the case of *Roper v. Simmons* (543 U.S. 551), the United States Supreme Court ruled, by a vote of 5 to 4, that the U.S. Constitution's Eighth and Fourteenth Amendments prohibited the execution of capital offenders under the age of 18. However, while the practice existed, juveniles, like women, were filtered from the process. They accounted for about:

- 8 percent of murder arrests,

- 3 percent of death sentences imposed at trial (before March 1, 2005),

- .03 percent of persons on death row (as of January 1, 2007), and

- 2 percent of persons executed under post-*Furman* statutes (1,070 executions as of April 12, 2007).[66]

Only 23 juveniles—all but one of whom were 17 years old at the time they committed their crimes—have been executed under post-*Furman* statutes.[67] The one exception was Sean Sellers, who was executed in Oklahoma on February 4, 1999, for a crime he committed when he was 16 years old.[68] The last executed juvenile in the United States who was younger than 17 at the time of his crime before Sellers was 16-year-old Leonard Shockley, who was executed in Maryland on April 10, 1959.[69] The first juvenile executed under post-*Furman* statutes was Charles Rumbaugh, who was executed in Texas on September 11, 1985; the last was Scott Hain, who was executed in Oklahoma on April 3, 2003.[70] The age at execution of the 23 juveniles ranged from 23 to 38, reflecting the time they spent on death row.[71] Since 1990, the United States was one of only eight countries that had executed anyone under 18 years of age at the time of the crime; the others were China, the Democratic Republic of the Congo, Iran, Nigeria, Pakistan, Saudi Arabia, and Yemen.[72] During the mid-1980s, Psychiatrist Dorothy Lewis and her colleagues evaluated 14 (40 percent) of the then 37 juvenile death row inmates in the United States.[73] They found that all of them had suffered head injuries as children, twelve of them had been abused either physically, sexually, or both, twelve of them had IQ scores of 90 or less, eleven of them had below-average reading abilities, nine of them had major neuropsychological problems, seven of them had psychotic disorders since early childhood, seven of them had serious psychiatric disturbances, and five of them reported being sodomized by relatives. As of this writing and since 1973, jurisdictions in the United States had imposed death sentences on 228 offenders under the age of 18 at the time of their crime,[74] but the chances of any of those juveniles actually being executed were remote. The reversal rate for juveniles sentenced to death under post-*Furman* statutes was about 90 percent.[75]

Whether or not juveniles should be subjected to capital punishment had been a controversial issue before the *Simmons* decision. A Gallup poll conducted in 2002 found that 72 percent of Americans favored the death penalty for people convicted of murder, 25 percent opposed it, and 3 percent didn't know or refused to answer. However, as noted in Chapter 2, only 26 percent of respondents in that poll favored the death penalty for juveniles, 69 percent opposed it, and 5 percent didn't know or refused to answer. Among subgroups, only 31 percent of males, 21 percent of females, 25 percent of whites, and 29 percent of nonwhites favored the death penalty for juveniles.[76] The level of support (or lack thereof) of the death penalty for juveniles in 2002 represented a dramatic change from the results of a Gallup poll conducted in 1994. In the 1994 poll, 60 percent of Americans thought that when a teenager commits a murder and is found guilty by a jury, he (the survey item did not address female teenage killers) should get the death penalty (compared with 80 percent who favored the death penalty for adults), 30 percent opposed the death penalty for teenagers, and 10 percent had no opinion.[77] Seventy-two percent of those who favored the death penalty for adults also favored it for teenage killers.

Among the reasons for not subjecting juveniles to capital punishment are the following:

- our society, as represented by our legislatures, prosecutors, judges, and juries, has rejected the juvenile death penalty;

- other nations, including many that share our Anglo-American heritage, have rejected the juvenile death penalty;

- the threat of the death penalty does not deter potential juvenile murderers because juveniles often do not consider the possible consequences prior to committing their murderous acts and because, even if they did consider these consequences, they would realize that very few juveniles actually receive the death penalty;

- juveniles are especially likely to be rehabilitated or reformed while in prison, thus rendering the juvenile death penalty especially inappropriate;

- the juvenile death penalty does not serve a legitimate retributive purpose, since juveniles are generally less mature and responsible than adults, and should therefore be viewed as less culpable than adults who commit the same crimes.[78]

An additional reason for treating juveniles differently than adults in the administration of justice is that juveniles are already treated legally differently than adults in other areas of life, such as driving, voting, gambling, marriage, and jury service.[79]

On the other hand, some of the reasons for subjecting juveniles to capital punishment are:

- the evidence of a societal consensus against the juvenile death penalty is nonexistent or at least too weak to justify a constitutional ban (this no longer may be the case);

- the views of other nations are irrelevant to the proper interpretation of our Constitution, at least absent a consensus within our own society;

- the threat of the death penalty can deter potential juvenile murderers, or at least the judgments of legislatures and prosecutors to that effect deserve deference;

- the most heinous juvenile murderers, who are the only ones likely to receive the death penalty, are not good candidates for rehabilitation or reform;

- there are some juvenile murderers who are sufficiently mature and responsible to deserve the death penalty for their crimes, and thus the juvenile death penalty serves a legitimate retributive purpose.[80]

As for other areas of the law that distinguish between adults and juveniles, proponents of capital punishment for juvenile offenders stress that while juveniles may not vote conscientiously or drive safely, they do know that killing other human beings is wrong.[81]

Another reason for supporting the death penalty for at least some juvenile capital offenders, and what makes the current practice of excluding death-eligible juveniles from the death penalty discriminatory, is that the designation of "juvenile" is arbitrary and only a proxy for more relevant characteristics. It was not until the sixteenth and seventeenth centuries that the young began to be viewed other than as miniature adults or property.[82] Before that time, juveniles as young as five or six were expected to assume the responsibilities of adults and, when they violated the law, were subjected to the same criminal sanctions as adults. Moreover, is there a significant difference on any relevant social characteristic between a 17- and 18-year-old, other than what has been created by law? Is it really meaningful to consider a 17-year-old a juvenile and an 18-year-old an adult?

In considering whether a person deserves the death penalty from a retributive standpoint, Law Professor Joseph Hoffmann points out that age is largely irrelevant. It is used because it serves as an imperfect proxy for more relevant social characteristics. Whether a murderer, regardless of age, deserves the death penalty depends, not on age, argues Hoffmann, but on maturity, judgment, responsibility, and the capability to assess the possible consequences of his or her actions.[83] Some juveniles possess those characteristics in greater quantity than some adults, or in sufficient quantities to be death-eligible; some do not. The use of age as a basis for determining who is or is not death-eligible is therefore discriminatory. Thus, the *Simmons* decision did nothing more than change the age at which death penalty states are allowed to discriminate.

Age plays a role in death penalty administration in another way. Research from Ohio shows that death-eligible offenders who were over 25 years old were more than twice as likely to be sentenced to death than were death-eligible offenders who were 25 years old or younger.[84]

Racial Discrimination. Post-*Furman* statutes also have failed to end racial discrimination in the imposition of the death penalty. In the past, discussions of racial discrimination have focused almost entirely on the race of those executed, and while race of offender is not the only form of racial discrimination, that issue is considered first.

As noted in Chapter 1, by 1860, no northern state punished by death any crime except for murder and treason. In the antebellum South, there was never much debate about abolishing the death penalty entirely but, by the Civil War, few whites were executed for any crime other than murder, even though penal codes continued to list other capital felonies.[85] In the case of southern blacks, on the other hand, the death penalty was imposed for many crimes. For example, in 1856, Virginia had 66 capital crimes for slaves but only one (murder) for whites; Mississippi had 38 capital crimes that applied exclusively to slaves.[86] In Texas prior to the Civil War, the crimes of insurrection, arson, and, if the victim were white, attempted murder, rape, attempted rape, robbery, attempted robbery, and assault with a deadly weapon were capital crimes if committed by slaves but were not capital crimes if committed by whites. Capital punishment in Texas was also reserved for free blacks that committed the crimes listed above as well as for the crime of kidnapping a white woman.[87] In Virginia, slaves were eligible to be executed for any crime for which a free person could be sentenced to prison for three years or more. If the victim were white in Virginia, rape, attempted rape, kidnapping a woman, and aggravated assault were capital crimes when committed by free blacks but were not when committed by whites.[88] The attempted rape of a white woman was a capital offense exclusively for blacks in Florida, Louisiana, Mississippi, South Carolina, Tennessee, Texas, and Virginia.[89] Black slaves were executed for the deterrent effect that southerners reasoned could not be achieved by either incarceration or forced labor. It was widely believed that the latter two punishments were not much worse and sometimes better than slavery itself.[90] Free blacks were executed for numerous crimes because, it appears, they were simply black. Whatever the reason, blacks were executed in the South disproportionately to their numbers in the population.

Between 1930 and 1980, 3,862 prisoners were executed under civil authority in the United States: 1,754 (45 percent) were white and 2,066 (53 percent) were black.[91] Blacks constituted around 10 percent of the population during that period. Among the 3,862 persons executed were 455 convicted of rape. Of those, 48 (11 percent) were white and 405 (89 percent) were black. Ninety-seven percent (443) were executed in the South.[92] Professors Wolfgang and Riedel reported in a 1975 study of 361 rape convictions from a sample of 25 Georgia counties from 1945-1965, "that the most important predictor of which among the 361 rapists would be sentenced to death was the racial combination of offender and victim. . . . [b]lack offenders who raped white victims . . . were significantly more likely to be sentenced to death in comparison to rapes involving all other racial combinations."[93]

The statistics on executions for the crime of rape indicate that the case for racial discrimination in the imposition of the death penalty is strongest for the South.[94] Recall that between 1930 and 1980, 60 percent of all executions in the United States occurred in the South. Of those executed, 28 percent were white and 72 percent were black.[95] Again, those figures do not necessarily indicate an undesirable form of racial discrimination if blacks committed a disproportionately greater number of death-eligible murders or rapes, but that was unlikely the case. From roughly 1973 through 1977, for example, 617 persons were arrested or suspected by police of death-eligible murder in Florida, 535 in Georgia, and 702 in Texas.[96] In Florida, 49 percent of the death-eligible murderers were black, in Georgia, 63 percent, and in Texas, 42 percent.[97] Racial distributions for rape were similar. Those figures suggest the unlikelihood that 89 percent of the death-eligible rapists and 72 percent of the death-eligible murderers in the South were black.

According to an "evaluation synthesis" of 28 post-*Furman* studies prepared by the U.S. General Accounting Office (GAO) and published in 1990, "more than half of the studies found that race of defendant influenced the likelihood of being charged with a capital crime or receiving the death penalty . . . [and in] more than three-fourths of the studies that identified a race-of-defendant effect . . . black defendants were more likely to receive the death penalty."[98] An update of the GAO study prepared for the American Bar Association (ABA) by the premier researchers in this area, Law Professor David Baldus and Statistician George Woodworth, showed that in nearly half of the death penalty states race of defendant was a significant predictor of who would receive a death sentence. In all but two of those states (Florida and Tennessee), black defendants were more likely to receive a death sentence.[99] Likewise, a 1994 study by the *Houston Post* found that in Harris County—which accounts for more post-*Furman* executions than any state other than Texas itself and more death sentences than most states—blacks were sentenced to death twice as often as whites.[100] In another study, Professor Baldus and his colleagues studied a sample of death-eligible murderers in Philadelphia, Pennsylvania, between 1983 and 1993. They found that African Americans had a nearly four times greater chance of receiving a death sentence than similarly situated defendants, even after controlling for a variety of factors including severity of offense and background of defendant.[101] They also discovered that race made the most difference in "mid-range" of severity or aggravation cases in which prosecutors and jurors exercise the most discretion in seeking and imposing the death penalty.[102] However, not all studies have discovered a race-of-defendant effect.[103]

In some cases,[104] but, interestingly, not in capital cases,[105] the Supreme Court has allowed racially discriminatory intent to be inferred from "a clear pattern, unexplainable on grounds other than race." Criteria of proof are more restricted in capital cases, but short of public admission of racially discriminatory intent or other unlikely happenstance, it is not clear how such intent on the part of participants in the administration of capital punishment could be shown.[106] Even when overt racially offensive remarks are made in capital trials, racial discriminatory intent is not always inferred. For example, in a 1985 capital case in Florida, the trial judge referred to the family of a black defendant as "niggers." The Florida Supreme Court did not strongly reprimand the judge for his remark; the Court only reminded him that he must always maintain an "image of impartiality."[107] In Utah, two black men were sentenced to death by an all-white jury and executed, "even though jurors received a note which contained the words 'Hang the Nigger's' [*sic*] and a drawing of a figure hanging on a gallows."[108] According to attorney Stephen Bright, "No court, state or federal, even had a hearing on such questions as who wrote the note, what influence it had on the jurors, and how widely it was discussed by the jurors."[109] In a 1989 capital trial in Georgia, both the judge and the defense attorney referred to the black defendant as "colored" and "colored boy." The defense attorney stated that he used the racial slur, "nigger," jokingly. Two of the jurors who sentenced the defendant to death admitted after the trial to using the word "nigger" to describe the defendant. Again, appellate courts found no fault.[110] It may be that racially discriminatory outcomes are not generally the product of a conscious process and that participants in the administration of capital punishment do not "know" that their behavior is racially motivated.

Available evidence indicates that post-*Furman* statutes have not eliminated a second, less obvious form of racial discrimination: *victim-based racial discrimination*. Whether the death penalty is imposed continues to depend on the race of the victim. Research shows that the killers of whites, regardless of their race, are much more likely to be sentenced to death than are the killers of non-whites. This is especially the case for the killers of white females.[111] For example, between 1973 and 1977, under a post-*Furman* statute in Florida, the probability of a black person receiving the death penalty for the aggravated murder of a white was 32 percent (143 offenders; 46 persons sentenced to death). The probability of a white person receiving the death penalty for the aggravated murder of a white was 21.5 percent (303 offenders; 65 persons sentenced to death). The probability for a black who killed a black was 4 percent (160 offenders; 7 persons sentenced to death), and the probability for a white who killed a black was 0 percent (11 offenders; no persons sentenced to death).[112]

In other words, a black person convicted of an aggravated murder of a white in Florida between 1973 and 1977 was more than seven times more likely to receive a death sentence than was a black who killed a black. A white person convicted of an aggravated murder of a white was almost five times more likely to receive a death sentence than was a black who killed a black. A person convicted of aggravated murder of a white, whether the killer was a black or a white, was more likely to receive the death penalty than was a person of either race convicted of aggravated murder of a black. Moreover, a white person convicted of aggravated murder of a black almost never received a death sentence (the total of such cases for Florida, Georgia, and Texas was 54; in three (5.5 percent) there was a death sentence).[113] A similar pattern was found in Georgia,[114] Texas,[115] South Carolina,[116] North Carolina,[117] Louisiana,[118] Alabama,[119] Mississippi,[120] Tennessee,[121] Kentucky,[122] California,[123] Illinois,[124] Missouri,[125] Oklahoma,[126] Maryland,[127] Virginia,[128] New Jersey,[129]

316 DEATHQUEST

Connecticut,[130] Ohio,[131] and Pennsylvania (Philadelphia).[132] The ABA study found evidence of race-of-victim disparities in 93 percent of death penalty states, and in all but one of those states (Delaware) white-victim cases were more likely to receive death sentences.[133]

The GAO evaluation synthesis further revealed that "in 82 percent of the studies, race of victim was found to influence the likelihood of being charged with capital murder or receiving the death penalty. . . . This finding was remarkably consistent across data sets, states, data collection methods, and analytic techniques."[134] The report also noted that "the race of victim influence was stronger for the earlier stages of the judicial process (e.g., prosecutorial decision to charge defendant with a capital offense, decision to proceed to trial rather than plea bargain) than in later stages."[135]

In the classic study used in the *McCleskey* case, Professor Baldus and his colleagues found that in Georgia under its post-*Furman* statute "race-of-victim effects [as was the case with race-of-defendant effects in their more recent Philadelphia study] were particularly strong in the midrange of cases when prosecutors and juries have the greatest room for the exercise of discretion."[136] They estimated that the outcomes in more than one-third of the midrange (in aggravation) cases were determined by the race of the victim. At least in the aforementioned states, these findings suggest that the life of a black victim is valued less than the life of a white victim, regardless of the race of the offender.[137]

More recent data do not indicate any change in the situation. As of January 1, 2007, defendant-victim racial combinations for post-*Furman* executions were as follows (based on 1,578 victims):[138]

Combination	Percent
white defendant/white victim	53.64
white defendant/black victim	1.42
white defendant/Asian victim	.28
white defendant/Latino(a) victim	.95
black defendant/white victim	20.62
black defendant/black victim	10.88
black defendant/Asian victim	.66
black defendant/Latino(a) victim	1.42
Latino defendant/white victim	3.31
Latino defendant/Latino(a) victim	2.65
Latino defendant/Asian victim	.09
Latino defendant/black victim	.19
Native American defendant/white victim	1.23
Native American defendant/Native American victim	.19
Asian defendant/Asian victim	.47
Asian defendant/white victim	.19

The data reveal that about 80 percent of the victims of those persons executed under post-*Furman* statutes have been white, and that only about 14 percent have been black. Yet, 57 percent of defendants executed have been white, 34 percent have been black, 6.5 percent have been Latino(a), 1.4 percent have been Native American and .66 percent have been Asian.[139] Discrimination seems apparent because, historically, capital crimes have generally been intraracial.[140] For example, in 2005, 83 percent of white victims were murdered by white offenders, and 91 percent of black victims were murdered by black offenders (when race of victim and offender were known).[141] Still, uncertainty remains about whether the data show discrimination because only about 20 percent of murders and nonnegligent manslaughters are capital crimes.[142] It seems likely that the percentage of interracial murders may be somewhat greater for capital murders than it is for noncapital murders. In any event, two major implications of these data are: (1) "in places that currently treat black defendants more punitively than similarly situated non-black defendants, an evenhanded system would reduce the absolute number of black defendants sentenced to death . . . [and] the proportion of black defendants on death row," and (2) "if an evenhanded policy were applied to the black and white victim cases (at the current rate for either black or white victim cases), the 'proportion' of black defendants on death row would increase."[143]

Sources of Racial Disparity/Discrimination. Studies that have found post-*Furman* racial disparity/discrimination have located the source of it predominately in the discretionary actions of prosecutors and juries. (Evidence suggests that prosecutors and juries are also sources of arbitrariness in the death penalty's application.) Professor Baldus and his colleagues declare that "the exercise of prosecutorial discretion [in seeking a death sentence] is the principal source of the race-of-victim disparities observed in the system."[144] In Georgia (and in other states) a capital sentencing hearing is a preliminary stage in the process that leads to a capital trial. Baldus and colleagues report that under Georgia's post-*Furman* statute, black defendants whose victims were white were advanced to a capital sentencing hearing by prosecutors at a rate nearly five times that of black defendants whose victims were black, and more than three times the rate of white defendants whose victims were black.[145] Other research found that prosecutors have sought the death penalty in 70 percent of cases involving black defendants and white victims and in only 35 percent of the cases involving other racial combinations.[146] A recent study of Maryland's death penalty found that, after controlling for relevant case characteristics, the killers of white victims, especially if they were black, were substantially more likely than the killers of non-whites to be charged by prosecutors with a capital crime and for the charge to "stick," that is, not be withdrawn by the prosecutor once the death notification was filed.[147]

In Florida, prosecutors have "upgraded" and "downgraded" potential capital cases under post-*Furman* statutes by alleging aggravating circumstances, charging defendants with an accompanying felony, ignoring evidence in police reports, and withholding an accompanying charge depending on the race of the offender and of the victim.[148] Professors Radelet and Pierce report that "cases in which blacks were accused of killing whites were the most likely to be upgraded and least likely to be downgraded."[149] Prosecutors have engaged in similar actions in South Carolina,[150] Kentucky,[151] and other states.[152] Prosecutors also have reduced death-eligible white-defendant or black-victim cases to noncapital ones through plea bargaining, or they have foregone a penalty trial and thus waived the death penalty, even when a defendant had been convicted by a jury of a capital offense.[153]

Historically, blacks are the demographic group most likely to oppose the death penalty[154] and thus are the group most likely to be excluded from jury service in capital cases. Even if blacks are not opposed to the death penalty categorically, they also can be underrepresented on capital juries by the prosecutor's exercise of peremptory challenges.[155] For example, if jurors express some opposition to the death penalty but not enough to exclude them for cause, they still can be eliminated through the prosecutor's peremptory challenge. In Texas, prosecutors have recently been found to have "shuffled" the venire panel (rearranging the order in which venire panel members were seated and questioned) to reduce the chances of blacks serving on a jury.[156] They also asked different questions to black and nonblack panel members about their views on the death penalty and minimum acceptable sentences to provide a basis for eliminating potential black jurors.[157] Finally, they used their peremptory challenges to exclude black venire members from juries—the latter a decades-old practice of the Dallas County District Attorney's Office.[158]

Data from the Capital Jury Project show that prosecutors are about twice as likely to ask the white co-victims of white murder victims to present victim-impact evidence at trial than they are to ask the black co-victims of black murder victims to do so.[159] Post-*Furman* evidence from two judicial circuits in Georgia show that blacks play only a small role in capital cases, except, of course, as defendants—a category in which they are overrepresented.[160] In the words of former Georgia state senator Gary Parker, "The classic death penalty case in Georgia remains a black person prosecuted by a white district attorney before a white judge and an all-white jury for a crime against a prominent white person."[161]

How black defendants in Georgia counties and other jurisdictions with black populations often exceeding 40 percent continue to be tried by all-white juries in light of the Supreme Court's *Batson* decision also points to racial discrimination. Recall from the discussion in Chapter 2 that *Batson v. Kentucky* (1986) requires trial judges to determine whether prosecutors intended to discriminate against black defendants by using their peremptory jury strikes to eliminate black jurors. However, the relationship between many prosecutors and trial judges may make this determination a meaningless exercise. Many trial judges are former prosecutors who, themselves, may have violated *Batson* as prosecutors and are sympathetic to the illegal actions of current prosecutors. Many trial judges, when they were prosecutors, hired the prosecutors that appear before them. Trial judges also may be beholden to prosecutors who contribute money to their re-election campaigns. Thus, it may be difficult for judges with such relationships with prosecutors to reject a prosecutor's reasons for striking black jurors.[162] The evidence is quite clear that racial disparities continue to be produced through the exercise of prosecutorial discretion in capital or potentially capital cases.

These findings are truly ironic in light of the majority's response in *Gregg* that:

> Petitioner's argument that the prosecutor's decisions in plea bargaining or in declining to charge capital murder are standardless and will result in the wanton or freakish imposition of the death penalty condemned in *Furman*, is without merit, for the assumption cannot be made that prosecutors will be motivated in their charging decisions by factors other than the strength of their case and the likelihood that a jury would impose the death penalty if it convicts.[163]

Although perhaps not as critical as the prosecutor, juries also play a role in racial disparities (and arbitrary sentencing decisions) produced under post-*Furman* statutes. Many potential jurors are biased from the onset of a capital case because of exposure to the media's typical one-sided coverage.[164] The media provide potential jurors with a "framework for understanding" a capital crime.[165] The media tend to focus on the most dramatic and heinous aspects of the crime. Rarely are the offender and his or her crime put in historical or social context. The offender's personal history and background—factors that might "humanize" the offender and mitigate the crime—generally are ignored. Thus, potential jurors are exposed to portrayals of capital offenders as "animals" or "monsters," as something less than human, something to fear and despise. Not surprisingly, then, research shows that the more negative information about a capital offender a potential juror was exposed to by the media, the more likely the potential juror was willing to convict the offender prior to his or her death penalty trial.[166] The irony is that most murderers are not like the media portrayals of them. As Law Professor David Dow, who, as previously noted, has represented more than 30 death row inmates, relates, "What is arresting about nearly all murderers is how ordinary they are, how unremarkable they appear."[167]

A remedy for the influence of pretrial publicity is a change of venue, but judges are reluctant to grant them even when prejudicial publicity has been extensive, community awareness of the crime is very high, and there is significant prejudgment of the case in the communities where the trial is to be held.[168] Judges are reluctant to grant change of venue motions because a change of venue is expensive when the trial is not held in the jurisdiction where most trial participants live. This is particularly true in capital cases, which are typically more complex and lengthy than other types of cases. The political risk of changing venues in capital cases is also a reason why elected judges are reluctant to grant them. When a highly publicized capital crime has been committed, judges, for political reasons, generally are more responsive to community sentiment to hold the trial in the jurisdiction where the crime was committed than they are to the constitutional rights of defendants.[169]

Another solution to the influence of pretrial publicity is the elimination of potential jurors affected by it during voir dire. However, biased jurors are hard to detect. This is especially true of ADP jurors (jurors who would automatically vote for the death penalty following a guilty verdict in a capital case). Evidence from the Capital Jury Project suggests that an average of 14 to 30 percent of capital jurors—between about 2 and 4 persons on a 12-person jury—are ADPs.[170] Research reveals that potential jurors (ADPs and others) often claim that they can be impartial, even when they know they have been exposed to negative pretrial publicity that has prejudiced their opinion of the defendant.[171] Research also indicates that the biasing effects of pretrial publicity are not reduced by judicial instructions to ignore it.[172]

Research conducted by Psychology Professor Craig Haney and others demonstrates that voir dire and death qualification (as noted in Chapter 2, the process of excluding death penalty opponents from capital juries because they are opposed to the death penalty under any circumstances),[173] themselves, are independent sources of bias in capital cases (especially when jurors are questioned in a group rather than individually after being sequestered). These processes have been found to "'condition' jurors to a particular point of view or set of expectations."[174] Research shows, for example, that potential jurors can be prejudiced by the responses of other potential jurors during voir dire and, in an effort to be seated or excused, may structure their answers to questions based on the reactions of judges and trial attorneys to the responses to the same questions asked of other potential jurors.[175]

Haney and his colleagues also found that the prolonged discussion of penalty at the very start of the trial during voir dire and death qualification, a unique aspect of capital trials, predisposed potential jurors to believe that the defendant was guilty and that he would be convicted and sentenced to death, that judges and attorneys shared their guilt-prone views, and that the judge in the case favored the death penalty. These beliefs, in turn, divert jurors' attention from the presumption of innocence. The discussion of penalty at the onset of the trial also desensitized potential jurors to the prospect of imposing the death penalty. Additionally, because death penalty opponents are excluded from participating in capital trials, many potential jurors believed that the law disfavors death penalty opponents. Finally, because they are required to publicly affirm their commitment to capital punishment during voir dire, potential jurors were more likely to believe that the death penalty was the appropriate punishment when confronted with a hypothetical capital case. They also were more likely to vote to impose it.[176]

Another source of bias is the capital trial, itself. Capital trials are unique among criminal trials because only in capital trials are juries required to make the sentencing decision. Professor Haney contends that "normal, law-abiding persons," who become jurors in capital cases, must overcome a deep-seated inhibition to sentence someone to death. To do so, according to Haney, jurors must be able to "morally disengage" from the realities of their decision. The trial structure and sequencing of evidence, the formal, legalistic atmosphere of the trial, and various legal doctrines allow them to do that.[177]

Moral disengagement is facilitated by the dehumanization of the capital defendant. As noted previously, this starts with typical media portrayals of the capital offender as a "monster" or an "animal." The trial is structured so that the first opportunity to "humanize" the capital defendant comes at the end of the trial, during the penalty phase when mitigation evidence can be presented. Even then, court rules give the prosecution the opportunity to present its evidence of aggravation first. As noted previously, data from the Capital Jury Project show that jurors are more likely to be influenced by the victim-impact testimony of the white co-victims of white murder victims than they are by the victim-impact testimony of the black co-victims of black murder victims.[178] During the guilt phase, the jury hears only the prosecution's description of the crime's brutal details. Moreover, the prosecution's typical theory of the crime—that the defendant is an inherently evil person entirely responsible for his or her crime—usually coincides with jurors' stereotypical beliefs about crimes and punishment. Not surprisingly, then, before jurors are exposed to any mitigating evidence, they become frightened of the defendant (assuming they were not already frightened of him), which provokes punitive and vengeful feelings and a concern about the defendant's future dangerousness, whether or not that issue was explicitly raised at trial.

Oftentimes the defendant unwittingly jeopardizes his or her own chances during the trial. Many jurors pay more attention to a defendant's appearance, demeanor, and reactions than the evidence presented. For example, when jurors see a clean-cut defendant in a suit and tie at the defense table, they may conclude that the defendant is trying to deceive them following the prosecution's presentation of photos showing the defendant as a totally different person being booked into jail with long hair, scruffy beard and tattoos everywhere.[179] Also, a defendant frequently does a disservice to himself or herself in the eyes of jurors by failing to show signs of remorse and repentance during the trial. When a prosecutor, for instance, shows photos of the victims' bodies and the defendant fails to show any emotion, jurors may decide there is little hope for redemption. A few tears shed by a defendant may mean the difference between a life and death sentence.[180] All of this helps explain why many capital jurors believe the defendant should be sentenced to death, *before the penalty phase of the trial begins*. To effectively deal with this structural barrier, defense attorneys must be able to make a strong case for mitigation during the penalty phase and overcome what many jurors believe is commonsense. However, as noted in the last chapter, many defense attorneys in capital cases lack the training, professional experience, time, and resources to do the job properly.[181] The "emotionally distant and decontextualized legal language by which the process proceeds" makes efforts at humanizing the capital defendant even more difficult.[182]

Also working against the capital defendant and contributing to moral disengagement is legal doctrine that forbids detailed discussion during the penalty phase of prison conditions or future prospects should the defendant be sentenced to life imprisonment without opportunity of parole (LWOP).[183] If jurors were made aware of the high level of security characteristic of modern maximum security prisons, the pains of imprisonment, as well as evidence that the death penalty is no greater deterrent than LWOP, defendants sentenced to LWOP only rarely engage in violent acts in prison, almost never escape or are released in error, sometimes are rehabilitated and make positive contributions while in prison, and that LWOP is nearly always less expensive than the death penalty with all it entails, they might feel more comfortable sentencing convicted capital defendants to LWOP. Furthermore, legal doctrine prohibits telling jurors of the details of the execution the defendant may experience if sentenced to death and how that execution may affect his family and friends. This, too, contributes to moral disengagement. Haney points to the asymmetry this prohibition creates because there is no prohibition to exposing jurors to the violence and, oftentimes, gore of the capital crime and the consequences of the crime to surviving family and friends.[184] Prosecutors also are allowed to introduce evidence about a defendant's prior criminal convictions during the penalty phase to show the defendant poses a future danger and the current crime was not an isolated event. Such evidence is generally not allowed during the guilt phase unless it has a direct bearing on the current crime.[185] Knowledge of the execution process, incidentally, may not matter anyway because research shows that most jurors are skeptical about an execution ever being carried out after a death sentence is imposed.[186] This skepticism is justified in states such as California, for example, where only 10 out of 717 defendants (1.4%) sentenced to death between 1977 and 2004 have been executed.[187]

Moral disengagement may also be the product of jurors misunderstanding or confusion about their sentencing responsibilities. As described earlier in this chapter, a considerable amount of research shows that jurors frequently misapprehend judges' capital-sentencing instructions, particularly those that apply to mitigation. Rather than correcting those misapprehensions, established legal doctrine presumes that jurors understand and follow judges' instructions, even when they do not. And when jurors ask questions, legal doctrine presumes that they understand the judge's answers, however unhelpful they may be, Many judges refuse to clarify instructions even when jurors make it clear they are confused and need help. At most, they simply repeat the original instructions. Long-standing legal doctrine also prohibits jurors from researching on their own the meanings of key terms about which they are confused.[188] In an attempt to overcome this latter problem some courts or legislatures have provided juries with definitions of confusing terms. However, in many cases, this has not helped. For example, the Virginia Supreme Court has provided the following definition for the term, "depravity," in the phrase "depravity of mind": "a degree of moral turpitude and psychical debasement surpassing that inherent in the definition of ordinary malice and premeditation."[189]

One of the issues about which jurors often seek clarification is the meaning of the phrase "life without parole." How a judge answers a jury's request for clarification can determine whether a jury returns a sentence of life or death. If a judge responds in unambiguous language that a defendant sentenced to life without parole will spend the rest of his or her natural life in prison, a jury is often likely to sentence a defendant to life without parole—frequently in a matter of minutes after receiving the judge's answer. On the other hand, if the judge responds in an ambiguous way by refusing to answer the question or by explaining to the jury that a governor has the power to commute sentences, the jury usually is quick to sentence a defendant to death.[190] Most jurors are reluctant to take risks with dangerous offenders.

The cumbersome and intimidating procedures in the way the court handles jurors' questions also are a disincentive for jurors to seek clarification. For example, in one case a juror during deliberations requested a witness's testimony to be reread to the jury. Before the judge granted the request, he first consulted with the prosecutor and defense attorney and then reconvened the court with all participants present, including the defendant, the lawyers, jurors, and court personnel. This process is typical, as judges guard against possible reversal on appeal by ensuring the defendant and attorneys are present whenever the jury is in the courtroom.[191] Such a time-consuming procedure discourages jurors from asking questions, assuming, of course, jurors even know they are confused and need help.

The misapprehension of jury instructions causes at least two significant and related problems. The first is that jurors may simply ignore the parts of the sentencing instructions they do not understand. For example, they may ignore mitigating evidence if they do not understand what mitigation means. Second, lacking guidance and left on their own, jurors are likely to resort to stereotypes and impermissible factors that, in turn, lead to arbitrary and discriminatory decisionmaking—the very outcomes the sentencing instructions were supposed to help eliminate.[192] For example, Professor Haney, reporting the results of his own research, observed that "being confused about the [judge's] instructions seemed to allow a greater amount of prejudice to come into play in the death-sentencing process, while high levels of comprehension appear to reduce or eliminate its effect."[193] Specifically, according to Haney, "our jurors regarded exactly the same mitigating and aggravating evidence very differently depending on whether it was offered in a case in which the defendant was white as opposed to one in which he was African American" (less so for aggravating evidence).[194] For instance, testimony that the defendant was abused as a child, had untreated psychological problems, and was a drug abuser was found to be significantly more mitigating for white defendants than it was for black defendants.[195] Furthermore, in some black defendant cases some jurors "inappropriately converted some of the mitigating factors [e.g., the defendant was abused as a child and had untreated psychological problems] into aggravating factors (by indicating that their presence in the case inclined them toward a death rather than life sentence)."[196]

The dynamics of jury deliberations also play a major role in capital case sentencing decisions. The law in most death penalty jurisdictions requires a jury to decide unanimously whether a capital defendant lives or dies. If it does not reach a unanimous decision, the result is a hung jury, following which the judge declares a mistrial and the prosecutor must decide whether to retry the case. Judges want to avoid hung juries, if at all possible. In fact, they have jury instructions, variously referred to as "shotgun charges," "hammer charges," "third-degree charges," "dynamite charges," and "nitroglycerine charges" intended to encourage jurors to continue deliberating and reach a unanimous verdict.[197] Many jurors consider a hung jury as a failure on their part. The most heinous cases and the least heinous cases rarely present problems for juries. In the former, juries almost always return death sentences and, in the latter, they almost always return life sentences, regardless of the individual characteristics of jurors.[198] It is usually only the "middle-range" cases, those that are less clear-cut, that present problems.

When jurors begin deliberations, one of the first things they do is take a vote to determine where the jury stands on sentence. In most cases, jurors are not unanimous on the initial ballot. This is not surprising because jurors, although death-qualified, still bring unique perspectives, experiences, and beliefs to jury deliberations often resulting in their reacting differently to the same evidence.[199] Consequently, it is always possible that another jury, with a different group of jurors, might decide the case differently.[200] Research shows that the initial vote often foretells the final vote. For example, as part of the Capital Jury Project, a study of South Carolina capital jurors by Law Professor Theodore Eisenberg and his colleagues discovered that if eight or more jurors vote for death on the first ballot, the jury invariably returns a death sentence. On the other hand, if fewer than eight jurors vote for death on the first ballot, the jury is almost guaranteed to choose a life sentence. In this study, a life sentence was easier to obtain than a death sentence.[201] The study also found that a juror's first vote is influenced by the juror's race, religion, and how strongly the juror believes death is the appropriate sentence in the case.[202] Black jurors were more likely than white jurors to vote for life on the first ballot, but not on the final one. In the end, all jurors generally voted with the initial majority and because black jurors rarely comprised a majority of jurors, majority rules usually meant white rule.[203] Additionally, jurors who identified themselves as Southern Baptists, of whom almost all are white, usually voted for death on the first ballot, as did jurors who felt strongly that death was the appropriate sentence in the case.[204]

In another study using data from the Capital Jury Project, Professors Bowers, Steiner, and Sandys found the influence of race in jury decisionmaking to be strongest in black defendant/white victim cases.[205] The racial composition of the jury made a difference. For example, on the first ballot in black defendant/white victim cases, two of every three white jurors believed the punishment should be death, while two of every three black jurors believed the punishment should be life imprisonment.[206] On the final vote, the jury was three times more likely to impose a death sentence if there were five or more white males on the jury than if there were four or fewer white males on the jury.[207] However, if there were at least one black male on the jury, the jury was twice as likely to impose a life sentence compared to juries that had no black members. Additional black male jurors only reduced the chances of a death sentence slightly.[208] The study revealed that white and black jurors in black defendant/white victim cases saw the same defendants, the same evidence, and the same arguments in the same cases very differently.[209] For instance, white jurors more often than black jurors saw black defendants as likely to pose a future danger to society and to return to the streets if not sentenced to death. Black jurors, on the other hand, were more likely than white jurors to see black defendants as remorseful and deserving of mercy. Black jurors were also more likely to wonder whether the black defendant was the actual killer or whether the killing was death-eligible in the first place. On each of these issues, males of each race took a more extreme position than females; still, black females were closer in position to black males and white females were closer in position to white males. These findings were independent of socio-economic status.[210] A reason that the presence of at least one male black juror significantly increases the likelihood of a life sentence in black defendant/white victim cases is that the black juror is sometimes able to help white jurors better understand and appreciate the defendant's life history and how it mitigates the crime.[211]

Research confirms that the way a jury ultimately reaches unanimity on sentence involves a complex social-psychological process. Classic psychological research shows that people have a desire to conform and fear being wrong.[212] People tend to trust a confident majority even when it is wrong because they do not trust their own judgment. However, if a person is joined by just one other person in his or her judgment, the power of the majority to alter a person's correct position is significantly reduced. If that one other person deserts to the majority's incorrect position, the other person's ability to resist the majority declines dramatically. This dynamic is especially likely to occur when people must announce their positions publicly and there are only two options from which to choose, as occurs in death penalty cases. The study of South Carolina jurors found that the more serious the crime, the less willing a juror was to switch his or her initial vote from death to life; conversely, the less serious the crime, the more willing a juror was to switch from death to life.[213] Also the more strongly a juror supported the death penalty, the less likely he or she would abandon his or her first vote, and the less strongly a juror supported the death penalty, the more likely he or she would abandon his or her initial vote.[214] Ironically, when asked, most people respond that they could resist the majority's influence and give the correct response. Yet, as noted, research shows that is not true in many cases.

The ability to resist a majority's position, which is believed to be wrong, is further complicated by mental and physical fatigue, stress, depression, insomnia, nightmares, a sense of isolation, and other maladies as jury deliberations are drawn out.[215] Other jurors, in an attempt to get a holdout to change positions, may try to make the holdout feel guilty by demanding the holdout switch his or her focus from the defendant to the victim and the victim's family.[216] Some holdout jurors are subject to personal attacks, both physical and mental. Black jurors have complained of being ostracized, deceived, and intimidated by white jurors.[217] When a holdout juror succumbs to the pressure and changes position to conform to the majority, the juror sometimes describes the process as being "brainwashed." According to Law Professor

Scott Sundby, life holdouts typically differ from death holdouts on their reasons for changing positions. To change positions, life hold-outs generally have to be convinced by the majority that a death sentence is the only appropriate sentence and to holdout for life violates the law and his or her oath as a juror. If they view their position as a product of an honest understandable difference of opinion, life holdouts will rarely change position.[218] Death holdouts, on the other hand, are likely to change their positions to avoid a hung jury. They do not want to make the taxpayer finance another trial and do want to guarantee that the defendant will at least spend the rest of his life in prison. They rarely con-cede that a life sentence is a just outcome and often view their fellow jurors as "gutless" or "wimps."[219] If a juror later realizes he or she voted wrongly for death instead of life, there is little he or she can do to cor-rect the mistake except petition the governor for clemency, an option which seldom succeeds.[220] Courts have an aversion to second guessing jury decisions and allowing jurors to cast doubt on a verdict that has been rendered. Short of some external influence, such as an attempt to bribe a juror, courts do not allow participants in a legal proceeding to challenge a verdict.[221] As the preceding discussion reveals, structural and social-psychological factors create corrupting biases in the way the death penalty is administered. These biases affect all capital defen-dants to varying degrees, but they adversely affect black capital defen-dants even more, particularly when their victims are white.

   Theories of Racial Discrimination in the Administration of the Death Penalty. There are several plausible theories of racial discrim-ination in the administration of the death penalty. The first and more obvi-ous theory is that prosecutors, judges, jurors, and even defense attorneys intentionally discriminate against black defendants and victims because blacks are feared, disliked, or both. Such an explanation certainly is believable, given the history of race relations in the United States, par-ticularly in the South.[222] Recent evidence shows that death penalty support by many whites continues to be associated with prejudice against blacks.[223]

   A second theory is that many actors in the legal system today, even in the South, believe they are not racially prejudiced or are not conscious that they are. Yet racially discriminatory outcomes are produced through a sometimes unconscious psychological process of racial identifica-tion.[224] Professor Haney calls the same phenomenon the "empathic divide."[225] Professors Gross and Mauro describe the process of vic-tim–based racial identification:

>   We are more readily horrified by a death if we empathize or
>   identify with the victim, or if we see the victim as similar to our-
>   selves or to a friend or relative, than if the victim appears to
>   us as a stranger. In a society that remains segregated socially

if not legally, and in which the great majority of jurors are white, jurors are not likely to identify with black victims or to see them as family or friends. Thus jurors are more likely to be horrified by the killing of a white than of a black, and more likely to act against the killer of a white than the killer of a black. This reaction is not an expression of racial hostility but a natural product of the patterns of interracial relations in our society.[226]

Victim–based racial identification, or the empathic divide, also may affect judges, prosecutors, and defense attorneys.[227] Thus, if victim–based racial identification affects all of the actors in the administration of capital punishment and, further, if nearly all of those actors are white, then it follows that racial discrimination against black defendants, particularly those who are the killers of whites, may be a real, albeit unintended outcome of the process.[228]

A third theory is that racial disparities are the result of institutional racism. Institutional racism occurs when members of a race are subordinated, disadvantaged, or overrepresented in negative outcomes through the normal functioning of social institutions, whether or not that subordination, disadvantage, or overrepresentation is consciously or deliberately intended.[229] It is possible that the racial disparities are not so much a product of overt racial animus as they are of the pragmatic goals of the courtroom participants. Consider two prosecutor examples. First, prosecutors may not underrepresent blacks in capital jury pools because of racial prejudice *per se*, but rather because of the belief that blacks are more likely than whites to oppose the death penalty and to acquit capital defendants if they are jurors, particularly when the defendant is black and the victim is white. As noted previously, evidence from the Capital Jury Project shows that in black defendant/white victim cases, a death sentence is imposed more than twice as often if there are at least five white males on the jury. On the other hand, the presence of only one black male on the jury reduces the chances of a death sentence by nearly one-half.[230] Because prosecutors are constrained by limited resources and highly motivated to win their trials, they increase their odds of winning by excluding as many blacks as possible.

The second example may not be the result of overt racial enmity but rather of a political consideration. Elected prosecutors may believe that their key constituencies want their limited resources expended on white victim cases and not on black ones.[231] Prosecutors themselves may not be racially prejudiced (they would focus their efforts on the prosecution of any social group if it would win them votes), but they may bow to the racial prejudices of their voters. In sum, whether racial discrimination is the product of institutional racism or of intentional or purposeful action, its existence in the administration of capital punishment is odious and intolerable.

The Supreme Court has implicitly recognized the existence of institutional racism in some types of cases (e.g., housing, public accommodations, jury selection, and employment) and has held it to be impermissible. The Court has not been equally responsive to institutional racism in death penalty cases but, instead, requires proof of intentional or purposeful discrimination in individual cases. One reason for this was given by Justice Powell in the *McCleskey* decision:

> McCleskey's claim, taken to its logical conclusion, throws into serious question the principles that underlie our entire criminal justice system. . . . [I]f we accepted McCleskey's claim that racial bias has impermissibly tainted the capital sentencing decision, we could soon be faced with similar claims as to other types of penalty.[232]

Professors Baldus and Woodworth provide two additional reasons why the Court may have rejected the claim of racial discrimination in McCleskey's particular case. First, "as a convicted murderer, McCleskey did not enjoy the same status of an 'oppressed minority' as would a blameless claimant seeking equal access to housing, employment, or schools."[233] Second, "McCleskey's claim primarily pointed not to discrimination on the basis of his race (over which he had no control) but rather to discrimination on the basis of the victim's race. . . . [I]t was McCleskey [however] who 'chose' his victim, a fact that weakened the moral appeal of his claim."[234] Finally, Professor Hoffmann argues that in *McCleskey* the Court, in effect, conceded that comparative injustice (that is, discrimination) was inevitable in any sentencing scheme, but decided that "none of the available alternative approaches to capital sentencing would be more 'just' than the guided discretionary approach employed in Georgia."[235]

Another theory suggests that the continuing practice of racial discrimination in the administration of the death penalty is evidence that capital punishment serves other latent purposes. According to this theory, it serves (1) as an instrument of minority group oppression ("to keep blacks in the South in a position of subjugation and subservience"), (2) as an instrument of majority group protection ("to secure the integrity of the white community in the face of threats or perceived challenges from blacks"), and (3) as a repressive response ("to conditions of dislocation and turmoil in . . . time of economic hardship").[236] From this viewpoint, the death penalty as administered devalues the lives of blacks—particularly in the South—by using them as tools in a social (racial) and economic power struggle. Advocates of the theory contend that the death penalty in the United States is, at least in part, a race relations mechanism that controls blacks by extermination or, perhaps even more importantly, by threat of extermination.

Counterarguments to Claims of Racial Discrimination. Many proponents of capital punishment claim that there is no longer any racial discrimination in its administration. The more sophisticated among them concede that there may have been racial discrimination in the past, but that evidence under post–*Furman* statutes reveals racial disparities and not discrimination.[237]

Concerning victim-based racial discrimination, Judge Paul Cassell believes it is implausible "that a racist criminal justice system would look past minority defendants and discriminate solely on the more attenuated basis of the race of their victims." He asks, "If racists are running the system, why wouldn't they just discriminate directly against minority defendants?"[238] Furthermore, according to Cassell, what appears to be victim-based racial discrimination simply may be an artifact of the nature of interracial murders. As noted previously, the vast majority of murders are intraracial and occur in circumstances where the death penalty is likely inappropriate. Black-on-white murders, on the other hand, frequently occur during the course of a serious felony. For example, in Georgia, fewer than ten percent of the black-on-black murders involve armed robbery compared to two-thirds of the black-on-white murders.[239] Compared to murders involving other racial combinations, black-on-white murders are more likely to involve aggravating factors such as the killing of a law enforcement officer (75-80 percent of whom are white), kidnapping and rape, mutilation, execution-style killing, and torture.[240] Other factors that could explain what appears to be victim-based racial discrimination are the victim's socioeconomic status, defendants' failure to accept plea bargains in such cases, black victims' families not insisting on the state's pursuing the death penalty, and the victim's role in the prosecutor's decision not to seek the death penalty. In the latter case, the victim may have been a drug dealer, who was robbed and killed, or a rival gang member killed in a drive-by shooting.[241] Not all research has shown victim-based discrimination. For example, an examination of capital murders in Texas between 1974 and 1988 showed that prosecutors were more likely to seek the death penalty in white-victim cases when the defendant was white, and not when the victim was black.[242] Another study in Texas found that even if victim-based discrimination were a problem in the past, it has decreased significantly. The study revealed that the percentage of defendants sentenced to death for killing white victims in Texas has declined from more than 90 percent in the 1970s to less than 50 percent by 2003.[243] Research also has shown that the proportion of black-victim cases and white-victim cases resulting in death sentences was nearly identical when death-sentenced inmates were compared to homicide arrests in Texas between 1994 and 2001, and legally relevant variables were controlled.[244]

Perhaps most damning from a death penalty proponent's perspective is the judgment of U.S. District Court Judge J. Owen Forrester.[245] In reviewing Baldus's Georgia study, Judge Forester observed that a race-of-victim effect was only evident in Baldus's summary models, ones that included only a few control variables. When additional control variables were added, he further noted, no statistically significant race-of-victim effects were found. When Baldus's model included all 430 control variables for which he had data, Forrester continued, no statistically significant evidence of racial discrimination was observed.[246] According to Professor Baldus, however, Judge Forrester was wrong.[247] In personal correspondence to this author, Baldus wrote, "the race of victim effect was robust across all analyses of death sentences imposed among all death eligible cases."[248] He also noted that there was no 430 variable model. The largest model had 230 variables.

Another argument is that even if some post–*Furman* death sentences are a product of racial discrimination, society's interests in retribution, justice, and concern for crime victims and their families are more important, so that racial discrimination in the death penalty's application can be and should be ignored.[249] A related argument suggests that even if there is racial discrimination in the application of the death penalty, that in no way reduces either the blameworthiness of the guilty defendants who are sentenced to death for racial reasons or society's justification for executing them.[250] A final argument is that racial discrimination is inevitable and that it infects all social institutions, the death penalty being no exception. Hence, there is nothing that can be done about such racial discrimination short of abolishing the death penalty.[251] A problem with abolishing the death penalty for that reason, according to Professor Louis Pojman, is that by the same logic it would also require the abolition of traffic laws and laws against murder, rape, and theft, for example, because those laws are applied to only some people who violate them.[252] He continues: "We should reform our practices as much as possible to eradicate unjust discrimination wherever we can, but if we are not allowed to have a law without perfect application, we will be forced to have no laws at all.[253] Proponents of capital punishment who make this argument clearly believe that the death penalty's administration can be reformed to significantly reduce discrimination, or that the merits of capital punishment outweigh any racial discrimination in its application.

Conclusion. The vote in the *McCleskey* decision was 5 to 4. Justice Lewis Powell who wrote the majority opinion cast the deciding vote. It was Powell's last year on the Court. Four years later, Powell's biographer asked him if he wished he could change his vote in any single case. Powell answered yes, in the *McCleskey* case. Powell, who had dissented in *Furman* and had regularly supported the death penalty in cases decided by the Supreme Court, opined, "I have come to think that capital punishment should be abolished . . . [because] it serves no useful purpose."[254]

The counterarguments of death penalty proponents, notwith-standing, the Supreme Court has not and likely cannot rid the imposition of the death penalty from repugnant forms of racial discrimination. Yet, in *Zant v. Stephens* (1983), *McCleskey v. Kemp* (1987), and other cases, it has clearly indicated that either defendant-based or victim-based racial discrimination in the administration of capital punishment, whether overt or covert, is constitutionally impermissible.[255] Even under post-*Furman* statutes, Professors Bowers and Pierce observe that:

> race is truly a pervasive influence on the criminal justice processing of potentially capital cases, one that is evident at every stage of the process . . . it is an influence that persists despite separate sentencing hearings, explicitly articulated sentencing guidelines, and automatic appellate review of all death sentences. . . .[256]

The same could also be said about social class, gender, and age discrimination.

Discussion Questions

1. What does it mean to say that the death penalty has been imposed in an arbitrary and discriminatory way?

2. Are arbitrariness and discrimination acceptable in the administration of capital punishment?

3. Has the death penalty been administered in an unacceptably arbitrary and discriminatory way?

4. Is the death penalty currently administered in an unacceptably arbitrary and discriminatory way?

5. If the answer to the former question is yes, what are the sources of arbitrariness and discrimination?

6. Should powerful and wealthy capital offenders be able to escape capital punishment?

7. Should any of the harmful actions described in this chapter, e.g., the production and distribution of known-lethal products, that are not now capital crimes be made capital crimes?

8. Should the administration of capital punishment be different for females and males?

9. Is there a significant difference in any relevant social characteristic between a 17- and 18-year-old, other than what has been created by law?

10. Is it really meaningful to consider a 17-year-old a juvenile and an 18-year-old an adult?

11. Have post-*Furman* death penalty statutes and Court decisions had the effect desired by the Court's majority in *Furman*? Can death penalty statutes be made constitutionally acceptable?

Notes

[1] Nakell and Hardy, 1987:16.

[2] Ibid.

[3] Bowers, 1984:191.

4 Tizon, 2003; also see McCord, 2005, who provides examples in both categories.

[5] Amsterdam, 1982:351.

[6] Death Penalty Information Center, April 20, 2007.

[7] Ibid.

[8] Ibid.

[9] Bowers, op. cit.

[10] Death Penalty Information Center, op. cit.

[11] Meltsner, 1973:224.

[12] See Bedau, 1982:56-57. Banner (2002:208) claims that before 1950 executions were primarily a northern phenomenon.

[13] Calculated from data at Death Penalty Information Center, op. cit.

[14] Ibid.

[15] Bowers, 1984, op. cit., p. 236, Table 7-5, from the effective dates of those states' respective post-*Furman* statutes through 1977. Keil and Vito (2006) also found similar variation in Kentucky.

[16] Joint Legislative Audit and Review Commission, 2002; also see Willing and Fields, 1999.

[17] Federal Bureau of Investigation, 2004.

[18] Baldus et al., 2001:18-19.

[19] Governor's Commission on Capital Punishment, 2002:88 and 196; also see Willing and Fields, op. cit.

[20] For Ohio, see Roberts, 2005; Seewar, 2005; Welsh-Huggins, 2005; Williams and Holcomb, 2001; for Maryland, see Paternoster and Brame, 2003.

[21] Dieter, 2005.

[22] Willing and Fields, op. cit,.; also see Bright, 2004:163-164

[23] Bowers, op. cit., p. 189.

[24] Bowers and Foglia, 2003; Haney, 2003:475-477; Garvey et al., 1999-2000; Sandys, 1998:304; Acker and Lanier, 1998:105; Bowers and Steiner, 1998:311, 321, 323; Frank and Applegate, 1998; Blankenship et al., 1997; Haney et al., 1994; Eisenberg and Wells, 1993-1994. Sentencing instructions in at least one California case were 30 pages long, see Sundby, 2005:49.

[25] Bowers and Steiner, 1999; Bowers and Steiner, 1998, p. 328; Bowers, 1995. "The Capital Jury Project (CJP) is organized as a consortium of university-based investigators . . . specializing in the analysis of data collected in their respective states and collaborating to address the following objectives of the Project: (1) to examine and systematically describe jurors' exercise of capital sentencing discretion; (2) to identify the sources and assess the extent of arbitrariness in jurors' exercise of capital discretion; and (3) to assess the efficacy of the principal forms of capital statutes in controlling arbitrariness in capital sentencing." "Lengthy, in-person interviews with capital jurors are the chief source of data for this research," see Bowers and Steiner, 1999, p. 643, n. 185.

[26] Bowers et al., 1998; Bowers and Foglia, 2003, op. cit.

[27] Bowers and Steiner, 1999; also see Eisenberg and Wells, 1993-1994; Haney, 2005:85; Hood, 1989; Paduano and Smith, 1987; Bowers and Foglia, 2003, op. cit.

[28] See, for example, *Simmons v. South Carolina*, 512 U.S. 154, 1994; *Ramdass v. Angelone*, 530 U.S. 156, 2000; *Weeks v. Angelone*, 528 U.S. 225, 2000. Georgia was the first state to bar jury consideration of parole or pardon by statute in 1955. Keeping such information from jurors has been justified by the separation of powers doctrine, the likely arbitrariness of unreliable speculation, and legislative intent. Such prohibitions have generally been considered a desirable protection for capital defendants and may have contributed to the decline in executions during the period. However, by the mid-1980s, this view began to be challenged. The claim was that jurors were substantially underestimating how long a person would remain in prison if not sentenced to die and the misperception made jurors more likely to impose the death penalty. Still, informing capital jurors about how long a capital defendant not sentenced to death would usually serve in prison also has its problems. In noncapital cases, the Supreme Court requires that jurors fully understand all available sentencing options. See Bowers and Steiner, 1999, pp. 633-634, 715-716, and 717, n. 324.

[29] Haney, 2005, op. cit., pp. 179-180; Sundby, op. cit.; Bowers and Foglia, 2003, op. cit.; Weisberg, 1983.

[30] Acker and Lanier, op. cit.; Bowers and Steiner, 1998, pp. 320-321; Hoffmann, 1995.

[31] Amsterdam, op. cit., p. 350.

[32] Ibid.

[33] See ibid.

[34] Quoted in ibid.

[35] Quoted in Bedau, op. cit., p. 190.

[36] See Bowers, 1984, op. cit., pp. 368-370.

[37] Ibid., p. 372; also see Burnett, 2002:Chap. 6.

[38] Bedau, op. cit.; Bowers, 1984, op. cit.; Schneider and Smykla, 1991.

[39] But see, Haney, 2003, op. cit., for a discussion of the importance of antecedent factors in the penalty phase of capital trials.

[40] Reiman, 2007; Simon, 2006.

[41] *Furman v. Georgia*, 1972, at 251-252.

[42] Meltsner, op. cit., p. 70.

[43] Stevenson, 2004:95.

[44] Dow, 2005:7.

[45] See Reiman, op. cit.; Tifft, 1982.

[46] See Marquart et al., 1994, for an examination of class effects on the death penalty in Texas.

[47] Federal Bureau of Investigation, 2005 at www.fbi.gov/ucr/05cius/offenses/expanded_information/data/shrtable_03.html.

[48] Schneider and Smykla, op. cit., p. 6, Table 1.1.

[49] From data in Bedau, op. cit.

[50] Rapaport, 1993:147.

[51] Streib, 2006. The largest number of women sentenced to death in one year during the modern era was 11 in 1989.

[52] Ibid.; Death Penalty Information Center, op. cit.

[53] Ibid.

[54] Extrapolated from Strieb, 2003:304

[55] Death Penalty Information Center, op. cit.

[56] Streib, 2006, op. cit.

[57] Ibid.; also see Gillespie, 2003:28-30.

[58] Streib, 1993:144.

[59] See Marquart et al., 1994, op. cit., for an examination of gender effects on the death penalty in Texas. Also see Rapaport, 1993:151, who argues "that the undervaluation of the heinousness of domestic murder is the most serious form of gender discrimination."

[60] Streib, 1993, op. cit., p. 142.

[61] Ibid., pp. 142-143.

[62] Ibid., p. 143.

[63] Ibid.

[64] Streib, 2003, op. cit., p. 322; also see Rapaport, 1993, op. cit., p. 146.

[65] Jones, 2002.

[66] Federal Bureau of Investigation, 2005, op. cit.; Streib, 2003, op. cit.; Death Penalty Information Center, op. cit.; *Death Row, U.S.A.*, 2007. The one remaining juvenile on death row reported here had not had his death sentence vacated by court order or other official action before January 1, 2007.

[67] There is some dispute over Jose High's age at the time he committed the crime for which he was executed in Georgia on November 6, 2001. It is believed he was 17 years old at the time of his crime.

[68] *Death Row, U.S.A.*, ibid.

[69] Streib, 1998, op. cit., p. 207.

[70] *Death Row, U.S.A.,* op. cit.

[71] Streib, 2005, op. cit.

[72] Death Penalty Information Center, op. cit.

[73] Lewis et al., 1988.

[74] Streib, 2005, op. cit.

[75] Ibid.

[76] Jones, 2002; also see Vogel and Vogel, 2003.

[77] Moore, 1994.

[78] Hoffmann, 1993:117; also see Bradley, 2006.

[79] Hoffmann, ibid.

[80] Ibid., pp. 117-118; also see Blecker, 2006.

[81] Hoffmann, ibid., p. 118; also see Blecker, 2006, ibid.

[82] See Bohm and Haley, 2007:475.

[83] Hoffmann, op. cit., pp. 118-119.

[84] Williams and Holcomb, 2001, op. cit.

[85] Banner, 2002:139-140.

[86] Ibid., p. 141; also see Vandiver et al., 2003, for a description of the Tennessee situation.

[87] Banner, 2002, ibid.

[88] Ibid.

[89] ibid.

[90] Ibid., p. 142.

[91] See Bedau, op. cit., pp. 58–59.

[92] Ibid., pp. 58–61.

[93] Cited in Paternoster, 1991:127. As noted in Chapter 2, in *Coker v. Georgia* (433 U.S. 584, 1977), the Supreme Court effectively ended the possibility of a death penalty for rape of an adult woman where the victim is not killed.

[94] See Marquart et al., 1994, op. cit.; Kleck, 1981; Hagan, 1974.

[95] See Bedau, op. cit.

[96] See Bowers, 1984, op. cit., pp. 221–222 for methodology.

[97] Ibid., p. 230.

[98] U.S. General Accounting Office, 1990:6.

[99] Baldus and Woodworth, 1997.

[100] Bright, 1997, op. cit., p. 4; also see Marquart et al., 1994, op. cit., for an examination of race effects on the death penalty in Texas.

[101] Baldus et al., 1998.

[102] Ibid.

[103] For example, in a recent study of Maryland's death penalty, no significant race-of-defendant effect was found, Paternoster and Brame, 2003, op. cit.; also see Williams and Holcomb, 2001, op. cit., who found no significant race-of-defendant effect in Ohio; Brock et al., 2000, who found similar results in four Texas counties.

[104] See *Village of Arlington Heights v. Metropolitan Hous. Dev. Corp.*, 429 U.S. 252, 266, 1977.

[105] See *McCleskey v. Kemp*, 481 U.S. 279, 1987; also see the discussion in Chapter 2,

[106] Lawrence (1987:387) has argued that "the intent requirement is a centerpiece in an ideology of equal opportunity that legitimizes the continued existence of racially and economically discriminatory conditions and rationalizes the superordinate status of privileged whites."

[107] Radelet and Pierce, 1985:32.

[108] Bright, 1998:131.

[109] Ibid.

[110] Bright, 2002:47-48.

[111] Williams and Holcomb, 2004; but see Stauffer et al., 2006 for a different finding. For a discussion of a gendered form of racism in the treatment of capital rape–murders, see Crocker, 2002.

[112] Bowers, 1984, op. cit.; also cf. Baldus et al., 1986; Foley, 1987; Gross and Mauro, 1989, 1984; Radelet and Pierce, 1991, 1985; Radelet and Vandiver, 1983; Radelet, 1981; Zeisel, 1981; Arkin, 1980.

[113] Bowers, 1984, ibid.

[114] Baldus et al., 1990, 1986, op. cit.; 1983; Barnett, 1985; Bowers, 1984, ibid.; Gross and Mauro, 1984, op. cit.

[115] Baldus et al., 1986, ibid.; 1983; Bowers, 1984, ibid.; Ekland–Olsen, 1988; Brock et al., 2000.

[116] Paternoster, 1991, op. cit.; 1984; 1983; Paternoster and Kazyaka, 1988; McCord, 2002.

[117] Gross and Mauro, 1984, op. cit.; Nakell and Hardy, 1987, op. cit.; but see Paternoster, 1991, ibid.; Unah and Boger, 2001; Stauffer et al., 2006, op. cit.

[118] Smith, 1987.

[119] Baldus et al., 1986, op. cit.

[120] Baldus et al., 1986, ibid.; Gross and Mauro, 1989, op. cit.; 1984, op. cit.

[121] Baldus et al., 1986, ibid.; also see Scheb II and Lyons, 2001, who found that race of victim in relation to that of the defendant significantly predicted the prosecutor's decision to seek the death penalty but not the jury's decision to impose a death sentence.

[122] Keil and Vito, 1995; Keil and Vito, 1990, 1989; Vito and Keil, 1988.

[123] Baldus et al., 1986, op. cit; Klein and Rolph, 1991.

[124] Baldus et al., 1986, ibid.; Governor's Commission on Capital Punishment, 2002; Gross and Mauro, 1989, op. cit., 1984, op. cit.; Murphy, 1984.

[125] Baldus et al., 1986, ibid.

[126] Gross and Mauro, 1989, op. cit., 1984, op. cit.

[127] Baldus et al., 1986, op. cit.; Paternoster and Brame, 2003, op. cit.

[128] Baldus et al., 1986, ibid.

[129] Bienen et al., 1988.

[130] *State v. Cobb*, 663A.2nd 948, 1995.

[131] Roberts, 2005, op. cit.; Seewar, 2005, op. cit.; Welsh-Huggins, 2005, op. cit.; Williams and Holcomb, 2001, op. cit.

[132] Baldus et al., 1998.

[133] Baldus and Woodworth, 1997.

[134] U.S. General Accounting Office, 1990, op. cit., p. 5.

[135] Ibid.; also see Paternoster and Brame, 2003, op. cit., who found the same pattern in Maryland.

[136] Baldus et al., 1990, op. cit., p. 185.

[137] See, for example, McAdams, 1998:165.

[138] *Death Row, U.S.A.*, op. cit.

[139] Ibid.

[140] See Zahn, 1989, for homicide trends during the twentieth century; also see Federal Bureau of Investigation, 2000, op. cit., p. 14.

[141] Federal Bureau of Investigation, 2005, op. cit.

[142] Baldus and Woodworth claim that "in most death sentencing states only about 10 to 15 percent of defendants arrested for homicide have committed death–eligible crimes," see Baldus and Woodworth, 1998:395-396. Note that Baldus and Woodworth are referring to homicide arrests and not to murders and nonnegligent manslaughters committed.

[143] Baldus and Woodworth, ibid., p. 402.

[144] Baldus et al., 1990, op. cit., p. 403.

[145] Baldus et al., 1983.

[146] Bright, 1997, op. cit.

[147] Paternoster and Brame, 2003, op. cit.

[148] Bowers, 1984, op. cit., pp. 340-341; Radelet, 1981, op. cit.; Radelet and Pierce, 1985, op. cit. Dow (2005, op. cit., p. 120) reports that circumstantial evidence has been the basis for about one-sixth of all death penalty convictions. Circumstantial evidence is based on inference and not on personal knowledge or observation. It is evidence not provided by testimony

[149] Radelet and Pierce, 1985, ibid., p. 601.

[150] Jacoby and Paternoster, 1982; Paternoster, 1984, op. cit.; Paternoster and Kazyaka, 1988, op. cit. .

[151] Vito and Keil, 1988, op. cit.

[152] Baldus et al., 1990, op. cit.; Gross and Mauro, 1989, op. cit.; Sorensen and Wallace, 1999.

[153] Baldus et al., ibid., p. 398.

[154] Bohm, 1991.

[155] See Bright, 1995; Hans, 1988.

[156] *Miller-El v. Dretke* (125 S. Ct. 2007, 2005).

[157] Ibid.

[158] Ibid.

[159] Karp and Warshaw, 2006:284.

[160] Bohm, 1994; also see Pokorak (1998) who shows that 98 percent of chief district attorneys in death penalty states are white.

[161] Parker, 1991:505.

[162] Bright, 2002, op. cit., pp. 54-55.

[163] *Gregg v. Georgia*, 1976 at 157.

[164] The following discussion is not limited to just racial prejudices.

[165] Haney, 2005, op. cit.

[166] Ibid., p. 62.

[167] Dow, 2005, op. cit., p. 183.

[168] Ibid.

[169] Ibid., pp. 97-98 and 113.

[170] Ibid., p. 287, n. 53.

[171] Ibid., p. 63.

[172] Ibid.

[173] See *Lockhart v. McCree*, 1986, and the discussion in Chapter 2.

[174] Haney, 2005, op. cit., p. 117; also see Bowers and Foglia, 2003, op. cit.

[175] Haney. 2005, ibid.

[176] Ibid., pp. 120-132.

[177] Ibid., pp. 141-143; also see Weisberg, 1983.

[178] Karp and Warshaw, 2006, op. cit,, p. 287.

[179] Sundby, op. cit., p. 31.

[180] Ibid., pp. 32-33.

[181] Haney, 2005, op. cit., pp. 146-147 and 151.

[182] Ibid., p. 146.

[183] Ibid., p. 154.

[184] Ibid., pp. 156 and 159.

[185] Sundby, op. cit., p. 17.

[186] Ibid., p. 157.

[187] Sundby, op. cit., p. 38.

[188] Ibid., pp. 183-184; also see Sundby, op. cit., p. 50.

[189] Sundby, op. cit., pp. 10-11.

[190] Ibid., pp. 147-148.

[191] Ibid., p. 66.

[192] Haney, op. cit., pp. 187-188.

[193] Ibid., p. 206.

[194] Ibid.; also see Bowers et al., 2001.

[195] Haney, ibid., p. 206.

[196] Ibid., pp. 206-207; also see Bowers et al., 2001, op. cit.

[197] Sundby, op. cit., p. 154.

[198] Eisenberg, 2001:278.

[199] Sundby, op. cit., pp. 133-134.

[200] Ibid., p. 134.

[201] Eisenberg et al., 2001, op. cit., pp. 303-304.

[202] Ibid., p. 277.

[203] Ibid.

[204] Ibid., pp. 303-304.

[205] Bowers et al., 2001, op. cit.

[206] Ibid., p. 260.

[207] Ibid., p. 259.

[208] Ibid.

[209] Ibid., p. 260.

[210] Ibid.

[211] Sundby, op. cit., p. 151.

[212] Ibid., pp. 81-84, citing the research of Solomon Asch and others.

[213] Eisenberg et al., 2001, op. cit., p. 304.

[214] Ibid., 2001, op. cit., pp. 303-304.

[215] Sundby, op. cit., pp. 87 and 168-169.

[216] Ibid., p. 88.

[217] Bowers et al., 2001, op. cit., p. 261.

[218] Sundby, op. cit., p. 156.

[219] Ibid., pp. 156-157.

[220] Ibid., p. 102.

[221] Ibid., pp. 100-101.

[222] Although the prevalence of racial discrimination in the United States probably has declined over the past few decades, it has not disappeared. A 1979 study by the National Conference of Christians and Jews found that 74 percent of blacks felt that they were discriminated against in white collar jobs, 68 percent in blue collar jobs, and 58 percent in finding decent housing; only 39 percent of blacks believed that the government was committed to equality, see *Facts on File*, 1979. The National Opinion Research Center's 1988 General Social Survey shows that 25 percent of white respondents believed that there should be laws against interracial marriages, 37 percent would not attempt to change the rules of racially segregated social clubs so that blacks could join, 24 percent agreed (strongly (8 percent) or slightly (16 percent)) that white people have a right to keep blacks out of their neighborhoods, 46 percent are living in racially segregated neighborhoods, and 44 percent of all respondents attended racially segregated churches, see Niemi, 1989.

[223] Barkan and Cohn, 1994; Soss et al., 2003. Young (2004) discovered that racially prejudiced white Americans are more likely to favor executing innocent people than freeing the guilty.

[224] See, for example, Baldus et al., 1990, op. cit., p. 79 fn. 59. For two explanations (one based on Freudian theory, the other on cognitive psychology) of the unconscious nature of racially discriminatory beliefs and actions in American society today, see Lawrence, 1987, op. cit., pp. 329–344.

[225] Haney, 2005, op. cit., p. 203.

[226] Gross and Mauro, 1989, op. cit., p. 113; also see Sundby, op. cit., p. 40. At least theoretically, the process of victim–based racial identification may apply as well to the white killers of white victims, though white actors in the legal system may show more sympathy for white killers than for black killers. The possibility of offender–based racial identification is a potentially fertile area for future research. For a discussion of "villain identification" by the capital offender, see Bowers, 1988:54. For a review of the extensive literature on the process of identification, see Gross and Mauro, 1989, op. cit., Chap. 7.

[227] Gross and Mauro, 1989, ibid, p. 114; regarding prosecutors, see Baldus et al., 1990, op. cit., p. 184.

[228] The discussion of victim-based racial identification is not intended to imply that intentional discrimination does not operate in the process. It is likely that some combination of the two account for racial discrimination where it exists. Either way, white hegemony in the administration of capital punishment could produce the same results through either process.

[229] See Carmichael and Hamilton, 1967.

[230] Bowers and Foglia, 2003, op. cit.

[231] See, for example, McAdams, 1998:166; Willing and Fields, 1999; Schoenfeld, 2005.

[232] *McCleskey v. Kemp*, 1987 at 315-16.

[233] Baldus and Woodworth, 1998, op. cit., p. 408.

[234] Ibid.

[235] Hoffmann, 1993, op. cit., p. 125.

[236] Bowers, 1984, op. cit., pp. 131-132; also see Douglas in *Furman v. Georgia*, 1972; Rusche and Kirchheimer, 1968; Baldus and Woodworth, 1998, op. cit., p. 386.

[237] See, for example, Wilbanks, 1987. For a graphic example of blatant post-*Furman* racial discrimination, see the description of the Walter McMillian case, Stevenson, op. cit., pp 79-82.

[238] Cassell, 2004:203.

[239] Ibid.

[240] Ibid., pp. 203-204.

[241] Sorensen, 2004.

[242] Ibid.

[243] Ibid.

[244] ibid.

[245] See *McCleskey v. Zant*, 580 F. Supp. 338, 368. M.D. Ga. 1984.

[246] See Cassell, 2004, op. cit., p. 204.

[247] See Baldus et al., 1990: Appendix B.

[248] Baldus, 2006.

[249] See, for example, Van den Haag, 1982.

[250] Ibid.

[251] Apparently this was the position of Justice Scalia, as indicated by a memo he wrote while *McCleskey* was pending in the Court, see Baldus and Woodworth, 1998, op. cit., p. 409.

[252] Pojman, 2004:71.

[253] Ibid.

[254] Cited in Radelet and Borg, 2000:48.

[255] See Baldus et al., 1990, op. cit.; Baldus and Woodworth, ibid., p. 389.

[256] Bowers and Pierce, 1982:220; also see Gross and Mauro, 1989, op. cit., 1984, op. cit.

CHAPTER 9

Retribution, Religion, and Capital Punishment

Retribution appears to be the primary basis of support for the death penalty in the United States.[1] In a recent Gallup poll, "An eye for an eye/They took a life/Fits the crime/They deserve it" was the reason given by the largest percentage of death penalty proponents (50 percent).[2] The next–favored reasons (11 percent each) were cost: "Save taxpayers money/Cost associated with prison," and deterrence: "Deterrent for potential crimes/Set an example." Law Professor Joseph Hoffmann claims that the basic principles of retributive justice are now the principal guide by which the Supreme Court evaluates whether the death penalty, either in a single case or in a category of cases, is cruel and unusual punishment in violation of the Eighth Amendment.[3]

Retributive motives or feelings are, at least to some extent, a product of religious teachings. This chapter examines the subjects of retribution, religion, and capital punishment. In the section on retribution, the effects of the death penalty on the families of murder victims and death row and executed inmates are also addressed.

Retribution and Capital Punishment

As a theoretical term, the concept of retribution is imprecise.[4] Philosopher John Cottingham argues that "the term 'retributive' as used in philosophy has become so imprecise and multivocal that it is doubtful whether it any longer serves a useful purpose."[5] Justice Thurgood Marshall, in *Furman v. Georgia* (1972), writes that "the concept of retribution is one of the most misunderstood in all of our criminal jurisprudence."[6] As a result, Law Professor Margaret Radin notes that "ret-

341

ributivism is espoused by both [political] liberals and conservatives; it is seen as both a new way to limit inhumane practices and to exorcise permissiveness and coddling of criminals."[7]

The different meanings of retribution cause two problems: (1) disagreements over retribution's effects on death penalty opinions, and (2) disagreements about the acceptability of retribution as a justification for capital punishment. Justice Potter Stewart, who voted with the majority in the *Furman* decision, held that retribution was psychologically necessary for maintaining social stability,[8] while Justice Marshall equated retribution with vengeance and argued that neither was compatible with decent and civilized conduct.[9] Did the Justices really have in mind the same definition of retribution?

Meanings of Retribution. Some scholars believe retribution and revenge are virtually synonymous.[10] Others say there is an important difference between the two terms. Professor Radin maintains that "revenge occurs when one person, with the idea of retaliation, injures someone she believes is responsible for an injury either to herself or to someone she cares about."[11] Revenge, for Radin, "is a private act between one person or group and another" and may or may not be justified.[12] On the other hand, she defines retribution as "a public act" or, more specifically, "the formal act of a community against one of its members, and is carried out in the manner and for the reasons that are justified under the political constitution of the community."[13] The purpose of retribution, argues Radin, is to prevent personal revenge, which she calls "revenge–utilitarianism."[14]

Law Professor Herbert Packer describes two versions of retribution: "revenge theory" and "expiation theory."[15] Revenge theory is captured in the idea of *lex talionis* ("an eye for an eye"), while expiation theory is based on the premise that only through suffering punishment can an offender atone for his or her crime.[16]

Criminologist James Finckenauer similarly distinguishes two versions of retribution.[17] In one version (the bad version, in some people's view), the criminal is paid back. This is retribution as revenge and vindictiveness. In a second version (the seemingly acceptable one according to the Supreme Court and some scholars of punishment philosophy), retribution means that the criminal pays back for the harm he or she has done. The desert theorists call this "just deserts." What is confusing, explains Finckenauer, is that in research examining the relationship between retributive feelings and death penalty support, the concepts of desert and retribution have generally been employed interchangeably.[18]

Professor Cottingham has prepared the most exhaustive list of meanings, identifying and critiquing nine "theories" of punishment that have been labeled retributive.[19] First, and the one he argues captures the fundamental notion of retribution is repayment theory. Although ostensibly similar to Packer's expiation theory (with elements of revenge theory), Cottingham claims that there can "not be an atonement theory of punishment; atonement is something voluntarily undertaken, punishment something exacted."[20] Another problem Cottingham has with a repayment theory of punishment is the unexplained question of "how or why suffering something unpleasant . . . should count as payment for an offence?"[21]

A second variety of retribution is desert theory: the idea that punishment is imposed because it is deserved.[22] This theory, taken literally, rests on the idea that an offender receives punishment as a reward for wrongdoing.[23] Recall Finckenauer's assertion that just deserts is one of two versions of retribution, the other being revenge.[24] Finckenauer argues that the principal difference between just deserts and revenge has to do with who repays whom, that is, whether the offender repays society (just deserts) or society repays the offender (revenge).[25] The distinction is specious for at least three reasons. First, just deserts, as Finckenauer defines it, is indistinguishable from restitution. Second, Finckenauer's conception of just deserts appears very similar to Packer's expiation theory and, as Cottingham reasons, as long as punishment is not voluntarily undertaken, it is not atonement. Few offenders volunteer to repay society. Third, Finckenauer proposes that in just deserts the offender is the subject, that is, "the active party," and in revenge the offender is the object, that is, "the passive target of society's actions."[26] It is not clear, however, how the punished offender can be, except perhaps in a hypothetical way, the subject or active party. The offender does not voluntarily seek to be punished to repay society in most cases; the offender is coerced. Moreover, how are the intentions of the offender in regard to punishment to be discerned? In either case, as Cottingham points out, it is not clear why suffering punishment should count as repayment for an offense.

A variation of desert theory, as some death penalty proponents interpret it, holds that "some crimes are so heinous [and] some criminals so evil, that no other sentence can satisfy justice."[27] In other words, justice simply requires capital punishment for some crimes and some offenders. This view, of course, begs the question, why? Why can't justice be achieved by a punishment other than death? Non-death penalty jurisdictions in the United States and throughout the world apparently are able to achieve justice without capital punishment. Why can't current death penalty jurisdictions do likewise?

A third variety of retribution is penalty theory, which is associated with the classical Kantian notion that an offender is punished automatically simply because he or she has committed a crime.[28] This idea implies both proportionality and deserts in punishment. In other words, a "punishment must fit the crime and must not be more or other than the person deserves" in order to respect a person's status as an autonomous moral entity.[29] Despite the emphasis on respecting a person's autonomy, penalty theory is still based on repayment, albeit circumscribed repayment.

Fourth is minimalism, which refers to the idea that "no one should be punished 'unless' he is guilty of a crime and culpable."[30] Minimalism is dismissed by Cottingham, who asks, "What on earth is supposed to be distinctly 'retributivist' about [this] thesis?"[31]

Fifth is satisfaction theory, which is similar to repayment theory and rests on a view of reciprocity: "A man is rightly punished because his punishment brings satisfaction to others."[32] However, as Cottingham notes, "if the underlying idea here is that the penal system provides a substitute for private revenge," then satisfaction theory is not a theory of retribution at all but rather one of social utility, furthering the goal of social stability.[33]

A sixth variety is fair play theory, which assumes that "failure to punish is unfair to those who practise self-restraint and respect the rights of others."[34] This theory, however, turns out to be a form of repayment theory as the offender is made to pay "for the unfair advantage he has obtained" by his or her criminal acts.[35]

Seventh is placation theory, which is captured by Kant's famous passage that "even if a civil society were to dissolve itself by common agreement . . . the last murderer remaining in prison must first be executed so that . . . the blood guilt thereof will not be fixed on the people."[36] Cottingham points out that this theory "looks forward to the desired result of appeasing the wrath of God" and, thus, "is unlikely to have much appeal to present-day thinkers concerned to provide a secular justification for punishment."[37]

An eighth variety is annulment theory, which, according to Cottingham confuses retribution with restitution. Annulment theory is based on the idea that "we are obliged to punish because to do so is 'to annul the crime which otherwise would have been held valid, and to restore the right.'"[38]

A ninth and final variety of retribution is denunciation theory, that is, punishment is inflicted to denounce a crime.[39] Cottingham maintains that denunciation theory is not uniquely retributivist since there are other ways, besides punishment, of denouncing crime.[40] At the end of his exercise, Cottingham admits that most of the theories that he has described share much in common with the notion of retribution as repayment. Indeed, one must strain to identify differences.

Sources of Retribution. Because of the presumed universality of retributive emotions, some writers have suggested that retributive motives have a biological basis.[41] Others have argued that retributive emotions are derived from the socialization process and "are the psychological representations of more overt social and socialpsychological processes."[42]

Professors Vidmar and Miller are among those who believe that the socialization process is the principal source of retributive emotions. They argue that retribution "derives from the individual's attachment to the group, internalization of group values, and perception of the offense as a threat to those values."[43] Retribution also may be a means of obtaining social acceptance about the moral rightness of the violated rule.[44] Vidmar and Miller found that retributive punishment reactions increased with the increasing importance of the violated rule and the increasing seriousness of the outcome.[45] Thus, for example, a greater retributive punishment would be expected in a case in which a murderer cannibalized or otherwise mutilated the victim's body than in a case in which the murderer did not.

Problems with Retribution as Revenge. Revenge for death-eligible crimes is an emotional, though quite understandable, reaction. A problem with revenge as a justification for capital punishment is that a decision as important as the intentional taking of a life by the state should be based more on reason than on emotion. Opponents of the death penalty point out that it is largely emotion that makes people want to punish in kind. As the father of a murder victim expressed it: "For many months after the bombing I could have killed Timothy McVeigh myself. Temporary insanity is real, and I have lived it. You can't think of enough adjectives to describe the rage, revenge, and hate I felt."[46] The brother of a murder victim put it this way: "Murder drives even the most loving and compassionate people to the edge of that fine line that separates our respect for life from our violent potentials."[47] As for punishing in kind, no other crime is punished in kind; the literal interpretation of the eye-for-an-eye maxim is not imposed for any other offense. For example, the state does not burn down the homes of arsonists, cheat people who defraud, or rape people who rape.[48] Why, then, opponents ask, is it necessary to kill people who kill? Their answer is that it is not. In practice, only a select few among all those who are death-eligible are executed in the name of revenge.

Criminologist Edna Erez claims that the eye-for-an-eye (*lex talionis*) formula has frequently been misinterpreted[49]—that the famous formula was never intended to be taken literally but was meant as a warning against applying punishment in a discriminatory way. The conclusion to the Biblical dictate of "an eye for an eye" is "You shall have one manner of law, as well for the stranger, as for your own country."[50] This has been interpreted to mean that the eye of a peasant is just as worthy as the eye of a noble; thus, the victim and the offender should be treated alike, without consideration of social status. The eye-for-an-eye formula was intended to require monetary compensation and not the trading of body parts.[51] Similarly, Law Professor Joseph Hoffmann points out that proportional punishment—a goal of retributive justice—does not require payment in kind, but instead needs only to "be defined in terms of whatever the particular society views as appropriate for the crime."[52] The key is that the proportional punishment be applied proportionately and not in a discriminatory way.

Thus, even assuming that revenge is a legitimate rationale, opponents of the penalty argue that there is no reason why revenge could not be served by another noncapital punishment. On this point rests what may be the quintessential difference between proponents and opponents of the death penalty: Proponents sometimes misunderstand that opponents of the penalty do not want capital offenders to escape punishment or justice; indeed, most of them want such offenders to be punished to the severest degree allowed by law. The only difference between the two groups is what the severest punishment allowed by law should be.

Supporters of capital punishment maintain that by allowing the state to seek revenge, relatives and friends of the victim(s) are relieved of the need to do so. An implication is that with the abolition of capital punishment, relatives and friends of a victim are more likely to seek personal revenge. However, as Justice Brennan observed in his *Furman* decision, "There is no evidence whatever that utilization of imprisonment rather than death encourages private blood feuds and other disorders."[53] During the hiatus in capital punishment in the United States between 1968 and 1977, there was no apparent increase in personal revenge, nor do states without capital punishment have elevated levels of personal revenge. The 128 countries that have abolished capital punishment in law or practice suffer no apparent problems either.[54] This seems proof that a need for revenge can be satisfied by an alternative punishment, such as life imprisonment.

Vindictiveness notwithstanding, the family or the friends of a victim—the "co-victims"—as well as others, may support capital punishment for the catharsis, finality, or closure it may bring to their loss.[55] However, whether executions provide co-victims closure is a controversial issue. On the one hand, a 2001 public opinion poll shows that 60 percent of Americans believed that the death penalty was fair because "it gives satisfaction and closure to the families of murder victims."[56] Describing his decision to grant clemency to all Illinois death-row inmates following discussions with co-victims, Governor George Ryan said, "To a family they talked about closure. . . . They pleaded with me to allow the state to kill an inmate in its name to provide the families with closure."[57] On the other hand, the meager research on capital crime victims' families reveals co-victims, including some who support capital punishment, who bristle at the contention that executions bring closure. For them, executions produce an outcome, but never closure.[58] As the daughter of a murder victim explained, "I get sick when death-penalty advocates self-righteously prescribe execution to treat the wounds we live with after homicide. . . . Those who hold out an event—execution—as the solution to pain have no understanding of healing. Healing is a process, not an event."[59] Similarly, the mother of a murder victim complains, "I don't know why the powers that be have come up with the word 'closure.' There is no closure, and there never, never will be."[60]

Law Professor Franklin Zimring maintains that in the past couple of decades "closure" has replaced "revenge" as a primary purpose of capital punishment.[61] It was not until 1989, he discovered, that the term "closure" was first used by the printed mass media to describe a major objective of the death penalty.[62] This symbolic and linguistic shift in emphasis from revenge to closure, according to Zimring, has been a "public relations godsend" for death penalty proponents that has transformed capital trials and executions, at least in the minds of the public, into politically palatable processes that serve the personal interests of homicide survivors.[63] He observes that the penalty stage of death penalty trials, for example, has become a "status competition" between the offender and those who were injured by the crime.[64] This shift in rhetoric has been especially important in retaining the support of people who distrust government because, for them, it is much easier to support executions as a public service, such as garbage collection or street cleaning, than it is to contend with arguments that executions represent the excessive use of power by and for the government.[65] As a public service, the death penalty is a private right and not a show of governmental power, which, for Zimring, is consistent with the American tradition of community control of punishment and vigilante justice.[66]

Research on co-victims emphasizes their immense suffering and loss.[67] Professor Margaret Vandiver summarizes some of the results of that research:

- The loss of a close relative to homicide is a shatteringly traumatic event. The pain, disruption, and trauma caused by homicide cannot be overstated.

- The trauma and difficulty of adjusting to loss due to homicide is such that survivors often experience Post–Traumatic Stress Disorder-like symptoms. Many survivors report losing their sense that there is any justice or safety in the world; many feel that life itself has lost all meaning.

- Survivors can expect to encounter difficulties in many other areas of their lives, including their marriages, relationships with children, friendships, and work.

- The experience of bereavement moves through several stages, including denial, anger, grief, and ultimately, resolution. These stages are necessarily distinct and do not always occur in the same sequence.

- The process of recovery takes years, if not decades. Expectations of quick grieving and recovery are unrealistic and damaging. Even after survivors resolve their grief, it is unlikely that their emotional lives will ever be the same as before the crime.

- Survivors often are not helped, and sometimes are further victimized, by the criminal justice system. Both formal and informal supports for homicide victims' survivors are dreadfully inadequate.

- The experience of isolation is very common—at the time they most need contact and support, families often feel the most isolated. The opposite situation of intrusion is often a problem as well, with unwelcome contacts from the criminal justice system, the media, and curiosity-seekers.

- There seems to be much potential for advancing the process of healing through nonjudgmental, ongoing, emotionally involved listening, without suggestions as to how the survivors should feel or what they should do.[68]

Some family members do not want their relative's killer executed. Among their reasons are the following:

- a general opposition to the death penalty;

- an execution would diminish or belittle the memory of their relative;

- a desire to avoid the prolonged contact with the criminal justice system that the death penalty requires;

- a desire to avoid the public attention an impending execution bestows on the condemned prisoner;

- a preference for the finality of a sentence of life imprisonment without the possibility of parole and the obscurity into which the defendant will quickly fall, over the continued uncertainty and publicity of the death penalty;

- a desire for the offender to have a long time to reflect on his or her deed, and perhaps to feel remorse for it;

- a hope that someday there can be some sort of mediation or reconciliation between the family and the offender;

- and if the offender is a relative, for obvious reasons.[69]

Another reason co-victims do not want their relative's murderer executed is that they do not want the murderer to "win." As the daughter of a murder victim explains, "If we let murderers turn us to murder, we give them too much power. They succeed in bringing us to their way of thinking and acting, and we become what we say we abhor."[70]

Some death penalty proponents argue that life imprisonment or a lesser punishment, rather than execution, may not provide the psychological relief deserved by victims' suffering survivors. For some families, anything less than an execution may be taken as a slight, "an indication that society does not value their relative or understand the magnitude of their loss."[71] For them, it is unfair that their loved one's killer will continue to experience many of the small joys of life, such as seeing the sun rise and set, celebrating birthdays, experiencing Christmases, and visiting with loved ones, while their loved one cannot.[72] Opponents respond in three ways. First, they acknowledge that an execution may indeed relieve feelings of profound loss, but assume that, in many cases, the relief may be only temporary. In the long run, they presume (there is no systematic research on the subject), an execution may make the burden more difficult to bear because the desire for revenge appeases only the basest and most primitive characteristics of human beings.

It is instructive that only a quarter of the approximately 1,100 people eligible to view Timothy McVeigh's execution was willing to do so. (U.S. Attorney General John Ashcroft approved closed-circuit television viewing for the survivors and relatives of victims of the 1995 Oklahoma City bombing.) Reasons for not viewing the execution included being opposed to capital punishment and not wanting to watch someone die. Many of those choosing not to watch the execution believed that they had healed physically, psychologically, and spiritually. Viewing the execution for them was an unnecessary diversion. They also feared that McVeigh's final statement might haunt them.[73]

Second, opponents note that the family members and friends of many criminal homicide victims are likely to be disappointed and, in many cases, offended by the "justice" they receive. Very few of them will receive any of the presumed benefits of capital punishment because 98-99 percent of criminal homicide offenders are never executed. In the vast majority of criminal homicides, a death sentence is not even sought. Thus, many homicide victims' family members and friends will feel that they and the homicide victim are unworthy and have been devalued by the justice system because the killer of their loved one or friend did not receive the maximum penalty allowed by law.[74]

Third, opponents point out that even if an execution did make a loss easier to endure for the relatives of the victim, that advantage would have to be weighed against the effects of the execution on the relatives of the perpetrator. This attempt to balance the death penalty's effects on both families raises two key questions posed nicely by Professor Vandiver:

> Given that the crime cannot be undone, what can the criminal justice system offer to the victim's family? And what kind of sentence can be imposed on a defendant found guilty of first degree murder that is commensurate to the crime, protects society, and yet does not destroy the defendant's family in turn?[75]

There is even less research on the families of death row or executed inmates than there is on victims' families. The research that is available, though, indicates that the effects of capital punishment on death row or executed inmates' families can be as profound as it is for victims' families. Families of death row or executed inmates are different from the families of victims of any other kind of violent death in some important ways. Professor Vandiver lists four of the differences:

- The families of condemned prisoners know for years that the state intends to kill their relatives and the method that will be used. They experience a prolonged period of anticipatory grieving, complicated by the hope that some court or governor will grant relief.

- Their relatives' deaths will come about as the result of the actions of dozens of respected and powerful persons. Their deaths will not be caused by a breakdown in social order but by a highly orchestrated and cooperative effort of authority.

- Their relatives are publicly disgraced and shamed; they have been formally cast out of society and judged to be unworthy to live.

- The deaths of their relatives are not mourned and regretted the way other violent deaths are; rather, the death is condoned, supported and desired by many people, and actively celebrated by some.[76]

In a footnote, Professor Vandiver adds a fifth important difference and its ironic consequence:

> Family members of capital defendants frequently have been victims of violent crime themselves; indeed, it is not unusual for these families to have lost relatives to homicide. Yet,

because of class and racial inequities in sentencing, it is unlikely their relatives' deaths were punished with much severity. How ironic for these families that when a relative encounters the criminal justice system as a defendant rather than a victim, the system turns from leniency to severity.[77]

Other problems experienced by families of death row inmates (some of which they share with the families of victims) are stress (both economic and psychological), grief (only the families of death row inmates experience anticipatory grief), depression and other medical illnesses, self–accusation, social isolation, powerlessness, demoralization, and family disorganization.[78] Since the families of both the victim and the perpetrator are usually "innocent," the infliction of pain and suffering on one group to relieve the pain and suffering of the other group is hard to justify.

The death penalty also affects police officers, attorneys, judges, jurors, witnesses, correctional personnel, and other persons who find themselves involved in the process by choice or by duty. Unfortunately, there is a dearth of research on the death penalty's impact on those people's lives.[79]

Supporters of capital punishment cite retributive grounds in suggesting that legal vengeance is a way of enhancing social solidarity and of sanctifying the importance of innocent life.[80] Assuming the argument has merit, there would seem to be other ways than capital punishment of achieving those ends (e.g., noncapital punishments or, better yet, more positive measures). Moreover, it is difficult to understand how the taking of a life, even of a person guilty of aggravated murder, in any way sanctifies life. Henry Schwarzschild, former Director of the Capital Punishment Project of the American Civil Liberties Union, asked, "How can a thoughtful and sensible person justify killing people who kill people to teach that killing is wrong?"[81]

Research shows that the public supports the death penalty primarily for vindictive revenge.[82] This raises two important questions. First, is the satisfaction of the desire for vindictive revenge a legitimate penal purpose? And second, does legitimizing this desire for vindictive revenge contribute to the violent social relationships that pervade our nation? Justice Marshall observed in his *Furman* decision:

> Retaliation, vengeance, and retribution have been roundly condemned as intolerable aspirations for a government in a free society. Punishment as retribution has been condemned as intolerable by scholars for centuries, and the Eighth Amendment itself was adopted to prevent punishment from becoming synonymous with vengeance.[83]

A principal source of the desire for vindictive revenge (the eye-for-an-eye variety) is religion; however, religious support for vindictive revenge and for the death penalty is puzzling, since the Bible is ambiguous on both subjects. (This discussion applies only to those religions that use the Bible, either the Old or the New Testament, as their basis of authority.)

Religion and Capital Punishment

The leaders of most organized religions in the United States no longer support the death penalty, and many actually openly favor its abolition.[84] For example, the National Conference of Catholic Bishops has declared its opposition, arguing that capital punishment is "uncivilized," "inhumane," "barbaric," and an assault on the sanctity of human life.[85] Religious leaders have argued that capital punishment is inconsistent with efforts "to promote respect for human life, to stem the tide of violence in our society and to embody the message of God's redemptive love."[86] Capital punishment is believed to institutionalize retribution and revenge and to exacerbate violence by giving it official sanction.[87]

A recent survey of religious organizations in the United States found that of the 126 religious organizations that responded to the survey, 61 percent (77) officially oppose capital punishment, 17 percent (22) officially support capital punishment, and 21 percent (27) leave it up to individual congregations or individual religious leaders to determine their own position on capital punishment.[88] The religious organizations that officially oppose capital punishment are: African Methodist Episcopal Church, African Methodist Episcopal Zion Church, American Association of Lutheran Churches, American Baptist Association, American Ethical Union, American Unitarian Conference, Anabaptist Groups, Anglican Catholic Church, Anglican Church, Anglican Church in America, Apostolic Christian Churches of America, Apostolic Faith Mission of Portland, OR, Apostolic Lutheran Church of America, Association of Free Lutheran Congregations, Brethren in Christ Church, Buddhist Information Network, Catholic Apostolic Church in North America, Christ Catholic Church International, Christian Methodist Episcopal Church, Church of All Worlds, Church of the Brethren, Church of God (Cleveland), Church of God of Prophecy, Church of the Lutheran Brethren, Church of the Lutheran Confession, Church of the United Brethren in Christ, Creation 7th Day Adventist Church, Disciples of Christ, Episcopal Church, Episcopal Missionary Church, Evangelical Community Church-Lutheran, Evangelical Covenant Church, Evangelical Friends International, Evangelical Lutheran Church in America, Evangelical Methodist Church, Friends General Conference, Friends United Meeting, Greek Orthodox Archdiocese of America, Holy Eastern Orthodox

Catholic and Apostolic Church in North America, The Independent Celtic Church, International Church of the Foursquare Gospel, Lutheran Church–Missouri Synod, official, Lutheran Orthodox Church, Malankara Archdiocese of the Syrian Orthodox Church in North America, Mennonite Brethren Churches, United States Conference, Mennonite Church USA, Mennonite–Conservative Mennonite Conference, Mennonite–The Evangelical Mennonite Conference, Mennonite Information Center, Missionary Church USA, Moravian Church in America, National Association of Evangelicals, National Council of Churches, National Spiritualist Association of Churches, Old Roman Catholic Church in North America, Orthodox Catholic Church of America, Orthodox Church in America, Orthodox Presbyterian Church, The Pagan Federation, Presbyterian Church in America, Presbyterian Church (U.S.A.), Primitive Baptist Church, Primitive Methodist Church in the U.S.A., Reform Judaism–Union for Reformed Judaism, Reformed Church in America, Reformed Episcopal Church, Religious Society of Friends, Roman Catholic, US Catholic Conference, Seventh Day Adventists, Sikhism Home Page, The Southern Episcopal Church, Swedenborgian Church, Taoism Information Page, Unitarian Universalist Association, United Church of Christ, United Methodist Church.

The religious organizations that officially support capital punishment are: American Carpatho-Russian Orthodox Diocese of the U.S.A, American Evangelical Christian Churches, Association of Reformed Baptist Churches of America, Baha'i–The Baha'i Faith, Church of Illumination, Church of Jesus Christ of Latter-day Saints, Conservative Judaism–United Synagogue of Conservative Judaism, Conservative Baptist Association of America, Conservative Congregational Christian Conference, Evangelical Congregational Church, Evangelical Presbyterian Church, Free Methodist Church of North America, General Association of Regular Baptist Churches, Islamic Society of North America, Nation Of Islam, Russian Orthodox Church outside of Russia, Separate Baptists in Christ, Southern Baptist Convention, Sovereign Grace Baptist Association, Syrian Orthodox Church: Eastern Vicariate of North America, United Synagogue of Conservative Judaism, Wisconsin Evangelical Lutheran Synod.

It is important to note that, despite the official positions of their religious organizations, a majority of people in the United States who profess a religious belief, whether Protestant, Catholic, or Jewish, appear to support capital punishment. According to a 2006 Gallup poll, for example, 67 percent of all Christians were in favor of the death penalty for a person convicted of murder, as were 68 percent of Protestants, 67 percent of Christians other than Protestants, 67 percent of Catholics, 55 percent of non-Christians, and 56 percent of those who had no religious preference.[89] However, a survey conducted among more than 1,000 U.S. Catholics in March 2005, found that 48.5 percent supported capital punishment and 48.4 percent opposed it.[90]

The relationship between religious belief and death penalty opinion is more complex than the general poll data suggest. For example, recent research by Professor James Unnever and his colleagues revealed that Americans with a personal relationship with a loving-forgiving God are less likely to support the death penalty for convicted murderers than are those who believe in a wrathful-punitive God.[91] Professor Harold Grasmick and his colleagues discovered that "evangelical/fundamentalist" Protestants were more likely to favor the death penalty than were "liberal/moderate" Protestants.[92] And Professor Chester Britt found that black fundamentalists were less likely to support the death penalty than were white fundamentalists.[93]

Capital Punishment in the Old Testament. Religious leaders who oppose capital punishment concede that the Old Testament prescribes the death penalty for many offenses. They are:

- murder (Exodus 21.12-13; Leviticus 24.17; Numbers 35.16ff; Deuteronomy 19.11ff)

- manslaughter (Numbers 35.9-28)

- bearing false witness on a capital charge (Deuteronomy 19.18-21)

- kidnapping or stealing a man (Exodus 21.16; Deuteronomy 24.7)

- cursing God (Exodus 22.28; Leviticus 24.10-16)

- idolatry (Exodus 20.3-5, 22.20; Deuteronomy 13.1-11, 17.2-7)

- disobedience of religious authority (Deuteronomy 17.8-13)

- laboring on the Sabbath (Exodus 31.14-15, 35.2)

- false prophecy in the name of God (Deuteronomy 18.20-22)

- child sacrifice (Leviticus 20.2)

- striking, cursing or rebelling against a parent (Exodus 20.12ff, 21.17; Leviticus 19.3, 20.9; Deuteronomy 21.18-21)

- adultery and unnatural vice (Leviticus 18.23, 20.10-16; Deuteronomy 22.22)

- prostitution or harlotry under certain circumstances (Leviti~~~ ?¹.9; Deuteronomy 22.20-24)

- sorcery (Exodus 22.18; Leviticus 20.27)

- incest (Leviticus 18.6-18, 20.14; Deuteronomy 27.20, 23)

- sodomy and bestiality (Leviticus 18.22ff, 20.13ff); and

- keeping an ox known to be dangerous, if it kills a person (Exodus 21.29)[94]

Offenders were executed by stoning—the standard method of judicial execution in Biblical times (Leviticus 24.14, 16; Deuteronomy 22.24; 1 Kings 21.13; Numbers 15.35)—and, in some cases, burning (Leviticus 20.14, 21.9; Genesis 38.24), beheading (2 Kings 6.31-32; 2 Samuel 16.9), strangling (not listed in the Old Testament, but contained in the Tractate on the Sanhedrin in the Mishnah), and shooting with arrows (Exodus 19.13). Occasionally, corpses of executed lawbreakers were hung in public as an example to others (Deuteronomy 21.22, 23), and sometimes, the corpse of the executed person was mutilated (2 Samuel 4.12).[95]

More scriptural support for capital punishment in the Old Testament includes Genesis 9.6, which commands, "Who sheddeth man's blood, by man shall his blood be shed," and 25 verses after "Thou shalt not kill," in Exodus 21.12, one finds, "He that smiteth a man so that he may die, shall be surely put to death."[96] Leviticus 24.17 states, "He who kills a man shall be put to death," and in Numbers 35.30-31, "If anyone kills a person, the murderer shall be put to death on the evidence of witnesses. . . . Moreover, you shall accept no ransom for the life of a murderer who is guilty of death; but he shall be put to death. . . ."[97]

It appears that the ancient Hebrews were a vengeful and barbaric people; however, in practice, Hebrew law made it very difficult to execute a capital offender. Some of the legal requirements and procedures were:

- the court was composed of 23 members (as opposed to three members in monetary matters): a majority of one was needed to acquit the defendant, but a majority of two was needed to convict;

- men lacking in compassion and mercy were not to be appointed to the court (among those excluded were the very old, the impotent or castrated, or the childless, all of whom were believed to have good reason for their lack of compassion and mercy);

- adjudication had to begin and be completed in the daytime;

- adjudication could be completed the same day if the defendant were acquitted, but was to be postponed until the following day if the defendant were convicted (to provide the opportunity of discovering favorable evidence);

- two capital cases could not be adjudicated on the same day, to allow enough time to thoroughly present the defendant's case;

- the court was expected to act in the defendant's defense (an adversarial system was not employed in capital cases);

- if members of the court witnessed the capital crime, they could not be involved in the case's adjudication because they could not argue in favor of the defendant;

- if the court began its adjudication process with a unanimous vote against the defendant, acquittal was mandated because such a vote could only mean that the court had not done its job defending the defendant (it was assumed that at least one argument could always be made on behalf of the defendant);

- adjudication began with arguments in favor of the defendant;

- those who argued against the defendant were allowed to change their minds; those who argued in favor of the defendant could not;

- everyone was allowed to argue in favor of the defendant, but only certain people could argue against the defendant;

- the defendant was not allowed to argue against himself or herself (conviction in capital cases could not be based solely on a confession);

- ignorance of the law was a valid defense (the death penalty could not be imposed unless witnesses warned the offender just prior to the commission of the crime that the act was punishable by death *and* the offender acknowledged the warning and admitted knowing the punishment for the crime) (originally this was a means of distinguishing between intentional and accidental murder);

- trustworthy testimony had to be given by two qualified eyewitnesses, who were together at the time and scene of the crime and observed the crime from the same place (witnesses had to be free adults, of sound mind and body, of unquestioned integrity, and have no personal interest in the case);

- evidence from those people related by blood or marriage was not admissible;

- circumstantial evidence was excluded;

- witnesses were warned not to testify to anything that was based on inference or hearsay;

- witnesses were interrogated separately about the exact time, place, and persons involved in the offense, and any material discrepancies resulted in an acquittal;

- witnesses were warned that false testimony would make them liable to the accused's penalty if the accused were convicted.[98]

Further, according to one authority:

> there was a saying that a Sanhedrin [in ancient times, the supreme council and highest court of the Hebrew nation] which put one man to death in seven years might be called murderous. Rabbi Eliezer ben Azarya said that it [the Sanhedrin] would be called murderous if it executed one man in seventy years. And Rabbi Akiba and Rabbi Tryphon said if they had been present, they would always have had some way of making it impossible to pass the death sentence.[99]

Two additional points about capital punishment in the Old Testament relevant to contemporary practice are important. First, the majority of the capital offenses of the ancient Hebrews are not capital offenses today, and few Americans would sanction the death penalty for most of them. Second, rabbis have concluded that the Torah ("the five books of Moses") suggests that different and more appropriate punishments may be used, as historical circumstances dictate.[100]

Finally, there is the Sixth Commandment's admonishment in the Old Testament, "Thou shalt not kill." Death penalty opponents who base their opposition primarily on their religious beliefs cite the Sixth Commandment as a scriptural basis for their position. Proponents of the penalty counter that in the original Hebrew, the Sixth Commandment translates as "Thou shalt not commit murder."[101] Thus, the Sixth Commandment presumably prohibits only murder and not capital punishment or killing in "just" wars. Catholic scholar Father James Reilly indicates that, according to the Roman Catechism of the Council of Trent promulgated by Pope Pius V in 1566, the death penalty is a morally permissible way to punish murderers.[102] That view, as noted previously, has since been superseded.

Capital Punishment in the New Testament. The New Testament provides many references that ostensibly argue against capital punishment. Followers of Jesus were asked to love their enemies (Matthew 5.44) and to forgive those who trespass against them (Matthew 6.14–15), and while he was on the cross, Jesus forgave his executioners because of their lack of knowledge and understanding. In Matthew 5.38–40, he provided an alternative to violence: "You have heard the commandment, 'An eye for an eye, a tooth for a tooth,' but what I say to you is: Offer no resistance to injury. When a person strikes you on the right cheek, turn and offer him the other." As evidenced by his ministry to outcasts and his acceptance of sinners, Jesus expressed a love and mercy for all people, regardless of their worth or merit. He was not, however, "soft on crime," but believed that ultimate judgment rested with God (Matthew 25.31–46). As St. Paul warned in Romans 12.19, "Vengeance is mine, says the Lord. I will repay."[103]

During the twelfth and thirteenth centuries (the Middle Ages) when the Catholic Church dominated social life in Western Europe, capital punishment began to be used widely for religious crimes—despite New Testament references seemingly against it. Before then, pre-Christian legal codes listed fewer crimes and milder punishments than those imposed later under religious auspices.[104]

Religious authorities created some of the more barbaric methods of execution. They included the rack, the wheel, the iron maiden, burning at the stake, and impaling in the grave. A primary purpose of those execution methods was to cause prolonged suffering before death so that in the interim, heretics had the opportunity to confess, repent, and receive salvation.[105]

Thus, even though the official position of the Catholic Church today is against capital punishment, traditional Catholic teaching supported it. Thomas Acquinas cited the following passage from Corinthians:

> Now every individual person is compared to the whole community, as part to whole. Therefore, if a man be dangerous and infectious to the community on account of some sin [crime], it is praiseworthy and advantageous that he be killed in order to safeguard the common good, since "little leaven corrupts the whole lump."[106]

Traditional thinking of the Catholic Church further held that capital punishment is the best deterrent to crime.[107] Paul wrote in Romans 13.4, "It is not without purpose that the ruler carries the sword. He is God's servant, to inflict his avenging wrath upon the wrongdoer."[108] Therefore, if capital punishment is the *only* effective way to protect society from predatory behavior, it is considered both legitimate and necessary. The arguable issue, of course, is whether capital punishment is the *only* effective way to prevent crime.

Protestant scholar and journalist Reverend G. Aiken Taylor states that "most Christians tend to confuse the Christian personal ethic with the requirements of social order . . . we tend to apply what the Bible teaches us about how we—personally—should behave toward our neighbors with what the Bible teaches about how to preserve order in society."[109] This presumed difference between a personal and a social ethic is what may ultimately divide Christians on the subject of capital punishment. But before the ethical division is accepted, several questions must be addressed: (1) "Does God, then, have two different sets of rules by which he wants people to live?" (2) "Does he have one code for individuals as Christians and another for persons acting together, as they do in government?" (3) "Does he have one ethic for Christians and another for rulers and politicians?" (4) "What happens when Christians become part of their society's decision-making process, as in the case of a democracy?"[110] Answers to those questions may enable some Christians to reconcile their differences regarding capital punishment.

Protestant clergyman and scholar Reverend Reuben Hahn writes, "Not to inflict the death penalty is a flagrant disregard for God's divine law which recognizes the dignity of human life as a product of God's creation. Life is sacred, and that is why God instituted the death penalty— as a way to protect innocent human life."[111] The problem with this argument, counters legal scholar Charles Black, is that, "though the justice of God may indeed ordain that some should die, the justice of man is altogether and always insufficient for saying who these may be."[112]

Conclusion

The public's retributive feelings toward capital offenders are what ultimately may sustain the institution of capital punishment in the United States. The reason many people support the death penalty is vindictive revenge—they want to pay back offenders for what they have done. Death penalty opponents ask why capital offenders cannot be paid back with a noncapital punishment such as life imprisonment without opportunity of parole. They point out that no other crime is punished in kind.

A principal source of vindictive revenge is religion: The phrase, an eye-for-an-eye, comes from the Bible. Yet, religious support for vindictive revenge, and for the death penalty, is puzzling because the Bible appears to be ambiguous on both subjects. An interesting question is how people, particularly people whose lives are governed by the Bible, can endorse revenge, support or oppose capital punishment, and use the Bible as a basis of their support or opposition, when they know the Bible is ambiguous on the subjects. Apparently not many people base their death penalty opinions on the Bible. When asked why they favored the death penalty for persons convicted of murder, only five percent of death penalty proponents in a recent Gallup poll responded, "Biblical reasons," while 13 percent of death penalty opponents answered, "Punishment should be left to God/religious belief."[113]

Still, religious support for capital punishment may be underestimated because public opinions, established over a long period of time, are difficult to change and probably lag behind changes in the official doctrines of organized religions. Moreover, in certain regions of the United States, religion may have more influence over death penalty opinions than in other regions. In the South, for example, religion may continue to exert an extraordinary influence on support for the death penalty, especially since the Southern Baptist Convention is one of the religious organizations that continues to support capital punishment.

Continued support for the death penalty, at least among some Christian groups, may be related to capital punishment's key role in the creation of Christianity. As New York State Senator James Donovan is reported to have asked in a letter to a church group opposed to the state's enactment of a death penalty statute, "Where would Christianity be today had 'Jesus got 8 to 15 years with time off for good behavior'."[114]

Discussion Questions

1. What is retribution?

2. Is retribution an acceptable basis for supporting the death penalty?

3. Why do so many people seek retribution for crimes, in general, and capital crimes, in particular?

4. How or why does suffering something unpleasant count as payment for a criminal offense?

5. How are the intentions of the offender in regard to punishment to be discerned?

6. Why is it necessary to kill people who kill?

7. Given that the crime cannot be undone, what can the criminal justice system offer to the victim's family?

8. What kind of sentence can be imposed on a defendant found guilty of first-degree murder that is commensurate to the crime, protects society, and yet does not destroy the defendant's family in turn?

9. How can a thoughtful and sensible person justify killing people who kill in order to teach that killing is wrong?

10. Is the satisfaction of the desire for vindictive revenge a legitimate penal purpose?

11. Does pandering to or legitimizing the desire for vindictive revenge contribute to the violent social relationships that pervade our nation?

12. Does the Bible (both Old and New Testaments) support the death penalty? Does it matter?

13. How can people, particularly people schooled in the Bible, endorse revenge, support or oppose capital punishment, and use the Bible as the basis of their support or opposition, when they know the Bible is ambiguous on these subjects?

14. Should a religious person support the death penalty?

Notes

[1] Bohm, Clark, and Aveni, 1991; Finckenauer, 1988; Harris, 1986; Lotz and Regoli, 1980; Kohlberg and Elfenbein, 1975; Sarat and Vidmar, 1976; Vidmar, 1974; Warr and Stafford, 1984; Firment and Geiselman, 1997. Most of the section on retribution is from Bohm, 1992b.
[2] Sourcebook of Criminal Justice Statistics 2003, p. 147, Table 2.55 (online). This is the latest national poll to address the issue.
[3] Hoffmann, 1993:124.
[4] Cottingham, 1979; Finckenauer, 1988; Packer, 1968; Radin, 1980.
[5] Cottingham, ibid., p. 238.
[6] *Furman v. Georgia* (408 U.S. 238, 1972) at 342.
[7] Radin, op. cit., p. 1165.
[8] *Furman v. Georgia*, op. cit. at 308.
[9] Ibid., at 332.
[10] For example, see Jacoby, 1983:1.
[11] Radin, op. cit., p. 1169.
[12] Ibid.
[13] Ibid.
[14] Ibid.
[15] Packer, op. cit., pp. 37–38.
[16] Ibid.
[17] Finckenauer, op. cit., p. 92.
[18] Ibid., p. 93.
[19] Cottingham, op. cit.
[20] Ibid., p. 238.
[21] Ibid.
[22] Ibid., p. 239; also see Finckenauer, op. cit.; Gale, 1985; Gibbs, 1978.
[23] Cottingham, ibid.
[24] Finckenauer, op. cit., p. 92.
[25] Ibid., p. 91.
[26] Personal correspondence with the author (1990).

[27] See, for example, Marquis, 2004:149.

[28] Cottingham, op. cit.

[29] Radin, op. cit., p. 1164; also see Hoffmann, op. cit., on retribution and the death penalty for juveniles.

[30] Cottingham, op. cit., p. 240.

[31] Ibid., p. 241.

[32] Ibid.

[33] Ibid., p. 242.

[34] Ibid.

[35] Ibid., p. 243.

[36] Ibid.

[37] Ibid., pp. 243–244. The need for a secular rather than a religious justification of punishment may not be as strong today as it was when Cottingham originally wrote his analysis.

[38] Ibid., p. 244.

[39] Ibid., p. 245.

[40] Ibid.

[41] On the universality of retributive emotions, see Heider, 1958; Kelsen, 1943; on the biological basis of retributive emotions, see Trivers, 1971.

[42] See, for example, Vidmar and Miller, 1980: 581.

[43] Ibid., p. 570.

[44] Ibid., p. 571.

[45] Ibid., p. 592.

[46] Cited in Levey, 2006:38.

[47] Ibid., p. 36.

[48] Amsterdam, 1982.

[49] Erez, 1981:32.

[50] Leviticus 24.22.

[51] Exodus 21.23; Erez, op. cit., p. 37.

[52] Hoffman, op. cit., p. 120.

[53] *Furman v. Georgia*, op. cit. at 303.

[54] More than half the world's countries (128) have now abolished capital punishment in law or practice. More than 40 countries have abolished the penalty since 1990. Sixty-nine countries have retained it although only a few execute in a given year. In 2005, for example, about 2,000 prisoners were executed in 22 countries. Amnesty International Website Against the Death Penalty, 2007.

[55] Vandiver reports the finding that approximately 16.4 million American adults have lost (1) immediate family members to homicide (5 million; includes vehicular homicide), (2) other relatives (6.6 million), or (3) close friends (4.8 million), see Vandiver, 2003:615. One co-victim observes that the resolution of a capital case provides three benefits: (1) it holds perpetrators accountable for their heinous crimes; (2) it provides some degree of "judicial closure," that is, at least the perpetrator is imprisoned during what may be a lengthy appellate process; and (3) "it allows victims to begin to construct a 'new sense of normal'," Levey, 2006, op. cit.

[56] Cited in Zimring, 2003:61.

[57] Cited in Sarat, 2006:220, n. 30.

[58] On the meager research on co-victims, see Acker and Karp, 2006; Vandiver, 2006. On the issue of closure, see Acker, 2006; Roper, 2006; Rosenbluth, 2006; Coleman, 2006; Levey, 2006, op. cit.; White, 2006.

[59] Cited in Levey, 2006, ibid., p. 44.

[60] Cited in Ellis et al., 2006:436.

[61] Zimring, op. cit., pp. 57-63.

[62] Ibid., p. 58.

[63] Ibid., pp. 51-52.

[64] Ibid., p. 55.

[65] Ibid., p. 62.

[66] Ibid.

[67] For a more detailed description of the effects of the death penalty on the families of homicide victims, see Vandiver, 2003, op. cit.

[68] Vandiver, ibid., pp. 616-617; also see Reed and Blackwell, 2006.

[69] Vandiver, ibid., pp. 635-636; for the personal accounts of "co-victims," see Coleman, 2006; Kimble, 2006; Levey, 2006, op. cit.; Roper, 2006, op. cit.; Rosenbluth, 2006, op. cit.; Wagner, 2006; White, 2006, op. cit.; Welch, 2002; Cushing, 2002. Professor Borg (1998) found significant variation in support of the death penalty among what she called "vicarious victims." Vicarious victims who were black, female, and non-evangelicals were less likely to support the death penalty than were whites, males, and evangelicals.

[70] Cited in Levey, 2006, op. cit., p. 44.

[71] Vandiver, op. cit., p. 638; King, 2006.

[72] Turow, 2003:52-53.

[73] "Some won't watch when McVeigh dies." *The Orlando Sentinel* (April 22, 2001), p. A3.

[74] Acker and Mastrocinque, 2006:149; also see Zimring, 2003, op. cit., pp. 55-57.

[75] Vandiver, 2003, op. cit., p. 613.

[76] Ibid., pp. 624-625.

[77] Ibid, p. 624.

[78] Smykla, 1987; Radelet et al., 1983; Vandiver, 2003, op. cit.; Vandiver, 1989, op. cit.; also see Kaczynski and Wright, 2006; King, 2006, op. cit.; Sharp, 2005; Eschholz et al., 2003; Prejean, 1993; Ingle, 1989.

[79] However, on correctional personnel, see Abramson and Isay, 2002; Johnson, 1998; Cabana, 1996; on judges, see Hintze, 2006; Leyte-Vidal and Silverman, 2006; Dickson, 2006; on prosecutors or state attorneys, see Hawkins, 2006; Gillette, 2006; on defense attorneys, see Walker, 2006; Ottinger, 2002; Stafford-Smith, 2002; on jurors, see Antonio, 2006.

[80] See Van den Haag and Conrad, 1983; Committee on the Judiciary, 1982; Vidmar and Miller, 1980, op. cit.

[81] Schwarzschild in Bedau, 1982.

[82] See Bohm, 1992. The desire for vindictive revenge is not shared by all co-victims. As the daughter of a murder victim explains, "I think people don't actually want vengeance. They would like to end their pain. Sometimes they think it's a zero-sum game: if they can make someone else feel pain, theirs will go away. I just don't think it works that way." Cited in Levey, op. cit., pp. 44-45. Also, research indicates that few jurors who return death sentences do so because of vengeful feelings. For example, in one study only 1 percent of death-returning jurors responded that "feelings of vengeance or revenge" were "very important" to their decision; an additional 4 percent stated it was "fairly important." Cited in Sundby, 2005:200, n. 5. These jurors are more likely to say that a defendant convicted of a capital crime creates a moral imbalance that can only be remedied by sentencing the defendant to death. A life sentence, on the other hand, cannot right the imbalance in part because prison life is too easy. Sundby, ibid., p. 127.

[83] *Furman v. Georgia*, 1972 at 343.

[84] Bedau, op. cit., pp. 305–306.

[85] Gow, 1986: 80.

[86] Religious Leaders in Florida, 1986: 87.

[87] Ibid.

[88] The survey was conducted in August and September of 2006. Originally, 193 religious organizations in the United States were identified from a listing provided by the Hartford Institute for Religion Research at http://hirr.hartsem.edu/org/faith_denominations_homepages.html. For various reasons, 67 of the organizations did not respond (22 of the organizations had invalid contact information), leaving 126 organizations that did respond (a 65 percent response rate, or a 74 percent response rate if the organizations with invalid contact information are excluded). My thanks to Gavin Lee for conducting the survey.

[89] Demographic data from the 2006 death penalty poll were obtained directly from The Gallup Organization. My thanks to Maura A. Strausberg, Data Librarian, for her help. Also see Carroll, 2004.

[90] Ostling, 2005.

[91] Unnever et al., 2006; also see Applegate et al., 2000.

[92] Grasmick et al., 1993.

[93] Britt, 1998; also see Young, 1992.

[94] Religious Leaders in Florida, op. cit., p. 88; Kehler et al., 1985:5–6. Haines (1996:103) claims that as many as 33 offenses in the Old Testament may have been punished by death.

[95] Religious Leaders in Florida, ibid.; Kehler et al., ibid., p. 6; Erez, op. cit., p. 29. Erez reports that Hebrew law forbade the mutilation of an executed person's body.

[96] Cited in Gow, op. cit., p. 84.

[97] Ibid.; also see Kania, 1999, for additional passages supporting capital punishment in the Old Testament, as well as in the Koran.

[98] Erez, op. cit., pp. 33–36; Kehler et al., op. cit., pp. 57–58.

[99] Cited in Kehler et al., op. cit., p. 8; also see Haines, 1996, op. cit., p. 104.

[100] Religious Leaders in Florida, op. cit.; also see Kehler, op. cit., pp. 1–2 for a similar Christian perspective.

[101] Koch in Gow, op. cit., p. 81.

[102] Gow, ibid., p. 82.

[103] Religious Leaders in Florida, op. cit., pp. 88–89; Kehler et al., op. cit.

[104] Bowers, 1984:132–133.

[105] Ibid., p. 133.

[106] Cited in Gow, op. cit., p. 83.

[107] Gow, ibid.

[108] Cited in Gow, ibid., p. 84.

[109] Ibid.

[110] Kehler et al., op. cit., p. 12.

[111] Cited in Gow, op. cit., p. 85.

[112] Black, 1974:96.

[113] Sourcebook of Criminal Justice Statistics 2003, p. 147, Table 2.55 (online).

[114] Quoted in Bedau, op. cit., p. 305.

CHAPTER 10

American Death Penalty Opinion[1]

Thirty-five years after the Supreme Court's decision in *Furman v. Georgia* (1972)—the ruling that temporarily halted capital punishment in the United States—65 percent of adult Americans indicated that they favor the death penalty for persons convicted of murder. This level of support is substantially lower than the 80 percent that favored the death penalty in a 1994 poll, which was the highest level of support in more than 70 years of scientific opinion polling.[2] However, it is considerably higher than in 1966—the year that death penalty support fell to 42 percent, its lowest level ever.[3] In 1994, only 16 percent of respondents opposed the death penalty, and 4 percent had no opinion; in 1966, 47 percent of respondents opposed the death penalty, and 11 percent had no opinion. In no year for which polls are available has a majority of Americans opposed capital punishment.

Why American Death Penalty Opinion Is Important

American death penalty opinion is important because such opinion, perhaps more than any other factor, probably accounts for the continued use of capital punishment in many jurisdictions in the United States. If most citizens in death penalty jurisdictions opposed capital punishment, it is unlikely the penalty would be employed. In the 1980s, attorney David Bruck predicted that the death penalty's "political potency" could be effectively neutralized if only a quarter to a third of death penalty proponents could be convinced to oppose the penalty.[4] Strong public support may contribute to the continued use of capital punishment in at least five ways. First, it probably sways legislators to vote in favor of death penalty statutes (and against their repeal).[5] Few politicians are willing to ignore the preferences of most of their constituents.[6] Support of capital punishment is also a rather easy way for politicians to signal and demonstrate their more conservative "law and order" credentials.

Second, strong public support likely influences some prosecutors to seek the death penalty for political rather than legal purposes in cases where they might ordinarily plea bargain. As Professor White relates from his interviews with defense attorneys:

> Some prosecutors are more reluctant to plea bargain now than they were a few years ago, because they feel that in today's climate failure to seek the death penalty in certain types of cases could have a devastating effect on their political careers.[7]

Third, to retain their positions, some trial-court judges feel public pressure to impose death sentences in cases in which such is inappropriate, and some appellate-court judges may uphold death sentences on appeal when they should not.[8] Among judges removed from office following their unpopular death penalty decisions were: Chief Justice Rose Bird and two other justices of the California Supreme Court, Tennessee Supreme Court Justice Penny White, Mississippi Supreme Court Justice James Robertson, Justice Charles Campbell of the Texas Court of Criminal Appeals, Texas district court judge Norman Lanford, and Washington Supreme Court Justice Robert Utter.[9]

Fourth, some governors may be dissuaded from vetoing death penalty legislation and commuting death sentences because of strong public support for the penalty. With regard to commutations, it is instructive to note that prior to 1970, governors in death penalty states "routinely commuted up to a third of the death sentences that they reviewed. . . . Today, however, commutations of death sentences by governors [and review boards] are rare events."[10] Few governors are willing to ignore what they perceive are their constituents' preferences.[11] Further, support of capital punishment generally defines for his or her constituents much of a governor's political agenda—at least the part that concerns crime.

Fifth, and arguably most important, strong public support might be used, at least indirectly, by justices of both state supreme courts and the United States Supreme Court as a measure of evolving standards of decency regarding what constitutes cruel and unusual punishment in state constitutions and under the Eighth Amendment of the United States Constitution.[12] Decline in public support was cited as such a measure in the *Furman* decision.[13]

This chapter is divided into three major sections. First is the history of American death penalty opinion. This section describes what is called here "the too simple and, therefore, misleading death penalty opinion question period." The second section surveys the present period and chronicles what is called "the more complex and revealing death penalty opinion question period." This section begins with a description of research that tested the hypothesis that death penalty support is largely a product of ignorance about the way capital punishment is actually administered. The final section addresses the future of American death penalty opinion and the effect it may have on the practice of capital punishment in the United States.

The History of American Death Penalty Opinion: The Too Simple and, Therefore, Misleading Death Penalty Opinion Question Period

The American Institute of Public Opinion, producer of the Gallup polls, conducted interviews for the first scientific death penalty opinion poll in the United States in December 1936.[14] The poll gauged public sentiment about the death penalty in light of the unprecedented media attention given to the execution of Bruno Hauptmann, the alleged kidnapper and murderer of the Lindbergh baby. The poll showed that 61 percent of the 2,201 adults interviewed "believe[d] in the death penalty for murder" and 39 percent did not.[15] The category of "no opinion" or "don't know" was not included as an option. Since that first poll, dozens of surveys of American death penalty opinion have been conducted.[16]

The most recent Gallup poll on death penalty opinion in the United States, conducted in 2006, found that 65 percent of Americans were in favor of the death penalty for a person convicted of murder, 28 percent were opposed, and 7 percent did not know or refused to respond.[17] Note the slight difference in the wording of the questions in the 1936 and 2006 polls. In the 1936 poll, respondents were asked, "Do you *believe* in the *death penalty* for murder?" (In the 1937 and later Gallup polls, respondents were asked, "Do you *favor or oppose capital punishment* for murder?") Respondents to the 2006 poll answered the question, "Are you *in favor* of the death penalty for a person *convicted* of murder?" It is doubtful that the subtle differences significantly altered the resulting opinions, but even a small change in the wording of questions and response categories can make an important difference in the distribution of opinions.[18]

Over the past 70 years or so, support of and opposition to capital punishment have varied substantially.[19] However, when the increases and decreases are plotted over time, a v-shape can be observed (with a slight downward tail in recent years). Viewing the v from left to right, in 1936, 61 percent of respondents favored the death penalty; in 1966, only 42 percent of respondents favored it; but, by 2006, 65 percent of respondents supported it. Put differently, between 1936 and 2006, there has been an overall 4 percentage point increase in support and 11 percentage point decrease in opposition to the death penalty. The 7 percentage point difference between overall support and opposition is a function of the respondents with "no opinion" or who refused to respond in the 2006 poll (the "no opinion" or "refused to respond" categories were not included in the 1936 poll). When the 70-year period is divided into the 1936 to 1966 and the 1966 to 2006 periods, the relatively precipitous decrease-then-increase in support (or increase-then-decrease in opposition) for the penalty is readily apparent. Support of capital punishment between 1936 and 1966 decreased 19 percentage points, while opposition increased 8 percentage points (the difference is due to the 11 percent of "no opinion" responses in the 1966 poll). On the other hand, between 1966 and 2006, support of the death penalty increased 23 percentage points, while opposition decreased 19 percentage points (again, the difference is attributable to changes in "no opinions" or "refused to responds").

A detailed analysis of the 55 percent increase in death penalty support since 1966 has yet to be written. It appears, however, that the *Furman* decision played an important part. As noted, 1966 marked the nadir in death penalty support in the United States, yet by 1967, support for the penalty had risen to 53 percent and opposition had decreased to 39 percent—an 11 percentage point increase in support and an 8 percentage point decrease in opposition.[20] The increase in support was relatively short-lived because by the end of 1971, death penalty support had fallen to 49 percent.[21] The Court's decision in *Furman v. Georgia* was announced on June 29, 1972. Two 1972 Gallup polls asked about death penalty opinions, one before the *Furman* announcement (interviews March 3 through 5) and one after it (interviews November 10 through 13).[22] In the pre-*Furman* poll, 50 percent of respondents favored the death penalty, 42 percent opposed it, and 9 percent had no opinion. The poll conducted post-*Furman* showed that 57 percent of respondents supported capital punishment, only 32 percent opposed it, and 11 percent had no opinion.[23] In short, between March and November, 1972, approximately four months before and four months after the announcement of the *Furman* decision, support for the death penalty increased 7 percentage points and opposition dropped 10 percentage points. Although other factors may have had an effect, it appears that significant public discontent with the *Furman* decision was decisive.

Demographic Characteristics of Respondents. Recent polls have included a greater variety of questions about death penalty opinions, whereas earlier polls focused primarily on the percentage distribution of opinions themselves and the percentage distribution of opinions by demographic characteristics of respondents.[24] Most of the Gallup polls provide information on the following ten demographic characteristics: (1) gender, (2) race, (3) age, (4) politics, (5) education, (6) income or socioeconomic status (SES), (7) occupation, (8) religion, (9) city size, and (10) region of the country.[25]

During the first half century of Gallup polling, between 1936 and 1986, five of the demographic characteristics varied substantially and five of them did not.[26] Characteristics showing greatest variation, in order of the magnitude of that variation, were race, income or SES, gender, politics, and region of the country. In other words, between 1936 and 1986, whites, wealthier people, males, Republicans, and Westerners tended to support the death penalty more than blacks, poorer people, females, Democrats, and Southerners.[27] The characteristics showing much less variation over the 50 years were age, education, occupation, religion, and city size.

A majority of people in all demographic categories, *except race,* supported the death penalty in the 1986 poll, but there was substantial variation within categories for all of the demographic characteristics except religion. City size was not a category in the 1986 poll. Blacks, females, people under 30, Democrats, college graduates, people in the bottom income or SES category, manual laborers, Easterners, and Southerners were less likely to support or more likely to oppose the death penalty than were whites, males, Republicans, high school graduates, people in the top income category, clerical and sales workers, Westerners, and Midwesterners.[28]

In the 2006 poll (the most recent one available), death penalty support exceeded 50 percent in every social category examined except race, with "only" 49 percent of nonwhites favoring the death penalty.[29] (67 percent of nonwhites favored the death penalty in the 2002 poll). Although separate data for blacks were not reported in the 2006 poll, nearly 60 percent of blacks have supported the penalty in recent years. Black support in the past has been much lower. A recent study found that black proponents are hardly distinguishable in other characteristics from their white counterparts. Black proponents tend to be male, married, politically conservative, have high incomes, come from middle- and upper–class backgrounds, live in urban areas and the South, are afraid of crime, have never been arrested, and perceive that the courts are too lenient with criminals.[30]

The 2006 poll included information about eight of the ten demographic characteristics reported in the earlier polls plus seven additional ones. The categories of occupation and city size were omitted. Characteristics showing the greatest variation, in order of the magnitude of that variation, were ideology, political party, race, sex/age, education, marital status, religion, sex, income, region of the country, age, and type of community. In other words, in 2006, conservatives, Republicans, whites, males 50 or older, people with some college, married people, Protestants, males, people with annual incomes of $30,000-$74,999, Southerners, people age 50-64, and rural residents favored the death penalty more than liberals, Democrats, nonwhites, females 50 or older, people with post-graduate educations, unmarried people, non-Christians, females, people with annual incomes of less than $20,000, Easterners, people age 65 or older, and urban residents. The characteristics with insignificant variation were whether employed, church attendance, and having children under 18.[31] The characteristics (for which there are comparable data) that have consistently distinguished death penalty opinions from 1936 through 2006 are race, sex, political party, and income. That is, over the 70 years from 1936 through 2006, whites, males, Republicans, and wealthier people have been more likely to support the death penalty than nonwhites, females, Democrats, and poorer people.

In a recent analysis, Professor Eric Baumer and his colleagues found that death penalty opinion was a function of both the characteristics of individuals and the social environment.[32] They discovered significant community-level variation in support of the death penalty, while controlling for standard demographic characteristics. Some areas had very high levels of support, other areas had more modest levels of support, and, in some areas, a majority of residents opposed the death penalty.[33] Residents of local areas with higher levels of homicide, a larger proportion of blacks (but much less than a majority), and a more conservative political climate were more likely to support the death penalty.[34] These data show there is much variation in death penalty opinions within various groups and not just between them.[35] Still, for the most part, the same sorts of people continue to favor the death penalty the most strongly. Based on findings from the most recent Gallup poll, then, it is not much of an exaggeration to state that most Americans favor the death penalty—or so it seems.

The Present: The More Complex and Revealing Death Penalty Opinion Question Period

Little critical scrutiny of the figures presented in various death penalty opinion polls existed prior to the *Furman* decision in 1972. The reported percentages of support and opposition were generally accepted as accurate indicators of public sentiment. One of the first people to question the validity of death penalty opinion poll results, albeit indirectly, while at the same time emphasizing their importance, was former Supreme Court Justice Thurgood Marshall.

The Marshall Hypotheses. Justice Marshall stressed in his opinion in *Furman v. Georgia* the importance of public opinion with respect to the constitutionality of the death penalty. He identified several standards by which to judge whether a punishment is cruel and unusual. One such standard was: "where a punishment is not excessive and serves a valid legislative purpose, it still may be invalid if popular sentiment abhors it."[36] Thus, wrote Marshall, "It is imperative for constitutional purposes to attempt to discern the probable opinion of an informed electorate."[37] He stressed that the public's choice about the death penalty must be "a knowledgeable choice."[38]

Like many other opponents, Marshall believed that, given information about it, "the great mass of citizens would conclude . . . that the death penalty is immoral and therefore unconstitutional."[39] He assumed that support of the penalty is a function of a lack of knowledge about it, and that opinions are responsive to reasoned persuasion. The one exception to his assumption was that if the underlying basis of support for the penalty were retribution, then knowledge would have little effect on opinions. Though some of his colleagues on the Court disagreed with him, Marshall maintained that retribution "is a goal that the legislature cannot constitutionally pursue as its sole justification for capital punishment."[40] He added, "I cannot believe that at this stage in our history, the American people would ever knowingly support purposeless vengeance."[41]

Social scientists did not take long to subject Marshall's assertions to empirical investigation. Two of the first three studies that systematically tested all or part of what have become known as "Marshall's hypotheses" were conducted in the United States; the third was conducted in Canada. A fourth study employing Stanford University undergraduates as subjects, although not a direct test of Marshall's hypotheses, is nevertheless relevant and will be discussed shortly. In one of the American studies, subjects were from the San Francisco Bay area, and the data were collected in 1974.[42] In the other, subjects were from Amherst, Massachusetts, and data were collected in 1975.[43] The Canadian study does not indicate when data were collected.[44] Three of the four studies support all or part of the Marshall hypotheses,[45] although possible problems relating to social conditions at the times data were collected and to methodology render the findings potentially inapplicable to current experience and generally invalid.

Following the *Furman* decision in 1972, there was a flurry of activity as 36 states moved to adopt new death penalty statutes that would meet the Supreme Court's requirements. Thus, at the times the Marshall hypotheses data were being collected in 1974 and 1975, the theory of the death penalty was receiving much media and public attention. A distorting factor in the research, though, was that no one had been executed in the United States since 1967, and no one in Canada since 1962. This moratorium made the issue of capital punishment "abstract" in that the respondents had no recent experience with it. Public opinion about the death penalty is sometimes dramatically different when people consider it in "concrete" situations (at times when people are being executed) rather than in the abstract.

A methodological dilemma for all studies of this type is operationalizing the concept of "informed" or "knowledgeable about the death penalty." According to Justice Marshall, for "the average citizen" (excepting those who base their opinion on retribution), some knowledge is "critical" to an informed opinion and "would almost surely convince [the average citizen] that the death penalty was unwise."[46] For Marshall, an informed citizen would know some of the following:

> that the death penalty is no more effective a deterrent than life imprisonment; that convicted murderers are rarely executed, but are usually sentenced to a term in prison; that convicted murderers usually are model prisoners, and that they almost always become law-abiding citizens upon their release from prison; that the costs of executing a capital offender exceed the costs of imprisoning him for life; that while in prison, a convict under sentence of death performs none of the useful functions that life prisoners perform; that no attempt is made in the sentencing process to ferret out likely recidivists for execution; and that the death penalty may actually stimulate criminal activity . . . capital punishment is imposed discriminatorily against certain identifiable classes of people; there is evidence that innocent people have been executed before their innocence can be proved; and the death penalty wreaks havoc with our entire criminal justice system.[47]

What Marshall fails to stipulate is how much of this information a citizen must know in order to be informed. Must one know all of it or will 50 to 60 percent suffice? Without setting a standard, Marshall leaves unanswered the key question of what it means to be informed or knowledgeable about the death penalty.

Results of the fourth study, the one using Stanford University undergraduates as subjects, differed dramatically from the results of the other three studies. The authors of the fourth study discovered that knowledge or information can have an entirely different effect on death penalty opinions than the one supposed by Marshall.[48] Professor Lord and his colleagues found that information about the death penalty polarized opinions, instead of changing them from in favor to opposed or vice versa.[49] In other words, subjects who initially favored the death penalty tended to favor it more strongly after receiving information about it, while subjects who initially opposed the death penalty tended to oppose it even more after becoming informed. The researchers attributed polarization to biased assimilation, that is, subjects interpreted evidence so as to maintain their initial beliefs:

> Data relevant to a belief are not processed impartially. Instead judgments about the validity, reliability, relevance, and sometimes even the meaning of proffered evidence are biased by the apparent consistency of that evidence with the perceiver's theories and expectations. Thus individuals will dismiss and discount empirical evidence that contradicts their initial views and will derive support from evidence, of no greater probativeness, that seems consistent with their views.[50]

Professors Ellsworth and Ross believe that biased assimilation is a probable explanation for the effect of knowledge on opinions in their study:

> [We] are tempted to infer that the attitude [opinion] comes first and the reasons second. . . . It looks very much as though our respondents simply went down the list of reasons, checking whatever side of the scale was compatible with their general attitude [opinion] toward capital punishment. The picture that emerges is one of an emotionally based attitude [opinion], tempered by a sense of social desirability.[51]

In short, contrary to expectations held by Justice Marshall and many other opponents, information about the death penalty may not significantly reduce the overwhelming public support that currently exists for capital punishment. Notwithstanding the support for Marshall's hypotheses, if the results of the Lord study are reliable, the effect of exposing people to information about the death penalty may be to polarize them on the issue.

Two other methodological problems with the studies are related to the validity of the experimental stimulus and the experimental manipulation. The first problem involves the form that "knowledge" takes, and the second has to do with the way "knowledge" is imparted to subjects. In the 1976 study by Sarat and Vidmar, the experimental conditions involved reading two 1,500 word essays that described "scientific and other information" about the death penalty. The experimental manipulation was preceded by a pretest and followed by a posttest. The entire operation took only one hour. Sarat and Vidmar are candid about the inadequacies of the manipulation:

> Without question our information manipulations had limited potential for developing truly informed opinion about the death penalty—the issues are intricate and complex while the essays are short and simple; furthermore, exposure to the information took place in a brief interview session without time for reflection, discussion, or clarification.[52]

The experimental manipulation proved somewhat successful, nevertheless. On the pretest, 62 percent of the (181 randomly selected adult) experimental subjects favored the death penalty, 27 percent opposed it, and 10 percent were undecided. On the posttest, 42 percent favored the death penalty, 38 percent opposed it, and 21 percent were undecided. The experimental stimulus did not produce a majority of subjects opposed to the death penalty, but it did decrease support and increase opposition and indecision.

The 1981 study by Vidmar and Dittenhoffer improved the validity of the experimental manipulation in Sarat and Vidmar by increasing the opportunity for subjects to assimilate information about the death penalty. In this study, subjects were asked to read a 3,500 word essay on the death penalty (emphasizing the Canadian experience) and a series of eight articles. The articles contained representative material intended to augment the essay. The subjects also had the option of reading two books—Sellin's *Capital Punishment* (1967) and Bedau's *The Death Penalty in America* (1967)—and were invited to pursue any other related reading. After two weeks, subjects met in small, unsupervised discussion groups to "freely discuss the facts and issues involved in the capital punishment debate and to try to reach a final decision within an hour."[53] The experimental manipulation was preceded by a pretest and was followed by a posttest.

The results of the Vidmar and Dittenhoffer study indicate that the experimental manipulation was effective. On the pretest, 48 percent of the experimental subjects favored the death penalty, 33 percent were opposed to it, and 19 percent were undecided. On the posttest, 24 percent were in favor, 71 percent were opposed, and 5 percent were undecided. Vidmar and Dittenhoffer's experimental stimulus, unlike the one used by Sarat and Vidmar, did produce a majority of subjects opposed to the death penalty.

Despite the improvement of Vidmar and Dittenhoffer's experimental manipulation over the one used by Sarat and Vidmar, the Vidmar and Dittenhoffer study still had serious deficiencies. First, the experimental group consisted of only 21 nonrandomly selected students (18 in the control group). Second, the experimenters had to assume that the subjects did indeed read the assigned material. Third, even if subjects did read the material, it was not possible to determine how much of the material was comprehended. As to the discussion groups, Vidmar and Dittenhoffer are probably correct that discussion should enhance conditions for opinion change, because active learning is presumed to be more conducive to opinion change than passive learning.[54] However, without supervision, the experimenters could not be sure of what happened in the groups. Was the death penalty in fact discussed? Did one member of the group dominate discussion? Were some of the group members intimidated or angered by others? Furthermore, a discussion of only one hour was probably not long enough for such an "intricate and complex" topic. Subjects were not given sufficient opportunity to reflect upon contradictory beliefs or to research information about which they disagreed. A discussion of only one hour also allowed a persuasive speaker to have extraordinary influence. In short, a discussion period of only one hour was probably not long enough to produce the intended effects of the experimental manipulation.

For those and other reasons, Professor Bohm and his colleagues, beginning in the mid–1980s, conducted a series of studies that used an experimental manipulation which provided subjects with more information, provided greater control over the circumstances in which the information was acquired, and allowed subjects more time to evaluate and integrate the information into their own systems of beliefs. The experimental stimulus employed by Bohm and his colleagues was a college class on the death penalty.[55]

A death penalty class generally met a total of 40 hours a semester. Bedau's *The Death Penalty in America*, Third Edition (1982) was the assigned text for the course. Coursework included lectures by the instructor, presentations by guest speakers, videos, and discussion. Topics discussed were the history of the death penalty in the United States, with special emphasis on relevant Supreme Court cases; public opinion; evidence about general deterrence and incapacitation; religious and retribution arguments; and information on the administration of the death penalty (e.g, sources of arbitrariness and discrimination, executions of innocent persons, costs, etc.).

In most of the experiments, subjects completed questionnaires at the beginning and the end of the semester. Although their content varied somewhat from semester to semester, the questionnaires, at minimum, generally sought information about the three principal variables in Marshall's hypotheses: opinions toward the death penalty, knowledge about the death penalty, and desire for retribution. The questionnaires also asked for demographic information about the subjects.

Bohm and his colleagues measured death penalty opinions with four questions because they believed that the general opinion question asked in the Gallup and other polls did not accurately reflect the complexity of public sentiment about the penalty. Each of the questions represented a different type of support or nonsupport for the death penalty. The first question was: "Which of the following statements best describes your position toward the death penalty for *all* persons convicted of first-degree murder?"[56] Only 28.3 percent of less-informed subjects opposed the death penalty for *all* persons convicted of first-degree murder (24.7 percent of males; 31.1 percent of females; 18.3 percent of whites; 37.6 percent of blacks), but 46.6 percent of more-informed subjects were opposed to it (41.2 percent of males; 51.1 percent of females; 32.3 percent of whites; 60 percent of blacks).[57]

A second question asked subjects whether they favored the death penalty for "*some* people convicted of first-degree murder." This question is the one that is most similar to the general death penalty opinion question asked in the Gallup and other polls. Results for this question are similar to those for the previous one: 28 percent of less-informed subjects opposed the death penalty (24.7 percent of males; 30 percent of females; 22.6 percent of whites; 30.6 percent of blacks), but 49.5 percent of more-informed subjects opposed it (49.5 percent of males; 50 percent of females; 40.9 percent of whites; 56.6 percent of blacks).[58]

The third and fourth questions were asked because prior research has found that support for the death penalty is greatly reduced when a distinction is made between support in the abstract and support in concrete situations.[59] The first concrete question was: "If you served on a jury in a trial where the defendant, if found guilty, would automatically be sentenced to death, could you convict that defendant?" Only 22.5 percent of less-informed subjects could not convict (14.4 percent of males; 30 percent of females; 5.4 percent of whites; 23.5 percent of blacks), while 34.4 percent of more-informed subjects could not convict (30 percent of males; 38 percent of females; 21.5 percent of whites; 47.1 percent of blacks).[60]

The second concrete question was: "If asked to do it, could you pull the lever that would result in the death of an individual convicted of first-degree murder?" On this question, 47.2 percent of less-informed subjects (45.4 percent of males; 55.5 percent of females; 37.6 percent of whites; 64.7 percent of blacks) and 49.6 percent of more-informed subjects could not pull the lever (50.5 percent of males; 62.2 percent of females; 40.9 percent of whites; 72.9 percent of blacks).[61]

Another reason for asking subjects four different death penalty questions was to ascertain whether subjects had a "coherent moral position" toward capital punishment. As Professor Radin explains:

> The reason it is often suggested that one ought to look to what people do rather than what they say, or even more pointedly, that those who favor the death penalty should be asked whether they would be willing to pull the switch themselves, is that a person is more likely to have reached a coherent moral position if she is going to be required to transform her beliefs into action.[62]

Although Bohm and his colleagues wondered how people could have a coherent moral position toward the death penalty when they were ignorant about the subject, they nevertheless examined whether responses to the four questions formed a Guttman scale and thus were indicative of a coherent moral position. To their surprise, their findings suggested that their subjects did indeed hold coherent moral positions toward the death penalty, whether they were informed or not.[63] When they used subjects' Guttman scale coefficients as measures of opposition to capital punishment, Bohm et al. found that while only 34.7 percent of less-informed subjects opposed capital punishment, 56.3 percent of more-informed subjects opposed it.[64] This was the only measure that produced a majority of all subjects opposed to the penalty.

In sum, results of this research provided at least qualified support for all three of Marshall's hypotheses.[65] Subjects generally lacked knowledge about the death penalty and its administration prior to exposure to the experimental stimulus but were more informed following it. To the degree that retribution provided the basis for support of the death penalty, knowledge had little effect on opinions. The hypothesis that an informed public would generally oppose the death penalty was supported in one test but not in others. (In some tests, a majority of black males and a majority of black and white females opposed the death penalty.) Thus, even though support for the death penalty might decline after subjects have been informed, the reduction may not be great enough to create a majority opposed to the death penalty.[66] This may hold true even when subjects are asked diverse death penalty opinion questions, such as "personal involvement" questions.[67]

Other findings of this research include the following:

- exposure to death penalty information may result in the polarization of opinions (favoring or opposing more strongly);[68]

- it may be more difficult for subjects to change their positions if they have to publicly announce their death penalty opinions;[69]

- initial beliefs about the death penalty and such issues as deterrence, revenge, and incapacitaton generally are not affected by giving people information about those issues;[70] and

- when opinions about the death penalty do change, it is most likely because of administrative reasons such as racial discrimination or execution of innocent people.[71]

However, when the death penalty opinions of subjects in the 1988 and 1989 classes were examined two and three years later, it was discovered that opinions on the two abstract death penalty opinion questions (that is, "Do you favor or oppose the death penalty *for all* and *for some* people convicted of first-degree murder?") had rebounded to near their initial pretest positions.[72] Opinions on the two concrete death penalty opinion questions (that is, could you convict? and could you pull the lever?) did not change significantly for the 1988 and 1989 classes at any of the three points in time (pretest, posttest, or follow-up).[73] Another follow-up study of the 1988 and 1989 death penalty classes more than ten years after students completed the class revealed small increases in support of the death penalty from the first follow-up period on the abstract opinion measures.[74] However, as was the case in the first follow-up study, the personal involvement measures did not change significantly in the second follow-up study.[75] Results of the follow-up studies also do not appear to be a function of a loss of knowledge, the irrelevancy of the death penalty class, or the influence of the instructor.[76] Why, then, did opinions rebound? Perhaps it was because death penalty opinions are based primarily on emotion rather than on cognition and that, in the long run, cognitive influences on death penalty opinions give way to emotional factors.

Results of the follow-up studies suggest that most death penalty opinions may not be significantly influenced by increased knowledge about the penalty or may be influenced only temporarily, at least if that knowledge is obtained in a college classroom.[77] If Justice Marshall had in mind a stimulus like the one employed in the research by Bohm and his colleagues, then Marshall's belief that death penalty opinions can be changed substantially (by increasing knowledge about the subject) may be wrong. This does not mean that the opinions are intransigent. Opinions do change, as evidenced by the more-than-70-year history of public opinion polls on the death penalty in the United States. It means only that classroom knowledge may not be an effective way of changing those opinions.

Asking about Alternatives to the Death Penalty. Perhaps more important than the amount of accurate knowledge a person has about the death penalty is the way in which the death penalty opinion question is asked. A critical problem with the general opinion question (e.g., Do you favor or oppose the death penalty for first-degree murder?) is that there is either no context to the question or the context is ambiguous. For example, when people are asked whether they favor or oppose the death penalty, or, for that matter, whether they favor or oppose the death penalty for *all* people or for *some* people convicted of first-degree murder, it is left to the imagination of each individual as to whether that means:

- the death penalty or no penalty at all;

- the death penalty or a too lenient alternative penalty such as five or ten years in prison;

- the death penalty or a severe penalty such as a lengthy prison sentence but with opportunity for parole;

- the death penalty or an alternative severe penalty such as life imprisonment with no possibility of parole; or perhaps

- the death penalty and some other alternative.

With the exception of their latest studies, Bohm and his colleagues did not fully anticipate this possibility.[78]

It still appears that many people support the death penalty because they fear an alternative penalty will not be punitive enough or that it may be inappropriate, given the severity of the crime. Several studies show that 25 to 60 percent of the public believes that the average prison term served by someone sentenced to life imprisonment is 10 years or less," even though the statement is false.[79] Another problem is that the public frequently fails to consider alternatives when asked the general death penalty opinion question because the media does a woeful job of publicizing them.[80]

Support of capital punishment drops, though, when the death penalty question is asked and a harsh and meaningful alternative is provided. In a 2006 Gallup poll, when respondents were given a choice of the death penalty or life imprisonment with absolutely no possibility of parole (LWOP) as the better penalty for murder, 47 percent preferred the death penalty, 48 percent favored LWOP, and five percent had no opinion.[81] In many polls less than one-half of the public supports the death penalty when given the options of it and LWOP.[82] When given the options of the death penalty and life imprisonment with absolutely no possibility of parole *and* the payment of restitution by the offender (who would work in prison industry) to the victim's family or the community (LWOP+), even less of the public (only 19 to 43 percent) prefers the death penalty over the alternative.[83] Thus, on the surface, a majority of the public appears receptive to replacing capital punishment with a harsh and meaningful alternative such as LWOP or LWOP+. This is especially true of nonwhites, people 65 years of age or older, women, especially women 50 years of age or older, Easterners, people with a post-graduate education, Democrats, and the unemployed.[84]

A reason why even a larger percentage of the public does not favor LWOP or LWOP+ over capital punishment is that many people are very skeptical about the ability of correctional authorities to keep capital murderers imprisoned for life. A national survey showed that only 11 percent of registered voters believed that an offender sentenced to life imprisonment without possibility of parole would never be released from prison.[85] So, although the public might say it prefers the alternative of LWOP or LWOP+ over capital punishment, in practice it may not want to make the substitution due to fears that the alternative cannot guarantee protection from the future actions of convicted capital murderers.

Another problem with the LWOP+ alternative is that many murder victims' families find the idea of restitution repugnant, especially if it is received directly from the murderer.[86] They view restitution as "blood money" and reject the idea that it could satisfy them or bring them closure.[87] However, some of them support the idea of forcing murderers to work in prison and requiring them to put their earnings into a fund to pay the social debt they owe society or into a general survivors' compensation fund. For some murder victim family members, forced labor and paying reparations are better alternatives than having murderers idling in prison at taxpayers' expense.[88]

Asking about Different Types of Death–Eligible Murders. Another ambiguity with general death penalty opinion questions is the type of murder, or first-degree murder, the pollsters have in mind.

Not all death-eligible murders are the same. To address this issue, Professors Durham, Elrod, and Kinkade presented people with 34 different murder scenarios, which varied by aggravating and mitigating circumstances.[89] Murders in some scenarios were death-eligible, and murders in others were not. Respondents were asked what they thought was the appropriate punishment.

The researchers found that people's willingness to impose the death penalty may be greater than public opinion polls indicate. Only 13 percent of respondents would sentence all of the murderers to death, but about 95 percent would sentence at least one to death.[90] There was also a huge variation in the willingness of people to impose the death penalty on different types of murderers. For one scenario, more than 90 percent of respondents thought death was the appropriate punishment, while for another, fewer than 25 percent of respondents so believed.[91] Even people in groups historically most opposed to the death penalty were likely to believe the death penalty was appropriate for at least some types of murderers. Although people's willingness to impose the death penalty was generally greatest for first-degree and felony murders, an unexpected finding was that several felony murders drew little death penalty support.[92] Durham and his colleagues also discovered that aggravating circumstances were more influential on sentencing decisions than were mitigating circumstances.[93] Finally, when the researchers compared their data with information obtained from the prosecutor's office, they found that the people they surveyed were more willing to impose the death penalty than was the prosecutor or than the law would have allowed.[94] These data suggest that death penalty support in the United States, for at least some types of murders, may be every bit as strong as recent public opinion polls suggest, and it may be even stronger for specific types of death-eligible murders.

Other Death Penalty Opinion Questions. As noted previously, recent polls have included a greater variety of questions about the death penalty than did earlier polls. In fact, much more information is available about annual death penalty opinions today than at any time in the history of death penalty opinion polling. Some of that information was explored in previous chapters of this book. Besides questions about the death penalty versus LWOP and different types of death-eligible murders, recent polls have included questions about the administration of the death penalty, such as whether it is applied fairly, how often an innocent person has been executed, and whether poor people are more likely to receive the death penalty than people of average or above average income. Questions have been asked about the frequency with which the death penalty is imposed (too often, not enough, right amount) and whether the death penalty should be imposed on certain categories of offenders, such as the mentally retarded, the mentally ill, juveniles, and women. Additional questions address whether the death penalty is morally acceptable, whether it acts as a deterrent, and whether there should be a moratorium on it. Reasons for favoring the death penalty also have been sought. Poll questions asked about George W. Bush's handling of death penalty cases as governor of Texas and how that would affect whether a person would vote for him as president. Finally, death penalty polls have included questions about the appropriateness of the death penalty for specific offenders, such as Timothy McVeigh, Terry Nichols, Juan Raul Garza, Andrea Yates, and Osama bin Laden.

Conclusion: The Future of American Death Penalty Opinion and the Death Penalty

One of the more ambitious attempts to explain death penalty opinion in the United States was based on the results of a 20-year longitudinal study of the development of moral judgment in American males. From that study, Professors Kohlberg and Elfenbein concluded that "nonfactual cognitive components of attitudes [opinions] toward capital punishment are determined by developing moral standards," as opposed to "irrational, purely emotional factors."[95] Since the American public generally is not well informed about the death penalty, then one might assume, following Kohlberg and Elfenbein, that death penalty opinions are primarily the product of "developing moral standards." Kohlberg and Elfenbein posited six moral stages and explained that as society progressed "through the universal, invariant sequence of moral stages," there is "a radical decline in support for capital punishment."[96] At Stage 6, to which society had yet to "progress," no person could support capital punishment.[97]

Kohlberg and Elfenbein observed that:

> A gradual socio-moral evolution is evidently taking place in the United States that can be described and theoretically explained as moral stage development across social institutions and individuals over time. In large part, this evolution takes the form of a movement from Stage 4 to Stage 5.[98]

According to Kohlberg and Elfenbein, then, society is morally developing to a stage where the public will not support the death penalty. This observation, however, was published in 1975 during the hiatus on capital punishment in the United States and after a period of decline in support. Subsequent developments, such as increasing public support for the death penalty (until recently) and an increase in the number of death sentences and executions (until recently), indicate either that Kohlberg and Elfenbein relied on a faulty theory, that they were wrong in their assessment of the moral evolution of American society, or that the American public is/was regressing in its moral development.

Public opinion about capital punishment, or at least public support, may prove to be irrelevant if and when the penalty is ever abolished in the United States. As Zimring and Hawkins have observed, "Successful and sustained abolition [of capital punishment] has never been a result of great popular demand."[99] Most countries that have abolished the death penalty continued to have a majority of citizens who supported retention at the time of abolition and shortly thereafter. Only gradually did death penalty support decline until opposition dominated public opinion.[100] In short, abolition of capital punishment, where it has occurred, generally has been achieved despite relatively strong public support for retention. In a sense, then, as Judge Cassell has observed, European countries do not have the death penalty because they are less democratic, or at least more insulated from public opinion, than the United States.[101] Zimring and Hawkins surmise that politicians and other opinion-makers probably will have to lead the public on this issue if capital punishment is ever to be abolished in the United States.

Based on my own analysis of the dramatic reversal in death penalty opinion in the United States beginning in the 1966 to 1967 period, I have concluded that "the key to understanding temporal variations in death penalty opinions probably lies in the fear and anxiety engendered by the social events of an era."[102] The strength of death penalty support and opposition appears to be both a psychological barometer of the level of dread and angst in a society and a symbolic marker of the social landscape. In particular, levels of support and opposition seem to demarcate the threshold level of people's tolerance of media-reported crime, and, at the same time, serve as an indicator of people's threshold tolerance of social change. As one student of the subject put it, death penalty support declined in the 1960s because, "as practiced, many people found [the death penalty] to be glaringly inconsistent with the ascendant ideas of the times."[103] It seems reasonable to assume "that historical changes, such as a political shift away from the conservative social policies of the last [two and a half decades or so], are apt to either produce a dramatic shift in future death penalty opinions or to be marked by changed death penalty opinions as the political shift passes a certain threshold level."[104] Either way, it is unlikely that the practice of capital punishment could be sustained if a majority of American citizens were to oppose it.

Discussion Questions

1. How strongly does the American public support the death penalty?

2. Do you support the death penalty for *all* persons convicted of first-degree murder? Why or why not?

3. Do you support the death penalty for *some* people convicted of first-degree murder? Why or why not?

4. If you served on a jury in a trial where the defendant, if found guilty, would automatically be sentenced to death, could you convict that defendant? Why or why not?

5. If asked to do it, could you pull the lever that would result in the death of an individual convicted of first-degree murder? Why or why not?

6. Would you support the death penalty if the alternative were life imprisonment with absolutely no possibility of parole? Why or why not?

7. Would you support the death penalty if the alternative were life imprisonment with absolutely no possibility of parole *and* the payment of restitution by the offender (who would work in prison industry) to the victim's family or the community (LWOP+)? Why or why not?

8. Should public opinion be used in determining whether capital punishment is an acceptable or a constitutional form of punishment?

9. Does the public's opinion about the death penalty matter? Should it matter?

10. Have the new death penalty statutes and their procedural reforms rid the death penalty's administration of the problems cited in *Furman*?

11. Can death penalty statutes be made constitutionally acceptable?

12. Why do people oppose capital punishment? How could they be so wrong?

13. Why do people support capital punishment? How could they be so wrong?

14. Will the death penalty ever be abolished in all jurisdictions in the United States? If yes, what will cause its abolition?

Notes

[1] A version of this chapter appeared as "American Death Penalty Opinion: Past, Present, and Future," in J. R. Acker, R. M. Bohm, and C. Lanier (eds.) (2003) *America's Experiment with Capital Punishment: Reflections on the Past, Present and Future of the Ultimate Penal Sanction*, 2nd ed. Durham, NC: Carolina Academic Press. Reprinted with permission.

[2] See Jones, 2006, for the most recent poll data. Unless indicated otherwise, figures reported in this chapter are from the Gallup polls, which are the oldest and most sustained effort to measure American death penalty opinion, see Bohm, 1991. However, see the Appendix to Ellsworth and Gross, 1994, for a list of 90 death penalty opinion surveys conducted in the United States between 1936 and July 1993, the text of the ques-

tions asked, and the proportions of respondents providing each recorded answer. For more recent polls, see the Death Penalty Information Center web site. Although some of those polls measure opinions about the death penalty for certain other categories of persons, such as juveniles and the mentally retarded, for certain other types of crimes, such as rape or kidnapping, and for certain kinds of death sentences, such as mandatory versus discretionary, this chapter focuses primarily on death penalty opinions for capital or aggravated murder. All post-*Furman* executions have involved capital or aggravated murderers.

[3] Erskine cites a Harris Survey released on July 3, 1966, that showed that only 38 percent of respondents favored the death penalty, 47 percent were against, and 15 percent had no opinion, see Erskine, 1970:295.

[4] Cited in Haines, 1996:164.

[5] On Tennessee legislators, see Whitehead, 1998; on Indiana legislators, see McGarrell and Sandys, 1996; but see Sandys and McGarrell, 1994. Evidence indicates that public opinion has affected policymaking in the United States in other areas, such as civil rights, see Oskamp, 1977:241; also cf. Page et al., 1987; Page and Shapiro, 1983; Monroe, 1979; Erikson, 1976; Weissberg, 1976.

[6] See Dieter, 1996. With regard to the death penalty, former New York Governors Hugh Carey and Mario Cuomo and former California Governor Jerry Brown are three notable exceptions. Each governor vetoed death penalty legislation despite strong public support for the penalty.

[7] White, 1987:17; also see Dieter, 1996, op. cit.; Callahan et al., 2000.

[8] Bright, 1998; Dieter, 1996, op. cit.; Bright and Keenan, 1995; Dickson, 2006:281.

[9] Bright, ibid., pp. 123-124; Dieter, ibid., pp. 2-4.

[10] Baldus and Woodworth, 1998:388-389; also see Burnett, 2002; Kobil, 1998; Dieter, 1996, ibid.

[11] A recent study found that "states are approximately 25 percent more likely to conduct executions in gubernatorial election years than in other years." It also discovered that "elections have a larger effect on the probability that an African-American defendant will be executed in a given year than on the probability that a white defendant will be executed and that the overall effect of elections is largest in the South." See Kubik and Moran, 2003.

[12] On state constitutions, see Bedau, 1987, Chap. 8; on the Eighth Amendment, see Marshall in *Furman v. Georgia,* 1972:329; also in *Furman*: Douglas, p. 242, Brennan, pp. 269-270; Burger, p. 383, and Powell, p. 409; *Trop v. Dulles*, 1958:101; *Weems v. United States*, 1910:349, 373; *Robinson v. California*, 1962:666; also cf. *Estelle v. Gamble*, 1976:102; *Roberts v. Louisiana*, 1976:336, 352; *Woodson v. North Carolina*, 1976:301; *Gregg v. Georgia*, 1976:173, 227. But see Justice Rehnquist's dissent in *Atkins v. Virginia*, 2002, where he is highly critical of using public opinion as a measure of evolving standards of decency.

[13] *Furman v. Georgia*, ibid., p. 329.

[14] Bohm, op. cit.

[15] Ibid., p. 115.

[16] See n. 2, supra.

[17] Jones, 2006.

[18] Unnever et al., 2005; McGarrell and Sandys, 1996, op. cit.; Sandys and McGarrell, 1995; Jones, 1994; Bowers, 1993; Bohm et al., 1991; Williams et al., 1988; Harris, 1986; Ellsworth and Ross, 1983; Sarat and Vidmar, 1976.

[19] The six most volatile short-term periods between 1936 and 2006 were: (1) 1953-1957 (23 percent decrease in support, 5 percent increase in opposition, and 17 percent increase in "no opinions" or "don't knows"), (2) 1960-1966 (11 percent decrease in support and 11 percent increase in opposition), (3) 1966-1967 (11 percent increase in support and 8 percent decrease in opposition), (4) 1971-1976 (16 percent increase in support and 12 percent decrease in opposition), (5) 1978-1995 (15 percent increase in support, 14 percent decrease in opposition, and 9 percent decrease in "no opinions"), and (6) 1995-2003 (13 percent decrease in support, 19 percent increase in opposition, and 6 percent decrease in "no opinions" or "don't knows") , see Bohm 1991, op. cit. and recent Gallup polls. With the exception of an analysis of the 1966-1967 period, see Bohm 1992a, there have been no attempts, of which this author is aware, to explain the volatile periods.

[20] See Bohm, 1991, ibid., p. 116. For an analysis of the historical circumstances, that is, the social events and economic trends, that contributed to the dramatic reversal in death penalty support and opposition between 1966 and 1967, see Bohm, 1992a, ibid.

[21] See Bohm 1991, ibid.

[22] Ibid.

[23] Ibid.

[24] Death penalty opinion research published prior to 1975, when death penalty support was more moderate than it generally has been since then, frequently attributed support of capital punishment to some rather unflattering social psychological characteristics such as dogmatism, authoritarianism, and racism. Proponents of capital punishment were less likely than opponents to approve of gun registration laws or to favor open housing legislation and more likely to favor restrictive abortion laws, approve of the John Birch Society, move if blacks moved into their neighborhoods, and support such things as restrictions on civil liberties, discrimination against minority groups, and violence for achieving social goals, see Vidmar and Ellsworth, 1974; also see Bohm, 1987. However, in light of the dramatic increase in death penalty support since 1975 (until recently), one might have hoped that such a distinctive personality profile of death penalty proponents no longer applied. Unfortunately, recent evidence suggests otherwise. Support of capital punishment by many whites continues to be associated with prejudice against blacks, see Barkan and Cohn, 1994; Bobo and Johnson, 2004; Bohm, 1994; Borg, 1997; U. S. General Accounting Office, 1990; Johnson, 2003, 2001.

[25] Bohm, 1991, op. cit.; also see Boots et al., 2003; Longmire, 1996; Fox et al., 1990-1991.

[26] See Bohm, 1991, ibid.

[27] Professor Borg (1997) found significant variation among Southerners' views of the death penalty. Southerners who were racially prejudiced toward blacks, religious fundamentalists, and politically conservative were more likely to support the death penalty than Southerners who did not possess those characteristics.

[28] Bohm, 1991, op. cit.

[29] Demographic data from the 2006 death penalty poll were obtained directly from The Gallup Organization. My thanks to Maura A. Strausberg, Data Librarian, for her help.

[30] Arthur, 1998. For one interesting and detailed position on the death penalty offered by a black man, see Jackson, 1996. Cochran and Chamlin (2006) found that the race/ethnicity difference in death penalty opinions held after controlling for the effects of socioeconomic status, religion/religiosity, political ideology, positions on right-to-life and other social issues, fear of crime and victimization experience, experience with the criminal justice system, philosophies of punishment, and attribution styles. Also see Bobo and Johnson, op. cit.; Johnson, 2003, op. cit., 2001, op. cit.

[31] See note 29.

[32] Baumer et al., 2003.

[33] Ibid., p. 866.

[34] Ibid., p. 844; also see Soss et al., 2003.

[35] This appears to hold true even among prison inmates, see Wilcox and Steele, 2003; Steele and Wilcox, 2003.

[36] *Furman v. Georgia*, 1972 at 332.

[37] Ibid., at 362, fn. 145.

[38] Ibid. Elaborating on this point, Marshall wrote that "the question with which we must deal is not whether a substantial proportion of American citizens would today, if polled, opine that capital punishment is barbarously cruel, but whether they would find it to be so in the light of all information presently available," see *Furman v. Georgia*, 1972:362. For Marshall, however, "this is not to suggest that with respect to this test of unconstitutionality people are required to act rationally; they are not [and often do not—author's addition]. With respect to this judgment, a violation of the Eighth Amendment is totally dependent on the predictable subjective, emotional reactions of informed citizens" (at 362). Even if the American people were adequately informed about the death penalty and its effects, Radin is but one scholar who believes that public opinion polls should not be relied on in constitutional adjudication, see Radin, 1978. She argues that public opinion polls should not be used because they (1) "show that the majority of the public favors few of the protections embodied in the Bill of Rights" . . . [and] "the purpose of the Bill of Rights is to protect certain rights of individuals from an overreaching majority," (2) "are subject to methodological errors," and (3) "may record frivolous or ill-considered answers, or answers influenced by intrinsic factors," see Radin, op. cit., pp. 1035–1036.

[39] *Furman v. Georgia*, 1972 at 363. In his dissent in *Furman*, Justice Powell disagreed with Marshall and argued that the public would not oppose the death penalty if it were informed about its administration, see *Furman v. Georgia*, 1972 at 430–446.

[40] *Furman v. Georgia*, 1972 at 363. In *Furman*, Justice Stewart, who voted with the majority, opined that retribution was psychologically necessary for maintaining social stability, see *Furman v. Georgia*, 1972 at 308.

[41] *Furman v. Georgia*, 1972 at 363. Disagreement over the legitimacy of retribution as a purpose of capital punishment may be the product of confusion over what retribution actually means. For a discussion of the different meanings of retribution, see Chapter 9.

[42] Ellsworth and Ross, 1983, op. cit.

[43] Sarat and Vidmar, 1976, op. cit.

[44] Vidmar and Dittenhoffer, 1981.

[45] The study by Ellsworth and Ross, 1983, op. cit., examined only opinions and knowledge about the death penalty. It did not examine whether knowledge about the death penalty would change opinions. Also see Longmire, 1996, op. cit., for the effects of knowledge about the death penalty on the opinions of death penalty proponents, opponents, and undecideds.

[46] *Furman v. Georgia,* 1972 at 362–363.

[47] Ibid., at 362–364.

[48] Lord et al., 1979.

[49] Lord et al. presented 24 proponents and 24 opponents of the death penalty (all subjects were undergraduate students) "first with the results and then with procedural details, critiques, and rebuttals for two studies dealing with the deterrent efficacy of the death penalty—one study confirming their initial beliefs and one study disconfirming their initial beliefs," see Lord et al., op. cit., pp. 2100–2101, for more detail.

[50] Ibid., p. 2099.

[51] Ellsworth and Ross, op. cit., p. 152; also see Roberts, 1984; Tyler and Weber, 1982. The concepts "attitudes" and "opinions" are often used synonymously, especially when discussing the death penalty. However, according to at least one authority, see Oskamp, 1977, opinions should be equated with beliefs, which are primarily cognitive, while attitudes are more emotion-laden. That distinction is ignored in this chapter, which employs the concepts "opinion" or "opinions" except in direct quotes (in which case the concepts are bracketed).

[52] Sarat and Vidmar, op. cit., p. 183, fn. 59.

[53] Vidmar and Dittenhoffer, op. cit., p. 49.

[54] Ibid., pp. 45–46.

[55] There are at least two potential problems with Bohm and his colleague's experimental design. First is the use of student subjects. Whether students are representative of the general public with regard to death penalty opinion is questionable. In the 2006 Gallup poll, 65 percent of all respondents supported the death penalty, 66 percent of respondents with a high school education or less supported it, 69 percent of respondents with some college supported it, and 62 percent of respondents with a college education supported it. Only respondents with post-graduate educations deviated significantly from the percentage of all respondents who favored the death penalty (only 54 percent of respondents with post-graduate educations supported the death penalty), see note 29. Variation in other years, however, has been both greater and smaller, see Bohm 1991, op. cit., pp. 131–132 and more recent polls. In any case, the reason for using student subjects was that it was one of the only ways to employ a prolonged stimulus experimentally. Brevity of exposure to the experimental stimulus was a weakness of previous research (cf. Sarat and Vidmar, 1976; Lord et al., 1979; Vidmar and Dittenhoffer, 1981). A second potential problem with Bohm and his colleague's experimental design is the influence of the instructor. A charismatic teacher could have a significant influence over his or her students' opinions. The instructor in the death penalty classes was always forthright about his strong opposition to the death penalty but emphasized that his opinion should not influence the opinion of anyone else. Despite his personal opinion, both sides of all issues were presented, and no preference was shown intentionally for either side. Also, the instructor played "devil's advocate" to the positions taken by students to provoke thoughtful consideration of the issues. Students were fully aware from the outset that their grade in the class was independent of their views. Informal feedback from all the classes and results of two and three year and more than ten year follow-up studies of the 1988 and 1989 classes indicate that "demand characteristics" had negligible effects, Bohm et al., 1993:42; Bohm and Vogel, 2002.

[56] As discussed in Chapter 2, although, in 1976, in the cases of *Woodson v. North Carolina* and *Roberts v. Louisiana*, the Supreme Court rejected mandatory statutes that automatically imposed death sentences for defined capital offenses, a question about the death penalty for all persons convicted of first-degree murder remains instructive. Not only does it give an indication of people's opinions in light of the Supreme Court decisions, but it also serves as a basis of comparison for other questions about the death penalty considered in this research.

[57] Bohm et al., 1991, op. cit., pp. 373-375, Tables 2, 3 & 4.

[58] Ibid.

[59] See Ellsworth and Ross, 1983, op. cit.; Jurow, 1971. The distinction made between abstract questions and questions involving concrete situations is somewhat artificial. As is well known, what people say and what people do are often very different. Research indicates that correlations between people's attitudes [opinions] and their behavior are "rarely above .30, and often are near zero," see Wicker, 1969. The largest correlations are typically found when the researcher focuses on a specific attitude [opinion] toward a well-defined situation. Conversely, when the attitude [opinion] is a very general one that is presumed to influence a variety of different situations, much less consistency between attitude [opinion] and behavior is found, see Crespi, 1971. Thus, what people say about the death penalty in general, and what they would do as jurors in a capital murder trial, for example, probably are not the same. For that matter, what people say they would do if they served as jurors in a capital murder trial, and what they would do if they actually served, may not be the same. This, of course, is a problem with all survey research.

[60] Bohm et al., 1991, op. cit.

[61] Ibid.

[62] Radin, 1978, op. cit., p. 1041.

[63] Bohm et al., 1991, pp. 368-369.

[64] Ibid., p. 375.

[65] See Bohm et al., 1991, ibid.; also see Bohm, 1989; Bohm, 1990; Bohm et al., 1990; Bohm and Vogel, 1994.

[66] Bohm, 1989, ibid.; Bohm et al., 1991, ibid.; Bohm and Vogel, 1994, ibid; Lambert and Clarke, 2001.

[67] Bohm et al., 1991, ibid.; Bohm et al. 1993, op. cit.; but see Murray, 2003.

[68] Bohm et al., 1990, op. cit.; Bohm 1990, op. cit.

[69] Bohm, 1990, ibid.

[70] Bohm et al., 1993, op. cit.; Bohm and Vogel, op. cit., 1994.

[71] Bohm, 1989, op. cit.; Bohm and Vogel, 1994, ibid.; Bohm et al., 1991, op. cit.; Bohm et al., 1993, ibid.; Sandys, 1995; Clarke et al., 2000-2001; Lambert and Clarke, op. cit.

[72] Bohm et al., ibid., 1993.

[73] Ibid. There was some significant change in opinions on the concrete questions in some of the tests.

[74] Bohm and Vogel, 2004.

[75] Ibid.

[76] Bohm et al., 1993, op. cit., p. 42; Bohm and Vogel, 2004, op. cit.

[77] Also see Patenaude, 2001, but see Sandys, op. cit.; Cochran and Chamlin, 2005, for different results.

[78] See Wright et al., 1995; Bohm and Vogel, 2004, op. cit.

[79] Bohm et al., 1991, op. cit., p. 371; Ellsworth and Ross, 1983, op. cit.; Paduano and Smith, 1987; Hood, 1989; Wright et al., ibid.; also see Bowers, 1993, op. cit.; McGarrell and Sandys, 1996, op. cit.; Bowers and Steiner, 1998.

[80] See, for example, Niven, 2002.

[81] Jones, 2006.

[82] See, for example, Gallup and Newport, 1991:44; also see Bowers et al., 1994; Ellsworth and Gross, 1994, op. cit.; Bowers, 1993, op. cit.; Boots et al., op. cit.

[83] See Bowers, 1993, ibid.; Sandys and McGarrell, 1995, op. cit.; McGarrell and Sandys, 1996, op. cit. Bowers notes that there is evidence suggesting that "a majority of the public would also be willing to accept parole after a fixed term of at least 25 years in preference to the death penalty on the condition that it was coupled with a restitution requirement and that the defendant had fully met the restitution requirement," see Bowers, 1993, op. cit., p. 168.

[84] Jones, 2006, op. cit.; Jones, 2002, op. cit. Professor Vogel (2003) found that the only demographic characteristic (that she examined) that distinguished the views of death penalty supporters about LWOP was wealth. Wealthier death penalty supporters were less likely to favor LWOP than other death penalty supporters.

[85] Cited in McGarrell and Sandys, 1996, ibid., p. 509.

[86] Kay, 2006:335.

[87] Ibid., p. 338.

[88] Ibid., pp. 340-342.

[89] Durham et al., 1996; also see Boots et al., op. cit.

[90] Durham et al., ibid., p. 726.

[91] Ibid., p. 727.

[92] Ibid.

[93] Ibid.

[94] Ibid.

[95] Kohlberg and Elfenbein, 1975: 617.

[96] Ibid., pp. 637–638.

[97] Ibid., p. 637.

[98] Ibid., p. 638.

[99] Zimring and Hawkins, 1986:12. Zimring (2003:23-24) notes that death penalty abolition in most European countries came during politically liberal administrations but, when they were replaced with politically conservative administrations, the death penalty was never reinstated. After abolition, he adds, the death penalty ceased to be an important political issue.

[100] Ibid.

[101] Cassell, 2004:200.

[102] Bohm 1992a, op. cit., p. 539.

[103] Haines, 1996, op. cit., p. 161.

[104] Bohm, op. cit.; also see Zimring, 2003.

APPENDIX A

American Bar Association
2003 Guidelines for the Appointment and Performance
of Defense Counsel in Death Penalty Cases*

Despite some overlap, Guidelines 1.1–10.1 primarily describe how jurisdictions should create a capital case defense services delivery system, and Guidelines 10.2-10.15.2 primarily provide performance standards outlining counsel's duties in those cases.

GUIDELINE 1.1—OBJECTIVE AND SCOPE OF GUIDELINES

A. The objective of these Guidelines is to set forth a national standard of practice for the defense of capital cases in order to ensure high quality legal representation for all persons facing the possible imposition or execution of a death sentence by any jurisdiction.

B. These Guidelines apply from the moment the client is taken into custody and extend to all stages of every case in which the jurisdiction may be entitled to seek the death penalty, including initial and ongoing investigation, pretrial proceedings, trial, post-conviction review, clemency proceedings and any connected litigation.

GUIDELINE 2.1—ADOPTION AND IMPLEMENTATION OF A PLAN TO PROVIDE HIGH QUALITY LEGAL REPRESENTATION IN DEATH PENALTY CASES

A. Each jurisdiction should adopt and implement a plan formalizing the means by which high quality legal representation in death penalty cases is to be provided in accordance with these Guidelines (the "Legal Representation Plan").

B. The Legal Representation Plan should set forth how the jurisdiction will conform to each of these Guidelines.

---

* "American Bar Association Guidelines for the Appointment and Performance of Defense Counsel in Death Penalty Cases," Revised February 2003, A Joint Project by the American Bar Association's Standing Committee on Legal Aid & Indigent Defendants and the Special Committee on Death Penalty Representation, published online at www.abanet.org/legalservices/downloads/sclaid/indigentdefense/deathpenalty guidelines2003.pdf © 2003 by the American Bar Association. Reprinted with permission.

C. All elements of the Legal Representation Plan should be structured to ensure that counsel defending death penalty cases are able to do so free from political influence and under conditions that enable them to provide zealous advocacy in accordance with professional standards.

GUIDELINE 3.1—DESIGNATION OF A RESPONSIBLE AGENCY

A. The Legal Representation Plan should designate one or more agencies to be responsible, in accordance with the standards provided in these Guidelines, for:

1. ensuring that each capital defendant in the jurisdiction receives high quality legal representation, and
2. performing all the duties listed in Subsection E (the "Responsible Agency").

B. The Responsible Agency should be independent of the judiciary and it, and not the judiciary or elected officials, should select lawyers for specific cases.

C. The Responsible Agency for each stage of the proceeding in a particular case should be one of the following:

Defender Organization

1. A "defender organization," that is, either:

    a. a jurisdiction-wide capital trial office, relying on staff attorneys, members of the private bar, or both to provide representation in death penalty cases; or
    b. a jurisdiction-wide capital appellate and/or post-conviction defender office, relying on staff attorneys, members of the private bar, or both to provide representation in death penalty cases; or

Independent Authority

2. An "Independent Authority," that is, an entity run by defense attorneys with demonstrated knowledge and expertise in capital representation.

D. Conflict of Interest:

1. In any circumstance in which the performance by a defender organization of a duty listed in Subsection E would result in a conflict of interest, the relevant duty should be performed by the Independent Authority. The jurisdiction should implement an effectual system to identify and resolve such conflicts.
2. When the Independent Authority is the Responsible Agency, attorneys who hold formal roles in the Independent Authority should be ineligible to represent defendants in capital cases within the jurisdiction during their term of service.

E. The Responsible Agency should, in accordance with the provisions of these Guidelines, perform the following duties:

1. recruit and certify attorneys as qualified to be appointed to represent defendants in death penalty cases;
2. draft and periodically publish rosters of certified attorneys;
3. draft and periodically publish certification standards and procedures by which attorneys are certified and assigned to particular cases;
4. assign the attorneys who will represent the defendant at each stage of every case, except to the extent that the defendant has private attorneys;
5. monitor the performance of all attorneys providing representation in capital proceedings;
6. periodically review the roster of qualified attorneys and withdraw certification from any attorney who fails to provide high quality legal representation consistent with these Guidelines;
7. conduct, sponsor, or approve specialized training programs for attorneys representing defendants in death penalty cases; and
8. investigate and maintain records concerning complaints about the performance of attorneys providing representation in death penalty cases and take appropriate corrective action without delay.

GUIDELINE 4.1—THE DEFENSE TEAM AND SUPPORTING SERVICES

A. The Legal Representation Plan should provide for assembly of a defense team that will provide high quality legal representation.

1. The defense team should consist of no fewer than two attorneys qualified in accordance with Guideline 5.1, an investigator, and a mitigation specialist.
2. The defense team should contain at least one member qualified by training and experience to screen individuals for the presence of mental or psychological disorders or impairments.

B. The Legal Representation Plan should provide for counsel to receive the assistance of all expert, investigative, and other ancillary professional services reasonably necessary or appropriate to provide high quality legal representation at every stage of the proceedings. The Plan should specifically ensure provision of such services to private attorneys whose clients are financially unable to afford them.

1. Counsel should have the right to have such services provided by persons independent of the government.
2. Counsel should have the right to protect the confidentiality of communications with the persons providing such services to the same extent as would counsel paying such persons from private funds.

GUIDELINE 5.1—QUALIFICATIONS OF DEFENSE COUNSEL

A. The Responsible Agency should develop and publish qualification standards for defense counsel in capital cases. These standards should be construed and applied in such a way as to further the overriding goal of providing each client with high quality legal representation.

B. In formulating qualification standards, the Responsible Agency should insure:

1. That every attorney representing a capital defendant has:

   a. obtained a license or permission to practice in the jurisdiction;
   b. demonstrated a commitment to providing zealous advocacy and high quality legal representation in the defense of capital cases; and
   c. satisfied the training requirements set forth in Guideline 8.1.

2. That the pool of defense attorneys as a whole is such that each capital defendant within the jurisdiction receives high quality legal representation. Accordingly, the qualification standards should insure that the pool includes sufficient numbers of attorneys who have demonstrated:

   a. substantial knowledge and understanding of the relevant state, federal and international law, both procedural and substantive, governing capital cases;
   b. skill in the management and conduct of complex negotiations and litigation;
   c. skill in legal research, analysis, and the drafting of litigation documents;
   d. skill in oral advocacy;
   e. skill in the use of expert witnesses and familiarity with common areas of forensic investigation, including fingerprints, ballistics, forensic pathology, and DNA evidence;
   f. skill in the investigation, preparation, and presentation of evidence bearing upon mental status;
   g. skill in the investigation, preparation, and presentation of mitigating evidence; and
   h. skill in the elements of trial advocacy, such as jury selection, cross-examination of witnesses, and opening and closing statements.

GUIDELINE 6.1—WORKLOAD

The Responsible Agency should implement effectual mechanisms to ensure that the workload of attorneys representing defendants in death penalty cases is maintained at a level that enables counsel to provide each client with high quality legal representation in accordance with these Guidelines.

GUIDELINE 7.1—MONITORING; REMOVAL

A. The Responsible Agency should monitor the performance of all defense counsel to ensure that the client is receiving high quality legal representation. Where there is evidence that an attorney is not providing high quality legal representation, the Responsible Agency should take appropriate action to protect the interests of the attorney's current and potential clients.

B. The Responsible Agency should establish and publicize a regular procedure for investigating and resolving any complaints made by judges, clients, attorneys, or others that defense counsel failed to provide high quality legal representation.

C. The Responsible Agency should periodically review the rosters of attorneys who have been certified to accept appointments in capital cases to ensure that those attorneys remain capable of providing high quality legal representation. Where there is evidence that an attorney has failed to provide high quality legal representation, the attorney should not receive additional appointments and should be removed from the roster. Where there is evidence that a systemic defect in a defender office has caused the office to fail to provide high quality legal representation, the office should not receive additional appointments.

D. Before taking final action making an attorney or a defender office ineligible to receive additional appointments, the Responsible Agency should provide written notice that such action is being contemplated, and give the attorney or defender office opportunity to respond in writing.

E. An attorney or defender office sanctioned pursuant to this Guideline should be restored to the roster only in exceptional circumstances.

F. The Responsible Agency should ensure that this Guideline is implemented consistently with Guideline 2.1(C), so that an attorney's zealous representation of a client cannot be cause for the imposition or threatened imposition of sanctions pursuant to this Guideline.

GUIDELINE 8.1—TRAINING

A. The Legal Representation Plan should provide funds for the effective training, professional development, and continuing education of all members of the defense team.

B. Attorneys seeking to qualify to receive appointments should be required to satisfactorily complete a comprehensive training program, approved by the Responsible Agency, in the defense of capital cases. Such a program should include, but not be limited to, presentations and training in the following areas:

1. relevant state, federal, and international law;
2. pleading and motion practice;

3. pretrial investigation, preparation, and theory development regarding guilt/innocence and penalty;
4. jury selection;
5. trial preparation and presentation, including the use of experts;
6. ethical considerations particular to capital defense representation;
7. preservation of the record and of issues for post-conviction review;
8. counsel's relationship with the client and his family;
9. post-conviction litigation in state and federal courts;
10. the presentation and rebuttal of scientific evidence, and developments in mental health fields and other relevant areas of forensic and biological science.

C. Attorneys seeking to remain on the roster or appointment roster should be required to attend and successfully complete, at least once every two years, a specialized training program approved by the Responsible Agency that focuses on the defense of death penalty cases.

D. The Legal Representation Plan should insure that all non-attorneys wishing to be eligible to participate on defense teams receive continuing professional education appropriate to their areas of expertise.

GUIDELINE 9.1—FUNDING AND COMPENSATION

A. The Legal Representation Plan must ensure funding for the full cost of high quality legal representation, as defined by these Guidelines, by the defense team and outside experts selected by counsel.

B. Counsel in death penalty cases should be fully compensated at a rate that is commensurate with the provision of high quality legal representation and reflects the extraordinary responsibilities inherent in death penalty representation.

1. Flat fees, caps on compensation, and lump-sum contracts are improper in death penalty cases.
2. Attorneys employed by defender organizations should be compensated according to a salary scale that is commensurate with the salary scale of the prosecutor's office in the jurisdiction.
3. Appointed counsel should be fully compensated for actual time and service performed at an hourly rate commensurate with the prevailing rates for similar services performed by retained counsel in the jurisdiction, with no distinction between rates for services performed in or out of court. Periodic billing and payment should be available.

C. Non-attorney members of the defense team should be fully compensated at a rate that is commensurate with the provision of high quality legal representation and reflects the specialized skills needed by those who assist counsel with the litigation of death penalty cases.

1. Investigators employed by defender organizations should be compensated according to a salary scale that is commensurate with the salary scale of the prosecutor's office in the jurisdiction.

2. Mitigation specialists and experts employed by defender organizations should be compensated according to a salary scale that is commensurate with the salary scale for comparable expert services in the private sector.

3. Members of the defense team assisting private counsel should be fully compensated for actual time and service performed at an hourly rate commensurate with prevailing rates paid by retained counsel in the jurisdiction for similar services, with no distinction between rates for services performed in or out of court. Periodic billing and payment should be available.

D. Additional compensation should be provided in unusually protracted or extraordinary cases.

E. Counsel and members of the defense team should be fully reimbursed for reasonable incidental expenses.

GUIDELINE 10.1—ESTABLISHMENT OF PERFORMANCE STANDARDS

A. The Responsible Agency should establish standards of performance for all counsel in death penalty cases.

B. The standards of performance should be formulated so as to insure that all counsel provide high quality legal representation in capital cases in accordance with these Guidelines. The Responsible Agency should refer to the standards when assessing the qualifications or performance of counsel.

C. The standards of performance should include, but not be limited to, the specific standards set out in these Guidelines.

GUIDELINE 10.2—APPLICABILITY OF PERFORMANCE STANDARDS

Counsel should provide high quality legal representation in accordance with these Guidelines for so long as the jurisdiction is legally entitled to seek the death penalty.

GUIDELINE 10.3—OBLIGATIONS OF COUNSEL RESPECTING WORKLOAD

Counsel representing clients in death penalty cases should limit their caseloads to the level needed to provide each client with high quality legal representation in accordance with these Guidelines.

GUIDELINE 10.4—THE DEFENSE TEAM

A. When it is responsible for designating counsel to defend a capital case, the Responsible Agency should designate a lead counsel and one or more associate counsel. The Responsible Agency should ordinarily solicit the views of lead counsel before designating associate counsel.

B. Lead counsel bears overall responsibility for the performance of the defense team, and should allocate, direct, and supervise its work in accordance with these Guidelines and professional standards.

   1. Subject to the foregoing, lead counsel may delegate to other members of the defense team duties imposed by these Guidelines, unless:

      a. The Guideline specifically imposes the duty on "lead counsel," or

      b. The Guideline specifically imposes the duty on "all counsel" or "all members of the defense team."

C. As soon as possible after designation, lead counsel should assemble a defense team by:

   1. Consulting with the Responsible Agency regarding the number and identity of the associate counsel;

   2. Subject to standards of the Responsible Agency that are in accord with these Guidelines and in consultation with associate counsel to the extent practicable, selecting and making any appropriate contractual agreements with non-attorney team members in such a way that the team includes:

      a. at least one mitigation specialist and one fact investigator;

      b. at least one member qualified by training and experience to screen individuals for the presence of mental or psychological disorders or impairments; and

      c. any other members needed to provide high quality legal representation.

D. Counsel at all stages should demand on behalf of the client all resources necessary to provide high quality legal representation. If such resources are denied, counsel should make an adequate record to preserve the issue for further review.

GUIDELINE 10.5—RELATIONSHIP WITH THE CLIENT

A. Counsel at all stages of the case should make every appropriate effort to establish a relationship of trust with the client, and should maintain close contact with the client.

B. Barring exceptional circumstances, an interview of the client should be conducted within 24 hours of initial counsel's entry into the case.

   1. Promptly upon entry into the case, initial counsel should communicate in an appropriate manner with both the client and the government regarding the protection of the client's rights against self-incrimination, to the effective assistance of counsel, and to preservation of the attorney-client privilege and similar safeguards.

   2. Counsel at all stages of the case should re-advise the client and the government regarding these matters as appropriate.

C. Counsel at all stages of the case should engage in a continuing interactive dialogue with the client concerning all matters that might reasonably be expected to have a material impact on the case, such as:

1. the progress of and prospects for the factual investigation, and what assistance the client might provide to it;
2. current or potential legal issues;
3. the development of a defense theory;
4. presentation of the defense case;
5. potential agreed-upon dispositions of the case;
6. litigation deadlines and the projected schedule of case-related events; and
7. relevant aspects of the client's relationship with correctional, parole or other governmental agents (e.g., prison medical providers or state psychiatrists).

GUIDELINE 10.6—ADDITIONAL OBLIGATIONS OF COUNSEL REPRESENTING A FOREIGN NATIONAL

A. Counsel at every stage of the case should make appropriate efforts to determine whether any foreign country might consider the client to be one of its nationals.

B. Unless predecessor counsel has already done so, counsel representing a foreign national should:

1. immediately advise the client of his or her right to communicate with the relevant consular office; and
2. obtain the consent of the client to contact the consular office. After obtaining consent, counsel should immediately contact the client's consular office and inform it of the client's detention or arrest.

    a. Counsel who is unable to obtain consent should exercise his or her best professional judgment under the circumstances.

GUIDELINE 10.7—INVESTIGATION

A. Counsel at every stage have an obligation to conduct thorough and independent investigations relating to the issues of both guilt and penalty.

1. The investigation regarding guilt should be conducted regardless of any admission or statement by the client concerning the facts of the alleged crime, or overwhelming evidence of guilt, or any statement by the client that evidence bearing upon guilt is not to be collected or presented.
2. The investigation regarding penalty should be conducted regardless of any statement by the client that evidence bearing upon penalty is not to be collected or presented.

B. Counsel at every stage have an obligation to conduct a full examination of the defense provided to the client at all prior phases of the case. This obligation includes at minimum interviewing prior counsel and members of the defense team and examining the files of prior counsel.

2. Counsel at every stage have an obligation to satisfy themselves independently that the official record of the proceedings is complete and to supplement it as appropriate.

GUIDELINE 10.8—THE DUTY TO ASSERT LEGAL CLAIMS

A. Counsel at every stage of the case, exercising professional judgment in accordance with these Guidelines, should:

1. consider all legal claims potentially available; and
2. thoroughly investigate the basis for each potential claim before reaching a conclusion as to whether it should be asserted; and
3. evaluate each potential claim in light of:

    a. the unique characteristics of death penalty law and practice; and
    b. the near certainty that all available avenues of post-conviction relief will be pursued in the event of conviction and imposition of a death sentence; and
    c. the importance of protecting the client's rights against later contentions by the government that the claim has been waived, defaulted, not exhausted, or otherwise forfeited; and
    d. any other professionally appropriate costs and benefits to the assertion of the claim.

B. Counsel who decide to assert a particular legal claim should:

1. present the claim as forcefully as possible, tailoring the presentation to the particular facts and circumstances in the client's case and the applicable law in the particular jurisdiction; and
2. ensure that a full record is made of all legal proceedings in connection with the claim.

C. Counsel at all stages of the case should keep under consideration the possible advantages to the client of:

1. asserting legal claims whose basis has only recently become known or available to counsel; and
2. supplementing claims previously made with additional factual or legal information.

GUIDELINE 10.9.1—THE DUTY TO SEEK AN AGREED-UPON DISPOSITION

A. Counsel at every stage of the case have an obligation to take all steps that may be appropriate in the exercise of professional judgment in accordance with these Guidelines to achieve an agreed-upon disposition.

B. Counsel at every stage of the case should explore with the client the possibility and desirability of reaching an agreed-upon disposition. In so doing, counsel should fully explain the rights that would be waived, the possible collateral consequences, and the legal, factual, and contextual considerations that bear upon the decision. Specifically, counsel should know and fully explain to the client:

1. the maximum penalty that may be imposed for the charged offense(s) and any possible lesser included or alternative offenses;
2. any collateral consequences of potential penalties less than death, such as forfeiture of assets, deportation, civil liabilities, and the use of the disposition adversely to the client in penalty phase proceedings of other prosecutions of him as well as any direct consequences of potential penalties less than death, such as the possibility and likelihood of parole, place of confinement and good-time credits;
3. the general range of sentences for similar offenses committed by defendants with similar backgrounds, and the impact of any applicable sentencing guidelines or mandatory sentencing requirements;
4. the governing legal regime, including but not limited to whatever choices the client may have as to the fact finder and/or sentencer;
5. the types of pleas that may be agreed to, such as a plea of guilty, a conditional plea of guilty, or a plea of nolo contendere or other plea which does not require the client to personally acknowledge guilt, along with the advantages and disadvantages of each;
6. whether any agreement negotiated can be made binding on the court, on penal/parole authorities, and any others who may be involved;
7. the practices, policies and concerns of the particular jurisdiction, the judge and prosecuting authority, the family of the victim and any other persons or entities which may affect the content and likely results of plea negotiations;
8. concessions that the client might offer, such as:
    a. an agreement to waive trial and to plead guilty to particular charges;
    b. an agreement to permit a judge to perform functions relative to guilt or sentence that would otherwise be performed by a jury or vice versa;
    c. an agreement regarding future custodial status, such as one to be confined in a more onerous category of institution than would otherwise be the case;
    d. an agreement to forego in whole or part legal remedies such as appeals, motions for post-conviction relief, and/or parole or clemency applications;
    e. an agreement to provide the prosecution with assistance in investigating or prosecuting the present case or other alleged criminal activity;
    f. an agreement to engage in or refrain from any particular conduct, as appropriate to the case;
    g. an agreement with the victim's family, which may include matters such as: a meeting between the victim's family and the client, a

promise not to publicize or profit from the offense, the issuance or delivery of a public statement of remorse by the client, or restitution;

    h. agreements such as those described in Subsections 8(a)-(g) respecting actual or potential charges in another jurisdiction;

9. benefits the client might obtain from a negotiated settlement, including:

    a. a guarantee that the death penalty will not be imposed;

    b. an agreement that the defendant will receive a specified sentence;

    c. an agreement that the prosecutor will not advocate a certain sentence, will not present certain information to the court, or will engage in or refrain from engaging in other actions with regard to sentencing;

    d. an agreement that one or more of multiple charges will be reduced or dismissed;

    e. an agreement that the client will not be subject to further investigation or prosecution for uncharged alleged or suspected criminal conduct;

    f. an agreement that the client may enter a conditional plea to preserve the right to further contest certain legal issues;

    g. an agreement that the court or prosecutor will make specific recommendations to correctional or parole authorities regarding the terms of the client's confinement;

    h. agreements such as those described in Subsections 9(a)-(g) respecting actual or potential charges in another jurisdiction.

C. Counsel should keep the client fully informed of any negotiations for a disposition, convey to the client any offers made by the prosecution, and discuss with the client possible negotiation strategies.

D. Counsel should inform the client of any tentative negotiated agreement reached with the prosecution, and explain to the client the full content of the agreement along with the advantages, disadvantages and potential consequences of the agreement.

E. If a negotiated disposition would be in the best interest of the client, initial refusals by the prosecutor to negotiate should not prevent counsel from making further efforts to negotiate. Similarly, a client's initial opposition should not prevent counsel from engaging in an ongoing effort to persuade the client to accept an offer of resolution that is in the client's best interest.

F. Counsel should not accept any agreed-upon disposition without the client's express authorization.

G. The existence of ongoing negotiations with the prosecution does not in any way diminish the obligations of defense counsel respecting litigation.

GUIDELINE 10.9.2—ENTRY OF A PLEA OF GUILTY

A. The informed decision whether to enter a plea of guilty lies with the client.

B. In the event the client determines to enter a plea of guilty:

    1. Prior to the entry of the plea, counsel should:

        a. make certain that the client understands the rights to be waived by entering the plea and that the client's decision to waive those rights is knowing, voluntary and intelligent;

        b. ensure that the client understands the conditions and limits of the plea agreement and the maximum punishment, sanctions, and other consequences to which he or she will be exposed by entering the plea;

        c. explain to the client the nature of the plea hearing and prepare the client for the role he or she will play in the hearing, including answering questions in court and providing a statement concerning the offense.

    2. During entry of the plea, counsel should make sure that the full content and conditions of any agreements with the government are placed on the record.

GUIDELINE 10.10.1—TRIAL PREPARATION OVERALL

As the investigations mandated by Guideline 10.7 produce information, trial counsel should formulate a defense theory. Counsel should seek a theory that will be effective in connection with both guilt and penalty, and should seek to minimize any inconsistencies.

GUIDELINE 10.10.2—VOIR DIRE AND JURY SELECTION

A. Counsel should consider, along with potential legal challenges to the procedures for selecting the jury that would be available in any criminal case (particularly those relating to bias on the basis of race or gender), whether any procedures have been instituted for selection of juries in capital cases that present particular legal bases for challenge. Such challenges may include challenges to the selection of the grand jury and grand jury forepersons as well as to the selection of the petit jury venire.

B. Counsel should be familiar with the precedents relating to questioning and challenging of potential jurors, including the procedures surrounding "death qualification" concerning any potential juror's beliefs about the death penalty. Counsel should be familiar with techniques: (1) for exposing those prospective jurors who would automatically impose the death penalty following a murder conviction or finding that the defendant is death-eligible, regardless of the individual circumstances of the case; (2) for uncovering those prospective jurors who are unable to give meaningful consideration to mitigating evidence; and (3) for rehabilitating potential jurors whose initial indications of opposition to the death penalty make them possibly excludable.

C. Counsel should consider seeking expert assistance in the jury selection process.

GUIDELINE 10.11—THE DEFENSE CASE CONCERNING PENALTY

A. As set out in Guideline 10.7(A), counsel at every stage of the case have a continuing duty to investigate issues bearing upon penalty and to seek information that supports mitigation or rebuts the prosecution's case in aggravation.

B. Trial counsel should discuss with the client early in the case the sentencing alternatives available, and the relationship between the strategy for the sentencing phase and for the guilt/innocence phase.

C. Prior to the sentencing phase, trial counsel should discuss with the client the specific sentencing phase procedures of the jurisdiction and advise the client of steps being taken in preparation for sentencing.

D. Counsel at every stage of the case should discuss with the client the content and purpose of the information concerning penalty that they intend to present to the sentencing or reviewing body or individual, means by which the mitigation presentation might be strengthened, and the strategy for meeting the prosecution's case in aggravation.

E. Counsel should consider, and discuss with the client, the possible consequences of having the client testify or make a statement to the sentencing or reviewing body or individual.

F. In deciding which witnesses and evidence to prepare concerning penalty, the areas counsel should consider include the following:

1. Witnesses familiar with and evidence relating to the client's life and development, from conception to the time of sentencing, that would be explanatory of the offense(s) for which the client is being sentenced, would rebut or explain evidence presented by the prosecutor, would present positive aspects of the client's life, or would otherwise support a sentence less than death;

2. Expert and lay witnesses along with supporting documentation (e.g., school records, military records) to provide medical, psychological, sociological, cultural or other insights into the client's mental and/or emotional state and life history that may explain or lessen the client's culpability for the underlying offense(s); to give a favorable opinion as to the client's capacity for rehabilitation, or adaptation to prison; to explain possible treatment programs; or otherwise support a sentence less than death; and/or to rebut or explain evidence presented by the prosecutor;

3. Witnesses who can testify about the applicable alternative to a death sentence and/or the conditions under which the alternative sentence would be served;

4. Witnesses who can testify about the adverse impact of the client's execution on the client's family and loved ones.

5. Demonstrative evidence, such as photos, videos, and physical objects (e.g., trophies, artwork, military medals), and documents that humanize the client or portray him positively, such as certificates of earned awards, favorable press accounts, and letters of praise or reference.

G. In determining what presentation to make concerning penalty, counsel should consider whether any portion of the defense case will open the door to the prosecution's presentation of otherwise inadmissible aggravating evidence. Counsel should pursue all appropriate means (e.g., motions in limine) to ensure that the defense case concerning penalty is constricted as little as possible by this consideration, and should make a full record in order to support any subsequent challenges.

H. Trial counsel should determine at the earliest possible time what aggravating factors the prosecution will rely upon in seeking the death penalty and what evidence will be offered in support thereof. If the jurisdiction has rules regarding notification of these factors, counsel at all stages of the case should object to any non-compliance, and if such rules are inadequate, counsel at all stages of the case should challenge the adequacy of the rules.

I. Counsel at all stages of the case should carefully consider whether all or part of the aggravating evidence may appropriately be challenged as improper, inaccurate, misleading or not legally admissible.

J. If the prosecution is granted leave at any stage of the case to have the client interviewed by witnesses associated with the government, defense counsel should:

1. carefully consider

a. what legal challenges may appropriately be made to the interview or the conditions surrounding it, and

b. the legal and strategic issues implicated by the client's co-operation or non-cooperation;

2. insure that the client understands the significance of any statements made during such an interview; and

3. attend the interview.

K. Trial counsel should request jury instructions and verdict forms that ensure that jurors will be able to consider and give effect to all relevant mitigating evidence. Trial counsel should object to instructions or verdict forms that are constitutionally flawed, or are inaccurate, or confusing and should offer alternative instructions. Post-conviction counsel should pursue these issues through factual investigation and legal argument.

L.   Counsel at every stage of the case should take advantage of all appropriate opportunities to argue why death is not suitable punishment for their particular client.

GUIDELINE 10.12—THE OFFICIAL PRESENTENCE REPORT

A.   If an official presentence report or similar document may or will be presented to the court at any time, counsel should become familiar with the procedures governing preparation, submission, and verification of the report. In addition, counsel should:

1.   where preparation of the report is optional, consider the strategic implications of requesting that a report be prepared;
2.   provide to the report preparer information favorable to the client. In this regard, counsel should consider whether the client should speak with the person preparing the report; if the determination is made to do so, counsel should discuss the interview in advance with the client and attend it;
3.   review the completed report;
4.   take appropriate steps to ensure that improper, incorrect or misleading information that may harm the client is deleted from the report;
5.   take steps to preserve and protect the client's interests where the defense considers information in the presentence report to be improper, inaccurate or misleading.

GUIDELINE 10.13—THE DUTY TO FACILITATE THE WORK OF SUCCESSOR COUNSEL

In accordance with professional norms, all persons who are or have been members of the defense team have a continuing duty to safeguard the interests of the client and should cooperate fully with successor counsel. This duty includes, but is not limited to:

A.   maintaining the records of the case in a manner that will inform successor counsel of all significant developments relevant to the litigation;

B.   providing the client's files, as well as information regarding all aspects of the representation, to successor counsel;

C.   sharing potential further areas of legal and factual research with successor counsel; and

D.   cooperating with such professionally appropriate legal strategies as may be chosen by successor counsel.

GUIDELINE 10.14—DUTIES OF TRIAL COUNSEL AFTER CONVICTION

A. Trial counsel should be familiar with all state and federal post-conviction options available to the client. Trial counsel should discuss with the client the post-conviction procedures that will or may follow imposition of the death sentence.

B. Trial counsel should take whatever action(s), such as filing a notice of appeal, and/or motion for a new trial, will maximize the client's ability to obtain post-conviction relief.

C. Trial counsel should not cease acting on the client's behalf until successor counsel has entered the case or trial counsel's representation has been formally terminated. Until that time, Guideline 10.15.1 applies in its entirety.

D. Trial counsel should take all appropriate action to ensure that the client obtains successor counsel as soon as possible.

GUIDELINE 10.15.1—DUTIES OF POST-CONVICTION COUNSEL

A. Counsel representing a capital client at any point after conviction should be familiar with the jurisdiction's procedures for setting execution dates and providing notice of them. Post-conviction counsel should also be thoroughly familiar with all available procedures for seeking a stay of execution.

B. If an execution date is set, post-conviction counsel should immediately take all appropriate steps to secure a stay of execution and pursue those efforts through all available fora.

C. Post-conviction counsel should seek to litigate all issues, whether or not previously presented, that are arguably meritorious under the standards applicable to high quality capital defense representation, including challenges to any overly restrictive procedural rules. Counsel should make every professionally appropriate effort to present issues in a manner that will preserve them for subsequent review.

D. The duties of the counsel representing the client on direct appeal should include filing a petition for certiorari in the Supreme Court of the United States. If appellate counsel does not intend to file such a petition, he or she should immediately notify successor counsel if known and the Responsible Agency.

E. Post-conviction counsel should fully discharge the ongoing obligations imposed by these Guidelines, including the obligations to:

1. maintain close contact with the client regarding litigation developments; and

2. continually monitor the client's mental, physical and emotional condition for effects on the client's legal position;

3. keep under continuing review the desirability of modifying prior counsel's theory of the case in light of subsequent developments; and

4. continue an aggressive investigation of all aspects of the case.

GUIDELINE 10.15.2—DUTIES OF CLEMENCY COUNSEL

A. Clemency counsel should be familiar with the procedures for and permissible substantive content of a request for clemency.

B. Clemency counsel should conduct an investigation in accordance with Guideline 10.7.

C. Clemency counsel should ensure that clemency is sought in as timely and persuasive a manner as possible, tailoring the presentation to the characteristics of the particular client, case and jurisdiction.

D. Clemency counsel should ensure that the process governing consideration of the client's application is substantively and procedurally just, and, if it is not, should seek appropriate redress.

References

Abramson, Stacy and David Isay (2002) "The Stopping Point: Interview with a Tie-Down Officer," pp. 169-173 in D.R. Dow and M. Dow (eds.) *Machinery of Death: The Reality of America's Death Penalty Regime.* New York: Routledge.

"Accusations Cost Chemist Job." *The Orlando Sentinel* (September 26), p. A13.

Acker, James R. (2006) "The Myth of Closure and Capital Punishment," pp. 167-175 in R.M. Bohm and J.T. Walker (eds.) *Demystifying Crime and Criminal Justice.* Los Angeles, CA: Roxbury.

Acker, James R. (1996) "The Death Penalty: A 25-Year Retrospective and a Perspective on the Future." *Criminal Justice Review* 21:139-60.

Acker, James R. and David R. Karp (2006) "Introduction," pp. 3-14 in J.R. Acker and D.R. Karp (eds.) *Wounds That Do Not Bind: Victim-Based Perspectives on the Death Penalty.* Durham, NC: Carolina Academic Press.

Acker, James R. and Charles S. Lanier (2000) "May God—or the Governor—Have Mercy: Executive Clemency and Executions in Modern Death-Penalty Systems." *Criminal Law Bulletin* 36:200-237.

Acker, James R. and Charles S. Lanier (1999) "Ready for the Defense? Legislative Provisions Governing the Appointment of Counsel in Capital Cases." *Criminal Law Bulletin* 35:429-477.

Acker, James R. and Charles S. Lanier (1998) "Death Penalty Legislation: Past, Present, and Future," pp. 77-115 in J.R. Acker, R.M. Bohm, and C.S. Lanier (eds.) *America's Experiment with Capital Punishment: Reflections on the Past, Present and Future of the Ultimate Penal Sanction.* Durham, NC: Carolina Academic Press.

Acker, James R. and Charles S. Lanier (1995) "Matters of Life or Death: The Sentencing Provisions in Capital Punishment Statutes." *Criminal Law Bulletin* 31:19-60.

Acker, James R. and Jeanna Marie Mastrocinque (2006) "Causing Death and Sustaining Life: The Law, Capital Punishment, and Criminal Homicide Victims' Survivors," pp. 141-160 in J.R. Acker and D.R. Karp (eds.) *Wounds That Do Not Bind: Victim-Based Perspectives on the Death Penalty.* Durham, NC: Carolina Academic Press.

"Alabama Inmate Becomes Oldest Executed Since '41" (2004) *The Orlando Sentinel* (August 6), p. A4.

Alter, Jonathan (2000) "A Reckoning on Death Row." *Newsweek* (July 3), p. 31.

Alter, Jonathan (2000) "The Death Penalty on Trial." *Newsweek* (June 12), pp. 24-34.

Alter, Jonathan and Mark Miller (2000) "A Life or Death Gamble." *Newsweek* (May 29), pp. 23-27.

"A Matter of Life and Death: The Effect of Life-Without-Parole Statutes on Capital Punishment," (2006) *Harvard Law Review* 119:1838-1854 at www.harvardlawreview. org/issues/119/april06/notes/capital_punishment.pdf.

American Bar Association (2006) *Evaluating Fairness and Accuracy in State Death Penalty Systems: The Georgia Death Penalty Assessment Report.* The report can be found at the Death Penalty Information Center website, www.deathpenalty info.org.

American Bar Association (2003) "Guidelines for the Appointment and Performance of Defense Counsel in Death Penalty Cases in the Summer 2003." *Hofstra Law Review* 31(4):913-1090. (accessed online.).

American Correctional Association 2005 Directory:Adult and Juvenile Correctional Departments, Institutions, Agencies and Probation and Parole Authorities (Lanham, MD: American Correctional Association, 2005),

Amnesty International Website Against the Death Penalty, 2002, "Facts and Figures on the Death Penalty," www.amnesty.org.

Amsterdam, Anthony G. (1982) "Capital Punishment," pp. 346-358 in H.A. Bedau (ed.) *The Death Penalty in America*, Third Ed. New York: Oxford University Press.

Ancel, Marc (1967) "The Problem of the Death Penalty," pp. 3-21 in T. Sellin (ed.) *Capital Punishment*. New York: Harper & Row.

Andersen, Kurt (1983) "An Eye for an Eye." *Time* (January 24), pp. 28-39.

Antonio, Michael E. (2006) "Jurors' Emotional Reactions to Serving on a Capital Trial." *Judicature* 89:282-288.

Applegate, Brandon K., Francis T. Cullen, Bonnie S. Fisher, and Thomas Vander Ven (2002) "Forgiveness and Fundamentalism: Reconsidering the Relationship Between Correctional Attitudes and Religion." *Criminology* 38: 719-753.

Archer, Dane, Rosemary Gartner, and Marc Beittel (1983) "Homicide and the Death Penalty: A Cross-National Test of a Deterrence Hypothesis." *Journal of Criminal Law and Criminology* 74:991-1013.

Arkin, Stephen D. (1980) "Discrimination and Arbitrariness in Capital Punishment: An Analysis of Post-Furman Murder Cases in Dade County, Florida, 1973-1976." *Stanford Law Review* 33:75-101.

Armbrust, Shawn (2002) "Chance and the Exoneration of Anthony Porter," pp. 157-166 in D.R. Dow and M. Dow (eds.) *Machinery of Death: The Reality of America's Death Penalty Regime*. New York: Routledge.

Arthur, John (1998) "Proximate Correlates of Black's Support for Capital Punishment." *Journal of Crime and Justice* 21:159-172.

Atwell, Mary Welek (2004) *Evolving Standards of Decency: Popular Culture and Capital Punishment*. New York: Peter Lang.

Bailey, William C. (1998) "Deterrence, Brutalization, and the Death Penalty: Another Examination of Oklahoma's Return to Capital Punishment." *Criminology* 36:711-733.

Bailey, William C. (1991) "The General Prevention Effect of Capital Punishment for Non-Capital Felonies," pp. 21-38 in R.M. Bohm (ed.) *The Death Penalty in America: Current Research*. Cincinnati, OH: Anderson Publishing Co.

Bailey, William C. (1990) "Murder and Capital Punishment: An Analysis of Television Execution Publicity." *American Sociological Review* 55:1308-1333.

Bailey, William C. (1984a) "Disaggregation in Deterrence and Death Penalty Research: The Case of Murder in Chicago." *Journal of Criminal Law and Criminology* 74:827-859.

Bailey, William C. (1984b) "Murder and Capital Punishment in the Nation's Capital." *Justice Quarterly* 1:211-233.

Bailey, William C. (1983) "The Deterrent Effect of Capital Punishment during the 1950s." *Suicide* 13:95-107.

Bailey, William C. (1980) "Deterrence and the Celerity of the Death Penalty: A Neglected Question in Deterrence Research." *Social Forces* 58:1308-1333.

Bailey, William C. (1979a) "The Deterrent Effect of the Death Penalty for Murder in California." *Southern California Law Review* 52:743-764.

Bailey, William C. (1979b) "The Deterrent Effect of the Death Penalty for Murder in Ohio: A Time-Series Analysis." *Cleveland State Law Review* 28:51-81.

Bailey, William C. (1979c) "Deterrence and the Death Penalty for Murder in Oregon." *Willamette Law Review* 16:67-85.

Bailey, William C. (1979d) "An Analysis of the Deterrent Effect of the Death Penalty in North Carolina." *North Carolina Central Law Journal* 10:29-52.

Bailey, William C. (1978) "Deterrence and the Death Penalty for Murder in Utah: A Time-Series Analysis." *Journal of Contemporary Law* 5:1-20.

Bailey, William C. (1977a) "Imprisonment v. the Death Penalty as a Deterrent to Murder." *Law and Human Behavior* 1:239-260.

Bailey, William C. (1977b) "Deterrence and the Violent Sex Offender: Imprisonment vs. the Death Penalty." *Journal of Behavioral Economics* 6:107-144.

Bailey, William C. (1974) "Murder and the Death Penalty." *Journal of Criminal Law and Criminology* 65:416-423.

Bailey, William C. and Ruth D. Peterson (1994) "Murder, Capital Punishment, and Deterrence: A Review of the Evidence and an Examination of Police Killings." *Journal of Social Issues* 50:53-74.

Bailey, William C. and Ruth D. Peterson (1989) "Murder and Capital Punishment: A Monthly Time-Series Analysis of Execution Publicity." *American Sociological Review* 54:722-743.

Bailey, William C. and Ruth D. Peterson (1987) "Police Killings and Capital Punishment: The Post-*Furman* Period." *Criminology* 25:1-25.

Baldus, David C. (2006) Personal correspondence with the author (April 26).

Baldus, David C. and James W.L. Cole (1975) "Statistical Evidence on the Deterrent Effect of Capital Punishment: A Comparison of the Work of Thorsten Sellin and Isaac Ehrlich on the Deterrent Effect of Capital Punishment." *Yale Law Journal* 85:17-186.

Baldus, David C. and George Woodworth (1998) "Racial Discrimination and the Death Penalty: An Empirical and Legal Overview," pp. 385-415 in J.R. Acker, R.M. Bohm, and C.S. Lanier (eds.) *America's Experiment with Capital Punishment: Reflections on the Past, Present and Future of the Ultimate Penal Sanction*. Durham, NC: Carolina Academic Press.

Baldus, David C. and George Woodworth (1997) "Race Discrimination in America's Capital Punishment System Since *Furman v. Georgia* (1972): The Evidence of Race Disparities and the Record of Our Courts and Legislatures in Addressing This Issue." Report prepared for the American Bar Association. Cited in Dieter, Richard C. (1998) "The Death Penalty in Black & White: Who Lives, Who Dies, Who Decides." Death Penalty Information Center, www.deathpenaltyinfo.org/racerpt.html.

Baldus, David C., George G. Woodworth, and Charles A. Pulaski (1990) *Equal Justice and the Death Penalty: A Legal and Empirical Analysis*. Boston: Northeastern University Press.

Baldus, David C., Charles Pulaski, Jr., and George Woodworth (1986) "Arbitrariness and Discrimination in the Administration of the Death Penalty: A Challenge to State Supreme Courts." *Stetson Law Review* 15:133-261.

Baldus, David C., Charles Pulaski, and George Woodworth (1983) "Comparative Review of Death Sentences: An Empirical Study of the Georgia Experience." *Journal of Criminal Law and Criminology* 74:661-753.

Baldus, David C., George Woodworth, Gary L. Young, and Aaron M. Christ (2001) "The Disposition of Nebraska Capital and Non-Capital Homicide Cases (1973-1999): A Legal and Empirical Analysis." The Nebraska Commission on Law Enforcement and Criminal Justice, www.nol.org/home/crimecom/homicide/homicide.htm.

Baldus, David C., George Woodworth, David Zuckerman, Neil Alan Weiner, and Barbara Broffitt (1998) "Race Discrimination and the Death Penalty in the Post-*Furman* Era: An Empirical and Legal Overview, with Preliminary Findings from Philadelphia." *Cornell Law Review* 83:1638-1770.

Banner, Stuart (2002) T*he Death Penalty: An American History*. Cambridge: Harvard University Press.

Barkan, Steven E. and Steven F. Cohn (1994) "Racial Prejudice and Support for the Death Penalty by Whites." *Journal of Research in Crime and Delinquency* 31:202-209.

Barnett, Arnold (1985) "Some Distribution Patterns for the Georgia Death Sentence." *University of California Davis Law Review* 18:1327-1374.

Barnett, Arnold (1981) "The Deterrent Effect of Capital Punishment: A Test of Some Recent Studies." *Operations Research* 29:346-370.

Baumer, Eric P., Steven F. Messner, and Richard Rosenfeld (2003) "Explaining Spatial Variation in Support for Capital Punishment: A Multilevel Analysis." *American Journal of Sociology* 108:844-875.

Beccaria, Cesare (1975) *On Crimes and Punishments*. Translated, with an introduction by Harry Paolucci. Indianapolis, IN: Bobbs-Merrill.

Bedau, Hugo Adam (2004) "An Abolitionist's Survey of the Death Penalty in America Today," pp. 15-50 in H.A. Bedau and P.G. Cassell (eds.) *Debating the Death Penalty: Should America Have Capital Punishment? The Experts on Both Sides Make Their Best Case*. New York: Oxford.

Bedau, Hugo Adam (1999) "Abolishing the Death Penalty Even for the Worst Murderers," pp. 40-59 in A. Sarat (ed.) *The Killing State: Capital Punishment in Law, Politics, and Culture*. New York: Oxford University Press.

Bedau, Hugo Adam (1997) *The Death Penalty in America: Current Controversies*. New York: Oxford University Press.

Bedau, Hugo Adam (1987) *Death is Different: Studies in the Morality, Law, and Politics of Capital Punishment*. Boston: Northeastern University Press.

Bedau, Hugo Adam (ed.) (1982) *The Death Penalty in America*, Third Ed. New York: Oxford University Press.

Bedau, Hugo Adam (ed.) (1967) *The Death Penalty in America: An Anthology*, Rev. Ed. Chicago: Aldine.

Bedau, Hugo Adam and Michael L. Radelet (1988) "The Myth of Infallibility: A Reply to Markman and Cassell." *Stanford Law Review* 41:161-170.

Bedau, Hugo Adam and Michael L. Radelet (1987) "Miscarriages of Justice in Potentially Capital Cases." *Stanford Law Review* 40:21-179.

Berk, Richard (2005) "New Claims about Executions and General Deterrence: Déjà vu All Over Again?" http://preprints.stat.ucla.edu/download.php?paper=396

Berlow, Alan (2003) "The Texas Clemency Memos." *The Atlantic Monthly* (July/August), pp. 91-96.

Beyleveld, Deryck (1982) "Ehrlich's Analysis of Deterrence." *The British Journal of Criminology* 22:101-123.

Bienen, Leigh B. (1996) "The Proportionality Review of Capital Cases by State High Courts After Gregg: Only 'The Appearance of Justice'?" *Journal of Criminal Law and Criminology* 87:130-314.

Bienen, Leigh B., Neil Alan Weiner, Deborah W. Denno, Paul D. Allison, and Douglas Lane Mills (1988) "The Reimposition of Capital Punishment in New Jersey: The Role of Prosecutorial Discretion." *Rutgers Law Review* 41:27-372.

"Birmingham News Criticizes Costly, Arbitrary Death Penalty," (2005) *The Birmingham News* (December 7) at www.deathpenaltyinfo.org/article.php?scid=7&did=851.

Blankenship, Michael B., James Luginbuhl, Francis T. Cullen, and William Redick (1997) "Jurors' Comprehension of Sentencing Instructions: A Test of the Death Penalty Process in Tennessee." *Justice Quarterly* 14:325-346.

Blecker, Robert (2006) "A Poster Child For Us." *Judicature* 89:297-301.

Blecker, Robert (2001) "The U.S. Needs to Rethink How It Applies Death Penalty." *The Orlando Sentinel* (from *The Washington Post*) (January 7), p. G1.

Bobo, Lawrence D. and Devon Johnson (2004) "A Taste for Punishment: Black and White Americans' Views on the Death Penalty and the War on Drugs." *Du Bois Review* 1:151-180.

Bohm, Robert M. (1994) "Capital Punishment in Two Judicial Circuits in Georgia: A Description of the Key Actors and the Decision-Making Process." *Law and Human Behavior* 18:319-338.

Bohm, Robert M. (1992a) "Toward an Understanding of Death Penalty Opinion Change in the United States: The Pivotal Years, 1966 and 1967." *Humanity and Society* 16:524-542.

Bohm, Robert M. (1992b) "Retribution and Capital Punishment: Toward a Better Understanding of Death Penalty Opinion." *Journal of Criminal Justice* 20:227-236.

Bohm, Robert M. (1991) "American Death Penalty Opinion, 1936-1986: A Critical Examination of the Gallup Polls," pp. 113-145 in R.M. Bohm (ed.) *The Death Penalty in America: Current Research*. Cincinnati: Anderson Publishing Co.

Bohm, Robert M. (1990) "Death Penalty Opinions: Effects of a Classroom Experience and Public Commitment." *Sociological Inquiry* 60:285-297.

Bohm, Robert M. (1989) "The Effects of Classroom Instruction and Discussion on Death Penalty Opinions: A Teaching Note." *Journal of Criminal Justice* 17:123-131.

Bohm, Robert M. (1987) "American Death Penalty Attitudes: A Critical Examination of Recent Evidence." *Criminal Justice and Behavior* 14:380-396.

Bohm, Robert M. and Keith N. Haley (2007) *Introduction to Criminal Justice*, Fourth Ed. Update. New York: McGraw-Hill.

Bohm, Robert M. and Brenda L. Vogel (2004) "More Than Ten Years After: The Long-Term Stability of Informed Death Penalty Opinions." *Journal of Criminal Justice* 32:307-327.

Bohm, Robert M. and Ronald E. Vogel (1994) "A Comparison of Factors Associated with Uninformed and Informed Death Penalty Opinions." *Journal of Criminal Justice* 22:125-143.

Bohm, Robert M., Ronald E. Vogel, and Albert A. Maisto (1993) "Knowledge and Death Penalty Opinion: A Panel Study." *Journal of Criminal Justice* 21:29-45.

Bohm, Robert M., Louise J. Clark, and Adrian F. Aveni (1991) "Knowledge and Death Penalty Opinion: A Test of the Marshall Hypotheses." *Journal of Research in Crime and Delinquency* 28:360-387.

Bohm, Robert M., Louise J. Clark, and Adrian F. Aveni (1990) "The Influence of Knowledge on Death Penalty Opinions: An Experimental Test." *Justice Quarterly* 7:175-188.

Bonczar, Thomas P. and Tracy L.Snell (2005) "Capital Punishment 2004." U.S. Department of Justice, *Bureau of Justice Statistics Bulletin* (November).

Boots, Paquette Denise, John K. Cochran, and Kathleen M. Heide (2003) "Capital Punishment Preferences for Special Offender Populations." *Journal of Criminal Justice* 31:553-565.

Borg, Marian J. (1998) "Vicarious Homicide Victimization and Support for Capital Punishment: A Test of Black's Theory of Law." *Criminology* 36:537-567.

Borg, Marian J. (1997) "The Southern Subculture of Punitiveness? Regional Variation in Support for Capital Punishment." *Journal of Research in Crime and Delinquency* 34:25-46.

Bowers, William J. (1995) "The Capital Jury Project: Rationale, Design, and Preview of Early Findings." *Indiana Law Journal* 70:1043-1102.

Bowers, William J. (1993) "Capital Punishment and Contemporary Values: People's Misgivings and the Court's Misperceptions." *Law and Society Review* 27:157-175.

Bowers, William J. (1988) "The Effect of Executions is Brutalization, Not Deterrence," pp. 49-89 in K.C. Haas and J.A. Inciardi (eds.) *Challenging Capital Punishment: Legal and Social Science Approaches*. Newbury Park, CA: Sage.

Bowers, William J. and Wanda D. Foglia (2003) "Still Singularly Agonizing: Law's Failure to Purge Arbitrariness from Capital Sentencing." *Criminal Law Bulletin* 39:51-86.

Bowers, William J. and Glenn L. Pierce (1980) "Deterrence or Brutalization: What Is the Effect of Executions?" *Crime and Delinquency* 26:453-484.

Bowers, William J. and Glenn L. Pierce (1975) "The Illusion of Deterrence in Isaac Ehrlich's Research on Capital Punishment." *Yale Law Journal* 85:187-208.

Bowers, William J. and Benjamin D. Steiner (1999) "Death by Default: An Empirical Demonstration of False and Forced Choices in Capital Sentencing." *Texas Law Review* 77:605-717.

Bowers, William J. and Benjamin D. Steiner (1998) "Choosing Life or Death: Sentencing Dynamics in Capital Cases," pp. 309-349 in J.R. Acker, R.M. Bohm, and C.S. Lanier (eds.) *America's Experiment with Capital Punishment: Reflections on the Past, Present and Future of the Ultimate Penal Sanction.* Durham, NC: Carolina Academic Press.

Bowers, William J. with Glenn L. Pierce and John F. McDevitt (1984) *Legal Homicide: Death as Punishment in America, 1864-1982.* Boston: Northeastern University Press.

Bowers, William J., Marla Sandys, and Benjamin D. Steiner (1998) "Foreclosed Impartiality in Capital Sentencing: Jurors' Predispositions, Guilt-Trial Experience, and Premature Decision Making." *Cornell Law Review* 83:1476-1556.

Bowers, William J., Benjamin D. Steiner, and Marla Sandys (2001) "Death Sentencing in Black and White: An Empirical Analysis of the Role of Jurors' Race and Jury Racial Composition." *University of Pennsylvania Journal of Constitutional Law* 3:171-274.

Bowers, William J., Margaret Vandiver, and Patricia H. Dugan (1994) "A New Look at Public Opinion on Capital Punishment: What Citizens and Legislators Prefer." *American Journal of Criminal* Law 22:77-150.

Bradley, Craig M. (2006) "The Right Decision on the Juvenile Death Penalty." *Judicature* 89:302-303, 305.

Brier, Stephen and Stephen Feinberg (1980) "Recent Econometric Modeling of Crime and Punishment: Support for the Deterrence Hypothesis?" *Evaluation Research* 4:147-191.

Bright, Stephen B. (2004) "Why the United States Will Join the Rest of the World in Abandoning Capital Punishment," pp. 152-182 in H.A. Bedau and P.G. Cassell (eds.) *Debating the Death Penalty: Should America Have Capital Punishment? The Experts on Both Sides Make Their Best Case.* New York: Oxford.

Bright, Stephen B. (2002) "Discrimination, Death, and Denial: Race and the Death Penalty," pp. 45-78 in D.R. Dow and M. Dow (eds.) *Machinery of Death: The Reality of America's Death Penalty Regime.* New York: Routledge.

Bright, Stephen B. (1998) "The Politics of Capital Punishment: The Sacrifice of Fairness for Executions," pp. 117-135 in J.R. Acker, R.M. Bohm, and C.S. Lanier (eds.) *America's Experiment with Capital Punishment: Reflections on the Past, Present and Future of the Ultimate Penal Sanction.* Durham, NC: Carolina Academic Press.

Bright, Stephen B. (1997) *Capital Punishment on the 25th Anniversary of Furman v. Georgia.* Atlanta, GA: Southern Center for Human Rights.

Bright, Stephen B. (1997b) "Neither Equal Nor Just: The Rationing and Denial of Legal Services to the Poor When Life and Liberty Are at Stake." *Annual Survey of American Law* 1997:783-836.

Bright, Stephen B. (1995) "Discrimination, Death and Denial: The Tolerance of Racial Discrimination in the Infliction of the Death Penalty." *Santa Clara Law Review* 35:433–483.

Bright, Stephen B. and Patrick J. Keenan (1995) "Judges and the Politics of Death: Deciding Between the Bill of Rights and the Next Election in Capital Cases." *Boston University Law Review* 75:759–835.

Brock, Deon, Nigel Cohen, and Jonathan Sorensen (2000) "Arbitrariness in the Imposition of Death Sentences in Texas: An Analysis of Four Counties by Offense Seriousness, Race of Victim, and Race of Offender." *American Journal of Criminal Law* 28:43–71.

Britt, Chester L. (1998) "Race, Religion, and Support for the Death Penalty: A Research Note." *Justice Quarterly* 15:175–191.

Bronson, Edward J. (1970) "On the Conviction Proneness and Representativeness of the Death-Qualified Jury: An Empirical Study of Colorado Veniremen." *University of Colorado Law Review* 42:1–32.

Brooks, Justin and Jeanne Huey Erikson (1996) "The Dire Wolf Collects His Due While the Boys Sit by the Fire: Why Michigan Cannot Afford to Buy into the Death Penalty." *Thomas M. Cooley Law Review* 13:877–905.

Brumm, Harold J. and Dale O. Cloninger (1996) "Perceived Risk of Punishment and the Commission of Homicides: A Covariance Structure Analysis." *Journal of Economic Behavior and Analysis* 31:1–11.

Brunsvold, Michelle L. (2004) "Medicating to Execute: *Singleton v. Norris*." *Chicago-Kent Law Review* 79:1291–1311.

Burnett, Cathleen (2005) "Restorative Justice and Wrongful Capital Convictions: A Simple Proposal." *Journal of Contemporary Criminal Justice* 21:272–289.

Burnett, Cathleen (2002) *Justice Denied: Clemency Appeals in Death Penalty Cases*. Boston: Northeastern University Press.

Bye, Raymond T. (1919) *Capital Punishment in the United States*. Philadelphia: The Committee of Philanthropic Labor of Philadelphia Yearly Meeting of Friends.

Cabana, Donald A. (1996). *Death at Midnight:The Confession of an Executioner*. Boston: Northeastern University Press.

California Department of Corrections and Rehabilitation, "Lethal Injection Procedures" at www.cya.ca.gov/ReportsResearch/lethalInjection.html (accessed March 31, 2006).

Callahan, Lisa, James R. Acker, and Catherine Cerulli (2000) "Accommodating Death Penalty Legislation: Personal and Professional Views of Assistant District Attorneys Toward Capital Punishment." *American Journal of Criminal Justice* 25:15–29.

Camp, Camille Graham and George M. Camp (1994) *The Corrections Yearbook 1994*. South Salem, NY: Criminal Justice Institute.

Canan, Russell F. (1989) "Burning at the Wire: The Execution of John Evans," pp. 60–80 in M.L. Radelet (ed.) *Facing the Death Penalty: Essays on a Cruel and Unusual Punishment*. Philadelphia: Temple University Press.

Carmichael, Stokely and Charles V. Hamilton (1967) *Black Power: The Politics of Liberation in America*. New York: Vintage Books.

Carroll, Joseph (2004) "Who Supports the Death Penalty?" The Gallup Organization (November 16) at www.deathpenaltyinfo.org/article.php?scid=23&did=1266

Carter, Dan T. (1969) *Scottsboro: A Tragedy of the American South*. New York: Oxford University Press.

Cassell, Paul G. (2004) "In Defense of the Death Penalty," pp. 183-217 in H.A. Bedau and P.G. Cassell (eds.) *Debating the Death Penalty: Should America Have Capital Punishment? The Experts on Both Sides Make Their Best Case*. New York: Oxford.

Cavender, Gray (1995) "Joining the Fray: An Interview with William J. Bowers." *American Journal of Criminal Justice* 20:113-136.

Cheatwood, Derral (1993) "Capital Punishment and Deterrence of Violent Crime in Comparable Counties." *Criminal Justice Review* 18:165-181.

Clarke, Alan W., Eric Lambert, and Laurie Anne Whitt (2000-2001) "Executing the Innocent: The Next Step in the Marshall Hypotheses." *Review of Law and Social Change* 26:309-345.

Clary, Susan (2001) "Killer's Defense Cost Will Set Record." *The Orlando Sentinel* (December 1), p. C1.

Cloninger, Dale O. (1977) "Death and the Death Penalty: A Cross-Sectional Analysis." *Journal of Behavioral Economics* 6:87-106.

Cloninger, Dale O. and Roberto Marchesini (2001) "Execution and Deterrence: A Quasi-Controlled Group Experiment." *Applied Economics* 33:569-576.

Cochran, John K. and Mitchell B. Chamlin (2006) "The Enduring Racial Divide in Death Penalty Support." *Journal of Criminal Justice* 34:85-99.

Cochran, John K. and Mitchell B. Chamlin (2005) "Can Information Change Public Opinion?: Another Test of the Marshall Hypotheses." *Journal of Criminal Justice* 33:573-584.

Cochran, John K. and Mitchell B. Chamlin (2000) "Deterrence and Brutalization: The Dual Effect of Executions." *Justice Quarterly* 17:685-706.

Cochran, John K., Mitchell B. Chamlin, and Mark Seth (1994) "Deterrence or Brutalization? An Impact Assessment of Oklahoma's Return to Capital Punishment." *Criminology* 32:107-134.

Cohen, Sharon (1999) "Mistakes Refocus Death-Penalty Debate." *The Orlando Sentinel* (August 15), p. A-4.

Cole, Richard (1984) "Florida's Execution Lead Is Attributed to History." *The Anniston* [AL] *Star* (November 22).

Coleman, Charisse (2006) "Matters of Life or Death," pp. 17-32 in J.R. Acker and D.R. Karp (eds.) *Wounds That Do Not Bind: Victim-Based Perspectives on the Death Penalty*. Durham, NC: Carolina Academic Press.

Committee on the Judiciary, U.S. Senate (1982) "Capital Punishment as a Matter of Legislative Policy," pp. 311-318 in H.A. Bedau (ed.) *The Death Penalty in America*, Third Ed. New York: Oxford University Press.

"Convicted Killer Put to Death by Electric Chair in Virginia." (2006) *The Orlando Sentinel* (July 21), p. A15.

Cook, Philip J. and Donna B. Slawson with Lori A. Gries (1993) *The Costs of Processing Murder Cases in North Carolina*. Raleigh, NC: North Carolina Administrative Office of the Courts.

"Costly Death Penalty Takes Toll on State Budgets," (2003) *Lakeland Ledger* (December 14) at www.deathpenaltyinfo.org/article.php?scid=7&did=851.

Cottingham, John (1979) "Varieties of Retributivism." *Philosophical Quarterly* 29:238-246.

"Court Backs Death-Row Man." (2001) *The Orlando Sentinel* (August 14), p. A7.

Cowan, Claudia, William C. Thompson, and Phoebe C. Ellsworth (1984) "The Effects of Death Qualification on Jurors' Predisposition to Convict and on the Quality of Deliberation." *Law and Human Behavior* 8:53-79.

Cox, David (1999) "Provenzano Loses Again." *The Orlando Sentinel* (September 4), p. D-1.

Cox, Archibald (1987) *The Court and the Constitution*. Boston: Houghton Mifflin.

Coyle, Marcia, Fred Strasser, and Marianne Lavelle (1990) "Fatal Defense: Trial and Error in the Nation's Death Belt." *The National Law Journal* 12 (No. 40, June 11):30-44.

Coyne, Randall and Lyn Entzeroth (2001) *Capital Punishment and the Judicial Process*, 2nd ed. Durham, NC: Carolina Academic Press.

Coyne, Randall and Lyn Entzeroth (1998) *Capital Punishment and the Judicial Process: 1998 Supplement*. Durham, NC: Carolina Academic Press.

Coyne, Randall and Lyn Entzeroth (1994) *Capital Punishment and the Judicial Process*. Durham, NC: Carolina Academic Press.

Crespi, Irving (1971) "What Kinds of Attitude Measures Are Predictive of Behavior?" *Public Opinion Quarterly* 35:327-334.

Crocker, Phyllis L. (2002) "Is the Death Penalty Good for Women?" pp. 195-224 in D.R. Dow and M. Dow (eds.) *Machinery of Death: The Reality of America's Death Penalty Regime*. New York: Routledge.

Culver, John H. (1985) "The States and Capital Punishment: Executions from 1977–1984." *Justice Quarterly* 2:567-578.

Cushing, Renny (2002) "Amazing Grace: Reflections on Justice, Survival, and Healing," pp. 283-287 in D.R. Dow and M. Dow (eds.) *Machinery of Death: The Reality of America's Death Penalty Regime*. New York: Routledge.

Dann, Robert H. (1935) "The Deterrent Effect of Capital Punishment." *Friends Social Service Series* 29:1-20.

Davey, Monica and Steve Mills (2003) "Illinois Governor Sweeps Inmates from Death Row." *The Orlando Sentinel* (January 12), p. A1.

Davis, Kevin (1998) "Hope Sought for Innocents Sentenced to Die." *USA Today* (November 13), p. 14A.

Death Penalty Information Center, www.deathpenaltyinfo.org.

"Death Penalty Expenses Adding Up," *New York Daily News* (October 20, 1999) at www.th-record.com/1999/10/20/executio.htm.

"Death Penalty Has Cost New Jersey Taxpayers $253 Million" (2005) *Newsday* (November 21) at www.deathpenaltyinfo.org/article.php?scid=7&did=85.

"Death Penalty in California Is Very Costly" (2006) *Lodi News-Sentinel* (March 11) at www.deathpenaltyinfo.org/newsanddev.php?scid=7.

"Death Penalty Prosecutions May Be Halted if Funding Is Inadequate," (2005) *ABA Journal* (April 15) at www.deathpenaltyinfo.org/article.php?scid=7&did=851.

Death Row, U.S.A. (2007) Criminal Justice Project, NAACP Legal Defense and Educational Fund, Inc. New York, NY 10013-2897 (99 Hudson St., Suite 1600) (Winter).

Death Row, U.S.A. (2006) Criminal Justice Project, NAACP Legal Defense and Educational Fund, Inc. New York, NY 10013-2897 (99 Hudson St., Suite 1600) (Winter).

Death Row, U.S.A. (2006) Criminal Justice Project, NAACP Legal Defense and Educational Fund, Inc. New York, NY 10013-2897 (99 Hudson St., Suite 1600) (Summer).

Death Row, U.S.A. (2002) Criminal Justice Project, NAACP Legal Defense and Educational Fund, Inc. New York, NY 10013-2897 (99 Hudson St., Suite 1600) (Spring).

Death Row, U.S.A. (1998) NAACP Legal Defense and Educational Fund, Inc. New York, NY 10013-2897 (99 Hudson St., Suite 1600) (Spring).

Death Row, U.S.A. (1996) NAACP Legal Defense and Educational Fund, Inc. New York, NY 10013-2897 (99 Hudson St., Suite 1600).

Decker, Scott H. and Carol W. Kohfeld (1990) "The Deterrent Effect of Capital Punishment in the Five Most Active Execution States: A Time-Series Analysis." *Criminal Justice Review* 15:173-191.

Decker, Scott H. and Carol W. Kohfeld (1988) "Capital Punishment and Executions in the Lone Star State: A Deterrence Study." *Criminal Justice Research Bulletin* 3:1-6.

Decker, Scott H. and Carol W. Kohfeld (1987) "An Empirical Analysis of the Effect of the Death Penalty in Missouri." *Journal of Crime and Justice* 10:23-45.

Decker, Scott H. and Carol W. Kohfeld (1986) "The Deterrent Effect of Capital Punishment in Florida: A Time Series Analysis." *Criminal Justice Policy Review* 1:422-437.

Decker, Scott H. and Carol W. Kohfeld (1984) "A Deterrence Study of the Death Penalty in Illinois, 1933-1980." *Journal of Criminal Justice* 12:367-379.

DeFronzo, J. (1979) "In Search of the Behavioral and Attitudinal Consequences of Victimization." *Sociological Spectrum* 25:23-39.

Denno, Deborah W. (2002) "When Legislatures Delegate Death: The Troubling Paradox Behind State Uses of Electrocution and Lethal Injection and What it Says about Us." *Ohio State Law Journal* 63:63-260 at http://moritzlaw.osu.edu/lawjournal/issues/volume63/number1/denno.html.

Denno, Deborah W. (1998) "Execution and the Forgotten Eighth Amendment," pp. 547-577 in J.R. Acker, R.M. Bohm, and C.S. Lanier (eds.) *America's Experiment with Capital Punishment: Reflections on the Past, Present and Future of the Ultimate Penal Sanction*. Durham, NC: Carolina Academic Press.

Denno, Deborah W. (1997) "Getting to Death: Are Executions Constitutional?" *Iowa Law Review* 82:319-464 (citations are from a draft copy).

Denno, Deborah W. (1994) "Is Electrocution an Unconstitutional Method of Execution? The Engineering of Death over the Century." *William and Mary Law Review* 35:551–692.

Dezhbakhsh, Hashem, Paul H. Rubin, and Joanna Mehlop Shepherd (2003) "Does Capital Punishment Have a Deterrent Effect? New Evidence from Post–Moratorium Panel Data." *American Law and Economic Review* 5:344-376.

Dickson, Brent E. (2006) "Effects of Capital Punishment on the Justice System: Reflections of a State Supreme Court Justice." *Judicature* 89:278-281.

Dieter, Richard C. (2006) Executive Director, The Death Penalty Information Center,. Personal communication (September 27, 2006).

Dieter, Richard C. (2005) "Costs of the Death Penalty and Related Issues," Testimony before the New York State Assembly: Standing Committees on Codes, Judiciary, and Correction (January 25) at www.deathpenaltyinfo.org ("Costs").

Dieter, Richard C. (2004) *Innocence and the Crisis of the American Death Penalty.* Washington, DC: The Death Penalty Information Center.

Dieter, Richard C. (1996) *Killing for Votes: The Dangers of Politicizing the Death Penalty Process.* Washington, DC: The Death Penalty Information Center.

Dieter, Richard C. (1993) *Sentencing for Life: Americans Embrace Alternatives to the Death Penalty.* Washington, DC: The Death Penalty Information Center.

Dieter, Richard C. (1992) *Millions Misspent: What Politicians Don't Say About the High Costs of the Death Penalty.* Washington, DC: The Death Penalty Information Center.

Dillehay, Ronald C. and Marla R. Sandys (1996) "Life Under *Wainwright v. Witt*: Juror Dispositions and Death Qualification." *Law and Human Behavior* 20:147-165.

Dinnerstein, Leonard (1968) *The Leo Frank Case.* New York: Columbia University Press.

Dow, David R. (2005) *Executed on a Technicality: Lethal Injustice on America's Death Row.* Boston: Beacon Press.

Dow, David R. (2002a) "Introduction: The Problem of 'Innocence'," pp. 1-8 in D.R. Dow and M. Dow (eds.) *Machinery of Death: The Reality of America's Death Penalty Regime.* New York: Routledge.

Dow, David R. (2002b) "How the Death Penalty Really Works," pp. 11-35 in D.R. Dow and M. Dow (eds.) *Machinery of Death: The Reality of America's Death Penalty Regime.* New York: Routledge.

Drizin, Steven A. and Richard A. Leo (2004) "The Problem of False Confessions in the Post-DNA World." *North Carolina Law Review* 82:891-1007.

Durham, Alexis M., H. Preston Elrod, and Patrick T. Kinkade (1996) "Public Support for the Death Penalty: Beyond Gallup." *Justice Quarterly* 13:705-736.

Ehrlich, Isaac (1982) "On Positive Methodology, Ethics, and Polemics in Deterrence Research." *British Journal of Criminology* 22:124-139.

Ehrlich, Isaac (1977) "Capital Punishment and Deterrence: Some Further Thoughts and Additional Evidence." *Journal of Political Economy* 85:741-788.

Ehrlich, Isaac (1975) "The Deterrent Effect of Capital Punishment: A Question of Life and Death." *American Economic Review* 65:397–417.

Ehrlich, Isaac and Zhiqiang Liu (1999) "Sensitivity Analysis of the Deterrence Hypothesis: Let's Keep the Econ in Econometrics." *Journal of Law and Economics* 42:455–488.

Einwechter, Jack E. (1998) Material graciously provided to the author in August. (Major Einwechter is a professor of Criminal Law at The Judge Advocate General's School, Charlottesville, VA.)

Eisenberg, Theodore, Stephen P. Garvey, and Martin T. Wells (2006) "Victim Characteristics and Victim Impact Evidence in South Carolina Capital Cases," pp. 297-321 in J.R. Acker and D.R. Karp (eds.) *Wounds That Do Not Bind: Victim-Based Perspectives on the Death Penalty*. Durham, NC: Carolina Academic Press.

Eisenberg, Theodore, Stephen P. Garvey, and Martin T. Wells (2001) "Forecasting Life and Death: Juror Race, Religion, and Attitude Toward the Death Penalty." *Journal of Legal Studies* 30:277-311.

Eisenberg, Theodore and Martin T. Wells (1993–1994) "Deadly Confusion: Juror Instructions in Capital Cases." *Cornell Law Review* 79:1–17.

Ekland-Olson, Sheldon (1988) "Structured Discretion, Racial Bias and the Death Penalty: The First Decade after *Furman* in Texas." *Social Science Quarterly* 69:853–873.

Ellis, Carroll Ann, Karin Ho, and Anne Seymour (2006) "The Impact of the Death Penalty on Crime Victims and Those Who Serve Them," pp. 431-444 in J.R. Acker and D.R. Karp (eds.) *Wounds That Do Not Bind: Victim-Based Perspectives on the Death Penalty*. Durham, NC: Carolina Academic Press.

Ellsworth, Phoebe C. and Samuel R. Gross (1994) "Hardening of the Attitudes: Americans' Views on the Death Penalty." *Journal of Social Issues* 50:19–52.

Ellsworth, Phoebe C. and Lee Ross (1983) "Public Opinion and Capital Punishment: A Close Examination of the Views of Abolitionists and Retentionists." *Crime and Delinquency* 29:116–169.

Erez, Edna (1981) "Thou Shalt Not Execute: Hebrew Law Perspective on Capital Punishment." *Criminology* 19:25–43.

Erikson, R.S. (1976) "The Relationship between Public Opinion and State Policy: A New Look at Some Forgotten Data." *American Journal of Political Science* 20:25–36.

Erskine, Helen (1970) "The Polls: Capital Punishment." *Public Opinion Quarterly* 34:290–307.

Eschholz, Sarah, Mark D. Reed, Elizabeth Beck, and Pamela Blume Leonard (2003) "Offenders' Family Members' Responses to Capital Crimes: The Need for Restorative Justice Initiatives." *Homicide Studies* 7:154-181.

Espy, M. Watt and John O. Smykla (1987) *Executions in the United States, 1608-1987: The Espy File*. Machine-readable data file. Ann Arbor, MI: Inter-University Consortium for Political and Social Research.

"Executions by Lethal Injection Being Challenged around the Country" (2005) The Death Penalty Information Center at www.deathpenaltyinfo.org/newsanddev.php ?scid=8&scyr=2005.

Facts on File (1979) *Facts on File Yearbook*, edited by L.A. Sobel. New York: Facts on File, Inc.

Facts on File (1961) *Facts on File Yearbook*, edited by L.A. Sobel. New York: Facts on File, Inc.

Facts on File (1960) *Facts on File Yearbook*, edited by L.A. Sobel. New York: Facts on File, Inc.

Facts on File (1959) *Facts on File Yearbook*, edited by L.A. Sobel. New York: Facts on File, Inc.

Facts on File (1958) *Facts on File Yearbook*, edited by L.A. Sobel. New York: Facts on File, Inc.

Facts on File (1957) *Facts on File Yearbook*, edited by L.A. Sobel. New York: Facts on File, Inc.

Facts on File (1956) *Facts on File Yearbook*, edited by L.A. Sobel. New York: Facts on File, Inc.

Facts on File (1955) *Facts on File Yearbook*, edited by L.A. Sobel. New York: Facts on File, Inc.

Fagan, Jeffrey (2005) "Deterrence and the Death Penalty: A Critical Review of New Evidence." Testimony to the New York State Assembly Standing Committee on Codes, Assembly Standing Committee on Judiciary and Assembly Standing Committee on Correction, Hearings on the Future of Capital Punishment in the State of New York (January 21), http://www.deathpenaltyinfo.org/article.php?scid=12&did=167.

Fan, David P., Kathy A. Keltner, and Robert O. Wyatt (2002) "A Matter of Guilt or Innocence: How News Reports Affect Support for the Death Penalty." *International Journal of Public Opinion Research* 14:439-451.

Federal Bureau of Investigation (2005) *Crime in the United States 2004*. U.S. Department of Justice, Washington, DC:GPO at www.fbi.gov/ucr/05cius/.

Federal Bureau of Investigation (2001) *Crime in the United States 2000*. U.S. Department of Justice, Washington, DC:GPO.

Federal Bureau of Investigation (1997) *Crime in the United States 1996*. U.S. Department of Justice, Washington, DC:GPO.

"Federal Judge Requires Medically Trained Personnel for North Carolina Lethal Injection." (2006) The Death Penalty Information Center at www.deathpenaltyinfo.org/news anddev.php?scid=8.

Federman, Cary and Dave Holmes (2005) "Breaking Bodies Into Pieces: Time, Torture and Bio-Power." *Critical Criminology* 13:327-345.

Ferrero, Eric (2006) Director of Communications, The Innocence Project. Personal Communication (September 27, 2006).

Filler, Louis (1967) "Movements to Abolish the Death Penalty in the United States," pp. 104–122 in T. Sellin (ed.) *Capital Punishment*. New York: Harper & Row.

Finckenauer, James O. (1988) "Public Support for the Death Penalty: Retribution as Just Deserts or Retribution as Revenge?" *Justice Quarterly* 5:81-100.

Firment, Kimberley A. and Edward Geiselman (1997) "University Students' Attitudes and Perceptions of the Death Penalty." *American Journal of Forensic Psychology* 15:65-89.

Fitzgerald, Robert and Phoebe C. Ellsworth (1984) "Due Process vs. Crime Control: Death Qualification and Jury Attitudes." *Law and Human Behavior* 8:31-51.

Foley, Linda (1987) "Florida after the *Furman* Decision: The Effect of Extralegal Factors on the Processing of Capital Offense Cases." *Behavioral Sciences & the Law* 5:457-465.

Forst, Brian E. (1977) "The Case Against Capital Punishment: A Cross-State Analysis of the 1960's." *Minnesota Law Review* 61:743-767.

Fox, James Alan, Michael L. Radelet, and Julie L. Bonsteel (1990-1991) "Death Penalty Opinion in the Post-*Furman* Years." *New York University Review of Law and Social Change* 18:499-528.

Frank, James and Brandon K. Applegate (1998) "Assessing Juror Understanding of Capital-Sentencing Instructions." *Crime and Delinquency* 44:412-433.

Freedman, Eric M. (1998) "Federal Habeas Corpus in Capital Cases," pp. 417-436 in J.R. Acker, R.M. Bohm, and C.S. Lanier (eds.) *America's Experiment with Capital Punishment: Reflections on the Past, Present and Future of the Ultimate Penal Sanction*. Durham, NC: Carolina Academic Press.

Freedman, Monroe H. (2003) "The Professional Obligation To Raise Frivolous Issues in Death Penalty Cases." *Hofstra Law Review* 31:1167-1180.

French, Howard W. (2002) "Japanese Keep Executions Secret." *The Orlando Sentinel* (June 30), p. A25.

Friedman, Lee (1979) "The Use of Multiple Regression Analysis to Test for a Deterrent Effect of Capital Punishment: Prospects and Problems," pp. 61-87 in S. Messinger and E. Bittner (eds.) *Criminology Review Yearbook*. Beverly Hills, CA: Sage.

Furillo, Andy (2005) "Life of Gang Founder in Schwarzenegger's Hands." *The Orlando Sentinel* (November 21), p. A6.

Gaddis, Thomas (1979) *Birdman of Alcatraz*. Ithaca, NY: Comstock Book Distributors.

Gale, M.E. (1985) "Retribution, Punishment, and Death." *University of California, Davis Law Review* 18:973-1035.

Galliher, John F., Larry W. Koch, David Patrick Keys, and Teresa J. Guess (2002) *America without the Death Penalty: States Leading the Way*. Boston: Northeastern University Press.

Galliher, John F., Gregory Ray, and Brent Cook (1992) "Abolition and Reinstatement of Capital Punishment during the Progressive Era and Early 20th Century." *The Journal of Criminal Law and Criminology* 83:538-576.

Gallup, George, Jr. (1995) *The Gallup Poll Monthly*, No. 357. Princeton, NJ: The Gallup Poll (June).

Gallup, Alec and Frank Newport (1991) "Death Penalty Support Remains Strong." *The Gallup Poll Monthly* (June).

Gallup Report (1985) "Support for Death Penalty Highest in Half-Century." Princeton, NJ: The Gallup Report.

Garey, Margot (1985) "The Cost of Taking a Life: Dollars and Sense of the Death Penalty." *University of California, Davis Law Review* 18:1221-1273.

Garner, Bryan A. (ed.) (2000) *Blacks Law Dictionary*, abridged seventh edition. St. Paul, MN: West.

Garvey, Stephen P., Sheri Lynn Johnson, and Paul Marcus (1999-2000) "Correcting Deadly Confusion: Responding to Jury Inquiries in Capital Cases." *Cornell Law Review* 85:627-655.

Gearan, Anne (2002) "Supreme Court Takes Up Claim of Poor Defense in Death Cases." *The Orlando Sentinel* (March 26), p. A11.

Gelineau, Kristen (2006) "DNA Confirms Guilt of Man Executed in '92." *The Orlando Sentinel* (January 13), p. A5.

"Georgia Judge Notes Expensive Bottom Line in Capital Cases," (2002) *Atlanta Journal-Constitution* (May 12) at www.deathpenaltyinfo.org/article.php?scid=7&did=851.

"Georgia Killer Is Granted His Wish to be Executed." (1998) *The Orlando Sentinel* (October 14), p. A-14.

Gibbs, Jack P. (1978) "The Death Penalty, Retribution and Penal Policy." *Journal of Criminal Law and Criminology* 69:291-299.

Gibson, William E. (2002) "Justices Weigh Case that Could Affect Up to 870 on Death Row." *The Orlando Sentinel* (April 23), p. A1.

Gillespie, L. Kay (2003) *Inside the Death Chamber: Exploring Executions.* Boston: Allyn and Bacon.

Gillette, Dane R. (2006) "Defending Death Penalty Judgment." *Judicature* 89:262-264.

Glaser, Daniel (1979) "Capital Punishment—Deterrent or Stimulus to Murder? Our Unexamined Deaths and Penalties." *University of Toledo Law Review* 10:317-333.

Goldberg, Faye (1970) "Toward Expansion of Witherspoon: Capital Scruples, Jury Bias, and Use of Psychological Data to Raise Presumptions in the Law." *Harvard Civil Rights-Civil Liberties Law Review* 5:53-69.

Gorecki, Jan (1983) *Capital Punishment: Criminal Law and Social Evolution.* New York: Columbia University Press.

Gottlieb, Gerald H. (1961) "Testing the Death Penalty." *Southern California Law Review* 34:268-281.

Governor's Commission on Capital Punishment (2002) State of Illinois. www.idoc.state.il.us/ccp/ccp/reports/commission_reports.html.

Gow, Haven Bradford (1986) "Religious Views Support the Death Penalty," pp. 79-85 in B. Szumski, L. Hall, and S. Bursell (eds.) *The Death Penalty: Opposing Viewpoints.* St. Paul, MN: Greenhaven.

Grasmick, Harold G., John K. Cochran, Robert J. Bursik, Jr., and M'Lou Kimpel (1993) "Religion, Punitive Justice, and Support for the Death Penalty." *Justice Quarterly* 10:289-314.

Grimes, Ruth-Ellen M. (1996) "Walnut Street Jail," pp. 493-497 in M.D. McShane and F.P. Williams III (eds.) *Encyclopedia of American Prisons.* New York and London: Garland.

Groner, Jonathan I. (2005) "Inadequate Anaesthesia in Lethal Injection for Execution." *The Lancet* 366 (accessed through www.sciencedirect.com).

Gross, Samuel R. (1998) "Lost Lives: Miscarriages of Justice in Capital Cases." *Law and Contemporary Problems* 61:125-152.

Gross, Samuel R. (1996) "The Risks of Death: Why Erroneous Convictions Are Common in Capital Cases." *Buffalo Law Review* 44:469-500.

Gross, Samuel R. (1984) "Determining the Neutrality of Death-Qualified Juries: Judicial Appraisal of Empirical Data." *Law and Human Behavior* 8:7-30.

Gross, Samuel, Kristen Jacoby, Daniel J. Matheson, Nicholas Montgomery, Sujata Patil (2004) "Exonerations in the United States, 1989 through 2003 at www.umich.edu/NewsAndInfo/exonerations-in-us.pdf.

Gross, Samuel R. and Robert Mauro (1989) *Death and Discrimination: Racial Disparities in Capital Sentencing*. Boston: Northeastern University Press.

Gross, Samuel R. and Robert Mauro (1984) "Patterns of Death: An Analysis of Racial Disparities in Capital Sentencing and Homicide Victimization." *Stanford Law Review* 37:27-153.

"Growing Elderly Population on Death Row" (2005) *USA Today* (February 10) at www.deathpenaltyinfo.org/article.php?&did=1708.

Guin, Cecile C. (2002) "An Eagle Soars: The Legacy of Mr. Smile," pp. 225-240 in D.R. Dow and M. Dow (eds.) *Machinery of Death: The Reality of America's Death Penalty Regime*. New York: Routledge.

Haas, Kenneth C. and James A. Inciardi (eds.) (1988) *Challenging Capital Punishment: Legal and Social Science Approaches*. Newbury Park, CA: Sage.

Hagan, John (1974) "Extra-Legal Attributes and Criminal Sentencing: An Assessment of a Sociological Viewpoint." *Law and Society Review* 8:357-383.

Haines, Errin (2006) "Civil-Rights-Era Crimes Receive Renewed Focus." *The Orlando Sentinel* (April 29), p. A25.

Haines, Herbert H. (1996) *Against Capital Punishment: The Anti-Death Penalty Movement in America, 1972-1994*. New York: Oxford University Press.

Hammel, Andrew (2002) "Jousting with the Juggernaut," pp. 107-126 in D.R. Dow and M. Dow (eds.) *Machinery of Death: The Reality of America's Death Penalty Regime*. New York: Routledge.

Haney, Craig (2005) *Death By Design: Capital Punishment As A Social Psychological System*. New York: Oxford University Press.

Haney, Craig (2003) "Mitigation and the Study of Lives: On the Roots of Violent Criminality and the Nature of Capital Justice," pp. 469-500 in J.R. Acker, R.M. Bohm, and C.S. Lanier (eds.) *America's Experiment with Capital Punishment: Reflections on the Past, Present and Future of the Ultimate Penal Sanction*, 2nd ed. Durham, NC: Carolina Academic Press.

Haney, Craig (1984) "On the Selection of Capital Juries: The Biasing Effects of the Death-Qualification Process." *Law and Human Behavior* 8:121-132.

Haney, Craig and Deana Dorman Logan (1994) "Broken Promise: The Supreme Court's Response to Social Science Research on Capital Punishment." *Journal of Social Issues* 50:75-100.

Haney, Craig, Lorelei Sontag, and Sally Costanzo (1994) "Deciding to Take a Life: Capital Juries, Sentencing Instructions, and the Jurisprudence of Death." *Journal of Social Issues* 50:149-176.

"'Hanging Judge' Calls for End to the Death Penalty" (2005) *Orange County Register* (June 24) at www.deathpenaltyinfo.org/article.php?scid=7&did=851.

Hans, Valerie P. (1988) "Death by Jury," pp. 149-175 in K.C. Haas and J.A. Inciardi (eds.) *Challenging Capital Punishment: Legal and Social Science Approaches.* Newbury Park, CA: Sage.

Hansen, Mark (2000) "Dearth of Volunteers: 16 States Require Civilian Witnesses to Ensure Dignity at Execution." *American Bar Association Journal*, www.abanet.org/journal/current/nwitns.html (July 21).

Harmon, Talia Roitberg (2001) "Predictors of Miscarriages of Justice in Capital Cases." *Justice Quarterly* 18:949-968.

Harmon, Talia Roitberg and William S. Lofquist (2005) "Too Late for Luck: A Comparison of Post-Furman Exonerations and Executions of the Innocent." *Crime & Delinquency* 51:498-520.

Harries, Keith and Derral Cheatwood (1997) *The Geography of Execution: The Capital Punishment Quagmire in America.* Lanham, MD: Rowman and Littlefield.

Harris, Philip W. (1986) "Oversimplification and Error in Public Opinion Surveys on Capital Punishment." *Justice Quarterly* 3:429-455.

Harris, Ron (2000) "Former Gangster Nominated for Peace Prize." *The San Francisco Examiner* (November 19), p. C-2.

Harrison, Paige M. and Allen J. Beck (2006) "Prison and Jail Inmates at Midyear 2005," U.S. Department of Justice, Bureau of Justice Statistics Bulletin (May).

Hastings, Deborah (2001) "Facts Disputed in Execution Case." *The Orlando Sentinel* (August 30), p. A3.

Hawkins, Bill (2006) "Capital Punishment and the Administration of Justice: A Trial Prosecutor's Perspective." *Judicature* 89:258-261.

Healy, Thomas (2001) "Swing Justice O'Connor Expresses Qualms about Death Penalty." *The Orlando Sentinel* (July 4), p. A4.

Heath, Mark J.S., Donald R. Stanski, and Derrick J. Pounder (2005) "Inadequate Anaesthesia in Lethal Injection for Execution." *The Lancet* 366 (accessed through www.sciencedirect.com).

Heider, F. (1958) *The Psychology of Interpersonal Relations.* New York: Wiley.

Heilbrun, Jr., Alfred B., Lynn C. Heilbrun, and Kim L. Heilbrun (1978) "Impulsive and Premeditated Homicide: An Analysis of Subsequent Parole Risk of the Murderer." *Journal of Criminal Law and Criminology* 69:108-114.

Herbert, Bob (2000) "What If You're Not Guilty?" *The New York Times* (April 16).

Hintze, Michael (2006) "Tinkering with the Machinery of Death: Capital Punishment's Toll on the American Judiciary." *Judicature* 89:254-257.

Hoffmann, Joseph L. (1995) "Where's the Buck?—Juror Misperception of Sentencing Responsibility in Death Penalty Cases." *Indiana Law Journal* 70:1137-1160.

Hoffmann, Joseph L. (1993) "On the Perils of Line-Drawing: Juveniles and the Death Penalty," pp. 117-132 in V.L. Streib (ed.) *A Capital Punishment Anthology.* Cincinnati: Anderson Publishing Co.

Holmes, William L. (2004) "Man is Cleared in 1984 Slaying." *The Orlando Sentinel* (April 17), p. A9.

Hood, Roger (2002) *The Death Penalty: A Worldwide Perspective*, Third Ed. New York: Oxford University Press.

Hood, William W. III (1989) "The Meaning of 'Life' for Virginia Jurors and Its Effect on Reliability in Capital Sentencing." *Virginia Law Review* 75:1605-1637 at web.lexis-nexis.com.ucfproxy.fcla.edu/universe/document?_m=41ffaeccc13ad4707b82ddbeb 9613e00&_docnum=1&wchp=dGLbVzz-zSkVA&_md5=ce4ed8343380 cb42d1d64b9aa47cfee3.

Hoppe, Christy (1992) "Life in Jail, or Death? Life Term is Cheaper." *The Charlotte* [North Carolina] *Observer* (March 22), p. 12A.

Howstuffworks: "How Lethal Injection Works" (2002) www.howstuffworks.com/lethal-injection2.htm.

Howard, Jr., Roscoe C. (1996) "The Defunding of the Post Conviction Defense Organizations as a Denial of the Right to Counsel." *West Virginia Law Review* 98:863-921.

Huff, C. Ronald, Arye Rattner, and Edward Sagarin (1986) "Guilty Until Proven Innocent: Wrongful Conviction and Public Policy." *Crime and Delinquency* 32:518-544.

"Indiana Editorial Calls For End to 'Costly; Death Penalty," (2005) *Fort Wayne Journal Gazette* (June 22) at www.deathpenaltyinfo.org/article.php?scid=7&did=85.

The Indiana Law Blog (2005) "Ind. Law – How in the Modern Media Age Can a Notorious Defendant Accused of a Heinous Crime Get a Constitutionally Fair Trial?" (November 29) at http://indianalawblog.com/archives/2005/11/ind_law_how_in.html.

"Indiana Taxpayers Charged Over $2 Million for Defense of Three Capital Cases." (1999) *Indianapolis Star/News* (February 7) at www.deathpenaltyinfo.org/article.php?scid=7&did=851.

Ingle, Joseph B. (1989) "Ministering to the Condemned: A Case Study," pp. 112-122 in M.L. Radelet (ed.) *Facing the Death Penalty: Essays on a Cruel and Unusual Punishment*. Philadelphia: Temple University Press.

Innocence Project at www.innocentproject.org.

Jackson, Rev. Jesse with Jesse Jackson, Jr. (1996) *Legal Lynching: Racism, Injustice and the Death Penalty*. New York: Marlowe.

Jacoby, Joseph and Raymond Paternoster (1982) "Sentencing Disparity and Jury Packing: Further Challenges to the Death Penalty." *Journal of Criminal Law and Criminology* 73:379-387.

Jacoby, Susan (1983) *Wild Justice: The Evolution of Revenge*. New York: Harper and Row.

Johnson, Robert (2003) "Life under Sentence of Death: Historical and Contemporary Perspectives," pp. 647-671 in J.R. Acker, R.M. Bohm, and C.S. Lanier (eds.) *America's Experiment with Capital Punishment: Reflections on the Past, Present and Future of the Ultimate Penal Sanction*, 2nd ed. Durham, NC: Carolina Academic Press.

Johnson, Robert (1998) *Death Work: A Study of the Modern Execution Process*, Second Ed. Belmont, CA: West/Wadsworth.

Johnson, Robert (1990) *Death Work: A Study of the Modern Execution Process*. Pacific Grove, CA: Brooks/Cole.

Johnson, Robert (1989) *Condemned to Die: Life Under Sentence of Death*. Prospect Heights, IL: Waveland.

Johnson, Devon (2003) "Set in Stone? Support for Capital Punishment among White and Black Americans." Paper presented at the annual meeting of the Academy of Criminal Justice Sciences.

Johnson, Devon (2001) "Punitive Attitudes on Crime: Economic Insecurity, Racial Prejudice, or Both?" *Sociological Focus* 34:33-54.

Joint Legislative Audit and Review Commission of the Virginia General Assembly (2002) Final Report (January 15), http://jlarc.state.va.us/pubs_rec.htm.

Jones, Jeffrey M. (2006) "Two in Three Favor Death Penalty for Convicted Murderers." The Gallup Organization, http://poll.gallup.com/content/?ci=23167asp.

Jones, Jeffrey M. (2002) "Slim Majority of Americans Say Death Penalty Applied Fairly." The Gallup Organization, www.gallup.com/poll/releases/pr020520.asp.

Jones, Jeffrey M. (2001) "Two-Thirds of Americans Support the Death Penalty." The Gallup Organization, www.gallup.com/poll/releases/pr010302.asp.

Jones, Peter R. (1994) "It's Not What You Ask, It's the Way that You Ask It: Question Form and Public Opinion on the Death Penalty." *The Prison Journal* 74:32-50.

Jurow, George L. (1971) "New Data on the Effect of a 'Death Qualified' Jury on the Guilt Determination Process." *Harvard Law Review* 84:567-611.

"Jury: Freed Inmate to Get $2.25 Million" (2006) *The Orlando Sentinel* (May 6), p. A2.

"Justice for All Act of 2004: Section-By-Section Analysis" at http://leahy.senate.gov/press/200410/SectionbySectionDNA.htm.

Kaczynski, David and Gary Wright (2006) "Building a Bridge," pp. 85-101 in J.R. Acker and D.R. Karp (eds.) *Wounds That Do Not Bind: Victim-Based Perspectives on the Death Penalty*. Durham, NC: Carolina Academic Press.

Kania, Richard R.E. (1999) "The Ethics of the Death Penalty." *The Justice Professional* 12:145-157.

"Kansas Study Concludes Death Penalty Is Costly Policy" (2003) Performance Audit Report: Cost Incurred for Death Penalty Cases: A K-Goal Audit of the Department of Corrections (December) at www.deathpenaltyinfo.org/article.php?scid=7&did=851.

Kaplan, John (1983) "The Problem of Capital Punishment." *University of Illinois Law Review* 3:555-577.

Karp, David R. and Jarrett B. Warshaw (2006) "Their Day in Court: The Role of Murder Victims' Families in Capital Juror Decision Making," pp. 275-295 in J.R. Acker and D.R. Karp (eds.) *Wounds That Do Not Bind: Victim-Based Perspectives on the Death Penalty*. Durham, NC: Carolina Academic Press.

Katz, Lawrence, Steven D. Levitt, and Ellen Shustorovich (2003) "Prison Conditions, Capital Punishment, and Deterrence," *American Law and Economics Review* 5:318-343.

Kay, Judith W. (2006) "Is Restitution Possible for Murder?—Surviving Family Members Speak," pp. 323-347 in J.R. Acker and D.R. Karp (eds.) *Wounds That Do Not Bind: Victim-Based Perspectives on the Death Penalty*. Durham, NC: Carolina Academic Press.

Kehler, Larry, Sharon Sawatzky, Harry Huebner, Louise Dueck, Edgar Epp, and Clarence Epp (1985) *Capital Punishment Study Guide: For Groups and Congregations*. Winnipeg: Mennonite Central Committee Canada.

Keil, Thomas J. and Gennaro F. Vito (2006) "Capriciousness or Fairness? Race and Prosecutorial Decisions to Seek the Death Penalty in Kentucky." *Journal of Ethnicity in Criminal Justice* 4:27-49.

Keil, Thomas J. and Gennaro F. Vito (1995) "Race and the Death Penalty in Kentucky Murder Trials: 1976-1991." *American Journal of Criminal Justice* 20:17-36.

Keil, Thomas J. and Gennaro F. Vito (1990) "Race and the Death Penalty in Kentucky Murder Trials: An Analysis of Post-*Gregg* Outcomes." *Justice Quarterly* 7:189-207.

Keil, Thomas J. and Gennaro F. Vito (1989) "Race, Homicide Severity, and Application of the Death Penalty: A Consideration of the Barnett Scale." *Criminology* 27:511-535.

Kelsen, H. (1943) *Society and Nature*. Chicago: University of Chicago Press.

Kimble, Marsha (2006) "My Journey and the Riddle," pp. 127-138 in J.R. Acker and D.R. Karp (eds.) *Wounds That Do Not Bind: Victim-Based Perspectives on the Death Penalty*. Durham, NC: Carolina Academic Press.

King, David R. (1978) "The Brutalization Effect: Execution Publicity and and the Incidence of Homicide in South Carolina." *Social Forces* 57:683-687.

King, Glen D. (1982) "On Behalf of the Death Penalty," pp. 308-311 in H.A. Bedau (ed.) *The Death Penalty in America*, Third Ed. New York: Oxford University Press.

King, Rachel (2006) "The Impact of Capital Punishment on Families of Defendants and Murder Victims' Family Members." *Judicature* 89:292-296.

Kleck, Gary (1981) "Racial Discrimination in Criminal Sentencing: A Critical Evaluation of the Evidence with Additional Evidence of the Death Penalty." *American Sociological Review* 46:783-805.

Klein, Lawrence R., Brian Forst, and Victor Filatov (1982) "The Deterrent Effect of Capital Punishment: An Assessment of the Evidence," pp. 138-159 in H.A. Bedau (ed.) *The Death Penalty in America*, Third Ed. New York: Oxford University Press.

Klein, Stephen P. and John E. Rolph (1991) "Relationship of Offender and Victim Race to Death Penalty Sentences in California." *Jurimetrics* 32:33-48.

Kobil, Daniel T. (2003) "The Evolving Role of Clemency in Capital Cases," pp. 673-692 in J.R. Acker, R.M. Bohm, and C.S. Lanier (eds.) *America's Experiment with Capital Punishment: Reflections on the Past, Present and Future of the Ultimate Penal Sanction*, 2nd ed. Durham, NC: Carolina Academic Press.

Kohfeld, Carol W. and Scott H. Decker (1990) "Time Series, Panel Design and Criminology: A Multi-State, Multi-Wave Analysis of the Effect of the Death Penalty in Contiguous States," pp. 198-240 in K.L. Kempf (ed.) *Measurement Issues in Criminology*. New York: Springer-Verlag.

Kohlberg, Lawrence and Daniel Elfenbein (1975) "The Development of Moral Judgments Concerning Capital Punishment." *American Journal of Orthopsychiatry* 45:614-640.

Koniaris, Leonidas G., Teresa A. Zimmers, David A. Lubarsky, and Jonathan P. Sheldon (2005) "Inadequate Anaesthesia in Lethal Injection for Execution." *The Lancet* 365 (accessed through www.sciencedirect.com).

Kravets, David (2006) "Doctors Refuse to Help Execute California Killer." *The Orlando Sentinel* (February 22), p. A3.

Kroll, Michael A. (1989) "The Fraternity of Death," pp. 16–26 in M.L. Radelet (ed.) *Facing the Death Penalty: Essays on a Cruel and Unusual Punishment*. Philadelphia: Temple University Press.

Kubik, Jeffrey D. and John R. Moran (2003) "Lethal Elections: Gubernatorial Politics and the Timing of Executions." *The Journal of Law and Economics* 46 (accessed through http://web.lexis-nexis.com).

Kunerth, Jeff (2000) "Lethal Injection Has Its Problems, Too." *The Orlando Sentinel* (January 3), p. A-1.

Lambert, Eric and Alan Clarke (2001) "The Impact of Information on an Individual's Support of the Death Penalty: A Partial Test of the Marshall Hypothesis Among College Students."*Criminal Justice Policy Review* 12:215-234.

Lanier, Charles S. and Beau Breslin (2006) "Extinguishing the Victims' *Payne* or Acquiescing to the 'Demon of Error': Confronting the Role of Victims in Capital Clemency Proceedings," pp. 179-201 in J.R. Acker and D.R. Karp (eds.) *Wounds That Do Not Bind: Victim-Based Perspectives on the Death Penalty*. Durham, NC: Carolina Academic Press.

Larranaga, Mark A. and Donna Mustard (2004) "Washington's Death Penalty System: A Review of the Costs, Length, and Results of Capital Cases in Washington State" at www.deathpenaltyinfo.org/article.php?scid=7&did=85.

Lawrence, Charles R., III (1987) "The Id, the Ego, and Equal Protection: Reckoning with Unconscious Racism." *Stanford Law Review* 39:317–388.

Layson, Stephen K. (1985) "Homicide and Deterrence: A Reexamination of the United States Time–Series Evidence." *Southern Economy Journal* 52:68–89.

Leahy, Patrick (2004a) "Statement of Senator Patrick Leahy: The Justice For All Act of 2004," (October 9, 2004) at http://leahy.senate.gov/press/200410/100904B.html.

Leahy, Patrick (2004b) "Justice For All Act of 2004: Section-By-Section Analysis" at http://leahy.senate.gov/press/200410/100904E.html.

Lehner, Patrick (1996) "Abolition Now!!!" www.abolition-now.com.

Leighton, Paul S. (1999) "Televising Executions: Primetime 'Live'?" *The Justice Professional* 12:191–207.

"Lethal Injections: Some Cases Stayed, Other Executions Proceed," (2006) The Death Penalty Information Center at www.deathpenaltyinfo.org/article.php?did=1686&scid=64.

Leusner, Jim (2006) "Horrors Relived." *The Orlando Sentinel* (October 22), p. A1.

Leusner, Jim and Nin-Hai Tseng (2006) "Execution Sends Message to Other Death-Row Inmates." *The Orlando Sentinel* (September 21), p. A1.

Levey, Dan (2006) "Feelings from the Heart," pp. 33-47 in J.R. Acker and D.R. Karp (eds.) *Wounds That Do Not Bind: Victim-Based Perspectives on the Death Penalty*. Durham, NC: Carolina Academic Press.

Lewis, Dorothy Otnow, Jonathan H. Pincus, Barbara Bard, Ellis Richardson, Leslie S. Prichep, Marilyn Feldman, and Catherine Yeager (1988) "Neuropsychiatric, Psychoeducational, and Family Characteristics of 14 Juveniles Condemned to Death in the United States." *American Journal of Psychiatry* 145:584–589.

Leyte-Vidal, Henry and Scott J. Silverman (2006) "Living with the Death Penalty." *Judicature* 89:270-273.

Liebman, James S., Jeffrey Fagan, and Valerie West (2000) "A Broken System: Error Rates in Capital Cases, 1973-1995." The Justice Project, www.justice.policy.net/jpreport.html.

Lilly, J. Robert (1997) "Military Justice: A Neglected Topic." *ACJS Today* 15:11.

Lilly, J. Robert (1996) "Dirty Details: Executing U.S. Soldiers During World War II." *Crime and Delinquency* 42:491-516.

Lilly, J. Robert (1993) "Race and Capital Punishment in the Military: WWII." Paper presented at the annual meeting the American Society of Criminology, Phoenix, AZ, October.

Lilly, J. Robert, Peter Davies, and Richard A. Ball (1995) "Dirty Details: Executing U.S. Soldiers During World War II." Paper presented at the annual meeting the American Society of Criminology, Boston, MA, November.

Lindsey, Sue (2005) "Man Found Competent—Execution Set," *The Orlando Sentinel* (August 6), p. A20.

Liu, Zhiqiang (2004) "Capital Punishment and the Deterrence Hypothesis: Some New Insights and Empirical Evidence." *Eastern Economic Journal* 30:237-258.

Locke, John (1988, originally 1690) *Two Treatises of Government* (ed. by Peter Laslett). New York: Cambridge University Press.

Lofquist, William S. (2002) "Putting Them There, Keeping Them There, and Killing Them: An Analysis of State-Level Variations in Death Penalty Intensity." *Iowa Law Review* 87:1505-1557.

Logan, Wayne A. (2006) "Victims, Survivors, and the Decisions to Seek and Impose Death," pp. 161-177 in J.R. Acker and D.R. Karp (eds.) *Wounds That Do Not Bind: Victim-Based Perspectives on the Death Penalty*. Durham, NC: Carolina Academic Press.

Longmire, Dennis R. (1996) "Americans' Attitudes About the Ultimate Sanction Capital Punishment," pp. 93-108 in T.J. Flanagan and D.R. Longmire (eds.) *Americans View Crime and Justice: A National Public Opinion Survey*. Thousand Oaks, CA: Sage.

Lord, Charles G., Lee Ross, and Mark R. Lepper (1979) "Biased Assimilation and Attitude Polarization: The Effects of Prior Theories on Subsequently Considered Evidence." *Journal of Personality and Social Psychology* 37:2098-2109.

Lotz, Roy and Robert M. Regoli (1980) "Public Support for the Death Penalty. *Criminal Justice Review* 5:55-66.

Luginbuhl, James and Kathi Middendorf (1988) "Death Penalty Beliefs and Jurors' Responses to Aggravating and Mitigating Circumstances in Capital Trials." *Law and Human Behavior* 12:263-281.

Lytle, Tamara and John Kennedy (2006) "Top Court Halts Killer's Execution." *The Orlando Sentinel* (January 26), p. A1.

Maguire, Kathleen and Ann L. Pastore (eds.) (2006) *Sourcebook of Criminal Justice Statistics* [Online]. Available http://www.albany.edu/sourcebook [accessed September 15, 2006].

Maguire, Kathleen and Ann L. Pastore (eds.) (2001) *Sourcebook of Criminal Justice Statistics 2000*. U.S. Department of Justice, Bureau of Justice Statistics. Washington, DC: GPO.

Maguire, Kathleen and Ann L. Pastore (eds.) (1997) *Sourcebook of Criminal Justice Statistics 1996*. U.S. Department of Justice, Bureau of Justice Statistics. Washington, DC: GPO.

Mailer, Norman (1979) *The Executioner's Song*. Boston: Little, Brown.

"Man Executed in Mississippi is Oldest to Die Since 1970s" (2005) *The Orlando Sentinel* (December 15), p. A8.

Mandery, Evan J. (2005) *Capital Punishment: A Balanced Examination*. Sudbury, MA: Jones and Bartlett.

Markman, Stephen J. and Paul G. Cassell (1988) "Protecting the Innocent: A Response to the Bedau-Radelet Study." *Stanford Law Review* 41:121-160.

Markon, Jerry (2006) "Wrongfully Jailed Man Wins Suit: Va. Officer Falsified Confession, Jury Rules." *Washingtonpost.com* (May 6) at www.washingtonpost.com/wp-dyn/content/article/2006/05/05/AR2006050501617.html.

Marquart, James W. and Jonathan R. Sorensen (1989) "A National Study of the *Furman*-Commuted Inmates: Assessing the Threat to Society from Capital Offenders." *Loyola of Los Angeles Law Review* 23:101-120.

Marquart, James W. and Jonathan R. Sorensen (1988) "Institutional and Postrelease Behavior of *Furman*-Commuted Inmates in Texas." *Criminology* 26:677-693.

Marquart, James W., Sheldon Ekland-Olson, and Jonathan R. Sorensen (1994) *The Rope, The Chair, and the Needle: Capital Punishment in Texas, 1923-1990*. Austin: University of Texas Press.

Marquis, Joshua (2005) "The Myth of Innocence." *The Journal of Criminal Law & Criminology* 95:501-521.

Marquis, Joshua K. (2004) "Truth and Consequences: The Penalty of Death," pp. 117-151 in H.A. Bedau and P.G. Cassell (eds.) *Debating the Death Penalty: Should America Have Capital Punishment? The Experts on Both Sides Make Their Best Case*. New York: Oxford.

McAdams, John C. (1998) "Racial Disparity and the Death Penalty." *Law and Contemporary Problems* 61:153-170.

McCaffrey, Shannon (2002) "Justices Refuse to Review Execution of Juveniles." *The Orlando Sentinel* (October 22), p. A3.

McCarthy, Michael (2006) "Lethal Injection Challenged as 'Cruel and Unusual' Fate." *The Lancet* 367 (accessed through www.sciencedirect.com).

McCord, David (2006) "If Capital Punishment Were Subject to Consumer Protection Laws." *Judicature* 89:304-305.

McCord, David (2005) "Lightning Still Strikes: Evidence from the Popular Press That Death Sentencing Continues to Be Unconstitutionally Arbitrary More Than Three Decades After *Furman*." *Brooklyn Law Review* 71:797-927.

McCord, David (2002) "A Year in the Life of Death: Murders and Capital Sentences in South Carolina, 1998." *South Carolina Law Review* 53:250-359.

McCord, David (2000) "State Death Sentencing for Felony Murder Accomplices Under the Enmund and Tison Standards." *Arizona State Law Journal* 32:843-896.

McFarland, Sam G. (1983) "Is Capital Punishment a Short-Term Deterrent to Homicide? A Study of the Effects of Four Recent American Executions." *Journal of Criminal Law and Criminology* 74:1014-1030.

McGarrell, Edmund F. and Marla Sandys (1996) "The Misperception of Public Opinion Toward Capital Punishment: Examining the Spuriousness Explanation of Death Penalty Support." *American Behavioral Scientist* 39:500-513.

McGovern, James R. (1982) *Anatomy of a Lynching: The Killing of Claude Neal.* Baton Rouge: Louisiana State University Press.

Mello, Michael (1989) "Another Attorney for Life," pp. 81-91 in M.L. Radelet (ed.) *Facing the Death Penalty: Essays on a Cruel and Unusual Punishment*. Philadelphia: Temple University Press.

Mello, Michael and Paul J. Perkins (1998) "Closing the Circle: The Illusion of Lawyers for People Litigating for Their Lives at the Fin de Siecle," pp. 245-284 in J.R. Acker, R.M. Bohm, and C.S. Lanier (eds.) *America's Experiment with Capital Punishment: Reflections on the Past, Present and Future of the Ultimate Penal Sanction.* Durham, NC: Carolina Academic Press.

Meltsner, Michael (1973) *Cruel and Unusual: The Supreme Court and Capital Punishment*. New York: Random House.

Michel, Lou and Dan Herbeck (2001) *American Terrorist: Timothy McVeigh & the Oklahoma City Bombing*. New York: Regan Books.

Miller-Potter, Karen S. (2002) "Death by Innocence: Wrongful Convictions in Capital Cases." *The Advocate: A Journal of Criminal Justice Education and Research* 24:21-29.

Miller, Kent S. and Michael L. Radelet (1993) *Executing the Mentally Ill: The Criminal Justice System and the Case of Alvin Ford*. Newbury Park, CA: Sage.

Mintz, Howard (2002) "Public Has Right to See Executions, Court Rules," *The Orlando Sentinel* (August 3), p. A12.

Mocan, H. Naci and R. Kaj Gittings (2003) "Getting Off Death Row: Commuted Sentences and the Deterrent Effect of Capital Punishment." *Journal of Law and Economics* 46:453-478.

Mocan, H. Naci and R. Kaj Gittings (2001) "Pardons, Executions and Homicide." http://econ.cudenver.edu/mocan/papers.htm.

Monroe, A.D. (1979) "Consistency between Public Preferences and National Policy Decisions." *American Politics Quarterly* 7:3-19.

Montgomery, Lori (1994) "Rising Outrage Over Crime Puts U.S. Back in the Execution Business." *The Charlotte [NC] Observer* (April 3), p. 2A.

Moore, David W. (1994) "Majority Advocate Death Penalty for Teenage Killers." *The Gallup Poll Monthly*, September: 2-5.

Moran, Gary and John Craig Comfort (1986) "Neither 'Tentative' nor 'Fragmentary': Verdict Preference of Impaneled Felony Jurors as a Function of Attitude Toward Capital Punishment." *Journal of Applied Psychology* 71:146-155.

Murphy, Elizabeth (1984) "The Application of the Death Penalty in Cook County." *Illinois Bar Journal* 93:90-95.

Murray, Gregg R. (2003) "Raising Considerations: Public Opinion and the Fair Application of the Death Penalty." *Social Science Quarterly* 84:753-770.

Muwakkil, Salim (1989) "The Death Penalty and the Illusion of Justice." *In These Times*, Vol. 13, No. 26 (May 24–June 6), p. 6.

Nakell, Barry and Kenneth A. Hardy (1987) *The Arbitrariness of the Death Penalty*. Philadelphia: Temple University Press.

The National Coalition to Abolish the Death Penalty (2002) www.ncadp.org/html/factsandstats.html.

"New York Death Penalty Trial 3.5 Times More Costly than Non-Capital Trial," (1999) *Newsday* (July 12) at www.deathpenaltyinfo.org/article.php?scid=7&did=851.

New York State Defenders Association (1982) *Capital Losses: The Price of the Death Penalty for New York State*. Albany, NY: New York State Defenders Association, Inc.

"New York Times Series Examines Life Sentences" (2005) *New York Times* (October 2-3) at www.deathpenaltyinfo.org/article.php?&did=1708.

Niemi, Richard (1989) *Trends in Public Opinion: A Compendium of Survey Data*. New York: Greenwood Press.

Niven, David (2002) "Bolstering an Illusory Majority: The Effects of the Media's Portrayal of Death Penalty Support." *Social Science Quarterly* 83:671-689.

Online Sunshine View Statutes (2006) "The 2006 Florida Statutes." http://www.leg.state.fl.us/statutes/index.cfm?mode=View%20Statutes&SubMenu=1&App_mode=Display_Statute&Search_String=aggravating+circumstances&URL=CH0921/Sec141.HTM

Oskamp, Stuart (1977) *Attitudes and Opinions*. Englewood Cliffs, NJ: Prentice-Hall.

Ostling, Richard N. (2005) "Bishops Rally Against Death for Inmates." *The Orlando Sentinel* (March 22), p. A3.

Ottinger, Sarah (2002) "Representing Robert Sawyer," pp. 249-266 in D.R. Dow and M. Dow (eds.) *Machinery of Death: The Reality of America's Death Penalty Regime*. New York: Routledge.

Owens, Sherri M. (2002) "Execution May Hinge on Killer's Mental Condition." *The Orlando Sentinel* (January 29), p. D1.

Packer, Herbert L. (1968) *The Limits of the Criminal Sanction*. Stanford: Stanford University Press.

Paduano, Anthony and Clive A. Stanford Smith (1987) "Deathly Errors: Jurors Misperceptions Concerning Parole in the Imposition of the Death Penalty." *Columbia Human Rights Law Review* 18:211-257.

Page, Benjamin I. and Robert Y. Shapiro (1983) "Effects of Public Opinion on Policy." *American Political Science Review* 77:175-190.

Page, Benjamin I., Robert Y. Shapiro, and Glenn R. Dempsey (1987) "What Moves Public Opinion?" *American Political Science Review* 81:23-43.

Palacios, Victoria (1996) "Faith in Fantasy: The Supreme Court's Reliance on Commutation to Ensure Justice in Death Penalty Cases." *Vanderbilt Law Review* 49:311-372.

Parker, Gary (1991) "Prepared Statement of Gary Parker, Georgia State Senator, Fifteenth Senatorial District, Columbus, GA." Hearing before the Subcommittee on Civil and Constitutional Rights of the Committee on the Judiciary, House of Representatives, One Hundred First Congress, Second Session on H.R. 4618 Racial Justice Act of 1990, etc., May 3 and 9, 1990. Serial No. 125, U.S. Government Printing Office: Washington, DC.

"Partial Costs in the Virginia trials of John Muhammad and Lee Malvo," (2004) *Washington Post* (February 14) at www.deathpenaltyinfo.org/article.php?scid=7&did=851.

Passell, Peter (1975) "The Deterrent Effect of Capital Punishment: A Statistical Test." *Stanford Law Review* 28:61-80.

Passell, Peter and John B. Taylor (1977) "The Deterrent Effect of Capital Punishment: Another View." *American Economic Review* 67:445-451.

Patenaude, Allan L. (2001) "May God Have Mercy on Your Soul! Exploring and Teaching a Course on the Death Penalty." *Journal of Criminal Justice Education* 12:405-425.

Paternoster, Raymond (1991) *Capital Punishment in America*. New York: Lexington.

Paternoster, Raymond (1984) "Prosecutorial Discretion in Requesting the Death Penalty: The Case of Victim-Based Discrimination." *Law and Society Review* 18:437-478.

Paternoster, Raymond (1983) "Race of Victim and Location of Crime: The Decision to Seek the Death Penalty in South Carolina." *Journal of Criminal Law and Criminology* 74:754-785.

Paternoster, Raymond and Robert Brame (2003) "An Empirical Analysis of Maryland's Death Sentencing System with Respect to the Influence of Race and Legal Jurisdiction." Final Report. Study commissioned by the Maryland governor at www.urhome.umd.edu/newsdesk/pdf/finalrep.pdf.

Paternoster, Raymond and AnnMarie Kazyaka (1988) "The Administration of the Death Penalty in South Carolina: Experiences Over the First Few Years." *South Carolina Law Review* 39:245-414.

Perez-Pena, Richard (2000) "The Death Penalty: When There's No Room for Error." *The New York Times* (February 13), p. 3.

Petersilia, Joan (1990) "Death Penalty Resolution Debated and Endorsed." *The Criminologist* 15:1.

Peterson, Ruth D. and William C. Bailey (2003) "Is Capital Punishment an Effective Deterrent for Murder? An Examination of Social Science Research," pp. 251-282 in J.R. Acker, R.M. Bohm, and C.S. Lanier (eds.) *America's Experiment with Capital Punishment: Reflections on the Past, Present and Future of the Ultimate Penal Sanction*, 2nd ed. Durham, NC: Carolina Academic Press.

Peterson, Ruth D. and William C. Bailey (1991) "Felony Murder and Capital Punishment: An Examination of the Deterrence Question." *Criminology* 29:367-395.

Peterson, Ruth D. and William C. Bailey (1988) "Murder and Capital Punishment in the Evolving Context of the Post-*Furman* Era." *Social Forces* 66:774-807.

Phillips, David P. (1980) "The Deterrent Effect of Capital Punishment: New Evidence on an Old Controversy." *American Journal of Sociology* 86:139-147.

Pokorak, Jeffrey J. (1998) "Probing the Capital Prosecutor's Perspective: Race of the Discretionary Actors." *Cornell Law Review* 83:1811-1820.

Pojman, Louis P. (2004) "Why the Death Penalty Is Morally Permissible," pp. 51-75 in H.A. Bedau and P.G. Cassell (eds.) *Debating the Death Penalty: Should America Have Capital Punishment? The Experts on Both Sides Make Their Best Case*. New York: Oxford.

Post, Leonard (2004) "ABA Death Penalty Guidelines Languish." *The National Law Journal* 26 (accessed online, address not reproduced because of its length).

Prejean, Helen (1993) *Dead Man Walking: An Eyewitness Account of the Death Penalty in the United States*. New York: Random House.

Radelet, Michael L. (2006) Personal communication to Robert M. Bohm, April 24.

Radelet, Michael L. (2006b) "Some Examples of Post-Furman Botched Executions." The Death Penalty Information Center at www.deathpenaltyinfo.org/article. php?scid=8&did=478.

Radelet, Michael L. (1981) "Racial Characteristics and the Imposition of the Death Penalty." *American Sociological Review* 46:918-927.

Radelet, Michael L. and Marian J. Borg (2000) "The Changing Nature of Death Penalty Debates." *Annual Review of Sociology* 26:43-61.

Radelet, Michael L. and Ronald L. Akers (1996) "Deterrence and the Death Penalty: The View of the Experts." *Journal of Criminal Law and Criminology* 87:1-16.

Radelet, Michael L. and Hugo Adam Bedau (2003) "The Execution of the Innocent," pp. 325-344 in J.R. Acker, R.M. Bohm, and C.S. Lanier (eds.) *America's Experiment with Capital Punishment: Reflections on the Past, Present and Future of the Ultimate Penal Sanction*, 2nd ed. Durham, NC: Carolina Academic Press.

Radelet, Michael L. and Glenn L. Pierce (1991) "Choosing Those Who Will Die: Race and the Death Penalty in Florida." *Florida Law Review* 43:1-34.

Radelet, Michael L. and Glenn L. Pierce (1985) "Race and Prosecutorial Discretion in Homicide Cases." *Law and Society Review* 19:587-621.

Radelet, Michael and Margaret Vandiver (1983) "The Florida Supreme Court and Death Penalty Appeals." *Journal of Criminal Law and Criminology* 74:913-926.

Radelet, Michael L. and Barbara A. Zsembik (1993) "Executive Clemency in Post-*Furman* Capital Cases." *University of Richmond Law Review* 27:289-314.

Radelet, Michael L., William S. Lofquist, and Hugo Adam Bedau (1996) "Prisoners Released From Death Rows Since 1970 Because of Doubts About Their Guilt." *Thomas M. Cooley Law Review* 13:907-966.

Radelet, Michael L., Hugo Adam Bedau, and Constance E. Putnam (1992) *In Spite of Innocence: Erroneous Convictions in Capital Cases*. Boston: Northeastern University Press.

Radelet, Michael L., Margaret Vandiver, and Felix M. Barado (1983) "Families, Prisons, and Men with Death Sentences." *Journal of Family Issues* 4:593-612.

Radin, Margaret Jane (1980) "Cruel Punishment and Respect for Persons: Super Due Process for Death." *Southern California Law Review* 53:1143-1185.

Radin, Margaret Jane (1978) "The Jurisprudence of Death: Evolving Standards for the Cruel and Unusual Punishment Clause." *University of Pennsylvania Law Review* 126:989-1064.

Ralph, Paige H. (1996) "Benjamin Rush," pp. 412–413 in M.D. McShane and F.P. Williams III (eds.) *Encyclopedia of American Prisons*. New York and London: Garland.

Rankin, Joseph H. (1979) "Changing Attitudes Toward Capital Punishment." *Social Forces* 58:194–211.

Rapaport, Elizabeth (1993) "The Death Penalty and Gender Discrimination," pp. 145–152 in V.L. Streib (ed.) *A Capital Punishment Anthology*. Cincinnati: Anderson Publishing Co.

Recer, Paul (1994) "Professional Groups Want Doctors Out of Executions." *The Charlotte* [NC] *Observer* (March 20), p. 17A.

Reckless, Walter C. (1969) "The Use of the Death Penalty." *Crime and Delinquency* 15:43–56.

Reed, Mark D. and Brenda Sims Blackwell (2006) "Secondary Victimization Among Homicide Families of Homicide Victims: The Impact of the Justice Process on Co-Victims' Psychological Adjustment and Service Utilization," pp. 253-273 in J.R. Acker and D.R. Karp (eds.) *Wounds That Do Not Bind: Victim-Based Perspectives on the Death Penalty*. Durham, NC: Carolina Academic Press.

Reidy, Thomas J., Mark D. Cunningham, and Jon R. Sorensen (2001) "From Death to Life: Prison Behavior of Former Death Row Inmates in Indiana." *Criminal Justice and Behavior* 28:62–82.

Reiman, Jeffrey (2007) *The Rich Get Richer and the Poor Get Prison: Ideology, Class, and Criminal Justice*, Eighth Ed. Boston: Allyn and Bacon.

Reinhold, Robert (1982) "Chemical Injection Executes Texas Killer." *The Anniston* [AL] *Star* (December 7), p. 1A.

Religious Leaders in Florida (1986) "Religious Views Denounce the Death Penalty," pp. 86–91 in B. Szumski, L. Hall, and S. Bursell (eds.) *The Death Penalty: Opposing Viewpoints*. St. Paul, MN: Greenhaven.

Roberts, Julian V. (1984) "Public Opinion and Capital Punishment: The Effects of Attitudes Upon Memory." *Canadian Journal of Criminology* 26:283–291.

Roberts, Kate, (2005) "Capital Cases Hard for Smaller Counties." *Associated Press* (May 8) retrieved from the Death Penalty Information Center website at www.death penaltyinfo.org/newsanddev.php?scid=71&scyr=2005.

Roper, Roberta, (2006) "Finding Hope: One Family's Journey," pp. 111-125 in J.R. Acker and D.R. Karp (eds.) *Wounds That Do Not Bind: Victim-Based Perspectives on the Death Penalty*. Durham, NC: Carolina Academic Press.

Rosenbluth, Stanley and Phyllis (2006) "Accidental Death Is Fate, Murder Is Pure Evil," pp. 103-109 in J.R. Acker and D.R. Karp (eds.) *Wounds That Do Not Bind: Victim-Based Perspectives on the Death Penalty*. Durham, NC: Carolina Academic Press.

Rothman, David J. (1980) *Conscience and Convenience: The Asylum and its Alternatives in Progressive America*. Boston: Little, Brown.

Rusche, Georg and Otto Kirchheimer (1968) *Punishment and Social Structure*. New York: Russell and Russell.

Sandys, Marla (1998) "Stacking the Deck for Guilt and Death: The Failure of Death Qualification to Ensure Impartiality," pp. 285–307 in J.R. Acker, R.M. Bohm, and C.S. Lanier (eds.) *America's Experiment with Capital Punishment: Reflections on the Past, Present and Future of the Ultimate Penal Sanction*. Durham, NC: Carolina Academic Press.

Sandys, Marla (1995) "Attitudinal Change Among Students in a Capital Punishment Class: It May Be Possible." *American Journal of Criminal Justice* 20:37–55.

Sandys, Marla and Edmund F. McGarrell (1995) "Attitudes Toward Capital Punishment: Preferences for the Penalty or Mere Acceptance?" *Journal of Research in Crime and Delinquency* 32:191–213.

Sandys, Marla and Edmund F. McGarrell (1994) "Attitudes Toward Capital Punishment Among Indiana Legislators: Diminished Support in Light of Alternative Sentencing Options." *Justice Quarterly* 11:651–677.

Santich, Kate (2001) "Last Man to Die: Who was Victor Feguer." *The Orlando Sentinel* (June 9), p. E1.

Sarat, Austin (2006) "Putting a Square Peg in a Round Hole; Victims, Retribution, and George Ryan's Clemency," pp. 203-232 in J.R. Acker and D.R. Karp (eds.) *Wounds That Do Not Bind: Victim-Based Perspectives on the Death Penalty*. Durham, NC: Carolina Academic Press.

Sarat, Austin (2005) *Mercy on Trial: What It Means to Stop an Execution*. Princeton, NJ: Princeton University Press.

Sarat, Austin (2002) *When the State Kills: Capital Punishment and the American Condition*. Princeton, NJ: Princeton University Press.

Sarat, Austin (ed.) (1999) *The Killing State: Capital Punishment in Law, Politics, and Culture*. New York: Oxford University Press.

Sarat, Austin and Neil Vidmar (1976) "Public Opinion, the Death Penalty, and the Eighth Amendment: Testing the Marshall Hypothesis." *Wisconsin Law Review* 17:171–206.

Savitz, Leonard (1958) "A Study in Capital Punishment." *Journal of Criminal Law, Criminology and Police Science* 49:338–341.

Scalia, John (1997) "Prisoner Petitions in the Federal Courts, 1980-96." U.S. Department of Justice, Office of Justice Programs, Bureau of Justice Statistics. Washington, DC: GPO.

Scheb II, John M. and William Lyons (2001) "Race, Aggravating Factors and Prosecutorial Discretion: Analyzing the Death Penalty in Tennessee." Paper presented at the annual meeting of the Academy of Criminal Justice Sciences, Washington, D.C. (April).

Scheck, Barry, Peter Neufeld, and Jim Dwyer (2001) *Actual Innocence: When Justice Goes Wrong and How to Make It Right*. New York: Penguin Putnam.

Schneider, Victoria and John Ortiz Smykla (1991) "A Summary Analysis of Executions in the United States, 1608-1987: The Espy File," pp. 1–19 in R.M. Bohm (ed.) *The Death Penalty in America: Current Research*. Cincinnati, OH: Anderson Publishing Co.

Schoenfeld, Heather (2005) "Violated Trust: Conceptualizing Prosecutorial Misconduct." *Journal of Contemporary Criminal Justice* 21:250-271.

Schuessler, Karl F. (1952) "The Deterrent Effect of the Death Penalty." *The Annals* 284:54–62.

Schwarz, Janet B. (1999) Personal Correspondence. Associate Reference Librarian, Virginia Historical Society (from the Minutes of the Council and General Court of Colonial Virginia (for June 14, 1632), edited by H.R. McIlwaine).

Schwarzschild, Henry (1982) "In Opposition to Death Penalty Legislation," pp. 364–370 in H.A. Bedau (ed.) *The Death Penalty in America*, Third Ed. New York: Oxford University Press.

Sellin, Thorsten (ed.) (1967) *Capital Punishment*. New York: Harper & Row.

Sellin, Thorsten (1959) *The Death Penalty*. Philadelphia: The American Law Institute.

Seewar, John (2005) "Two Killers; One Spared." *Associated Press* (May 9) retrieved from the Death Penalty Information Center website at www.deathpenaltyinfo.org/newsanddev.php?scid=71&scyr=2005.

Sharp, Susan F. (2005) *Hidden Victims: The Effects of the Death Penalty on Families of the Accused*. Piscataway, NJ: Rutgers University Press.

Shepherd, Joanna M. (forthcoming) "Deterrence versus Brutalization: Capital Punishment's Differing Impacts Among States." *Michigan Law Review*.

Shepherd, Joanna M. (2004) "Murder of Passion, Execution Delays, and the Deterrence of Capital Punishment." *Journal of Legal Studies* 33:283-321.

Simon, David R. (2006) *Elite Deviance*, Eighth Ed. Boston: Allyn and Bacon.

Simon, Jonathan and Christina Spaulding (1999) "Tokens of Our Esteem: Aggravating Factors in the Era of Deregulated Death Penalties," pp. 81–113 in A. Sarat (ed.) *The Killing State: Capital Punishment in Law, Politics, and Culture*. New York: Oxford University Press.

Smith, M. Dwayne (1987) "Patterns of Discrimination in Assessments of the Death Penalty: The Case of Louisiana." *Journal of Criminal Justice* 15:279-286.

Smith, Tom W. (1975) "A Trend Analysis of Attitudes Toward Capital Punishment, 1936-1974," pp. 257-318 in J.E. Davis (ed.) *Studies of Social Change Since 1948*, Volume II. Chicago: University of Chicago National Opinion Research Center.

Smykla, John O. (1987) "The Human Impact of Capital Punishment: Interviews with Families of Persons on Death Row." *Journal of Criminal Justice* 15:331-347.

Snell, Tracy L. (2006) "Capital Punishment 2005." U.S. Department of Justice, *Bureau of Justice Statistics Bulletin* (December).

Snell, Tracy L. (1997) "Capital Punishment 1996." U.S. Department of Justice, *Bureau of Justice Statistics Bulletin* (December).

Sorensen, Jon (2004) "The Administration of the Capital Punishment," *ACJS Today* 29 (2):1, 4, 5, and 7.

Sorensen, Jonathan R. and Rocky L. Pilgrim (2000) "An Actuarial Risk Assessment of Violence Posed by Capital Murder Defendants." *Journal of Criminal Law and Criminology* 90:1251-1270.

Sorensen, Jon and Donald H. Wallace (1999) "Prosecutorial Discretion in Seeking Death: An Analysis of Racial Disparity in the Pretrial Stages of Case Processing in a Midwestern County." *Justice Quarterly* 16:559-578.

Sorensen, Jon and Robert D. Wrinkle (1996) "No Hope for Parole: Disciplinary Infractions Among Death-Sentenced and Life-Without-Parole Inmates." *Criminal Justice and Behavior* 23:542-552.

Sorensen, Jon, Robert Wrinkle, Victoria Brewer, and James Marquart (1999) "Capital Punishment and Deterrence: Examining the Effect of Executions on Murder in Texas." *Crime and Delinquency* 45:481-493.

Soss, Joe, Laura Langbein, and Alan R. Metelko (2003) "Why Do White Americans Support the Death Penalty?" *Journal of Politics* 65:397-421.

Spangenberg, Robert L. and Elizabeth R. Walsh (1989) "Capital Punishment or Life Imprisonment? Some Cost Considerations." *Loyola of Los Angeles Law Review* 23:45-58.

Stack, Steven (1987) "Publicized Executions and Homicide, 1950-1980." *American Sociological Review* 52:532-540.

Stafford-Smith, Clive (2002) "Killing the Death Penalty with Kindness," pp. 269-273 in D.R. Dow and M. Dow (eds.) *Machinery of Death: The Reality of America's Death Penalty Regime*. New York: Routledge.

Stauffer, Amy R., M. Dwayne Smith, John K. Cochran, Sondra J. Fogel, and Beth Bjerregaard (2006) "The Interaction between Victim Race and Gender on Sentencing Outcomes in Capital Murder Trials." *Homicide* 10:98-117.

Steele, Tracey and Norma Wilcox (2003) "A View from the Inside: The Role of Redemption, Deterrence, and Masculinity on Inmate Support for the Death Penalty." *Crime & Delinquency* 49:285-312.

Steiker, Carol and Jordan Steiker (2006) "The Effect of Capital Punishment on American Criminal Law and Policy." *Judicature* 89:250-253.

Steiker, Carol S. and Jordan M. Steiker (1998) "Judicial Developments in Capital Punishment Law," pp. 47-75 in J.R. Acker, R.M. Bohm, and C.S. Lanier (eds.) *America's Experiment with Capital Punishment: Reflections on the Past, Present and Future of the Ultimate Penal Sanction*. Durham, NC: Carolina Academic Press.

Stephan, James J. and Tracy L. Snell (1996) "Capital Punishment 1994." *Bureau of Justice Statistics Bulletin*, U.S. Department of Justice. Annapolis Junction, MD: BJS Clearinghouse.

Stephens, Gene (1990) "High-Tech Crime: The Threat to Civil Liberties." *The Futurist* (July-August), pp. 20-25.

Stern, Andrew (2006) "Ex-Illinois governor gets prison sentence." *M and C News* at http://news.monstersandcritics.com/northamerica/article_1198669.php/Ex-Illinois_governor_gets_prison_sentence.

Stevenson, Bryan (2004) "Close to Death: Reflections on Race and Capital Punishment in America," pp. 76-116 in H.A. Bedau and P.G. Cassell (eds.) *Debating the Death Penalty: Should America Have Capital Punishment? The Experts on Both Sides Make Their Best Case*. New York: Oxford.

Stinchcombe, Arthur L., Rebecca Adams, Carol A. Heimer, Kim Lane Scheppele, Tom W. Smith, and D. Garth Taylor (1980) *Crime and Punishment—Changing Attitudes in America*. San Francisco: Josey-Bass.

Streib, Victor L. (2006) "Death Penalty for Female Offenders January 1, 1973, Through December 31, 2005." www.law.onu.edu/faculty/streib/femdeath.htm.

Streib, Victor L. (2005) "The Juvenile Death Penalty Today: Death Sentences and Executions for Juvenile Crimes, January 1, 1973–December 31, 2004." www.law.onu.edu/faculty/streib/juvdeath.htm.

Streib, Victor L. (2003) "Executing Women, Juveniles, and the Mentally Retarded: Second Class Citizens in Capital Punishment," pp. 301-323 in J.R. Acker, R.M. Bohm, and C.S. Lanier (eds.) *America's Experiment with Capital Punishment: Reflections on the Past, Present and Future of the Ultimate Penal Sanction*, 2nd ed. Durham, NC: Carolina Academic Press.

Streib, Victor L. (1998) "Executing Women, Children, and the Retarded: Second Class Citizens in Capital Punishment," pp. 201-221 in J.R. Acker, R.M. Bohm, and C.S. Lanier (eds.) *America's Experiment with Capital Punishment: Reflections on the Past, Present and Future of the Ultimate Penal Sanction*. Durham, NC: Carolina Academic Press.

Streib, Victor L. (1993) "Death Penalty for Female Offenders," pp. 142-145 in V.L. Streib (ed.) *A Capital Punishment Anthology*. Cincinnati: Anderson Publishing Co.

Streib, Victor L. (1989) "Juveniles' Attitudes Toward Their Impending Executions," pp. 38-59 in M.L. Radelet (ed.) *Facing the Death Penalty: Essays on a Cruel and Unusual Punishment*. Philadelphia: Temple University Press.

Streib, Victor L. (1988) "Imposing the Death Penalty on Children," pp. 245-267 in K.C. Haas and J.A. Inciardi (eds.) *Challenging Capital Punishment: Legal and Social Science Approaches*. Newbury Park, CA: Sage.

Sturrock, Tim (2006) "Man behind historic death penalty case back in jail." Macon.com at www.macon.com/mld/macon/15568709.htm (accessed September 25, 2006).

Sundby, Scott E. (2005) *A Life and Death Decision: A Jury Weighs the Death Penalty*. New York: Palgrave Macmillan.

Surette, Ray (1992) *Media, Crime, and Criminal Justice: Images and Realities*. Pacific Grove, CA: Brooks/Cole.

Supreme Court of the United States, "About the Supreme Court," "A Brief Overview of the Supreme Court" at www.supremecourtus.gov/about/about.html

Supreme Court of the United States, "About the Supreme Court," "The Court and Constitutional Interpretation" at www.supremecourtus.gov/about/about.html

The Supreme Court Historical Society, "History of the Court," "The Chase Court, 1864-1873" at www.supremecourthistory.org/02_history/subs_history/02_c06.html

Sutherland, Edwin H. (1925) "Murder and the Death Penalty." *Journal of Criminal Law and Criminology* 15:522-529.

Tabak, Ronald J. (2001) "Finality Without Fairness: Why We are Moving Towards Moratoria on Executions and the Potential Abolition of Capital Punishment." *Connecticut Law Review* 33:733-763.

"Table of Compensation Statutes" (2006) Life After Exoneration Program at www.exonerated.org/legal.php. (accessed June 24).

Taylor, Gary (2000) "Dozens Seek Front-Row Seat for Executions." *The Orlando Sentinel* (May 8), p. C-3.

Taylor, Gary and Rene Stutzman (2000) "Appeals Run Out—Sims Set For Death." *The Orlando Sentinel* (February 23), p. A-1.

Texas Defender Service (2004) "Deadly Speculation: Misleading Texas Capital Juries with False Predictions of Future Dangerousness." Houston and Austin, TX: Texas Defender Service at www.texasdefender.org/publications.htm.

The Constitution Project (2005) *Mandatory Justice: The Death Penalty Revisited* (Washington, D.C.: The Constitution Project Death Penalty Initiative) at www.constitutionproject.org/deathpenalty/article.cfm?messageID=136&categoryId=2.

Thomas, Charles W. and Samuel C. Foster (1975) "A Sociological Perspective on Public Support for Capital Punishment." *American Journal of Orthopsychiatry* 45:641-657.

Thompson, Don (2006) "California Executes Man Despite Protests About Age." *The Orlando Sentinel* (January 18), p. A4.

Thompson, E.P. (1975) *Whigs and Hunters: The Origin of the Black Act.* New York: Pantheon.

Thompson, Ernie (1999) "Effects of Execution on Homicides in California." *Homicide Studies* 3:129-150.

Thompson, Ernie (1997) "Deterrence Versus Brutalization: The Case of Arizona." *Homicide Studies* 1:110-128.

Thompson, William C. (1989) "Death Qualification After *Wainwright v. Witt* and *Lockhart v. McCree*." *Law and Human Behavior* 13:185-215.

"Three Men Facing Federal Execution Receive Stays," (2006) The Death Penalty Information Center at www.deathpenaltyinfo.org/newsanddev.php?scid=8.

Tifft, Larry (1982) "Capital Punishment Research, Policy, and Ethics: Defining Murder and Placing Murderers." *Crime and Social Justice* 17:61-68.

Tizon, Tomas Alex (2003) "'I killed the 48 women'. *The Orlando Sentinel* (November 6), p. A1.

Trivers, Robert L. (1971) "The Evolution of Reciprocal Altruism." *Quarterly Review of Biology* 46:35-57.

Turney, Paul H. (2000) "New Developments in Military Capital Litigation: Four Cases Highlight the Fundamentals." *The Army Lawyer* (May):103-114.

Turow, Scott (2003) *Ultimate Punishment: A Lawyer's Reflections on Dealing with the Death Penalty.* New York: Picador

Tyler, Tom R. and Renee Weber (1982) "Support for the Death Penalty: Instrumental Response to Crime, or Symbolic Attitude?" *Law and Society Review* 17:21-45.

Unah, Isaac and John Charles Boger (2001) "Race and the Death Penalty in North Carolina, An Empirical Analysis: 1993-1997." www.deathpenaltyinfo.org/NCRaceRpt.html.

Unnever, James D. and Francis T. Cullen (2005) "Executing the Innocent and Support for Capital Punishment Implications for Public Policy." *Criminology & Public Policy* 4:3-38.

Unnever, James D., Francis T. Cullen, and John P. Bartkowski (2006) "Images of God and Public Support for Capital Punishment: Does a Close Relationship with a Loving God Matter?" *Criminology* 44: 835-866.

Unnever, James D., Francis T. Cullen, and Julian V. Roberts (2005) "Not Everyone Strongly Supports the Death Penalty: Assessing Weakly-Held Attitudes About Capital Punishment." *American Journal of Criminal Justice* 29:187-216.

U.S. General Accounting Office (1990) *Death Penalty Sentencing: Research Indicates Pattern of Racial Disparities*. Report to Senate and House Committees on the Judiciary. Washington, DC:GAO.

Van den Haag, Ernest (1998) "Justice, Deterrence and the Death Penalty," pp. 139-156 in J.R. Acker, R.M. Bohm, and C.S. Lanier (eds.) *America's Experiment with Capital Punishment: Reflections on the Past, Present and Future of the Ultimate Penal Sanction*. Durham, NC: Carolina Academic Press.

Van den Haag, Ernest (1982) "In Defense of the Death Penalty: A Practical and Moral Analysis," pp. 323-341 in H.A. Bedau (ed.) *The Death Penalty in America*, Third Ed. New York: Oxford University Press.

Van den Haag, Ernest and John P. Conrad (1983) *The Death Penalty: A Debate*. New York: Plenum.

Vandiver, Margaret (2006) "The Death Penalty and the Families of Victims: An Overview of Research Issues," pp. 235-252 in J.R. Acker and D.R. Karp (eds.) *Wounds That Do Not Bind: Victim-Based Perspectives on the Death Penalty*. Durham, NC: Carolina Academic Press.

Vandiver, Margaret (2003) "The Impact of the Death Penalty on the Families of Homicide Victims and of Condemned Prisoners," pp. 613-645 in J.R. Acker, R.M. Bohm, and C.S. Lanier (eds.) *America's Experiment with Capital Punishment: Reflections on the Past, Present and Future of the Ultimate Penal Sanction*, 2nd ed. Durham, NC: Carolina Academic Press.

Vandiver, Margaret (1989) "Coping with Death: Families of the Terminally Ill, Homicide Victims, and Condemned Prisoners," pp. 123-138 in M.L. Radelet (ed.) *Facing the Death Penalty: Essays on a Cruel and Unusual Punishment*. Philadelphia: Temple University Press.

Vandiver, Margaret, David J. Giacopassi, and Mazie S. Curley (2003) "The Tennessee Slave Code: A Legal Antecedent to Inequities in Modern Capital Cases." *Journal of Ethnicity in Criminal Justice* 1:67-89.

Vick, Karl (1996) "Delaware Readies Gallows as Rare Form of Execution Draws Near." *The Washington Post* (January 21), p. B4.

Vidmar, Neil (1974) "Retributive and Utilitarian Motives and Other Correlates of Canadian Attitudes Toward the Death Penalty." *Canadian Psychologist* 15:337-356.

Vidmar, Neil and Tony Dittenhoffer (1981) "Informed Public Opinion and Death Penalty Attitudes." *Canadian Journal of Criminology* 23:43-56.

Vidmar, Neil and Phoebe Ellsworth (1974) "Public Opinion and the Death Penalty." *Stanford Law Review* 26:1245-1270.

Vidmar, Neil and Dale T. Miller (1980) "Socialpsychological Processes Underlying Attitudes Toward Legal Punishment." *Law and Society Review* 14:565-602.

Vila, Bryan and Cynthia Morris (eds.) (1997) *Capital Punishment in the United States: A Documentary History*. Westport, CT: Greenwood.

Villa, Judi (2005) " Aged Inmates' Care Puts Stress on State," *The Arizona Republic* (May 8) at www.azcentral.com/specials/special21/articles/0508prisonaging01.html.

444   DEATHQUEST

Visger, Mark A. (2005) "The Impact of *Ring v. Arizona* on Military Capital Sentencing." *The Army Lawyer* (September):54-77.

Vito, Gennaro and Thomas Keil (1988) "Capital Sentencing in Kentucky: An Analysis of the Factors Influencing Decision Making in the Post-*Gregg* Period." *Journal of Criminal Law and Criminology* 79:483-508.

Vito, Gennaro F. and Deborah G. Wilson (1988) "Back from the Dead: Tracking the Progress of Kentucky's *Furman*-Commuted Death Row Population." *Justice Quarterly* 5:101-111.

Vito, Gennaro F., Pat Koester, and Deborah G. Wilson (1991) "Return of the Dead: An Update on the Status of *Furman*-Commuted Death Row Inmates," pp. 89-99 in R.M. Bohm (ed.) *The Death Penalty in America: Current Research*. Cincinnati, OH: Anderson Publishing Co.

Vogel, Brenda L. (2003) "Support for Life in Prison Without the Possibility of Parole Among Death Penalty Supporters." *American Journal of Criminal Justice* 27:263-275.

Vogel, Brenda L. and Ronald E. Vogel (2003) "The Age of Death: Appraising Public Opinion of Juvenile Capital Punishment. *Journal of Criminal Justice* 31:169-183.

Vold, George B. (1952) "Extent and Trend of Capital Crimes in the United States." *The Annals* 284:1-7.

Vold, George B. (1932) "Can the Death Penalty Prevent Crime?" *Prison Journal* 12:3-8.

Wagner, Shane (2006) "The Death Sentence: For Criminals or Victims?" pp. 69-83 in J.R. Acker and D.R. Karp (eds.) *Wounds That Do Not Bind: Victim-Based Perspectives on the Death Penalty*. Durham, NC: Carolina Academic Press.

Waldo, Gordon P. (1981) "The Death Penalty and Deterrence: A Review of Recent Research," pp. 169-178 in I.L. Barak-Glantz and C.R. Huff (eds.) *The Mad, the Bad, and the Different: Essays in Honor of Simon Dinitz*. Lexington, MA: Heath.

Walker, R. Neal (2006) "How the Malfunctioning Death Penalty Challenges the Criminal Justice System." *Judicature* 89:265268.

Warr, Mark and Mark Stafford (1984) "Public Goals of Punishment and Support for the Death Penalty." *Journal of Research in Crime and Delinquency* 21:95-111.

Weinstein, Henry (2002) "Court Backs Inmate with Sleepy Lawyer." *The Orlando Sentinel* (June 4), p. A5.

Weisman, Robyn S., Jeffrey N. Bernstein, and Richard S. Weisman (2005) "Inadequate Anaesthesia in Lethal Injection for Execution." *The Lancet* 366 (accessed through www.sciencedirect.com).

Weisberg, Robert (1983) "Deregulating Death," pp. 305-395 in P.B. Kurland, G. Casper, and D.J. Hutchinson (eds.) *The Supreme Court Review, 1983*. Chicago: University of Chicago Press.

Weissberg, R. (1976) *Public Opinion and Popular Government*. Englewood Cliffs, NJ: Prentice-Hall.

Welch, Bud (2002) "Speaking Out Against the Execution of Timothy McVeigh," pp. 275-281 in D.R. Dow and M. Dow (eds.) *Machinery of Death: The Reality of America's Death Penalty Regime*. New York: Routledge.

Welch, Mandy and Richard Burr (2002) "The Politics of Finality and the Execution of the Innocent: The Case of Gary Graham," pp. 127-143 in D.R. Dow and M. Dow (eds.) *Machinery of Death: The Reality of America's Death Penalty Regime*. New York: Routledge.

Welsh-Huggins, Andrew (2005) "Death Penalty Unequal." *Associated Press* (May 7) retrieved from the Death Penalty Information Center website at www.death penaltyinfo.org/newsanddev.php?scid=71&scyr=2005.

White, Linda L. (2006) "A Tiger by the Tail: The Mother of a Murder Victim Grapples with the Death Penalty," pp. 49-68 in J.R. Acker and D.R. Karp (eds.) *Wounds That Do Not Bind: Victim-Based Perspectives on the Death Penalty*. Durham, NC: Carolina Academic Press.

White, Welsh S. (1987) *The Death Penalty in the Eighties: An Examination of the Modern System of Capital Punishment*. Ann Arbor: University of Michigan Press.

Whitehead, John T. (1998) "Good Ol' Boys and the Chair: Death Penalty Attitudes of Policy Makers in Tennessee." *Crime and Delinquency* 44:245-256.

"White House: Bush Thinks Death Penalty is Deterrent." (2005) *The Orlando Sentinel* (December 3), p. A10.

Wicker, A.W. (1969) "Attitudes Versus Actions: The Relationship of Verbal and Overt Behavioral Responses to Attitude Objects." *Journal of Social Issues* 25:41-78.

Wilbanks, William (1987) *The Myth of a Racist Criminal Justice System*. Monterey, CA: Brooks/Cole.

Wilcox, Norma and Tracey Steele (2003) "Just the Facts: A Descriptive Analysis of Inmate Attitudes Toward Capital Punishment. " *The Prison Journal* 83:464-482.

Williams, Frank P., Dennis R. Longmire, and David B. Gulick (1988) "The Public and the Death Penalty: Opinion as an Artifact of Question Type." *Criminal Justice Research Bulletin* 3:1-5.

Williams, Kenneth (2005) "Ensuring the Capital Defendant's Right to Competent Counsel: It's Time for Some Standards." *The Wayne Law Review* 51:129-161 at http://web.lexis-nexis.com. (full address to long to reproduce here}.

Williams, Marian R. and Jefferson E. Holcomb (2004) "The Interactive Effects of Victim Race and Gender on Death Sentence Disparity Findings." *Homicide Studies* 8:350-376.

Williams, Marian R. and Jefferson E. Holcomb (2001) "Racial Disparity and Death Sentences in Ohio." *Journal of Criminal Justice* 29:207-218.

Willing, Richard and Gary Fields (1999) "Geography of the Death Penalty." *USA Today* (December 20), p. 1A.

Wilson, Richard J. (2003) "The Influence of International Law and Practice on the Death Penalty in the United States," pp. 147-165 in J.R. Acker, R.M. Bohm, and C.S. Lanier (eds.) *America's Experiment with Capital Punishment: Reflections on the Past, Present and Future of the Ultimate Penal Sanction*, 2nd ed. Durham, NC: Carolina Academic Press.

Wolfgang, Marvin E. and Marc Riedel (1975) "Rape, Race and the Death Penalty in Georgia." *American Journal of Orthopsychiatry* 45:658-668.

Wolfson, Wendy Phillips (1982) "The Deterrent Effect of the Death Penalty upon Prison Murder," pp. 159-173 in H.A. Bedau (ed.) *The Death Penalty in America*, Third Ed. New York: Oxford University Press.

Wollan, Laurin A., Jr. (1989) "Representing the Death Row Inmate: The Ethics of Advocacy, Collateral Style," pp. 92-111 in M.L. Radelet (ed.) *Facing the Death Penalty: Essays on a Cruel and Unusual Punishment*. Philadelphia: Temple University Press.

Wolpin, Kenneth I. (1978) "Capital Punishment and Homicide in England: A Summary of Results." *American Economic Review* 68:422-427.

Woodward, Bob and Scott Armstrong (1979) *The Brethren: Inside the Supreme Court*. New York: Simon and Schuster.

Word, Ron (2004) "Killer Put to Death After Delay." *The Orlando Sentinel* (May 27), p. B5.

Word, Ron (2004b) "Death Row Not Too Hot for Inmates." *The Orlando Sentinel* (August 10), p. B5.

Word, Ron (2002) "Federal Cases Rarely End in Death Penalty." *The Orlando Sentinel* (November 18), p. B3.

Wright, Harold O., Jr., Robert M. Bohm, and Katherine M. Jamieson (1995) "A Comparison of Uninformed and Informed Death Penalty Opinions: A Replication and Expansion." *American Journal of Criminal Justice* 20:57-87.

Wyble, D.W. (1985) "Capital Punishment in the Military." *Military Police* (Winter):36-37.

Yardley, Jim (2001a) "Oklahoma Takes Close Look at Evidence in Capital Cases." *The Orlando Sentinel* (September 2), p. A5.

Yardley, Jim (2001b) "Oklahoma Inquiry Focuses on Scientist Used by Prosecutors." *The New York Times* (May 2), p. A1.

Yardley, Jim (2000) "On the Record: Texas' Busy Death Chamber Helps Define Bush's Tenure." *The New York Times* (January 7), www.crimelynx.com/bushdp.html.

Young, Robert L. (2004) "Guilty Until Proven Innocent: Conviction Orientation, Racial Attitudes, and Support for Capital Punishment." *Deviant Behavior* 25:151-167.

Young, Robert L. (1992) "Religious Orientation, Race and Support for the Death Penalty." *Journal for the Scientific Study of Religion* 31:76-87.

Yunker, James A. (2002) "A New Statistical Analysis of Capital Punishment Incorporating U.S. Postmoratorium Data." *Social Science Quarterly* 82:297-311.

Yunker, James A. (1976) "Is the Death Penalty a Deterrent to Homicide: Some Time-Series Evidence." *Journal of Behavioral Economics* 5:1-32.

Zahn, Margaret A. (1989) "Homicide in the Twentieth Century: Trends, Types, and Causes," pp. 216-234 in T.R. Gurr (ed.) *Violence in America: The History of Crime*, Vol. 1. Newbury Park, CA: Sage.

Zeisel, Hans (1982) "The Deterrent Effect of the Death Penalty: Facts v. Faith," pp. 116-138 in H.A. Bedau (ed.) *The Death Penalty in America*, Third Ed. New York: Oxford University Press.

Zeisel, Hans (1981) "Race Bias in the Administration of the Death Penalty: The Florida Experience." *Harvard Law Review* 95:456-468.

Zerwick, Phoebe (2004) "Hunt Case Leads to Legal Reform." *Winston-Salem Journal* (December 16) at http://darrylhunt.journalnow.com/epilogue.html.

Zimmerman, Paul R. (forthcoming) "Estimates of the Deterrent Effect of Alternative Execution Methods in the United States: 1978-2000." *American Journal of Economics and Sociology*.

Zimmerman, Paul R. (2004) "State Executions, Deterrence, and the Incidence of Murder." *Journal of Applied Economics* 7:163-193.

Zimmers, Teresa A., David A. Lubarsky, Jonathan P. Sheldon, and Leonidas G. Koniaris (2005) "Inadequate Anaesthesia in Lethal Injection for Execution—Authors' reply." *The Lancet* 366 (accessed through www.sciencedirect.com).

Zimring, Franklin E. (2003) *The Contradictions of American Capital Punishment*. New York: Oxford University Press.

Zimring, Franklin E. and Gordon Hawkins (1986) *Capital Punishment and the American Agenda*. Cambridge: Cambridge University Press.

Zinn, Howard (1990) *A People's History of the United States*. New York: Harper Perennial.

Index

Victim-based racial discrimination, 315, 330
Victim-based racial identification, 327-328, 339n226
Victim Compensation Fund (2001), 280
Victim-impact statements, 83-84, 112n160
Victim-impact testimony, racial discrimination and, 321
Victims, family or friends of. *See* Co-victims
Videotaping interrogation, 271
Vidmar, Neil, 345, 373-374
Vinson, Fred M. (Chief Justice), 16
Violent Crime Control and Law Enforcement Act (1994), 76, 117, 126
Virginia
  abolition of death penalty, 13
  appellate review, 74
  Atkins v. Virginia, 96-97, 98, 141, 282, 303
  capital crimes in early, 6-7
  capital crimes and racial discrimination, 313
  choice of means of execution, 155, 165
  clemency for condemned prisoners in 18th century, 266
  compensation for wrongly convicted, 278
  conviction rate of capital murder defendants, 217
  cost of appointed defense in capital trial, 219
  death sentencing practices, 300
  executions of death-eligible offenders, 299
  Innocence Commission, 276
  lethal injection executions, 163
  racial discrimination in death sentencing, 315
  structured discretion statute, 72-73
  Supreme Court denial of *certiorari* in rape case, 21
Virginia Supreme Court, definition of depravity, 323
Voir dire, in capital cases, 218

Wainwright v. Witt, 88
Walker, Herbert V. (Judge), 18
Walton v. Arizona, 78-79
War, law of, "grave breaches" of, 131
Warren, Earl (Chief Justice), 22, 25

Washington
  abolition of capital punishment, 12
  choice of means of execution, 165
  Craemer v. Washington, 42
  Earl, Jr., 276
  economic costs of capital punishment, 213
  hanging, 153
  moratoria bill, 282
  reinstatement of death penalty, 13
  Strickland v. Washington, 98-99, 263
Washington Post, expose of racial disparities of Maryland's death row, 283
Watkins, Pamela, 190
Watts v. Indiana, 52-53
Weeks v. Angelone, 93
Weems v. United States, 20, 146-147
Wells, William, 36-37
West, Valerie, 283
West Virginia
  abolition of death penalty, 13
  abolition of death penalty, 19
  indemnifying wrongly convicted, 277
White, Byron (Justice), 60, 62-66
Whitman, Walt, 8
Whittier, John Greenleaf, 8
Wiggins v. Smith, 99-100
Wilkerson v. Utah, 38, 146
Wilkins v. Missouri, 97
Will, George, 284
Williams, Stanley "Tookie," 207
Williams, Wayne, 244
Williams (Terry) v. Taylor, 86
Williams v. New York, 43
Wilmore, Curtis Reese, 276
Wilson, George, 35-37
Winston v. United States, 44
Wisconsin
  costs of capital punishment seminar, 227
  costs of death row and execution chamber, 227
  homicide death rates, 178
  indemnifying wrongly convicted, 277
  restoration of death penalty, 15
Witchcraft, colonial hangings for, 5
Witherspoon v. Illinois, 25, 57-58, 88, 303
"Without capital punishment," 44

About the Author

Robert M. Bohm is a Professor of Criminal Justice and Legal Studies at the University of Central Florida in Orlando. He has also been a faculty member in the Departments of Criminal Justice at the University of North Carolina at Charlotte (1989–1995) and at Jacksonville State University in Alabama (1979–1989). In 1973-1974, he worked for the Jackson County Department of Corrections in Kansas City, Missouri, first as a corrections officer and later as an instructor/counselor in the Model Inmate Employment Program, a Law Enforcement Assistance Administration sponsored work-release project. He received his PhD in Criminology from Florida State University in 1980.

Professor Bohm has published numerous journal articles and book chapters in the areas of criminal justice and criminology. In addition to being the author of *Deathquest III: An Introduction to the Theory and Practice of Capital Punishment in the United States,* 3rd ed. (LexisNexis/Anderson Publishing, 2007), he is the author of *A Concise Introduction to Criminal Justice* (McGraw-Hill, 2008) and *A Primer on Crime and Delinquency Theory,* 2nd ed. (Wadsworth, 2001). He is co-author (with Keith N. Haley) of *Introduction to Criminal Justice,* 5th ed. (McGraw-Hill, 2009). He is also the editor of *The Death Penalty in America: Current Research* (Anderson Publishing Co., 1991) and co-editor (with James R. Acker and Charles S. Lanier) of *America's Experiment with Capital Punishment: Reflections on the Past, Present, and Future of the Ultimate Sanction,* 2nd ed. (Carolina Academic Press, 2003) and (with Jeffery T. Walker) *Demystifying Crime and Criminal Justice* (Oxford University Press, 2006). Professor Bohm has been active in the American Society of Criminology, the Southern Criminal Justice Association, and especially the Academy of Criminal Justice Sciences, having served in the latter organization as Trustee-at-Large (1987–90), Second Vice-President (1990–91), First Vice-President (1991–92), and President (1992–93). In 1989, the Southern Criminal Justice Association selected him as the *Outstanding Educator of the Year.* In 1999, he became a Fellow of the Academy of Criminal Justice Sciences and, in 2001, he was presented with the Founder's Award of the Academy of Criminal Justice Sciences.